PUBLIC SPEAKING

THIRD EDITION

Michael Osborn

UNIVERSITY OF MEMPHIS

Suzanne Osborn

UNIVERSITY OF MEMPHIS

6, 7, 9, 13, 14

HOUGHTON MIFFLIN COMPANY • BOSTON • NEW YORK

*We dedicate this edition of Public Speaking to the fond memory of
H. P. Constans, our "Prof" at the University of Florida, who many
years ago introduced us to the tradition of great nineteenth and
twentieth century textbooks in public speaking.*

Sponsoring Editor: George Hoffman
Basic Book Editor: Karla Paschkis
Senior Project Editor: Susan Westendorf
Senior Production/Design Coordinator: Jill Haber
Senior Manufacturing Coordinator: Marie Barnes
Marketing Manager: Pamela J. Laskey

Cover design: Diana Coe
Cover image: Diana Coe

Printed in the U.S.A.
Library of Congress Catalog Card Number: 96-76943
Student Edition ISBN: 0-395-80882-0
Instructor's Annotated Edition: 0-395-80883-9

3 4 5 6 7 8 9—DOC—00 99 98

Contents

PART ONE
The Foundations of Public Speaking 1

CHAPTER 1
You as a Public Speaker 2

CHAPTER 2
Your First Speech 34

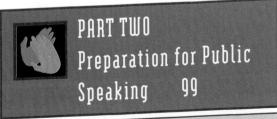

CHAPTER 6

Using Supporting Materials in Your Speech   172

CHAPTER 7

Structuring Your Speech   202

CHAPTER 10

Using Language Effectively 310

CHAPTER 11

Presenting Your Speech 342

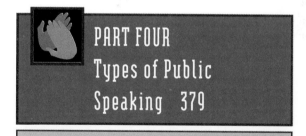

**PART FOUR
Types of Public
Speaking 379**

CHAPTER 12

Informative Speaking 380

CHAPTER 13

Persuasive Speaking   414

CHAPTER 14

Evidence, Proof, and Argument   448

CHAPTER 15

Ceremonial Speaking   486

APPENDIX A

Group Communication   A1

APPENDIX B

Speeches for Analysis   B1

Preface

Over the past decade *Public Speaking* has enjoyed wide acceptance in colleges and universities as a comprehensive textbook for the public speaking course. When we approached this revision, our first impulse was to be conservative, to aim simply at updating the information and freshening the examples. However, *Public Speaking* gained its acceptance by taking chances, not by being timid. In that spirit we offer here not so much a revision as a renewal. Preparing this edition has been a voyage of discovery in which both we and our book have grown and changed. We have not hesitated to be bold when we thought that change might benefit our student readers.

We began our work with two major goals. A constant theme of our book is our respect and affection for the undergraduate student. We know how challenging this class can be, and we have renewed our effort to reach out to them. Thus, a primary goal of this edition is to make our book accessible to an even wider range of students. We also wished to improve certain sections of the book that have never quite satisfied us. These sections present perplexing problems that all authors must confront. How best to present an initial overview of the public speaking process that is understandable, and yet does not reduce the subject to an oversimplified model? How to write meaningfully about such rich topics as the language of public speaking, or the nature of persuasive speaking, in just one or two chapters that beginning students can understand and apply? We are satisfied that this edition of our book comes closer than before to meeting these goals. In the process of reaching for them, we have made some discoveries that we are eager to share with users of this book.

 ## CHANGES AND CONTINUING THEMES IN THE FOURTH EDITION

The changes, discoveries, and continuing themes that characterize this edition include a strong new emphasis on the personal development of the student, diversity as an emerging challenge for contemporary communication, values and ethics as a central concern and obligation for the modern speaker, listening as a creative activity, unified models of persuasion and practical reasoning, and the impact of new technologies on the basic course.

The Student's Personal Development

Previous users will recognize that Chapter 1 is essentially a new chapter. In it, we talk more directly to student readers, engaging and motivating their interest. We have developed a new transformational model that gives both speakers and listeners an enlarged sense of their role in the creation of public knowledge. We are convinced that interference generated by speaker fears, audience distrust and distraction, and cultural differences creates barriers between speakers and listeners. To emphasize the power of public speaking to lower these barriers, our new model dramatizes victory over what we call "Interference Mountain." We also relate more closely to our student readers through the increased use of personal examples.

Developing Chapter 1 and the sections beyond it led us to a remarkable discovery. We found that three key metaphors representing three major dimensions of skill emerged within the text as central to the student's learning experience. The first of these metaphors was *the student as climber:* both as speakers and listeners, students must learn to climb the barriers of interference that separate them in order to enjoy genuine communication interactions. This metaphor seems especially appropriate in the context of cultural diversity. The second metaphor, which we develop in Chapters 6–8, is *the student as builder.* The student must learn how to arrange attractive and well-supported structures of thought. This metaphor emphasizes the mastery of logic and the orderly development of ideas. The third metaphor, which we develop in Chapters 9–11 and 14, is *the student as weaver.* Students must learn to weave symbols into the fabric of communication, and to fashion a tapestry of argument out of evidence and proof. This metaphor emphasizes the creativity of public speaking as a practical art form. By focusing on these central metaphors of climbing, building, and weaving, we want to help our students develop abilities that are critical to communication and to successful living.

Diversity as Challenge and Opportunity

The public speaking class provides an ideal laboratory to explore and discover the multitude of cultures that make up our country. Students must learn to respect the many voices that make up what Lincoln once described as "the chorus of the Union." They also must learn to recognize and accept the different voices within themselves, for most of us have been fashioned by many cultures. The diversity of cultures in most audiences presents the speaker with a formidable practical problem of speech adaptation: *How can we speak in a manner that invites shared understanding?* The ancient writers on rhetoric never had to contend with the idea or reality of such an audience. A time of growing cultural diversity only magnifies the ideal of public speaking as a social force that can recreate the enlightened community in the face of cultural fragmentation.

For these reasons, the theme of cultural diversity continues to expand in our Fourth Edition. Chapter 1 enlarges its discussion of "cultural benefits," introduces cultural diversity as a potential source of interference, and offers universal values as a means of transcending cultural differences. We also emphasize that cultural diversity offers opportunity as well as challenge. To experience the different cultures of others is to be enriched by their perspectives. As the book proceeds, topics such as the self-awareness inventory in Chapter 2, listening through the static of different cultures in Chapter 3, audience analysis in Chapter 4, the selection of supporting materials in Chapter 6, and the speaker's language in Chapter 10, offer opportunities to heighten the speaker's concern and appreciation for cultural diversity and to study its impact on communication.

Centrality of Values and Ethics

We have always felt that our major ethical obligation is to make students sensitive to the possible impact of public speaking on the lives of others. Our words can affect how others see themselves and their worlds, and how they react to what they see. We have renewed and strengthened our emphasis on values and ethics: a diverse society heightens the importance of basic human values that can join people of different races and cultural backgrounds. Because of the pervasive importance of values and ethics, we have chosen not to confine ethics to a single chapter, but rather to seek the specific application of ethical considerations throughout the book.

Early in the book we discuss plagiarism and challenge each class to develop its own code of ethical conduct for speaking. Chapter 5 introduces the concept of *responsible knowledge* as an ethical requirement for all public speakers, and tells students how to acquire such knowledge. We direct the attention of students to ethical concerns as we consider listening, audience analysis and adaptation, cultural variations, topic selection, research, certain ways of structuring speeches, presentation aids, uses of language, and the consequences of informing and persuading others. Throughout the text, we warn against abuses of supporting materials, evidence, proofs, arguments, and potent stylistic forms. We encourage students to respect cultural differences both in themselves and others, and to engage in thorough deliberation of public issues. In short, we seek to raise the ethical sensitivity of student-readers.

Listening as a Creative Activity

We recently worked with the National Issues Forums Institute on a project to improve public communication. This work resulted in the publication of the book, *Alliance for a Better Public Voice: The Communication Discipline and the National Issues Forums*. That experience has led us to develop a fresh approach to listening in the public speaking class. In the past, textbooks—including our own—have focused more on critical listening as a defensive skill for protection from exploitive or defective communication. While useful, this emphasis shortchanges the creative, constructive dimension of listening that makes the audience a vital partner in communication. The balanced ideal of critical and constructive listening invites audiences to participate more fully in the co-creation of meaning. We translate this ideal into practical terms in Chapter 3.

Unified Models of Persuasion and Practical Reasoning

Past users will remember that we have grounded our explanation of persuasion in a simplified version of McGuire's account of the persuasive process. In this edition we continue to make this comprehensive explanation useful to beginning students. We have also sought in previous editions to study the relationships among evidence, proof, and argument as an interactive process, so that students can get a good overall grasp of the role of reasoning in persuasion. This edition extends this effort by showing how deductive, inductive, and analogical modes of reasoning also work together when persuasion is logical, based in reality, and informed by practical experience. Making these complex processes accessible and useful to beginning students is the major business of Chapters 13 and 14, and results in a new, unified model of practical reasoning.

New Technologies

We live in a time in which new technologies are transforming the possibilities of human communication. Chapter 5's emphasis on the changing nature of the library and on the research resources now brought into our homes through computer networks reflects our excitement over these technologies. Even more dramatic is the transformation of Chapter 9, which we now call "Presentation Aids." This change reflects our response to the expanding presentational resources made possible by the computer, and to the new horizons of multimedia presentations.

FEATURES OF THE TEXT

To help us reach out to the beginning student, we develop two special features: an emphasis on the how and why of public speaking and a step-by-step presentation of practical information and useful guidelines.

The How and Why of Public Speaking

Ancient educators thought public speaking belonged at the center of liberal education, and we wholeheartedly agree. What other discipline, they argued, requires students to think clearly, to organize their thoughts, to select and combine words artfully and judiciously, and to express themselves with power and conviction, all under the direct scrutiny of a live audience? The study of public speaking should empower us in the many social, economic, and political situations that require open discussion. Not only personal success but the fate of our communities may depend upon the outcomes of such discussions.

For these reasons we believe that a college or university course in public speaking should offer both practical advice and an understanding of why such advice is practical. Therefore we continue to emphasize both the *how* and the *why* of public speaking—*how* so that beginners can achieve success as quickly as possible, and *why* so that they can manage their new skill wisely. The Roman educator, Quintilian, held forth the ideal of "the good person speaking well" as the goal of all such instruction. We follow in his path as we stress the value of speech training in the development of the whole person. We also emphasize that successful public speaking is leadership-in-action and that improving one's speaking skills is excellent training for leadership roles. In addition, understanding the basics of public communication can make students more resistant to unethical speakers and more intelligently critical of daily communication. We want to help students become both better producers and better consumers of public communication.

Consistent with our "how and why" philosophy, we base our practical advice on underlying principles of human communication. As we offer advice on structuring speeches, we show how various speech designs connect with basic concepts of "good form," explaining why some speeches succeed and others fail. We ground our advice on informative speaking in tried-and-true principles of learning theory, and our suggestions on persuasive speaking on research findings in social psychology and the communication discipline. We show further how evidence, proof, and argument function together as an integrated system that makes persuasion work. As we consider ceremonial speaking, we show how two basic principles, one derived from classical and the other from contemporary rhetorical theory, provide essential techniques for successful communication. We draw from the past and present and from the social sciences and the humanities in our effort to help students understand and manage the powerful techniques described in this book.

Step-by-Step Presentation

Our presentation of topics helps students build knowledge and skills step-by-step to achieve positive results. It is especially important for beginners to have a successful first speaking experience. For this reason, Chapter 2 offers an elementary overview of required skills so that students can plan good initial speeches. This kind of overview, pioneered by our book, helps students present introductory speeches that build a sense of classroom community and trust. In the chapters that follow, students learn how to listen critically and constructively, to analyze their audiences, to select, refine, and research speech topics, to develop supporting materials, to arrange these materials in appropriate structures, to outline their thinking in disciplined patterns, and to create effective presentation aids. They also learn how to manage words and how to present their messages. They become acquainted with the nature of information and how to present it, the process of persuasion and how to engage it, and the importance of ceremonial speaking in its various forms. Appendix A, "Group Communication," offers concise practical advice on how to participate effectively in small groups. Individual instructors may rearrange this pattern to suit different syllabi and course strategies.

PLAN OF THE BOOK

Our book is both logical and flexible. We begin with an overview of what the student can expect from the course and gradually build toward more complex skills and deeper understanding. Teachers may adapt the sequence of chapters to any course plan, because each chapter covers a topic thoroughly and completely.

Part One, "The Foundations of Public Speaking," provides basic information that students need for their first speaking and listening experiences. Chapter 1 highlights the personal, social, and cultural benefits of speaking effectively, introduces the nature of public speaking as communication, and emphasizes the ethical responsibilities speakers must always bear in mind. The new transformational model developed in the chapter shows how good speaking can have a desirable impact on the speaker, the audience, and public knowledge. Chapter 2 offers students procedures for inventing, planning, outlining, practicing, and presenting their first speeches. Focusing on how the first speech functions to introduce the self or others, the chapter helps students develop credibility for later speeches and cope with communication apprehension. An annotated student speech of self-introduction completes the chapter. Chapter 3, on critical and constructive listening, redefines the role of the audience in public communication. The chapter identifies common listening problems and explores ways to overcome these problems, helps students sharpen their critical thinking skills, and develops criteria so that they may become more constructive speech evaluators. The chapter concludes by emphasizing ethical responsibilities of listeners.

Part Two, "Preparation for Public Speaking," provides in-depth coverage of the basic skills needed to prepare an effective speech: audience analysis, topic selection, research techniques, the development of supporting materials, and structuring and outlining. Chapter 4 emphasizes the importance of the audience one anticipates when preparing a speech. The chapter has been rearranged to explore first the motivations listeners bring to speech situations, how to adapt a message to audience characteristics, and how to adjust to factors in the immediate speech situation. Chapter 5 provides systematic ways to select and refine topics for successful speeches. We emphasize the ethical and practical importance of having *responsible knowledge* before one speaks. We identify library resources most useful for public speaking, including computer access to electronic databases. The chapter concludes by offering suggestions for interviewing and for recording the information one discovers. Chapter 6 covers the types of supporting materials speakers must gather as they research their topics. The chapter discusses facts and statistics, examples, and testimony. Responding to recent research, it introduces the narrative as another basic form of supporting material. It also tells students how to select the best supporting materials for their speeches, and how to bring these materials to life through comparison, contrast, and analogy. Chapter 7 shows students how to develop simple, balanced, and orderly speech designs, how to select and shape their main points, how to use transitions to move smoothly from point to point, and how to prepare effective introductions and conclusions. Chapter 8 explains why outlining is so important, how to develop working outlines in which speeches take form, how to complete a formal outline, and how to fashion a key-word outline for use during presentation.

Part Three, "Developing Presentation Skills," brings a speech to the point of presentation. It covers the use of presentation aids, language, voice, and body to make a speech come alive before an audience. Chapter 9 explains the development and appropriate use of presentation aids to augment the message of a speech; examples illustrate the strengths and weaknesses of each type of aid. This chapter's discussion of how to use the computer both to generate aids and in the actual presentation of the speech is distinctive. So is its discussion of the role of color in the visual communication of ideas. Chapter 10 provides a comprehensive understanding of the powerful role language plays in communication and offers many practical suggestions for using words effectively. In this edition, more and better explanations help students understand why the examples offered work or don't work. The chapter has been streamlined and focused for easier learning. Chapter 11 helps students develop presentation skills, offering useful exercises to develop both voice and body as instruments of communication. The aim of this chapter is to help students build an extemporaneous style that is adaptable to most public speaking situations. The chapter offers a section on how to make video presentations, and adds a new section on how to handle question-and-answer sessions.

Part Four, "Functions of Public Speaking," discusses informative, persuasive, and ceremonial functions of public speaking. Chapter 12 covers the principles and practices of speeches designed to share information and increase understanding, including new coverage of briefings. The chapter explains how to motivate listeners to learn, discusses the different types of informative speeches, and presents designs suitable for structuring such speeches. The chapter concludes with an annotated student speech. Chapter 13 describes the principles underlying the persuasive process. The chapter focuses on how to meet the challenge of persuasion and how to adapt to different audiences. The chapter also discusses designs that are appropriate for building persuasive speeches, and offers an annotated student speech for illustration and analysis. In Chapter 14 we explain the uses of evidence, proof, and argument and how to combine them in effective persuasion. The object is to show students how to form powerful arguments that support their positions on policies or proposals. The chapter concludes by identifying the major forms of fallacy that can discredit persuasion, so that students can avoid such errors in their own speeches and detect them in the messages of others. Chapter 15 discusses speaking on ceremonial occasions. The chapter shows how to use the important techniques of identification and magnification to best advantage. We consider many types of ceremonial speeches, such as speeches of introduction, tribute, acceptance, inspiration, eulogy, and celebration, including the after-dinner speech. This edition adds coverage of presenting awards and how to function as a master of ceremonies. The chapter features interesting annotated speech excerpts by and about Olympic track and field legends Jesse Owens and Wilma Rudolph.

Appendix A, "Group Communication," introduces students to the problem-solving process and the responsibilities of group participants. This appendix also provides guidelines for managing informal and formal meetings, and introduces students to the basic concepts of parliamentary procedure. Appendix B contains sample speeches by professional and student speakers for classroom analysis and discussion.

Highlights of Specific Changes

Throughout the Fourth Edition, the reader will encounter fresh writing and examples, new sample speeches, and a number of specific improvements. Chief among these specific changes are the following:

- Giving more attention in Chapter 1 to the similarities and differences between public speaking and conversation.
- Expanding self-awareness inventory in Chapter 2 to include "cultural background."
- Moving our discussion of "Evaluating Speeches" from Chapter 1 to Chapter 3, so that speech evaluation criteria are linked more closely to critical and constructive listening.
- Restructuring Chapter 4 so that we build from general audience dynamics to specific audience demographics to certain situational factors that can shape the immediate adaptation of a message.
- Developing a clearer conception of the general function, specific purpose, thesis statement, and preview as we tell students how to select, narrow, and refine speech topics in Chapter 5.
- Emphasizing an environmental theme as we selected fresh examples of student speeches for this edition.
- Adding modes of selecting and using speech materials and the uses of humor to our discussion of supporting materials.
- Streamlining our discussion of outlining in Chapter 8 so that we discuss the process of developing working, formal, and key word outlines.

- Simplifying Chapter 10's discussion of "the speaker's language" so that we focus more on the essentials of what language can do for us, how it works, and the standards by which we measure its effectiveness.
- Adding material on how to handle questions and answer sessions as we discuss how to present a speech in Chapter 11.
- Adding "briefings" to Chapter 12 as an important subtype of informative speaking to make our discussion more useful to speaking in applied settings.
- Presenting new speeches and new figures illustrating the interrelationships of proofs and forms of reasoning in Chapter 14.
- Updating our discussion of group communication in Appendix A to include ways to deal with cultural gridlock, electronic brainstorming, and new approaches to group leadership.

Learning Tools

To help the student master the material presented in the book, we have developed a number of special learning tools.

- Every chapter opens with a motivating epigram and vignette. Learning objectives cue students to the chapter content and prepare them for productive reading.
- We were the first to develop Speaker's Notes, highlighted internal summaries that help students grasp, remember, and apply the essential concepts.
- Recognizing that our students are increasingly "eye-minded" in an age of visual communication, we have enriched the illustration program to engage student interest. We have added many enlivening figures and summary tables. Attractive photographs and a new design add to the book's visual appeal.
- Because this book is optimistic and ambitious, respecting students' ability to learn a wide range of vital subject matter, we have accepted our responsibility to provide bountiful examples that illustrate and apply the content in a clear, lively, often entertaining way. We want students to learn a great deal from our book, and we want them to enjoy the experience.
- We conclude each chapter with a summary and a list of "terms to know" that remind students of what they have learned and to reinforce and focus the educational experience. A glossary at the end of the book defines all the "terms to know," offering further assurance against confusion as the student navigates the book.
- End materials for each chapter offer important food for thought in the form of discussion and application exercises and questions. Instructors can make use of these materials for in-class discussion or individual projects.

- Recognizing that students often learn best from the speeches of other students, we emphasize the use of in-class examples to illustrate important concepts in the book. The book abounds with entire speeches, both from student and professional speakers, often annotated so that student readers will recognize these concepts as they take form in actual speeches. One such example extends over several chapters, as we follow the development of a speech on the greenhouse effect from topic selection in Chapter 5 to formal outline and final presentation in Chapter 8. Other selections from speeches contrast effective and ineffective uses of the same speech techniques. Texts of entire speeches are found at the ends of Chapters 2, 8, 12, 13, 14, and 15, and in Appendix B. They represent an interesting array of topics, contexts, and speakers, and illustrate the major functions of self-introductory, informative, persuasive, and ceremonial speeches.

SUPPLEMENTARY MATERIALS

For Instructors

The Instructor's Resource Manual was written by Randall Parrish Osborn and Suzanne Osborn. The Osborn/Osborn manual is the most comprehensive of its kind available, and can be used as a text for training teaching assistants. Part I includes sections on the purpose and philosophy of the course, preparing a syllabus, a discussion of grading and evaluating speeches, a troubleshooting guide, teaching tips for new instructors, and an extensive bibliography of resource readings. Part II offers a chapter-by-chapter guide to teaching public speaking, including learning objectives, lecture/discussion outlines, guidelines for using end-of-chapter items, additional activities, transparency masters and handouts, and a bibliography of readings for enrichment.

The Annotated Instructor's Edition includes general and ESL teaching tips for every chapter.

Printed Test Bank

The Computerized Test Bank includes all the test items from the printed test bank.

Transparencies

Student Speeches Video and Guide   New to this edition, this video includes 15 student speeches that reflect our commitment to diversity. The accompanying *Guide to the Video Program*, prepared by the authors, contains the text of each student speech, an evaluation, suggested discussion questions, and a commentary. Two additional tapes of student speeches released with the third edition are also available to adopters.

Using Presentation Aids Video
Speech Assessment Video and Guide
ESL Teaching Guide
Speech Evaluator Software
CD-ROM Multimedia Presentation

For Students

Speech Designer Software
Multicultural Workbook
Speech Preparation Workbook
Classical Origins of Public Speaking

ACKNOWLEDGEMENTS

Many people have helped improve *Public Speaking* as it has passed through its revisions. For this edition, we wish to thank Margaret Seawell, Sponsoring Editor during the first months of the revision. Margaret has been our editor and close friend for many years. Margaret's successor, George Hoffman, has attacked our project with dedication, zeal, and insight, and we are grateful for how he has handled this transition. Another dear person on the Houghton Mifflin editorial staff, Jeanne Herring, has been supportive in ways too numerous to mention. Finally, we would especially like to acknowledge our basic book editor, Karla Paschkis. More than an editor, Karla has been a collaborator and co-conspirator. Her creative hand is on this book from cover to cover.

In addition, this edition has benefitted from the special help of a number of able persons. Steve Baker, librarian at Union University in Jackson, Tennessee, opened our eyes to the incredible array of electronic research resources that have developed since our last edition. Don Ochs, Professor Emeritus at the University of Iowa, and Kathryn Wylie-Marques, chair of the Communication Department at the John Jay College of Criminal Justice, have developed respectively the annotations and ESL annotations for our instructor's edition. Glen Williams and Roy Schwartzman, basic course directors at Texas A & M University and the University of South Carolina respectively, have transcended their roles as reviewers to become valued advisers and consultants on this revision. Glen has helped us grasp the potential of computers to both generate presentation aids and enlarge presentation options through multimedia. Roy assumed responsibility for revising and improving our test bank questions. Captain Frank Loveridge, basic course director at West Point, demonstrated to us during an unforgettable morning in San Antonio how CD-ROMs might enrich the teaching of our textbook.

At the University of Memphis, Kathryn Hendrix and Brooke Quigly have co-produced the videotape of student speeches for this edition, and David Liban has been the technical coordinator of the project. Dan Lattimore, chair of the Journalism Department, went out of his way to help us, and John Bakke, chair of the Department of Communication, and Dick Ranta, dean of the College of Communication and Fine Arts, continue to support us in ways too numerous to mention, not the smallest of which is their total and unquestioned friendship. Randall Osborn has assumed major responsibility for updating the Instructor's Resource Manual: Randy has worked on this project with both professional and family pride. These are just some of the many who have helped us fashion a better book.

We thank our colleagues listed below, whose thoughtful and helpful critical readings guided our revisions for the Fourth Edition.

Elizabeth Berry, California State University—Northridge

Ferald J. Bryan, Northern Illinois University

Susan Cody, Ryerson Polytechnic University

Charity Granata, Fresno City College

Jim Hasenauer, California State University—Northridge

Lynn O'Neal Heberling, University of Akron

Shirley Jones, Salt Lake Community College

Nancy Yake Kerr, Dean College

Meg Kreiner, Spokane Community College

Sherry T. LaBoon, University of Missouri at St. Louis

Julie Ann Larson, University of Texas at Brownsville

George M. Lawson, Jr., University of Nebraska at Kearney

Ronald Lee, University of Nebraska—Lincoln

Giacomo R. Leone, Illinois Valley Community College

Edith LeFebvre, California State University—Sacramento

William K. Loftus, Austin Community College

Clark McMillion, University of Missouri at St. Louis

Dr. Richard Quianthy, Broward Community College

Roy Schwartzman, University of South Carolina

Deanna Sellnow, North Dakota State University

Deborah Smith-Howell, University of Nebraska at Omaha

Kimberly M. Spiezch, Iowa State University

Glynis Holm Strause, Bee County College

Thomas Veenendall, Montclair State University

Beth M. Waggenspack, Virginia Polytechnic Institute

Robert E. White, Black Hawk College

Glen Williams, Texas A & M University

Kathryn Wylie-Marques, John Jay College of Criminal Justice

Our continuing gratitude goes also to reviewers too numerous to mention of the previous editions. Many of you have lavished much time and energy on this book, and have been candid with your impressions and generous with your suggestions. You have taught us well, and we hope that you are pleased by the continuing growth of this book that you have helped to nurture.

List of Speeches

PUBLIC SPEAKING

PART ONE

The Foundations of Public Speaking

CHAPTER 1

You as a Public Speaker

THIS CHAPTER WILL HELP YOU

■ understand how a course in public speaking can help you personally.

■ discover the social and cultural benefits of the course.

■ grasp the nature of public speaking as communication.

■ appreciate your responsibilities as an ethical speaker.

Speeches are
actions among
people, and, indeed,
most effective ones.
— Georg Wilhelm
Friedrich Hegel

For a long time Mary had worried about taking public speaking.
She had never thought of herself as a public speaker. She was not
sure she could carry it off, so she avoided the class as long as possible. Finally the time came when she simply had to take the course.
She entered the first class meeting with dread and discovered
about twenty-four other stony-faced students who looked as uncomfortable as she felt. Later, her teacher confessed to the class
that he also felt discouraged when he saw the sullen group. Mary
thought about dropping the class but realized that was not really
an option. So she decided to stick it out and try to survive as best
she could.

Her first oral assignment was a speech of self-introduction. Preparing for this, it dawned on Mary why marine biology was so fascinating to her. As she spoke on this subject and became involved
in her presentation, she forgot much of her nervousness. While
certainly not perfect, Mary's first speech did some things quite
well. It helped others get to know her as a person, and it built respect for her later informative and persuasive speeches on the fate
of the oceans. She was pleased when her classmates emphasized
the positive things she had done.

As she listened to other speakers, Mary found to her surprise that
she was starting to enjoy the class. Some of the speeches were
quite stimulating, and she joined in the discussion of how they had
worked well and how they might be improved. The "great stone
faces" began to chip away to reveal the colorful, warm human beings they had masked, and she found herself liking many of her
classmates.

As the term went on and Mary gave additional speeches, she discovered that others would listen to her and take her seriously. She learned to care about her classmates and to rejoice in their small successes as they improved. As she researched her speeches, she learned to keep her audience constantly in mind. She sought out facts, opinions, examples, and stories her listeners would find useful and interesting. Toward the end of the term it dawned on her: *she was a public speaker!* She also could now recognize the strategies, techniques, and even manipulations in the world of communication surrounding her. She knew she would be ready to accept the challenges of public speaking and careful listening whenever the need for these should arise in her life.

Perhaps by now you have guessed the point of our story. There is not one Mary, but there are many Marys. Mary represents all the successful students we have known in many years of teaching public speaking. Her story is their story, and it can be yours as well.

To write your own success story, you need five essential ingredients. The first is your own *commitment:* you must want to succeed and be willing to work toward that goal. The second is *experience:* you must give speeches and learn from the constructive suggestions of your classmates and instructor. Third is a helpful *instructor,* who will encourage your growth as a speaker. Fourth is a *supportive audience* of classmates, who will encourage you and whom you can help in return. Fifth is this *textbook,* to guide and enrich your learning process by pointing out the "hows" and "whys" of public speaking.

While all these ingredients are important, perhaps the most important is your commitment. You must *determine* that you will learn the art of public speaking, that you will find topics that deserve your best effort, that you will treat listeners ethically and responsibly, and that you will be a constructive listener for other speakers. In this chapter we will explain why this class deserves your commitment, help you understand the nature of the art you will soon be learning, and prepare you to meet the ethical challenges of public speaking.

HOW A PUBLIC SPEAKING COURSE CAN HELP YOU

A college course in public speaking offers benefits in three important dimensions of your life. These include personal benefits, social benefits, and cultural benefits. Each area of benefits becomes a powerful argument justifying your commitment to this class.

Personal Benefits

You should benefit personally from this class in two ways. First, you will have an opportunity to grow into a sensitive, creative, and skilled communicator. Second, you will enjoy the practical advantages brought about by improved communication skills.

Growth as a Public Speaker.   The most basic benefits of this class, those that make all the rest possible, are the sensitivity and creativity you should develop as you learn to be an effective speaker. Public speaking encourages you to look inside yourself and explore what really matters to you so that you can share these convictions and concerns. Additionally, the class teaches you how to consider the welfare and needs of your listeners. What issues concern them? Are these the issues that *ought* to concern them? How might the audience react when you speak on these issues? What personal experiences can you draw upon to make them come alive for listeners? How can you build a base of knowledge so that you can speak responsibly?

One special sensitivity you also should acquire is an appreciation for the power of speech. The biggest lie we ever learn is that "Sticks and stones can break my bones, but words can never hurt me." Sometimes words can hurt more than sticks or stones. But words can also create, build, and transform. There is a magic to the art of speaking that has been acknowledged since civilization began. From the time of Homer, nearly three thousand years ago, poets have marveled over the forces that move speakers to eloquence. The Oglala Sioux, for example, think that speaking must have divine origins. They believe that "the ability to make a good speech is a great gift to the people from their Maker, Owner of all things."[1]

As you speak before a group, you will become aware of how people respond to you. A responsive audience can make your thoughts and feelings come alive in ways you have never experienced before. One of your authors experienced this phenomenon in a dramatic way:

> When he moved to Memphis in 1966, Michael was asked by a friend to speak at a campaign kickoff for the first black candidate for mayor in Memphis. The organizers wanted to emphasize the candidate's appeal across racial lines but could get no other white person to speak at the event. He agreed, with some apprehension. "What would happen to him?" — that concern for the self rather than for others that Martin Luther King shamed as he told the parable of the Good Samaritan in his speeches — bothered him as well. Yet he agreed to speak. The audience was huge, and he stood up among the parade of black speakers, an unknown person before an unfamiliar audience, significant only because of his race. His opening lines were, "Long ago a man far wiser than any of us said, 'A house divided against itself cannot stand.'" He paused, and from that audience there came a thunderous "AMEN!" He was startled, but he smiled, and they smiled, and then he went on. As he spoke, it occurred to him what their acceptance meant, how supported he felt by their encouragement, and how strong and vital his

message seemed, as he talked about opening the rusted doors of opportunity to those who had been left on the outside.[2]

There is a mystery here that is hard to penetrate, but it has to do with the joint creation of meaning, an awareness that the speaker and listener work together to make sense of the uncertainty that surrounds them. Such moments can be unforgettable and significant to all who experience them.

There are other important skills you will acquire as you grow into a successful speaker. You will learn how to find a worthwhile topic, how to research it to strengthen your message, how to structure and order your presentation, how to use language that will etch your thoughts on the minds of listeners, and how to present a speech that commands attention. These are not only arts of speaking but arts of living as well. They can make you more effective, not just as a speaker but as a person.

You will also learn to be a more effective listener. Listening is often the forgotten part of the communication process, though most of us listen far more than we speak. Education in public speaking can help you critically evaluate what you hear. Becoming a sophisticated consumer of messages is increasingly important in our society. The daily barrage of media messages directed at us makes the ability to sort out honest from dishonest public communication a basic survival skill. People who cannot make such distinctions are open to exploitation. You will also learn how to become a constructive listener who plays an essential role in the creation of meaning. We examine listening in more detail in Chapter 3.

A final personal bonus of your public speaking class is that it makes you an active participant in the learning process. You don't just sit in a class, absorbing lectures. *You* put communication to work. The speeches you give illustrate the strategies, the possibilities, and the problems of human communication. As you join in the discussions that follow these speeches, you learn to identify elements that can promote or block communication. In short, you become a vital member of a learning community. It is no accident that the words *communication* and *community* have a close relationship: they both derive from the Latin word for *common,* meaning "belonging to many" or "shared equally."

Practical Benefits. The personal growth you experience in a public speaking class also makes possible a number of practical benefits. The skills you build in this class can help you in other classes, in campus activities, and in whatever career you undertake. The reasons for these practical benefits are clear: studies indicate that, on average, we spend 75 percent of each day communicating with others. Of this time, we spend about 45 percent listening and 30 percent speaking.[3] No wonder, then, that the public speaking class applies so closely to vital arts of living.

The practicality of learning how to communicate better extends into the world of business. Corporate managers report that they spend 60 percent of their day communicating face-to-face. A Wisconsin Office of Academic Affairs study identified oral communication skills as a basic factor in the evaluation of job candidates. The study also found that these skills correlate highly with success at work. Similarly, 250 companies surveyed by the Center for Public Resources rated speaking and listening skills among the most critical areas in need of improvement for people entering the work force. An American Council on Education report, *Employment Prospects for College Graduates,* advises readers that "good oral and written skills can be your most prized asset" in getting and holding a desirable position.[4]

The abilities you develop in this class also can help you in life beyond the workplace. Picture the following scenarios:

> **The local school board has just announced that it may remove *A Catcher in the Rye, Huckleberry Finn, Of Mice and Men,* and *To Kill a Mockingbird* from the high school library. It will hold a public hearing on this issue at its next regular meeting. Because you feel strongly about this issue and others refuse to step forward, you decide that you must attend the meeting and speak out for the sake of your children and your principles and beliefs.**

> **A real estate developer is planning to build a shopping center and office complex on fifteen acres of undeveloped land near your home. You believe that such a development will not only devalue your property but also destroy the beauty and serenity of your neighborhood. The Land Use Control Board has scheduled a public hearing next week. To protect your pocketbook as well as your lifestyle, you need to speak at that hearing.**

At such moments, important family and personal values may depend on your ability to speak effectively in public.

Clearly, the study of public speaking offers important personal benefits. This class should help you develop sensitivity and creativity, understand the power of spoken words, begin to master the art of effective oral expression, become a more effective listener, and share the excitement of an interactive learning community. As a result of these benefits, many students experience an incredible sense of personal growth in the public speaking class. What they learn and what they become prepares them for the opportunities and challenges they will encounter later in life.

Social Benefits

Studies of ancient life have made it clear that we are social beings. From the beginning of time we have lived in societies that make our lives possible. It is natural for us to belong to groups and to seek out the company of others. We draw much of our personal identity from the groups we belong to, and our status and effectiveness within these groups depends largely on our communication skills.

Anna Aley, a student at Kansas State University, found herself living in substandard off-campus housing. She brought that problem to the attention of her classmates in a persuasive speech. Anna felt exploited and

The United States Constitution and Bill of Rights protect rights to assemble and speak out on issues without fear of retaliation. Public speaking is vital to the survival of a free society.

endangered by that situation and cared deeply about others who shared her fate. Her persuasive speech (the text of which follows Chapter 13) was selected by her classmates for presentation in a public forum on campus. During that presentation she made such an impression that the local newspaper printed the text of her speech and launched an investigation of the off-campus housing problem. The paper then followed up with a strong editorial, and the mayor established a rental inspection program in the community. Anna's experience is a dramatic example of how speeches, even those given in a classroom, can benefit society.

Although not all the speeches we give and hear are so momentous, our words create ripples of meaning that can spread far beyond the time and place in which we speak. We never know how the speeches we give might ultimately affect the lives of others. Even now, we recall brave classroom speeches given by students thirty years ago supporting civil and human rights in our nation. Their words continue to resonate in our memories and in our lives.

Clearly, the personal benefits of public speaking are tied to social benefits. It is part of our nature to care about the groups we value. When we can help them, we also feel deeply confirmed as human beings. Richard Sennett in *The Fall of Public Man* argues that civilization, serving the best interests of the many, cannot survive without the active participation of citizens.[5] Those who are confident in their public speaking skills are ready to take active roles whenever social problems or crises arise.

The effectiveness of our political system depends on our ability to deliberate and make wise judgments on issues of public policy. At the very least, we must be able to listen critically to those who represent us in government, advise them concerning our positions, and evaluate their performance come election time. We should be able to take part in public discussions in which we learn from others, develop responsible convictions on important issues, and speak our minds for the benefit of others. The entire democratic system is built on open public communication. America's founders realized the importance of freedom of speech when they wrote the First Amendment to the Constitution:

> **Congress shall make no law respecting an establishment of religion, or prohibiting the free exercise thereof; or abridging the freedom of speech, or of the press; or the right of the people peaceably to assemble, and to petition the government for a redress of grievances.**

Such freedom is not without its risks, as noted by Supreme Court Justice William Brennan:

> **Rulers always have and always will find it dangerous to their security to permit people to think, believe, talk, write, assemble and particularly to criticize the government as they please. But the language of the First Amendment indicates that the founders weighed the risks involved in such freedoms and deliberately chose to stake this Government's security and life upon preserving the liberty to discuss public affairs intact and untouchable by the government.**[6]

To be able to speak without fear of retaliation, to have the opportunity to hear all sides of an issue, and to be free to make informed judgments that affect our lives are rights basic to our social system. Acquiring the presentation and evaluation skills you need to keep this freedom alive is a profound social benefit of this course.

Cultural Benefits

Several generations ago, if you listened to the radio (in those days before television) or read magazines, you would find one striking assumption: America was the best of all possible worlds. The attitude typified **ethnocentrism,** the tendency of any nation, race, religion, or organized group to believe that its way of looking at and doing things is the right and proper way, and that other perspectives and behaviors are less valuable. Ethnocentrism can touch everything from the values we affirm and the God we worship to the clothes we wear and the food we eat. Clearly, ethnocentrism is a human, not an American trait, as we shall see more clearly in Chapter 4. But we Americans certainly have had our share of it. Forty years ago, Richard M. Weaver, a noted conservative intellectual and scholar of communication, suggested:

> The Western World has long stood as a symbol for the future; and accordingly there has been a very wide tendency in this country, and also I believe among many people in Europe, to identify that which is American with that which is destined to be. . . . The typical American is quite fatuous in this regard: to him America is the goal toward which all creation moves; and he judges a country's civilization by its resemblance to the American model.[7]

How we talk about ourselves, especially the images we select to represent ourselves, are often the key to such cultural arrogance. In the first half of this century, the "melting pot" was an especially popular metaphor that expressed American ethnocentrism. This theory, which originated in the great steel mills of the industrial East, suggested that as various ethnic and national groups came to this country, they would be blended and melted down in a vast cultural cauldron into "the American Character." While it held out the promise that all the immigrants who had come to our shores might be absorbed easily into our national life and forged into a powerful new unity, the "melting pot" also said quite clearly — to ourselves and to anyone else who would listen — "American is best."

Another problem with the "melting pot" metaphor was that it created a **stereotype**, a generalized picture of a race, gender, or nationality that supposedly represented the essential character of a group. We may have stereotypes of Latinos, or of athletes, or of "rednecks." If we look inside ourselves and confront ourselves honestly, we may discover many such stereotypes. They stick in our minds and become habits of thinking. We may use them because they simplify human interactions or because they are endorsed by a group important to us. Unfortunately, stereotypes can be quite damaging. They may entail harsh prejudgments about others, and may block us from seeing the real value of a unique person who just happens to be Latino, or an athlete, or from the rural South. They may impede our ability to communicate with others in a genuine way.

The stereotype inherent in the "melting pot" theory seemed harmless on the surface. It offered an image of the ideal American citizen, but that citizen always had a decidedly white, definitely male face. Asians, Middle Easterners, and African Americans — just to mention some of the "out" groups — did not mix very readily into a common pot. There simply was no such pot. Moreover, often these people, joined by Native Americans and others, *did not wish* to lose their ethnic identities. Within the melting pot, women simply disappeared. It was hard to champion the economic and political rights of women when the ideal citizen was always a man. Elizabeth Lozano summarizes the shortcomings of the melting pot stereotype and begins to explore an alternative view of American character:

> The "melting pot" is not an adequate metaphor for a country which is comprised of a multiplicity of cultural backgrounds and traditions . . . we might better think of the United States in terms of a "cultural bouillabaisse" [stew] in which all ingredients conserve their unique flavor,

while also transforming and being transformed by the adjacent textures and scents.[8]

A public speaking class is an ideal place to savor this rich broth of many cultures. When a public speaking class encourages us to analyze ourselves and our audiences, we discover these many flavors of the American experience. It can help us open our minds to the valuable contributions our varied backgrounds make to our lives. Understanding our audience would be simple if we were all the same, but how dull that would be! And how exciting it can be when we discover *how* to appeal to and identify with the many cultures our audience represents. You will probably discover that you yourself are "multicultural." One of your authors describes herself as "part Swedish, part Welsh, part German, and all hillbilly." The other is Scotch, Irish, and English with a dollop of Creek Indian. Just imagine the complex cultural heritage of our children! Communication scholar Dolores V. Tanno describes her cultural background as an "unfolding ethnic identity" that includes, in order of her own realization, "I am Spanish," "I am Mexican American," "I am Latina," and "I am Chicana," and expresses her joy in discovering these various identities.[9]

As we strive to understand our own and others' unfolding identities, we must guard against the subtle intrusion of stereotypes into our thinking. Casey Man Kong Lum has pointed out that the main problem confronted by Chinese immigrants in New York City may not be relating to the American culture but to other Chinese. As he notes, there are seven major Chinese dialect groups, each with its own subgroups.[10] To the extent that different languages imply different cultures, any conclusion that "The Chinese feel . . ." or "The Chinese perspective on this problem is . . ." must surely be a distortion, if not a fiction.

Perhaps the best protection against such "creeping stereotyping" is to remember that we are, in the final analysis, talking to individuals. Navita Cummings James, a communication scholar at the University of South Florida, sums up the attitude we must preserve:

> **I am a child of the American baby boom. I am a person of color, and I am a woman. All of these factors have influenced the creation of the person I am today, just as the time and place of each of our births, our genders, races, and ethnicities influence the people we are today.**[11]

When all is said and done, we are all unique. But the many cultures you may encounter as you speak in your class can provide a liberating learning experience. In most such classes you can almost see ethnocentricism evaporating and hear stereotypes cracking and breaking.

Throughout this section, we have introduced the "melting pot" and "cultural bouillabaisse" as ways of thinking about American character. One of our favorite metaphors for the complex culture of the United States entered into public dialogue at the conclusion of Abraham Lincoln's first inaugural address, as he sought to hold the nation together on the eve of the Civil War:

> The mystic chords of memory, stretching from every battlefield, and patriot grave, to every living heart and hearthstone, all over this broad land, will yet swell the chorus of the Union, when again touched, as surely they will be, by the better angels of our nature.[12]

Lost in the immediate crisis of that war, Lincoln's image of America as a harmonious chorus implied that the individual voices of Americans not only can survive but, when heard together, can create a music that is more rich and beautiful than when heard alone.

Lincoln's image of a harmonious chorus may seem out of place beside the noisy contemporary American scene, but it holds forth a continuing dream of a society in which individualism and the common good can not only survive but enhance each other. In your class and within these pages you will hear many voices: Native Americans and new Americans, women and men, conservatives and liberals, Americans of all different colors and lifestyles. Sometimes these voices may seem bitter, alienated, dispossessed, but all of them are a part of the vital chorus of our nation. The public speaking class provides an opportunity to hear the voices in this chorus and add your voice to them.

PUBLIC SPEAKING AS COMMUNICATION

Picturing yourself as a public speaker may be difficult, just as it was for Mary in our opening vignette. At first Mary saw public speaking as a mysterious skill possessed only by the leaders in our society. But she soon realized that she had been practicing for public speaking for a long time. As an infant, Mary developed the most essential tool of communication — language. When her grandfather explained to her why flowers bloom and why she must stay away from fire, she was being introduced to two of the great functions of human communication, *informing* and *persuading*. Later, as she developed close friends and talked with them on every subject under the sun, she began practicing the interaction skills that are central to communication: when and how to listen as well as speak, and what kind of behaviors either advance or impede the flow of feelings and ideas as we interact.

What happens when three people become six, when six become twelve, or when twelve become twenty-four? Public speaking is really only an enlargement of the conversational skills we have been practicing all of our lives. On the other hand, there are some distinctive features of public speaking as communication which we must understand.

Public Speaking as Expanded Conversation

Public speaking retains three important characteristics of conversation. First, it preserves the natural directness and spontaneity of conversation. Second, it features the colorful, compelling qualities of good conversation. And third, it is tuned to the reactions of listeners.

Public Speaking Preserves the Directness and Spontaneity of Conversation. Even though a message has been carefully planned and prepared, it must come to life before the live audience. Consider the following opening to a self-introductory speech:

> It may seem hot today, but it's not near as hot as good ol' Plainview, Texas, where I was born and reared. I almost said "roasted." John has just told us about the joys of urban living. Now you're going to hear about another lifestyle, what you might call a "country-fried" lifestyle.

Compare that opening with:

> My name is Sam Johnson, and I come from Plainview, Texas.

The first version, because of its references to weather conditions and to an earlier speech, seems fresh and spontaneous. The "us" and "you," along with the casual humorous remarks, suggest that the speaker is reaching out to his audience. The second, unless presented with a great deal of oomph, will sound quite ordinary. The first opening invites listening: the second invites yawning.

Public Speaking Is Colorful and Compelling. We enjoy listening to good conversationalists because of their colorful speech. It naturally follows that we are often influenced by what they have to say. Consider the following development of the "heat" theme from the above example:

> That place was so hot it would make hell seem air-conditioned! It was so hot it would make an armadillo sweat! It was so hot that rattlesnakes would rattle just to fan themselves!

Compare those words with the following:

> The average summer day in Plainview was often over a hundred degrees.

The literal meaning of both statements is not that different, but the first contains the kind of vivid, lively conversational qualities that make audiences want to listen.

Public Speaking Is Tuned to Listeners. Public speakers must be aware of the reactions of listeners, and make both on-the-spot and carefully planned adjustments to their reactions. As you develop basic conversation skills, you learn how listeners react. Smiles and frowns, nodding heads, looks of boredom or confusion all are meaningful in conversations. The technical term for these reactions is **feedback**. Feedback is absolutely vital to a public speaker. Smiles and nods of agreement can raise your confidence and let you know that you are getting through to listeners. On the other hand, frowns or signs of confusion or disagreement should prompt you to rephrase or present more evidence that what you say is true. Imagine you were giving a speech about global warming, and some members of the audience looked angry or perplexed. You might add, as you monitor such negative signals:

> **I know it may be hard to accept the conclusion that we are responsible for global warming. But Dr. Tom Wigley, a climatologist at the National Center for Atmospheric Research, recently said in an interview with the *New York Times:* "I think the scientific justification for the statement is there, unequivocally." And Dr. Michael Oppenheimer, an atmospheric scientist with the Environmental Defense Fund, added: "The scientific community has discovered the smoking gun."**
>
> **For our own sakes, the sake of our children, and the sake of the human future, we'd better start believing it and asking what we can do about it.**

A wise speaker always has additional facts, figures, and expert opinions in reserve for such moments. We cover responding to audience feedback in greater detail in Chapter 11.

In addition to such impromptu adjustments, your entire speech should be designed to answer the questions that audiences — knowingly or unknowingly — will ask:

- *Why should I be interested in your topic?*
- *What do you mean?*
- *How do I know that is true?*
- *What can I do about it?*

You must answer "Why should I be interested?" in the introduction of your speech or you will lose your audience before you ever get started. "What do you mean?" suggests that your purpose and language must be clear and understandable. For example, if you said, "A pattern of climatic response to human activities is identifiable in the climatological record," listeners might well respond with, "Huh?" "How do I know that is true?" conveys the natural skepticism of listeners to startling information or conclusions. This question calls for evidence, like that offered above on global warming. "What can I do about it?" comes up in persuasive speeches. It challenges speakers to present a course of action that seems both practical and promising. If you can successfully answer these questions, the response to your speech may be more than immediate feedback: the lives of listeners may be enriched in some lasting way. Your speech and you will have made a difference.

It seems clear from this discussion that public speaking — far from being a mysterious skill — is a natural, but expanded, application of abilities and sensitivities we develop as we learn how to converse with one another. On the other hand, as we move from three to six, six to twelve, and twelve to twenty-four listeners, there are some striking changes in the patterns of communication that we must also understand.

Distinctive Features of Public Speaking

Conversations reflect a free-flowing, spontaneous, fluid process of communication. In this process the roles of speaker and listener are usually not well defined, because the conversationalist is *both* a speaker and a listener in an ongoing interaction. A conversation is a series of fragments that may or may not fit together into a meaningful whole. For example, conversationalists may talk at some length before realizing that they are talking about different things. When that happens, one is apt to hear, as T. S. Eliot's "That is not what I meant at all. That is not it, at all."[13] In contrast, public speaking defines the roles of speaker and listener more clearly. Speeches may seem fresh and spontaneous, but good speeches represent carefully considered research, audience analysis, design, wording, and practice. In public speaking, the medium of communication can affect the message, as in the case of speeches presented on radio or television. Finally, the environment in which public speaking occurs changes dramatically from the typical setting for conversation.

Speaker and Listener Roles Are Clearly Defined.   In conversation it is often hard to determine who is the speaker and who is the listener. In contrast, public speaking emphasizes the role of **speaker,** and there is no doubt who the speakers and listeners are. Whether speakers can take advantage of this prominent role depends on their ability to reward listeners with interesting and important messages. As Aristotle pointed out more than two thousand years ago, our impressions of speakers themselves affect how we

An extemporaneous presentation sounds natural and spontaneous. It allows speakers to adapt to their audience and elaborate on ideas that need further explanation.

respond to their messages. We are far more inclined, he observed, to react favorably when we think speakers are competent in their subject matter and when we trust them. These ancient qualities of competence and integrity form the basis of the modern term *credibility*. Aristotle also noted that audiences respond more favorably when speakers seem likable — when they seem to be people of good will. Modern researchers have uncovered still another important speaker characteristic, forcefulness (or dynamism).[14] Some speakers strike us as vital, action-oriented people. When important interests are at stake and action seems called for, we may turn to such people to lead the way. These qualities of likableness and forcefulness combine to form the basis for another modern term, *charisma*. Taken together, credibility and charisma provide an updated account of what Aristotle called the **ethos** of the speaker, a factor vital to our acceptance or rejection of a speech.[15] We consider ethos at greater length in Chapter 2.

In public speaking, the role of the **listener** is also quite important. As we will see in Chapter 3, ideal listeners are supportive, yet listen carefully and critically. Such listeners seek the value in all messages and listen actively and enthusiastically, rather than passively and apathetically. Finally, listeners help construct the meaning in messages. Because the fate of a message depends on how listeners respond to it, the audience must never be far from the speaker's mind. Indeed, Chapter 4 shows that intelligent speech preparation begins with audience analysis. What needs or problems are foremost in their minds? What subjects might interest them? What biases might distort their reception of certain messages? Such questions are crucial to the selection of your topic and to the way you frame your message.

Successful Public Speaking Offers Carefully Planned Messages. As we have indicated, conversations are fragmentary. They are often tentative explorations, taking many wrong turns — and sometimes even ending there. This drift of meaning can be unpredictable, which makes conversation quite exciting: "If that is true, then that must be true as well. Wow!" But the fragments of conversation don't always fit together into a meaningful pattern, and misunderstandings sometimes occur. In contrast, successful public speaking offers a **message** that is carefully designed to be internally consistent and complete. The message is based on responsible research and considered reflection. It is designed to guide the audience to give sympathetic attention to the speaker's ideas. It has been carefully worded and rehearsed so that it achieves maximum impact. The message is the product of the speaker's **encoding** processes, the effort to find words, tones, and gestures that will convey how he or she thinks and feels about the subject. Encoding is the invitation to meaning that the speaker offers an audience. Audience members respond by **decoding** the message, deciding what the speaker intended, and determining the value of the message for their lives.

Shaping a message is a basic public speaking skill. You begin by selecting and refining a worthwhile topic. Next, you build a message structure in which each point seems to follow naturally and appropriately from the point before it until an idea is completed. We cover the art of speech organization in Chapter 7, "Structuring Your Speech." Within this overall structure, supporting material — facts, examples, testimony, and narratives — give your message substance. We address finding such material in Chapter 5, "Selecting and Researching Your Topic," and using such material in Chapter 6, "The Use of Supporting Materials." To strengthen or clarify a message and add energy and variety to a speech, you may illustrate points with maps, models, or charts. We tell you how to develop such materials in Chapter 9, "Presentation Aids."

The wording of a message is very important. The right words can make a message memorable. For example, in 1994 Republicans effectively used the phrase "Contract with America" as a label for the legislative program they presented to the public. It caught the electorate's imagination and forwarded their cause. On the other hand, the wrong words can destroy a speaker's ethos and impair the effectiveness of a message. For example, one sympathetic senator did not help the cause when, speaking in support of a balanced federal budget, he declared: "We're finally going to wrassle to the ground this gigantic orgasm that is just out of control."[16] We discuss the effective use of language in Chapter 10, "The Speaker's Language."

Finally, you convey your message by the way you use your voice, facial expressions, and gestures. We cover these topics in Chapter 11, "Presenting Your Speech." Becoming a master of the message is a complicated process, but it is a goal you can achieve through practice and constructive advice from your teacher and classmates.

The Medium Can Affect the Message.   Sound travels through air, and that air is the **medium** of the message. In conversation we can usually take the medium for granted, unless someone mumbles indistinctly. In that case, the sound impulses sent by the communicator do not possess sufficient strength and precision to travel successfully to our ears and then to our brains for decoding. The remedy for the problem is very clear: "Speak up!" we are apt to say, "Speak more distinctly!" That kind of blunt, honest feedback usually helps the problem.

As we move to public speaking, the medium can present complications. When speaking before an audience, we are not as close to our listeners. We may discover that we are in a place with poor acoustics or "dead spots" that block sound waves. When such problems arise, the speaker must make immediate adjustments, such as speaking more loudly, distinctly, or slowly.

When speaking on radio or television or when taping a presentation, speakers quickly realize that the change to an electronic medium has profound effects on communication. Radio emphasizes the attractiveness, clarity, and expressiveness of the speaker's voice, but removes the speaker's visual impact. Television brings a speaker into a close relationship with unseen viewers, so personality and physical appearance are magnified. Moreover, either medium precludes monitoring the immediate response of the audience, so direct feedback is not possible. When speakers want news

| Conversation | Speech | Radio | Television |

FIGURE 1.1

Types of Media

coverage, they must often compress their ideas into twenty-second "sound bites" to fit the time constraints of newscasts. Their language must be immediately clear and colorful, so that casual listeners will be able to understand and remember the message. For speakers accustomed to eye contact, the impersonal microphone and the impassive eye of the camera may be unsettling. To be effective, speakers must be able to imagine the audience beyond the microphone and the camera, and speak to those listeners as individuals.

Although a change in the medium of presentation can complicate the speaker's job, effective speakers realize that the electronic media present a rare opportunity to extend their message to mass audiences. We cover media presentations in Chapter 11.

The Communication Environment Changes. Conversation can occur in a variety of settings, and the actual settings can influence the communication that takes place in them. One of the most profound discussions of the ethics of communication, Plato's *Phaedrus,* written in ancient Greece some twenty-four hundred years ago, takes place in a woodland setting that frames and colors its message appropriately. This setting is described by Socrates as

> . . . a fair resting-place, full of summer sounds and scents. Here is this lofty and spreading plane-tree and the [flowering vines] high and clustering, in the fullest blossom and the greatest fragrance; and the stream which flows beneath the plane-tree is deliciously cold to the feet. . . . But the greatest charm of all is the grass, like a pillow gently sloping to the head.[17]

In this setting of natural beauty Socrates envisions the loving nature of communication at its finest. Such communication, he argues, promotes spiritual growth for both listeners and speakers. Beyond the physical setting, the moods and immediate concerns of participants can also affect the fate of a message. Taken together, these physical and psychological factors make up the **communication environment.**

In public speaking the communication environment is both simple and more complex. In public speaking classes your speeches will most likely all be presented in one place — your classroom. This simplifies the problem of the physical setting: you can get used to speaking in one place. On the other hand, the move from three people to twenty-four complicates the psychological aspects of the communication environment. Both the events and the expectations that are part of this environment can encourage or discourage speech effectiveness. For example, your carefully planned presentation attacking "oppressive campus security" could be jeopardized if a major crime occurs on campus shortly before your speech. But a campus incident demonstrating the overreaction of security forces could be a real bonanza. You must be flexible enough to adapt to such events as you make your speech.

Audience expectations are another important part of the communication environment. If your listeners are anticipating an interesting self-introductory speech and instead hear a tirade against tax reform, the communication environment may become a bit chilly. In another time, another place, perhaps, your speech might work — but not in that particular circumstance.

The negative or challenging factors in the communication environment that can disrupt effectiveness are called **interference.** Interference, which we discuss further in Chapter 3, can range from physical noise that impedes the hearing of a speech, such as a plane flying over the building, to psychological "noise" within speakers and listeners that prevents them from connecting.

While conversationalists are often close acquaintances who feel comfortable with each other, public speakers and their audiences can seem like strangers to each other, especially during first encounters. At such times, they may raise psychological barriers to protect themselves from the risks of genuine communication. Speakers troubled by communication anxiety may see listeners as distant, unfriendly, or threatening. Even before beginning to speak, they have raised a barrier between themselves and their audience. Listeners may fear hidden agendas. They may be suspicious of a speaker's motives, cautious about accepting messages, or concerned that what a speaker asks of them may be costly or risky. They may fear the change, even the growth, that can result from genuine communication. They may believe that even desirable change can have unpredictable consequences that will present them with problems. Or, they may have been wounded by a previous communication encounter. Such suspicions and fears may raise the barrier even higher.

Moreover, listeners may be indifferent to a message or distracted by other concerns. Worries over money or an upcoming test, or dreams about the weekend ahead, can further block communication. Stereotypes that clutter our heads with prejudice may multiply interference and dramatically raise the barriers between speakers and listeners.

As these formidable barriers develop, the speaker may lose influence over the listener's decoding. As most of us have learned from hard experience,

FIGURE 1.2

FIGURE 1.2

**Blocked by Interfer-
ence Mountain**

what speakers intend and what listeners hear can be miles apart. Because of
interference, messages may have unintended, unexpected, and unfortunate
meanings. *The art of public speaking is an effort to overcome interference
so that listeners can accept the invitation to meaning offered by the message.*

At the beginning of a public speaking course, the barriers of fear, suspicion, indifference, distraction, and prejudice may seem quite formidable.
Figure 1.2 illustrates the frustration speakers and listeners may feel as they
first confront this "Interference Mountain." Figure 1.3 suggests that climbing this mountain is the first challenge students confront in the public
speaking class. It requires the best efforts of speakers and listeners to success-

FIGURE 1.3

**Climbing Interference
Mountain**

FIGURE 1.4
At the Summit

fully scale its slopes and meet at its summit. This book contains detailed instructions on how to climb above these barriers both as speaker and listener. As you meet the challenge of Interference Mountain, you should discover that you are also able to lower it, as Figure 1.4 indicates. Your communication anxiety will ebb, trust will begin to replace suspicion, involvement will overcome indifference, and respect will reduce prejudice. By the end of the course, you will have made Interference Mountain into a molehill.

Is this a realistic representation of the problem of interference? From our experience, we can say it is. One of your authors once ran for the Congress of the United States and, during that six-month experience, spoke before many audiences. On one occasion he was speaking at a meeting of mothers who were dependent on welfare benefits to support their families. He had a good message and was expecting a warm reception. But the speech fell flat. Later someone explained to him that the welfare checks were late. The women's concern over this delay raised such a barrier of interference that no one could have addressed them successfully that day. They simply were in no mood for a speech. Happily, however, that was a rare example on the campaign trail!

Communication as Transformation

If public speaking were always so difficult, few of us would be willing to try it. Efforts at communication would seem the height of folly. While communication can be challenging, successful communication offers so many rewards that it deserves our continued effort and our commitment to improve our public speaking skills. Such communication can go beyond the sharing of vital information, ideas, and advice.

At some basic level, successful communication implies the sharing of selves. In the introduction to *Bridges Not Walls,* John Stewart, an interpersonal communication scholar, notes: "Every time persons communicate, they are continually offering definitions of themselves and responding to definitions of the other(s) which they perceive." Therefore, Stewart suggests, communication is an ongoing transaction "in which *who we are* (our 'existence and nature') emerges out of the event itself."[18] We agree: *public speaking is a self-creative event in which we may discover ourselves as we communicate with others.* We can grow and expand when we communicate ethically with others. On the other hand, deceitful and dishonest communication will thwart the process of growth.

This is exactly what Plato told us long ago in the *Phaedrus*. Indeed, Plato went beyond the idea of communication as transaction — in which participants are constantly defining themselves — to communication as **transformation.** *Transformation is the dynamic effect of successful communication not only on the identities of speaker and listener, but on public knowledge as well.* Plato realized that ethical communication, which respects the humanity of listeners and nourishes it with truth, encourages the spiritual growth of both speaker and listeners.

While interference presented a few sad and perplexing moments during your author's congressional campaign, there were rewarding moments as well. Over the months of speaking, of meeting countless people and listening to their needs, convictions, and fears, an amazing thing began to happen. He found himself transforming from professor to congressman. By the end of that campaign, he was ready to assume a legislative role. As you grow and develop in your public speaking class, you may notice a similar phenomenon. Like Mary in our opening vignette, you may discover the public speaker in you!

Another amazing thing happened in that congressional campaign. As he learned more and more about the district and its needs, your author decided that the most fundamental problem in the district involved the fate of the many children who were victims of poor nutrition and inadequate prenatal care. Even now, he can remember his own words to those audiences:

> **If you are born in many areas of Memphis, you have a one-in-seven chance of being permanently brain-damaged from poor care and lack of an adequate diet. You and I — we allow this game of Russian roulette to go on all over our city. And do we pay the price! Just imagine the thousands who will never become productive citizens, who will never pay taxes, or who will drift into crime. Just imagine the lost humanity of all these people.**

Then he would plead with listeners to support programs for the reform of these problems. Many of them — he could tell by their looks and subsequent actions — began to see themselves as caring citizens. To sense their transformation was a deeply rewarding personal benefit of these public speaking experiences.

Well, you may say, "I won't be running for Congress." Perhaps not, but be prepared to see your classmates change in response to the good speeches you give throughout the term. The transformative effect of successful public speaking on listeners can be quite dramatic.

Finally, as rhetorical scholar Lloyd Bitzer has noted, successful communication builds public knowledge, what we as a community deem as worth knowing.[19] Public speaking expands and builds this knowledge base. It develops the scope and accuracy of our public awareness. Long after the campaign was over, and the author had finally reconciled himself to *not* being a congressman, a heightened awareness of child nutritional problems lingered in Memphis. The local newspapers launched a campaign to improve these conditions, and he had the satisfaction of seeing at least some of his ideas put into effect.

In these fundamental ways, then, for the speaker, listener, and the state of public knowledge, public speaking can be transformative. This is why Figure 1.3 shows both the speaker and the listener as having grown larger. They also have been drawn closer together. While Interference Mountain has now been lowered to a small hill, the overall communication environment has expanded with the growth of public knowledge fostered by the successful speaking experience.

YOU AS AN ETHICAL SPEAKER

We can hardly open our mouths without our words affecting others in important ways. The topics you select, the supporting materials and arguments you use, the way you structure your thoughts, and the words you choose can all have ethical consequences. When we speak of **ethics** we mean the moral dimension of human conduct, how we treat others and wish to be treated in return.

Because it is so important, you can't simply bottle up ethics in a chapter and then forget it. We shall return to ethics time and again as the book develops. Here we will develop two central themes: *(1) Ethics in public speaking emphasizes respect for the integrity of ideas, and (2) ethics in public speaking requires concern for the impact of our communication on listeners.* Listeners also must be willing to assume an important ethical role in the speaking situation. We shall examine this role in Chapter 3.

Respect for the Integrity of Ideas

Respect for the integrity of ideas means meeting the demands of responsible knowledge, carefully using communication techniques, and avoiding plagiarism.

Acquiring Responsible Knowledge. In another of his dialogues, the *Gorgias,* Plato launched an attack on the public speakers of his time. He charged that speakers, especially politicians, typically are ignorant of their subjects, but that they shamelessly parade their ignorance before the public anyway. Second, Plato charged that speakers pander to public tastes, making listeners feel satisfied with themselves when actually they should be made aware of the need for improvement.

The growing cynicism of Americans toward public affairs and politicians suggests that things haven't improved all that much in the last two thousand years. In October 1992, during the presidential campaign between George Bush and Bill Clinton, a poll conducted by *Time* magazine and CNN revealed that 63 percent of voting Americans "have little or no confidence that government leaders talk straight."[20] It is not a time of great faith in the spoken word.

"Great," you may be thinking. "That's all I need, a skeptical audience, adding more altitude to Interference Mountain. Besides, I'm no expert on many of the subjects I'm interested in, and my listeners will know I'm not. So how can I get them to listen to me with any respect at all?"

Fortunately, you do not have to be an expert on all the topics of public life to speak effectively and ethically about them. If you speak from **responsible knowledge**, your audience will listen to you with respect, especially if you are able to show listeners that they will benefit from your message.

What is responsible knowledge and what does it require of speakers? As we describe it in more detail in Chapter 5, responsible knowledge of a topic includes

- knowing the main points of concern.
- understanding what experts believe about these points.
- being aware of the most recent events or discoveries about these points.
- realizing how these points directly affect the lives of your listeners.

Responsible knowledge requires that you know more about a topic than your listeners, so that your speech has something to give them. *Responsible knowledge is adapted, useful knowledge that takes into account the needs and interests of your listeners.*

Let's consider how one of our students, Stephen Huff, gained responsible knowledge for an informative speech. Stephen knew little about earthquakes before his speech, but he did know that earthquakes were on the minds of his listeners after some recent disasters in California. He also knew that Memphis was sitting right on top of the New Madrid fault, and that this was not good news. Finally, he knew that a major earthquake research center was located at the University of Memphis.

Stephen telephoned the center and scheduled an interview with its director. During the interview, Stephen asked a series of strategic questions: Where was the New Madrid fault, and what was the history of its activity? What was the probability of a major quake in the near future in the Memphis area? How prepared was Memphis for a major quake? How extensive might damage be in the event of such a catastrophe? What could his listeners do to prepare for it? What readings would the director recommend that might shed additional light on such questions?

Notice that Stephen avoided such general questions as "what are earthquakes?" and "what makes them happen?" Such questions might well have prompted long, rambling answers that would simply have exhausted the time available for the interview. Rather, all his questions were designed to gain knowledge that would be of particular interest and value to his listeners. Armed with knowledge from the interview, Stephen was prepared to visit the library and track down the readings suggested by the director. He was well on his way to giving the good speech that appears at the end of Chapter 12. Acquiring responsible knowledge requires time and effort, but it is well rewarded when you are able to bring the gift of such knowledge to your listeners.

Carefully Using Communication Techniques. Respect for the integrity of ideas also requires that you handle the techniques of oral communication very carefully. For example, one frequently used technique is to quote respected authorities in support of your position. Used ethically, this technique helps establish the credibility of ideas by demonstrating that they are not just the dream-children of the speaker — that they are authenticated by experts. You must be careful, however, to avoid abusing this technique by **quoting out of context.** This unethical use of a quotation distorts its meaning. In effect, it is a form of lying and deception. *The New Yorker* describes an all-too-typical example:

> When Newt Gingrich's historical science-fiction novel, *1945,* goes on sale this summer, potential buyers will no doubt be impressed by the ringing praise offered up for the Speaker's maiden literary effort by luminaries of Gingrich's nemesis, the establishment press. "An instant classic!" Sam Donaldson says. . . . Gingrich's publisher, Jim Baen, of Baen Books, says that he intends to build a national advertising campaign around [such] quotes. . . . Baen happily admits that the quotes "may be taken a tiny, tiny bit out of context."
>   . . . Donaldson [and others] did say these things — more or less — but they meant to mock Gingrich, not to plug him. . . . Donaldson uttered his remarks recently on the ABC television show "Day One," and they . . . were meant to parody a particularly purple patch of Gingrichite prose: the Speaker's description of a "pouting sex kitten . . . sitting athwart" the hero's chest. Donaldson's quote in its entirety was "This is an instant classic which will be draped athwart the Speaker's neck by his opponents in every election he runs in from now on."[21]

In more serious policy arguments, quoting out of context can produce an entirely dishonest and misleading effect. In your speeches, quote people carefully and reflect the true spirit of their meaning.

As we talk about the use of supporting materials in Chapter 6 and then again about developing evidence and proofs for persuasive speeches in Chapter 14, we shall be especially attentive to the problem of the ethical and unethical uses of communication techniques.

Avoiding Plagiarism. Finally, respect for the integrity of ideas requires that a speech must be the original work of the speaker and must acknowledge major sources of information and ideas. *Presenting the ideas and words of others as though they were your own — without acknowledging their contribution — is called* **plagiarism.** While preparing to revise this textbook, we found it depressing to discover the extent of such intellectual theft in journalism, literature, scholarship, and scientific research as well as public speaking. As writer Paul Gray said in *Time:* "An author's worst dream is to be accused of plagiarism, of stealing ideas and language from someone else and parading them as original. This charge is a lightning bolt to the . . . writer's reason for being. . . ."[22]

Given the shame and ruin that come when plagiarism is discovered, why do writers and speakers do it? Perhaps it is the pressure of time, of deadlines in modern life, of the terrible temptation to "cut a few corners" in order to win recognition — or improve a grade. Whatever the answer, you should avoid plagiarism — or even the appearance of it — at all cost. Beyond the immorality of the practice, which should be reason enough to avoid it, remember that colleges and universities consider plagiarism a major infraction of the student code and impose penalties ranging from grade reduction to suspension.

So how should you avoid any hint of plagiarism? The most gross form of such theft, simply presenting someone else's speech word-for-word as though it were your own, is easy enough to avoid. On the other hand, there are more subtle forms of intellectual looting, which you can escape by observing certain rules of conduct.

You should not summarize an article from a newspaper or magazine and present it as your speech. For starters, the speech will probably not be very good, because it will not have been designed for your particular audience. Because it does not bear the stamp of your own thinking and feeling, it will not seem authentic. And because the speech is not really a part of you, it will be hard for you to present it effectively. Instead of nourishing listeners with your ideas and feelings, it will seem as though you have simply opened a can and warmed up its contents. Do not cheat yourself and disappoint an audience this way. You should also be careful about relying too much on any single source of information. Instead, gather facts and ideas from a variety of sources, develop your own thinking about what they mean to you and your listeners, and present them in your own words.

You should credit the sources of ideas in your speech. When you quote someone, directly or by paraphrase, let your listeners know. Also give credit to the sources of ideas and information in your speech. Rather than simply saying:

> **The dean of the College of Communication at Boston University resigned after he presented a commencement address that was plagiarized.**

say instead:

> **According to the *Boston Globe* of July 2, 1991, the dean of the College of Communication at Boston University presented a plagiarized speech**

How to Avoid Plagiarism

SPEAKER'S NOTES

1 Never summarize a single article for a speech. You should not simply parrot other people's language and ideas.

2 Get information and ideas from a variety of sources; then combine and interpret these to create an original approach to your topic.

3 Introduce your sources as lead-ins to direct quotations: "Studs Terkel has said that a book about work 'is, by its very nature, about violence — to the spirit as well as the body.' "

4 Identify your sources of information: "According to *The 1990 Information Please Almanac,* tin cans were first used as a means of preserving food in 1811" or "The latest issue of *Time* magazine notes that. . . ."

5 Credit the originators of ideas that you use: "John Sheets, director of secondary curriculum and instruction at Duke University, suggests that there are three criteria we should apply in evaluating our high school."

at the university's commencement ceremonies that year. Then on July 15, the *Washington Times* confirmed that the president of the university had accepted the dean's resignation, saying "It's the duty of all responsible scholars and writers to credit their sources."[23]

By the way, this sad story is true. To make it even worse, a reporter for the *New York Times,* when writing a story about the plagiarized speech, himself plagiarized from the *Globe* account and was placed on suspension.

It doesn't make sense not to credit the sources of your information and ideas. As the above example shows, citing your sources can strengthen your speech. It helps your ethos by demonstrating that you have carefully prepared. And it provides borrowed ethos by associating your thinking with that of respected others — experts, well-respected publications, or opinion-leaders.

Concern for Listeners

Recognizing the power of communication leads ethical speakers to a genuine concern for how words affect the lives of their listeners. We conclude this chapter by introducing two related ideas: how the "other" orientation of public speaking requires us to be more ethically sensitive, and how applying universal values may help us overcome the problems of audience diversity.

Developing an "Other" Orientation. Mary, in our opening story, begins her public speaking class with a great deal of concern about her personal fate. During the class, however, as she becomes more confident about her competence as a speaker, and as she comes to know and grow fond of her classmates, she increasingly designs her speeches with her audience in mind. In so doing, Mary develops an "other" orientation. Her thinking has expanded from a concern for self to a concern for her listeners. In the process she will have grown out of **egocentrism**, the tendency to believe that our thoughts, dreams, interests, and desires are or should be shared by others. Jaksa and Pritchard, in *Communication Ethics: Methods of Analysis*, offer a pertinent example:

> All too often we assume that others share our enthusiasm for a certain topic of conversation. This was once humorously brought to the attention of one of the authors of this text. After offering a lengthy explanation of the importance of egocentricity in Kohlberg's theory of moral development, he was greeted with this response from a student. "I think I understand what egocentric thinking is. Here's an example. You're interested in Kohlberg. So you assume we are, too."[24]

The double irony here is that the moral maturation from egocentric to other-centered thinking is the direction of the process that Kohlberg describes! The discipline of the public speaking class encourages this desirable growth into an "other" orientation, and into the expansion of the self that this growth implies.

Applying Universal Values. We have already noted that the public speaking class encourages us to counter ethnocentrism, which is the group parallel to egocentrism in that it holds up our own culture as the most desirable model. We learn to respect each other's cultures and to look through different cultural windows on the world. But this also presents us with a problem. If your class represents many cultures, each offering a different outlook, then how can you frame a speech that will communicate and appeal across these many audiences-within-an-audience?

One answer to this perplexing problem has been offered by Rushworth M. Kidder, former senior columnist for *The Christian Science Monitor* and president of the Institute for Global Ethics. In his book *Shared Values for a Troubled World,* Kidder reports interviews with leading moral representatives of many cultures that indicate the existence of a global code of ethical conduct, centering on the deeply and widely shared values of *love, truthfulness, fairness, freedom, unity, tolerance, responsibility, and respect for life.*[25] If Kidder is correct, appeals to these fundamental values should resonate in any culture, and should be well received across the many audiences-within-an-audience which may make up your public speaking class. We shall say more about how to effectively engage such values in Chapter 4.

IN SUMMARY

How a Course in Public Speaking Can Help You. This class deserves your commitment because of the significant benefits it offers. Personally, you should benefit from the opportunity to grow as a sensitive, skilled communicator, and from the practical advantages such growth makes possible. You should also become a more effective member of society. Self-government cannot work without responsible and effective public communication, and public speaking is the basic form of such communication. The public speaking class can expose you to different cultures as you hear others express their lifestyles, values, and concerns. Such exposure can counter *ethnocentrism,* the tendency to feel that our way to live is the right way.

Public Speaking as Communication.   Public speaking builds upon the basic communication skills we originally develop as we acquire language and learn how to converse with others. As expanded conversation, public speaking preserves the natural directness and spontaneity and the colorful and compelling qualities of good conversation. Like conversation, public speaking is tuned to the reactions of listeners and makes adjustments to this *feedback.* Speeches are also designed with the reactions of listeners in mind.

In contrast with conversation, public speaking defines the roles of speaker and listener more clearly. Public speaking gives prominence to the *speaker.* The *ethos* of a speaker, based on audience perceptions of the speaker's competence and integrity, likableness and forcefulness, can be critical to the success of a speech. A successful speech is carefully planned to be internally consistent and complete. Its *message,* the structure of ideas, words, presentation aids, vocal patterns, and body language, travels through a *medium* that connects the speaker with an *audience.* The speaker *encodes* the message, the listener *decodes* its meaning. Misunderstandings arise when message and meaning are far apart. The *communication environment* can promote or impede understanding. To achieve effective communication, the speaker must overcome *interference* that can block or distort the message. Successful communication can result in the *transformation* of speaker, audience, and the knowledge they share.

You as an Ethical Speaker.   Ethical considerations in public speaking are inescapable. Ethical public speaking emphasizes respect for the integrity of ideas, and concern for the impact of communication on listeners. Respect for the integrity of ideas means meeting the demands of *responsible knowledge,* carefully using communication techniques, and avoiding *plagiarism.* Responsible knowledge is useful knowledge. It requires having up-to-date information on the major points of a topic, what the most respected experts have to say about it, and how these points affect your immediate audience. Plagiarism is intellectual theft. Being convicted or even suspected of such a crime can damage your ethos beyond repair.

Concern for listeners comes as you develop an "other" orientation in your public speaking class to balance the *egocentrism,* or excessive preoccupation with the self, that you may bring to such a class. You can solve the problem of adapting to the many cultures that may be represented in your class if you base your appeals in a global code of ethics.

TERMS TO KNOW

ethnocentrism	interference
stereotype	decoding process
feedback	transaction
speaker	transformation
ethos	ethics
listener	responsible knowledge
message	quoting out of context
encoding process	plagiarism
medium	egocentrism
communication environment	

DISCUSSION

1. Look for symptoms of ethnocentrism and egocentrism among newsmakers of the day. What impact do these attitudes have on events and on the ethos of those who speak in connection with them? Share your ideas in class.

2. Identify some stereotypes at work in your own thinking and in your conversations with friends. Why do these stereotypes exist? What is the result of their existence?

3. Discuss how the ethics of communication might be applied to advertising. Bring to class an example of an advertisement that you think is unethical and explain why.

4. What personal and social benefits are lost in societies that do not encourage the free and open exchange of ideas?

5. Do you agree that it is better to think of American culture as a "chorus" rather than as a "melting pot"? What images of American identity do you prefer, and why?

APPLICATION

1. Develop your own personal statement of commitment. What do you hope to gain from your public speaking class? Plan time during your week so that you can work to achieve these benefits.

2. The Speech Communication Association has adopted the following code of ethics concerning free expression:

Credo for Free and Responsible
Communication in a Democratic Society

Recognizing the essential place of free and responsible communication in a democratic society, and recognizing the distinction between the freedoms our legal system should respect and the responsibilities our educational system should cultivate, we the members of the Speech Communication Association endorse the following statement of principles:

We believe that freedom of speech and assembly must hold a central position among American constitutional principles, and we express our determined support for the right of peaceful expression by any communicative means available.

We support the proposition that a free society can absorb with equanimity speech which exceeds the boundaries of generally accepted beliefs and mores; that much good and little harm can ensue if we err on the side of freedom, whereas much harm and little good may follow if we err on the side of suppression.

We criticize as misguided those who believe that the justice of their cause confers license to interfere physically and coercively with the speech of others, and we condemn intimidation, whether by powerful majorities or strident minorities, which attempts to restrict free expression.

We accept the responsibility of cultivating by precept and example, in our classrooms and in our communities, enlightened uses of communication; of developing in our students a respect for precision and accuracy in communication, and for reasoning based upon evidence and a judicious discrimination among values.

We encourage our students to accept the role of well-informed and articulate citizens, to defend the communication rights of those with whom they may disagree, and to expose abuses of the communication process.

We dedicate ourselves fully to these principles, confident in the belief that reason will ultimately prevail in a free marketplace of ideas.

Working in small groups, discuss how you would adapt this credo into a code of ethics for use in your public speaking class. Each group should present the code it proposes to the class, and the class should determine a code of ethics to be used during the term.

3. Begin keeping a speech evaluation notebook in which you record comments on effective and ineffective, and ethical and unethical speeches you hear both in and out of class. As you observe speeches, ask yourself the following twelve questions:

   (1) How did the speaker rate in terms of ethos?

   (2) Was the speech well adapted to its listeners' needs and interests?

   (3) Did the speech take into account the cultural complexity of its audience?

   (4) Did the speech make an effective connection with universal values?

   (5) Was the message clear and well structured?

   (6) Did the medium pose any problems?

   (7) Was the language and presentation of the speech effective?

   (8) How did listeners respond, both during and after the speech?

   (9) Did the communication environment have an impact?

(10) Did the speech overcome interference to achieve its goal?

(11) Did the speaker respect the integrity of ideas by developing an original speech that exhibited responsible knowledge and a careful use of communication techniques?

(12) Did the speaker exhibit proper concern for the impact of the message on listeners?

NOTES

1. "The Lakota Family," *Bulletin of Oglala Sioux Community College, 1980–81* (Pine Ridge, SD), p. 2.

2. Michael Osborn, "The Last Mountaintop of Martin Luther King, Jr.," *Martin Luther King, Jr., and the Sermonic Power of Public Discourse,* ed. Carolyn Calloway-Thomas and John Louis Lucaites (Tuscaloosa, AL: The University of Alabama Press, 1993), p. 148.

3. As reported by Roy Berko, "Adult Literacy and Lifelong Learning: A Communicative Perspective," *Rationale Kit: Information Supporting the Speech Communication Discipline and Its Programs* (Annandale, VA: Speech Communication Association, 1994), p. 1.

4. From "Statements Supporting Speech Communication," ed. Kathleen Peterson (Annandale, VA, Speech Communication Association, 1986).

5. Richard Sennett, *The Fall of Public Man* (New York: Knopf, 1977).

6. William Brennan, "Commencement Address," Brandeis University, 1986; cited in *Time,* 9 June 1986, p. 63.

7. Richard M. Weaver, "Ultimate Terms in Contemporary Rhetoric," *Language is Sermonic: Richard M. Weaver on the Nature of Rhetoric,* eds. Richard L. Johannesen, Rennard Strickland, and Ralph T. Eubanks (Baton Rouge: Louisiana State University Press, 1970), p. 95.

8. Elizabeth Lozano, "The Cultural Experience of Space and Body: A Reading of Latin American and Anglo American Comportment in Public," *Our Voices: Essays in Culture, Ethnicity, and Communication,* eds. Alberto Gonzalez, Marsha Houston, and Victoria Chen (Los Angeles: Roxbury Publishing Company, 1994), p. 141.

9. Dolores V. Tanno, "Names, Narratives, and the Evolution of Ethnic Identity," *Our Voices,* pp. 30–33.

10. Casey Man Kong Lum, "Regionalism and Communication: Exploring Chinese Immigrant Perspectives," *Our Voices,* pp. 146–51.

11. Navita Cummings James, "When Miss America Was Always White," *Our Voices,* p. 43.

12. T. Harry Williams, ed., *Abraham Lincoln: Selected Speeches, Messages, and Letters* (New York: Holt, Rinehart and Winston, 1964), p. 148.

13. From "The Love Song of J. Alfred Prufrock," *T. S. Eliot: Collected Poems, 1909–1935* (New York: Harcourt, Brace and Company, 1936), p. 16.

14. See the discussion summarizing ethos-related research in James C. McCroskey, *An Introduction to Rhetorical Communication* (Englewood

Cliffs, NJ: Prentice Hall, 1993), pp. 78–98, and a critique of such research in Gary Cronkhite and Jo Liska, "A Critique of Factor Analytic Approaches to the Study of Credibility," *Communication Monographs* 43 (1976): 91–107.

15. Book 2.1 of the *Rhetoric,* trans. Lane Cooper (New York: Appleton-Century-Crofts, 1932), p. 92.

16. Cited in *Newsweek,* 25 May 1992, p. 21.

17. *The Dialogues of Plato,* trans. Benjamin Jowett, in Great Books of the Western World, vol. 7 (Chicago: Encyclopaedia Britannica, Inc., 1952), p. 116. See the analysis by Richard M. Weaver, "The *Phaedrus* and the Nature of Rhetoric," *Language Is Sermonic,* pp. 57–83.

18. John Stewart, ed., *Bridges Not Walls: A Book About Interpersonal Communication,* 5th ed. (New York: McGraw-Hill Publishing Company, 1990), p. 22.

19. Lloyd F. Bitzer, "Rhetoric and Public Knowledge," *Rhetoric, Philosophy, and Literature: An Exploration,* ed. Don M. Burks (West Lafayette, IN: Purdue University press, 1978), pp. 67–93.

20. "Lies, Lies, Lies," *Time,* 5 October 1992, p. 32.

21. "The Talk of the Town," *The New Yorker,* 27 April 1995, p. 37.

22. "The Purloined Letters," *Time,* 26 April 1993, p. 59.

23. According to *Washington Times,* 15 July 1991, p. B10, and "Recycling in the Newsroom," *Time,* 29 July 1991, p. 59.

24. James A. Jaksa and Michael S. Pritchard, *Communication Ethics: Methods of Analysis,* 2nd ed. (Belmont, CA: Wadsworth Publishing Company, 1994), p. 94.

25. Rushworth M. Kidder, *Shared Values for a Troubled World: Conversations with Men and Women of Conscience* (San Francisco: Jossey-Bass Publishers, Inc., 1994).

CHAPTER 2

Your First Speech

THIS CHAPTER WILL HELP YOU

- understand the impressions you make on others as a speaker.
- select the best way to introduce yourself or someone else.
- develop an effective introduction, body, and conclusion for your first speech.
- compose full and key-word outlines for your first speech.
- build effective presentation skills, keeping the focus on ideas.
- control communication anxiety.

Without speech there would be no community. . . . Language, taken as a whole, becomes the gateway to a new world.

— Ernst Cassirer

Jimmy Green worried about his introductory speech. How could he give a speech about himself when nothing exciting had ever happened to him? Jimmy opened his speech on growing up in Decatur County by referring to a popular song, "A Country Boy Can Survive." Then he captivated his urban audience with delightful descriptions of jug fishing for catfish and night-long barbecues where "more than the pig got sauced." Jimmy was surprised that the class found his speech not only interesting but fascinating.

In the discussion following her introductory speech, Sandra Baltz told her classmates that she was taking the course on a pass-fail option. She had dreaded the class and had put it off as long as possible because she felt she wasn't good at talking to groups and was afraid she would do poorly. Her successful speech of self-introduction appears at the end of this chapter.

Anne Gilbert, an engineering student, introduced Spider Lockridge, defensive halfback on the football team. She told the class that although Spider was best known for his fierce tackles, there was another side to his personality. Spider's hobby was writing poetry. Anne read several of his poems to the class, revealing him as a sensitive and witty person. Later, Anne said she was surprised her audience was not more aware of how nervous she had felt.

Many of us do not appreciate the value of our experiences or realize that others can find us quite interesting. Most of us underestimate our speaking ability. Even though we spend a lot of time talking each day, the idea of "public speaking" seems intimidating. We worry that everyone will know how anxious we are and are amazed when we discover that listeners are so caught up with what we are saying that they don't even notice our nervousness. All the students just described surprised themselves by giving excellent introductory speeches.

The initial speeches in a class can help build a communication environment that nurtures effective speaking and listening. No matter what the exact nature of your assignment, your first challenge is to present yourself as a credible source of ideas. In this chapter we show you how to begin building credibility as you introduce yourself or others. We discuss how to find the best topic for such speeches and how to develop and present them convincingly.

Before the first speeches, you and your classmates are usually strangers. You may even be a stranger to yourself! Introductory speeches give you a chance to explore your personality. These speeches also serve as an icebreaker, giving members of the class a chance to know each other better. You will probably find that your classmates are a diverse and interesting group, and you should begin to develop an appreciation for them as individuals. What you learn about other class members also will help you prepare your later speeches. It will give you insights into the knowledge, interests, attitudes, and motivations of your listeners that you can use to adapt your messages. Because it is easier to communicate with people you know, you should also feel more comfortable about speaking before the class.

Even more important, regardless of the type of your introductory speech assignment, your first speech can be helpful in establishing your credentials for later messages. Indeed, whenever you speak to a new audience, you will have to establish your credibility on your topic. As we noted in Chapter 1, people are more likely to respond favorably to those they respect and like.

Gaining skill in introducing yourself also may help you in later life. Although formal speeches of self-introduction are rare in the world beyond the classroom, the skills you learn in this chapter will help you learn how to present your best self to others. They may enable you to make a favorable first impression at a job interview or at a social gathering. You deserve to make a good impression on others, just as people deserve to have their best cases presented in a court of law. The analogy is good, because others are constantly judging us from such impressions.

UNDERSTANDING THE IMPRESSIONS YOU MAKE

When you stand before others to offer information, ideas, or guidance, you are acting as a leader. The functions of public speaking and leading are closely connected. You may never have thought of yourself as a leader, but as you develop your speaking ability, you will also be growing in leadership potential.

Both leading and communicating begin with listeners forming favorable impressions based on perceptions of competence, integrity, likableness, and forcefulness. In this section we explore ways you can convey these desirable qualities of *ethos*.

Competence

Competent speakers seem informed, intelligent, and well prepared. You can appear to be competent only if you know what you are talking about. People listen more respectfully to those who speak from both knowledge and experience. You can build a perception of **competence** by selecting topics that you already know something about and by doing sufficient research to qualify yourself as a responsible speaker.

You can further enhance your competence by citing authoritative sources who are qualified by training or experience as experts on a topic. For example, if you are speaking on the link between nutrition and heart disease, you might quote a prominent medical specialist or a publication of the American Heart Association: "Dr. Milas Peterson heads the Heart Institute at Harvard University. Last week in his visit to our campus, he told me. . . ." Note the factors of effectiveness here:

- The speaker has cited the qualifications of the expert, including his connection with a prestigious institution.
- The quotation is recent, suggesting that it contains the latest information on the subject.
- The connection between the expert and the speaker is direct and personal, suggesting a favorable association.

When you cite authoritative sources in this way, you are in effect "borrowing" their ethos to enhance your own as you strengthen the points you make in the speech. Remember, though, that "borrowed" ethos enhances but does not replace *your* ethos. Personal experience related as stories or examples can also help a speech seem authentic, bring it to life, and make you seem more competent. "I lived this myself" can be a very dramatic technique. Your competence will be further enhanced if your speech is well organized, if you use language ably and correctly, and if you have practiced your presentation.

Integrity

A speaker who conveys **integrity** appears ethical, honest, and dependable. Listeners are more receptiv e when speakers are straightforward, responsible, and concerned about the consequences of their words. You can enhance your integrity by presenting all sides of an issue and then explaining why you have chosen your position. It also helps if you can show that you are willing to follow your own advice. In a speech that calls for commitment or action, it should be clear to listeners that you are not asking more of them than you would of yourself. The more you ask of the audience, the more important your integrity becomes.

Let us look at how integrity can be conveyed in a speech. Mona Goldberg was preparing a speech on welfare reform. The more she learned about the subject, the more convinced she became that budget cuts for welfare programs were unwise. In her speech Mona showed that she took her assignment seriously by citing many authorities and statistics. She reviewed arguments both for and against cutting the budget and then showed her audience why she was against reducing aid to such social programs. Finally, Mona revealed that her own family had had to live on unemployment benefits at one time. "I know the hurt, the loss of pride, the sense of growing frustration. I didn't have to read about them in the library." Her candor showed that she was willing to trust her listeners to react fairly to this sensitive information. The audience responded in kind by trusting her and what she had to say. She had built an impression of herself as a person of integrity.

This example also shows how a "halo effect" can cause competence and integrity to be linked in judgments of credibility.[1] Speakers who rank high in one quality may get positive evaluations in the other.

Likableness

Speakers who receive high marks for **likableness** seem to radiate goodness and good will and inspire audience affection in return. True likableness comes only when the speaker really cares about the audience and is willing and able to adapt his or her message to meet audience needs. Audiences are more willing to accept ideas and suggestions from speakers they like. A smile and direct eye contact can signal listeners that you want to communicate. Likable speakers share their feelings as well as their thoughts. They enjoy laughter at appropriate moments, especially laughter at themselves. Being able to talk openly and engagingly about your mistakes can make you seem more human and appealing.

The more likable speakers seem, the more audiences want to identify with them.[2] **Identification** is the feeling of sharing or closeness that can develop between speakers and listeners despite different cultural backgrounds. Audiences may identify with speakers who talk or dress the way they do. Audiences also respond well to speakers who use gestures, language, and facial expressions that are natural and unaffected. When talking to an audience, you should speak a little more formally than you do in everyday conversation, but not much more. Similarly, you should dress well for your speech, but not extravagantly, just simply and nicely. Although superficial, these identification factors can be important. You do not want to create distance between yourself and listeners by language or dress that seems either too formal or too casual.

The character and person-ality of a speaker can influ-ence how well a message is received. Speakers who seem competent, trust-worthy, warm, and dy-namic are most likely to be effective.

When there are obvious cultural differences between the audience and the speaker, identification may yet be built on shared experiences, values, or beliefs. In such situations, speakers can invite identification by telling stories or by using examples that help listeners focus on what they share in common. Such stories may also help the audience appreciate their differ-ences. For example, Jimmy Green's tales of his outdoor life helped his audi-ence understand both him and his background. By educating them and engaging their interest, he bridged the gap between his rural background and their urban experiences.

Forcefulness

Anne Gilbert, who introduced Spider Lockridge as both poet and football player, later confessed to us that before her speech she lacked confidence, was not sure how her speech would be received, and worried that she might make a mistake. But when Anne walked in front of the room to speak, she seemed confident, decisive, and enthusiastic. In short, she con-veyed the qualities of **forcefulness.** Whatever she might have secretly felt, her listeners responded only to what they saw and gave her high marks for her sense of command. You will also be forceful if you convey qualities of confidence, decisiveness, and enthusiasm.

At first you may not feel confident about public speaking, but it is im-portant for you to appear so. If you seem self-assured, listeners will respond to you as though you are, and you may find yourself becoming what you appear to be. In other words, you can trick yourself into developing a very desirable characteristic! When you appear in control of the situation, you also help put your listeners at ease. This feeling comes back to you as positive feedback and further reinforces your confidence. One of our students, John Scipio, was at first a bit intimidated by his public speaking class, but John was blessed with two natural virtues: he was a large, imposing person with a powerful voice. And then he found a subject he truly believed in. When John presented his impressive classroom tribute to Dr. Martin Luther King, Jr.'s final speech, he radiated force, in addition to competence, likability, and integrity:

> When I asked him during a telephone interview why he thought Dr. King was such an effective leader, Ralph Abernathy said, "He possessed a power never before seen in a man of color." What was this power that he spoke of? It was the power to persuade audiences and change opinions with his words. It was the power of speech. . . . In this speech, Dr. King had to give these people hope and motivate them to go on. . . . He spoke to all of us, but especially to those of us in the black community, when he said, "Only when it is dark enough can you see the stars." And when he talked of standing up to the firehoses in Birmingham, he said, "There's a certain kind of fire that no water can put out." And on the last night of his life, with less than twenty-four hours to live, he was still thinking of our nation: "Let us move on," he said, "in these powerful days, these days of challenge, to make America what it ought to be."

FIGURE 2.1
Components of Ethos

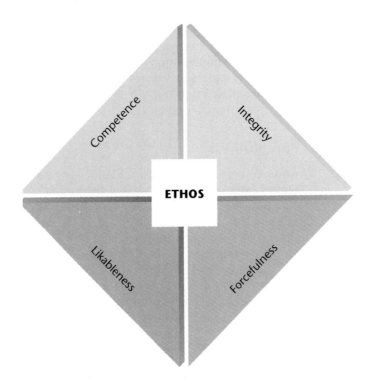

> Dr. King's oratorical brilliance is personified in this, his last speech. Many
> can be referred to as "speaker," but only a select few have earned the
> title of "orator." Dr. King was truly an orator.

To appear forceful, you must also be decisive. In persuasive speeches,
you should consider all the important options available to your audience,
but there should be no doubt by the end of the speech where you stand
and why. Your commitment to your position must be strong.

Finally, you gain forcefulness from the enthusiasm you bring to your
speech. Your face, voice, and gestures should indicate that you care about
your subject and about the audience. Your enthusiasm endorses your message. We discuss more specific ways of developing confidence, decisiveness, and enthusiasm in speech presentations at the end of this chapter
and in Chapter 11.

INTRODUCING YOURSELF AND OTHERS

A speech of introduction is often the first assignment in a public speaking
class because it helps warm the atmosphere, creates a sense of community,
and provides an opportunity to develop credibility. Of course there is no
way to tell your entire life history or another person's history in a short
speech. You have to be selective. What you should avoid is relating a few
superficial facts, such as where you went to high school or what your major
may be. Such information reveals very little about a person and is usually
not very interesting.

The method of introducing yourself or others that has worked best for
our students over the years is the following: *Isolate the one thing that best
defines and identifies you or your classmate.* Answer this question: *What
is it that describes you or the person you are introducing as a unique person?* Now, develop a speech around the answer that builds positive ethos
for later speeches. Jimmy Green introduced himself as a person with strong
outdoor interests and later gave interesting, effective speeches on environmental problems. Sandra Baltz's "My Three Cultures" prepared her audience for the speeches she would later give about Middle Eastern ideas,
customs, and issues. Anne Gilbert not only introduced Spider Lockridge as
a multidimensional person but also established a picture of herself as a tol-
erant person with wide-ranging interests.

To help you isolate the essential traits about yourself or the person you
will be introducing, conduct a **self-awareness inventory** in which you answer the following questions:

1. *Is your **cultural background** the most important thing about you?*
   How has it shaped you? How might you explain this influence to others? In her self-introductory speech (reprinted at the end of this chapter) Sandra Baltz described herself as a unique product of three cultures.
   She felt this cultural background widened her horizons. Note how she

As you plan your introductory speech, consider your experiences. Personal narratives can bring a speech to life and develop a sense of closeness between the speaker and the audience.

focused on food to represent clearly and concretely how these elements come together harmoniously in everyday experience:

In all, I must say that being exposed to three very difficult cultures — Latin, Arabic, American — has been rewarding for me and has made a difference even in the music I enjoy and the food I eat. It is not unusual in my house to sit down to a meal made up of stuffed grape leaves and refried beans and all topped off with apple pie for dessert.

2. *Is the most important thing about you the **environment** in which you grew up?* How were you shaped by it? What stories or examples demonstrate this influence? How do you feel about its effect on your life? Are you pleased by it, or do you feel that it limited you? If the latter, what new horizons would you like to explore? In his self-introductory speech about his life in rural Tennessee, Jimmy Green concluded by saying:

To share my world, come up to the Tennessee River some pleasant fall afternoon. We'll take a boat ride north to New Johnsonville, where Civil War gunboats still lie on the bottom of the river, and you will see how the sun makes the water sparkle. You will see the hills sloping down to the river, and the rocky walls, and I will tell you some Indian legends about them. We'll "bump the bottom" as we fish for catfish, just drifting with the current, and if we're lucky, we might see a doe and her fawn along the shoreline, or perhaps some Canada geese, or even an eagle soaring far overhead. These are the images of home that I carry with me wherever I go.

3. *Was there some particular **person** — a friend, relative, or childhood hero — who had a major impact on your life?* Why do you think this person had such influence? Often you will find that some particular person was a great inspiration to you. Here is a chance to share that inspiration, honor that person, and in the process, tell us much about yourself. In her self-introductory speech, Marty Gaines explained how her two grandmothers had meant so much to her:

> Margaret Hasty was my "Memma." She was the kind of grandmother that everybody knows and loves. The kind that when you visit her house, she's waiting for you at the back door, and you walk up the steps, and she grabs you and she gives you a big hug. And she's always got your favorite cookies hidden in the cabinet. . . .
>
> Martha Clark Akers . . . was my other grandmother. And that's what she was, my Grandmother. Grandmother was very formal, very strict, very well educated. And when you went to visit Grandmother's house, she was at the door. But she didn't yank you up and give you a big hug. She held the door open so that you could walk in, file past, and give her a gentle kiss on the cheek. And then you'd go to the couch and sit down. And when she was ready to speak, she would say "Well, how are your grades?" or "What books have you read lately?"
>
> I didn't understand Grandmother for years. I finally realized that she loved me just as much as Memma, but in a different way. Where Memma loved me for who I was, Grandmother loved me for what she knew I could become and for what she wanted me to be. Both have given me a great blessing.
>
> Now, when I come home from work, there are some days that I'll just grab my children up, and give them a big hug, and tell them I love them. And I think to myself, "Thank you, Memma." And then there are other days when I come home and there may be a nasty note from the teacher, and I know I'm going to have to be strong and strict. And I say to myself, "Give me strength, Grandmother."

4. *Have you been marked by some unusual **experience?*** Why was it important? How did it affect you? What does this tell us about you as a person? The experiences that shape people's lives are often dramatic. If you have had such an experience, it could provide the theme for a very effective speech. George Stacey, a student in an evening class, told of an incident that happened while he was working as a security guard at a bank:

> One afternoon shortly after I started working, a customer had a heart attack in the bank. I wasn't trained to handle anything like that and

he died before the paramedics arrived. I felt like my ignorance had killed him. As a result of that experience, I enrolled in first aid and CPR courses and now work as a volunteer with the county emergency services.

Not long ago, another customer lost consciousness while standing in line at the bank. Because of my training, I was able to render the proper first aid while someone else called 911. She lived, and I felt redeemed.

This speech gave the audience a glimpse of George's humanity and also established his credentials for presenting a later successful informative speech on CPR.

Experiences need not be this dramatic to be meaningful. Rod Nishikawa related how an encounter with prejudice at an early age changed his life and helped him develop personal inner strength. His self-introductory speech is outlined later in this chapter and reprinted in Appendix B. Sharing such experiences can help establish an atmosphere of trust in the classroom.

5. *Are you best characterized by an* **activity** *that brings meaning to your life?* Remember, what is important is not the activity itself but how and why it affects you. The person being introduced must remain the focus of the speech. Talk about the specific elements in the activity that relate to your personality, needs, or dreams. When you finish, the audience should have an interesting picture of you. When she conducted her self-awareness inventory, Laura Haskins realized that her entire life was best described as one frenetic activity. As she considered what it took to meet the demands of her family, home, work, and her university classes, she discovered a very apt image that became the central theme of her self-introductory speech:

Come one, come all, see the magnificent juggler! See her juggle family, home, work, college, whatever comes her way. I wasn't always this good. My juggling act began impromptu when I enrolled in nursing school. My children were preschoolers then and I had to learn fast. . . .

Experience has taught me to plan, prioritize, rearrange as necessary, and pass off to my assistant juggler, my husband, without missing a beat. The International Jugglers Association is reviewing my application for membership. I'm a shoo-in. I may not be June Cleaver, but I am a magnificent juggler.

6. *Is the* **work** *you do a major factor in making you who you are?* If you select this approach, focus on how your job has shaped you rather than simply describing what you do. What have you learned from your work that has changed you or made you feel differently about others? In introducing Mike Peterson, Carol Solomon told how his work as a bartender had influenced him. She explained that his job involved more than just mixing drinks — that it had made him an observer of people.

He sees them in their times of happiness, when they are celebrating a promotion or a grandson or an anniversary. He sees the sadness of lonely people trying to make a connection, and he sees the other people, the predators, who try to take advantage of them. He hears lots of good stories, both tragic and hilarious, and he thinks he may become a writer so that he can tell these stories. Maybe, if we're lucky, he'll tell us sometime about the land shark who got hooked by the hooker.

After her speech the audience saw both Mike and his work in a new light. Carol's introduction helped him gain the interest of listeners.

7. *Are you best characterized by your goals or purpose in life?* A sense of commitment to a purpose will usually fascinate listeners. If you choose to describe some personal goal, again be sure to emphasize why you have this goal and how it affects you. Tom McDonald had returned to school after dropping out for eleven years. In his self-introductory speech he described his goal of finishing college:

Finishing college means a lot to me now. The first time I enrolled, right out of high school, I "blew it." All I cared about was athletics, girls, and partying. Even though I have a responsible job that pays well, I feel bad about not having a degree. My wife's diploma hangs on our den wall as a constant reminder. All I have hanging on the den wall is a stuffed duck!

As he spoke, many of the younger students began to identify with Tom; they saw a similarity between what caused him to drop out of school and their own feelings at times. Although he wasn't "preachy," Tom's description of the rigors of working forty hours a week and carrying nine hours a semester in night school carried its own clear message.

8. *Are you best described by some value that you hold dear?* How did it come to have such meaning for you? Why is it important to you? Values are abstract, so you must rely on concrete applications to make them meaningful to others. As you introduce yourself or others, be careful not to appear preachy or morally superior to your listeners. As she worked through her self-awareness inventory, Beth Riley discovered that her passionate love of life and her strong sense of values were the most distinctive things about her. But how could she make these traits come to life for others? And how could she unify her speech? Beth found an ingenious way:

I think a good way to introduce myself is to look at the characteristics of my favorite color, red. Red is an emotional color. It feels things very deeply and loves to make people smile. Red is so full of emotion that it has to have an outlet. It loves to make music, to sing, and to write poetry. Most of all, red is deeply passionate. It is passionately devoted to principles like honesty, integrity, and compassion. It grieves over the

Self-awareness Inventory

1 Is your cultural background the most important thing about you?
2 Have you been influenced by your environment?
3 Did some person have an impact on your life?
4 Were you shaped by some unusual experience?
5 Is there some activity that reflects your personality?
6 Can you be characterized by the work that you do?
7 Do you have some special goal or purpose in life?
8 Does some value have great meaning for you?

SPEAKER'S NOTES

loss of these basic principles in our society, one in which it's okay to cheat on your taxes and the basic working principle of government seems to be "screw the poor." Red is passionate in its anger. It is angry over the needless suffering of the homeless in a nation of wealth and excess. . . . If you see me around campus, and you can't remember my name, just call me Red.

As you explore your own background or that of a classmate, we suggest that you ask all the probe questions within the self-awareness inventory. Don't be satisfied with the first idea that comes to you. You should find this thorough examination of yourself and others to be quite rewarding.

DEVELOPING YOUR FIRST SPEECH

The first speech that you give in class will usually be very brief. You may be asked to introduce yourself or a classmate, to describe a place or object, or to make a point and support it with information and an example or story. Whatever your first assignment, you must keep its design simple. Your speech must move quickly to its purpose and develop concisely. Plan carefully so that every word counts.

Designing Your Speech

The overall design of your speech will be shaped by the topic you select, your purpose, and the main points you wish to make. Different topics or purposes will suggest different kinds of designs. We discuss these options in Chapters 12 and 13, and you may wish to refer to these chapters as you plan your first speech. Let us look at how a design might develop in a self-introductory speech.

If you decide that the major factor in your life was environmental — the neighborhood in which you grew up — then you might select a *categorical* design. You could begin with the setting, a description of a street scene in which you capture the sights, sounds, and smells of the locale: "I can always tell a Swedish neighborhood by the smell of *lutefisk* on Friday afternoons." Next you might describe the people, focusing on a certain neighbor who influenced you — perhaps the neighborhood grocer, who loved America with a patriotic passion, helped those in need, and always voted stubbornly for the Socialist party. Finally, you might talk about the street games you played as a child and what they taught you about people and yourself. This "setting-people-games" categorical design structures your speech in an orderly manner.

The example also suggests how the introduction, body, and conclusion of your speech should be closely related. Your introduction could be the opening street scene that sets the stage for the rest of your speech. In the body of the speech you could describe the people, using the grocer as an extended example, then go on to describe the childhood games that reinforced the lessons of sharing. Your conclusion should make clear the point of the speech:

> I hope you have enjoyed this "tour" of my neighborhood, this "tour" of my past. If you drove down this street tomorrow, you might think it was just another crowded, gray, urban neighborhood. But to me it is filled with colorful people who care for each other and who dream great dreams of a better tomorrow. That street runs right down the center of my life.

Other topics and purposes might suggest other designs. If you select an experience that influenced you, such as "An Unforgettable Adventure," your speech might follow a *sequential* pattern as you tell the story of what happened. You would talk about events in the actual time sequence in which they occurred. Again, you could use the introduction to set the scene and the conclusion to summarize the effect this experience had on you. Should you decide to tell about a condition that has had a great impact on you, a *causation* design might be most appropriate. Maria One Feather, a Native American student, used such a design in her speech "Growing Up Red — and Feeling Blue — in White America." In this instance she treated the condition as the cause and its impact on her as the effect.

The stepping stones to success in your first speech are to select your topic, decide on your purpose, focus what you want to say, and determine the design best suited to develop the speech. The design you choose will suggest how you should proceed to open the speech, develop its body, and bring it to a satisfactory conclusion.

Let us consider some additional examples of how this process of developing the introduction, body, and conclusion may work in introductory speeches. Although we discuss these parts of the speech separately, keep in mind that they are part of a larger whole. To be effective, they must fit and work together in the finished product.

Introduction

The basic purposes of an **introduction** are to arouse the interest of your audience, to prepare them for the rest of the speech, and to build a good relationship between yourself and listeners. Randy Block captured the attention of his audience when he opened his introductory speech with this statement:

> **I want to tell you about a love affair of mine that won't upset my wife, even if she finds out about it!**

This opening startled his audience into listening and aroused curiosity about what would follow. Randy next revealed his **thesis statement:** his "love affair" was with a bicycle. He used a categorical design to explain the main reasons he was fond of his bicycle. Fortunately, Randy's speech was colorful and interesting, for any speaker who creates such intense curiosity in an introduction must justify that interest with the substance of the speech. An introduction should never upstage the message of a speech.

Eric Whittington engaged his listeners by reciting a list of place names, pausing after each name:

> **Guam . . . Hawaii . . . California . . . Washington . . . Michigan . . . Virginia . . . South Carolina . . . Florida . . . Tennessee. I'm twenty years old. I've lived in eight different states and one trust territory. I've moved eighteen times in my life and attended schools in nine different school systems. You might think that moving so much wouldn't be good for a person, but it provided me with the opportunity to get to know and appreciate many different lifestyles. Come with me on this journey through my life and share the experience.**

This introduction prepared the audience for the speech's *spatial* design; Eric showed how three of these areas in particular had enriched his life.

Suzette Carter opened her introductory speech by establishing a personal relationship with her listeners:

> **Last Monday Elizabeth told us how she enjoyed being an "obedient wife." I admire her honesty and her courage for saying that. I too was an obedient wife and daughter most of my life. But the result was that it took a long time to learn who I was and how I could be independent. I'd like to tell you about this quest for myself, in hopes that it may help some of you who have the same problem.**

Suzette's speech followed a sequential design, tracing major relevant events in her life. Introductions serve a vital function: they set the tone for the speech to come and give the audience a "mental map" of the design the speech will follow. The best introductions tend to be written after the body of the speech — after all, it is difficult to draw a map if you don't know where you are going. We provide other suggestions for preparing introductions in Chapter 7.

Body

The **body** is the most important part of your speech. It is here that you develop your main points, the most important ideas in your message. In a short presentation you cannot cover many main points and support them adequately. Limit their number so you can develop them in depth. For a three-to-five-minute assignment, you should restrict yourself to two or three main points. (Determining and wording main points is covered in more detail in Chapter 7).

Returning to our student examples, Randy developed two main points in explaining why he loved his bike: (1) biking gave him a sense of freedom, and (2) biking provided him with an opportunity for adventure. Eric explained his appreciation for diversity with three main points: (1) living in the relaxed multicultural society of Hawaii, (2) living in an industrial town in Michigan, and (3) living in Charleston, South Carolina — a city steeped in the tradition of the Old South. Eric's use of examples to develop these points provided interesting, specific detail that illustrated and enlivened his theme. Had he tried to talk about all the places he mentioned in his opening, he would have gone well over the time limit assigned by his teacher and might have bored his listeners as well. Suzette described three main phases in her quest for self: (1) her life in an overprotective home, (2) her life with a domineering husband, and (3) finally finding herself on her own. *Suzette managed this self-disclosure carefully so that she could control her materials emotionally and not embarrass her listeners with stories that were too private and painful.* Keep discretion in mind as you develop the body of your introductory speech — you are not on a tabloid talk show. If you are uncertain about what you wish to disclose, you should discuss it with your instructor, but the general rule to follow is: *When in doubt, leave it out!*

Every main point in your speech should be bolstered with some form of supporting material — facts and figures, testimony, examples, or narratives. Supporting materials provide content and substance to your message, especially in the body of your speech (see Chapter 6 for further information). Using facts and figures builds the impression that you know what you are talking about. For example, Randy might have mentioned the number of bicycles sold in the United States last year to suggest that others shared his passion for biking. These figures would not only have added an interesting bit of information: they would also have enhanced his perceived competency. Testimony involves citing what others, especially experts in the field, have to say about your subject. Had Eric cited child development experts on the connection between exposure to many cultures and the development of desirable qualities in children, he could have provided even more in-depth knowledge about his subject and himself.

Examples and narratives are especially useful in the introductory speech because they help develop a feeling of closeness between the audience and the speaker. They hold the interest of the audience while revealing some important truth about the speaker or the topic. Narratives should be short and to the point, moving in natural sequence from the beginning of the story to the end. The language of narration should be colorful, concrete, and active; the presentation, lively and interesting. Randy used a narrative effectively to show how his bicycle provided him with an opportunity for adventure. He told about the time he traveled 130 miles in fourteen hours of continuous biking, and of what happened when he crawled under a bridge to escape the blazing midafternoon sun.

By concentrating on two or three main points in the body of your speech and developing them with facts and figures, testimony, examples, or narratives, you can provide your audience with useful and appealing listening experiences.

Conclusion

These students all concluded by showing how the experiences they related had affected their lives. The **conclusion** often includes a **summary statement,** which restates the main points and the thesis statement, and **concluding remarks,** which often tie back to the introduction, apply the message to the audience, and end on a high or humorous note. Randy used these techniques to end his speech:

> Now you know why I have this "love affair" with my bike. I love the sense of freedom and the opportunity for adventure that it gives me. Perhaps you would also enjoy this kind of affair. Give it a fling!

Eric concluded his speech by explaining that moving so much had allowed him to develop an appreciation for different cultures. Suzette explained

---

Preparing Your First Speech

1 Select a design appropriate to your topic and purpose.

2 Develop an introduction that arouses attention and interest as it leads into your topic.

3 Limit yourself to two or three main points.

4 Develop each main point with narratives, examples, facts and figures, and/or testimony.

5 Prepare a conclusion that ties your speech together and reflects on your meaning.

SPEAKER'S
NOTES

that although she now considers herself liberated and independent, she does not think of herself as a stereotype. She is not so much a feminist as an individual. "I'm not Gloria Steinem," she said in her conclusion. "My name is Suzette Carter."

OUTLINING YOUR FIRST SPEECH

You should prepare an outline using complete sentences to help you organize your thoughts. The outline should contain your introduction, thesis statement, main ideas and supporting materials, and your conclusion so that you can see if all these vital elements work together as you plan to speak. In addition, your outline should contain transitions to help you move from one point to another. You should also prepare a **key-word outline**, to use as you practice and present your speech. As its name suggests, this abbreviated outline contains only key words and phrases to prompt your memory. It can also contain presentation cues, such as "pause here" or "talk slowly and softly." Although the full outline may require several pages to complete, the key-word outline often fits on one or two index cards. We say more about outlining in Chapter 8.

In the following outline for a self-introductory speech, several critical parts of the speech — the introduction, thesis statement, and conclusion — are written out word for word. They anchor the meaning you intend to convey and make your entrance into and exit from the speech both smooth and effective. Thus, it is important that they be planned carefully. Note, however, that the body of the speech is not written out, encouraging spontaneity in the actual presentation.

"FREE AT LAST"
by Rod Nishikawa

Introduction

> *Attention-arousing and orienting material:* Three years ago I presented the valedictory speech at my high school graduation. As I concluded, I borrowed a line from Dr. Martin Luther King's "I Have a Dream" speech: "Free at last, free at last, thank God almighty we're free at last!" The words had a joyful, humorous place in that speech, but for me personally, they were a lie.

> *Thesis statement:* I was not yet free, and would not be free until I had conquered an ancient enemy, both outside me and within me — that enemy was racial prejudice.

Body

Rod uses three main points to structure the problem-solution design of his speech. Each main

I. When I was eight years old I was exposed to anti-Japanese prejudice.

   A. I was a "Jap" who didn't belong in America.

   B. The bully's words burned into my soul.

point is supported with facts, examples, or narratives. Note how the outline uses roman numerals in the body to indicate main points, capital letters to indicate the subpoints that develop them, and Arabic numbers to indicate the sub-subpoints that in turn support the subpoints. These numerals and letters are indented progressively to signal the logical structure of the ideas in the speech.

    1. I was ashamed of my heritage.

    2. I hated having to live in this country.

      [Transition: "So I obviously needed some help."]

II. My parents helped me put this into perspective.

  A. They survived terrible prejudice in their youth during World War II.

  B. They taught me to accept the reality of prejudice.

  C. They taught me the meaning of *gaman:* how to bear the burden within and not show anger.

      [Transition: "Now, how has *gaman* helped me?"]

III. Practicing *gaman* has helped me develop inner strength.

  A. I rarely experience fear or anger.

  B. I have learned to accept myself.

  C. I have learned to be proud of my heritage.

Conclusion

Summary Statement: Practicing *gaman,* a gift from my Japanese roots, has helped me conquer prejudice.

Concluding Remarks: Although my Japanese ancestors might not have spoken as boldly as I have today, I am basically an American, which makes me a little outspoken. Therefore, I can talk to you about racial prejudice and of what it has meant to my life. And because I can talk about it, and share it with you, I am finally, truly, "free at last."

PRESENTING YOUR FIRST SPEECH

Once you have analyzed your topic and outlined your ideas for your first speech, you are ready to prepare for presentation. *An effective presentation spotlights the ideas, not the speaker, and is offered as though you were talking with the audience, not reading to them or reciting from memory.*

Spotlight the Ideas

The presentation of a speech is the climax of planning and preparation — the time you have earned to stand in the spotlight. Though presentation is important, it should never overshadow the speech. Have you ever had this kind of exchange?

    "She's a wonderful speaker — what a beautiful voice, what eloquent diction, what a smooth delivery!"

      "What did she say?"

      "I don't remember, but she sure sounded good!"

Practice your speech first using your formal outline, then switch to your key word outline.

Unfortunately, there are times when speakers use presentation skills to cover up a lack of substance or disguise unethical speaking. Lost in such moments is the basic purpose of public speaking — *the presentation of ideas in messages that have been carefully prepared so that they deserve the attention they receive from listeners.*

As you practice speaking from your outline and when you present your speech, concentrate on the thoughts you have to offer. *You should have a vivid realization of these ideas during the moments of actual presentation.*[3] In other words, the thoughts should come alive as you speak, joining you and your listeners.

Sound Natural

An effective presentation, we noted in Chapter 1, preserves many of the best qualities of conversation. It sounds natural and spontaneous, yet has a depth, coherence, and quality that are not normally found in social conversation. The best way to approach this ideal of improved conversation is to present your speech extemporaneously. An *extemporaneous presentation* is carefully prepared and practiced but not written out or memorized. If you write out your speech, you will be tempted either to memorize it word for word or to read it to your audience. Reading or memorizing usually results in a stilted presentation. **Do not read your speech!** That defeats the purpose of public communication because it robs the audience of its chance to participate in the creation of ideas. *Audience contact is more important than exact wording.* The only parts of a speech that might be memorized are the introduction, the conclusion, and a few other critical phrases or sentences, such as the wording of main points or the punch lines of humorous stories.

Key-Word Outline

To sound conversational and spontaneous, use your key-word outline while speaking. *Never make the mistake of using your full outline as you present your speech.* You may lapse into reading it and lose contact with your audience. (The following key-word outline is based on the outline presented earlier.)

"FREE AT LAST"

Attention: HIGH SCHOOL VALEDICTORY SPEECH

Thesis statement: NOT FREE — ENEMY WAS RACIAL PREJUDICE

> Rod felt that abbreviations and telegraphic notations would be enough to keep him on the track of the speech he had planned so carefully. He capitalized his key words to make them easier to see during his speech. Notice his reminders to himself indicating how he wants to present the speech at strategic moments.

    I. ENCOUNTER WITH BULLY
       A. "JAP": DIDN'T BELONG HERE   *Mime the bully*
       B. WORDS BURNED IN SOUL
          1. ASHAMED OF HERITAGE
          2. HATED LIVING IN AMERICA   *Pause and smile*
   II. PARENTS HELP
       A. SURVIVED MUCH WORSE
       B. TAUGHT ME TO ACCEPT REALITY
       C. TAUGHT ME *GAMAN*   *Pause and write on board*
  III. *GAMAN* — INNER STRENGTH
       A. NO FEAR OR ANGER   *Emphasize*
       B. ACCEPTED SELF
       C. PROUD OF HERITAGE   *Pause*

Summary: *GAMAN* — JAPANESE ROOTS — CONQUERS PREJUDICE.

Concluding Remarks: BUT I AM ALSO AMERICAN: CAN TALK ABOUT IT; THEREFORE, "FREE AT LAST"

Practice Your Speech

Speech classrooms often have a speaker's lectern mounted on a table at the front of the room. Lecterns can seem very formal and can create a barrier between you and your listeners. Therefore, if you are attempting to build identification and good feelings, standing behind a lectern may be inappropriate. Moreover, short people can almost disappear behind a lectern.

Because their gestures are hidden from view, their messages lose much of the reinforcing power of body language. For these reasons, you may wish to experiment in practice with speaking from the side of the lectern or even in front of it.

If you plan to use the lectern, place your outline high on its surface so that you do not have to noticeably lower your head to look at it. That way, you reduce the loss of direct eye contact with your listeners. Print your key-word outline in large letters that you can read easily with a glance. If you are using note cards, don't try to hide them or look embarrassed if you need to refer to them. Most listeners probably won't even notice it when you use them. Remember, your audience is far more interested in what you have to say than in any awkwardness you may feel.

As you practice, imagine your audience in front of you. Begin practicing from your full outline, then move gradually to your key-word outline as the other becomes imprinted in your mind. Maintain eye contact with your imaginary listeners, just as you will during the actual presentation. Look around the room so that everyone feels included in your message. Try to be enthusiastic about what you are saying. Let your voice suggest that you are confident. Strive for variety and color in your vocal presentation: avoid speaking in a monotone, which never changes pace or pitch. Pause to let important ideas sink in. Let your face, body, and voice respond to your ideas as you utter them.

CONTROLLING YOUR COMMUNICATION ANXIETY

Almost all speakers, veterans as well as rookies, have some degree of communication anxiety. International students, or students from marginalized cultural groups, often have a great deal of it.[4] As you give your first speech, you may experience it as well. In fact, there might be something wrong if you didn't have some feelings of anxiety. The absence of any nervousness could suggest that you do not care about the audience or your message. We once attended a banquet where an award was presented to the "Communicator of the Year." Before sitting down to eat, this recipient confessed privately to us, "I dread having to make this speech!" We were not surprised when this person, who is now governor of Tennessee, made an effective presentation.

There are many reasons why public speaking can be frightening. Speaking before large groups of people, where one is the center of attention, is not an everyday occurrence for most people. Moreover, the importance of communication in such moments is usually great; much depends on how well we speak. This element of risk, combined with the feeling of strangeness, can explain why many people dread public speaking. The important thing is not to be too anxious about your anxiety. Accept it as natural, and be assured that the general effect of the public speaking class is to reduce such anxiety.[5] Even more significant, you will learn how to convert these feelings into positive energy. *One of the biggest myths about public speaking classes is that they can or should rid you of any natural fears.* Instead, you should learn how to harness the energy generated by anxiety so that your speaking is more dynamic. No anxiety often means a flat, dull presentation. Transformed anxiety can make your speech sparkle. The late Edward R. Murrow, prize-winning radio and television commentator, once said: "The best speakers know enough to be scared. . . . The only difference between the pros and the novices is that the pros have trained the butterflies to fly in formation."

How can you train your butterflies to fly for you? If you find yourself building to an uncontrollable state of nervousness before a speech, don't stand around and discuss with your classmates how frightened you feel, especially with other speakers scheduled that day. You will only increase your own anxiety, and make theirs worse as well.[6] Instead, go off by yourself and practice relaxation exercises. While breathing deeply and slowly, concentrate on tensing and then relaxing your muscles, starting with your neck and working down to your feet. These relaxation techniques will help you control the physical symptoms of anxiety.[7] While you are relaxed, identify any negative thoughts you may harbor about yourself as a speaker, such as "Everybody will think I'm stupid" or "Nobody wants to listen to me." Replace them with positive messages that focus on your ideas and your audience, such as "These ideas are important and useful" or "Listeners will really enjoy this story." This approach to controlling communication anxiety by deliberately replacing negative thoughts with positive, constructive statements is called **cognitive restructuring**.[8] A final technique to help you control communication anxiety is **visualization**, in which you systematically picture yourself succeeding as a speaker, then practice and present your speech with that image in mind. Athletes often employ visualization to improve their performances.[9] Using this technique, you picture a day of success, from the moment you get up to the moment you enjoy the congratulations of classmates and teacher for an excellent speech.[10] To make visualization work best, you will have to develop and enact the kind of script we suggest in Application 4 at the end of this chapter.[11] You must have a vivid sense of your successful day for visualization to be effective.[12]

There are other things you can do to control communication anxiety. First, select a topic that interests and excites you, so that you will get so involved with it that there is little room in your mind for worry about yourself. Second, choose a topic that you already know something about so that you will be more confident. Then build on that foundation of knowledge. Visit the library and interview experts. The better prepared you are, the more confident you will be that you have something worthwhile to say. Third, consider whether you might use a presentation aid — a chart, graph, object, or model. Preparing a presentation aid helps you think through your speech. Referring to a visual aid during your speech encourages gesturing, and gesturing helps release excess energy in constructive ways. (For advice on preparing a presentation aid, see Chapter 9.) Fourth, practice, practice, and then practice some more. The more you master your message, the more comfortable you will be, and the more successful you can expect to be.[13] Fifth, develop a positive attitude toward your listeners. Don't think of them as "the enemy." Expect them to be helpful and attentive.

Finally, as we stated earlier, act confident, even if you don't feel that way. When it is your turn, walk briskly to the front of the room, look at your audience, and establish eye contact. If appropriate to your subject, smile before you begin your presentation. Whatever happens during your speech, remember that listeners cannot see and hear inside you. They know only what you show them. Show them a controlled speaker communicating well-researched and carefully prepared ideas. *Never place on your listeners the additional burden of sympathy for you as a speaker* — their job is to listen to what you are saying. Don't say anything like "Gee, am I scared!" Such behavior may make the audience uncomfortable. If you put your listeners at ease with your confident appearance, they can relax and provide the positive feedback that will make you a more assured and better speaker.

When you reach your conclusion, pause, and then present your summary statement and concluding remarks with special emphasis. Maintain eye contact for a moment before you move confidently back to your seat. This final impression is very important. *You should keep the focus on your message, not on yourself.* Even though you may feel relieved that the speech is over, don't say "Whew!" or "I made it!" and never shake your head to show disappointment in your presentation. Even if you did not live up to your aspirations, you probably did better than you thought.

Do these techniques really work, and is such advice helpful? Research on communication anxiety has established the following conclusions: *(1) such techniques do work, and (2) they work best in combination.* Keep in mind that controlling communication anxiety takes time. As you become more experienced at giving speeches and at practicing the suggestions in Speaker's Notes 2.3, you will find your fears abating and should improve your ability to convert communication anxiety into positive, constructive energy.[14]

Ten Ways to Control Communication Anxiety

1. Learn and use speech skills to develop confidence.
2. Practice relaxation exercises to control tension.
3. Replace negative, self-defeating statements with positive statements.
4. Visualize yourself being successful.
5. Select a topic that interests and excites you.
6. Select a topic you know something about and research it thoroughly.
7. Use a visual aid to release energy through movement.
8. Practice, practice, practice!
9. Expect your audience to be helpful and attentive.
10. Act confident, even if you don't quite feel that way.

SPEAKER'S NOTES

Thus far, we have discussed controlling communication anxiety in terms of what the speaker can do, but the audience also can help speakers by creating a positive communication climate. As an audience member, you should listen attentively and look for something in the speech that interests you. Even if you are not excited about the topic, you might pick up some techniques that will be useful when it is your time to speak. When you discuss or evaluate the speeches of others, be constructive and helpful. That's an attitude you will appreciate when others comment on your speech.

IN SUMMARY

Many of us underrate our potential for public speaking. Starting with your first speech, you can work to build a positive communication environment for yourself and others. You can also develop your ethos as a speaker.

Understanding the Impressions You Make. Listeners acquire positive impressions of you based on your ability to convey competence, integrity, likability, and forcefulness. You can build your perceived *competence* by citing examples from your own experience, by quoting authorities, and by organizing and presenting your message effectively. You can earn an image of *integrity* by being accurate and complete in your presentation of information. You can promote *likability* by being a warm and open person with whom your listeners can easily identify. *Forcefulness* arises from listeners' perceptions of you as a confident, enthusiastic, and decisive speaker.

Introducing Yourself and Others. The speech of introduction helps establish you or the person you introduce as a unique person. It may focus on cultural background, environmental influences, a person who inspired you, an experience that affected you, an activity that reveals your character, the work you do, your purpose in life, or some value you cherish.

Developing the Introductory Speech. In developing your introductory speech, determine the appropriate design to organize your thoughts. Organizational strategies include categorical divisions, sequences of events, cause-effect relationships, and spatial patterns. Your speech should begin with an *introduction* that gains attention as it leads into the *body* of your message and also reveals your *thesis statement*. The design you select determines how the body of your speech will be structured and developed. Narratives and examples are especially useful in developing speeches of introduction. Other forms of supporting material useful in developing the body are facts and figures and testimony. Finally, your speech should come to a satisfying conclusion. Your conclusion should include a *summary statement* and *concluding remarks* that highlight the meaning.

Outlining Your Introductory Speech. You can improve your chances for presenting a well-developed and well-structured speech by building an outline. As you practice and present the speech, use a *key-word outline* to jog your memory.

Presenting Your Introductory Speech. When presenting your first speech, keep the spotlight on the message and strive for a conversational presentation. Never let presentation skills overshadow your ideas.

Controlling Your Communication Anxiety. Use your nervousness as a source of energy. Cope with communication anxiety by using relaxation exercises before you speak. Use *cognitive restructuring* to replace negative messages to yourself with positive ones. Use *visualization* techniques to build a vivid image in your mind of yourself as a successful speaker. The skills training you receive in class will further increase your comfort and confidence. Select a topic that interests you and that you already know something about so that you can build on this foundation. Use visual aids to give your nervous energy a constructive outlet through gesture. Practice until your outline is imprinted on your mind. During actual presentation you should appear confident and avoid expressions of personal discomfort.

TERMS TO KNOW

competence	body
integrity	conclusion
likableness	summary statement
identification	concluding remarks
forcefulness	key-word outline
self-awareness inventory	communication anxiety
introduction	cognitive restructuring
thesis statement	visualization

DISCUSSION

1. Although we have defined ethos in terms of public speakers, other communicators also seek to create favorable impressions of competence, integrity, likableness, and forcefulness. Advertisers always try to create favorable ethos for their products. Bring to class print advertisements to demonstrate each of the four dimensions of ethos we have discussed. Explain how each ad uses ethos.

2. Select a prominent public speaker and analyze his or her ethos. On which dimensions is this speaker especially strong or weak? How does this affect the person's leadership ability? Present your analysis for class discussion.

3. Political ads often do the work of introducing candidates to the public and disparaging their opponents. Study the television or print ads in connection with a recent political campaign. Bring to class answers to the following questions:

a. What kinds of positive and negative identities do the ads establish?

b. Which of these ads are most and least effective in creating the desired ethos? Why?

c. Which of the self-awareness inventory questions discussed in this chapter might explain how the candidates are introduced?

APPLICATION

1. As the introductory speeches are presented in your class, build a collection of "word portraits" of your classmates as revealed by their speeches. At the end of the assignment, analyze these "bios" to see what you have learned about the class as a whole. What topics might they prefer? Did you detect any strong political or social attitudes to which you might have to adjust? Submit one copy of your analysis to your instructor, and keep another for your own use in preparing later speeches.

2. Prepare a full outline of your speech of introduction. On an attached page identify the design you are using and discuss why this design is most appropriate. Turn in a copy of your outline and this rationale to your instructor.

3. Identify any negative messages you might send yourself concerning public speaking. How might you change these messages, using the principles of cognitive restructuring?

4. To help visualize yourself succeeding as a speaker, write a script in which you describe specific details of an ideal experience of speaking. Start with getting up in the morning on the day of your speech and continue to the moments of satisfaction after you have concluded. Once you have completed your script, relax, concentrate on it, and bring it to life in your mind. As a model both for your own script and for your mental enactment of it, consider the following script and instructions for an informative speech developed by Professors Joe Ayres and Theodore S. Hopf:

> Close your eyes and allow your body to get comfortable in the chair in which you are sitting. Move around until you feel that you are in a position that will continue to be relaxing for you for the next ten to fifteen minutes. Take a deep, comfortable breath and hold it . . . now slowly release it through your nose (if possible). That is right . . . now take another deep breath and make certain that you are breathing from the diaphragm (from your belly) . . . hold it . . . now slowly release it and note how you feel while doing this . . . feel the relaxation fluidly flow throughout your body. And now, one more REALLY deep breath . . . hold it . . . and now release it slowly . . . and begin your normal breathing pattern. Shift around, if you need to get comfortable again.
>
> Now begin to visualize the beginning of a day in which you are going to give an informative speech. See yourself getting up in the

morning, full of energy, full of confidence, looking forward to the day's challenges. You are putting on just the right clothes for the task at hand that day. Dressing well makes you look and feel good about yourself, so you have on JUST what you want to wear, which clearly expresses your sense of inner well-being. As you are driving, riding, or walking to the speech setting, note how clear and confident you feel, and how others around you — as you arrive — comment positively regarding your fine appearance and general demeanor. You feel thoroughly prepared for the task at hand. Your preparation has been exceptionally thorough, and you have really researched the target issue you will be presenting today. Now you see yourself standing or sitting in the room where you will present your speech, talking very comfortably and confidentially with others in the room. The people to whom you will be presenting your speech appear to be quite friendly, and are very cordial in their greetings and conversations prior to the presentation. You feel ABSOLUTELY sure of your material and of your ability to present the information in a forceful, convincing, positive manner. Now you see yourself approaching the area from which you will present. You are feeling very good about this presentation and see yourself move eagerly forward. All of your audio visual materials are well organized, well planned, and clearly aid your presentation.

Now you see yourself presenting your talk. You are really quite brilliant and have all the finesse of a polished, professional speaker. You are also aware that your audience is giving head nods, smiles, and other positive responses, conveying the message that you are truly "on target." The introduction of the speech goes the way you have planned. In fact, it works better than you had expected. The transition from the introductory material to the body of the speech is extremely smooth. As you approach the body of the speech, you are aware of the first major point. It emerges as you expected. The evidence supporting the point is relevant and evokes an understanding response from the audience. In fact, all the main points flow in this fashion. As you wrap up your main points, your concluding remarks seem to be a natural outgrowth of everything you have done. All concluding remarks are on target. When your final utterance is concluded, you have the feeling that it could not have gone better. The introduction worked, the main points were to the point, your evidence was supportive, and your conclusion formed a fitting capstone. In addition, your vocal variety added interest value. Your pauses punctuated important ideas, and your gestures and body movements were purposeful. You now see yourself fielding audience questions with brilliance, confidence, and energy equal to what you exhibited in the presentation itself. You see yourself receiving the congratulations of your classmates. You see yourself as relaxed, pleased with your talk, and ready for the next task to be accomplished that day. You are filled with energy, purpose, and a sense of general well-being. Congratulate yourself on a job well done!

Now — I want you to begin to return to this time and place in which we are working today. Take a deep breath . . . hold it . . . and let it go. Do this several times and move slowly back into the room. Take as much time as you need to make the transition back.[15]

NOTES

1. W. H. Cooper. "Ubiquitous Halo." *Psychological Bulletin* 90 (1981): 218–224.

2. Kenneth Burke, *A Rhetoric of Motives* (Berkeley and Los Angeles: University of California Press, 1969), pp. 20–23.

3. Donald C. Bryant and Karl R. Wallace, *Fundamentals of Public Speaking,* 4th ed. (New York: Appleton-Century-Crofts, 1969), p. 233.

4. Marianne Martini, Ralph R. Behnke, and Paul E. King, "The Communication of Public Speaking Anxiety: Perceptions of Asian and American Speakers," *Communication Quarterly* 40 (1992): 280.

5. Heidi M. Rose, Andrew S. Rancer, and Kenneth C. Crannell, "The Impact of Basic Courses in Oral Interpretation and Public Speaking on Communication Apprehension," *Communication Reports* 6 (1993): 54–60.

6. Ralph R. Behnke, Chris R. Sawyer, and Paul E. King, "Contagion Theory and the Communication of Public Speaking State Anxiety," *Communication Education* 43 (1994): 246–251.

7. Gustav Friedrich and Blaine Goss, "Systematic Desensitization," in John A. Daly and James C. McCroskey, eds., *Avoiding Communication: Shyness, Reticence, and Communication Apprehension* (Beverly Hills, CA: Sage, 1984), pp. 173–188.

8. William J. Fremouw and Michael D. Scott, "Cognitive Restructuring: An Alternative Method for the Treatment of Communication Apprehension," *Communication Education* 28 (1979): 129–133.

9. Joe Ayres and Theodore S. Hopf, "Visualization: Is It More Than Extra-Attention?" *Communication Education* 38 (1989): 1–5.

10. Tim Hopf and Joe Ayres, "Coping with Public Speaking Anxiety: An Examination of Various Combinations of Systematic Desensitization, Skills Training, and Visualization," *Journal of Applied Communication Research* 20 (1992): 183–198.

11. The effectiveness of self-devised and enacted scripts has been demonstrated in Joe Ayres, "Comparing Self-constructed Visualization Scripts with Guided Visualization," *Communication Reports* 8 (1995): 193–199.

12. Joe Ayres, Tim Hopf, and Debbie M. Ayres, "An Examination of Whether Imaging Ability Enhances the Effectiveness of an Intervention Designed to Reduce Speech Anxiety," *Communication Education* 43 (1994): 252–258.

13. Kent E. Menzel and Lori J. Carrell, "The Relationship Between Preparation and Performance in Public Speaking," *Communication Education* 43 (1994): 17–26.

14. Mike Allen, John E. Hunter, and William A. Donohue, "Meta-Analysis of Self-Report Data on the Effectiveness of Public Speaking Anxiety Treatment Techniques," *Communication Education* 38 (1989): 54–76.

15. Ayres and Hopf, pp. 2–3. Copyright by the Speech Communication Association, January 1989. Reproduced by permission of the publisher.

My Three Cultures

Sandra Baltz

Sandra's introduction stirs interest and curiosity. Her awareness of public affairs and fluency in Spanish suggest that she is a competent, complex, and interesting individual.

This transition into the body of her speech establishes Sandra's integrity while foreshadowing the idea that serious problems can arise from cross-cultural misunderstandings. Sandra's thesis statement amplifies audience interest in her complex cultural background.

By comparing and contrasting the advantages and disadvantages of growing up bilingual, Sandra continues to build her ethos. We learn that she has traveled widely and is a premed student (competence). We find that she wants to serve people (integrity). As Sandra talks about her dialect problems and family reunions, the light humor increases her likableness. Her statement that "there really is no language barrier among family and friends" is the key to her deeper message, which invites acceptance and appreciation for those who may seem different from us.

Several years ago I read a newspaper article in the *Commercial Appeal* in which an American journalist described some of his experiences in the Middle East. He was there a couple of months and had been the guest of several different Arab families. He reported having been very well treated and very well received by everyone that he met there. But it was only later, when he returned home, that he became aware of the intense resentment his hosts held for Americans and our unwelcome involvement in their Middle Eastern affairs. The journalist wrote of feeling somewhat bewildered, if not deceived, by the large discrepancy between his treatment while in the Middle East and the hostile attitude that he learned about later. He labeled this behavior hypocritical. When I reached the end of the article, I was reminded of a phrase spoken often by my mother. "Sandra," she says to me, *"respeta tu casa y a todos los que entran en ella, trata a tus enemigos asi como a tus amigos."*

This is an Arabic proverb, spoken in Spanish, and roughly it translates into "Respect your home and all who enter it, treating even an enemy as a friend." This is a philosophy that I have heard often in my home. With this in mind, it seemed to me that the treatment the American journalist received while in the Middle East was not hypocritical behavior on the part of his hosts. Rather, it was an act of respect for their guest, for themselves, and for their home — indeed, a behavior very typical of the Arabic culture.

Since having read that article several years ago I have become much more aware of how my life is different because of having a mother who is of Palestinian origin but was born and raised in the Central American country of El Salvador.

One of the most obvious differences is that I was raised bilingually — speaking both Spanish and English. In fact, my first words were in Spanish. Growing up speaking two languages has been both an advantage and a disadvantage for me. One clear advantage is that I received straight A's in my Spanish class at Immaculate Conception High School. Certainly, traveling has been made much easier. During visits to Spain, Mexico, and some of the Central American countries, it has been my experience that people are much more open and much more receptive if you can speak their language. In addition, the subtleties of a culture are easier to grasp and much easier to appreciate.

I hope that knowing a second language will continue to be an asset for me in the future. I am currently pursuing a career in medicine. Perhaps by knowing Spanish I can broaden the area in which I can work and increase the number of people that I might reach.

Now one of the disadvantages of growing up bilingually is that I picked up my mother's accent as well as her language. I must have been about four years old before I realized that our feathered friends in the trees are called "birds" not "beers" and that, in fact, we had a "birdbath" in our back yard, not a "beerbath."

Family reunions also tend to be confusing around my home. Most of my relatives speak either Spanish, English, or Arabic, but rarely any combination of the three. So, as a result, deep and involved conversations are almost impossible. But with a little nodding and smiling, I have found that there really is no language barrier among family and friends.

In all, I must say that being exposed to three very different cultures — Latin, Arabic, and American — has been rewarding for me and has made a difference even in the music I enjoy and the food I eat. It is not unusual in my house to sit down to a meal made up of stuffed grape leaves and refried beans and all topped off with apple pie for dessert.

I am fortunate in having had the opportunity to view more closely what makes Arabic and Latin cultures unique. By understanding and appreciating them I have been able to better understand and appreciate my own American culture. In closing just let me add some words you often hear spoken in my home — *adios* and *allak konn ma'eck* — goodbye, and may God go with you.

CHAPTER **3**

Developing Your Listening Skills

THIS CHAPTER WILL HELP YOU

- understand effective listening and its importance.
- overcome the barriers to effective listening.
- improve your critical thinking skills.
- become a constructive speech evaluator.
- understand your ethical responsibilities as a listener.

When people talk, listen completely. . . . Most people never listen. Nor do they observe.

— Ernest Hemingway

You walk to the front of the room, ready to make your first presentation. You pause and make eye contact with your audience. This is what you see:

In a far corner of the room a student is frantically trying to finish her accounting homework. A ledger is open on her desk and a textbook is open on her lap. Her eyes move from the book to the ledger. She never stops writing and she never looks up.

In the other far corner a student is sleeping off the effects of last night's party. His eyes are closed most of the time. Occasionally his chin drops down onto his chest, and he jerks himself up trying to look alert, but alas, within twenty seconds he has wandered off to la-la land again.

The student immediately in front of you looks like she's in a dentist's office waiting for a root canal. When she looks up her eyes reflect worry and they do not focus on you. She glances away, her lips are moving forming silent words. She's next on the list of the day's scheduled speakers.

Finally, you spot a friendly face — someone who actually looks as though he's ready to listen. His desk is empty except for a notebook. He is sitting alert, a pencil poised in his hand. His eyes are on you. He is smiling. He looks interested in what you might have to say.

good listener can be hard to find. This is most obvious to people who must deal with the public all the time. Legend has it that President Franklin Delano Roosevelt was bemused by the poor listening behavior of people who attended social functions at the White House. To test his contention that people didn't really attend to what was said to them, he once greeted guests in a receiving line by murmuring, "I murdered my grandmother this morning." Typical responses ran along the lines of, "Thank you," "How kind of you," or other platitudes of polite approval. It was quite some time before he encountered someone who had actually listened and responded, "I'm sure she had it coming to her."[1]

Poor listening has its price. If you are not listening effectively in a classroom lecture or at new employee orientation at work, you may miss important information. When people in a group don't listen, the group may make poor decisions. When juries don't attend to the evidence presented, they cannot render a sound verdict. When people who care for each other don't listen to each other, relationships may suffer. At the very least, poor listening skills can create negative impressions of competence. One of your authors recalls talking to customer service representatives on the phone when she was single. After seeming to listen to a problem, they almost invariably asked, "Would you please spell that last name for me." She invariably replied, "S-M-I-T-H!" She always wondered, "If they can't remember or can't spell Smith, how can they remember or solve my problem?"

The listening skills you learn in this public speaking class should also serve you well in interpersonal and small group settings. In this chapter we will consider the nature of effective listening and its benefits to both listener and speaker. We will also discuss the external and internal sources of interference that impede effective listening and suggest ways to cope with these problems. We will then relate effective listening to the analysis and evaluation of speeches. Finally, we will consider what it means to be an ethical listener.

THE NATURE AND IMPORTANCE OF EFFECTIVE LISTENING

Although we spend the greatest amount of our communication time listening to others speak, we receive far less formal training in listening than we do in speaking, writing, or reading.[2] Why is this so? Perhaps educators assume that we know how to listen well by nature, despite a great deal of evidence to the contrary. They may undervalue listening because they associate it with following, while they associate speaking with leading. In the dominant American culture, leadership is admired more than "followership," even though being a judicious follower is one definition of a good citizen. We frequently emphasize speaking while neglecting the obvious fact that listening is essential to any communication transaction. Finally, in a society that admires being "on the move," we may think of speaking as an active, listening as a passive behavior. This ignores the fact that *effec-*

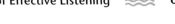

tive listening is a dynamic activity that seeks out the meaning intended in messages, considers their motivations, evaluates the soundness of their reasoning and the reliability of their supporting materials, calculates the value and risk of accepting their recommendations, and integrates them creatively into the world of the listener.

Other cultures place a higher premium on good listening behaviors. Some Native American tribes, for example, have a far better appreciation for their importance. The council system of the Ojai has three main rules for conducting business: "Speak honestly, be brief, and listen from the heart."[3] The Lakota also recognize the value of listening. In their culture:

> **Conversation was never begun at once, nor in a hurried manner. No one was quick with a question, no matter how important, and no one was pressed for an answer. A pause giving time for thought was the truly courteous way of beginning and conducting a conversation. Silence was meaningful with the Lakota, and his granting a space of silence to the speech-maker and his own moment of silence before talking was done in the practice of true politeness and regard for the rule that, "thought comes before speech."[4]**

We shall apply these lessons from the Ojai and Lakota people and regard listening as vital to successful communication.

What Constitutes Effective Listening?

The Chinese symbol for the verb "to listen" has four basic elements: undivided attention, ears, eyes, and heart.[5] This symbol points out some of the basic differences between simply hearing and actually listening. *Hearing* is an automatic process in which sound waves stimulate nerve impulses to the brain. *Listening* is a voluntary process that goes beyond the mere physical reaction to sounds. At the very least listening involves hearing, paying attention, comprehending, and interpreting:

- You must be able to hear a message in order to listen, even though you — don't necessarily listen to everything you hear. You must decide to listen.
- You must focus on the message and block out other noises, distractions, thoughts, or feelings that may compete for your attention.
- You need to comprehend what you hear. You must understand both the language and point of view of the speaker.
- You must interpret the meaning of what you hear in light of your own knowledge and experiences.

Effective listening takes the process even further into the realm of **critical listening.** Critical listeners analyze and evaluate what they hear, then respond appropriately with constructive feedback to the speaker. The analysis and evaluation stage of effective listening involves examining a message rather than accepting it at face value. It adds a fifth element, "mind," to the Chinese symbol. As you comprehend and evaluate, you may offer feedback — visual cues such as smiles or frowns, puzzled looks, or nods of agreement that let a speaker know how you are responding. In short, critical listening allows you to focus on the potential value of messages.

Truly effective listening goes beyond critical listening to **constructive listening.** Constructive listening involves seeking out the value in messages for ourselves and others. We often think of listeners as though they were merely the "unpackers" of meaning encoded in messages. But constructive listeners *add* to a message, sifting it for its special applications to their lives. As they listen to a speech on the importance of air bags in automobiles, they may be weighing their limited ability to buy a new car against the advantages of the new safety system. They may wonder whether there are differences in the quality of airbags from one automobile to another. If they don't hear the answers they seek in the speech, these aggressive listeners often question the speaker later, creating a dialogue that *extends the meaning of the speech.* Such dialogues often produce discoveries, better realizations of public values, and better answers to public questions. In this way constructive listeners join with the speaker in **participative communication**, a process in which both share responsibility for creating meaning.[6] As speakers offer messages and listeners respond, their different worlds interact to produce meaning.

Constructive listeners also look beyond the speaker's words for the motives and feelings that underlie them. They are able to empathize and identify with a speaker even when they disagree with the speaker's position. They "listen" with their hearts as well as with their ears.

The critical and constructive dimensions of effective listening work together. Just as constructive listening makes us want to listen more, and expands the horizons of our awareness, critical listening allows us to judge more carefully new subjects and issues that come to our attention. Effective listening makes possible the transformative effect of successful public speaking, in which speaker, listener, and the state of public knowledge improve because of the communication experience.

Benefits of Effective Listening

Effective listening benefits both listeners and speakers. Among the many speakers they receive, effective listeners learn to separate the honest from the exploitive and the valuable from the worthless. Speakers benefit from the feedback such listeners provide.

Benefits to the Listener. Good listening skills can help protect you from questionable persuasion. Effective listeners are less vulnerable to "snake-oil pitches."[7] Unethical persuaders often try to cover up a lack of substance or reasoned appeals with a glib presentation or with irrelevant appeals. How many times have you seen attractive, scantily clad young men and women appearing in ads to sell everything from soft drinks to automatic transmission repair services? Clearly, such advertising tries to con-

Familiarizing yourself with the subject helps you listen more effectively. It is especially helpful when information is new or the topic is technical or difficult to understand.

nect its products with totally unrelated basic needs. Moreover, consider ads that rely on celebrity endorsements. What are the ads really selling? The products — or the lifestyles and values of the celebrities?[8] Ads may also ask you to buy what "doctors" recommend without telling you anything about the credentials of these "doctors" — Ph.D.s in history may know very little about vitamins! Finally, political hucksters may hope that you won't notice their substitution of assertion for evidence, their appeals to prejudice in the place of sound reasoning. Effective listening skills help you ward off such deception.

Listening skills also have broad application to your academic and professional life. Students who listen effectively earn better grades and achieve beyond expectation.[9] The reasons would seem obvious: effective listeners learn to concentrate on what is being said and to identify what is important. They motivate their own learning process by exploring the value of information for their lives. The most effective student listeners read assignments ahead of time to familiarize themselves with the words that will be used and to provide a foundation for understanding. By listening well to the speeches presented in your class, you can discover the kinds of subjects that interest your classmates. You can also learn from their experience what techniques work best and the mistakes you should avoid. By observing carefully how they structure, support, and present their speeches, you can tell why one presentation was better received than another.

At work, improved listening skills may mean the difference between success and failure — both for individuals and for companies. A recent report from the Department of Labor included listening among the basic skill competencies needed to prepare young people for the world of work.[10] A survey of over 400 top-level personnel directors suggested that the two most important factors in helping graduates find jobs were speaking and listening ability.[11] Another survey of major American corporations reported that poor listening is "one of the [companies'] most important problems" and that "ineffective listening leads to ineffective performance. . . ."[12] If you listen effectively on the job, you will make fewer mistakes. You will improve your chances for advancement.[13] This is especially true in organizations that provide services rather than goods. Companies that encourage people at every level to develop effective listening skills enjoy many dividends. They suffer less from costly misunderstandings. Employees are more innovative when they sense that management will listen to new ideas. Morale improves, and the work environment becomes more pleasant and productive. For these reasons many Fortune 500 corporations provide listening training programs for their employees.[14]

Benefits to the Speaker.   Speakers also benefit from an audience of good listeners. When audiences don't listen well they can't provide useful feedback for speakers. Without such feedback, speakers can't adapt their messages so that audiences understand them better. The participative communication made possible by effective listening makes speaking meaningful.

Beyond allowing speakers to tailor more effective messages, a good audience can help alleviate some of the communication anxiety that all speakers experience by creating a supportive classroom environment.[15] Speakers need to realize that you, as a listener, want them to succeed. Public speaking in a classroom setting is not a zero-sum game in which if one person wins (or does well) another person loses (or does poorly). Rather, when it goes well, public speaking in the classroom becomes a win-win game for all concerned. You can convey your support nonverbally by being pleasant and responsive rather than dour and inattentive.[16] Smile encouragingly at speakers before they begin. Stop talking, clear your desk of anything other than a notebook and pen, sit up, and give them your undivided attention. Show them you're listening to their ideas rather than counting how many times they say "er." When appropriate, nod in agreement with what they say. Show respect for speakers as people, even when you may disagree with their ideas. Try not to overreact when you do disagree; otherwise, you may miss some value in what they say.

An audience of effective listeners also can boost a speaker's self-esteem. How many times have you had people *really listen* to you? How often have you had an opportunity to educate others? How frequently have your ideas and recommendations been taken seriously? If your answer to these questions is "seldom" or "never," then you may be in for a pleasant surprise when you make your presentations. You will soon discover that there are few things quite as rewarding as having people really listen to you and respect what you say. In this class you will learn how to substantiate your ideas with responsible knowledge, how to organize your thoughts so people find them easy to follow, and how to present them with poise and forcefulness. As you become more adept, your audience will listen more attentively and your self-confidence will grow accordingly.

OVERCOMING BARRIERS TO EFFECTIVE LISTENING

The first step in developing effective listening skills is to become aware of what may keep us from being good listeners. Some barriers to good listening arise from external sources of interference, such as a noisy room. But the most formidable barriers to effective listening are internal, based in the listener's own attitudes. At best, these barriers present a challenge; at worst, they may completely block communication. They form the listener's side of Interference Mountain — we must climb above them before we can join speakers in participative communication.

To become better listeners, we must recognize and understand our listening problems. Figure 3.1 will help you identify problems that require your attention. Study the list and place a check by statements that describe your listening attitudes and behaviors.

FIGURE 3.1

Listening Problems Checklist

_____ 1. I believe listening is an automatic process, not a learned behavior.
_____ 2. I stop listening and think about something else when a speech is uninteresting.
_____ 3. I find it hard to listen to speeches on topics about which I feel strongly.
_____ 4. I react emotionally to certain words.
_____ 5. I am easily distracted by noises when someone is speaking.
_____ 6. I don't like to listen to speakers who are not experts.
_____ 7. I find some people too objectionable to listen to.
_____ 8. I nod off when someone talks in a monotone.
_____ 9. I can be so dazzled by a glib presentation that I don't really listen to the speaker.
_____ 10. I don't like to listen to speeches that contradict my values.
_____ 11. I think up counterarguments when I disagree with a speaker's perspective.
_____ 12. I know so much on some topics that I can't learn from most speakers.
_____ 13. I believe the speaker is the one responsible for effective communication.
_____ 14. I find it hard to listen when I have a lot on my mind.
_____ 15. I stop listening when a subject is difficult.
_____ 16. I can look like I'm listening when I am not.
_____ 17. I listen only for facts and ignore the rest of a message.
_____ 18. I try to write down everything a lecturer says.
_____ 19. I let a speaker's appearance determine how well I listen.
_____ 20. I often jump to conclusions before I have listened all the way through a message.

External Sources of Interference

External sources of interference may arise from the environment, from the message, or from the presentation. Most of the time, these sources of interference are relatively minor contributors to poor listening — they are the foothills of Interference Mountain. External sources of interference are often better addressed by speakers than by listeners. For example, if a helicopter passes overhead, speakers may need to talk louder so that they can be heard. We cover how speakers can make such adjustments during their presentations in Chapter 4. Keep in mind, however, that communication is a joint enterprise. It is your responsibility as a listener to provide feedback so that speakers realize there is a problem. If there are simple things you can do to help speakers, like moving to a vacant seat closer to the front of the room, you should certainly do your part.

Environmental Problems. The most obvious source of environmental interference is noise that makes it difficult for you to hear what the speaker is saying. The noise may be constant or it may come and go throughout a presentation. If the general noise level is high, you will need to sit close enough to the speaker so that you can hear comfortably. If the noise is intermittent or comes from outside the room, you may need to close a window or a door. Obviously it is best to do this before speakers start their presentations. If you must do so while someone is speaking, be as quiet and unobtrusive as possible.

Message Problems. Messages that are full of jargon or unfamiliar words, or that are poorly organized, make it difficult for people to listen effectively. We provide suggestions to speakers on using language effectively in Chapter 10, and on how to organize a message clearly in Chapters 7 and 8. As a listener you have to put forth some effort to help overcome these problems. If you know the words in a presentation may be unfamiliar, such as a lecture in one of your other courses, try to acquaint yourself with that vocabulary ahead of time. Read assigned material in advance of the lecture and look up difficult words. If a message is poorly organized, taking notes can help. Often you can find a pattern in the speaker's rambling thoughts that will make them easier to remember and evaluate. Try to identify the main points or claims the speaker makes. Differentiate these from supporting materials such as examples or narratives. Figure 3.2 provides some helpful suggestions for taking notes.[17]

Presentation Problems. Speakers who talk too fast may be difficult to follow. On the other hand speakers who talk too slowly or too softly may lull you into sleep. Speakers may also have habits that are distracting. They may sway to and fro or fiddle with their hair while they are talking. Occasionally, you may even encounter speakers whose dress or hairstyle is so unusual that you find yourself concentrating more on them than on what they are saying. We advise speakers on how to minimize such distractions in Chapter 11. As a listener, sometimes just being aware that you are responding to such cues may be enough to help you listen more attentively. If

FIGURE 3.2

Guidelines for Taking Notes

1. Prepare to listen by studying background material ahead of time and having a notebook and a pen or pencil.
2. Leave a large margin on the left and take notes in outline form (see Chapter 8). Align the main points with the left-hand margin and indent supporting material. Leave spaces between main points.
3. Don't try to write down everything you hear. Use a telegraphic writing style that omits nonessential words.
4. Be alert for signal words such as the following:
    A. *for example* or *case in point* suggests supporting material will follow.
    B. *the three causes* or *the four steps* suggests a list you should number.
    C. *before* or *after* suggests that the time sequence is important.
    D. *therefore* or *consequently* suggests a causal relationship.
    E. *similarly* or *on the other hand* suggests a comparison or contrast will follow.
    F. *above all* or *keep in mind* means this is an important idea.
5. Review your notes as soon as possible. Use the large left-hand margin to paraphrase, summarize, or write out questions you may have.

you find yourself drifting away because of such problems, remind yourself that what speakers say is usually the most important part of their message.

Internal Sources of Interference

The most serious listening problems stem from sources of interference within the listener. Fortunately, some of these problems can be anticipated by the speaker and most are under the listener's control. These problems may be caused by reactions to words, personal concerns, attitudes, or bad listening habits you have acquired in the past.

The key to this problem of drifting attention and loss of focus is a certain condition of our minds. It is a simple fact that our minds can process information far faster than people usually speak. Most people speak at about 125 words per minute in public, but can process information at about 500 words per minute.[18] This time lapse provides an opportunity for listeners to drift away to more delightful or difficult personal concerns. Too often daydreamers will smile and nod encouragingly even though they haven't heard a thing the speaker has said. This deceptive feedback is a major cause of failed communication.

Reactions to Words. As you listen to a message, you react to more than just the objective meanings of words. You respond to their emotional meanings as well. Some **trigger words** may set off such powerful emotional reactions that they dominate the meaning of the discourse in which they occur. After a speech one time before a group of conservative business executives, one of your authors mentioned the words "labor union" in response to a question. He learned the hard way that any favorable or even neutral use of "labor union" immediately raised a high barrier of interference for that group. Conversely, before certain union audiences any like use of "management" might also create suspicion.

While some words are certainly ugly, and deserve condemnation whenever they are used, we remain convinced that people should control words and not the opposite. We should not let trigger words prevent us from hearing and evaluating the entire message within its overall context. Let's consider another example. For you, the use of the term "girls" to refer to adult females may be a negative "trigger word." You simply can't help despising what you regard as demeaning and disrespectful language. Now suppose a recruiter visiting your campus is describing opportunities for advancement in his company. As an example he tells you about "one of the girls from the office" who was recently promoted to a management position. His use of the term "girls" makes you think this must surely be a sexist organization. As you sit there stewing over his word choice, you miss his later statement that over the past three years two-thirds of all promotions into management have gone to women, and that an aggressive affirmative action program aimed at promoting more females and minority employees is in effect.

How can you demystify the power of such language over your reactions? Our suggestion is that you train yourself to look at the overall message and to analyze the individual case. For example, would it make any difference if the recruiter were a woman rather than a man? Ask yourself: Why is this person using such language? Is he personally insensitive, or is he testing me? Does he represent an attitude that is widespread in the company? By concentrating on such questions, you can defuse some of the power of trigger words and distance yourself from your own emotions. You can then decide whether you wish to confront the recruiter in order to clarify these questions. For example, you might tactfully say, "I'm extremely impressed by what you have told me, and I can certainly see myself succeeding with your company. But I'm troubled by your use of the term 'girls.' Sometimes that word is a sign that women are not really respected in a company. Can you help me with this problem?" There is a risk in such confrontational strategy: you might offend the recruiter and not get a highly desirable position. But there is also a risk in committing to a job situation that might be bad for you. You simply will have to make the judgment to confront or not to confront, based on your reading of the situation at the moment.

Trigger words can be positive as well as negative and can blind you to flawed, even dangerous messages. How many times have people been deceived by such trigger words as "freedom," "democracy," or "progress."[19] Such techniques are often used in advertisements where the products or services are paired with words like "American" and "Mom" or associated with traditional cultural heroes. For example, Chevrolet trucks sound the "heartbeat of America," Qantas is the airline "your mother would prefer you to fly," and the Franklin/Templeton mutual fund uses a currency-type picture of Ben Franklin as its logo.

Your attention also can be disrupted by chance associations with words. The speaker mentions the word "desk," which reminds you that you need a better place to study in your room, which reminds you that you have to buy a new lamp, which starts you thinking about where you should shop for the lamp, which gets you thinking about the good fried mushrooms at Friday's restaurant in the mall, which reminds you that you didn't eat breakfast and you're hungry. By the time your attention drifts back to the speaker, you have lost the gist of what is being said.

One of the most common barriers to effective listening is simply not paying attention. How many times have you found yourself daydreaming, even when you know you should be listening to what is being said? One reason for this problem is that our minds can process information far faster than people usually speak. Most people speak at about 125 words per minute in public, but can process information at about 500 words per minute.[18] This time lapse provides an opportunity for listeners to drift away to more delightful or difficult personal concerns. Too often day-dreamers will smile and nod encouragingly even though they haven't heard a thing the speaker has said. This deceptive feedback is a major cause of failed communication. Both personal reactions to words and distractions can set off such reactions.

To improve your ability to concentrate, keep a listening log for a week in your lecture classes. As you take class notes, put an "X" in the margin each time you notice your attention wandering. By each "X" jot down a few words pinpointing the cause, for example, "used *girls* for women." After class, count the times your mind drifted and note the causes. Can you identify a pattern of inattention? This exercise will help you identify the conditions that induced your inattention and will make you more consciously aware of your tendency to daydream. Once you realize how often and why you are drifting away, you can more easily guard against this tendency.

Personal Concerns. If you are tired, hungry, angry, worried, or pressed for time, you may find it difficult to concentrate. Your personal problems may take precedence over listening to a speaker. You can control inattention caused by internal distractions. Come to your classes well rested and well fed. Remind yourself that you can't really do your homework for another class when someone is talking. Leave your troubles at the door even if it means scheduling a time to worry later in the day. Clear your mind and your desk of everything except paper on which to take notes. Sit erect, establish eye contact with the speaker, and get ready to listen!

Attitudes. You may have strong positive or negative attitudes toward the speaker or the topic that can diminish your listening ability. All of us have biases of one kind or another. Listening problems arise when our biases prevent us from receiving messages accurately. Some of the ways that bias can distort messages are through filtering, assimilation, and contrast effects.[20]

Filtering means that you simply don't process all incoming information. You hear what you want to hear. You unconsciously screen the speaker's words so that only some of them reach your brain. Listeners who filter will hear only one side of "good news, bad news" speeches — the side

A questioning look from a listener suggests a lack of understanding. Try to rephrase what you have said or add an example to make your meaning more clear.

that confirms their preconceived notions. **Assimilation** means that you see positions similar to your own as being closer to it than they actually are. Assimilation most often occurs when listeners have a strong positive attitude toward a speaker or topic. For example, if you believe that the president can do no wrong, you may be tempted to assimilate everything he says so that it seems consistent with all your beliefs. A **contrast effect** occurs when you see positions that differ from yours as being more distant than they actually are. For example, if you are a staunch Democrat, you may think anything Republicans say will be different from what you believe, even if that is not true. Biases can make you put words in a speaker's mouth, take them away, or distort them.

The attitudes that cause most listening problems are those related to the speaker or the topic. If you know a speaker or have heard something about him or her, you may have developed attitudes that cause listening problems. The more competent, interesting, and attractive you expect speakers to be, the more attentive you will be and the more likely you will be to accept what they have to say. If your positive feelings are extremely strong, you may accept anything you hear from such speakers without considering the merits of the message. But if you anticipate an incompetent, uninteresting, or unattractive speaker, you may be less attentive and less likely to accept his or her ideas. You may dislike speakers because of positions they have previously defended or groups with which they are associated. Such biases may impair your listening ability.

Your attitudes toward certain topics also can affect how well you listen. If you believe that a topic is relevant to your life, you may listen more carefully than if you are indifferent. Speeches about retirement planning usually fall on deaf ears with young audiences. You may listen more attentively, although less critically, to speeches that support positions you already hold. If you feel strongly about a subject and oppose the speaker's position, you may find yourself rehashing counterarguments instead of listening. For example, if you have strong feelings against gun control, you may find yourself silently reciting the Second Amendment to the U.S. Constitution instead of listening to a speaker's arguments in favor of gun control. When you engage in such behaviors, you may miss much of what the speaker actually has to say. Finally, you may think that you already know enough about a topic. In such cases, you are not likely to listen effectively and may miss out on new, potentially useful information.

Attitudes are not easy to control. The first step in overcoming biases is to admit you have them. Next, decide that you will listen as objectively as you can, and that you will delay judgment until you have heard the entire message. Being objective does not mean that you must agree with a message — only that you believe that it deserves to be heard on its own terms. What you hear may help you see clearly the faults or the virtues of an opposing position. As a result, you may feel confirmed in what you already believe, or you may decide to reevaluate your position. Finally, determine that you will find value in listening. Even if you are not interested in a topic, look for something in the speech that will benefit you personally. Even poor speeches can provide examples of what not to do when you are presenting your own speech.

Habits.   Many listening problems are simply the result of bad habits. You may have watched so much television that you expect all messages to be fast moving and entertaining. You may have learned how to pretend you are listening to avoid dull or difficult materials. Your experiences as a student may have conditioned you to listen just for facts. You may jump to conclusions before hearing a complete message. Such habits can interfere with effective listening.

Some poor listening habits stem from heavy television viewing. Television messages are characterized by fast action and the presentation of short bits of information. Habitual television viewing may lead us to want all messages to follow this format. William F. Buckley has commented that "the television audience . . . is not trained to listen . . . to 15 uninterrupted minutes."[21] Our television-watching experiences may also lead us into "the entertainment syndrome," in which we demand that speakers be lively, interesting, funny, and charismatic to hold our attention.[22] Unfortunately, not all subjects lend themselves to such treatment, and we can miss much if we listen only to those who put on a "dog and pony show."

Although honest feedback is important to speech effectiveness, we all have learned how to pretend we are paying attention. We may sit erect, gaze at the speaker, even nod or smile from time to time (although not always at the most appropriate times), and not listen to one word that is being said! You are most likely to feign attention when you are daydreaming or when a message is difficult to understand. If the speaker asks, "Do you understand?" you may nod brightly, sending false feedback just to be polite or to avoid seeming dimwitted.

Our fear of failure may cause us to avoid listening to difficult material. If we are asked questions later, we can always say "I wasn't really listening" instead of "I didn't understand." We may believe that asking questions would make us look less than intelligent — that our questions may be "dumb," when the truly "dumb question" is the one that is not asked. Additionally, our desire to have things simplified so that we can understand them without much effort makes us susceptible to "snake oil" pitches, those oversimplified remedies for everything from fallen arches to failing government policies.

Your experiences as a student may contribute to another bad habit: listening only for facts. If you do this, you may miss the forest because you are so busy counting the leaves on the trees. Placing too much emphasis on facts can keep you from attending to the nonverbal aspects of a message. Effective listening includes integrating what you hear and what you see. Gestures, facial expressions, and tone of voice communicate nuances that are vital to the message of a speech.

Overcoming bad habits requires effort. When you find yourself feigning attention, remember that honest feedback helps speakers, but that inappropriate feedback deceives them. Don't try to remember everything or write down all that you hear. Instead, listen to the main ideas and identify supporting materials. Paraphrase what you hear so that it makes sense to you. Try to build an overall picture of the meaning in your mind. Attend to the nonverbal cues as well. Does the speaker's tone of voice change the meaning of the words? Are the gestures and facial expressions consistent with the words? If not, what does this tell you?

Improving Your Listening Skills

SPEAKER'S NOTES

1 Identify your specific listening problems and work to correct them.
2 Motivate yourself to get everything you can out of messages.
3 Put problems and biases aside so that you can be more attentive and open to new ideas.
4 Control your reactions to trigger words and other distractions.
5 Postpone judgments until you have heard all the speaker has to say.
6 Don't get wrapped up in details or try to write down everything a speaker says.
7 Listen for the main ideas and get an overall sense of meaning.

FIGURE 3.3

Differences Between
Good and Poor
Listeners

Good Listeners	Poor Listeners
1. focus attention on the message.	1. allow their minds to wander.
2. control reactions to trigger words.	2. respond emotionally to trigger words.
3. set aside personal problems when listening.	3. let personal problems interfere with listening.
4. work to overcome distractions.	4. succumb easily to distractions.
5. don't let their biases interfere with listening.	5. let their biases interfere with listening.
6. don't let speaker mannerisms interfere with listening.	6. allow speaker mannerisms to interfere with listening.
7. listen for things they can use.	7. tune out dry topics.
8. recognize the role of the listener in communication.	8. hold the speaker responsible for communication.
9. listen actively.	9. listen passively.
10. reserve judgment until a speaker is finished.	10. jump to conclusions before a speaker is finished.
11. provide honest feedback to speakers.	11. feign attention, giving false feedback to listeners.
12. become familiar with difficult material ahead of time.	12. avoid listening to difficult material.
13. listen for main ideas.	13. listen only for facts.
14. don't demand that all messages be entertaining.	14. want all messages to be entertaining.

Practice extending your attention span. If your original listening log shows that you drifted away from a lecturer twenty times in one class session, see if you can reduce this to fifteen, then to ten, then to five. The Speaker's Notes on "Improving Your Listening Skills" summarize how you might listen more effectively to messages.

This discussion of external and internal barriers to effective listening yields the profile offered in Figure 3.3, which contrasts many good and poor listening behaviors. Work to become the listener profiled in the left column by avoiding behaviors described in the right.

DEVELOPING YOUR CRITICAL THINKING AND LISTENING SKILLS

Developing your critical thinking and listening skills will further increase your effectiveness as a listener. **Critical thinking and listening** is an integrated process of examining information, ideas, and proposals. It involves

- questioning and exploring what you hear, accepting nothing at face value.
- developing your own position on issues by examining competing ideas.

Effective listeners provide feedback for speakers through body language and facial expressions. Without effective listeners the dynamic circle of communication is broken.

- being receptive to new thoughts and new perspectives on old subjects.
- evaluating evidence and reasoning.
- discussing with others the meanings of events.[23]

Throughout this course the skills and knowledge you acquire as you learn to prepare speeches will be useful also for analyzing and evaluating the messages you receive. You will learn how to evaluate and use supporting materials and different language resources in speeches. As you learn to prepare responsible arguments, you will also be learning how to evaluate the arguments of others. Although these topics will be covered in more depth in later chapters, here we will preview some questions important to critical listening.

Does the speaker support ideas or claims with facts and figures, testimony, and examples or narratives? Whenever speakers claim, "This statement is beyond dispute!" it is a good time to start a dispute. Listen for what is *not* said, as well as to what is said. No supporting material equals no proof. No proof should equal no acceptance. Don't hesitate to ask such speakers challenging questions.

Does the speaker use supporting materials that are relevant, representative, recent, and reliable? Supporting materials should relate directly to the issue in question. They should be representative of the situation as it exists rather than exceptions to the rule. The speaker who shouts, "Television is destroying family values!" and then offers statistics that demonstrate a rising national divorce rate, has not demonstrated a causal relationship between television and family values. Facts and figures should be the most recent ones available. This is particularly important when knowledge about a topic is changing rapidly. Supporting materials should come from sources that are trustworthy and competent in the subject area. Controversial material, especially, should be verified by more than one source, and the sources should represent different perspectives on the issue.

Does the speaker cite credible sources? Ethical speakers specify the credentials of their sources. When credentials are left out or described in vague terms, their testimony may be questionable. We recently found an advertisement for a health food product that contained "statements by doctors." A quick check of the current directory of the American Medical Association revealed that only one of the six "doctors" cited was a member of AMA and that his credentials were misrepresented. Always ask yourself, "Where does this information come from?" and "Are these sources qualified to speak on the topic?" We cover the use of supporting materials in greater detail in Chapters 6 and 14.

Does the speaker clearly distinguish among facts, inferences, and opinions? Facts are verifiable units of information that can be confirmed by independent observations. Inferences make projections based on facts. Opinions add personal interpretations or judgments to facts: they tell us what someone thinks about a subject. For example, "Mary was late for class today" is a fact. "Mary will probably be late for class again tomorrow" is an inference. "Mary is an irresponsible student" is an opinion. It may sound easy to make these distinctions among facts, inferences, and opinions, but you must be constantly alert to detect confusions of them in the messages you hear. Facts, opinions, and inferences all have a legitimate place in public discourse, but all can be misused. Facts and opinions (in the form of testimony) are covered in more detail in Chapter 6. Inferences are discussed as part of the reasoning process in Chapter 14.

Does the speaker use language that is concrete and understandable or purposely vague? When speakers have something to hide, they often use incomprehensible or vague language. Introducing people who are not physicians as "doctors" to enhance their testimony on health subjects is one form of such vagueness. Another trick is to use pseudoscientific jargon such as "This supplement contains a gonadotropic hormone similar to pituitary extract in terms of its complex B vitamin-methionine ratio." If it sounds impressive but you don't know what it means, be careful. We cover other problems relating to language use in Chapter 10.

Does the speaker ask you to ignore reason? Vivid examples and stories often express the speaker's deep passion for a subject and invite the listener to share such feeling. When this happens, speakers should also include sound information and reasons to justify their feelings. In politics, those who try to inflame feelings in order to promote their own programs, without regard to the accuracy or adequacy of their claims, are called **demagogues.** We should always ask, *what are these speakers asking us to forget?* As we write, Republican leaders who are attempting to reform the Medicare program charge that their Democratic opponents are asking voters to forget that unless there is significant change, the entire program will soon collapse. Democratic leaders charge in return that the Republicans are asking voters to forget the fate of the poor and elderly who will be affected by their reforms. In the face of such conflicting claims, the critical thinker will cultivate healthy skepticism and investigate the conflicting claims carefully before coming to a conclusion.

Does the speaker rely too much on facts and figures? Although we have just cautioned you to be wary of speakers who rely solely on emotional appeals, you also should be wary of speakers who exclude emotional appeals. You can never fully understand an issue unless you understand how it affects others, how it makes them feel, how it colors the way they view the world. Suppose you were listening to a speech on environmental pollution that contained the following information: "The United States has 5 percent of the world's population but produces 22 percent of the world's carbon dioxide emissions, releases 26 percent of the world's nitrogen oxides, and disposes of 290 million tons of toxic waste."[24] Although these numbers are impressive, what do they really tell you about the human problem of pollution? Consider how much more meaningful this material might be if accompanied by the story of Colette Chuda, a five-year-old California girl who died recently from cancer many feel resulted from exposure to a polluted environment.[25]

Does the speaker use plausible reasoning? When reasoning is plausible, conclusions appear to follow from the points and supporting materials that precede them. In other words, they make good sense. The basic assumptions that support arguments should be those on which most rational people agree. Whenever reasoning doesn't seem plausible, ask yourself why, and then question the speaker or consult with independent authorities before you make decisions or commit yourself. We cover the use of appeals and reasoning in more detail in Chapter 14.

Does the message promise too much? If an offer sounds too good to be true, it probably is. The health-food advertisement previously described contained the following claims: "The healing, rejuvenating and disease-fighting effects of this total nutrient are hard to believe, yet are fully documented. Aging, digestive upsets, prostrate [sic] diseases, sore throats, acne, fatigue, sexual problems, allergies, and a host of other problems have been successfully treated. . . . [It] is the only super perfect food on this earth. This statement has been proven so many times in the laboratories around the world by a chemical analyst that it is not subject to debate nor challenge." Maybe the product is also useful as a paint remover and gasoline additive.

Does this message fit with what I already know? Although we have stressed the importance of being open to new knowledge, inconsistent information should set off an alarm in your mind. You should always very carefully evaluate information that is inconsistent with your beliefs before you accept it. Yet keep in mind that what you think you know might not necessarily be so. Apply your critical thinking skills. Ask the speaker tough questions as suggested in the Speaker's Notes "Guides for Critical Thinking and Listening." Use the library to further verify information.

What other perspectives might there be on this issue? How would people from a different cultural background perceive the problem? How would

Guides for Critical Thinking and Listening

SPEAKER'S NOTES

1 Require all claims to be supported with facts and figures, testimony, examples, or narratives.

2 Evaluate supporting materials with regard to relevance, representativeness, recency, and reliability.

3 Assess the credibility of information sources for competence and trustworthiness.

4 Differentiate among facts, inferences, and opinions.

5 Be wary of language that is purposely vague or incomprehensible.

6 Look for a balance between rational and emotional appeals.

7 Be on guard against claims that promise too much.

8 Check the consistency of what you hear against what you know.

9 Consider alternate perspectives on the issue.

10 Ask questions whenever you have problems understanding or accepting a message.

someone older see it? How might someone of the other gender see it? Why might these people see it differently from you? Would their solutions or suggestions be different? Whenever a message addresses a serious topic, try to examine the issue from several points of view. New and better ideas often emerge when we look at the world from a different angle.

These questions provide a framework for critical thinking. When we add these skills to the improved listening behavior that comes when we solve our listening problems, we are on the way to becoming effective listeners.

EVALUATING SPEECHES

The communication process we describe in Chapter 1 suggests the importance of feedback from listeners. Up to now, we have been discussing the immediate feedback you give speakers during their presentations. Many instructors provide an additional opportunity for you to offer oral feedback after speakers have made their presentations. You may ask questions, comment on effective techniques, or offer suggestions for improvement. Such feedback should be aimed at helping the speaker improve.

There is a difference between criticizing a speaker and giving a **critique**, or evaluation, of a speech. Criticism can suggest emphasizing what someone did wrong. It can create a negative, competitive communication environment. In contrast, when you give a critique, your manner should be helpful and supportive. Give credit where credit is due. Point out strengths as well as weaknesses. Whenever you point out a weakness or problem, do so tactfully and try to suggest remedies or solutions. This type of interaction creates a classroom environment that stresses the willingness of students to help each other.

To participate in the evaluation of speeches, you need a set of standards to help you answer the question *What is a good speech?* Your instructor may have a special set of criteria for grading your presentations, and the criteria may be weighted differently from one assignment to another. For example, your instructor may assess your informative speeches primarily in terms of their structure and the adequacy of information and examples, and may evaluate your persuasive speeches based on your use of evidence and reasoning. Regardless of these special criteria, there are four general categories of guidelines you can use to evaluate speeches:

- *overall considerations* that apply to all aspects of a speech.
- *substance* factors that apply to the ideas and evidence.
- *structural* factors that apply to the way the speech is organized.
- *presentation* factors that apply to the way the speaker presents the speech.

Overall Considerations

Some aspects of speech evaluation apply across the factors of substance, structure, and presentation. These include commitment, adaptation, purpose, freshness, and ethics. Figure 3.4 illustrates these general guidelines for evaluating a speech. Your instructor may use this or a similar form for grading your presentations. You may wish to use it as a guide for critiquing the speeches that you hear.

Commitment.   In Chapter 1 we mentioned that your own commitment was essential to success in this course. It is also essential to an effective public speech. Commitment means caring. You must feel that the speaker believes both in the subject and in your welfare as a listener. Commitment makes itself known in the substance of a message. Committed speakers will have invested the time and effort needed to gain responsible knowledge of their subject. Commitment also shows up in how well a speech is structured. A good speech cannot be prepared at ten-thirty the night before a presentation. It takes time to analyze an audience, select a topic and research it adequately, organize your message, and practice its presentation. Finally, commitment shows up in your presentation in terms of the energy, enthusiasm, and sincerity you project. Commitment is the spark in the speaker that can touch off fire in the audience.

Anna Aley's speech on substandard off-campus housing problems, reprinted at the end of Chapter 13, illustrates the importance of commitment. She believed in the importance of the topic both to herself and to other students. It took Anna more than two weeks to research her subject

FIGURE 3.4

Guidelines for
Evaluating Speeches

Overall Considerations

_____ Did the speaker seem committed to the topic?
_____ Did the speech meet the requirements of the assignment?
_____ Was the speech adapted to fit the audience?
_____ Did the speech promote identification among topic, audience, and
speaker?
_____ Was the purpose of the speech clear?
_____ Was the topic handled with imagination and freshness?
_____ Did the speech meet high ethical standards?

Substance

_____ Was the topic worthwhile?
_____ Had the speaker done sufficient research?
_____ Were the main ideas supported with reliable and relevant information?
_____ Was testimony used appropriately?
_____ Were the sources documented appropriately?
_____ Were examples or narratives used effectively?
_____ Was the reasoning clear and correct?

Structure

_____ Did the introduction spark your interest?
_____ Did the introduction adequately preview the message?
_____ Was the speech easy to follow?
_____ Could you identify the main points of the speech?
_____ Were transitions used to tie the speech together?
_____ Did the conclusion summarize the message?
_____ Did the conclusion help you remember the speech?

Presentation

_____ Was the language clear, simple, and direct?
_____ Was the language concrete?
_____ Were grammar and pronunciations correct?
_____ Was the speech presented extemporaneously?
_____ Were notes used unobtrusively?
_____ Was the speaker appropriately enthusiastic?
_____ Did the speaker maintain good eye contact?
_____ Did gestures and body language complement ideas?
_____ Was the speaker's voice expressive?
_____ Were the rate and loudness appropriate to the material?
_____ Did the speaker use pauses appropriately?
_____ Did presentation aids make the message clearer or more memorable?
_____ Were presentation aids skillfully integrated into the speech?
_____ Was the presentation free from distracting mannerisms?

and to prepare her speech for classroom presentation. Then she polished it some more before presenting the speech for the public forum on campus.

Adaptation.   For a speech to be effective it must meet the particular requirements of the assignment and be adapted to the listener's needs. An assignment will typically specify the **general function** of the speech: an **informative speech** that aims at extending your understanding of a topic; a **persuasive speech** that attempts to influence your attitudes or actions; or a **ceremonial speech** that celebrates shared values. The assignment may also specify time limits, the number of references required, and the manner of presentation (such as a required presentation aid or extemporaneous mode of speech). You should take account of these requirements in your critique.

An effective speech must also be adapted to the audience's interests and needs. Effective speakers are listener-centered. This means that as speakers plan and prepare their messages, they should weigh each technique and each piece of supporting material in terms of audience appropriateness. Will this example interest listeners? Is this information important for them to know? How can speakers best involve the audience with their topic? The close involvement of subject, speaker, and listener is called **identification.** It is vital for effective speaking. One way speakers can invite identification is to ask involving questions at the beginning of a speech: "Have you ever thought about what it would mean not to have electricity?" Also, the pronoun *we* used artfully throughout a speech seems to draw audience, speaker, and subject closer together.

Purpose.   Beyond a general function, speeches should also have a specific purpose. For example, an informative speech may have the specific purpose of increasing listeners' knowledge of the causes of the greenhouse effect. The specific purpose of a speech will typically be evident by the end of the introduction, and must be unmistakably clear by the time the speaker begins the conclusion.

A speech that lacks a clear sense of purpose will seem to drift and wander as though it were a boat without a rudder, blown this way and that by whatever thought occurs to the speaker. Developing a clear purpose begins with the speaker considering audience needs. Speakers must decide precisely what they want to accomplish: what they want listeners to learn, think, or do as a result of their speeches.

Freshness.   Any speech worth listening to will bring something new to you. The topic should be fresh and interesting. If the topic has been overused, then the speech must be innovative to sustain attention. One frequently overused topic for persuasive speeches is drinking and driving. When speakers choose such topics, they can't simply reiterate the common advice "if you drink, don't drive" and expect to be effective. The audience will have heard that hundreds of times. To get through to listeners on that subject, speakers have to find a new way to present the material. One student of ours gave a speech on "responsible drinking and driving" that stressed the importance of understanding the effects of alcohol and of knowing your own tolerance limits. Her fresh approach and important information gave us a new perspective on an old problem.

Ethics. Perhaps the most important measure of a speech is whether it is good or bad for you. Although we have considered ethics in Chapter 1, the subject is important enough to bear repeating here. An ethical speech demonstrates respect for the audience, responsible knowledge, and concern for the consequences of exposure to the message.

Respect for the audience means that speakers are sensitive to the cultural composition of their audience and are aware that well-meaning people often hold varying positions on an issue. Ethical speakers take care not to offend others even as they dispute their arguments or question their information. We discuss additional audience considerations in Chapter 4.

Ethical speakers base their messages on responsible knowledge of their subject. They assess the accuracy and objectivity of their sources of information in terms of potential bias. They recognize their own prejudices and try to be accurate and objective in their presentation of information. Ethical speakers do not off opinions and inferences as facts. An ethical speaker will report the sources of factual data and ideas, all the more fully when the information runs counter to what is generally believed. Finally, ethical speakers do not fabricate data or present the ideas or words of others without acknowledging their contributions.

Ethical speakers are aware that words have consequences. Inflammatory language can arouse strong feelings in audience members that sometimes block constructive deliberation. Ethical speakers think through the possible ramifications of their messages before they present them. The greater the possible consequences, the more carefully speakers must assess the potential effects of their messages, support what they say with credible evidence, and temper their conclusions with regard for listener sensitivities.

Evaluating Substance

An effective speech has **substance.** This means the speech has a worthwhile message that is supported by facts and figures, testimony, examples and/or narratives. The starting point for a substantive presentation is a well-chosen topic. The topic should interest both the speaker and listeners, once they are shown how it affects their lives. Generally, speakers should already know something about the topics they select. This knowledge serves as the foundation for further research that enables them to speak responsibly and authoritatively. While personal experiences are a valid source of information, speakers should always validate, update, and broaden such experience with library-based research or interviews with knowledgeable people. We discuss selecting and researching topics in more detail in Chapter 5.

Speakers add substance by interweaving reliable information into the fabric of their speeches. *Facts and figures* give precise focus to a speaker's points. *Testimony* adds the authority and prestige of knowledgeable, respected others to the speaker's claims. Such testimony can add expert opinions or eloquent quotations to the speech substance. At other times speakers may rely on lay testimony from ordinary people with whom the audience might identify. For example, the opinions of other students might be meaningful on issues that pertain to campus life. *Examples* can help listeners understand better what speakers are talking about. *Narratives* can engage the audience by telling some colorful story that illustrates the speaker's message.

Skillful speakers often combine different types of supporting material to make their points more accessible to listeners. Combining statistical data with an example can make ideas more clear and compelling. For instance, a speaker might say, "The base of the Great Pyramid at Giza measures 756 feet on each side." While precise, this may be difficult to visualize. But what if the speaker adds, "More than eleven football fields could fit in its base." Aha! This example gives a concrete point of reference by comparing the unfamiliar or hard-to-understand concept with something you might relate to. We discuss the use of supporting materials in greater detail in Chapter 6.

Evaluating Structure

A good speech is carefully planned so that it carries you through an orderly progression of ideas, making it easy to follow. Without a good design a speech may seem to consist of random ideas that have been thrown together willy-nilly. A worthwhile message can get lost in the confusion.

There are three main parts to every message: an introduction, the body of the speech, and a conclusion. The introduction should arouse interest in the topic and preview the message to follow. The body of the speech presents a speaker's main ideas and the supporting material needed to develop them. The conclusion should summarize the main points, reflect upon the meaning of the message, and provide a sense of closure.

The introduction may begin with an example, a quotation, or a question that draws you into the topic, such as "So you think there's no need to worry about global warming?" Once speakers gain attention, they will usually prepare listeners for what is to come by previewing the main points. More suggestions for developing introductions can be found in Chapter 7.

The organization of the body of the speech will vary according to the subject and purpose. If a speech tells you how to do something — for instance, how to mat and frame a picture — its main points should follow the order of the process which it describes. If the subject breaks naturally into parts, such as the three major causes of global warming, the speaker can use a categorical design to present them. Chapters 12 and 13 discuss these and other designs for speeches.

A variety of concluding techniques can be used to end a speech. If speakers have covered several main points in the body, they should summarize them and then make a final statement that will help listeners re-member the essence of the message. Chapter 7 provides additional infor-mation on developing conclusions.

Effective speeches also contain transitions that link the various parts of the speech. They signal you that something different is coming and help the speech flow better. Transitions should be used between the introduc-tion and body of a speech, between the body and conclusion, and between the main points within the body. Transitions can be a single word, such as *next* or *finally*. They also can be whole sentences, such as "Now that you can see the problem clearly, let's turn to how we can solve it." Transitions bridge ideas and aid understanding. You will learn more about them in Chapter 7.

Evaluating Presentation Skills

No speech can be good unless it is presented effectively. Both the actual words speakers use and the way they convey these words are important fac-tors in presentation.

The oral language of speeches must be instantly intelligible. You don't have an instant-replay button to push if you don't understand what the speaker has said. The train of meaning simply leaves the station without you aboard. Therefore, speakers' sentences should be simple and direct. They should avoid complex chains of dependent clauses. Compare the fol-lowing examples:

> **Working for a temporary employment service is a good way to put yourself through school because there are always jobs to be found and the places you get to work in are interesting — besides, the people you work for treat you well, and you don't have to do the same thing day after day — plus, you can tailor the hours to fit your free time.**

> **Working for a temporary employment service is a good way to put yourself through school. Jobs are readily available. You can schedule your work to fit in with your classes. You don't stay at any one place long enough to get bored. And you meet a lot of interesting people who are glad to have your services.**

Which is easier to follow? The first example rambles on, the information is presented in no particular order, and the speaker pauses only to catch a breath. In the second example, the sentences are short, inviting the ef-fective use of pause to separate ideas. As a result, the meaning is more clear.

Concrete words are generally preferable to abstract ones because they create vivid pictures for you and enhance the speaker's meaning. Consider the following levels of abstraction:

most abstract	my pet
	my dog
	my puppy
	my eight-week-old puppy
	my eight-week-old black puppy
most concrete	my eight-week-old black Labrador puppy

As the language goes from abstract to concrete, you are better able to visualize what is being talked about, and there is less chance of misunderstanding. We discuss other language factors that help improve communication in Chapter 10.

An effective presentation sounds natural and enthusiastic. It draws attention to the speaker's ideas rather than to the speaker, and avoids distracting mannerisms. To achieve these qualities, most class assignments call for an **extemporaneous presentation.** In this style of speaking, the speech is carefully prepared and practiced but *not* written out or memorized. Extemporaneous speaking allows speakers to adapt to the audience during a presentation. If listeners look confused, speakers can rephrase what they have said or provide another example. This kind of speaking does require practice, however. Extemporaneous does *not* mean "off the top of the speaker's head."

Practice may not make perfect, but it certainly improves a speaker's chances of doing a good job. While rehearsing, a speaker may discover that a technique that looked good on paper sounds stilted or silly when spoken. It often helps if speakers can tape-record their speeches, leave them overnight, then play them back the next day. Supportive roommates or friends can listen to the speech and offer suggestions that further improve it before presentation. They should be able to identify the purpose and the main points of the speech. Speakers should imagine their audiences before them as they practice. If possible, they should find a time when the classroom is not being used so that they can try out the speech where it actually will be presented. The more they can practice under these conditions, the better the speech should flow when the class actually hears it.

During actual presentations speakers should talk loud enough to be heard in the back of the room. If speakers speak too softly, it will be hard for you to keep your attention focused on the speech. Body language is also an important part of effective presentation. The speaker's posture should be relaxed. Movements should seem natural and spontaneous. Speakers who point to their heads every time they say "think" or who spread their arms out wide every time they say "big" will seem artificial and contrived. Gestures should complement what a speaker has to say, not compete with it for attention.

Keep these points in mind as you prepare to offer constructive feedback after oral presentations. Additional suggestions for effective presentation can be found in Chapter 11.

YOUR ETHICAL RESPONSIBILITIES AS A LISTENER

In Chapter 1 we discussed the ethics of public speaking. As a listener, you have ethical responsibilities as well. Ethical listeners do not prejudge a speech and they keep an open mind. It is irresponsible to say or think, "My mind is made up on that issue. Don't try to persuade me." John Milton, a great English poet and intellectual of the seventeenth century, observed in *Areopagitica,* his treatise on freedom of speech, that listening to our opponents can be beneficial. We may learn something from them and gain a new and better perspective on an issue. Or, as we question and argue with them, we may discover *why* we believe as we do. When we protect ourselves from ideas, we deprive ourselves of the chance to exercise and strengthen our own convictions.

Just as we should be open to ideas, we should also be receptive to the lifestyles and cultural backgrounds of others. Prejudice can prevent us from realizing that people should be judged as individuals, not as members of races, classes, or cultural groups. Moreover, we may have misguided ideas about different races or cultures that keep us from appreciating their unique contributions. While we may *hear* others, we may not *listen* to them. When this happens, we are deprived not only of the chance to explore other worlds, but also of the opportunity to understand our own more clearly. In comparing and contrasting our lifeways with others, we learn more about ourselves.

While we believe that ethical listeners should remain open to ideas that may at first seem strange or even hostile, we do not suggest that you lower your interference barriers to all messages. Some ideas, after fair consideration, prove to be faulty, risky, or even evil. Not every speaker has our good at heart. Perhaps our best advice to you is to be an open but cautious listener, combining the best traits of ethical and critical listening.

Finally, remember the impact of your listening on others. Good listeners tend to grow good speakers. Good listeners seek out the value in ideas, often finding unexpected worth in a speech. Good listeners are also concerned about the ethical impact of messages on others who may not be present. Good listeners not only apply our variation of the Golden Rule: "Listen to others as you would have them listen to you." They extend it. Recognizing that their own preferences may not always transfer to other cultures, good listeners try to learn the communication values and norms of other people. They are then able to apply a variation of what Bennett has called the Platinum Rule: "Listen to others as *they* would have you listen to them."[26] The result should be a considerable development in understanding individuals from cultures other than your own. All sides benefit when speakers and listeners take their ethical roles seriously.

IN SUMMARY

Listening is as important to communication as speaking. Basic listening skills include hearing, paying attention, comprehending, and interpreting a message. *Critical thinking* adds analysis and evaluation to these skills. *Constructive listening* suggests the additional vital role of the listener in the creation of meaning. To become better listeners, we must first overcome our listening problems. To be truly effective listeners, we must combine the basic skills with critical thinking and a constructive orientation.

Benefits of Effective Listening. Effective listening benefits both listeners and speakers. Listeners become less vulnerable to unethical advertising or to dishonest political communication. Improved listening skills will help your performance as a student, and may mean the difference between success and failure at work. Speakers benefit from an audience of good listeners. The feedback from good listeners can make their messages more understandable. Effective, supportive listeners can help relieve some of the communication apprehension that all speakers experience, and can also boost a speaker's self-esteem.

Overcoming Listening Problems. Some listening problems may arise from external sources, such as a noisy environment. They may also result from a poorly organized message, language the audience does not understand, or speakers whose presentation skills are distracting. Most serious listening problems arise from factors internal to the listener, such as personal reactions to words, worries, attitudes, or bad listening habits. Personal reactions to *trigger words* may set off strong emotions that block effective listening. Biased attitudes toward the speaker or topic can interfere with listening. Bad habits, such as pretending we are listening when we are not or listening only for facts, can also impair our listening behavior.

Effective listening skills can be developed. The first step is to identify your listening problems. Concentrate on the main ideas and the overall pattern of meaning in the speech. Strive for objectivity, withholding value judgments until you are certain you understand the message.

Developing Critical Thinking Skills. *Critical thinking* skills help you analyze and evaluate messages more effectively. Critical listeners question what they hear, require support for assertions and claims, and evaluate the credentials of sources. Critical listeners differentiate among facts, inferences, and opinions. They become wary when language seems overly vague or incomprehensible, when inflammatory speech takes the place of cool reason, or when a message promises too much. When what they hear does not fit with what they know, critical listeners consider the message very carefully and ask questions.

Evaluating Speeches.   Speech evaluation in the classroom takes the form of a *critique,* a positive and constructive effort to help speakers improve. Criteria for speech evaluation include overall considerations, substance, structure, and presentation skills. Overall considerations encompass commitment, audience adaptation, clarity of purpose, freshness of perspective, ethical standards, and any particular requirements of the assignment. Substance factors take into account the value of the topic, the sufficiency of research, and the adequacy of supporting material and lines of reasoning. Structural factors include the presence of an effective introduction, a clearly organized body that includes the main points and supporting materials, and a conclusion that provides closure. Presentation factors consider the words speakers use and the way they convey their messages through voice and gesture.

Listeners have ethical responsibilities. Ethical listeners do not prejudge a speech but are open to ideas and receptive to different perspectives. Ethical listeners test what they hear and are sensitive to the impact of ideas on others. They represent all who might be affected by the message.

TERMS TO KNOW

constructive listening	critique
participative communication	general function
trigger words	informative speech
filtering	persuasive speech
assimilation	ceremonial speech
contrast effect	substance
critical thinking and listening	extemporaneous presentation

DISCUSSION

1. Complete the "Listening Problems Checklist" on page 73 of this chapter. Working in small groups, discuss your listening problems with the other members of the group. Develop a listening improvement plan for the three most common listening problems in your group. Report this plan to the rest of the class.

2. List three positive and three negative trigger words that provoke a strong emotional reaction when you hear them. Have someone write these words on the chalkboard. Try to group the words into categories, such as sexist or ethnic slurs, political terms, ideals, and so forth. Discuss why these words have such a strong impact on you. How might you control their effect?

3. Identify a speaker outside your class to whom you have difficulty listening. Identify the sources of interference in yourself that make it hard for you to listen. Do you feel such interference is justified?

APPLICATION

1. Review the notes you have taken in one of your lecture courses. Are you able to identify the main points, or have you been trying to write down everything that was said? Compare your note taking before and after studying listening behavior. Can you see any difference?

2. Read the following paragraph carefully:

Dirty Dick has been killed. The police have rounded up six suspects, all of whom are known criminals. All of them were near the scene of the crime at the approximate time that the murder took place. All had good motives for wanting Dirty Dick killed. However, Larcenous Lenny has been completely cleared of guilt.

Now determine whether each of the following statements is true (T), false (F), or is an inference (?).[27]

T F ? 1. Larcenous Lenny is known to have been near the scene of the killing of Dirty Dick.

T F ? 2. All of the rounded-up criminals were known to have been at the scene of the murder.

T F ? 3. Only Larcenous Lenny has been cleared of guilt.

T F ? 4. The police do not know who killed Dirty Dick.

T F ? 5. Dirty Dick's murderer did not confess of his own free will.

T F ? 6. It is known that the six suspects were in the vicinity of the cold-blooded assassination.

T F ? 7. Larcenous Lenny did not kill Dirty Dick.

T F ? 8. Dirty Dick is dead.

The answers are found following the Notes at the end of the chapter. Were you able to distinguish between inferences and facts?

3. With your classmates observe three minutes of silence. During this time write down all sounds or distractions heard in the classroom. Compile a list of these distractions on the chalkboard. Discuss (a) how much of a problem each might be for both speakers and listeners and (b) what speakers and listeners could do to minimize these distractions.

4. Use the guidelines on page 87 of this chapter to evaluate a speech you view on tape in class. Discuss the strengths and weaknesses of the presentation. Consider what type of constructive oral feedback you might offer this speaker to improve his or her next presentation. Discuss both critical and supportive ways of presenting the same type of feedback.

NOTES

1. Cited in Clifton Fadiman, ed., *The Little, Brown Book of Anecdotes* (Boston: Little, Brown, 1985), pp. 475–476.

2. Larry Barker, et al, "An Investigation of Proportional Time Spent in Various Communication Activities by College Students," *Journal of Applied Communications Research* 8 (1980): 101–109; Walter Pauk, *How to Study in College,* 4th ed. (Boston: Houghton Mifflin, 1989), pp. 121–133; and Larry L. Barker, *Listening Behavior* (Englewood Cliffs, NJ: Prentice-Hall, 1971), pp. 3–9.

3. Richard Bruce Hyde, "Council: Using a Talking Stick to Teach Listening," *The Speech Communication Teacher* Vol. 7.2 (Winter 1993): 1–2.

4. Luther Standing Bear, Oglala Sioux chief, cited in *Native American Wisdom: Photographs by Edward S. Curtis* (Philadelphia: Running Press, 1993), pp. 58–59.

5. Ronald B. Adler and George Rodman, *Understanding Human Communication,* 5th ed. (Fort Worth, TX: Harcourt Brace, 1994), p. 130.

6. We describe this concept further in Michael and Suzanne Osborn, *Alliance for a Better Public Voice: The Communication Discipline and the National Issues Forums* (Dayton, OH: National Issues Forums Institute, 1991).

7. Waldo Braden, "The Available Means of Persuasion: What Shall We Do About the Demand for Snake Oil?" in *The Rhetoric of Our Times,* ed. J. Jeffry Auer (New York: Appleton-Century-Crofts, 1969), pp. 178–184.

8. Jeffrey A. Trachtenberg, "Beyond the Hidden Persuaders: Psychological Aspects of Marketing," *Forbes* (23 Mar. 1987), pp. 134–137; and "Michael Jordan's Magical Powers," *The Economist,* 1 June 1991, p. A28.

9. W. B. Legge, "Listening, Intelligence, and School Achievement," in *Listening: Readings,* ed. S. Duker (Metuchen, NJ: Scarecrow Press, 1971), pp. 121–133.

10. U.S. Department of Labor, "What Work Requires of Schools" (U.S. Government Printing Office), 1991.

11. Dan B. Curtis, Jerry L. Winsor, and Ronald D. Stephens, "National Preferences in Business and Communication Education," *Communication Education* 38 (1989): 7–14.

12. Gary T. Hunt and Louis P. Cusella, "A Field Study of Listening Needs in Organizations," *Communication Education* 32 (1983): 399.

13. B. D. Sypher, R. N. Bostrom, and J. H Seibert, "Listening Communication Abilities and Success at Work," *Journal of Business Communication* (Fall 1989), 293–303.

14. Andrew D. Wolvin and Carolyn Gwynn Coakley, "A Survey of the Status of Listening Training in Some Fortune 500 Corporations," *Communication Education* 40 (1991): 152–164.

15. Lou Davidson Tillson, "Building Community and Reducing Communication Apprehension: A Case Study Approach," *The Speech Communication Teacher* (Summer 1995), 4–5.

16. Some material for this section was synthesized from William B. Gudykunst, Stella Ting-Toomey, Sandra Sudweeks, and Lea P. Stewart, *Building Bridges: Interpersonal Skills for a Changing World* (Boston: Houghton Mifflin, 1995), pp. 228–229.

17. Adapted from Walter Pauk, *How to Study in College* 4th ed. (Boston: Houghton Mifflin, 1989), pp. 136–161; and Dave Ellis, *Becoming a Master Student,* 7th ed. (Boston: Houghton Mifflin, 1994), pp. 136–150.

18. Andrew D. Wolvin and Carolyn Gwynn Coakley, *Listening,* 2nd ed. (Dubuque, IA: William C. Brown, 1985), p. 177.

19. Richard M. Weaver, "Ultimate Terms in Contemporary Rhetoric," *Language Is Sermonic: Richard M. Weaver on the Nature of Rhetoric,* eds. Richard L. Johannesen, Rennard Strickland, and Ralph T. Eubanks (Baton Rouge: Louisiana State University Press, 1970), p. 95.

20. J. J. Makay and W. R. Brown, *The Rhetorical Dialogue: Contemporary Concepts and Cases* (Dubuque, IA: William C. Brown, 1972), pp. 125–145.

21. William F. Buckley, "Has TV Killed Off Great Oratory?" *TV Guide,* 12 Feb. 1983, p. 38.

22. James J. Floyd, *Listening: A Practical Approach* (Glencoe, IL: Scott, Foresman, 1985), pp. 23–25.

23. John Chaffee, *Thinking Critically,* 2nd ed. (Boston: Houghton Mifflin, 1988), p. 59.

24. *Time,* 18 December 1989, cover.

25. Jim Motavalli, "In Memory of Colette," *E: The Environmental Magazine,* May/June 1994, pp. 30–31.

26. Milton J. Bennett, "Overcoming the Golden Rule: Sympathy and Empathy," in *Communication Yearbook 3,* ed. Dan Nimmo (New Brunswick, NJ: Transaction Books, 1979), pp. 407–422.

27. Answers to Application item #2: (1) ?, (2) T, (3) ?, (4) ?, (5) ?, (6) ?, (7) ?, (8) T.

PART TWO

Preparation for Public Speaking

CHAPTER 4

Adapting to Your Audience and Situation

- understand the dynamics of your audience.
- adapt your message to audience characteristics.
- meet the ethical challenges of audience diversity.
- adjust your speech to the situation of presentation.

Of the three elements in speech-making — speaker, subject, and person addressed, it is the last one, the hearer, that determines the speech's end and object.

— Aristotle

It's the beginning of the fall term and the president of Students for Environmental Action has a busy day ahead. At eight o'clock in the morning he will introduce SEA to the new students assembled at the soccer field. His major goals will be to inform them about SEA's projects for the coming year and to recruit new members. Later that day he faces a more daunting task. The director of the fifteen-member Coahoma County Industrial Development Board has asked him to speak at their monthly meeting to let them know "what you students are up to." He must reassure them that SEA's work will help, not hurt, the business climate in the area.

He will speak on the same general topic, but the different audiences will create different challenges and goals for him. The listeners he anticipates — their needs and interests — must be at the center of his thinking as he plans and develops his speeches. Moreover, the setting for his speeches can make a big difference in how he presents them. His manner of presentation, as well as the language he chooses, may vary from the soccer field to the board room.

In this chapter we consider both the audience you will address and the setting for your speech. Our purpose is to help you plan ways to adapt your messages so that they can be most effective. *The more you know about your audience and speaking situation, the more effective your speech should be.* Good audience analysis will indicate what topics your listeners might find most interesting, what they may already know about your topic, what they need to know, and how they may feel about it. Audience analysis can also help you select supporting materials to strengthen your speech, decide on its overall design and structure, and choose techniques to help listeners understand and relate to your topic.

You may have some ethical misgivings about adapting a message to fit a particular audience. But the spoken word is meant to be heard. The central question in assessing ethics is the speaker's motive: *do you use adaptation techniques to disguise your position, or to reveal it most effectively to a particular audience?* Adapting to your audience does not mean that you should change the essence of your message. That would be "waffling" — the unethical technique of taking one position with one group of listeners and a different position with another. Such tactics almost always come to light and damage speakers' reputations. However, you can ethically adapt your message to particular audiences in terms of the language you use, the examples you provide, the stories you tell, the authorities you cite, and your manner of presentation. To do this, you must develop a genuine sensitivity to your listeners.

This sensitivity begins with respect for people and an awareness of how the power of words can make a difference in their lives. Ethical speakers ask such questions as, "How can I tailor my message to reach my audience without compromising my convictions?" and "How can I give my ideas a chance for a fair hearing?"

In this chapter we take an in-depth look at *audience dynamics,* the needs, attitudes, and values that listeners may bring to the speaking situation. Second, we consider *demographic factors,* characteristics such as age, political and religious preferences, and gender. Third, we consider some of the major challenges of *audience diversity* that can make it difficult to overcome the barriers that separate people. Finally, we focus precisely on practical features of the *communication situation,* the "little things" that can make or break your speech.

 ## ADAPTING TO AUDIENCE DYNAMICS

We begin with an in-depth look at **audience dynamics,** the motivations, attitudes, beliefs, and values that influence behavior. An understanding of how these dynamics function is central to that sensitivity you must develop as you consider your listeners. The better you understand what makes people act as they do, the better you can adapt your message so that it serves their needs.

Motivation

Our needs and wants make up our **motivation,** the force that moves us to action and directs our actions toward specific goals. Motivation explains *why* people behave as they do.[1] When we think of applying motivation to public speaking, we may think first of its use in persuasive messages designed to move people to action. Making people aware of a need, and then showing them a way to satisfy it, is a major persuasive strategy (see Chapter 13). Motivational appeals are also important in informative speeches. *People will listen, learn, and retain your message only if you can relate it to their needs, wants, or wishes.* Finally, an understanding of motivation can help you identify the common ground that unites all of us regardless of our differences.

While all people share certain motivations, these can vary in importance according to the person, situation, and culture. People are motivated by what they don't have that they need, want, or value. For example, if you have recently moved to a new town, your need to make friends may lead you to seek out places where you can meet others. Even when your needs are met, you can still respond to wants. Suppose you have just eaten a very satisfying meal. If someone enters the room with a tray of warm, freshly baked cookies, the sight and smell can be enough to make you want some, even though you aren't really hungry.

In an extensive early study of human motivation, Henry A. Murray and his associates at the Harvard Psychological Clinic identified more than twenty-five different human needs.[2] They suggested that these needs varied in intensity according to each person's particular situation and that each individual arranges them in a personal hierarchy of importance. Figure 4.1 contains a list of twelve of these needs that seem especially relevant to motivating audiences.

The late psychologist Abraham Maslow was instrumental in popularizing the study of human needs by arranging them in a hierarchy with five different levels (see Figure 4.2). According to Maslow, the needs at the lower levels must be satisfied to some reasonable degree before the higher-level needs come into play. Although his basic works were published over twenty-five years ago, they are still considered to be "on the cutting edge."[3]

Physiological Needs. Maslow's most basic level are our **physiological needs** for food, water, air, and comfort, akin to the need for comfort identified in Figure 4.1. When these needs are aroused, they can dominate behavior. This explains why speeches concerning clean air to breathe and water to drink usually attract attention. Physiological needs also underlie the power of some advertising. An ad for a diet program might show a piece of chocolate cake, proclaiming, "You can have your cake and diet, too!" Storm window or furnace companies may contrast a warm interior scene with cold, snowy weather outside. If you can show listeners that your topic affects their physical well-being or will help satisfy their need for comfort, you'll have most of them sitting up and listening attentively. Speech topics such as "Meals in Your Room: The Alternative to Cafeteria Food" and "CPR Training Could Save Your Life" might appeal to this need level.

The SEA speaker we describe in our opening vignette might well appeal to physiological needs as he addresses both his student audience and the development board. The fact that we all share these needs could well become the common ground he establishes between himself and both groups.

FIGURE 4.1
Twelve Needs to Consider as Motivational Appeals

1. COMFORT	Having enough to eat and drink, keeping warm when it's cool and cool when it's warm, being free from pain.
2. SAFETY	Feeling secure in your surroundings, being protected from crime, surviving accidents and natural disasters, having an environment free of pollutants.
3. CONTROL	Having a hand in your own destiny, planning for the future, fixing things and people, influencing or directing others, controlling your environment.
4. TRADITION	Having a sense of roots, having a feeling of continuity with the past, doing things as they have always been done, honoring your forbears.
5. FRIENDSHIP	Establishing warm relations with others, being a member of a group or organization, being accepted by others, having someone to love and be loved by.
6. NURTURANCE	Taking care of others, comforting those in distress, aiding the helpless, caring for animals, giving to charitable organizations, providing volunteer service.
7. RECOGNITION	Being treated as valuable and important, having your achievements praised by others, receiving trophies or awards, being the center of attention.
8. SUCCESS	Accomplishing something of significance, overcoming obstacles to achieve your goals, doing better than expected, reaching the pinnacle of your profession.
9. INDEPENDENCE	Being able to stand on your own, being self-sufficient, making your own decisions, being your own person.
10. VARIETY	Longing for adventure, visiting new and unusual places, trying different things, changing jobs, moving to a new town, meeting new people.
11. CURIOSITY	Understanding the world around you, understanding yourself, understanding others, questioning why things happen or why people act as they do, finding out about the unusual.
12. ENJOYMENT	Doing something just for the fun of it, taking a vacation, pampering yourself, pursuing a hobby.

FIGURE 4.2

Maslow's Hierarchy of Needs

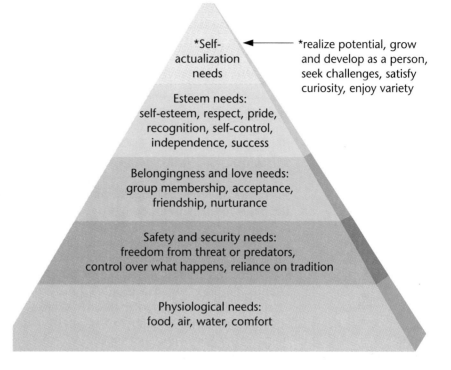

Safety and Security Needs. At the second level in Maslow's hierarchy are our **safety and security needs.** We seek protection from harm and some order or predictability in our lives. When crime runs rampant, when family values seem to be deteriorating, or when we feel we are not in control of our lives, our needs for safety and security come to the forefront. These needs may also explain our desire to control our fate and the importance of tradition in our lives, as shown in Figure 4.1.

Advertisements for home security systems often highlight personal vulnerability. Water filtration system ads promise to keep us safe from contaminants. Most advertisements related to this need level play on the fears of listeners. Such appeals may be justified, but you should use them carefully. If you arouse fear in listeners, you must also show how they can protect themselves from the dangers you describe.[4] When the news is bad, people sometimes blame the messenger. Or they may feel that you are manipulating their emotions. The student speech on earthquake preparedness at the end of Chapter 12 shows how needs for safety and security can be used effectively in an informative message. Additional topics that relate to these needs might include "Secrets of Time Management Experts: How to Take Control of Your Life" and "Crime on Our Campus: What You Can Do to Assure Your Safety."

The SEA speaker we introduced at the beginning of our chapter must recognize that in the eyes of many members of the development board, he and his organization may appear as a threat to their well-being. To the extent that he ethically can, he must reassure them that SEA seeks only good for the community and intends no harm. As a matter of fact, he should look for ways in which the board and SEA might work together to minimize *both* the threat of pollution and the impact of pollution control on area businesses.

Belongingness Needs. Most people are strongly moved to give and receive affection, companionship, loyalty, approval, and support. These **belongingness needs** are related to the needs for friendship and nurturance that Murray identified (Figure 4.1). The need to belong is probably the most prevalent appeal in contemporary American advertising.[5] How many ads have you seen that suggest that if you don't use the "right" deodorant, serve the "right" soft drink, or drive the "right" vehicle, you'll be left out in the cold?

Speakers who can relate their topics to the audience's needs for friendship, acceptance, or nurturance can improve their chances for success. Some possible topics related to this need include "New Interests, New Friends: Finding Your Place on Campus" and "Love Makes the World Go 'Round: A Look at Computer Dating Services." As he confronts his student audience in our chapter-opening vignette, our SEA speaker might well anticipate that many members of his audience might be seeking new friends and a sense of "place" in their new campus lives. If he can depict SEA as an organization of warm and caring people who welcome newcomers, he will be making a powerful appeal to belongingness needs.

Esteem Needs. Our needs for self-respect, prestige, and the respect of others — our **esteem needs** — are usually satisfied through accomplishment, praise, recognition, and status symbols. Everyone likes to be treated as valuable and important. People like others to acknowledge their achievements. They often place great value on trophies and other tangible signs of recognition. Esteem needs connect with Murray's needs for recognition and success (Figure 4.1). Advertisements frequently appeal to this need level by associating their products with elegant homes, expensive cars, or lavish vacations. When we buy such products, we are associating ourselves with these symbols of success and bolstering our self-esteem.

Speakers can use the need for esteem in a variety of ways. Speeches that show listeners how they can improve their lives or that give them a sense of pride are often well received. Some sample topics include "Preparing to Interview for the Job You Want" and "Six Tips for Better Studying: Ways to Improve Your Grades." As he addresses the development board on SEA activities, our student speaker might announce that his organization will make an annual award to the local business that has been most environmentally conscious during the previous year. In so doing he would be calling on listeners' needs for esteem and recognition to gain acceptance for his group.

Self-Actualization Needs. The highest needs in Maslow's hierarchy are our **self-actualization needs** to grow as people, fully realize our potential, and find our own identity. Self-actualization considers the importance of achievement for its own sake rather than for recognition. It includes meeting challenges, satisfying curiosity, and leaving our creative mark on the world. It relates to the needs for variety and independence identified by Murray (Figure 4.1). The U.S. Army's "Be All That You Can Be" ads and Nike's "Just Do It!" campaign appeal to self-actualization needs.

Appeals to self-actualization may be especially effective with people who are idealistic or whose identity is not firmly established. Some sample topics might include "Expanding Your Horizons Through the Campus Cultural Exchange" or "Independence: The Test of True Maturity." As he addresses his student audience, our SEA speaker could emphasize the importance of finding ourselves through our service to others.

Attitudes, Beliefs, and Values

While all people have needs, they don't all satisfy these needs in the same way. The specific ways people choose to satisfy their needs may be determined by their attitudes, beliefs, and values. **Attitudes** typically refer to our feelings about something — whether we like or dislike, approve or disapprove of people, events, or ideas. Attitudes also include our **beliefs** — what we know or think we know about something — and the way we are inclined to act toward it.[6] Most of the time our important social attitudes are anchored by our **values**, how we think we should behave or what we regard as an ideal state of being.[7] These ideals guide much of our thinking

People from diverse backgrounds often can be united around common attitudes and values.

and motivate much of our behavior. As we noted in Chapter 1, certain values transcend national and cultural boundaries. We will consider them more fully later in this chapter.

Information about your audience's beliefs, attitudes, and values can be vital to planning your speech. If their beliefs are built on faulty or incomplete understanding, you may be able to provide new and better information. Understanding their attitudes can suggest what strategies you might use to get a fair hearing. Suppose you are preparing a speech opposing capital punishment, and you know that most members of your audience strongly favor this policy. Audiences that have negative attitudes toward your position may distort your message, discredit you as a communicator, or even refuse to listen to you. Understanding these tendencies, how can you maintain your position and still reach listeners? One way to deal with a negative audience advises you to build identification between yourself and your audience, to avoid the use of emotion, relying instead on rational appeals, to limit what you hope to accomplish, and to acknowledge that others may believe differently.[8] Such strategies should be considered as you plan and prepare your message. These and other techniques for handling reluctant audiences are discussed in detail in Chapter 13.

How can you find out in advance about your audience's values, beliefs, and attitudes? In the classroom it is not difficult because people reveal this kind of information constantly as they speak and take part in class discussions. Outside the classroom such information may be harder to obtain. However, as you question the person who invites you to speak, ask about attitudes and values that may be related to your topic.

If advance knowledge of audience dynamics is critical to your presentation, conduct a survey to explore your listeners' knowledge of the subject, their relevant attitudes and values, and how they might respond to sources of information you might use in your speech. Classroom surveys can yield helpful results if you use the following guidelines to prepare your questionnaire:

- Use language that is concrete, clear, and easy to understand.
- Keep your questions short and to the point.
- Use simple rather than complex or compound sentences.
- Avoid words such as *all*, *always*, *none*, and *never*.
- Keep bias out of your questions so you don't skew the results.
- Provide room for comments.
- Keep the questionnaire short.

Ask your instructor's permission to hand out the survey at the beginning of a class period and to take it up at the end. Figure 4.3 shows a sample survey questionnaire on the subject of capital punishment that may be used as a guide to developing a questionnaire on your subject.

FIGURE 4.3

Sample Attitude Questionnaire

For each question, please circle the number that most clearly represents your position.

1. How interested are you in the topic of capital punishment?

Very Interested		Unconcerned				Not Interested
7	6	5	4	3	2	1

2. How important do you think the issue of capital punishment is?

Very Important		No Opinion				Very Unimportant
7	6	5	4	3	2	1

3. How much do you know about capital punishment?

Very Little		Average Amount				Very Much
7	6	5	4	3	2	1

4. How would you describe your attitude toward capital punishment?

Total Opposition		"On the Fence"				Total Support
7	6	5	4	3	2	1

5. Please place a check beside the sources of information on capital punishment that you would find the most acceptable.

_____ Attorney general's office

_____ FBI

_____ Local police department

_____ Criminal justice department of the university

_____ American Civil Liberties Union

_____ Local religious leaders

_____ Conference of Christians and Jews

_____ NAACP

_____ Other (please specify) _____

Comments:

ADJUSTING TO AUDIENCE DEMOGRAPHICS

From our in-depth look at the dynamics of human behavior, we turn now to **audience demographics**, those observable characteristics of your listeners that are important to successful audience adaptation. These characteristics include age, gender, education level, group affiliations, and sociocultural background. You need to gather as much information as you can about these factors as you plan and prepare your message. If you are not familiar with the group you are invited to address, seek such demographic information from the person who invites you to speak. You might also talk with group members or contact others who may have such knowledge.

During political campaigns, demographic analyses are used to help candidates identify audience concerns. In your speech class, such information can help you estimate interest in your topic and how much listeners may already know about it. When you combine this information with an understanding of audience dynamics you can get some idea of how they may feel about your subject, and how you might motivate them. Your instructor may conduct such an analysis early in the term and distribute the results to the class.

If introductory speeches are presented in your class, they should also provide useful demographic information. *Your own eyes and ears may be your best tools for audience analysis.* The information you get from really listening to your classmates, combined with insights from public opinion surveys, can help you adjust your message. Information on public opinions is readily available in popular periodicals: the *Washington Post National Weekly Edition* devotes one page of each issue to "What Americans Think"; *Harper's* magazine regularly includes "Harper's Index," a compilation of unusual and interesting statistics; *USA Today* provides tidbits of poll results on a daily basis; demographic data with a marketing orientation appears monthly in *American Demographics;* and each January, the American Council on Education releases the results of a national survey of attitudes of college freshmen that are usually reported in the *Chronicle of Higher Education.*

A word of caution is needed when it comes to interpreting and acting on demographic data. Note that in our discussion we have used words like "estimate" and "insights." Most information on audience demographics — as well as on attitudes and values — is gathered through surveys that rely on self-reports. Survey data is prone to error because people tend to give "socially appropriate" responses to questions. This doesn't necessarily mean people are lying, just that they will report what they "think they ought to say" rather than what they actually end up doing. For example, in a nationwide survey of college freshmen conducted in the early fall of 1992, over 75 percent of the students polled reported that they planned to vote in the presidential election that year. The election results painted a different picture of actual participation by young voters.[9]

Note finally that the relevance of specific demographic factors will vary from topic to topic. For example, if you were speaking on "Government

Services — Get What Your Taxes Pay For," age might be an important consideration, but gender or religious affiliation might be irrelevant.

Age

Age has been used to predict audience reactions since the time of Aristotle, who suggested that young listeners are pleasure loving, optimistic, impulsive, trusting, idealistic, and easily persuaded. Older people, he said, are more set in their ways, more skeptical, cynical, and concerned with maintaining a comfortable existence. Those in the prime of life, Aristotle suggested, present a balance between youth and age, being confident yet cautious, judging cases by the facts, and taking all things in moderation.[10]

Contemporary communication research supports the relationship between age and persuasibility that Aristotle described. Maximum susceptibility to persuasion occurs during childhood and declines as people grow older. Most research also suggests that younger people are more flexible and open to new ideas, but older people tend to be more conservative and less receptive to change. Some recent research, however, suggests that older adults may be more willing to change than previously thought.[11] You can change the minds of older adults, but you'll have to work harder to do it.

What expectations might you have about your classroom audience? To begin with, the average college student is getting older. In 1987, 16 percent of college students were over 35; by 1997 this figure is expected to rise to 22 percent.[12] Age can be an important factor in the selection of speech topics. For example, an audience consisting mainly of eighteen- and nineteen-year-olds might be interested in a speech on campus social activities. To an older audience, this topic could seem trivial or uninteresting.

What else does contemporary research tell us about today's college students? In 1994, first-year students at more than six hundred colleges and universities expressed less concern for political affairs than in any of the preceding twenty-nine years the Higher Education Research Institute at UCLA has conducted surveys. The 1994 survey of more than 300,000 students indicated that they also were less likely to participate in community action programs, environmental cleanup activities, or programs designed to help promote racial understanding. Politically, slightly over half of the students identified themselves as "middle-of-the-road," with the others split fairly equally between liberal and conservative. Although they are not activists, they do hold strong political and social attitudes. As Figure 4.4 shows, approximately 80 percent think the death penalty should not be abolished and about three quarters believe "there is too much concern in the courts for the rights of criminals." In other areas the students support greater government efforts to protect the environment (84 percent), control the sale of handguns (80 percent), protect consumers (72 percent), promote energy conservation (72 percent), and develop a national health care plan (70 percent)

Such survey information provides interesting discoveries, but keep in mind that these conclusions are based on national data and may not neces-

FIGURE 4.4

Some Sample Beliefs of Today's College Students

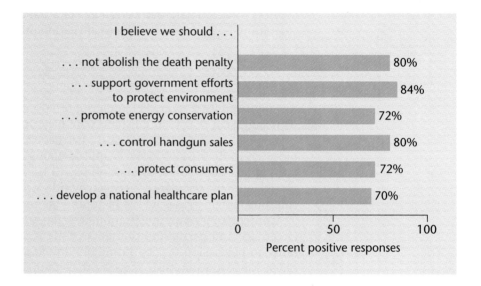

sarily describe *your* classmates. Your own observations may help you confirm or correct this portrait of the typical college student insofar as your listeners are concerned.

Gender

In our society, ideas about gender differences are changing rapidly. The changes are especially marked in the areas of "gender-appropriate" roles and interests. During the 1950s, when your authors were in undergraduate school, one of them could not participate in intercollegiate debate because she was female and debate was deemed more useful for the males who were more likely to be lawyers or politicians, and thus would benefit more from the experience. During that same time *Life* magazine interviewed five (male) psychiatrists who suggested that women's ambitions were the "root of mental illness in wives, emotional upset in husbands, and homosexuality in boys."[13] As late as 1981, this same publication introduced the first female Supreme Court justice, Sandra Day O'Connor, with the headline, "President Goes A-Courtin'."[14]

Some of the greatest changes in gender differences have been in education, work, and politics. In 1950 only 24 percent of all college degrees went to women; by 1990 women earned 53 percent of all degrees awarded.[15] In 1962, 43 percent of females between the ages of 25 and 54 were in the labor force; by 1990 this was up to 75 percent. Between 1980 and 1990 the number of female professionals rose 100 percent and the number of female managers just about doubled. These changes in education and work are beginning to show up in changes in women's perceived leadership potential. A 1994 study reported that, for the first time, women were slightly more likely to emerge as leaders than men in mixed sex groups.[16] Moreover, such female leaders do not simply take on "masculine" traits, such as dominance and control motives. Both they and the male leaders are likely to represent a blend of gender-related qualities: they are competitive and independent, yet sensitive and supportive.

The role of women in politics has also changed: in the 1992 American presidential election, 54 percent of the voters were women, and more females sought and won public office than ever before.[17] The 1977–79 Congress of the United States had 20 female members; the 1993–95 Congress had 55.[18] Once elected to office, females tend to vote more in favor of health care reforms, women's rights, and bills providing services for women and children than their male counterparts. Female legislators are also more likely to oppose the death penalty, nuclear power plants, and legislation prohibiting abortion. Similar changes in women's political power have been noted in Canada. In the 1993 election there were 245 female legislative candidates.[19] Women won 54 seats in the 295-member House of Commons, 16 more than in the 1988 election.[20]

As you consider gender, be careful not to fall into the trap of stereotypes. For example, many people still think of automobiles as a traditionally "male domain," yet in 1992 females bought approximately 50 percent of all new cars.[21] When purchasing cars, women tend to be more discriminating buyers. A *U.S. News/CNN* poll conducted in 1995 reported that women rated safety features, fuel economy, resale value, *Consumer Reports* ratings, and horsepower as more important factors in their purchasing decisions than did men. In fact, the only factor in the survey that men rated as more important was the color of the car.[22]

Given such rapid changes, is there any way you can use gender as a reliable factor in audience analysis? First, be sure that any differences reported *really make a difference*. Often the communication differences between genders, while statistically significant, can be so small that they have no practical significance.[23] Next, be certain that any assumptions you make are based on the most current data available because the differences are often a matter of "now you see them, now you don't." Differences that seem true even as we write may be outdated by the time you read this text. Finally, be careful to avoid sexism and gender stereotyping. These two topics are covered in detail later in this chapter.

Educational Level

You can better estimate your listeners' knowledge of and interest in a topic from their educational level than from their age or gender. The more educated your audience, the more you can assume they know about general topics and current affairs, and the broader their range of interests is apt to be. Research suggests that better-educated audiences are more interested in social, consumer, political, and environmental issues. They are more curious, and they enjoy learning about new ideas, new things, and new places. If your speech presents a fresh perspective on a familiar problem, they should be avid listeners. Finally, better-educated audiences tend to be more open minded. They are more accepting of social and technological changes and more supportive of women's rights and alternative lifestyles than are less-educated listeners.[24]

Educational differences can also affect the strategies you use in a speech. For example, if there are several positions on an issue, you should assume that a better-educated audience will be aware of them. Therefore, you should be especially careful to acknowledge alternative viewpoints and explain why you have selected your position.[25] Although you should always speak from responsible knowledge, knowing that your listeners are highly educated places even more pressure on you for careful preparation. A well-educated audience will require that you supply evidence and examples that can stand up under close scrutiny. If you are not well prepared, such listeners will question your credibility.

Group Affiliations

The groups people belong to reflect their interests, attitudes, and values. Knowing the occupations, political preferences, religious affiliations, and social group memberships of an audience can provide useful information. This knowledge can help you design a speech that better fits the interests and needs of your listeners. It can make your message more relevant and can help promote identification between listeners and your ideas.

Occupational Groups.   Members of occupational groups are united by special employment interests. For example, members of the Speech Communication Association share concerns about educational policies and practices, freedom of speech, and communication ethics. In business organizations, union members typically care about seniority, salary, benefits, and working conditions as well as the overall health of the company that provides their livelihood. Knowing your listeners' occupational affiliations, or in the case of your classmates their work aspirations, can suggest the kinds of examples that will best illustrate your ideas or the authorities they will find most credible. If many of your classmates are business majors, for instance, they may place more credence in information drawn from the *Wall Street Journal* than from *USA Today*.

Occupational group membership can also provide insight into how much your listeners know about a topic and which aspects of it should be more interesting to them. Use this information to guide your selection of topics and choice of examples. It may even suggest the kind of language you should use. For example, speeches on tax-saving techniques given to professional writers and then to certified public accountants should not have the same focus or use the same language. With the writers you might stress record keeping and business deductions and avoid using technical jargon. With the CPAs you might concentrate on factors that invite audits by the IRS, and you would not have to be so concerned about translating technical terms into lay language.

Political Groups.   Members of organized political groups are generally quite interested in problems of public life. Knowing how interested in politics your listeners are and their political party preferences can be useful in planning and preparing your speech.[26] For example, Democrats and Republicans often have different political agendas. During the 1992 presidential campaign Perot supporters emerged as the "radical middle," that 20 to 30 percent of the electorate at the center of the political spectrum, disdainful of the traditional parties, and ready to try something new.[27]

People with strong political ties usually make their feelings known. Some of your classmates may be members of the Young Democrats or Young Republicans. Your college may conduct mock elections or take straw votes on issues of political interest, reporting the results in the campus newspaper. Be on the alert for such information.

Religious Groups. Knowing the religious affiliations of listeners can provide useful information because religious training often underlies many of our social and cultural attitudes and values. Members of fundamentalist religious groups are likely to have conservative social and political attitudes. Baptists tend to be more conservative than Episcopalians, who in turn are often more conservative than Unitarians. In addition, a denomination may advocate specific beliefs that many of its members accept as a part of their religious heritage.

A word of caution needs to be added here. You can't always assume that because an individual is a member of a particular religious group, he or she will embrace all of the teachings of that group. For example, you might expect audiences that are primarily Roman Catholic to have negative attitudes toward abortion and birth control. A 1995 *Time/CNN* survey reported that 79 percent of American Catholics believe they should make up their own minds on moral issues such as birth control and abortion and 80 percent believe it is possible to disagree with the Pope on official moral issues and still be a good Catholic.[28]

One thing you can count on, however, is that audiences are usually quite sensitive concerning topics related to their religious convictions. As a speaker you should be aware of this sensitivity and be attuned to the religious make-up of your anticipated audience. Appealing to "Christian" values before an audience that includes members of other religious groups may offend listeners and diminish the effectiveness of your message. The classroom audience of today will likely be made up of students from different religious backgrounds. Since religious affiliation may be a strong indicator of values, it is wise not to ignore its potential importance.

Social Groups. Membership in social groups can be as important to people as any other kind of affiliation. Typically, we are born into a religious group, raised in a certain political environment, and end up in an occupation as much by chance as by design. But we choose our social groups on the basis of our interests. Photographers join the Film Club, business people become involved with the Chamber of Commerce, environmentalists may be members of the Sierra Club, and feminists may join the National Organization for Women.

Knowing which social groups are represented in your audience and what they stand for is important for effective audience adaptation. A speech favoring pollution control measures might take a different focus depending on whether it is presented to the Chamber of Commerce or to the Audubon Society. With the Chamber of Commerce you might stress the importance of a clean environment in inducing businesses to relocate in your community; with the Audubon Society you might emphasize the effects of pollution on wildlife. People tend to make their important group memberships known to others around them. Be alert to such information from your classmates and consider it in planning and preparing your speeches.

Sociocultural Background

People often are grouped by sociocultural background, a broad category that can include everything from the section of the country in which they live to their racial or ethnic identity. There is a wealth of survey data available on such groups. For example, a recent article in *Marketing Power* described some of the characteristics of Texans, who spend more than the average American on deodorant, diet pills, and disposable diapers.[29] While such reports may be fascinating to read, they often do not provide a speaker with the kind of insight that is helpful in planning and preparing presentations. One thing you can count on, however, is that your classroom audience will probably represent many different cultures. Data from the 1990 census shows that almost 25 percent of Americans have an African, Asian, Hispanic, or Native American heritage.[30] If you live in New Mexico, California, Hawaii, New York, or the District of Columbia, there is a greater than 50 percent chance that any two individuals you encounter will differ ethnically or racially.[31]

People from different sociocultural backgrounds often have different experiences, interests, and ways of looking at things. Consider, for example, the different perspectives that urban and rural audiences may have on gun control. Urban audiences may associate guns with crime and violence in the streets, and rural audiences may associate guns with hunting and recreation. A white, middle-class audience might have difficulty understanding what it means to grow up as a member of a minority. Midwesterners and southerners may have misconceptions about each other.

Since most college classes represent a variety of backgrounds, you must strive to reach the majority without ignoring or offending the minority. Remember that two of the major pillars of ethical speaking are respect for your audience and concern for the consequences of your words. With diverse audiences your appeals and examples should relate to those experiences, feelings, values, and motivations that people hold in common. It also may be helpful to envision smaller audiences within the larger group. You may even want to direct specific remarks to these smaller groups. You might say, for example, "Those of you majoring in the liberal arts will find computer skills just as important in your work as they are for business majors," or "Those of you majoring in business may discover that large corporations are looking for employees with the breadth of perspective that comes from a liberal arts education." Direct references to specific subgroups within the audience can keep your speech from seeming too general.

If your classmates gave introductory speeches or responded to one another in class, you should have a good idea of the diversity of their backgrounds and interests. This specific information will be much more valuable than anything you can learn from reading about college students in magazines or books. *They* are the listeners you will address. When you accept invitations to speak outside the classroom, ask questions about the demographic make-up of your anticipated audience. The more information you have about listeners, the better you should be able to adapt your message and the better it should be received.

MEETING THE CHALLENGES OF AUDIENCE DIVERSITY

Some thirty years ago Marshall McLuhan, an English professor at the University of Toronto, suggested that technological changes in the media of communication were turning the world into a "global village."[32] Today we live in the global village that McLuhan envisioned.[33] Instantaneous satellite transmissions bring news into your living room as it happens. PCs, modems, the Internet, and commercial on-line services provide immediate access to information previously available only in the libraries of prestigious colleges and universities. Speeches that once were dusty relics in the pages of anthologies come to life through the wizardry of videotape and CD-ROMS. Jury trials and peace negotiations take place under the watchful electronic eye. Teleconferences and computer conferencing make it possible for executives in Singapore to "meet" with executives in New York without having to travel. National boundaries are dissolving as time and space no longer impede the flow of information and ideas. Today's media have the power to penetrate ideological walls.[34]

As we move into the twenty-first century, we must adapt to this changing technology and the diverse cultural world in which we all live. There is no alternative. Although speaking to a diverse audience always represents a challenge, we choose to look upon it more as an opportunity than as an obstacle. In fact, learning how to communicate with a diverse audience can be one of the most rewarding experiences of your public speaking class. This skill will also help you in the world of work. National and international companies now invest heavily in training their executives and employees to communicate more effectively within and across cultures.[35]

To make the most of the opportunities of addressing varied audiences, you must be able to avoid some pitfalls. You must understand the power of stereotypes and bias and of the problematic "isms" — ethnocentrism, sexism, and racism. Finally, you should know how to find and build common ground with your listeners.

Stereotypes and Bias

We inevitably use past experience — either our own or that of others — to interpret new information and to guide our interactions with other people. To use past experience most efficiently, we think and react in terms of categories. For example, having read and heard many stories about poisonous reptiles, we may decide to be careful around all creatures that fall into the category of snakes. Problems can arise, however, when we start categorizing people. Such categories can easily harden into stereotypes. **Stereotypes** are rigid sets of beliefs and expectations that prepare and predispose us toward good or bad, desirable or undesirable encounters with others. Our positive or negative stereotypes reflect the attitudes or biases we have toward the group.[36] When stereotypes dominate our thinking, we react more to them than to the people we meet who seem to fit within them.

People form stereotypes based on easily visible characteristics such as gender, race, or age.[37] Other factors on which stereotypes are often based include a person's ethnic identity, religion, occupation, or place of residence. Our stereotypes may arise from many sources. We can form them from direct experiences with a few individuals who we then assume to be representative of a group. Most stereotypes, however, are formed indirectly from our families and friends, schools and churches, or media exposure. For example, our stereotype of Native Americans may fall into the "Tonto syndrome" often portrayed in Western movies, or our stereotype of Japanese businessmen may be shaped by watching derogatory films like "Rising Sun."[38] As we noted in Chapter 3, such biases or stereotypes can impair our listening ability. As we will see in Chapter 6, they may also intrude on our selection and evaluation of supporting materials.

Whatever their origin, stereotypes can have a powerful influence on our thinking. Too often, we judge the people we meet by our stereotypes and not upon their own merits as individuals. Stereotypes are also persistent: we are reluctant to give them up, especially when they agree with the stereotypes possessed by our friends and families. When we encounter people who do not fit our stereotypes, we may discount them as "exceptions to the rule." Beyond their obvious unfairness, stereotypes can also lead to disastrous behaviors. In their most extreme form they can justify the genocide that took place in Hitler's Germany or the more recent "ethnic cleansing" in places like Bosnia.

Ethnocentrism, Sexism, and Racism

Ethnocentrism, sexism, and racism represent the most common types of problems that impede effective communication with a diverse audience.

Ethnocentrism.   As we noted in Chapter 1, **ethnocentrism** is the belief that our way of life is the "right" and superior way. Actually, ethnocentrism is not always bad. In its milder form ethnocentrism expresses itself in patriotism and national pride. It helps people unite and work toward common goals. It satisfies our need for esteem by picturing us as members of a valued group. It encourages immigrants to assimilate into a new national identity that provides common ground for living and getting along with one another.

But ethnocentrism can have a darker side. Charles De Gaulle, who led the French people during the mid-twentieth century, once noted: "Patriotism is when love of your own people comes first; nationalism, when hate for people other than your own comes first."[39] As we noted in Chapter 1, the "melting pot" metaphor of our American heritage may have exaggerated ethnocentrism and expressed something of its darker side. It made people want to forsake their roots and origins. *When ethnocentrism goes beyond pride in one's own group to the rejection or derogation of others, it becomes a real problem in human relations and a formidable barrier to cross-cultural communication.*

One of your authors' grandparents immigrated from Sweden. Only the eldest child in their family learned the Swedish language and all that got passed down to your author was the ability to insult someone in Swedish. In like manner, other immigrants and Native Americans were encouraged to become "Americanized." They were urged to give up their language and their cultural beliefs and practices. Some even gave up their "foreign sounding" names, especially if they went into show business or politics. In short, they were pressured into becoming amalgamated American citizens in the vast "melting pot." In contrast, Canadians historically viewed their culture as a "mosaic" and tolerated greater ethnic diversity.[40]

The first step in controlling ethnocentrism is to recognize any tendencies you may have to undervalue other cultures. *We must learn to look for and respect the humanity in all people, and to recognize that this humanity transcends race and culture.* Obviously, you should avoid offensive language that puts others down on the basis of their race or group affiliation. Also, keep in mind that any group may suffer the pains of ethnocentrism. As Southerners, your authors were offended during the 1992 presidential campaign when the Clinton-Gore ticket was referred to by journalists on national news shows as the "Bubba" ticket. In northern New Mexico, Native Americans sometimes use the term "Tejanos," which literally means "Texans," as an insult for all newcomers — regardless of their race — who are neither of Spanish nor American Indian ancestry.[41]

Sexism. Sexism occurs when we allow gender stereotypes to control our interactions with members of the opposite sex. **Gender stereotyping** involves making broad generalizations about men or women based on outmoded assumptions, such as "men don't know how to take care of children" or "women don't understand business." Such beliefs transcend national boundaries and have been reported in over thirty countries in North and South America, Europe, Africa, Asia, and Australia.[42] Gender stereotyping is especially problematic when it implies that differences between men and women justify discrimination. As you plan and prepare your message, try to be aware of any gender stereotypes you might have that could interfere with effective communication. Be especially careful not to portray gender roles in ways suggesting superiority or inferiority. For instance, when you use examples or stories to illustrate a point, don't make all your authority figures male.

Gender stereotyping often reveals itself in the use of sexist language. As you plan and prepare your speeches, you must carefully consider the language that you use so that you can avoid such problems. **Sexist language** involves making gender references in situations where the gender is unknown or irrelevant. It may involve the generic use of masculine nouns or pronouns, such as referring to "man's advances in science" or using *he* when the intended reference is to both sexes. You can avoid this problem simply by saying "she or he" or by using the plural "they." Some people have criticized this practice, saying that it makes the wording of messages awkward. They scoff at the seriousness of the problem. In her book on gender and communication, Julia Wood demonstrated how important such language practices can be through the experience of a skeptical male student who suddenly found the situation reversed:

> For a long time I thought all this stuff about generic *he* was a bunch of junk. I mean it seemed really clear to me that a word like *mankind* obviously includes women or that *chairman* can refer to a girl or a guy who chairs something. I thought it was pretty stupid to hassle about this. Then last semester, I had a woman teacher who taught the whole class using *she* or *her* or *woman* whenever she was referring to people as well as when she meant just women. I realized how confusing it is. I had to figure out each time whether she meant women only or women and men. And when she meant women to be general, I guess you'd say generic for all people, it still made me feel left out. A lot of the guys in the class got pretty hostile about what she was doing, but I kind of think it was a good way to make the point.[43]

Racism.   Just as gender stereotyping and sexist language can block communication, so can racism. Although blatant racism and discrimination are no longer socially acceptable in most circles, a subtle form of such prejudice can still infect our thinking. While we may pay lip service to the principles of racial equality, we may still engage in **symbolic racism.**[44] In some contexts, when we say, "In our [white] neighborhood we believe in family values," the unspoken message may be "therefore, we are superior to your race." Or we might say, "We believe in hard work and earning our pay," when we really mean, "Why don't you [black] people get off welfare!" Thus we may cling to and excuse the vestiges of racial stereotypes by appeals to values like family stability or the Protestant work ethic.[45] In such cases our accusatory message may be, our race honors such values and yours doesn't.

It may be helpful to view the impact that racism can have from the perspective of someone on the receiving end. NBC's "Today" show co-host, Bryant Gumbel, commented on how it feels:

> It is very hard for any white person to appreciate the depth of what it means to be black in America. . . . Racism isn't only being called a nigger and spit on. It's being flipped the bird when you're driving, or walking into a store and being asked to check your bag, or being ignored at the checkout counter, or entering a fine restaurant and being stared at.[46]

As you take the factor of race into consideration in your audience analysis, examine your thinking for biases and stereotypes that you may rationalize as value or lifestyle differences. Be sensitive about the language you use. When you are referring to a different racial or ethnic group, use the terms *they* prefer and avoid using the trigger words we discussed in Chapter 3. Stay away from examples that cast members of a particular ethnic group into stereotypical roles that imply inferiority. And of course, avoid racist humor.

One language problem that relates to all three of these negative "isms" is **marking**, adding an irrelevant reference to gender, ethnicity, race, or sexual preference when none is needed. For example, if you referred to "Thompson, the African-American engineer," you might be trivializing her contribution by drawing attention to race when it is irrelevant. Some audience members may interpret your remarks as suggesting that "Thompson is a pretty good engineer *for a person of color,*" whether you intend that or not. The following excerpt from a speech by Martina Navratilova, who was named the world's top-rated female tennis player for seven years, shows how marking affects people:

> Labels, labels, labels — now, I don't know about you, but I hate labels. Martina Navratilova, the lesbian tennis player. They don't say Joe Montana, the heterosexual football player. One's sexuality should not be an issue. . . . I did not spend over 30 years of my life working my butt off trying to become the very best tennis player that I can be, to then be

Avoiding Racist and Sexist Language

1 Do not use slang terms to refer to racial, ethnic, religious, or gender groups.
2 Avoid using the generic *he* and gender-specific titles such as chair*man*.
3 Avoid "markers" that introduce irrelevant references to race, gender, or ethnicity.
4 Avoid stereotypic references that imply inferiority or superiority.
5 Do not use sexist, racist, ethnic, or religious humor.

SPEAKER'S
NOTES

called Martina, the lesbian tennis player. Labels are for filing. Labels are for bookkeeping. Labels are for clothing. Labels are not for people.[47]

Finding Common Ground

A recent study sponsored by the National Conference of Christians and Jews demonstrated that stereotypes and prejudice are present in all groups in our culture. The survey revealed that people of color see whites as "bigoted, bossy, and unwilling to share power."[48] Although each of the minority groups surveyed also demonstrated negative stereotypes of and feelings toward other people of color, they were united by a collective sense of being victims of discrimination. Fully 80 percent of African Americans, 60 percent of Latino Americans, and 57 percent of Asian Americans are convinced that their opportunities in work, housing, and education are not equal to those enjoyed by whites. On the other hand, over 50 percent of all whites believe that people of color enjoy equal opportunities. The survey concluded that "most whites simply do not acknowledge the tangible effects that discrimination has on the daily lives of minorities."

Lest you think the situation is hopeless, we should also point out that there were some positive results in this research. More than 80 percent of all groups polled expressed admiration of Asian Americans for the value they presumably place on intellectual and professional achievement and for having strong family ties and respecting their elders. Similarly large majorities felt that Latino Americans take pride in their culture, work hard to attain a better life, and have deep religious and family ties. Equally sizable majorities agreed that African Americans work hard when given a chance, believe strongly in American ideals and the American Dream, are deeply religious, and have made valuable contributions to American society. Over 90 percent of all groups surveyed also agreed that learning to understand and appreciate the lifestyles, tastes, and contributions of each other's groups was either "very important" or "important." *The most heartening finding of the study was the indication that nine out of ten Americans from all groups would be willing to work with each other to try to solve the most pressing problems in their neighborhoods and communities.* They expressed a willingness to work together to help protect each other's children from gangs and violence, to help improve schools, including teaching understanding and respect for the cultural heritage of all groups, and to look for ways to ease racial, religious, and ethnic tensions.

In her book, *The Mismeasure of Women,* Carol Tarvis suggests that focusing on differences between the sexes strengthens the myths that perpetuate misunderstandings.[49] This insight is probably equally applicable in terms of ethnic and racial differences. In Chapter 1 we noted that the Institute for Global Ethics identified eight **universal human values** that transcend cultural differences: love, truthfulness, fairness, freedom, unity, tolerance, responsibility, and respect for life.[50] Contemporary social scientific research has also demonstrated the existence of transcendent social values. Shalom Schwartz and his associates at the Hebrew University of

Jerusalem conducted a study of values in twenty different countries. They identified ten universal values: achievement, tradition, power, enjoyment, self-direction, security, universalism, benevolence, conformity, and stimulation.[51] Although these two lists of values are not identical, the differences are more a matter of terminology and approach than of substance. The Institute for Global Ethics emphasized what Schwartz and his colleagues identified as benevolence and universalism. The Schwartz study defined values more broadly to include motivational concepts. Figure 4.5 lists these universal values and shows how they appear to come together.

If you can appeal to these common values in your speeches to a diverse audience, you can often unite your listeners behind your ideas or suggestions. Senator Carol Moseley-Braun turned the tide of congressional support against endorsing the United Daughters of the Confederacy's use of the Confederate battle flag in their emblem by appealing to the more universal values of freedom, unity, and tradition:

> The only issue is whether or not this body is prepared to put its imprimatur on the Confederate insignia used by the United Daughters of the Confederacy. . . . [T]hose of us whose ancestors fought on a different side in the Civil War, or who were held, frankly, as human chattel under the Confederate flag, are duty bound to honor our ancestors as well by asking whether such recognition by the U.S. Senate is appropriate.

FIGURE 4.5
Universal Values

POWER	Social power, authority, recognition from others, wealth
ACHIEVEMENT	Success, ambition, influence
TRADITION	Accepting one's fate, devout, humble, respect for cultural heritage
ENJOYMENT	Pleasure
SELF-DIRECTION	Freedom, independence, choice of own goals, self-respect, curiosity, creativity
SECURITY	National security, social order, family security, sense of belonging, personal health and cleanliness, reciprocity in personal relationships
UNITY	Unity with nature, protecting the environment, inner harmony, social justice, equality, tolerance, world peace
BENEVOLENCE	Honesty, helpfulness, forgiveness, loyalty, responsibility, friendship, love, spiritual life, meaning in life
CONFORMITY	Politeness, obedience, self-discipline, honoring parents and elders
STIMULATION	Variety, excitement, daring

> So I submit, as Americans we have an obligation . . . to make a statement that we believe the Civil War is over. . . . Whether we are black or white, Northerners or Southerners, all Americans share a common flag. The flag which is behind you right now, Mr. President, is our flag. . . .[52]

ADJUSTING TO THE COMMUNICATION SITUATION

Finally, we come to the actual situation of your speech. It would be a shame if, after considering carefully the dynamics that might drive audience behavior, the demographics that might affect your particular audience, and the challenges of diversity that might enrich or diminish your interaction with listeners, you should stumble over some pitfalls in the situation itself. To make your final successful adjustment to your audience and situation, you must consider the time, place, occasion, size of the audience, and overall context of your speech.

Time

The time of day, day of the week, time of the year, and amount of time allotted for speaking may all call for careful consideration.[53] If you are speaking early in the morning, you may need to be more forceful to awaken listeners. The vigor of your voice and manner of presentation must carry the idea that you have an important message to bring. Since all of us have a tendency to yawn — at least mentally — after a good meal, after-dinner speeches (discussed in detail in Chapter 15) almost always need lively examples and humor to keep listeners from nodding off. Speeches scheduled for the evening present a similar problem. Often listeners will have already completed a day at work and will have left the comforts of home to hear what you have to say. Your speech must justify their attendance with good ideas presented in artful ways.

Check List for Analyzing the Communication Situation

1 Will the time or timing of my speech present any challenges?
2 Will room arrangements be adequate? Will I have the equipment I need for presentation aids?
3 What does the audience expect on this occasion?
4 Is there any late-breaking news on my topic?
5 Will I possibly have to adjust to previous speakers?
6 How large will the audience be?

SPEAKER'S NOTES

Elie Wiesel, recipient of the 1986 Nobel Peace Prize, had to overcome many distractions when speaking at this Holocaust memorial service. A compelling message and a forceful presentation can help speakers cope with problems of traffic noise and inclement weather.

If your speech is scheduled on a Monday, when people have not yet resigned themselves to the weekend being over, or on a Friday, when listeners may drift to the weekend ahead, you may have to plan some especially interesting materials to gain and hold attention. Similarly, gloomy winter days or balmy spring weather can put people in different frames of mind and their moods can color how they receive your speech.[54] Your materials and presentation style will have to be bright and engaging to overcome audience blahs or prevent their daydreaming.

The amount of time allotted for your presentation is also critical. *A short speech does not necessarily mean shorter preparation time.* Short speeches require you to focus your topic so that it can be handled in the time allotted (see Chapter 5). Short presentations also demand that you restrict yourself to no more than two or three main points, and that you be very selective as you decide on supporting materials (see Chapters 6 and 7). Choose the most relevant and impressive facts, statistics, and testimony, the most striking examples and stories. Structure your speech so that you begin with a burst and end with a bang. To make these selections, you must be able to draw from a wide range of materials. Even the short speech requires that you have a thorough grasp of your subject.

Place

The place where you will be speaking can also affect your planning. When speaking outside, you may have to cope with unpredictable distractions. When speaking inside, you need information concerning the size and layout of the room and the availability of a lectern or electronic equipment your presentation aids may require.

Even in the classroom, speakers must learn to cope with distractions — construction and traffic noises may filter in from outside or students in the hall may be raucous and loud. How can you handle such problems? If the noise is temporary, you should pause and wait until it stops, then repeat your last words and go on with your message. If the noise is constant you may have to speak louder to be heard. You may even have to pause and close a window or door. The important thing is to take such problems in stride and not let them distract you or your audience from your message. Sometimes a light remark can signal listeners that you are not flustered by the interruption: "This is the first time I've ever been heckled by a jack-hammer!" Then you can go on to command attention.

Occasion

As you plan and prepare your message, you need to take into account *why* people have gathered to listen. When an audience is required to attend a presentation, as in a mandatory employee meeting or a public speaking class, you may have to work hard to arouse interest and sustain attention. When members of an audience voluntarily attend a presentation, they usually have a good reason for doing so and are more motivated to listen. But you must know why they are there and what they expect to get from your speech. When a speaker does not offer the kind of message listeners expect, they may be puzzled or even annoyed. For example, if they are expecting an informative presentation on investment strategies and instead get a sales pitch for a mutual fund, they may feel exploited. This could result more in irritation than in persuasion.

Size of Audience

The size of your audience can affect how you speak. A small audience usually offers more direct feedback and the chance for more interactive communication. As a rule of thumb, a smaller audience invites a more casual presentation. You could easily overwhelm a small audience if you spoke with a formal oratorical style, an overly loud voice, or grandiose gestures. Such a presentation would be at best inappropriate, at worst ridiculous.

On the other hand, larger audiences offer less direct feedback. Because you cannot make or sustain eye contact with everyone, you should choose representative listeners in various sections of the audience and change your visual focus from time to time. Establishing eye contact with listeners in all sections of the room helps more people feel included. With large audiences you also should speak more deliberately and distinctly. Your gestures should be more emphatic so that everyone can see them, and any visual aids used must be large enough for those in the back of the audience to see without strain. We discuss such presentation factors in more detail in Chapter 11.

Context

Anything that happens near the time of your presentation becomes part of the context of your speech. Both recent speeches and recent events can influence how the audience responds to you.

The Context of Recent Speeches. Any speeches presented immediately before yours create an atmosphere in which you must work. This atmosphere has a **preliminary tuning effect** on listeners, preparing them to respond in certain ways to you and your message.[55] At political rallies, patriotic music and introductions prepare the audience for the appearance of the featured speaker. At concerts, warm-up groups put listeners in the mood for the star.

Preliminary tuning may also affect classroom presentations. Instructors may encourage an effective speaker to lead off, hoping to create a positive effect that stimulates others to do their best. Good speeches also help listeners become a more receptive audience. On the other hand, less successful speeches, especially if they come one after another, can create a downward spiral that both speakers and listeners must work to reverse.

Previous speeches also may affect the mood of an audience. If the speech right before yours covered a sensitive topic, it may have aroused strong emotions. In such a case you may need to ease the tension before you can expect listeners to give you favorable attention. One way of handling such a problem is to acknowledge the reactions and use them as a springboard into your own speech:

> **Obviously, many of us feel very strongly about the legalization of marijuana. What I'm going to talk about is also very important — but it is something I think we can all agree on — the challenge of finding a way to stop children from killing other children in our community.**

Another technique might be to begin with a story that involves listeners and refocuses their attention. At times humor can help relieve tension, but people who are upset may be in no mood for laughter. Your decision on whether to use humor must be based on your reading of the situation: the mood of listeners, the subject under discussion, and your own ability to use the technique effectively. We cover the use of narratives and humor in greater detail in Chapter 6.

In addition to dealing with the mood created by earlier speeches, you may also have to adapt to their content. Suppose you have spent the past week preparing a speech on the *importance* of extending endangered species legislation. Then the speaker before you makes a convincing presentation on the *problems* of extending endangered species legislation. What can you do? Try to turn this negative preliminary tuning to your advantage by adjusting your introduction. Point out that the earlier speech has established the importance of the topic but that — as good as that effort was — it did not give the total picture: "Now you will hear the *other* side of the story."

FIGURE 4.6
Audience Analysis
Worksheet

Topic: _____

Audience: _____

	Factor Description	Adaptations Needed
Audience Dynamics	Audience Attitude: _____	_____
	_____	_____
	Relevant Values: _____	_____
	_____	_____
	Motivational Appeals: _____	_____
	_____	_____
Audience Demographics	Age: _____	_____
	Gender: _____	_____
	Education: _____	_____
	Group Affiliations: _____	_____
	_____	_____
	Sociocultural Background: _____	_____
	_____	_____
	Interest in Topic: _____	_____
	_____	_____
	Knowledge of Topic _____	_____
	_____	_____
Speaking Situation	Time: _____	_____
	Place: _____	_____
	Occasion: _____	_____
	Audience Size: _____	_____
	Context: _____	_____

The Context of Recent Events. When listeners enter the room the day of your speech, they bring with them information about recent events. They will use this knowledge to evaluate what you say. If you are not up on the latest news about your topic, your credibility can suffer. A student in one of our classes once presented an interesting and well-documented speech comparing public housing in Germany with that in the United States. Unfortunately, she was unaware of a current scandal involving local public housing. For three days before her presentation, the story had made the front page of the local paper and was the lead story in area newscasts. Everyone expected her to mention it. Her failure to discuss this important local problem weakened her credibility.

In contrast, Rod Nishikawa used current events to lead into a persuasive speech urging support of gun control legislation. Shortly before his presentation, a crazed gunman had injured and killed a number of children in a school yard in Stockton, California. Rod presented an effective speech urging his classmates at the University of California — Davis to contact their local representatives in support of a pending gun-control bill. Because Stockton is near Davis, his references to the nearby massacre evoked vivid images.

At times the context of events to which you must adjust your speech may be totally unexpected. When that happens you must make on-the-spot adjustments so that things work in your favor. During the 1985 graduation ceremony at Loyola Marymount University, the school's president fell off the platform immediately before the commencement address. While the only thing injured was his dignity, the fall certainly distracted the audience. The speaker, Peter Ueberroth, organizer of the 1984 Los Angeles summer Olympic Games, recaptured their attention and brought down the house by awarding the president a 4.5 in gymnastics.[56]

Figure 4.6 provides an Audience Analysis Worksheet that will help you consider all the factors we have discussed in this chapter as you plan for the audience and situation of your speech.

IN SUMMARY

Both the audience you anticipate and the setting of your speech are critical to your planning. The central ethical question as you design your speech is whether you use adaptation techniques to disguise your real purpose or to reveal it more effectively to a particular audience. Successful audience adaptation requires that you understand audience dynamics, have important information concerning audience demographics, be sensitive to the challenges posed by audience diversity, and be able to adjust to situational factors.

Adapting to Audience Dynamics. *Motivation* explains why people behave as they do. People will listen, learn, and retain your message only if you can relate it to their needs, wants, or wishes. Some motives you may call on include comfort, safety, friendship, recognition, variety, control, independence, curiosity, tradition, success, nurturance, and enjoyment. Your audience's attitudes, beliefs, and values will affect the way they receive and interpret your message. If your listeners are initially negative toward your topic, you will have to adjust your presentation to receive a fair hearing.

Adjusting to Audience Demographics. *Audience demographics* include information about more specific characteristics of your listeners, such as their age, gender, educational level, group membership, and sociocultural make-up (race, social class, etc.). The more you know about such factors, the better you can tailor your speech so that it serves your listeners' interests and needs.

Meeting the Challenges of Audience Diversity. Today we live in a global village composed of many diverse groups. Learning to understand and adapt to diversity will help you prepare more effective messages. Examine your thinking for stereotypes that categorize people inflexibly and attribute positive or negative traits to them. Be on guard against ethnocentrism, sexism, and racism as you plan and prepare your presentations. When speaking to a diverse audience, search for common ground based on universal values.

Adjusting to the Communication Situation. You must be flexible enough to adjust to particular features of the speaking situation. The time in which you speak, the place of your speech, the constraints of the occasion, and the size of your audience can all pose challenges. In addition, you will be speaking in a context of other speeches and recent events, to which you must adjust as you make your presentation.

TERMS TO KNOW

audience dynamics	audience demographics
motivation	stereotypes
physiological needs	ethnocentrism
safety and security needs	sexism
belongingness needs	gender stereotyping
esteem needs	sexist language
self-actualization needs	symbolic racism
beliefs	marking
attitudes	universal human values
values	preliminary tuning effect

DISCUSSION

1. How might the following situations affect a speech you are about to give, and how would you adapt to them?

   a. You are the last speaker during the last class period before spring break.

   b. A lost student walks into the class right in the middle of your speech, looks around, says, "Excuse me," and walks out.

   c. The speaker right before you gives an incredibly successful speech, which brings spontaneous applause from the class and high praise from the instructor.

    d. The speaker right before you bombs badly. The speech is poorly prepared, the speaker is very nervous and simply stops in the middle and sits down, visibly upset.

    e. (It rarely happens, but . . .) The speaker right before you gives a speech on the same topic, taking the same general approach.

2. Rank the ten universal human values in Figure 4.5 in terms of their importance to you. Discuss how the three values you ranked highest might make you susceptible to certain speech topics and approaches.

3. Construct a demographic portrait of the average student at your school with respect to age, gender, educational background, group affiliations, and sociocultural background. What speech topics might this listener find most interesting? What motives, values, and attitudes might he or she bring to these topics?

4. Consider the following situation:

> **A Boston couple decided to spend their vacation in Memphis where they grew up and had families. On their way they stopped at the Shiloh Civil War Battleground where the guide extolled the virtues of the Northern forces in that battle. When their tour was finished, they thanked the guide and told her they wanted to get back home to Memphis before dark. She looked surprised and said, "From your license plate I assumed you were Yankees. I should have given you the 'Southern' tour."**

Working in small groups, discuss the ethical ramifications of this "adaptation." Have a spokesperson for your group present your conclusions to the class as a whole.

APPLICATION

1. Explain how you would tailor a speech on the general topic of recycling for an audience composed of

    a. high school sophomores.

    b. the local Chamber of Commerce.

    c. your college administration.

    d. your classmates.

2. If you were to speak on the general topic of recycling, what kinds of examples might you develop to appeal to the following audience needs?

    a. safety

    b. nurturance

    c. comfort

    d. recognition

3. Imagine for the moment that *you* are the speaker we mentioned at the beginning of this chapter. You are the president of Students for Environ-

mental Action. To refresh your memory, you have been asked to attend a meeting of new students at the soccer field at eight o'clock in the morning and to introduce them to SEA. Your major goals will be to inform them about SEA's projects for the coming year and to recruit new members. That evening, you have been invited to address the Coahoma County Industrial Development Board on "what you students are up to." Your task is to reassure them that SEA's work will help, not hinder, the business climate in the area.

Like every good speaker, you have carefully constructed a demographic analysis of both groups and have also identified some pertinent situational factors. Your task is to analyze the data that follows in light of what we have said in this chapter in order to plan an overall speech strategy. Develop a one-page written report for each speech that will outline a plan for adaptation to each audience and situation.

The audience for the morning speech consists of students attending the college for the first time. There are 4,526 first-year students and 803 transfer students, but not all of them will be at this student activities program. Most of them are from out of town and know very little about SEA. The average first-year student is nineteen years old. Fifty-five percent of the students are female and 45 percent are male. They come mainly from the small towns and rural areas within a 200-mile radius of the campus. Seventy percent of the students are white, twelve percent are African Americans, eight percent are Latinos, six percent are Asian Americans, and the rest are classified as "other." Most have been raised in blue-collar homes with traditional values and moderate political beliefs. About half are Democrats and half are Republicans. Over thirty percent of the students will be working to help pay for their education. You will be the seventh speaker on the program. You have been asked to hold your remarks to five minutes.

The audience for the second speech is the fifteen-member Industrial Development Board. All of them plan to attend the presentation in the executive board room of a local chemical manufacturing company at seven-thirty in the evening. You will make a fifteen-minute presentation, then answer questions. The board members represent a broad spectrum of business interests from service organizations to manufacturing. Thirteen members of the board are white, one is a Latino American, and one is an Asian American. Only one is a female. All are college educated and hold high-level technical or executive positions. Their average age is forty-seven. They are politically conservative and active in local politics. Nine are Republicans, four are Democrats, and two consider themselves Independents. Eight are members of the Junior Chamber of Commerce, four belong to the National Rifle Association, one is the president of Coahoma Bass Masters, and one is active in the Sierra Club. Hunting and fishing are the major recreational activities in the area. You are the only person scheduled to speak at the meeting. Last week the local paper printed an article outlining SEA's plans for the year, which include efforts to ban the dumping of industrial wastes into the Coahoma River and to lobby the state legislature to designate 300 acres of land owned by the college as a wildlife preserve.

This is the third year that SEA has been active on campus. The first year the group had twenty members. They assessed campus environmental problems and started a successful campus recycling effort. Last year SEA had over fifty members. They continued the recycling program and assessed environmental problems in the county. SEA's major project last year was to stop the poisoning of pigeons on campus. To call attention to the problem, the group had to take drastic action. They found out from someone in the grounds department when the poison was going to be set out. At five o'clock the next morning thirty SEA members collected the carcasses of dead pigeons and dumped them on the steps of the administration building, where they held a demonstration. The campus and local papers published pictures of the demonstrating students. The Associated Press picked up the story and called SEA "a junior Greenpeace."

You, the speaker, are a twenty-five-year-old junior pre-law major who served six years in the Navy. Your high school record was "undistinguished" and your successes in the military surprised you. While in the service you completed three courses at a junior college. You are a member of the African-American Students' Association and the Pre-Law Club in addition to being the president of SEA. A picture of you leading last year's demonstration was on the front page of the local paper. You care very strongly about this year's SEA projects. Although you are a hunter, you don't think campus land should be used for that purpose. You also believe that the dumping of wastes in the river can cause health problems in addition to spoiling recreational activities.

NOTES

1. Barbara Engler, *Personality Theories: An Introduction,* 4th ed. (Boston: Houghton Mifflin, 1995), pp. 273–280, 340–363; Edward Hoffman, "The Last Interview of Abraham Maslow," *Psychology Today* (Jan.-Feb. 1992): 68–74; Abraham H. Maslow, *Motivation and Personality* (New York: Harper, 1970).

2. Henry A. Murray, *Explorations in Personality* (New York: Oxford University Press, 1938).

3. Hoffman, pp. 68–74.

4. F. Gleicher and R. E. Petty, "Expectations of Reassurance Influence the Nature of Fear-Stimulated Attitude Change," *Journal of Experimental Social Psychology* 28 (1992): 86–100; Kim Witte, "Fear Control and Danger Control: A Test of the Extended Parallel Process Model (EPPM)," *Communication Monographs* 61 (1994): 113–134; Kim Witte and Kelly Morrison, "Using Scare Tactics to Promote Safer Sex Among Juvenile Detention and High School Youth," *Applied Communication Research* 23 (1995): 128–142.

5. Jib Fowles, "Advertising's Fifteen Basic Appeals," *Et Cetera* 39 (1982); reprinted in Robert Atwan, Barry Orton, and William Vesterman, *American Mass Media: Industries and Issues,* 3rd ed. (New York: Random House, 1986), pp. 43–54.

6. James M. Olson and Mark P. Zanna, "Attitudes and Attitude Change," *Annual Review of Psychology* 44 (1993): 117–154.

7. Rushworth M. Kidder, *Shared Values for a Troubled World* (San Francisco: Jossey-Bass, 1994); Milton Rokeach, *Beliefs, Attitudes and Values: A Theory of Organization and Change* (San Francisco: Jossey-Bass, 1970) and *The Nature of Human Values* (New York: Free Press, 1973); Shalom H. Schwartz and Wolfgang Bilsky, "Toward a Theory of the Universal Content and Structure of Values: Extensions and Cross-Cultural Replications," *Journal of Personality and Social Psychology* 58 (1990): 878–891; Shalom H. Schwartz, Sonia Roccas, and Lilach Sagiv, "Universals in the Content and Structure of Values: Theoretical Advances and Empirical Tests in Twenty Countries," *Advances in Experimental Social Psychology* 25 (1992): 1–65.

8. Herbert W. Simons, *Persuasion: Understanding, Practice, and Analysis,* 2nd ed. (Reading, MA: Addison-Wesley, 1986), pp. 121–139.

9. Attitude survey results were reported in Michele N.-K. Collison, "More Freshmen Say They Are Choosing Colleges Based on Costs," *Chronicle of Higher Education,* 22 Jan. 1991, pp. 33–37, and Mary Jordan, "More Freshmen Lean to the Left," *Washington Post National Weekly Edition,* 20–26 January 1992, p. 37. Actual voting records were reported in *The 1994 Information Please Almanac* (Boston: Houghton Mifflin, 1993), p. 644.

10. *The Rhetoric of Aristotle,* trans. George Kennedy (New York: Oxford University Press, 1992), pp. 163–169 (Book 2, Chs. 11–14).

11. William J. McGuire, "Attitudes and Attitude Change," in *The Handbook of Social Psychology,* vol. 2, eds. Gardner Lindzey and Elliot Aronson (New York: Random House, 1985), pp. 287–288; J. A. Krosnick and D. F. Alwin, "Aging and Susceptibility to Attitude Change," *Journal of Personality and Social Psychology* 57 (1989): 416–25; Milton Rokeach, *The Open and Closed Mind* (New York: Basic Books, 1960); T. R. Tyler and R. A. Schuller, "Aging and Attitude Change," *Journal of Personality and Social Psychology* 61 (1991): 689–97.

12. The information in this section was drawn from Anita Manning, "Adults Are Giving the Old College Try," *USA Today,* 12 Sept. 1989, pp. D1–D2; Nicholas Zill and John Robinson, "The Generation X Difference," *American Demographics,* April 1995, pp. 26–33; "The American Freshman: National Norms for Fall 1994," Higher Education Research Institute (project summary report available from the University of California, Los Angeles, Graduate School of Education and Information Studies); Paula Mergenhagen, "Finding a Place in the World," *Marketing Power,* June 1995, p. 14; Geoffrey Meredith and Charles Schewe, "The Power of Cohorts," *American Demographics,* Dec. 1994, pp. 22–31.

13. Cited in Allison Adato and Melissa G. Stanton, "If Women Ran America," *Life,* June 1992, p. 40.

14. James R. Gaines, "A Note from the Editor," *Life,* June 1992, p. 6.

15. The data in this section comes from Lisa DiMona and Constance Herndon, eds., *The 1995 Information Please Women's Sourcebook* (Boston: Houghton Mifflin, 1994).

16. Russell L. Kent and Sherry E. Moss, "Effects of Sex and Gender Role on Leader Emergence," *Academy of Management Journal,* October 1994, pp. 1335–1346.

17. "Exit Poll Results 1992," *Newsweek: Special Election Issue,* Nov./Dec. 1992, p. 10.

18. DiMona and Herndon, p. 424.

19. Bruce Wallace, "Playing Gender Politics: Female Politicians Are Changing Canadian Politics," *Maclean's,* 4 October 1993, pp. 16–19.

20. "Women, Minorities Gain in Canadian Election," *The Washington Times,* 31 Oct. 1993, p. A12.

21. Eric Hollreiser, *Adweek's Marketing Week,* 10 Feb. 1992, pp. 14–18.

22. "New Wheels," *U.S. News & World Report,* 5 June 1995, p. 70.

23. Daniel J. Canary and Kimberley S. Hause, "Is There Any Reason to Research Sex Differences in Communication?" *Communication Quarterly* 41 (1993): 129–144.

24. James Atlas, "Beyond Demographics," *Atlantic Monthly,* Oct. 1984, pp. 49–58; Arnold Mitchell, *The Nine American Lifestyles: Who We Are and Where We're Going* (New York: Macmillan, 1983); P. Schonback, *Education and Intergroup Attitudes* (London: Academic Press, 1981); Rockeach, 1960.

25. McGuire, pp. 271–72.

26. For a detailed analysis of this topic, see Donald R. Kinder and David O. Sears, "Public Opinion and Political Action," in *The Handbook of Social Psychology*, vol. 2, pp. 659–741.

27. Joe Klein, "Who Are These People: Perot's Odd Fawn-athon Highlights the Growing Anger of the Radical Middle," *Newsweek,* 21 Aug. 1995, p. 31; David S. Broder, "The Perot People," *The Washington Post,* 15 Aug. 1995, p. A17; "Radical Middle Feels the Squeeze: Perot's Disaffected Decry Special Interests on Both Sides," *The Washington Post,* 14 Aug. 1995, p. A1.

28. Paul Gray, "The Catholic Paradox," *Time,* 9 Oct. 1995, pp. 64–68.

29. Marcia Mogelonsky, "Texas Tastes," *Marketing Power,* June 1995, p. 18.

30. Felicity Barringer, "Census Shows Profound Change in Racial Makeup of the Nation," *New York Times,* 11 Mar. 1991, p. A1.

31. "Measuring Diversity: How Does Your State Rate?" *National Education Association Today,* Sept. 1992, p. 8.

32. Marshall McLuhan, *Understanding Media: The Extensions of Man* (New York: McGraw-Hill, 1964).

33. Lewis Lapham, "Prime-Time McLuhan," *Saturday Night,* Sept. 1994, pp. 51–54.

34. "Mass Communication: Mass Culture, Global Culture," *The New Grolier Multimedia Encyclopedia,* CD-ROM, (Novato, CA: Software Toolworks, 1993).

35. Some articles representative of this recent trend include Gary Bonvillian and William A. Nowlin, "Cultural Awareness: An Essential Element of Doing Business Abroad," *Business Horizons,* Nov.–Dec. 1994, pp. 44–50; Anthony P. Carnevale and Susan C. Stone, "Diversity Beyond the Golden Rule," *Training and Development,* Oct. 1994, pp. 22–39; E. K. Miller, "Diversity and Its Management: Training Managers for Cultural Competence Within the Organization," *Management Quarterly,* Summer 1994, pp. 17–23; Mary Munter, "Cross-Cultural Communication for Managers," *Business Horizons,* May-June 1993, pp. 69–78; Charlene Marmer Solomon, "Managing Today's Immigrants," *Personnel Journal,* Feb. 1993, pp. 56–65.

36. R. C. Gardner, "Stereotypes as Consensual Beliefs," in Mark P. Zanna and James M. Olson, eds., *The Psychology of Prejudice: The Ontario Symposium,* vol. 7, (Hillsdale, NJ: Erlbaum, 1994), pp. 1–32.

37. Susan T. Fiske, "Social Cognition and Social Perception," *Annual Review of Psychology* 44 (1993): 155–194.

38. Leah Eskin, "The Tonto Syndrome," *Scholastic Update,* 26 May, 1989, pp. 21–22, and Nisid Hajari, "The Dark Side of the Sun: Stereotypes in 'Rising Sun,'" *Entertainment Weekly,* 6 Aug. 1993, pp. 26–28.

39. Cited in *The Merriam-Webster Dictionary of Quotations* (Springfield, MA: Merriam-Webster, Inc., 1992), p. 309.

40. Brian Bergman, "A Nation of Polite Bigots? Poll of Canadians' Views on Race and Ethnic Relations," *Maclean's,* 27 Dec. 1993, pp. 42–43.

41. Tony Hillerman, *The Great Taos Bank Robbery and Other Indian Country Affairs* (Albuquerque: University of New Mexico Press, 1973), pp. 145–146.

42. Sharon S. Brehm and Saul M. Kassin, *Social Psychology,* 2nd ed. (Boston: Houghton Mifflin, 1993), p. 164.

43. Julia T. Wood, *Gendered Lives: Communication, Gender, and Culture* (Belmont, CA: Wadsworth, 1994), p. 126.

44. Brehm and Kassin, p. 176, and Bergman, pp. 42–43.

45. Olson and Zanna, pp. 117–154.

46. G. Plaskin, "Bryant Gumbel," *Us,* 5 Sept. 1988, pp. 29–35.

47. From a speech presented April 4, 1993, reprinted in DiMona and Herndon, pp. 344–345.

48. The data in this section comes from The National Conference of Christians and Jews, "Taking America's Pulse: A Summary Report of the National Conference Survey on Inter-Group Relations," undated, available from The National Conference, 71 Fifth Avenue, New York, NY 10003.

49. Carol Tarvis, *The Mismeasure of Women* (New York: Simon & Schuster, 1992).

50. Rushworth M. Kidder, *Shared Values for a Troubled World,* (San Francisco: Jossey-Bass, 1994), pp. 1–19.

51. Shalom H. Schwartz, Sonia Roccas and Lilach Sagiv, "Universals in the Content and Structure of Values: Theoretical Advances and Empirical Tests in Twenty Countries," *Advances in Experimental Social Psychology* 25 (1992): 1–65.

52. Carol Moseley-Braun, "Debate on Design Patent for the United Daughters of the Confederacy," delivered in the U.S. Senate, 22 July 1993, reprinted in DiMona and Herndon, pp. 429–430.

53. James W. Gibson and Michael S. Hanna, *Audience Analysis: A Programmed Approach to Receiver Behavior* (Englewood Cliffs, NJ: Prentice-Hall, 1976), pp. 25–26.

54. N. Schwarz, H. Bless and G. Bohner, "Mood and Persuasion: Affective States Influence the Processing of Persuasive Communications." *Advances in Experimental Social Psychology* 24 (1991): 161–199.

55. For more about preliminary tuning, see Theodore Clevenger, Jr., *Audience Analysis* (Indianapolis: Bobbs-Merrill, 1966), pp. 11–12.

56. Reported in *Time*, 17 June 1985, p. 68.

CHAPTER 5

Selecting and Researching Your Topic

■ find and focus your speech topic.
■ determine the general and specific purposes of your speech.
■ develop a clear thesis statement.
■ obtain responsible knowledge on your topic.

Learn, compare,
collect the facts! . . .
Always have the
courage to say to
yourself — I am
ignorant.

— Ivar Petrovich
Pavlov

"I have to speak for *five whole minutes*? Why, I don't know that much about anything!" Your instructor has just given you your assignment. You are to prepare an informative speech on a subject of your choice. Your stomach starts to tighten as you worry. "Speech about what? How do I *begin*?"

Preparing to speak before an audience can seem overwhelming, especially if you've never done it before. Simply getting started may be the most difficult part of speech preparation. If the task before you seems overwhelming, take it in small steps, advises Robert J. Kriegel, a performance psychologist who has counseled many professional athletes. While working as a ski instructor, Kriegel found that beginners would look all the way to the bottom of a slope. The hill would seem too steep, the challenge too difficult, and the beginning skiers would back away. However, if he told them to think only of making the first turn, this would change their focus from something they thought they could not do to something they knew they could do.[1]

The "first turn" you must make is finding a good topic in light of what you know about your audience and yourself. Fortunately, there are systematic ways to help you meet this challenge successfully. We will then talk about the "second turn," developing a clear purpose. Finally, we will discuss the "third turn," expanding your knowledge so that you can make an informed presentation that will be useful to others. This chapter will help you negotiate these first turns.

Together, they form the initial phase of the flow chart introduced in Figure 5.1: Major Steps in Speech Preparation. As the chart indicates, you will work back and forth between these steps in the first phase of speech preparation. In later chapters, we will deal with the

FIGURE 5.1

Major Steps in the
Preparation of a
Speech

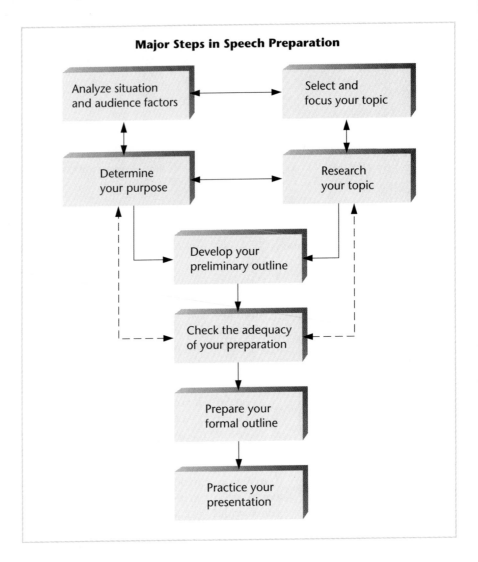

But for now, back to that first turn. What is a good topic? It is one that involves you, that allows you to express something important to you, or to explore something that fascinates you. It should also allow you to make a contribution to listeners, to enrich their lives with useful information or advice. Finally, a good topic is one that you can speak about responsibly, given the time allowed for your speech and the preparation time available.

A good topic involves you. Fix in your mind an ideal picture of yourself speaking. It may look something like the following:

You're really excited about what you are saying. Your face reflects your deep concern and interest in the subject. Your voice expresses your

feelings as you share your thoughts with listeners. Your gestures reinforce your intense engagement with your speech: they help interpret your message and reach out to listeners. Everything about you says, "This is important!" "You're going to love this!" or "This will make a real difference in your lives."

Now, let's work backwards from this image. What kind of subject might make this image a reality? That's the topic we want! If your topic is not important to you, you will find it hard to invest the time and effort needed to speak responsibly and effectively. The enthusiasm you generate when you speak on topics to which you are committed is contagious. It gets listeners involved as well.

A good topic involves your listeners. Now imagine an audience of ideal listeners.

They are leaning forward in their seats, intent on what you are saying. Their faces are alive with interest. They laugh and frown appropriately in response to your message. At key moments, they nod their heads in agreement. You enjoy their entire attention. At the end of your speech, they can't help themselves: they break out in spontaneous applause. They can't wait to ask you questions about your ideas or to express their reactions. They really don't want to let you sit down!

Working backwards from this image, the question is clear: what kind of topic will help you attain this ideal? By now, you may have heard the first speeches of your classmates, and you will have begun collecting information concerning the dynamics and demographics of your audience. So you can ask yourself, "What are the interests and concerns of my listeners? What is happening that they should know about?" A good topic should be formed in terms of such questions.

Earlier class discussions may help you find such a topic. Perhaps one of your classmates gave a speech honoring his family doctor's sense of caring. The speech sparked a lively discussion and started you thinking about your own less pleasant experiences with doctors. Then the lights come on in your mind. You could develop an informative speech on the relationship between personal physician care and patient recovery or a persuasive speech advocating training in interpersonal skills for physicians. Whatever topic you select, you can't take audience involvement for granted. Your introduction will be critical for arousing their interest. You must show listeners how the topic affects them personally and what they stand to gain from your message. For this topic to be really effective, it must also fit the time, place, and occasion for the speech, as we noted in Chapter 4. A celebration in honor of a friend, for example, is *not* the time to present a political tirade.

The final test of a good topic is whether you can acquire the knowledge you need to speak responsibly on it. The time you have for the preparation and presentation of your speech is limited. Consequently, you should select a topic area you already know something about, then con-

Criteria for a Good Speech Topic

1 Have I selected a topic that will enrich the lives of listeners?
2 Does the topic concern me deeply?
3 Will the topic fulfill the assignment or expectation for my speech?
4 Have I narrowed the topic so that it fits the time allotted to me?
5 Can I develop responsible knowledge on this topic?

SPEAKER'S NOTES

centrate on developing some *manageable part* of it for your presentation. Instead of trying to cover all the problems involved in the disposal of nuclear waste, it would be better to limit yourself to discussing your state's role in nuclear waste disposal or to focus on whether your community has an adequate plan to cope with the problem. The limited topic would be more manageable, could be adapted more precisely to your audience, and should lend itself to responsible preparation.

FINDING A GOOD TOPIC

One way to go about finding a good topic is to chart your personal interests, then those of your listeners so that you can analyze topic ideas in terms of their appropriateness and practicality.

Charting Interests

Begin your search for a good topic by listing your own interests and those of your listeners in order to determine points of convergence. To develop these **interests charts**, use a system of prompt questions similar to the self-awareness inventory introduced in Chapter 2:

1. What *places* do you find interesting?
2. What *people* do you find fascinating?
3. What *activities* do you enjoy?
4. What *objects* do you find interesting?
5. What *events* are foremost in your mind?
6. What are your long- and short-range *goals*?
7. What *values* are important to you?
8. What *problems* concern you most?
9. What *campus concerns* do you have?

As you ask these questions, write down brief responses. Try to develop at least five responses for each question. Your interests chart might look like that in Figure 5.2.

Getting Ideas from the Media.   Sometimes it is hard to come up with a list of potential topic areas out of the blue. If your mind goes blank, you can sometimes jump-start it by using newspapers, magazines, or television to generate ideas. Go through the Sunday paper, scan *Time* or *Newsweek*, or watch the evening news. Study the headlines, titles, advertisements, and pictures. What catches your attention? Add these responses to your interests chart.

One student developed an idea for a topic after seeing an advertisement for bank services. The ad stirred some unpleasant memories of a personal event — writing a check that bounced! This in turn suggested an eventual speech on keeping better personal financial records. His problem was getting listeners to see the importance of this topic to their lives. His solution was to develop an introduction that startled the audience into attention.

> Last month I committed a crime! I wrote a bad check, and it bounced. The check was for $4.67 to a local grocery store where I bought the fixings for a spaghetti supper. The bank charged me $15.00 for the overdraft, and the store charged me $10.00 to retrieve my bad check. That was the most expensive spaghetti dinner I've ever eaten!

FIGURE 5.2
Your Interests Chart

Places	People	Activities
Yellowstone Park	Pancho Villa	hiking
Freeport, Maine	Maria Tallchief	playing chess
San Antonio, Texas	Martina Navratilova	watching basketball
Avenue of the Giants	Charles Lindbergh	drying flowers
San Francisco	Sojourner Truth	traveling

Objects	Events	Goals
quilts	Olympic games	start a business
Western art	hurricanes	work in NYC
antique fishing lures	float trip on Snake River	visit Switzerland
political cartoons	Mardi Gras	live on a houseboat
graffiti	Pioneer Days Festival	have a family

Values	Problems	Campus Concerns
close family ties	air and water pollution	race relations
tolerance	televised trials	off-campus housing
physical fitness	substance abuse	date rape
respect	Internet regulation	campus security
family of humanity	public prayer in schools	parking

Similarly, the headline "Travel Money Tips Offered" might inspire you to speak on "Champagne Travel on a Beer Budget." Or the personals section in the classified ads might prompt your speech on "The Dangers of Computer Dating Services."

Be careful not to misuse media sources. The media can suggest ideas for speeches, but you can't simply summarize an article and serve it up as your speech. Use the article as a starting point for your own thinking and be especially careful not to plagiarize. Search out more information about the topic. *Your* speech must be *your* message, designed to appeal to *your* specific audience. You should always bring something new to your subject — a fresh insight or an application to the lives of listeners.

Matching Your Interests to Your Audience.   Make a similar chart of apparent audience interests as revealed by class discussion and your demographic analysis. What places, people, events, activities, objects, goals, values, problems, and campus concerns seem to spark their attention? Now study the two charts together, looking for points of shared interest in order to pinpoint your best topic possibilities. To do this systematically, make a three-column **topic area inventory chart.** In the first column (your interests), list the subjects you find most appealing. In the second column (audience interests) list the subjects that seem uppermost in the minds of listeners. In the third column, match columns one and two to find the most promising areas of speech topics. Figure 5.3 shows a sample topic area inventory chart.

In this example, your interests in travel and hiking are matched with the audience's interest in unusual places and developed into a possible speech topic area: "Weekend Adventures Within Two Hours of Campus." Similarly, your concern for physical fitness is paired with the audience's interest in deceptive advertising to generate another possible topic area: "Ex-

FIGURE 5.3

Topic Area Inventory Chart

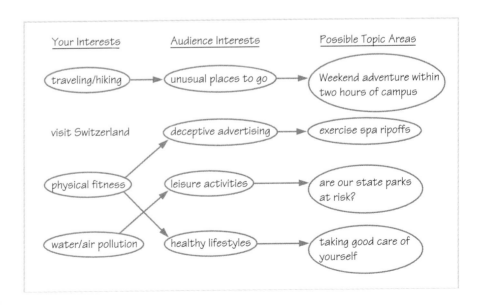

ercise Spa Rip-offs." Your interest in water and air pollution could combine with audience interests in leisure to lead to the topic area: "Are Our State Parks at Risk?"

Analyzing Your Topic

The problem with these topic areas is precisely that: they are *areas* of topics, but they are not yet refined into actual topics for speeches. They are probably too broad for the kind of short speech you will usually be assigned. So you need to narrow them to make them more specific and concrete. You also need to be sure you are taking the right approach to them. In short, what you need is a *system of analysis*. One such system includes the questions beginning reporters are taught to ask in order to assure that they investigate a story thoroughly. This system, which is especially useful for the analysis of informative speech topics, was described by the writer Rudyard Kipling as follows:

> **I keep six honest serving-men**
> **(They taught me all I knew);**
> **Their names are What and Why and When**
> **And How and Where and Who.**[2]

Not all these questions will apply to every topic area, but by working through the list systematically, you should be able to develop a number of possible topics. Let's take "Exploring National Parks" as a topic area and see where these "six honest serving-men" might lead us:

Who started the national park system? Who works in the parks? Who uses the parks?

What are national parks? Are they mainly for entertainment, public education, or environmental preservation? What are the most popular parks? What are the least-known parks? What do people like best in our parks? What is the difference between a national park and a national forest?

When was the first national park established? When was the most recent national park opened? When are the parks most crowded? When are they least crowded?

Where is the closest national park? Where are the major attractions in that park? Where can you go to escape the crowds of tourists in the parks? Where can you see the most wildlife in the park?

Why were national parks established? Why do people go to national parks? Why are some campgrounds closed to tent campers?

How are our national parks financed? How do people train to be park rangers? How can students get summer work in a park?

As you consider the six prompts, write down as many specific connections to your topic area as you can. You may notice that certain clusters of ideas emerge: some entries may center on the history of the parks, some on park attractions, others on wildlife and ecological concerns. What would be the best topic for your speech on national parks? That depends a great deal on your audience and locale. Some of your listeners might be interested in summer jobs at the park. If you live near a park and most audience members have already visited there, a speech on the park's major attractions would offer little new information. Such an audience, however, might be interested in the history of the park or in current ecological problems there, such as the impact of acid rain. On the other hand, if you live far from the nearest park and most audience members have never been there, a speech on its major attractions could be quite engaging.

Your final choice of a topic should be made in light of your purpose: what you hope to accomplish in your speech for the benefit of your listeners. We shall discuss purpose in the next section, and defer the final selection process until then.

Our example thus far describes a search for an informative speech topic. The same system of analysis, slightly amended, can be used to analyze topics for persuasive speeches. Because persuasion often addresses problems, you simply change the focus of the questions and add a few that are specific to persuasive situations:

Who is involved in or affected by this problem?

What issues are most important?

Why did the problem arise?

Where is this problem happening?

When did the problem begin?

How is this problem like or unlike previous problems?

How extensive is the problem?

What options are available for dealing with the problem?

Selecting Your Topic

After you have completed the interests charts and analyzed the topic areas they suggest, two or three specific topics should emerge as important and appealing possibilities. Now you should ask of each:

- Does this topic fit the assignment?
- Could I give a speech on this topic in the time available?
- Can I learn enough about this topic to give a responsible speech?
- Why would I want to speak on this topic?

As you consider your options in light of these questions, a final choice should become clear.

DETERMINING YOUR PURPOSE

"Why would I want to speak on this topic?" To answer this final question you must know the general function of your speech, determine your specific purpose, and develop a clearly worded thesis statement and preview.

General Function

The invitations you receive to speak outside class will usually indicate an appropriate **general function** for your speech. In class, the general function is often assigned. The most basic functions of speeches are **to inform** your listeners, **to persuade** them, or **to celebrate** an event with them. *The general function of a speech to inform is to share knowledge with your listeners or to expand their competence in an area. If your general function is to persuade, you will show listeners how they should believe or act, and you will give them sound reasons to accept your advice. A speech of celebration emphasizes the importance of some occasion, whether it is a marriage, the death of some notable person, or a grand accomplishment.* Speeches of celebration occur in a wide variety of forms, including "toasts," eulogies, after-dinner speeches, and commencement addresses.

As you will discover in class, these functions may sometimes overlap; for example, a speech celebrating an event, such as the end of the twentieth century, may also inform you of the major events of the century and persuade you to support certain goals for the twenty-first century.

As we noted earlier, people who invite you to speak outside the classroom will usually imply the kind of general function expected of your speech. As we write these words, one of your authors has been invited to speak to the local historical society on his work with the Tennessee Humanities Council. He knows that these listeners will be most interested in the grants programs made available through the council to encourage local initiatives in the humanities. His speech will be largely informative, and he will also introduce himself and try to create good will for the council. Were he to come to the meeting and launch instead an attack on those in Congress who are attempting to reduce federal support for the arts and humanities, he would be violating the unspoken terms of his invitation by presenting a persuasive message. That would be his last invitation to address the Decatur County Historical Society! On the other hand, if his speech is successful, then members of the society may come to value the THC. His next invitation might then be to tell members how they could help the endangered national and state humanities councils. A persuasive speech would be the proper response to such an invitation.

There are times when the general function of an invited speech may be left to your discretion. You may be asked to speak because you are a specialist on a subject, because you are a respected member of the community, or simply because you have a good reputation as a speaker. When this happens, you will have to select your general function according to the audience, subject, and occasion. This calls for a careful audience analysis. For example, if you discover that your listeners know very little about your topic, you might decide that your general function should be to inform them. If you feel the situation demands a change in public policy, you may feel morally obligated to persuade your listeners. Good sense and a good sense of ethics will usually point you in the right direction.

Specific Purpose

Your **specific purpose** is what you would like to accomplish in your speech. It identifies *precisely* what you want listeners to understand, believe, feel, or do. Having a specific purpose clearly in mind helps direct your research toward relevant information so that you don't waste valuable time.

You should be able to state your specific purpose clearly and succinctly as a single idea. Let's look at how a specific purpose statement gives focus to your speech:

Topic:	**National parks**
General function:	**To inform**
Specific purpose:	**To inform my audience about hiking trails in Shenandoah National Park**

Topic:	**Greenhouse effect**
General function:	**To persuade**
Specific purpose:	**To persuade my audience that the greenhouse effect poses a serious threat to our environment**

How can you tell if you have a good specific purpose? Your specific purpose should offer an approach to your topic that will offer listeners new and useful information or advice. You bore your listeners and waste their time when you tell them something they already know. Audiences appreciate speakers who avoid trivial or stale topics. Finally, your specific purpose should be manageable in the time allotted to you. In a five-minute speech you have only about seven hundred words to get your message across. If you can't cover the material in the time allowed, then you must narrow your focus to something you can handle. Referring back to Figure 5.1, note that many of the arrows point in two directions. This suggests that preparing a speech is a process and that you should move back and forth among the different activities until you are satisfied with the results.

Let's look at some examples of poor specific purpose statements and see how they might be improved:

Poor:	**To inform my audience about our national parks**
Improved:	**To inform my audience of the lesser-known attractions in Yellowstone Park**

Poor:	**To persuade my audience that driving while drinking is dangerous**
Improved:	**To persuade my audience to accept the idea of *responsible* drinking and driving**

In our first example, the specific purpose to inform the audience about "our national parks" is poor because it is too general. It does not narrow the topic sufficiently. With this *nonspecific* purpose you could prepare a speech on the fate of grizzly bears in Yellowstone Park, on the differences between national parks and national forests, on national parks in urban areas, or on a multitude of other subjects. The *improved* version limits the topic so that it can be handled within the time permitted. This helps you concentrate your research on those materials most useful to your speech.

The second *poor* specific purpose is also too general, and it would not enrich the audience. Who would argue that driving while drinking is not dangerous? Unless the speaker can offer a fresh perspective on the subject, maintaining attention or motivating the audience will be difficult. The *improved* version is more limited and offers what could be a new perspective: the idea of *responsible* drinking and driving.

Thesis Statement and Preview

Most of the time your specific purpose will be reflected in your speech in the **thesis statement.** The thesis statement condenses your message into a single declarative sentence. It is usually offered as you introduce your speech so that listeners will understand your intentions. Notice how the following speaker presents his thesis statement:

> **Today I want to discuss a moral blight on our campus — the epidemic of date rape, and what we can do about it .**

The thesis statement should be followed by a preview. The **preview** signals the main points that will develop in the body of the speech. In effect, it presents an oral agenda for the speech:

> **I will first define date rape, then show its causes and consequences, and conclude with some good advice on how to prevent and avoid it.**

In this example, listeners have been alerted to three main points in the speech:

  I. The nature of date rape.

 II. Its causes and effects.

III. Prevention of date rape.

Now the audience has a blueprint to help them follow the speech. In long or complicated speeches especially, the preview makes it easier for audience members to listen and reduces chances for misunderstanding.

In ethical speaking, the thesis statement will fully reflect the speaker's specific purpose. *But let the listener beware!* At times speakers will not be totally candid. Deep in her heart of hearts, the speaker may have the following specific purpose: "I want to sell these listeners an encyclopedia." But in the speech itself, the thesis statement may put forth a different intention:

> "I want to help you improve the quality of your lives by offering you — free of charge — this wonderful encyclopedia set [*thesis statement*].
> Your only obligation is to help us demonstrate this encyclopedia in your neighborhood. We only ask that you keep your set up to date by purchasing at a special discount rate the annual supplements for the next ten years."

Such disguises of a speaker's true intention may be fairly trivial (unless you buy the set!), but substitute a political philosophy or a religious cause for an encyclopedia, and you can see just how serious the problem can be. The greater the distance between the hidden specific purpose and the thesis statement that surfaces in the speech, the larger the ethical problem.

At times speakers may leave the thesis statement unstated, to be constructed by listeners from cues within the speech. Note, for example, how Cecile Larson left the thesis statement implicit in her speech, "The 'Monument' at Wounded Knee," which appears in Appendix B. Speakers may leave the thesis statement unstated in order to create a dramatic effect as listeners discover it for themselves. This, however, is a high-risk technique — listeners may miss the point! In most instances speakers should reveal the thesis statement as they introduce their speeches.

As it surfaces within the speech, the thesis statement should give to your specific purpose a sharp focus, and the preview should point listeners in a clear direction.

Specific purpose:	To inform my audience about the less well-known attractions in Yellowstone Park.
Thesis statement:	Many visitors leave Yellowstone Park without seeing some of its most interesting attractions.
Preview:	Today I want to introduce you to three of the less well-known attractions in Yellowstone: the Fountain Paint Pots, the Grand Canyon of the Yellowstone, and the Firehole River.
Specific purpose:	To persuade my audience to accept the idea of *responsible* drinking and driving.
Thesis statement:	*Responsible* drinking and driving can solve a serious social problem and might even save your life.
Preview:	You can join my "responsible drinking and driving club" by knowing your tolerance for alcohol, having a designated driver, and not letting friends drive while intoxicated.

Let us now look at the entire process of moving from general topic area to preview to see how these steps may evolve in speech preparation:

Topic area:	Vacations in the United States
Topic:	Camping in the Rockies
General function:	To inform
Specific purpose:	To inform my audience that there are beautiful, uncrowded places to camp in the Rockies
Thesis statement:	You can get off the beaten path and find some wild and wonderful places to camp in the Rockies.
Preview:	Three beautiful yet uncrowded camping areas in the Rockies are Bridger-Teton National Forest in Wyoming, St. Charles Canyon in Idaho, and Dinosaur National Monument in Utah.

A speech titled "Camping in the Rockies: Getting Off the Beaten Path" might then take the following form:

Introduction:	Page 43 of the tour guide to Grand Teton National Park reveals this idyllic picture of camping [display enlarged picture]. As you can see, the area is beautiful and uncrowded. With a picture like this in mind, I started my first camping trip to the Rockies two summers ago. Was I ever disappointed! After a long drive I arrived at Jenny Lake campground about two in the afternoon — early enough to set up camp, take a hike, and prepare a leisurely dinner. But, no! All the campsites had been taken since eight-thirty that morning. Not only were no sites available, but after driving through the campground, I realized I wouldn't have wanted to camp there anyway. Hundreds of tents were crowded on top of one another. It looked like a refugee relocation center after a disaster. And it wasn't only the crowding that was bad, but the noise! Radios and televisions blasted you with an unholy mixture of music and game shows and soap operas. I might just as well have been back in our freshman dorm.
Transition:	Not every camping area in the Rockies is like this.
Thesis statement:	You can get off the beaten path and find some wild and wonderful places to camp in the Rockies.
Preview:	Three of the most interesting, beautiful, and uncrowded are Bridger-Teton National Forest in Wyoming, St. Charles Canyon in Idaho, and the Dinosaur National Monument in Utah.

Main points:	1. Bridger-Teton National Forest at Slide Lake has a magnificent view of the Tetons. [Show enlarged photo, audiotape background of bird sounds.]
	2. St. Charles Canyon, on a white-water stream, offers the ultimate in seclusion. [Show enlarged photo; stream sounds.]
	3. At Dinosaur National Monument you can watch the excavation of gigantic skeletons that are millions of years old. [Photo; sounds of excavation.]
Transition and conclusion:	There are interesting, beautiful, and uncrowded places to camp if you know where to look. Try the National Forest Service campgrounds or national monuments rather than the overcrowded national parks. Last summer I enjoyed the peace and serenity of Slide Lake while reveling in its view of the Tetons. I caught native cut-throat trout in secluded St. Charles Canyon, and saw the ancient petroglyphs at Dinosaur National Monument. I can't wait to get back!

Although the thesis statement appears in the foregoing example, you will note that the speaker *does not* begin with "My thesis statement is. . . ." Rather, it appears naturally in the introduction as a lead into the preview. Both thesis statement and preview suggest that this speech may give us interesting facts, vivid examples, and engaging stories. The thesis statement indicates what kind of informative speech we will hear (descriptive), and the preview implies the overall design or pattern the speech will follow (categorical).

With a clear thesis statement in mind, speakers can focus their research to acquire responsible knowledge of the topic. In this case the speaker might use pamphlets, brochures, or books purchased at the sites mentioned; national recreation area attendance figures from almanacs; and materials available in the government documents section of the library.

ACQUIRING RESPONSIBLE KNOWLEDGE

Although we have discussed selecting and framing your topic before we have taken up research, your background reading for a speech will often begin before you form your thesis statement. Indeed, in order to determine your approach and the main points you will develop, you will probably have to find out more about your topic. Once you have your specific purpose and thesis statement clearly in mind, you can move on to that concentrated phase of research that will provide you with **responsible knowledge** for your speech. Responsible knowledge of a topic implies that you have a good grasp of

- its main issues or points of interest.
- what the most respected authorities say.
- the latest major developments.
- local concerns or applications of special interest to *your* audience.

Although you cannot become an authority on most topics with ten hours or even ten days of research, you can learn enough to speak responsibly. Your research should result in your knowing more than the rest of the class about your topic. Responsible knowledge allows you to enrich the lives of listeners with good information or advice. It places you in a sound ethical position. The major sources of information available to you are your own knowledge and experiences, library resources, and interviews. Each of these sources can supply facts, testimony, examples, or narratives to use as supporting materials in your speech.

As you pursue your quest for responsible knowledge, keep in mind the checklist offered in Figure 5.4, "Quest for Responsible Knowledge." It offers

FIGURE 5.4

Quest for Responsible Knowledge

_____ I have developed personal knowledge of my topic from which I can draw authentic examples.

_____ I have expanded my background knowledge of the topic by reading general and/or specialized encyclopedias.

_____ I have sought the advice of a librarian in forming an overall research strategy.

_____ I have checked newspaper indexes and recent news magazines to assure that my information is up to date.

_____ I have used on-line search services to form a short list of the most promising books and articles on my subject.

_____ I have used CD-ROM databases to explore specialized periodicals and journals that might enrich my speech.

_____ I have considered the possible usefulness of the following specialized sources:

    _____ atlases

    _____ biographical resources

    _____ books of quotations

    _____ almanacs

    _____ government documents

_____ I have looked for local applications of my topic by using the library's own indexing services and by searching newspaper computerized indexes and abstracts.

_____ I have interviewed local experts to see how my topic applies locally and to customize the knowledge in my speech.

a comprehensive view of resources you might utilize. Not every item will be appropriate for every speech, and for any speech, some will be much more appropriate than others. But by checking off the items one-by-one as they apply in your situation, you can be assured that you have conducted the research phase of your speech preparation thoroughly and systematically.

Personal Experience

You should begin your research by taking stock of what you already know about your topic. Personal experience adds credibility, authenticity, and freshness to a speech. As valuable as personal knowledge is, however, you should not depend on it as your *sole* source of information because it may be limited or unreliable. Your experiences may not be truly representative, or may be representative only of your cultural background. As you read or hear what others have to say on your topic, you should be willing to expand or correct your previous impressions if they prove to be narrow or distorted.

You also can actively seek out personal experience that will add credibility to your speech. Suppose you want to deliver a speech on how television news shows are put together. You could arrange to visit a nearby station

First hand experience adds authenticity to a speech. It is a good starting point for developing responsible knowledge.

that produces a live newscast. Take in the noise, the action, and the excitement that occur before and during a show — this atmosphere can enrich your speech.

You must take the initiative to arrange such experiences. For example, if you want to give a speech on the boredom of assembly line work, you might phone a local union for help in gaining firsthand exposure. To test this recommendation, we phoned the local Labor Council headquarters and talked with a union leader, who said the problem of worker boredom was acute in many local industries. We then asked if his office would help student speakers who wanted to arrange interviews with workers or make visits to plants. He responded enthusiastically, "Just tell the students to give us a call." Such willingness to cooperate is understandable. Any large organization likes favorable publicity. As a speaker, you control part of that publicity. You will never be more aware of the power of public speaking than when people "roll out the red carpet" to make the kind of favorable impression they hope will surface in your speech. Just don't be so flattered by the attention you receive that you forget to be on guard against bias on controversial issues.

Although personal experience is often a good starting point for your research, it is rarely enough to support an entire speech. To fill in the gaps and verify your knowledge and information, you should turn next to library resources.

Library Research

Although knowledge obtained from the library may lack the excitement and immediacy that personal experience provides, it has definite advantages. Library research can give you a broad perspective and a sound basis for speaking responsibly. It can extend, correct, and enrich your experience by acquainting you with others' experiences and knowledge.

When your authors were in college, "doing library research" meant a long, manual search through the card catalog and journal indexes. One then had to retrieve the books or periodicals, read them (most often in the library), and take copious hand-written notes on index cards. There were no copying machines or electronic databases. Even as recently as when the first edition of this textbook appeared, computerized topic searches had to be run at great expense by library specialists. Today, seventy-five miles from any college library, we can gather a wealth of information from our home offices by accessing the Internet, CD-ROM databases, and on-line services. Even the concept of the library seems to be undergoing revolutionary change: from a repository of books and written materials, the library has expanded to a site of dynamic access to the world's information.[3]

Given the wide variations among libraries, our best advice is to *take the guided tour usually offered at the beginning of each academic year at your college or university*. Become acquainted with your own library's resources. Many college and large municipal libraries have the following major research resources to help you:

1. *On-line catalog* of books and major publications
2. *Reference area* containing timely information and bound or computerized indexes to magazines, newspapers, and journals
3. *Government documents area* containing federal, state, and local government publications
4. *Nonprint media archives* of films, videotapes, recordings, and microfilms
5. *Special collections areas* with materials that can help you adapt your topic to local needs and interests
6. *CD-ROM databases* that offer concentrated access to large bodies of information
7. *Computerized search services* to provide bibliographic assistance
8. *Holding areas,* or stacks, where books and bound volumes of periodicals are shelved
9. An *interlibrary loan service* that offers access to specific materials that may not be available in your library

With such a multitude of resources available, it can be difficult to know where to begin. *The most valuable resource in any library is the professional librarian, who can steer you to the most appropriate sources of information.* The following review of library resources focuses on the special needs of student speakers, who must spend their limited research time to best advantage.

Library research is the key to acquiring responsible knowledge. Reading selected books on your topic can give you a deeper understanding and make your speech more authoritative.

Reference Area. The reference area offers concentrated sources of information. Some of the materials you may find useful are described below.

Encyclopedias. Encyclopedias can either be general or about a specific subject area. They are often a useful *first step* for your research, in that they provide a basic overview of background information. Encyclopedias should not be used, however, as your major source of information. They are of especially limited use for fast-breaking topics on which knowledge is developing rapidly. You will need the more specific and timely information that you can get from other sources to bring your message up to date.

Among the more respected general encyclopedias are *Encyclopaedia Britannica, World Book Encyclopedia,* and *Encyclopaedia Americana.* Some of the subject-specific encyclopedias you might find in your library include:

> *Encyclopedia of Religion and Ethics*
> *Encyclopedia of African Amerian Culture and History*
> *International Encyclopedia of the Social Sciences*
> *Encyclopedia of Islam*
> *Encyclopedia of Education*
> *Dictionary of Asian American History*

Sources of Current Facts. Up-to-date information is important to many topics. If you are not aware of recent events related to your topic, your credibility will be damaged. For the most recent information, start with a newspaper index, such as the *New York Times Index* or *Black Newspapers Index,* which guides you to leading African-American newspapers. Who won this year's Nobel Peace Prize? How did Hurricane Opal affect the economy of the Southeast? Why was the jury decision in the O. J. Simpson trial received differently by African-Americans and European-Americans? These indexes will direct you to articles related to such questions and may even provide summaries of what they say. Other sources of up-to-date information include current issues of popular news magazines such as *Time* or *Newsweek.* Another easy-to-use source of recent information is *Facts on File,* which reports weekly on current events and is indexed by topics.

Additional Indexes and Abstracts. Periodical indexes direct you to magazine and journal articles on your topic. These articles may not always be current, but they provide depth of information. They often reduce situations, issues, and arguments to their essentials. In addition, the books and authors mentioned in the articles can lead you to other sources of information. Abstracts provide a summary of the articles that help you determine their relevance to your purpose.

Indexes and abstracts range from the highly specialized to the very general. The following, all of which are available in CD-ROM as well as print format, are frequently used:

Reader's Guide to Periodical Literature contains author and subject references to articles in over 175 popular periodicals. This source is especially useful for speakers because the articles are written for a general readership that is probably similar to the type of audience you will have in class. The magazines indexed attract reputable writers and will add credibility to your speech when cited. When you need answers to questions such as "Where is acid rain a problem?" or "How is increased attendance affecting the environment in our national parks?" *Reader's Guide* can direct you to articles that might help answer these questions.

Business Periodicals Index covers a wide range of business and economic magazines and journals and is helpful for speeches on topics such as career choices, sales techniques, or advertising appeals.

Public Affairs Information Service (PAIS) publishes an index that covers periodicals, pamphlets, and other documents reporting on civic and governmental issues that range from land use policy to tax reform.

Congressional Information Service (CIS) is a comprehensive index to the publications of the U.S. Congress.

Social Sciences Index covers articles you may find useful on topics involving social problems.

Index to Journals in Communication Studies includes references to topics of interest to communication students. What made Abraham Lincoln an effective speaker? What can be done about communication apprehension? Articles addressing these and similar questions are indexed here (now available both in print and in CommSearch '95, an annually updated CD-ROM format distributed by the Speech Communication Association).

Atlases. If your topic calls for geographical information or comparisons among regions and areas, you may wish to consult an atlas like the *National Atlas of the United States of America,* the *New International Atlas,* the *Times Atlas of the World,* and the *Commercial Atlas and Marketing Guide.* Such resources contain more than just maps; they often include information on issues such as religious preference by state, population density of countries, or the agricultural or industrial production of a given area. These atlases may also suggest ideas for presentation aids.

Biographical Information. You can find out about noteworthy people by consulting one of the many biographical resources found in most libraries. The *Who's Who* series provides brief information on important living people; the *Dictionary of American Biography* covers famous Americans of the past. *Current Biography* contains longer essays on people who are prominent in the news. *Notable American Women* contains information on women "whose work in some way took them before the public." *Reference Library of Black America* is probably the most comprehensive source of information about prominent African-Americans. It also includes interesting articles that are not strictly biographical.

Books of Quotations. Quotations are especially useful in speeches. Quotations from famous sources are indexed by topic and author in such books as *Bartlett's Familiar Quotations, The Oxford Dictionary of Quotations,* and *The Harper Book of American Quotations.* Sources that are particularly applicable for speeches on cultural themes include *The New Quotable Woman, A Treasury of Jewish Quotations,* and *My Soul Looks Back, 'Less I Forget: A Collection of Quotations by People of Color.* Some compilations of quotations are also available through commercial on-line computer services such as CompuServe.

Almanacs, Yearbooks, and Directories.   Almanacs provide compilations of facts and figures on a wide range of topics. What movies were the biggest hits in the 1940s? What was the strongest earthquake ever to rock the United States? Who is the conductor of the Boston Pops? You can find this kind of information in an almanac like *The Information Please Almanac, The World Almanac,* or the *Book of Facts.* Specialized almanacs such as *The Hispanic Almanac, The Hispanic-American Almanac,* and *The Native North American Almanac* can inform speeches on cultural themes. Yearbooks such as the *Statistical Abstract of the United States* provide data on everything from the annual catch of abalone to the yearly production of zinc.

Directories like the *Encyclopedia of Associations* tell you about the members, leaders, and functions of organizations. *Indian Reservations* provides descriptions of 276 Native American reservations located in 32 states. *Asian Americans Information Directory* covers 19 ethnic groups from east or southeast Asia which have significant representation in the United States.

Local Resources.   Many libraries maintain a clipping and filing service on topics of local interest, or may index local newspapers by subject. These resources can help you adapt your topic to the specific local concerns of your listeners. Such services might also suggest prominent and knowledgeable people who live nearby that you might interview. Still another pertinent resource is *Lexis Nexis,* an online service which indexes the contents of major newspapers and other scholarly and lay publications. Through this service and other newspaper databases, you might discover local, state, or regional applications of your topic. Ask your librarian about the availability of these resources.

Government Documents.   Most government documents are housed in their own section of the library. These documents provide more in-depth information than that found in most almanacs. Such material includes reports on congressional hearings, legislation, and proceedings; the proclamations, orders, and other formal statements of the president; and opinions and decisions of the Supreme Court. Some of the major government publications include:

Congressional Record: daily account of the proceedings of Congress

Federal Register: proclamations and orders of the president and regulations of various departments of government

United States Reports: opinions and decisions of the Supreme Court

Monthly Catalog of United States Government Publications: the master list of government documents (*GPO* is the electronic version of this catalog.)

American Statistics Index: a master guide to government statistical publications

Index to U.S. Government Periodicals: covers 150 of the major U.S. serial publications

Undex (United Nations Document Index): covers publications issued by the United Nations

Many of the above resources are now available on line through Internet or commercial services such as CompuServe. In addition, some private publications provide insight into various political perspectives on issues being debated in Congress or reviewed in the federal courts, and on controversial federal regulations. One of the best of these is the *Congressional Quarterly Weekly Report.* The more specialized *Editorials on File* may also prove useful on such issues.

Electronic Databases. Almost all libraries now have electronic databases. Your library may offer the following:

On-line catalogs, which will allow you to search your library's book holdings by author, title, or subject; *Books in Print,* the most comprehensive listing of books currently available from publishers; and the *OCLC Online Union Catalog,* which contains more than 23 million bibliographic records for books, serials, sound recordings, musical scores, audiovisual media, maps, archives, manuscripts, and computer files.

Students are often advised to start their research with the subject listings in such catalogs. This advice may not always be best for speakers because on popular subjects you might find fifty or even five hundred books listed, and you have no way to determine which are most relevant or helpful. However, in the articles you read on your topic, you may encounter references to books that sound particularly interesting. Reading the best books on your topic can give you a deeper understanding that will make your speech more authoritative and impressive.

Computerized newspaper indexes such as *Lexis Nexis,* which we mentioned above under Local Resources. Other prominent newspaper indexes include *Newsbank,* which indexes and abstracts articles from over 500 newspapers in the United States with an emphasis on topics of current interest; *Ethnic Newswatch,* which indexes more than 100 magazines and newspapers, including Spanish-language publications; and *Newspaper Abstracts,* which concentrates on ten major U.S. newspapers since 1985, including the *Atlanta Constitution,* the *New York Times, USA Today, Wall Street Journal,* and *Washington Post.*

Periodical indexes, including such resources as *Periodical Abstracts,* which indexes and abstracts articles from about 1000 selected magazines and professional journals in all fields; *ABI/Inform,* containing abstracts and indexing to articles from over 800 business and management journals; *Hispanic American Periodicals Index,* which indexes publications especially relevant to topics involving Hispanic American interests; and *ERIC,* which indexes articles and documents in all areas of education. Of special interest is *FirstSearch,* a massive on-line search service which provides access to about fifty major databases, including — just to name a few — the *Social Sciences Index, Humanities Index, Reader's Guide to Periodical Literature,* and *OCLC Catalog.*

Access to the **Internet,** the most comprehensive source of data. Using the Internet, you are able to conduct electronic conversations and even interviews with others who share your interests and to retrieve information from countless sources. The only problem is one of quality control: sometimes it can be hard to tell experts from pseudo-experts, or information from bogus information, when you communicate on the Internet. If you are relying on material from the Internet for your speech, be sure to verify the credentials of the source.

CD-ROM databases which store enormous amounts of data on disks similar to those used by stereo music systems. For example, the thirteen-volume *Oxford English Dictionary* can be stored on just one CD-ROM disk. Many other databases, such as the *Art Index, Biography Index, Humanities Index, Social Sciences Index, Periodical Abstracts,* and *Index to Journals in Communication Studies* (as CommSearch '95) are also available on CD-ROM disks. In addition to the indexing and abstracting services offered by CD-ROM databases, you can often download the articles you want to read directly from them.

You do not have to be a computer whiz to use these resources. Simply read any of the opening screens or help menus that are designed to guide you through the search procedures for the particular database. Many libraries also place quick reference guides to the databases next to the computer workstations. A printer attached to the computer allows you to print your references, or you may download the articles directly. Using such a service, you can find your references, copy the bibliographic information, read the article, and make a copy — all in the same place.

Interviewing for Information

Interviewing experts can give you credibility similar to what you acquire through personal experience. If you can say, "Prof. Michelle Nussbaum, who holds the Chair of Excellence here in environmental studies, told me during an interview that . . . ," listeners will sit up and take notice. Like personal experience, however, interviewing has its limitations. Finding the right person to interview can be the first problem. Or you may feel so grateful to someone for granting you an interview that you simply accept that person's word without further investigation. If you know little about the subject, it may be difficult for you to evaluate what you hear.

To minimize these problems, check your library's local clipping and indexing services or its available newspaper indexing and abstracting services to help you identify nearby prospects for interviews. If you are on the Internet, you may put out a call for suggestions in one of the forum discussions. What

Plan your interview to make maximum use of your expert's time. Avoid questions that can be answered with a *yes* or *no* and let the expert do most of the talking.

you discover from these sources can also help you frame questions to ask during the interview. Do as much reading as you can before the interview.

Establishing Contact. If time permits, write a letter requesting the interview. Then follow up with a telephone call to set a time and place. If you are pressed for time, you may have to call the person directly. In your letter or call, introduce yourself and explain your purpose. Explain why you are calling: you know that the expert has knowledge that will be valuable to your listeners. (A little judicious flattery may go a long way — especially when it is deserved!) Indicate the kinds of questions you would like to ask during the interview. This communicates that you are a serious person who has some knowledge already, and also sketches an agenda that you would like the interview to follow. Don't be shy. A request for an interview is a compliment. Interview prospects are usually quite pleased to think that their ideas may have impact on a larger audience through your speech.

Designing the Interview. In your telephone call or letter or at the beginning of the interview, establish why you are there and what you hope to learn. Plan **open questions** that invite your expert to discuss the meaning of events. In general, avoid **closed questions** that constrain responses into brief answers, such as "Is air pollution a problem in our city?"[4] Ask such questions only as follow-ups to open questions, or when you need to pin your expert down. Never supply the answer you want in your question, as in "Don't you think that air pollution is a crisis that demands our attention?" Design your questions in a sequence so that the answers form a coherent line of thought:

> What are the causes of air pollution in Silver City?
>
> What is the impact of air pollution on people's lives?
>
> Is there a serious effort underway to minimize air pollution?
>
> Are polluters cooperating in this campaign? Why or why not?
>
> What can students do to help the effort?

Allow the person you are interviewing to complete the answer to one question before you ask another. Don't interrupt and jump in with another question every time your expert pauses. Your expert may go from one point to another and may even answer a question before you ask it. You should be flexible enough to adapt to the spontaneous flow of conversation.

Design your questions so that your expert is not made defensive by the way they are worded. Questions such as "When are you intellectuals going to climb down from the ivory tower and get involved in the campaign for a better environment?" are not only argumentative but offensive. Save any controversial but necessary questions for later in the interview after you have established rapport. Ask such questions honestly but tactfully: "Some

The Art of Interviewing

1. Locate and contact an expert on your topic.
2. Research the topic so that you can develop effective questions.
3. Dress neatly and arrive on time.
4. Let the expert do most of the talking. Do not interrupt.
5. Ask your questions diplomatically and sincerely.
6. Avoid questions that call for yes or no answers. Do not ask leading questions. Save controversial questions until late in the interview.
7. Use probes, mirror questions, verifiers, and reinforcers to follow up on answers.
8. Summarize what you have heard so that your expert can verify it.
9. Go over your notes as soon as possible to assure that you have recorded vital information and quotations correctly.
10. Send a thank-you note as a professional courtesy.

SPEAKER'S NOTES

people say that experts like you need to 'dirty their hands more' in the day-by-day effort to improve the environment. How do you respond to such criticism?" If asked with sincerity rather than hostility, this kind of question may produce the most interesting part of your interview.

Should you plan to tape-record your interview? Although a tape recorder can free you from note taking and help you get the exact wording of answers, setting up and running it can be a nuisance that interferes with establishing rapport. Also, many people dislike being tape-recorded. Never attempt to record interviews without obtaining prior consent. A good time to seek such consent is in your initial contact. If your expert seems reluctant, don't press the point.

Conducting the Interview.   Arrive for the interview on time. Dress nicely to show that you take the interview seriously and as a sign of respect for the person you are interviewing. When you meet your expert, take time for a little small talk before you get into your prepared questions. Try to establish common ground. On one occasion, as we were interviewing the late Supreme Court Justice Hugo Black, the justice discovered during small talk before the interview that one branch of the Osborn family hailed originally from the hill country of north Georgia. Since these were also his family roots, he felt rapport with us. This reduced the tension, and we went on to have a productive interview.

Let the expert do most of the talking while you do the listening. Be alert for opportunities to follow up on responses by using probes, mirror questions, verifiers, or reinforcers.[5] **Probes** are questions that ask the expert to elaborate on a response: "Could you tell me more about the part played by auto emissions?" **Mirror questions** reflect back part of a response to encourage further discussion. The sequence might go as follows:

> **"So I told Joan, 'If we want people to change their attitudes, we're going to have to start marching in the front of the movement.' "**

> **"You felt you were moving toward a leadership role?"**

A **verifier** confirms the meaning of something that has just been said, such as "If I understand you correctly, you're saying. . . ." Finally, a **reinforcer** is verbal or nonverbal encouragement for the person to communicate further. A smile, a nod, or a comment such as "I see" are reinforcers that can keep the interview moving.

If you feel the interview beginning to drift off course, you can often steer it back with a transition. As your expert pauses, you can say, "I believe I understand now the causes of air pollution. But can you tell me more about how this level of pollution affects our lives?"

Do not overstay your welcome. As the interview draws to a close, summarize the main points you have learned and how you think they may be useful in your speech. A summary allows you to verify what you have heard and reassures the expert that you intend to use the information fairly and accurately. Show your gratitude for the interview as you conclude, then follow up with a telephone call or thank-you letter in which you report the successful results of your speech.

After the interview is concluded, find a quiet place, go over the notes you have taken, and get down the wording of important answers while they are still fresh in your mind. Nothing is more frustrating than to recall that your expert made a striking statement that would be perfect for the conclusion of your speech, but you can't remember what it was.

As you draw near the end of the search phase of your research, consider once again the checklist in Figure 5.4 "Quest for Responsible Knowledge" (pg. 153). Have you touched all the main bases in gathering potentially useful information? If so, then you will be ready to move on to the next steps in speech preparation.

RECORDING INFORMATION

In the course of your research, you will come across facts and statistics, examples, stories, and quotations, all of which might be useful in your speech. It is impossible to remember all of these items, or even to remember where you saw them, unless you keep notes. Many researchers use index cards — usually 5" x 8" — to record the information they discover. Even if you photocopy or download your research material, you may find it is useful to prepare such cards because they are easy to handle and sort by categories. Information cards focus precisely on facts and figures, quotations, or examples you might use in your speech and indicate where they were obtained. Source cards provide full information on where your information comes from.

Information Cards

Information cards are used to record ideas and material from an article or book, one item of information to a card. For any single article or book you may have several cards. While you are doing your research, you will not always know whether something will be useful in your speech. When in doubt, write it out! The more information you have to select from, the more responsible your knowledge will be. Avoid getting into situations in which you remember that you read something important but can't remember what it was, and — worse still — you can't remember where you read it.

Each card should contain a *heading* describing the type of information on the card, an abbreviated *source* reference, and the *information* itself, which may be either a direct quotation or a paraphrase of what the author said. Figure 5.5 shows a sample information card.

FIGURE 5.5
Information Card

Heading	Yellowstone Grizzlies in "Fragile" Condition
Source	Chadwick, "Grizzly Country," p. 12.
Information	"Today, the entire 6-million-acre greater Yellowstone ecosystem is estimated to hold just 200 to 250 grizzlies. Isolated as if on an island, they have become vulnerable to inbreeding as well as to catastrophic wildfire, drought or disease epidemics. The word <u>fragile</u> doesn't seem to go with <u>horribilis</u>, yet it describes their future in Yellowstone all too well at the moment."

FIGURE 5.5
Information Card

Source Cards

You should also prepare a **source card** for each article or book you use. The source card contains information about the author, the title of the publication, where the material was published, and the date of publication. This information permits you to document precisely your sources when you introduce them in your speech. Establishing who said something and where and when it was said is important to the credibility of your information.

The source card for a book typically takes the following specific form: author, title, place of publication, publisher, and date of publication. A source card for an article lists the author, article title, name of the periodical, volume number, date, and pages (see Figure 5.6). On your source card write out a brief summary of the material, including comments on its quality and significance. You can also record information about the author, book, or periodical that might be helpful as you support points during your speech.

Testing Information

When you find material that you think might be usable, you must test it carefully. As you research your topic, ask yourself: Does this article contain

FIGURE 5.6
Source Card

Bibliographic information	Douglas H. Chadwick, "Grizzly Country," <u>Nature Conservancy,</u> 45 (July/August 1995): 11–15.
Summary and comments	Draws disturbing picture of the fate in the lower 48 of the grizzly bear, described as "the untamed soul of the Rockies." Explains what is being done to help the dwindling population. The author, a wildlife biologist, wrote <u>The Fate of the Elephant.</u> The Nature Conservancy is one of the most effective environmental action groups.

relevant and useful information? Does it cite experts I might quote in my speech to support my ideas or position? Are there any interesting examples that I could use to make my ideas clearer? Are there any stories that will bring my ideas to life? Your quest for responsible knowledge should help you find nuggets of information that add value to your message.

Once you have found such material, you must test its reliability, thoroughness, recency, and precision. **Reliability** refers to the trustworthiness of information. Ask yourself:

> *Are these sources qualified by education or experience to make these claims?*
>
> *Do these sources have a reputation for competency and integrity?*
>
> *Are these sources relatively free from bias on this topic?*
>
> *Is there general agreement among the best sources on these points?* (If your experts disagree, then you must pan the streams of research more carefully.)

Thoroughness of information is also an important consideration. Don't be satisfied with reading just one or two articles on your subject. Read until you stop being surprised by what you discover. **Recency** is essential when knowledge is changing rapidly on a subject. Last year's readings on the state of the economy are today's old news. If someone in your audience points out that more recent data contradicts your point, you'll have to pick your credibility up off the floor. **Precision** is important if you are speaking on a topic that varies widely from place to place, such as unemployment rates or the incidence of AIDS. You must be certain that your information applies in the locale where you are speaking. We show you in the next chapter how to apply such tests specifically to the different types of supporting materials.

IN SUMMARY

To give a successful speech, you must find a good topic, realize the general function and specific purpose of your speech, frame a clear thesis statement, and expand your knowledge so that you can speak responsibly. A good topic is one that involves and fascinates both you and your audience. A good topic will be limited so that you can research it adequately and develop a speech that will fit within the allotted time.

Finding a Good Topic. One way to discover promising topic areas is to chart your interests by using a system of prompt questions and by scanning the media. Next, chart audience interests as disclosed in previous speeches and class discussions and match them with your own. To develop topic possibilities, use a system of analysis based on six key questions: who, what, when, where, why, and how. When applied to a topic area, these questions can guide you to specific topics. As you move toward your selection, consider whether a given topic fits the assignment, whether you can speak on it within the time limits, and why you would want to speak on it.

Determining Your Purpose. The *general function* of your speech might be to inform listeners, to persuade them, or to celebrate some occasion with them. Your *specific purpose* identifies the kind of response you would like to evoke, what you want to accomplish. Your *thesis statement* is the hub of your message, expressed within a single sentence. It is followed by the *preview*, which sketches the main points you will develop in the body of your speech.

Acquiring Responsible Knowledge. *Responsible knowledge* implies that you have a good grasp of the main issues surrounding a topic, what the most noted experts say about it, the most recent developments, and how it applies specifically to your listeners and their locale. You can acquire responsible knowledge from personal experience, library resources, and interviews. Personal experience can make your speech seem highly credible and authentic, but you should not rely on it as your only source of information. Library research can add objective, authoritative information to your speech. The knowledge you obtain through interviews can add freshness, vitality, and local relevance to your speech.

Recording Information. As you conduct research, record what you learn on index cards. Use *information cards,* which pinpoint exact quotations and precise bits of information, and *source cards* for each article, book, or interview. The source card identifies the author, date, and place of publication. It may be used to record background information about the source and to summarize and evaluate the material. As you collect research for your speech, you should ask four basic questions: does this material satisfy the tests of *reliability, thoroughness, recency,* and *precision* so that I can use it responsibly in my speech?

TERMS TO KNOW

interests charts	CD-ROM databases
topic area inventory chart	open questions
general function	closed questions
informative function	probes
persuasive function	mirror questions
celebratory function	verifiers
specific purpose	reinforcers

thesis statement   information card

preview   source card

responsible knowledge   reliability

on-line catalog   thoroughness

computerized newspaper indexes   recency

periodical indexes   precision

Internet

DISCUSSION

1. Working in small groups, exchange your personal interests charts. Discuss the most promising areas for speech topics that emerge across these charts. Report these to the class.

2. Using the system of analysis described in this chapter, analyze the most promising topic areas identified in item 1. As you consider these topic possibilities, discuss what general functions they might serve.

3. As a follow-up to items 1 and 2, develop specific purposes and thesis statements for the three topics that interest you most. Evaluate them in class, using the criteria for selecting good topics and determining specific purposes described in this chapter.

4. In what ways might personal experience limit and distort your knowledge as well as enrich it? Discuss such limitations in class, drawing on examples from your own experience.

APPLICATION

1. Working in small groups, scan a variety of media resources to generate topic areas for speeches. Each group should be responsible for checking one of the following materials:

a. the local Sunday newspaper

b. a television news program over a week's time

c. a recent issue of a weekly news magazine

d. a recent issue of a general-interest magazine

In the first part of a class period, meet as groups to generate a list of topic ideas. Each group should select five topic ideas. In the second part of the class period, a representative should present each group's recommendations to the class and explain how and why the topics were chosen. Which kind of media resource produced the best speech topics? What are the strengths and limitations of each?

2. Choose one of the topics you selected from Application 1 and identify the most likely sources of information you could use to develop it.

3. Take a walking tour of your library and locate the various resources described in this chapter. While you are there, try to find the answers to the following questions. Do not ask the librarian for assistance. Record the source of each answer.

a. What was the population of the city in which you were born in the year of your birth?

b. What television show had the highest ratings when you were six years old?

c. What contemporary public figure do you admire most? When and where was he or she born? What is he or she most noted for?

d. Who won the Nobel prize for literature in the year your most admired public figure (MAPF) was born? What was the author's nationality? most noted work(s)?

e. What actress won the Academy Award for best supporting actress in the year your MAPF was born? What movie was she in?

f. Who were the U.S. senators of the state in which you were born during the year of your birth?

g. Who were the Republican presidential and vice-presidential candidates during the election held nearest the birth year of your MAPF?

h. What noteworthy event took place during the month and year of your birth? When and where did this happen?

4. Discuss the following thesis statements in terms of their effectiveness:

a. You ought to protect yourself from date rape.

b. The role of superstitions in our lives.

c. Young children should not be admitted to horror movies.

d. Weekend trips are preferable to long vacations.

e. Nutritious meals you can cook in your dorm room.

Improve those that do not meet the criteria for effective thesis statements.

NOTES

1. Robert J. Kriegel, *If It Ain't Broke . . . Break It!* (New York: Warner, 1991), pp. 167–68.

2. Rudyard Kipling, *Just So Stories* (Garden City, NY: Doubleday, 1921), p. 85.

3. Tibbett L. Speer, "I Sing the Library Electric," *American Demographics,* Oct. 1995, pp. 19–21.

4. See the discussion in Jeanne Tessier Barone and Jo Young Switzer, *Interviewing Art and Skill* (Boston: Allyn and Bacon, 1995), pp. 89–99.

5. Lois J. Einhorn, Patricia Hayes Bradley, and John E. Baird, Jr., *Effective Employment Interviewing: Unlocking Human Potential* (Glenview, IL: Scott, Foresman, 1982), pp. 135–139.

CHAPTER **6**

Using Supporting Materials in Your Speech

- understand the forms of supporting materials.
- select the best supporting materials for your speeches.
- learn how to use supporting materials to best advantage.

The universe is
made of stories, not
of atoms.
— Muriel Rukeyser

Our home on the Tennessee River stands at the top of a ridge-line several hundred feet above the river. It is built upon terrain that slopes down at about a 45-degree angle, so that while the front of the home rests upon solid earth, the back of it rises on posts some thirty feet above the ground. You might think that the structure is flimsy, but actually it is quite strong. Our builders selected the finest wood, concrete, plastics, and steel available. And they knew how to fashion and combine these materials into powerful supports.

Up to now, we have characterized your speeches primarily as a journey over Interference Mountain in which you and your listeners work to overcome the barriers that separate you. In these next chapters, we use a different metaphor. We look at your speeches as a structure of ideas raised up on solid pillars of supporting materials. Like our builders, you must know your materials and what they can support. You need to know how to select them and how to use them wisely. Just as our home is built to withstand storms and high winds, your speech must be built to withstand doubt and even controversy. When you stand to speak upon it, you must be absolutely confident of its structural integrity.

Facts and statistics, testimony, examples, and narratives are the major forms of **supporting materials** used in the building of speeches. These materials provide the substance, strength, credibility, and appeal a speech must have before listeners will place their faith in it. *Their essential functions are to arouse interest, to elaborate and explain the meaning of your ideas, to emphasize* *their importance to listeners, and to verify controversial or surprising statements you might make.* Your personal experience, library research, and interviews with experts, described in Chapter 5, should have provided you with a good stockpile of such materials.

As we examine each type of supporting material, we will discuss its nature and significance, how to evaluate it, and how to put it to work in your speeches.

FACTS AND STATISTICS

Facts and statistics are the most objective forms of supporting material. To call them objective is to say that — in comparison with other forms of supporting material — they can stand alone, independent of any one person's experience of them. Examples, stories, and testimony are more subjective, in that they depend more on the experience of a person or a certain group of people. This relatively independent nature of facts and statistics means that you can count on them to add credibility to your ideas. If "the facts are in your favor," this creates a presumption that what you are saying is true. Therefore, facts and statistics are especially important when your topic is unfamiliar or your ideas are controversial.

Facts

Facts are verifiable units of information, which means that independent observers see and report them consistently. Richard Weaver, a prominent

Facts and figures add substance to a speech. Presentation aids, discussed in Chapter 9, can help a speaker explain information more effectively.

communication critic writing in the 1950s, suggested that Americans honor facts as the highest form of knowledge. He further noted that Americans respect scientific facts and numbers in the way that other societies often respect divine revelation.[1] Although we may believe we are more sophisticated consumers of communication than the audiences of the '50s, a recent survey conducted by the Gallup organization revealed that 86 percent of the people polled agreed that "references to scientific research in a story increased its credibility."[2] We still worship at the altar of science.

The following statements are factual because they can be verified as either true or false:

Chevrolet Tahoe is an American-made utility vehicle.
Most students at our school earn their degrees in five years.
Television ads often rely on emotional appeals.

While factual statements can stand by themselves, speakers rarely use them without interpreting them. Interpretations often are simply a few additional words that transform factual statements into claims:

Chevrolet Tahoe is a *superior* American-made utility vehicle.
Most *hard-working* students at our school earn their degrees in five years.
Television ads often rely on *unethical* emotional appeals.

There is nothing essentially wrong with providing interpretations or making claims. We often must shape factual statements to fit our purpose. The problem comes when speakers and audiences forget that these are no longer just factual statements that can stand alone without further demonstration. The addition of such words as "superior," "hard-working," or "unethical" means that these speakers have added another burden of support to their speeches. They must now introduce other facts or statistics, examples, testimony, or stories to prove that the claims are justified — that they are more than just opinions. Claims that are allowed to go forward as factual statements introduce bias, distortion, and confusion into speeches.

We usually cannot verify directly the accuracy of facts. We have no idea how we might proceed on our own to verify whether Chevrolet Tahoes actually are "superior." We would have to look to independent authorities who are competent to verify such claims and who have no economic axe to grind. So we might say in a speech, "According to the latest issue of *Consumer Reports*, which did extensive tests with many utility vehicles, the Chevrolet Tahoe is superior." If our reading of *Consumer Reports* is correct, we have introduced a factual statement in support of a claim. Because this factual statement comes from an expert source, we have combined fact and expert testimony, which we discuss later in this chapter. Incidentally, note also how we reassure careful listeners: our source is the "latest," and *CR* was responsible in its work ("did extensive tests").

Sources of information have ethos just as speakers do. For example, *Consumer Reports* enjoys a reputation for responsible, objective testing of products. On social or political issues, the ideological position of the source may be important. For example, if you cited William F. Buckley's *National Review* in support of a claim, skeptical listeners might respond, "Well, that's a conservative magazine. Of course Buckley will support this right-wing claim!" On the other hand, if you also cite *The New Republic,* a more liberal publication, then skeptical listeners might think, "Well, if both left and right agree, then maybe what she's saying is true."[3]

Even seemingly neutral sources present "factual" information that is colored by its cultural environment. Compare the following excerpts from the same encyclopedia in its 1960 and 1990 editions:

> *1960:* Kiowa Indians hunted buffalo on the southwestern plains of the United States. The Kiowa and their allies, the Comanche, raided many Texas ranches. They probably killed more whites than any other Indian tribe. . . . By [a] treaty signed in 1868, the Kiowa agreed to go with the Comanche to a reservation in Indian territory (now Oklahoma). But only the Kiowa chiefs had signed the treaty, and no chiefs could force their young men to make such a sacrifice. Many struggles and arrests occurred before the Kiowa finally went to live on the reservation. When trouble broke out in 1874, Satanta, one of the most daring Kiowa leaders, was arrested and sentenced to prison. There he committed suicide. The Kiowa then "put their hands to the plow." They now live peacefully as farmers. Several have become well-known artists.

> *1990:* Kiowa Indians are a tribe that lives largely in Oklahoma and elsewhere in the Southwestern United States. The tribe has about 8,000 members, most of whom live in rural communities near Anadarko, Carnegie, and Mountain View, Oklahoma. Other tribal members live in urban areas and work in law, medicine, teaching, and other professions. . . . [In] 1970 the Kiowa adopted their own tribal constitution. The tribe is governed by the Kiowa Indian Council, which consists of all members who are at least 18 years old. The Kiowa Business Committee, an elected group, manages tribal programs in such fields as business, education, and health.[4]

Both of these accounts are "factual," but the first dwells upon past conflict, defining the Kiowas as adversaries of the dominant culture, while the second emphasizes assimilation. The contrast reminds us that even relatively objective descriptions are selective and incomplete. We should always ask ourselves what any given description is leaving out, and whether that omission is critical to our understanding.

Statistics

Statistics are numerical facts that can describe the size of something, make predictions, illustrate trends, or show relationships. Americans are almost as much in awe of numbers as they are of science. In the same Gallup study cited earlier in this chapter, 82 percent of those surveyed said that statistics increased a story's credibility.[5] These figures suggest that statistics can be one of the most powerful forms of supporting material that can be used in speeches.

The following example from a student speech demonstrates how statistical information can appear in speeches:

> The Environmental Protection Agency is saying that secondhand smoke causes 3,000 lung cancer deaths a year; 35,000 heart disease deaths a year; and contributes to 150,000 to 300,000 respiratory infections in babies, mainly bronchitis and pneumonia, resulting in 7,500 to 15,000 hospitalizations. It triggers 8,000 to 26,000 new cases of asthma in previously unaffected children and exacerbates symptoms in 400,000 to 1 million asthmatic children.

When presented orally, statistics can be rather baffling. Using a brief explanation, example, or presentation aid (see Chapter 9) can make numerical information more understandable in your speeches. Compare the above example with the way a physician used similar figures to help his listeners understand the extent of medical problems caused by smoking:

> I ask you to check your watches. Because in this hour, by the time I'm done speaking, 50 Americans will die from smoke-related diseases. By the time you sit down to breakfast in the morning, 600 more will have joined them: 8,400 by the end of the week — every week, every month, every year — until it kills nearly half-a-million Americans, year in, year out. That's more than all the other preventable causes of death combined. Alcohol, illegal drugs, AIDS, suicide, car accidents, fires, guns — all are killers. But tobacco kills more than all of them put together.
>
> These are hard, cold realities, defined by hard, cold statistics. But I'd ask you to remember this most important fact. Every statistic is an encoded memorial to what was once a living, breathing — loving and loved — mother, father, sister, brother. Not numbers, real people, and the toll is as terrible as the most horrific war.[6]

The contrast provided by these two examples is revealing. In the first example, the speaker almost drowns the listener with a deluge of numbers. While the magnitude of the problem is made undeniable, the mere recitation of statistics may overwhelm the audience. In the second example, the speaker uses fewer numbers, but by connecting the numbers so that they form a pattern, he makes them more comprehensible. Moreover, by comparing smoking to other forms of preventable death, he builds its importance in the minds of listeners. Finally, in order to increase the impact of his message, he transforms his numbers by describing the people they represent. We shall discuss these techniques of comparison and description in more detail later in this chapter.

Evaluating Facts and Statistics

Your research notes should contain a wide assortment of facts and statistics on most of the topics you select. Before you decide which of these materials will actually appear in your speeches, use the critical thinking skills we discussed in Chapter 3 to evaluate them. Ask the following questions:

- Is this information relevant?
- Is this information the most recent available?
- Are the sources of this information credible?
- Is this information reliable?

As you review your research notes, you may discover much interesting information about your topic that does not directly relate to your specific purpose. No matter how fascinating it seems, if the information is not relevant, don't use it. A speech that is cluttered with interesting digressions is difficult for listeners to follow. You should also be certain that any statistics you cite are relevant to your locale. If you talk about the "crisis of unemployment" in your area, basing your claim on a national average of 7 percent, you could have a problem if someone points out that the local rate is only 4 percent.

You must also consider how current the information is, especially when your topic is one on which information changes rapidly. On certain subjects, such as *who* is doing *what* to *whom* in the Bosnian crisis, yesterday's news is already obsolete. When you speak on such topics, be sure you are up to date. Save yourself the embarrassment of having a listener point out that your claims are invalid because of what happened this morning!

It is also important to evaluate the sources of your information. Test even "factual" material for potential bias, distortions, or omissions. Don't be taken in by "scientific sounding" names, especially if the information contradicts common sense. Cynthia Crossen, a reporter and editor with the *Wall Street Journal*, exposes many instances of such deception in her book, *Tainted Truth*. For example, she presents the case of a study attributed to "the Cooper Institute for Aerobic Research" which concluded that "white bread will not make you gain weight." It turns out that the study that produced this amazing conclusion was funded by the makers of Wonder Bread.[7]

To guard against deceptive information, do not rely too heavily on any one source. Computerized access to information makes it easy to double-check your facts and statistics. Information confirmed by more than one authority should be more reliable. The more controversial your topic, the more critical the reliability of your information. Compare what different expert sources have to say, and look for areas of agreement.

As you weigh the use of facts and statistics, be careful not to read into information what you want to find or exaggerate the results. Be on guard against the tendency to distort facts and statistics by the way you word them. Don't ignore information that contradicts your claims by rejecting it

Using Facts and Statistics

1 Use the most recent, reliable facts and statistics.

2 Use information from unbiased sources who have no vested interest in the results they report.

3 Interpret information accurately. Do not stretch or twist its meaning.

4 When using statistics in speeches, round off numbers whenever you can without distorting results.

5 Make statistics understandable by amplifying them with examples or visual aids.

6 Don't overwhelm your audience with a barrage of facts and statistics.

SPEAKER'S NOTES

as atypical or irrelevant. And, obviously, don't put blind faith in what appear at first glance to be factual statements.

Be especially careful when using statistics. Remember that listeners place great faith in numbers. Keep in mind that statistical predictions are based on probability, not certainty, and that they are subject to misuse and abuse. Peter Francese, founder and president of *American Demographics*, has pointed out that while statistics are supposed to represent reality, they may also be used to create reality:

> **Politicians and lobbyists carefully select the numbers they use to talk about crime (it's always rampant) or immigration (it's always out of control). The numbers are typically used to prove there is a "big" problem. It's like rounding up vicious dogs to prove that all dogs bite. . . . No number can represent truth perfectly. Every survey has some error or bias. Data from public records, such as crime reports, can be underreported or misclassified. And even perfectly collected data are open to different interpretations.[8]**

Chapter 14's discussion of other possible misuses of facts and statistics as evidence in persuasive speaking will provide additional help in evaluating information and using it ethically.

Using Facts and Statistics

Information is useful when it is framed into strong supports that prevent a speech from collapsing under the weight of its claims. Three techniques for framing facts and statistics into powerful supporting materials are definitions, explanations, and descriptions.

Definitions. A definition helps your audience understand what you are talking about by translating your topic into words your listeners will understand. It helps assure that speaker and listeners are talking about the same thing. Your audience analysis should help you determine whether you need to provide definitions in your speech. As a general rule, you should provide definitions for any technical terms that are unfamiliar to your audience the first time you use them. For example, you might define *osteoporosis* as "a disease of older women that causes their bones to break easily and results in a humped back."

Definitions can be persuasive as well as informative. A persuasive definition reflects your way of looking at a controversial subject. It presents your perspective in such a way that your listeners will want to share it. A persuasive definition usually puts the subject in an emotional context. In a speech on domestic violence against women Donna Shalala, U.S. Secretary of Health and Human Services, provided the following persuasive definition of domestic violence: "Domestic violence is terrorism. Terrorism in the home. And that is what we should call it."[9]

Explanations.   Longer and more detailed than definitions, **explanations** combine facts and statistics to clarify a topic or demonstrate how it works. The following explanation of "old growth," combined perhaps with an enlarged photograph as a presentation aid, might work well in a speech on forest preservation:

> From a traditional forester's view, *old growth* forests are those in which wood production has reached its peak. . . . Old-growth forests contain many large, live, ancient trees. They are forests that have never been harvested. The Wilderness Society defines "classic" old growth as "containing at least eight big trees per acre exceeding 300 years in age or measuring more than 40 inches in diameter at breast height."[10]

Again, it is important to offer explanations early in your speech to help your listeners easily grasp your meaning.

Descriptions.   **Descriptions** are "word pictures" that help listeners visualize information. The best descriptions evoke vivid images in the minds of the audience. The great Roman rhetorician, Longinus, once said of images that they occur when, "carried away by enthusiasm and passion, you think you see what you describe, and you place it before the eyes of your hearers."[11] Images color information with the speaker's feelings: they establish a mood in addition to increasing understanding. Note how the following description of the monument at Wounded Knee, which commemorates the massacre of hundreds of Sioux men, women, and children (complete text of this speech is in Appendix B), both paints a picture and establishes a mood:

> Two red brick columns topped with a wrought iron arch and a small metal cross form the entrance to the grave site. The column to the right is in bad shape: cinder blocks from the base are missing; the brickwork near the top has deteriorated and tumbled to the ground; graffiti

on the columns proclaim an attitude we found repeatedly expressed about the Bureau of Indian Affairs: "The BIA sucks!" Crumbling concrete steps lead you to the mass grave. The top of the grave is covered with gravel, punctuated by unruly patches of chickweed and crabgrass. . . .

Such descriptions help bring information to life before an audience. But a word of caution is in order. The description above works well because it is *understated*. All too often beginning speakers indulge in emotional overkill. They add too many adjectives, too much emotional coloration. If "grave site" here were "lonely grave site," if "attitude" were "angry attitude," if "mass grave" were "abandoned mass grave," we would begin to think more about the speaker's feelings than about the subject being portrayed. *Let listeners supply the adjectives in their own minds.* That way, they will *participate* in creating the image. They will then be less likely to feel they are being manipulated.

TESTIMONY

You use **testimony** when you cite the words and ideas of others in support of your message. When you repeat the exact words of others, you are using a **direct quotation**. Direct quotations are useful when the material is brief, the exact wording is important, or the language is especially eloquent. When points are controversial, direct quotation can also seem authoritative and conclusive. You also may **paraphrase** material or restate in your own words what others have said. Keep in mind that when you paraphrase testimony you must still cite the source.

There are three types of testimony which you can use as supporting material. Expert testimony comes from sources who are authorities on the topic. Lay testimony involves citing ordinary citizens who may have firsthand experience. Prestige testimony comes from someone who is highly regarded but not necessarily an expert on the topic at hand.

Expert Testimony

Expert testimony comes from people who are qualified by training or experience to serve as authorities on a subject. As you review your research notes, you will probably discover statements by experts offering opinions, information, or simply interesting quotations. When you cite experts in your speeches, you are calling on them as qualified witnesses to support your case. In a sense, using expert testimony allows you to borrow ethos from them to make your speech more credible. Expert testimony is especially important when your topic is innovative, unfamiliar, highly technical, or controversial.

When using expert testimony, remember that competence is area-specific. That means that statements can be used as *expert testimony* only when they fall within the area in which your expert is qualified. For example, emergency room physicians who could provide expert testimony on the physical effects of gunshot wounds might not qualify as experts on gun control legislation.

As you introduce expert testimony in your speeches, be sure to present the credentials of your experts. You can further strengthen the value of testimony by emphasizing its recency or, when appropriate, by the fact that it was published by a prestigious journal or newspaper.

> **Dr. Lee Gonzales, chair of our Criminal Justice Department and former member of the Presidential Task Force on Inner-City Violence, said last week in the *Washington Post* that a law requiring the licensing of handguns would. . . .**

You may wish to say more about your experts' background or the nature of their research projects, depending on the circumstances of your speech.

Lay Testimony

Lay testimony representing the voice of the people is highly regarded in democratic societies. In the United States, people have become almost obsessed with public opinion polls, especially during political campaigns. Newspapers keep us informed of what "the people" think about issues. In fact *USA Today* features lay testimony along with that of experts on its editorial page.[12] Speakers often use lay testimony to provide an understanding of the real-life consequences of issues. If you were preparing a speech on assembly line boredom, you might quote factory workers to add an authentic note to your message.

Lay testimony cannot be used to establish the objective validity of ideas. But if your listeners can identify with the people you quote because they are "just like us," they may be more willing to accept the point you are making. While expert testimony deals primarily with the dispassionate determination of facts and carefully considered interpretations based upon them, lay testimony more often deals with direct personal experience and appeals to feelings. Such testimony can be extremely powerful when it is emotionally charged. For example, in a speech at the Center For National Policy, Congressman Richard Gephardt used lay testimony to illustrate the devastating impact of unemployment:

> **A few weeks ago, I met a man in Jefferson County, Missouri, who had lost his job and couldn't find a way to earn a living. His economic crisis shattered his marriage, as well as his self-confidence. He had loaded all of his worldly possessions into his car, and was headed down the road to nowhere. He looked at me with tears in his eyes, and said, "They took away more than my paycheck. They took away my *pride*.". . . Your job is more than what you *do* — it's who you *are*. It's your identity.[13]**

Prestige Testimony

Prestige testimony associates your message with the words of a respected public figure. This person is usually an eloquent writer or cultural hero or heroine who, while not necessarily an expert on your particular topic, has voiced some timeless truth that supports, illuminates, and elevates your ideas. Citing such testimony can add distinction to your speech. It allows you to associate your cause with the ethos of the revered person.

Prestige testimony is also one source of *mythos*, a form of proof discussed in Chapter 14 that summons the power of tradition in support of your message. In a speech on the "giveaway of our public lands," Brock Evans, a vice president of the Audubon Society, used prestige testimony to emphasize the depth of the problem:

> If there ever was a crisis for all our public lands and wildlife heritage, it is now. The words that keep running through my head, over and over again these terrible times, come from President Abraham Lincoln who in another time of crisis, 130 years ago, said:
>
> "Fellow countrymen, we cannot escape history . . . the dogmas of the quiet past will no longer suffice for the stormy present . . . as the occasion now before us is piled high with difficulties, so we must rise to that occasion . . . history will judge us if we fail."
>
> And that is how I feel about these times now. . . . These are frightening times for anyone who loves the American land and its biological treasures, for anyone who believes in that great tradition of public lands ownership, for anyone who shares the opinion of our forefathers that some lands should belong to *all* the people.[14]

In this example Evans used Lincoln's exact words so that he would not lose the elegance and force of the language. When the testimony is taken from a long passage or excerpted from a series of passages, you might find it advantageous to paraphrase the testimony. Just be sure that you cite the source, and that you reflect fairly the spirit of her or his words.

Evaluating and Using Testimony

Like facts and statistics, testimony must meet the test of *relevance*. And like facts and statistics, testimony must seem *free from bias*. For example, a doctor who promotes vitamin therapy may be the part-owner of a company that sells vitamins. Her expert advice to "start taking Nature Blessed vitamins today" may be somewhat suspect because of self-interest. The test of *recency* takes a strange twist when applied to testimony. If you are using expert or lay testimony, the conventional rule applies: *latest is best*. But if you are using prestige testimony, often *the older the better*. Wisdom ages well, and heroes and heroines glow brighter with the passage of time.

In addition to these basic tests, you must also consider whether the type of testimony is appropriate for your purpose. Lay testimony can humanize

Using Testimony

1 Select sources your audience will respect.
2 Be careful to quote or paraphrase material accurately.
3 Point out the qualifications of sources you are citing as experts.
4 Use only expert testimony to validate information.
5 Use lay testimony to build identification and add authenticity.
6 Use prestige testimony to enhance the general credibility of your message.

SPEAKER'S NOTES

a speech and promote identification among listeners, your message, and yourself. Prestige testimony can enhance the attractiveness of both speech and speaker, but only expert testimony can demonstrate that a statement is factually true. If you are using expert testimony, be sure your source is an authority in the specific topic area of the speech.

As you use testimony in your speeches, be sure that your paraphrase or quotation you select reflects the overall meaning and intent of its author. Never twist the meaning of testimony to make it fit your purposes. As we noted in Chapter 1, this unethical practice is called "quoting out of context." Political advertising is rife with examples of quoting out of context as candidates try to put a positive spin on their image. For example, during a recent political campaign in Illinois, one state representative sent out a fund-raising letter that claimed he'd been singled out for "special recognition" by *Chicago Magazine:* and indeed, he had. He had been cited as "one of the state's ten worst legislators."[15]

To assure accuracy, have quotations written out on note cards so that you can read them, rather than relying on memory. Use testimony from more than one source, especially when your topic is controversial or there is a possibility of bias. A transition, such as "According to . . ." or "In the latest issue of . . . ," leads gracefully into such material. And once again, be sure to introduce the credentials of your sources of testimony. That way, you help them have maximum impact in your speech. You can find much useful information about your sources in the biographical resources mentioned in Chapter 5.

EXAMPLES

Examples bring a speech to life. Just as pictures serve as graphic illustrations for a printed text, **examples** serve as verbal illustrations for an oral message. In fact, some scholars prefer the term *illustration* to *example.* The word *illustration* derives from the Latin *illustrare,* which means "to

Anfernee "Penny" Hardaway, all-star point guard for the Orlando Magic, often speaks for the NBA's "Stay in School" campaign. He is shown here with Bob Lanier, director of the NBA campaign and a former Detroit Piston, and Vice President Al Gore in such a program. Such prestige testimony is usuallly effective with young audiences.

shed light" or "to make bright." Good examples illuminate the message of your speech, making it clearer and more vivid for your audience.

In addition to clarifying ideas, examples can also arouse attention and sustain interest. A speech without examples is usually boring. Examples make ideas seem real by providing concrete applications. They demonstrate that what you have said either has happened or could happen. Speakers acknowledge these functions when they say, "Let me give you an example." Similarly, examples may be used to personalize your topic and to humanize both you and your message. Fred Krupp, executive director of the Environmental Defense Fund, used this personal example to open a speech presented at an Environmental Marketing Communications Forum:

> **Thank you for the kind introduction. I'm a little surprised that you left out my most important qualifying credential. I have three small sons — ages 7, 4, and 14 months. So I do know a great deal about cleaning up after environmental disasters.[16]**

Examples about people give the audience someone with whom they can identify, thus involving them in the speech. Personalized examples help the audience to *experience* the meaning of your ideas, not simply to *understand* them. Examples that point out common experiences, beliefs, or values also help to bridge gaps in cultural understanding. When Hillary

Clinton spoke at the United Nations Fourth World Conference on Women in Beijing, China, she used many brief examples to demonstrate that all women share common problems and face a common destiny:

> . . . Over the past two-and-a-half years, I have had the opportunity to learn more about the challenges facing women in my own country and around the world. I have met new mothers in Jojakarta, Indonesia, who come together regularly in the village to discuss nutrition, family planning, and baby care. . . . I have met women in South Africa who helped lead the struggle to end apartheid and are now helping build a new democracy. . . . I have met women in India and Bangladesh who are taking out small loans to buy milk cows, rickshaws, thread and other materials to create a livelihood for themselves and their families. I have met doctors and nurses in Belarus and Ukraine who are trying to keep children alive in the aftermath of Chernobyl. The great challenge of this conference is to give voice to women everywhere whose experiences go unnoticed, whose words go unheard.[17]

Examples also provide emphasis. When you make a statement and follow it with an example, you are pointing out that what you have just said is IMPORTANT. Examples amplify your ideas. They say to the audience, "This bears repeating." Examples are especially helpful when you introduce new, complex, or abstract material. Not only can they make such information clearer, they also allow time for the audience to process what you have said before you move on to your next point.

Types of Examples

Examples take different forms, and these forms have different functions. An example may be brief or extended and may be based either on an actual event or on something that might have happened.

Brief Examples. A **brief example** mentions a specific instance to demonstrate a more general statement. Brief examples are concise and to the point. Often a speaker will use several of them together, as did Ms. Clinton. Another speaker used the following brief example on the state of our culture as she addressed students at Hillsdale College:

> In *New York Magazine,* only weeks ago, a veteran TV anchorman is reported to lament . . . about the declining caliber of TV reporters. He cites as an example the newsbreak that the terrorists who sabotaged the *Achille Lauro* were to be tried in absentia, which caused one reporter to run through the newsroom asking, "Where is Absentia?"[18]

Extended Examples. An **extended example** contains more detail and allows you to dwell more fully on a single instance. The speaker cited above also used the following extended example in her speech:

> What is the current state of our culture? By way of a short answer, let me relate a true personal experience. A few years ago, while recovering from a tennis injury, I worked out regularly with a personal trainer. At that time, the new Broadway musical *Les Miz* had reawakened an interest in Victor Hugo's immortal book *Les Miserables* on which the play was based. New Yorkers were reading or rereading the book with fervor — on subways and buses, in bank lines, in doctors' offices and even on exercise bikes. One day at my "very upscale" gym, the woman next to me warmed up on her bike reading a paperback of that great, classic novel which she had propped up on the handlebars. A trainer wandered by — a male in his mid-thirties with a B.S. degree — and noted her reading material with visible surprise. He stopped short and asked in wonderment, "They made a book of it already?"[19]

Extended examples give us more detailed information about a subject. They allow the speaker to convey feeling about a topic that might be lost if the speech relied solely on brief examples.

Factual Examples. A **factual example** is based on an actual event or a real person as in the preceding extended example. Factual examples provide strong support for your ideas because they are grounded in reality. When you actually know the people involved, factual examples can be even stronger. If the factual examples you wish to use could be embarrassing, you can change the names of the people involved to protect their privacy. Mark Thompson used the following factual example in a classroom speech to define the meaning of generosity:

> Generosity? I'll tell you what it means. Last week, tennis champion Arthur Ashe died — one more innocent victim of AIDS. Yesterday, a retired secretary and grandmother who is dying of lung cancer in Brooklyn gave $400,000 to St. Jude Children's Research Hospital to help create the Arthur Ashe Chair for Pediatric AIDS Research. She wanted his name remembered, not hers. We know only that she is a person "of very modest means" who received the money in a malpractice suit when doctors failed to recognize her symptoms of cancer. She wanted to reach out to children who, like her, are fighting terminal illness.
>
> While she remains anonymous, this obscure woman is a champion too — a champion of the human spirit. She has given us a gift far more precious than her money.

Hypothetical Examples. Examples need not be real to be effective. A **hypothetical example** is a composite of actual people, situations, or events. Although created by the speaker, it represents reality. It is a fiction that may open the door to truth even better than a factual example. To be effective, hypothetical examples must seem plausible. Hypothetical examples are often introduced with a phrase such as, "Imagine yourself in the following situation. . . ." The following hypothetical example was used by a student speaker to illustrate the meaning of "cabin fever":

> Picture the following: you're in a room with five other people — four of them under ten years old, brimming with energy. It's been raining for six days — a cold, heavy rain. No one can go outside. The kids run in circles and fight with one another. The other adult nags at you when awake and snores when asleep. What kind of mood would you be in?

You should use hypothetical examples when the factual examples you find don't adequately represent the *truth* of a situation, or when a factual example might prove unnecessarily embarrassing to actual people. Be especially careful that your hypothetical examples are truly representative, and that they don't distort the truth just to make your point. Always alert your listeners to the hypothetical nature of your example: such introductory phrases as "imagine yourself," "picture the following," or "let's pretend that" should caution audiences that they will be hearing a hypothetical example that nevertheless purports to represent the truth. The standards of ethical speech require that you never present a hypothetical example as though it were factual.

Evaluating and Using Examples

Evaluate examples in terms of their relevance, representativeness, and believability. No matter how interesting an example may seem, if it does not advance your specific purpose, leave it out. Examples must also fairly represent situations as they actually exist. Remember, what works well with one audience may seem out of place with another. Examples must meet the tests of taste and propriety. They should fit the mood and spirit of the occasion. Risk offending listeners only when they must be shocked into attention before they can be informed or persuaded.

Examples often make a difference between a speech that is humdrum and one that is successful. Highlight their authenticity by providing the names of people, places, and institutions involved in them. It is much easier

Using Examples

1 Use examples to arouse and sustain attention, clarify abstract or technical ideas, and emphasize major points.
2 Make your examples specific by naming the people and places in them.
3 Use factual examples whenever possible.
4 Use examples that are believable and representative of a situation.
5 Keep examples brief and to the point; do not ramble.
6 Be selective in your use of examples. Save them for points of major importance.

SPEAKER'S NOTES

for a listener to relate to Matt Dunn of the local General Motors plant than to some anonymous worker in an unnamed company. Use transitions to move smoothly from statement to example and from example to statement. Phrases such as "For instance . . ." or "As you can see . . ." work nicely.

NARRATIVES

A **narrative** goes beyond an example by *telling a story* within the speech. Humans are story-telling animals. Most children are brought up on narratives — stories that entertain, fables that warn of dangers, and parables that teach virtues. People organize their experiences and memories of human happenings in terms of narratives.[20] Moreover, when information seems odd (i.e., Harvard-educated plumber), people look for the stories that will explain the phenomenon and satisfy their curiosity.[21]

Narratives are especially effective in speeches because they draw listeners into the action. Because listeners can often "see" themselves enacting certain roles within the stories, narratives can encourage those transformations of identity and behavior that ethical public speaking makes possible. Moreover, narratives stimulate the processes of constructive listening and participative communication that we discussed in Chapter 3. Because stories prompt listeners to create meaning from what they hear, the audience becomes involved in the creation of the message. It becomes *their* discovery, *their* truth. Such involvement enhances the impact of the message.

Personal narratives also increase the sense of identification between speakers and audiences. They can help bridge the cultural differences that separate people of diverse backgrounds. According to Vice President Gore, storytelling can even help old enemies make peace. When Palestinian, Israeli, Jordanian, and Syrian leaders met recently to discuss a peace treaty, Gore saw the negotiations coming to a stand-off. The situation looked unpromising until, in Gore's words, "The breakthroughs came when they told stories about their families. I have seen time and time again how storytelling brings people together."[22]

Narratives serve many of the same functions as examples. They make a speech livelier and help sustain attention. They clarify abstract or technical ideas. They emphasize a point through amplification. A narrative functions as a speech within a speech — beginning with an attention-getting introduction, continuing with a body in which the story develops, and ending with a conclusion that reinforces the message. Facts and statistics fade with time, but narratives leave the audience with something to remember.

Because they are so effective at involving the audience, narratives are often used in the introductions of speeches. Narratives that contain a light touch of humor also help make the audience comfortable.[23] One student, speaking on the importance of "selective disobedience," opened his speech with the following narrative:

Once when I was in high school our football team had a slim lead near the end of a big game. We had just taken possession of the ball on our own ten-yard line with no time outs left. The coach told the quarterback, "Run play 14 twice, then punt, NO MATTER WHAT HAPPENS!" The quarterback called play 14 and we gained 45 yards. He called it again and we gained 40 more yards. By now the ball was on our opponent's five-yard line, but the quarterback followed instructions and called for a punt. When our team came off the field as the ball changed hands the coach grabbed the quarterback and yelled at him, "Why did you do that? What were you thinking about?" The quarterback replied, "I was thinking — we really do have a dumb coach!" Today I'd like to talk with you about the importance of practicing "selective disobedience" — about knowing when and how to break the rules.

Concluding narratives leave the audience with something to remember and extend the impact of a message. They can establish a mood that will last long after the last words have been spoken. In a speech to the Rotarians of Murray, Utah, David Archambault, Lakota Sioux and president of the American Indian College Fund, used the following narrative as part of his conclusion:

More than 100 years ago, our great chief Sitting Bull was murdered. His people — frightened that they too would be killed — set out on foot across South Dakota along with Chief Big Foot. Carrying their children, they fled across the frozen prairie through the bitter subzero cold 200 miles to seek refuge on the Pine Ridge reservation in southwestern South Dakota.

On December 29, 1890, near a creek now known to all the world as Wounded Knee, Chief Big Foot and his followers were massacred. No one knows who fired first, but when the shooting was over, nearly 300 Indians — men, women, and children — lay dead and dying across the valley. Their bodies were dumped into a mass grave. The survivors were unable to hold a burial ceremony, a ceremony we call the wiping away of tears. It meant the living could never be free. On the 100th anniversary of the massacre at Wounded Knee, several hundred of us on horseback retraced the journey of Big Foot and his band during those final days. We arrived at dawn at the site of the mass grave at Wounded Knee and completed the wiping of tears ceremony. The Si Tanka Wokiksuye, the Chief Big Foot Memorial Ride, was a mourning ritual that released the spirits of our ancestors and closed a tragic chapter in our history.

We have the opportunity now to help rebuild our nation. And I do not mean just the Indian nations. On this 500th anniversary of Columbus's voyages, we together can build a better America, a nation enriched by the diversity of its people and strengthened by the values that bring us together as a community.[24]

In a narrative, dialogue is usually preferable to paraphrase. When speakers use dialogue, they reproduce conversation directly. Paraphrasing can save time, but it can also rob a narrative of power and a sense of immediacy. Let people speak for themselves in your narratives. The late Senator Sam Ervin of North Carolina was a master storyteller. Note how he used dialogue in the following narrative, which opened a speech on the Constitution and our judicial system:

> Jim's administrator was suing the railroad for his wrongful death. The first witness he called to the stand testified as follows: "I saw Jim walking up the track. A fast train passed, going up the track. After it passed, I didn't see Jim. I walked up the track a little way and discovered Jim's severed head lying on one side of the track, and the rest of his body on the other." The witness was asked how he reacted to his gruesome discovery. He responded: "I said to myself, 'Something serious must have happened to Jim.'"
>
> Something serious has been happening to constitutional government in America. I want to talk to you about it.[25]

Had "Mr. Sam" paraphrased this story as "The witness reported that he knew instantly that the victim had had a serious accident," he would have destroyed its effect. Dialogue makes a narrative come alive by bringing listeners close to the action. Paraphrase distances the audience.

Evaluating Narratives

Relevance is again a major criterion when you decide about using a narrative. Speakers sometimes "borrow" a narrative from anthologies of stories or jokes and then strain to connect it with their topic. Narratives should never be used simply to amuse your listeners. They must also help you make your point. An irrelevant narrative distracts your listeners and may even overpower your actual message. Stay away from narratives that foster negative stereotypes or contain language your audience might find offensive. Finally, ask yourself whether the narrative will seem fresh and original to your listeners. If they have already heard your story, they may decide you have nothing new to say.

Storytelling is an important folk art. Set off the story from the rest of your speech by pausing as you begin and end the story. Voice and dialect changes may signal listeners that a "character" is speaking. Your language should be colorful and active. Create a sense of anticipation and suspense as you build to the punchline or conclusion. If your story evokes laughter, wait for it to subside before going on. Since storytelling is an intimate form of communication, reduce the distance between you and listeners — either physically by moving toward them or psychologically by being less formal. Finally, you should practice telling your story to get the wording and tim-

Using Humor

1 Use humor to put the audience at ease.

2 Remember, the kind of humor you use reflects on your character. Avoid religious, ethnic, racist, or sexist humor.

3 Don't be funny at the expense of others. If you poke fun at anyone, let it be yourself.

4 Keep humor to a minimum in informative and persuasive speeches.

5 Avoid irrelevant humor: be sure that humorous stories fit into and complement the flow of meaning.

SPEAKER'S NOTES

ing just right. Get some friends to act as a surrogate audience to see if you can bring the story off.

Be especially careful as you introduce humor into a speech. Avoid stories that are funny at the expense of others. If you poke fun at anyone, let it be yourself. Speakers who tell amusing stories about themselves sometimes rise in the esteem of listeners. When this technique is effective, the stories that seem to put the speakers down are actually building them up.[26] Note how former President Jimmy Carter used this type of humor as he acknowledged his introduction as a speaker at commencement exercises at Rice University:

> I didn't know what Charles [the person who introduced him] was going to say. For those who have been in politics and who are introduced, you never know what to expect. There was a time when I was introduced very simply. "Ladies and gentlemen, the President of the United States," period. But then when I left office I was quite often invited by lowly Democrats who were in charge of a program at an event. Then when I got there with two or three TV cameras, the leaders of the organization — almost invariably Republicans — would take over the introduction of me, and quite often the introduction would be a very negative one derived primarily from President Reagan's campaign notes. I had to do something to heal my relationship with the audience before I could speak so I always would tell them after that, "Ladies and gentlemen, of all the introductions I've ever had in my life, that is the most recent."[27]

A well-told narrative can add much to a speech, but its use should be reserved for special occasions. Too many narratives can turn a speech into a rambling string of stories without a clear focus. Use narratives to arouse or sustain attention, to create a special mood for your message, or to demonstrate some important truth.

THREE TECHNIQUES FOR USING SUPPORTING MATERIALS

The best materials for building homes on hilltops are only as good as the builders who use them. Similarly, the best supporting materials for speeches depend for their effectiveness on the skill of speechmakers. Much of the art of building speeches depends upon the wise use of three major techniques. Just as definitions, explanations, and descriptions are special techniques for using facts and statistics, *comparison, contrast,* and *analogy* are general techniques for using *all* the forms of supporting materials — facts and statistics, testimony, examples, and narratives — to best advantage.

Comparison

A **comparison** makes an unfamiliar or controversial idea more understandable or acceptable by pointing out its similarities to something the audience already understands or accepts. Comparisons can strengthen facts and statistics, testimony, examples, and narratives by connecting them with each other. Consider how the following speaker used comparison in a classroom speech:

> **The proposal before us for licensing handguns is much like licensing drivers. You would have to take a written test to demonstrate that you know and understand the principles of handgun safety and regulations, just like you now have to take a written test to demonstrate your mastery of driving safety and regulations. You would have to take a "hands-on" test to demonstrate your ability to use a handgun safely and skillfully, just like you have to demonstrate your ability to drive a car. And finally, you would be subjected to a background check to determine your suitability to be licensed to have a handgun, just like your application for a driver's license is checked for DUIs and moving traffic violations.**

As this example may illustrate, comparisons can be especially helpful when they take the strangeness out of what might seem a radical new proposal. A good comparison can increase an audience's comfort level with an idea by reducing its sense of threat. Before you decide to use a comparison, ask yourself these questions:

- *Are there enough similarities to justify the comparison?* In the above example, there are three critical points of similarity. See if you can find them.
- *Are the similarities significant to the idea you wish to support?* In the above example, the fact that a computer would be used for background checks both for driving and gun licenses might be neither central nor significant.
- *Are there important differences that might invalidate the comparison?* Here you must imagine yourself as an unfriendly critic of the compari-

son. An unfriendly critic might argue that while driving automobiles is not constitutionally protected, owning weapons enjoys the sanction of the Bill of Rights. You will have to decide whether the comparison would be strong enough to overcome this objection.

Contrast

A **contrast** emphasizes the differences between things. One of our sentences in the description of comparison, "A good comparison can *increase* an audience's comfort level with an idea, and *reduce* its sense of threat," is a contrast. Just as a red cross stands out more vividly against a white background than an orange one, contrasts make facts and statistics, examples, testimony, and narratives stand out. At times, contrasts are subtle, depending on the audience members' sense of the difference between the reality presented in a speech and their own experience. Yukio Matsuyama, former chief writer and member of the editorial board of the *Asahi Shimbun* (newspaper), used a striking implicit contrast to emphasize the differences in the costs of living between Japan and the United States. Since he could safely assume that his American audience of professional journalists knew the costs of taxis in the United States, he did not need to provide that information:

> **Did you know that you have to pay nearly 150 dollars — not yen — for a taxi from the center of Tokyo to Narita Airport, and once there, a government toll of 15 dollars for using the airport facilities? If such a thing were to happen in Boston, it might cause another Boston Tea Party![28]**

As you consider whether to use a particular contrast, ask yourself the following:

- *Is the sense of contrast dramatic enough to help my case?*
- *Is the difference relevant to the point I wish to make?* If the above speaker's purpose were to demonstrate spiritual differences between Japanese and American cultures, the taxi fee contrast, while quite dramatic, would be irrelevant.
- *Are there other points of difference that might invalidate the point?* Again, take the point of view of an unfriendly critic. If such a critic were able to show that an enormous difference in income in both countries makes such costs quite bearable in Japan, then the speaker's point would be blunted.

Analogy

An **analogy** combines the principles of both comparison and contrast: *it points out the similarities between things or concepts that are essen-*

tially dissimilar. Analogies come in two forms: the first, literal analogies, are much the same as comparison in that they tie together subjects from the same realm of experience, such as football and soccer, in order to reinforce a point. The second form, **figurative analogy**, combines subjects from different realms of experience. Our opening to this chapter uses a figurative analogy between building homes and building speeches. We will return to this analogy over the next several chapters, because it seems a productive way of thinking about what we are describing. Analogies make concepts or ideas that are remote or poorly understood more immediate and comprehensible. They are especially useful near the beginnings of speeches, where they establish a perspective in which the speech can develop. M. George Allen, senior vice president of research and development for the 3M Company, combined comparison, contrast, and analogy as he established a perspective for his speech, "Succeeding in Japan:"

> I think of doing business in Japan as being like a game of football. But first, you need to know which game of football it is you are playing. Is it the American gridiron sport — or what the rest of the world calls football and what we call soccer?
>
> American football is a bruising battle. The players are huge and strong. They have nicknames like "Refrigerator." And the game is played in short bursts of intense energy. In soccer-football, the players are smaller, but faster. Play is continuous. And a soccer fullback weighs less than lunch for a gridiron fullback.
>
> In a nutshell, gridiron football is trench warfare: soccer football is the cavalry. Likewise, when it comes to business, the Japanese play a different game than we do.[29]

In this example Mr. Allen first draws a *comparison* with football, perhaps to emphasize the aggressive, competitive qualities of international business. He next proceeds to develop a *contrast* between the sports of football and soccer, in order to establish the basis for a *figurative analogy:* just as similar forms of sport can be quite different, so can styles of business reflect the fundamentally different lifestyles of their nations.

As you weigh the use of an analogy, ask yourself the following:

- *Will the analogy help me make some fundamental point about my subject?*
- *Will the analogy distract my listeners?* In the above example, Mr. Allen risked losing some listeners who would prefer to think more about soccer and football than about international business practices.
- *Does the analogy establish a beneficial association for my subject?* Some critics complain that the analogy of sports to politics, so popular among American journalists who describe the "horserace" of political campaigning, both trivializes politics and dehumanizes politicians.

DECIDING WHAT SUPPORTING MATERIAL YOU SHOULD USE

The following general guidelines may help you make wise choices as you select supporting materials for your speech and ways to combine them:

1. If an idea is *controversial,* rely primarily on facts, statistics, factual examples, or expert testimony from sources the audience will respect and accept.

2. If your ideas or concepts are *abstract,* use examples and narratives to bring them to life. Use comparisons, contrasts, or analogies so that your listeners grasp your ideas and develop appropriate feelings about them.

3. If an idea is highly *technical,* supplement facts and statistics with expert testimony. Use definitions, explanations, and descriptions to aid understanding. Use examples, comparisons, contrasts, and analogies to help listeners integrate information.

4. If you need to *arouse emotions,* use lay and prestige testimony, examples, or narratives. Excite listeners by using contrast and analogy.

5. If you need to *defuse emotions,* emphasize facts and statistics and expert testimony. Keep the focus on definitions and explanations.

6. If your topic is *distant* from the lives of your listeners, draw it closer to them through information, examples, and narratives, activated by descriptions, comparisons, and analogies with which they can identify.

Although the need for certain types of supporting material may vary with different topics and audiences, a good rule of thumb is to *support each main point with the most important and relevant facts and statistics available.* To clarify each point, use testimony, and provide sufficient definitions, explanations, and descriptions. Additionally, *support each main point with at least one interesting example or narrative.* To make your presentation more dramatic or memorable, emphasize examples and narratives, brought to life through striking comparisons, contrasts, or analogies.

IN SUMMARY

Facts and statistics, testimony, examples, and narratives are the major forms of *supporting materials.* These materials provide the substance, strength, credibility, and appeal a speech must have before listeners will place their faith in it.

Facts and Statistics. Information in the form of facts and statistics is the most objective form of supporting material, especially useful for unfamiliar or controversial topics. *Facts* are verifiable, which means that independent observers see and report them consistently. *Statistics* are numerical facts that describe the size of something, make predictions, illustrate trends, or show relationships. Be careful not to confuse factual statements with interpretations and claims. Be sure that your information meets the tests of relevance, recency, credibility, and reliability.

Use definitions, explanations, and descriptions to frame facts and statistics into powerful supports. A *definition* is a concise statement of meaning. An *explanation* more fully expands on what something is or how it works. *Descriptions* are word pictures that help the audience visualize what you are talking about.

Testimony.   *Testimony* cites the ideas or words of others in support of your message. When you repeat the exact words of others, you make use of *direct quotation.* When you summarize what others say, you *paraphrase* them. *Expert testimony* comes from recognized authorities who support the validity of your claims. *Lay testimony* represents "the voice of the people" on a topic. *Prestige testimony* connects your message with the general wisdom of some revered figure.

Be sure that the sources you cite are free from bias. State their credentials as you introduce their testimony, and never quote them out of context.

Examples.   *Examples* serve as verbal illustrations. They help arouse interest, clarify ideas, sustain attention, personalize a topic, emphasize your major points, demonstrate how your ideas can be applied, and make it easier for listeners to remember your message. *Brief examples* mention specific instances. *Extended examples* contain more detail and give the speaker more time to build impressions. *Factual examples* are based on actual events and persons. *Hypothetical examples* are invented by the speaker to represent reality. Use people's names to personalize examples and magnify their power.

Narratives.   A *narrative* tells a story that illustrates some truth about the topic. Good narratives draw listeners into the action and help establish a mood. They should be told in colorful, concrete language using dialogue and characterization. A lively and informal style of presentation can enhance narration. Avoid narratives that demean others and reinforce negative stereotypes.

Three Techniques for Using Supporting Materials.   Comparison, contrast, and analogy are general techniques used to make the most of supporting materials. *Comparison* points out the similarities of an unfamiliar, controversial topic to something the audience already understands or accepts. *Contrast* emphasizes the differences among things to make some important point. *Analogy* combines the principles of comparison and contrast to heighten awareness. In the form of *figurative analogy,* this technique creates an overall way of looking at a topic by relating subjects from different realms of experience. Analogies can result in creative, surprising moments for listeners.

TERMS TO KNOW

supporting materials	prestige testimony
facts	example
statistics	brief example
definition	extended example
explanation	factual example
description	hypothetical example
testimony	narrative
direct quotation	comparison
paraphrase	contrast
expert testimony	analogy
lay testimony	figurative analogy

DISCUSSION

1. Read a speech from a recent issue of *Vital Speeches of the Day*, looking closely for examples of statistics used as supporting materials. Were you convinced by the statistics? Did the speakers use definitions, explanations, or descriptions to increase their effectiveness? Apply the tests of relevance, recency, credibility, and reliability to determine whether the statistics might have been more convincing. Report your observations and conclusions in class.

2. In the same speech you examine for question 1, evaluate the use of testimony. Can you find instances in which the kind of testimony was inappropriate, or when testimony of a different or additional sort might have helped the speakers realize their purposes? Do these speakers establish adequately the credentials of those whom they quote or cite? Report your discoveries to the class.

3. Evaluate the use of supporting materials in one of the student speeches in Appendix B. Consider the following questions: Is there sufficient supporting material? What types are used? Are they appropriate to the purpose? Do they make the speech more effective for you? How and why?

4. Look in newspapers or magazines for recent statements by public officials that purport to be factual but that may actually contain distortion. What tips you off to the distortion? In your judgment, would most readers be likely to detect this bias?

APPLICATION

1. Develop a hypothetical example or narrative to illustrate one of the following abstract concepts:

love

compassion

peace

pain

justice

2. Note how television advertisements often give facts and statistics, testimony, examples, or narratives in combination with presentation aids. Using the criteria provided in this chapter and in Chapter 9, analyze and evaluate a current TV ad with respect to the techniques used.

3. Determine which types of testimony might best support the following statements:

a. Native Americans don't get a square deal in the United States.

b. Campus security measures are inadequate.

c. AIDS is spreading rapidly in the heterosexual community.

d. America should return to a system of open immigration.

e. Asian immigrant children are outperforming American-born children in public schools.

Defend your choices in class.

NOTES

1. Richard Weaver, "Ultimate Terms in Contemporary Rhetoric," in *The Ethics of Rhetoric* (Chicago: Henry Regnery, 1953), pp. 211–232.

2. Cynthia Crossen, *Tainted Truth: The Manipulation of Fact in America* (New York: Simon & Schuster, 1994), p. 36.

3. For similar commentary on other periodicals, see Howard Kahane, *Logic and Contemporary Rhetoric: The Use of Reason in Everyday Life* (Belmont, CA: Wadsworth, 1984), pp. 337–338.

4. Reprinted by permission of *World Book Encyclopedia*. This material was brought to our atttention by Professor Gray Matthews of the University of Memphis.

5. Crossen, p. 36.

6. Lonnie R. Bristow, "Protecting Youth from the Tobacco Industry," in *Vital Speeches of the Day,* 15 Mar. 1994, pp. 333–334.

7. Crossen, p. 42.

8. Peter Francese, "Editorial: Lies, Damned Lies . . . ," *American Demographics,* Nov. 1994, p. 2.

9. Donna E. Shalala, "Domestic Terrorism: An Unacknowledged Epidemic," in *Vital Speeches of the Day,* 15 May 1994, p. 451.

10. Adapted from *The 1992 Information Please Environmental Almanac* (Boston: Houghton Mifflin, 1992), p. 144.

11. Longinus, *On The Sublime,* trans. W. Rhys Roberts, in *The Great Critics: An Anthology of Literary Criticism,* eds. James Harry Smith and Edd Winfield Parks, 3rd ed. (New York: W. W. Norton & Company, 1951), p. 82.

12. The power of lay testimony is one possible implication of Michael Calvin McGee's "In Search of the People: A Rhetorical Alternative," *Quarterly Journal of Speech* 61 (1975): 235–249.

13. Richard A. Gephardt, "The Democratic Challenge in the 104th Congress," in *Vital Speeches of the Day,* 15 Jan. 1995, p. 199.

14. Brock Evans, "A Time of Crisis: The Giveaway of our Public Lands," in *Vital Speeches of the Day,* 1 Sept. 1995, p. 691.

15. "On the Campaign Trail," *Reader's Digest,* March 1992, p. 116.

16. Fred Krupp, "Business and the Third Wave: Saving the Environment," presented to the Environmental Marketing Communications Forum, New York, 12 March 1992, in *Vital Speeches of the Day,* 15 August 1992, p. 656.

17. Hillary Rodham Clinton, "Women's Rights are Human Rights," in *Vital Speeches of the Day,* 1 Oct. 1995, p. 739.

18. Alexandra York, "The State of the Culture," in *Vital Speeches of the Day,* 1 May 1993, p. 434.

19. York, p. 433.

20. Jerome S. Bruner, *Acts of Meaning* (Cambridge: Harvard Univ. Press, 1990), and "The Narrative Construction of Reality," *Critical Inquiry* 18 (1991): 1–21.

21. Z. Kunda, D. T. Miller, and T. Claire, "Combining Social Concepts: The Role of Causal Reasoning," *Cognitive Science* 14 (1990): 551–577.

22. Associated Press, "Gore Promotes Benefits of Good Storytelling," *The Memphis Commercial Appeal,* 8 Oct. 1995, p. B2.

23. Roger Ailes, *You Are the Message* (New York: Doubleday, 1988), p. 70–74.

24. David Archambault, "Columbus Plus 500 Years: Whither the American Indian," in *Vital Speeches of the Day,* 1 June 1992, p. 493.

25. Sam J. Ervin, Jr., "Judicial Verbicide: An Affront to the Constitution," presented at Herbert Law Center, Louisiana State University, Baton Rouge, 22 Oct. 1980, in *Representative American Speeches 1980–1981,* ed. Owen Peterson (New York: H. W. Wilson, 1981), p. 62.

26. Christie McGuffee Smith and Larry Powell, "The Use of Disparaging Humor by Group Leaders," *Southern Speech Communication Journal* 53 (1988): 279–292, and Charles R. Gruner, "Advice to the Beginning Speaker on Using Humor — What the Research Tells Us," *Communication Education* 34 (1985): 142–147.

27. Jimmy Carter, "Excellence Comes from a Repository that Doesn't Change: The True Meaning of Success," in *Vital Speeches of the Day,* 1 July 1993, p. 546.

28. Yukio Matsuyama, "Japan's Role in the New World Order," in *Vital Speeches of the Day,* 15 May 1992, p. 463.

29. M. George Allen, "Succeeding in Japan: One Company's Perspective," in *Vital Speeches of the Day,* 1 May 1994, p. 430.

CHAPTER 7

Structuring Your Speech

THIS CHAPTER WILL HELP YOU

- ■ develop a simple, balanced, and orderly speech design.
- ■ shape and arrange your main points.
- ■ use transitions to make your speech flow smoothly.
- ■ prepare introductions that capture attention, establish credibility, and focus your speech.
- ■ prepare conclusions that summarize your message, provide closure, and give the audience something to remember.

Every discourse ought to be a living creature; having a body of its own and head and feet; there should be a middle, beginning, and end, adapted to one another and to the whole.

— Plato

The greenhouse effect is a gradual warming of the earth caused by human activities that dump carbon dioxide into the atmosphere. Fossil fuel use has more than doubled since 1950. One cause of the greenhouse effect is industrial emissions. The summer of 1993 brought record-breaking heat waves and the winter of 1991–92 was the warmest in 97 years. Skin cancers could increase as much as 26 percent if the ozone level drops another 10 percent. This past winter a gigantic iceberg almost as large as Rhode Island broke off an ice shelf in the Antarctic Peninsula. The greenhouse effect is a danger to our world.

How much of this randomly scrambled information would you remember if you heard it presented this way? There seems to be important news here, but it gets lost in the hodgepodge organization. Although unstructured techniques like brainstorming ideas and free-writing can sometimes stimulate the flow of ideas,[1] when you want to communicate those ideas to others you must carefully plan and structure your message.

A well-organized presentation makes it easier for listeners to understand and remember what you have to say.[2] Suppose you must take an introductory physics course next semester and you got the following material from Students for Better Teaching concerning two instructors who will teach the course at times you can schedule it:

JOHNSON, DENISE   Professor Johnson is very entertaining. She tells a lot of funny stories and puts on demonstrations that seem like a "magic show." But she doesn't explain difficult material in any systematic fashion, so it's hard to take notes. When it's time for departmental examinations, you often don't know how or what to study.

MARTINEZ, JOAN   Professor Martinez is very business-like. She starts each lecture by reviewing the material covered in the last session and asks if anyone has questions. Her lectures are easy to follow. She points out what is most important for students to know and uses clear examples that make difficult ideas easier to understand and apply.

Which instructor would you choose? When the content of a message is important, most of us will choose the speaker who is well organized over the entertainer. In fact, a recent study indicated that some of the reasons college students dislike certain instructors are that they stray from the subject, go off on tangents, jump from one idea to another, ramble, or are generally disorganized.[3]

How well your presentation is organized clearly affects your ethos.[4] As we noted in Chapter 2, "competence" is an important part of credibility. It is hard for listeners to think you are competent when your speech is poorly organized. They are more likely to think that you have a muddled mind or that you didn't care enough to prepare carefully.

In this chapter we look at the principles that explain why people prefer well-organized messages. We then use these principles to explain how to structure the body of your speech. Next, we consider the importance of transitions to make a speech flow smoothly. Finally, we discuss how to prepare effective introductions and conclusions.

PRINCIPLES OF GOOD FORM

The structure of a speech should follow the ways people naturally see and arrange things in their minds. People rarely store information in individual bits. Instead they *cluster* material so that it can be more easily recalled. For example, people store and recall telephone numbers as two or three *groups* of numbers such as *909-647-2830*, not *9-0-9-6-4-7-2-8-3-0*.[5] Once grouped, information is organized according to a few basic principles.[6] When these principles are satisfied, a speech has **good form**. *To develop good form, you should present your material simply, balance the length of the parts of your speech, and arrange your main points so that they lead naturally from one to another.* In other words, good form depends on simplicity, balance, and order.

Simplicity

The more simple your speech design, the easier it will be for listeners to follow, understand, and remember your message. Simplicity is especially important in oral presentations because the audience doesn't have a manuscript that they can reread if material seems confusing. To achieve **simplicity** you should limit the number of main ideas in your speech and keep each direct and to the point.

Number of Main Points.   In general, *the fewer main points you have, the better.*[7] Remember, each main point of your message must be developed with supporting materials. It takes time to present information, examples, narratives, and testimony effectively. Short classroom speeches (under ten minutes) usually should have no more than four main points. Even longer speeches outside the classroom, those that may last up to an hour, should not normally attempt more than five main points. Look at what happens when a speech becomes overburdened with main points:

Thesis statement: Government welfare programs aren't working.

Main points: I. There are too many programs.

           II. The programs often duplicate coverage.

           III. Some people who really need help are left out.

           IV. The programs are underfunded.

           V. They waste money.

           VI. Recipients have no input into what is really needed.

           VII. The programs create dependence and stifle initiative.

           VIII. They rob the poor of self-respect.

All of these points are important, but presented in this way, they seem overwhelming. It would be hard for listeners to remember them because there are too many of them and they are not organized into a meaningful pattern. Let's see how these ideas might be clustered into a simpler structural pattern:

Thesis statement: Our approach to welfare in America is inadequate, inefficient, and insensitive.

Main point: I. Our approach is inadequate.

Subpoints: A. We don't fund it sufficiently.

           B. Some people who need help get left out.

Main point: II. Our approach is inefficient.

Subpoints: A. There are too many programs.

           B. There is too much duplication.

           C. There is too much waste of money.

Main point: III. Our approach is insensitive.

Subpoints: A. It creates dependence.

           B. It stifles initiative.

           C. It robs people of self-respect.

This simple structure makes the speech easy to follow. The ideas have been arranged so that the main points follow each other in a logical pattern of development. Each main point breaks down into more specific subpoints that extend and explain its meaning. Overlapping points have been combined and unnecessary ideas omitted. The audience can remember the ideas more easily.[8]

Phrasing Main Points.   You also should state your main points as simply as possible. In the preceding example, not only has the number of main points been reduced, but the wording of these points has been made clear and direct. Parallel phrasing ("Our approach is . . .") has been used for emphasis. This strategic repetition helps listeners remember the message. It also allows the speaker to refer to the "Three I's" (Inadequate, Inefficient, and Insensitive) of welfare in the introduction and conclusion, a strategy that would spotlight the message and tie the speech together.

To achieve simplicity, be sure your specific purpose, thesis statement, and main points are very clear to you so that you can express them succinctly. Think of simplicity as a major goal when building your speech.

Balance

Balance means that all the major parts of your speech — the introduction, body, and conclusion — receive the right amount of emphasis and development. Proper emphasis in turn depends largely upon timing. Instructors frequently specify time limits for your speeches, so you must plan your message with these in mind. It can be very disconcerting to find yourself finishing the first main point of your speech with only one minute left and two more main points plus your conclusion to cover. Keep timing in mind as you prepare your speech, cutting and adding material to maintain the proper balance. Time yourself as you rehearse the speech to be sure it fits within the allotted limits.

There is no absolute rule of thumb that establishes how the major parts of speeches should be balanced. However, the following suggestions may be helpful:

1. *The body should be the longest part.* The body contains the essence of your message — the major ideas you want to communicate. It's where you conduct the business of your speech. If you spend three minutes on your introduction, a minute and a half on the body, and thirty seconds on the conclusion, your speech will be badly out of balance.

2. *Allocate time according to your topic and audience.* Within the body, you should allocate time based upon the topic and upon where the audience stands in relation to your specific purpose. One way to balance your main points is to give each about the same amount of development, which suggests that the main points are equally important. This strategy might be appropriate for the speech attacking the "three I's" of welfare policy, in which each point merits about equal attention.

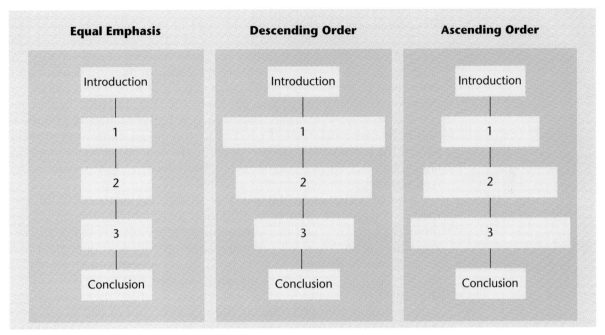

Equal Emphasis	Descending Order	Ascending Order
Introduction	Introduction	Introduction
1	1	1
2	2	2
3	3	3
Conclusion	Conclusion	Conclusion

FIGURE 7.1
Balanced Speeches

Another approach is to arrange your main points in the order of their importance. You could begin with your most important point and then list the other main points in *descending order* of importance, spending proportionately less time on each. For example, in a problem-solution persuasive speech, if listeners must be convinced there actually is a problem, you would devote most of your time to meeting the challenge of the first main point. On the other hand, if listeners generally agree there is a problem, but don't know what to do about it, then you should devote most of your time to discussing the second main point, your proposed solution. Your main points would then develop in *ascending order* of importance. Careful consideration of your topic and careful analysis of your audience will usually suggest how to allocate time within the body of your speech.

3. *The introduction and conclusion should be approximately equal in length.* For example, if you begin a brief story in your introduction leading into the body of your speech, you might end the story as you conclude the speech. That should strike listeners as a balanced introduction and conclusion, leading you gracefully into and out of your speech. Once again, the total amount of time spent on the introduction and conclusion should be less than that spent on the body of your speech. As a general rule, we advise our students that in a five-minute presentation the combined length of the introduction and conclusion should be about a minute long. This leaves them with four minutes to develop the main points of their messages.

Order

The parts of your speech should not only be well balanced; they should also fit and work well together. They should satisfy your listeners' need for **order.** An orderly speech follows a consistent pattern of development. At the most basic level, you must begin with an introduction, develop your main ideas in the body of your speech, then end with a conclusion. You should develop the body of your speech first so that your introduction and conclusion fit your message. Your speech will also fit together better, as well as be better balanced, if you can tie the introduction to the conclusion. If the introduction asked a question, the conclusion could supply an answer based on ideas from the speech. Or, if you began with a story of defeat, your conclusion might offer a related story of victory.

Order also applies to the way you arrange the main points in your speech. If you want to propose a solution to a problem, you should first present the problem and then the solution. Why? Because that is the way our minds work. We don't normally come up with solutions, then look for problems to fit them. Orderly thinking also governs the presentation of steps in a process. You begin with the step that starts the process, then cover the remaining steps in the order in which they occur. If you jump around in your presentation, the audience is apt to get lost on one of the jumps.

How well a speech fits together depends on the way the individual parts relate to each other and to the overall pattern they form. As you move from introduction to body, from point to point within the body, and from the body to the conclusion, you should use transitions to help listeners see the larger picture. We discuss the use of transitions in greater detail later in this chapter.

STRUCTURING THE BODY OF YOUR SPEECH

Because the body of your speech contains the major substance of your message, you should organize it first. In developing the body of your speech, you have three major tasks to accomplish:

1. You must determine your main points.
2. You must arrange your main points effectively.
3. You must decide how to use supporting materials.

Determine Your Main Points

In the course of your research, you will discover that certain themes are stressed or repeated. These themes are the most important concerns and issues connected with your topic. Look at them in terms of how they relate to your specific purpose, thesis statement, and the needs and interests of your listeners. They provide the raw material from which you will fashion the **main points** of your speech. Your main points are the most prominent ideas of your message, the ones you emphasize most, your principal points of focus. They are the columns that support the structure of your speech.

Let's look at how you might determine the main points for a speech on the causes of the greenhouse effect. To get the best overall picture of themes, prepare a **research overview.** List your main sources of information and then summarize the major ideas from each source identified on the information and source cards discussed in Chapter 5. Figure 7.2 presents a research overview based on four sources of information: general information from an encyclopedia entry, a discussion guide published by the National Issues Forums Institute, a magazine article from *Time,* and an article from the *Commercial Appeal* newspaper. Scan the overview, looking for repeated themes and concerns that emerge across the sources. You might come up with the following themes:

- The greenhouse effect is a gradual warming of the earth's atmosphere (GE 1, 3; CA 5, 6)
- The greenhouse effect may be caused by too much carbon dioxide in the atmosphere (GE 2; NIF 1A; CA 1)
- Increased carbon dioxide comes from energy consumption, industrial pollution, and loss of woodlands, especially in the industrialized nations (NIF 2; CA 2, 3)
- The greenhouse effect may cause serious health, environmental, and economic problems (NIF 1B, 1C, 1D; T 1, 3; CA 6)

Once you have identified the major themes from your research, you should determine how these relate to the specific purpose and thesis statement of your speech. You should also assess how relevant they are to the needs and interests of your audience. In this example your specific purpose

FIGURE 7.2
Sample Research Overview

Grolier Encyclopedia (GE)	NIF Pamphlet (NIF)	Time Article (T)	Commercial Appeal Newspaper (CA)

1. Melting ice caps and rise in sea level	1. Problem:
	  A. Carbon dioxide too high
	  B. Hole in ozone layer
	  C. Climate changes
	  D. Health problems
		1. Problem revealed in Antarctica	1. Too much carbon dioxide: 30% increase in past 200 years

2. Increased carbon dioxide from burning fossil fuels		2. CFCs gobble ozone	2. Increased methane and nitrous oxide

3. Rise in global temps in '80s and '90s	2. Causes
	  A. Loss of woodlands
	  B. Industriall pollution
	  C. Energy consumption
		3. Ozone depletion leads to
		  A. Cataracts
		  B. Mutations in DNA
		  C. Skin cancer
		  D. Impaired immunity
		  E. Reduced crop yields
			3. Half of problem emissions from 36 industrialized countries

4. Need to limit CFCs			4. Sea level rise/polar melting
			5. Increased global temperatures
			6. Could cause coastal floods, climate changes, storms
			7. Environmentalists vs. industry reps conflict

is "to inform my audience of the causes of the greenhouse effect." Your audience may have heard of the greenhouse effect, but their knowledge of the topic is probably vague and they may not be aware of its importance to their lives.

In light of these considerations, you realize that you must start by defining the greenhouse effect to establish a shared base of meaning. As a matter of fact, with this or any other technical topic you must be sensitive to the need for definitions throughout your speech. Such definitions must go beyond simple translations. You should use explanations and descriptions (discussed in Chapter 6) to bring the topic into the lives of listeners. If your purpose were to persuade listeners, you might develop the alarming consequences predicted for the greenhouse effect as main points to motivate your listeners to support changes in public policy. In your informative speech, however, you decide to mention these consequences in your introduction and as part of your definition to arouse interest and to motivate your audience to listen. Once you have their interest, you can proceed to discuss the causes. In this case, from the major themes revealed by your research overview, you might fashion the following main points:

- The greenhouse effect is a gradual warming of the earth from human activities.
- The loss of woodlands adds to the greenhouse effect.
- Industrial emissions accelerate the greenhouse effect.
- Increased energy consumption magnifies the greenhouse effect.

Arranging Your Main Points

Once you have determined your main points, you must decide how to arrange them. You need to come up with a way of ordering them that is appropriate for your audience, fits your material, and serves your specific purpose. For example, in the above case the first main point will provide needed definitions and heighten interest. The next three main points will establish, in increasing order of importance, the principal causes of the greenhouse effect. Following the balance requirement of good form, you will spend proportionately more time on each cause as your speech develops.

Beyond these important strategic considerations, other factors help explain why some patterns satisfy the principle of good form more than others. As we noted earlier in this chapter, people organize information into clusters or patterns that are easily recalled. These patterns become habits of the mind, expectations that predetermine how we process our experiences. They function like mental forms or templates into which we pour or fit new information. We see and experience the world through them. How we arrange our speeches must be in harmony with these expectations. *These principles are similarity, proximity, and closure.* In this section we discuss some basic speech designs that relate to these principles of orderliness. More detailed examples of speech designs may be found in Chapters 12 and 13, which discuss informative and persuasive speaking.

Principle of Similarity. The **principle of similarity** leads people to group things together that seem alike. This tendency underlies the *categorical design* for speeches. Speakers use categories when they discuss "three major causes of the greenhouse effect" or "the four basic components of a good stereo system." Categories can be based on the actual divisions of a topic, such as the symptoms of a disease. They also may be used to represent customary ways of thinking about a subject, such as the four basic food groups. *Such causes, components, symptoms, and groups go together because they seem alike in relation to their subjects.* Socrates may have been thinking of categories when he advised speakers to divide subjects "according to the natural formation, where the joint is, not breaking any part as a bad carver might."[9]

You also can use a categorical design to talk about a person. For example, you might believe that the public image of Gloria Steinem has been distorted by poor press coverage; therefore, you decide to present a speech that will help the audience understand her activism. You decide on a categorical design so that you can emphasize the factors leading to her activism. In such a design you might consider (1) personal and family events, (2) professional events, and (3) political events. These categories, related by their similarity as forces in her life, generate the main points of your speech:

Specific purpose: To inform my audience of critical events that contributed to Gloria Steinem's activism.

Thesis statement: To understand Gloria Steinem's activism we need to understand the forces that shaped her life.

Main points:
    I. Steinem's personal life laid the basis for her activism.
    II. Steinem's professional activities exposed her to sexual harassment.
    III. Steinem's political experiences subjected her to discrimination.[10]

Principle of Proximity. According to the **principle of proximity**, things that occur close together in time or space should be presented in the order in which they naturally occur. For example, a how-to speech should have a *sequential design* that presents the steps in the order in which they should be taken. If you want to discuss events that led to a present-day problem, you might use the sequential design to present a historical perspective of the situation. Your research may show that the major events occurred in 1955, 1970, and 1987. If you follow this chronological pattern, your speech will be easy to understand. But if you start talking about 1970, then jump back to 1955, then leap ahead to the present before doubling back to 1987, you will probably lose most of your listeners by violating the principle of proximity.

If you were preparing a speech describing the scenic wonders of Yellowstone Park, your speech might best follow a *spatial design*. Such a design is based on the closeness of physical relationships, such as east-west, up-down, or points around a circle. You might begin with your audience at the south visitor's center, take them up the west side to Old Faithful, continue north to Mammoth Hot Springs, then down the east side through the Grand Canyon of the Yellowstone. This way your audience gets a verbal map to follow as well as a picture of the major attractions in the park.

Principle of Closure.   The **principle of closure** is based on the natural tendency of people to seek completion.[11] We like to have patterns carried through to the end so that we feel we have the "whole picture," or know the "whole story." Have you ever gotten engrossed in a magazine article in a waiting room only to find that some previous reader has torn out the last page of the story? Can you remember the annoyance you felt? Your need for closure had been frustrated.

The principle of closure applies to several speech designs. For example, if you omit an important category when developing your topic, listeners may notice its omission. If you leave out a necessary step in a sequence, audiences may sense the flaw. Although all speeches should satisfy this need, there are two speech patterns for which closure is absolutely essential. These are *cause-effect* and *problem-solution* designs. Because we want the world to seem purposeful and controllable, we like for all events to have clear causes and for all problems to have satisfactory solutions.

A cause-effect speech can go in two directions: it can begin by focusing on some present situation as an effect and then seek its causes, or it can look at the present as a potential cause of future effects. Sometimes these variations can be combined. You might take a current situation such as the budget deficit and develop a speech tracing its origins. If you had enough time, you might continue by predicting the future effects of the deficit. Understanding the causes could help your listeners see what needs to be done to reduce the deficit. Predicting future effects might make them *want* to reduce it.

Determining and Arranging Your Main Points

SPEAKER'S NOTES

1   Prepare a research overview to identify repeated ideas and themes.
2   Frame main points in light of the function and purpose of your speech and the needs of your audience.
3   Limit your main points to four or fewer for a short speech.
4   Use the principle of similarity to develop categories.
5   Use the principle of proximity to arrange main points in sequential or spatial patterns.
6   Use the principle of closure to provide completeness in causation and problem-solution designs.

The problem-solution design focuses attention on a problem and then provides a solution for it. Such speeches often use motivational appeals to bring the problem home to listeners. Once you have aroused strong feelings, your solutions must show how to satisfy them, or the audience may feel frustrated and resentful. Returning to our previous example, the budget deficit could be presented as a problem, a threat to national security and the well-being of future generations. The speaker then should provide a solution. In either of these variations, speakers must discuss both cause and effect or problem and solution in order to satisfy listeners' need for closure.

Let these principles of similarity, proximity, and closure help you select the most effective design for your speech. The design you choose, in turn, helps you determine and arrange your main points. We consider the basic speech designs in more detail in Chapters 12 and 13.

Adding Supporting Materials

Once you have framed and arranged your main points, you must support them with facts and figures, testimony, examples, or narratives to make them sturdy and reliable. As you develop your main points, you should also consider whether you need to divide them into subpoints. The subpoints contain information or ideas that listeners need before they can understand or accept the main point. For example, assume that you have framed a main point: "The answer to environmental waste on campus is a recycling program." To support this main point, you realize that you must also support two subpoints: "My recycling plan will work" and "My recycling plan is affordable."

You strengthen both main points and subpoints by grounding them in supporting materials. In the instance just mentioned, you could support your subpoint on workability by citing *examples* of other campuses that successfully used a similar plan. You might even develop a before-and-after *narrative* to describe how one college dealt with its waste disposal problem. To convince listeners that your proposal is cost efficient, you might use *statistics* and *expert testimony*, being certain to cite the sources of your information and to introduce their credentials. Once you have developed these supporting materials, the main point should be acceptable to reasonable listeners.

In Chapter 6 we provided some general guidelines for selecting supporting materials. Here we show how to work supporting materials into the structure of your speech. Main points that are developed with supporting materials help fortify a message against the doubts or disagreements of reasonable listeners. Supporting materials answer the practical questions such listeners often ask, either aloud or silently in their minds:

1. *What is the basis of that idea?* (You answer with facts or statistics.)
2. *How do you know? Who else says so?* (You supply testimony.)
3. *How does it work? Where is it true?* (You offer an example.)
4. *So what? Why should I care?* (You develop a narrative that explains why.)

Although the situation will vary from topic to topic, speaker to speaker, and audience to audience, it is possible to set up an ideal model for the support of any main point or important subpoint. This model includes the point plus the following supporting materials:

- the most important relevant facts and statistics.
- the most authoritative judgments made by sources the audience respects.
- at least one interesting story or example that clarifies or brings the idea to life.

Figure 7.3 provides a model format for supporting a point. Let us look at how this format could work in a speech. Assume that you want to demonstrate a main point that suntans are not a sign of good health. Here is one way you could use supporting materials to develop this point:

Statement: Suntans are not as "good" for you as they look on you.

Transition: Let's examine some of the evidence.

FIGURE 7.3

Outline Format for Supporting a Point

Statement: _____

_____

Transition into facts or statistics: _____

    1. Factual information or statistics that support statement: _____

_____

_____

Transition into testimony: _____

    2. Testimony that supports statement: _____

_____

_____

Transition into example or narrative: _____

    3. Example or narrative that supports statement: _____

_____

_____

_____

Transition into restatement: _____

Restatement of original assertion: _____

_____

Facts/statistics:	According to a 1995 report by the American Cancer Society, prolonged exposure without protection is responsible for about 90 percent of all skin cancers.
Transition:	Moreover, exposure without protection also accelerates the aging process.
Expert testimony:	According to Dr. John M. Knox, head of dermatology at the Baylor University College of Medicine, "If you do biopsies on the buttocks of people ages seventy-five and thirty-five, you won't see any differences under the microscope . . . protected skin stays youthful much longer."
Transition:	Let's look at an example of one person who suffered from overexposure.
Example:	Jane was a fair-skinned blond-haired girl who loved the sun as a child and teen-ager. She would sunburn often but didn't think there would be any effects other than the short-term pain. Lying in the sun seemed so healthy and appealing, she didn't dream it could harm her. Now at forty-five, she knows better. She couldn't believe her ears when her doctor told her she had skin cancer. She felt that she took good care of herself. Now she cannot go out into the sun, even for a few minutes, without using a sunscreen and wearing a hat, a long-sleeved shirt, and long pants.
Transition:	What does all this mean?
Restatement:	A suntan may make you look healthy, but it is not healthy. Overexposure to the sun causes cancer and premature aging. Are you willing to take that risk just to look good for a brief time?

In this example three forms of supporting material — statistical information, expert testimony, and example — work together to establish the main point. Each contributes its special strength. If each of your main points is well supported, the structure of your speech should stand up even if questioned or challenged by critical listeners.

We shall have a great deal more to say about building the body of your speech as we discuss the designs of speeches further in connection with the general functions of informing and persuading listeners in Chapters 12 and 13.

USING TRANSITIONS

The example of using supporting materials also illustrates the important work of transitions in a speech. **Transitions** show your listeners how your ideas connect with each other. They help your listeners focus on the meaning of what you have already discussed and prepare them for what is still to come. They serve as signposts that help listeners see the overall pattern of your message. Transitions also connect your main points and tie the body of a speech to its introduction and conclusion.

Some transitions are simple, short phrases such as "Another point that must be made is. . . ." More often, however, transitions are worded as phrases that link ideas, such as "Having looked at why people don't pay compliments more often, let's consider. . . ." This type of transition sums up what you have just said while directing your audience to your next point.

Certain stock words or phrases can be used to signal changes in a speech. For example, words and phrases like *until now* or *only last week* can be used to point out time changes. Transitions such as *in addition* can be used to show that you are expanding on what you have already said. The use of the word *similarly* indicates that a comparison will follow. Phrases such as *on the other hand* cue listeners to a contrast. Cause-and-effect relationships can be suggested with words like *as a result* or *consequently*. Introductory phrases like *traveling north* can indicate spatial relationships. Phrases or words like *in short, finally,* or *in conclusion* can signal that the speech is coming to its end. Figure 7.4 contains a list of some commonly used transitions.

One special type of transition is the **internal summary.** An internal summary reminds listeners of the points you have already covered before you move on to the next part of your message. Internal summaries are especially useful in cause-effect and problem-solution speeches, where they can span the gap between the two dimensions of the design. An internal summary signals listeners that you have finished your discussion of the causes or problem and you are now ready to describe the effects or solution. In addition, an internal summary condenses and repeats your ideas, which can help your listeners remember your message. If listeners have somehow missed the point, the transition helps put them back on track. Consider the following example:

> **So now we see what the problem is. We know the cost in human suffering. We know the terrible political consequences and the enormous economic burden. The question is, what are we going to do about it? Let me tell you about a solution that many experts agree may turn things around.**

The speaker condensed the three subpoints concerning the human, political, and economic aspects of a problem into an internal summary that prepared the audience for the solution phase of the speech. Internal summaries should be brief and to the point so that they highlight the major features of your message.

The lack of planned transitions is often apparent when beginning speakers overuse words and vocalized pauses such as *well, you know, okay,*

FIGURE 7.4
Common Transitions

To indicate	Use
Time changes	until, now, since, previously, later, earlier, in the past, in the future, meanwhile, five years ago, just last month, tomorrow, following, before, at present, eventually
Additions	moreover, in addition, furthermore, besides
Comparison	compared with, both are, likewise, in comparison, similarly, of equal importance, another type of, like, alike, just as
Contrast	but, yet, however, on the other hand, conversely, still, otherwise, in contrast, unfortunately, despite, rather than, on the contrary
Cause-effect	therefore, consequently, thus, accordingly, so, as a result, hence, since, because of, due to, for this reason
Numerical order	first, second, third, in the first place, to begin with, initially, next, eventually, finally
Spatial relations	to the north, alongside, to the left, above, moving eastward, in front of, in back of, behind, next to, below, nearby, in the distance
Explanation	to illustrate, for example, for instance, case in point, in other words, to simplify, to clarify
Importance	most importantly, above all, keep this in mind, remember, listen carefully, take note of, indeed
The speech is ending	in short, finally, in conclusion, to summarize

or "er" to replace transitions. Plan a variety of transitions to help your speech flow smoothly. If you find that you can't develop effective transitions, you may need to rethink the structure of your message. Outline your thoughts to be sure that they move in a clear direction and an orderly sequence. We cover outlining more fully in Chapter 8.

Once you have identified and arranged your main points, decided how to develop them with supporting materials, and planned how to connect them with transitions, you can prepare your introduction and conclusion so that you have a balanced speech that begins and ends effectively. These parts of your speech are especially important because listeners generally are most affected by what they hear at the beginning and end of a message.[12] The introduction allows you to make a good first impression and to set the stage for how your audience will respond. The conclusion provides an opportunity for you to make a lasting impression.

INTRODUCING YOUR MESSAGE

The introduction to your speech is an invitation to listen. Consequently, the audience should be foremost in your mind as you plan your opening words. When you first begin to speak, the audience will have two basic concerns in mind: *Why should I listen to this speech?* and *Why should I listen to this speaker?* These questions relate to two of the three basic functions of an introduction. First, it should capture attention and excite interest so that your audience *wants* to listen to your message. Second, it should help establish your ethos as a competent, trustworthy, and likable person with whom the audience can identify. Finally, your introduction should help focus and preview your message to make it easier for the audience to follow.

A successful introduction also helps prepare you to present the rest of your speech. Such an introduction gets you off to a good start and helps allay any performance anxiety you might feel. Therefore, prepare your introduction carefully to assure a smooth entry into your speech. Practice it until you are confident and comfortable with it. If the context of your presentation requires it, you may vary it during the actual speaking situation (see Chapter 4). Establish good eye contact with listeners. *Do not read your introduction!*

Capturing Attention

All too often beginning speakers open their presentations with something like "Good evening. The topic of my speech is . . ." and then jump right into their message. Needless to say, this is not an effective way to begin a speech. It does not invite your audience to listen. Nor does it make them *want* to. There are several good ways to attract, build, and hold the interest of your audience. You may:

- involve the audience,
- relate your subject to personal experience,
- ask rhetorical questions,
- create suspense,
- tell a story,
- use humor,
- begin with a quotation, or
- startle listeners.

Involve the Audience.   You involve listeners when you connect them with your message. One of the most frequently used involvement techniques is to offer sincere, well-deserved compliments. Does the group, the location, or an audience member merit praise? People like to hear good things about themselves and their community. This technique is often used in formal speeches when custom requires a speaker to make such ac-

The introduction of your speech must immediately engage your audience. If you don't get their attention within the first minute of speaking, they may be lost to you forever.

knowledgements before moving into the actual presentation. These introductory remarks can be very brief, as illustrated by the opening words of President John F. Kennedy in a speech given at a White House dinner honoring Nobel Prize winners:

> **I think this is the most extraordinary collection of talent, of human knowledge, that has ever been gathered together at the White House, with the possible exception of when Thomas Jefferson dined alone.**[13]

With this elegant tribute Kennedy was able to honor his guests without embarrassing them or going overboard with praise. His witty reference to the genius of Thomas Jefferson also paid tribute to the past.

A less formal way to involve listeners is to relate your topic directly to their lives. When you can demonstrate that what you are talking about matters to them, your speech will be more effective.[14] This is especially important if your topic seems distant from the audience's immediate concerns or experiences. Beth Duncan wanted to speak to her classroom audience on Alzheimer's disease. She helped listeners relate to her topic with the following opening in which she read a letter directly from a piece of folded stationery:

> I'd like to share with you a letter my roommate got from her grand-
> mother, an educated and cultured woman. I watched her weep as she
> read it, and after she showed it to me, I understood why.
>
> "Dear Sally," she read. "I am finally around to answer your last.
> You have to look over me. ha. I am so sorry to when you called Sun-
> day why didn't you remind me. Steph had us all so upset leaving and
> not telling no she was going back but we have a good snow ha and
> Kathy can't drive on ice so I never get a pretty card but they have a
> thing to see through an envelope. I haven't got any in the bank until
> I get my homestead check so I'm just sending this. ha. When you was
> talking on the phone Cathy had Ben and got my groceries and I had
> to unlock the door. I forgot to say hold and I don't have Claudette's
> number so forgive me for being so silly. ha. Nara said to tell you she
> isn't doing no good well one is doing pretty good and my eyes. Love,
> Nanny."
>
> Sally's grandmother has Alzheimer's disease. Over 2.5 million older
> people in the United States are afflicted with it. It could strike someone
> in our families — a grandparent, an aunt or uncle, or even our mother
> or father.

When Beth finished this introduction, her classmates felt moved and
deeply involved. Realizing that this disease could affect their own families
made them want to hear the rest of Beth's speech. You also can involve
your listeners by relating your topic to their motivations or attitudes and
by using inclusive pronouns such as *we* and *our*. We discuss the use of inclusive pronouns in more detail in Chapter 10.

Relate Your Subject to Personal Experience.   An old adage suggests
that people are interested first in themselves, next in other people, then in
things, and finally in ideas. This may explain why relating a topic to personal experience heightens audience interest. When speakers have been
personally involved with a topic, they also gain credibility. We are more
willing to listen to others and take their advice if we know they have traveled the road themselves.

Relating your subject to personal experience also can establish common
ground between yourself and listeners. This can be very important when
you face a wary or unfriendly audience. Brock Evans, vice president of the
Audubon Society, recently addressed the Seattle Rotary Club on the Endangered Species Act. Because this speech was presented amid a controversy
concerning logging restrictions in that area, his introduction before this
skeptical group was especially critical. Evans combined the techniques of
involving the audience and relating the topic to personal experience in
this introduction:

> It is always a distinct honor to be invited to speak before a prestigious
> group like the Rotary Club of Seattle. I thank you for inviting me to be
> here today, and not just because of the opportunity to share a few

thoughts about this very important subject. Those of you who know me know that my roots here run very deep. It was 30 years ago that I moved here from the Midwest, because I wanted to live in what I thought then — and still do now — was the most beautiful part of the country.

And those of you who know me know that my passion for this special Northwest land, its unique blend of mountain and forest and sea, goes even deeper . . . for it caused me to leave a law practice here, in order to devote my life to fight to help keep our way of life, to keep the Northwest the special place it is. It has now become a life's work that has taken me many places, first all across the Northwest, and finally into "exile" as I now believe — in the nation's capital — that other Washington, where for better or worse, so many of the great issues of our time are finally resolved.[15]

In this example, the love of the area and its beauty unites the speaker and listeners. The fact that the speaker "adopted" the area lends special credence to his passion for it.

Ask Rhetorical Questions.   Most of the time you ask a question in order to get information. However a **rhetorical question** has a different purpose, especially when asked in the introduction of a speech. The speaker does not expect a spoken answer from the audience to a question such as, "Have you ever thought about what your life would be like if you were a different color?" Such a question focuses the audience on a vital issue. Its purposes are to arouse curiosity and to get listeners thinking. When speakers do solicit direct answers to such questions, they plan carefully so that the answers they receive set up the remainder of their speech. Their intention is to involve listeners with their message. James H. Carr, a vice president with a federal government mortgage funding group, opened a speech on the problems in American cities with the following rhetorical questions:

How many of you saw the chase of O.J. Simpson . . . down an L.A. freeway . . . on June 17? Did you watch any of the pretrial hearings that took place over the three weeks following that event? Who can tell me how many other people were murdered in America on June 12, the same night as Nicole Brown Simpson? Based on average national crime statistics, 63 other people lost their lives due to violent crime on the night of June 12. And during the next three weeks, while the major networks broadcast O.J. Simpson's pretrial hearings, more than 1,200 people were murdered. This tragedy did not attract the attention of the nation. But it should have.[16]

Rhetorical questions often tie in to recent dramatic events, as this example shows. However, they can be just as effective when they relate to everyday experiences. Annette Berrington opened her classroom speech on safety belts by asking the audience:

> How many of you buckled up your seat belts on your way to school this morning? How many of you didn't? How many of you almost never use your seat belts on short trips around town? How many of you don't buckle up because it's uncomfortable? Or because it will "mess up" your clothes? Or because you simply just don't think about it?
>
> Most people now do use their seatbelts on a regular basis. But even though Tennessee has a law requiring us to buckle up, too many of us just ignore it. We risk injury and death on a daily basis. Last week I called Nashville and talked to Ben Dailey at the State Department of Safety. What he told me really blew my mind. Of the 997 people killed in automobile accidents in our state in 1994, 772 were *not* using a seat belt at the time of the crash! How do you like those odds? You have a much greater chance of being killed in an auto accident if you don't buckle up.

These rhetorical questions provided a provocative opening. Several audience members lowered their eyes or looked away. They had been caught and they knew it. Needless to say, Annette had captured her audience's attention.

Develop Suspense. We can trace the human fascination with suspense and mystery far back into antiquity.[17] You can attract and hold your listeners' attention by arousing their curiosity, then making them wait before you satisfy it. The following introduction creates curiosity and anticipation:

> Getting knocked down is no disgrace. Champions are made by getting up just one more time than the opponent! The results are a matter of record about a man who suffered many defeats: Lost his job in 1832, defeated for legislature in 1832, failed in business in 1833, defeated for legislature in 1834, sweetheart died in 1835, had nervous breakdown in 1836, defeated for nomination for Congress in 1843, elected to Congress in 1846, lost renomination in 1848, rejected for land officer in 1849, defeated for Senate in 1854, defeated for nomination for Vice-President in 1856, defeated for Senate in 1858. In 1860 Abraham Lincoln was elected President of the United States. Lincoln proved that a big shot is just a little shot who keeps shooting. The greatest failures in the world are those who fail by not doing anything.[18]

The list of failures aroused the audience's curiosity. Who was this loser? Many were surprised when they discovered it was Abraham Lincoln. This effective introduction set the stage for the speaker's message that perseverance is the key to success.

Tell a Story. We humans began our love affair with stories around the campfires of ancient times. It is through stories that we remember the past and pass on our heritage to future generations. Stories also entertain and educate us — they depict abstract problems in human terms. In introductions, stories help capture audience attention and involve listeners in creating the meaning of the message. In a speech on domestic violence, Donna E. Shalala, U.S. Secretary of Health and Human Services, began with the following narrative:

> The day after Christmas last year, Marsha Brewer-Stewart was found with a knife in her chest. Police say she was murdered by her husband, Gregory. Just seven months earlier, Marsha had stood by her husband's side in a suburban Chicago courtroom to try to clear him of attempting to kill her. She had dismissed the episode as a drunken fit of rage. Police and prosecutors begged her not to post his bond, nor to move back with him, but like many women before her, she forgave him.
>
> Then, on December 26, Marsha called the police, desperate for help. The police called back, and the man who answered said nothing was wrong. By the time a squad car arrived to check on her, Marsha was dead. Hours later, her husband was charged with murder. It's a common story. Studies show us just how common. In this country, domestic violence is just about as common as giving birth — about four million instances of each. Think about that — hopelessness and hope, equally weighted in our society — and all too often, intermingled in the same woman's life.[19]

Narratives are also good at establishing a mood for your message. Sandra Baltz, a premed major, opened a speech on the dilemma of setting priorities for organ transplants with the following narrative:

> On a cold and stormy night in 1841 the ship *William Brown* struck an iceberg in the North Atlantic. Passengers and crew members frantically scrambled into the lifeboats. To make a bad disaster even worse, one of the lifeboats began to sink because it was overcrowded. Fourteen men were thrown overboard that horrible night. After the survivors were rescued, a crew member was tried for the murders of those thrown overboard.
>
> Fortunately, situations like this have been few in history, but today we face a similar problem in the medical establishment: deciding who will live as we allocate scarce medical resources for transplants. Someday, your fate — or the fate of someone you love — could depend on how we resolve this dilemma.

In the preceding examples, the stories set a somber mood for the serious messages that follow. Stories can also be used to establish a lighter mood through the use of humor.

Use Humor.   Humor can enliven an introduction and, when used appropriately, can put your audience in a receptive mood for your message. But humor may also be the most frequently misused technique of introducing speeches. Thinking that amusing listeners will assure success, beginning speakers often search through joke books to find something to make people laugh. Unless carefully adapted, such material often sounds canned, inappropriate, or only remotely relevant to the topic or occasion. If you wish to use humor in your introduction, be certain the material is fresh and pertinent.

Humor can sometimes help to thaw an audience, especially when speakers make themselves the object of the humor. Takakazu Kuriyama, Japanese ambassador to the United States, opened a speech at George Washington University with the following anecdote:

> Thank you. I'm delighted to be part of your Ambassador Lecture Series. I think it's very brave of you to invite ambassadors to speak. We are not especially known for our oratory or clarity. Someone once noted that a diplomat is a person who thinks twice before saying nothing. Someone else said that if a diplomat says yes, he means perhaps; if he says perhaps he means no; and if he says no, he's no diplomat.[20]

Be especially careful when using humor to open a speech. It can be grossly inappropriate for some topics and occasions. Also, don't let a humorous introduction "upstage" the rest of your speech. We once heard a student open a speech with a rather risque quotation from Mae West, "Is that a gun in your pocket, or are you happy to see me?" It drew an initial gasp followed by some hearty laughter. Unfortunately, as the speech continued, one student would chuckle over the remembered joke, then the audience would start laughing all over again even when nothing funny had been said. After the speaker finished, we questioned the audience about their "inappropriate" responses. Their reply? "We kept remembering that Mae West line. We just couldn't help it." And to this day, neither of your authors can remember the topic of the speech, just the opening humor.

Begin with a Quotation.   With the possible exception of quoting Mae West, starting your speech with a striking quotation or paraphrase from a well-known person or respected authority can both arouse interest and give you borrowed ethos. The person you cite should be someone the audience knows, respects, or can identify with.

The most effective opening quotations are brief and to the point. One of our students used the following quotation, attributed to the novelist William Faulkner, to introduce her classroom speech on job satisfaction:

> You can't eat for eight hours a day, nor drink for eight hours a day, nor make love for eight hours a day — all you can do for eight hours is work. Which is the reason why man makes himself and everybody else so miserable and unhappy.

She used this quotation to highlight the theme of her message, that work can be *the* great source of happiness or unhappiness in our lives, and that education should empower us to select our work rather than having it imposed upon us by accident or necessity.

Most books of quotations (see Chapter 5) are indexed by key words and subjects as well as by authors. Collections of quotations are also available on CD-ROMS. They are an excellent source of statements you might use to introduce your topic.

Startle the Audience.   Anything truly unusual draws attention to itself and arouses curiosity. Consider the headlines from the sensationalist tabloids: "BIGFOOT SPOTTED IN NORTHWEST ARKANSAS!" "WOMAN PREDICTS EARTHQUAKES WITH HER TOES!" Evita Moreno startled her audience into attention with the opening of her informative speech. Note how she combines startling the audience with the use of rhetorical questions:

> If the statistics hold true, more than half of us in this room have risked our lives in the past year. Indeed, millions of college students have willingly exposed themselves to a life-threatening disease in the past year. That disease is cancer. Do you think these numbers exaggerate? Do you believe you're not at risk? Let's see.
>
> How many of you smoke or use some form of tobacco? Raise your hands. Okay, that's six. Now, how many of you eat a lot of fatty fast food — hamburgers, french fries, pizza. Come on, raise your hands. Well, that's fourteen. Now, in the past year, how many of you took a sunbath — or went to a tanning parlor — or worked outside without using a sunscreen oil or lotion? That's seventeen! I guess my numbers were a little bit off, but I actually understated the probability. Today I want to tell you how you can lower your risk and avoid becoming a statistic in someone else's speech.

Capturing Attention

1 Show listeners how the topic involves them.
2 Call on personal experience with the topic.
3 Ask rhetorical questions to make the audience think.
4 Create suspense and anticipation.
5 Open with a story that relates to your topic.
6 Engage your listeners with humor.
7 Begin with a quotation from a well-known person.
8 Startle the audience with unusual information.

SPEAKER'S
NOTES

The startle technique must always be used with care. You don't want to arouse more interest in your introduction than the body of your speech can satisfy. If your opening is too sensational, it will "upstage" the rest of your speech. Similarly, be careful not to go beyond the bounds of propriety. You want to startle your listeners into attention, not offend them.

Establishing Your Credibility

The second major function of an effective introduction is to establish yourself as a competent, trustworthy, and likable person with whom the audience can identify. People tend to form first impressions of speakers that color their later perceptions.[21] In Chapter 2 we discussed the importance of the impressions you make on listeners in terms of your competence, integrity, likableness, and forcefulness — your ethos. As you make later presentations, you will carry over some of the initial ethos you established with your first presentation and from your interactions in class. You must confirm or strengthen this initial ethos in the introduction of your speech.

The most important thing you must establish is that you are qualified to speak on your subject. Establishing credibility is often difficult for beginning speakers. As we noted in Chapter 2, you can seem competent only if you know what you are talking about. People listen more respectfully to those who speak both from knowledge and personal experience.[22] As we noted in Chapter 5, the perception of competence can be fortified by selecting topics you already know something about and by doing research to qualify yourself as a responsible speaker. In your introduction you can *allude* to your research to reinforce your credibility:

> I was amazed to learn in psychology class that research does not support a strong link between exposure to persuasive communications and behavior. This discovery led me to do more reading on the relationship between advertising and consumer activity. What I found was even more surprising, especially when you consider that, according to the *Wall Street Journal,* companies were willing to pay 1.3 million dollars for a thirty-second spot commercial during the 1996 Super Bowl telecast.

Here the specific reference to the *Wall Street Journal* article suggests that you have done the research needed to make a responsible speech. Throughout the rest of your speech you can cite other respected sources to confirm this impression as you introduce your supporting materials. It would not be effective, however, to simply announce baldly at the beginning of your speech:

> The information for my speech comes from my psychology textbook, two articles from the *Journal of Applied Psychology,* and a feature story in the *Wall Street Journal.*

That would seem forced, awkward, and artificial. It would interrupt the natural flow of your introduction.

Your perceived competence will be further strengthened if your speech is well organized, if you use language ably and correctly, and if you have practiced so that your presentation flows smoothly.

To create a perception of integrity you must come across as an ethical and honest person. Convince listeners at the outset that all of your rhetorical cards are on the table. Audiences are more receptive when speakers are straightforward, sincere, and concerned with the consequences of their words.[23] You can enhance your integrity by showing respect for those who hold different opinions while still maintaining your personal commitment to your topic and position.

You should also present yourself as a likable and forceful speaker. Likable speakers are pleasant and tactful. They treat listeners as friends, inspiring affection in return.[24] Likable speakers also share their feelings and are able to laugh at themselves. To come across as a forceful speaker, you must project self-confidence. Although some communication anxiety is natural, as we noted in Chapter 2, you must train your butterflies to fly in formation. Your introduction should also display enthusiasm for your message. A smile and direct eye contact signals listeners that you want to communicate.

When you establish favorable ethos at the outset, you also create the grounds for one of the most powerful effects of communication: identification between yourself and listeners. **Identification** occurs when people successfully overcome the personal and cultural differences that separate them and share thoughts and feelings as though they were one.[25] When you seem likable, sincere, competent, and forceful, your listeners want to identify with you, and your effectiveness as a communicator is magnified.

Focus and Preview Your Message

The final function of an introduction is to focus on your thesis statement and preview the body of your speech. The **thesis statement**, as we noted in Chapter 5, signals the message of your speech in concentrated form. It is a one-sentence version of the speech. The **preview** foreshadows the main points you will cover and offers your listeners an overview of the speech to come. It follows the thesis statement near the end of the introduction.

Martha Radner offered the following thesis statement and preview for her speech on campus security problems.

> **This campus will be a much safer place if we adopt my plan to improve campus security [*thesis statement*]. First, I want to show you how dangerous our situation has become. Second, I'll explore the reasons why current security measures on our campus are ineffective. And third, I'll present my plan for a safer campus environment [*preview*].**

By informing her listeners of her intentions as well as her speech design, Martha helped her audience listen intelligently.

Selecting and Using Introductory Techniques

There are no hard and fast rules for determining exactly how you should open a speech. As you review your research notes, look for material that would make an effective introduction. The following guidelines may help you make a wise selection:

- Consider your audience. Use *your* introduction to tie *your* topic to *their* needs, interests, or well-being.
- Consider the mood you want to establish. Some topics will mandate a light touch, while others may call for more solemnity.
- Consider your time constraints. If you are to speak for seven minutes, you can't get bogged down in a five-minute introduction.
- Consider what you do best. Some people are effective storytellers, and others are better using striking statistics or quotations. Go with your strength!

DEVELOPING AN EFFECTIVE CONCLUSION

Many beginning speakers end their presentations awkwardly. "That's all, folks!" may be an effective closing for a film cartoon, but in a speech such conclusions violate the audience's need for closure. Saying "That's it, I guess" or "Well, I'm done," accompanied by a sigh of relief, suggests that you have not planned your speech very carefully. The final words of your speech should stay with listeners, remind them of your message, and, if appropriate, move them to action.

Summarizing Your Message

Your conclusion should begin with a **summary statement** of the main points you made in your speech. This summary often functions as a transition between the body and the final remarks. It signals the audience that you are about to finish. The following summary of main points appears in the speech on the greenhouse effect reprinted at the end of Chapter 8:

> **In conclusion, if you want to know why we have a greenhouse effect, listen for the falling trees, watch the industrial smoke darkening the air, smell the exhaust fumes we are pumping into the atmosphere.**

The transition "In conclusion" alerts listeners to the summary statement that follows. Note that the statement does not simply repeat the main

An effective conclusion summarizes your message and should leave the audience with something to remember.

points verbatim. Rather, the speaker rephrases these points artfully so that listeners can picture themselves actually experiencing the message.

Concluding Remarks

Although the summary statement itself can offer listeners a sense of closure, to seal that effect you need to provide some **concluding remarks** that stay with your listeners. Many of the techniques that create effective introductions can also be used to develop memorable conclusions. Using the same technique to close a speech that you used to open it can balance your speech.

Involve the Audience. At the beginning of a speech, you involve the audience by showing them how your message relates directly to their lives. At the conclusion of your speech, you should remind them of what they personally have at stake. In the speech on the greenhouse effect, the summary statement we have just analyzed was followed immediately by remarks that place the meaning of that statement in perspective for listeners:

> The greenhouse effect is a monster we all are creating. And if we don't stop, we and our children face more and more drastic climate changes and serious health problems.

These comments tie in to the beginning of the speech, reemphasizing the seriousness of the problem it describes. The reference to "children" underscores the point that listeners are involved very deeply. In persuasive speeches, concluding remarks also often urge listeners to take the first step to confirm their commitment to action and change.

Ask Rhetorical Questions.   When used in an introduction, rhetorical questions help arouse attention and curiosity. When used in a conclusion, such questions give your audience something to think about after you have finished. Annette Berrington opened her speech on the use of seat belts with a rhetorical question, "How many of you buckled up on your way to school this morning?" Her final words were "Now that you know what a lifesaver seat belts are, how many of you will buckle up on the way home?" This final question echoed the beginning and served as a haunting reminder to use seat belts. Had she closed with "Remember, seat belts save lives," the effect would not have been as dramatic and memorable.

When used at the end of a persuasive speech, concluding questions may be more than rhetorical. They may actually call for a response from the audience. During his 1988 presidential campaign, the Reverend Jesse Jackson often used this technique to register voters. He would end a speech by asking:

> How many of you are not registered to vote? Raise your hands. No, stand up so we can see you! Is that all of you who aren't registered? Stand up! Let me see you!

Such questioning and cajoling would be followed by on-site voter registration. Evangelists who issue an invitation to salvation at the end of their sermons often use concluding questions in a similar way. To be effective, this technique must be the climax of a speech that has prepared its audience for action.

End with a Story.   Stories are remembered long after facts and figures are forgotten. A concluding narrative can help your audience *experience* the essence of your message. To conclude her speech on domestic terrorism, which she opened with a narrative, Donna E. Shalala told the following story:

> Let me conclude by telling you about a child psychologist named Sandra Graham-Berman who took responsibility for doing even more [about the problem of domestic abuse]. Several years ago she became

aware of a support group for battered women. But she heard that there was no professional support for their children. On her own time and with her own money she began a support group for the children of these battered women. She began to see the girls and boys act out, talk out, and draw out their fears and their frustrations. She helped them learn they are not alone in their pain. And she taught them that when mommy is in trouble — when she is being hurt by daddy — it's possible to get help by dialing 9-1-1.

A few years later, a shy 8-year-old girl walked in on a fight. Her father — if you can believe it, a child psychiatrist — was beating her mother on the head with a hammer. Try to imagine that. Try to imagine what you would do. Well, that little girl knew what to do. She remembered the lesson taught to her by a caring adult. And so she went to that phone, picked it up, pressed 9-1-1, and saved her mother's life. The father is in prison now and the family's trying its best to build a new life. If that little girl can have the courage to pick up the telephone, surely we can have the courage to prevent such stories from happening.[26]

Close with a Quotation. Brief quotations that capture the essence of your message make effective conclusions. For example, if one literary quotation opens a speech, another on the same theme can provide an elegant sense of closure. Susie Smith opened her speech on job satisfaction with a quotation from William Faulkner that linked work and unhappiness. She closed the speech with a more positive quotation from Joseph Conrad that summed up the meaning of satisfying work:

> I like what is in work — the chance to find yourself. Your own reality — for yourself, not for others — what no other . . . can ever know.

These concluding remarks put the seal on Susie's message: that the search for work must be much more than finding a job; rather, that we must prepare ourselves for an occupation that will help us find, define, and create ourselves and our world.

End with a Metaphor. A striking **metaphor** can end your speech effectively.[27] As we will discuss at greater length in Chapter 10, metaphors combine things that are apparently unlike so that we see unexpected relationships. As a conclusion to a speech, an effective metaphor reveals a hidden truth about the speaker's subject in a memorable way. Melodie Lancaster, president of Lancaster Resources, used such a metaphor, combined with a narrative, as she concluded a speech to the Houston Council of the American Business Womens' Association:

> We recall the story of the three stonemasons who were asked what they were doing. The first said, "I am laying brick." The second replied,

"I am making a foundation." And the third said: "I am building a cathedral." Let's you and I set our sights that high. Let's build cathedrals of success today, tomorrow, and the day after tomorrow.[28]

Consider the many meanings this metaphor might evoke in the minds of listeners. First, the speaker suggests listeners must work as hard as stonemasons. Second, she suggests they must work with a vision of their goals in mind. Third, the connection with a cathedral suggests they must work with the zeal and dedication characteristic of religious commitment. All these meanings are packed into the metaphor, making it memorable for her audience.

Whatever closing technique you select should satisfy your audience that what was promised in the beginning has now been delivered. Plan your summary statement and concluding remarks very carefully, just as you did with your introduction. Practice it until you are confident you will end your speech impressively. After your final words, pause a moment to let them sink in, then take your seat.

IN SUMMARY

A speech that is carefully structured helps the audience understand your message and enhances the ethos of the speaker.

Good Form.   A well-structured speech has *good form:* it is simple, balanced, and orderly. *Simplicity* can be achieved by limiting the number of main points and using clear, direct language. A speech has *balance* when the major parts receive proper emphasis and when they work together. The requirement of *order* means that a speech follows a consistent pattern of development.

Structuring the Body of Your Speech.   You should structure the body first, so that you can build an introduction and conclusion that fit well with the principal part of your message. To develop the body, determine your main points, decide how to arrange them, then select effective supporting materials. To discover your main points, prepare a *research overview* of the information you have collected. This summary can help you spot major themes that can develop into main points.

Arrange your main points so that they follow natural mental patterns based on the principles of similarity, proximity, and closure. The *similarity* of objects or events may suggest a categorical design for structuring main points. *Proximity* suggests that things should be discussed as they happen together in space or time. If they occur in a time sequence, use a sequential design for your speech. If they occur in physical relationship to each other, a spatial design might be appropriate. The structure of the body satisfies the principle of *closure* when it completes the design it begins. Cause-effect and problem-solution designs require closure in order to be effective.

Supporting materials fill out the structure of the speech and buttress main points and subpoints. In an ideal arrangement, you should support each point with information, testimony, and an example or story that emphasizes its human aspects.

Using Transitions. Effective *transitions* point up the relationships among ideas in your speech and tie the speech together. *Internal summaries* remind listeners of the points you have made in one part of your speech before moving on to another.

Preparing an Effective Introduction. The introduction to a speech should arouse your listeners' interest, establish your credibility, and focus and preview your message. Some useful ways to introduce a speech include involving the audience, relating your subject to personal experience, asking rhetorical questions, creating suspense, telling a story, using humor, beginning with a quotation, or startling the audience. As you build credibility, you also make possible identification between you and the audience.

Developing an Effective Conclusion. An effective conclusion should summarize the meaning of your speech, provide a sense of closure, leave the audience with something to remember, and, if appropriate, motivate listeners to act. Techniques useful for conclusions include reinvolving the audience, asking questions, closing with a quotation, telling a story, and ending with a metaphor. Your speech will seem more symmetrical and satisfying to listeners if your conclusion ties into your introduction.

TERMS TO KNOW

good form

simplicity

balance

order

main points

research overview

principle of similarity

principle of proximity

principle of closure

transitions

internal summary

rhetorical question

identification

preview

summary statement

final reflections

metaphor

DISCUSSION

1. Working in small groups, share your research overviews for your next speeches. What major themes emerge, and how might these be framed

into main points in light of the function and purpose of your speech? Defend your analysis and your selection of main points.

2. Share the organizational plan of your next speech with a classmate so that you become consultants for each other. Help each other come up with alternative patterns for the main points, and optional introductions and conclusions. After the speeches are presented, each consulting team should explain the options it considered and why it chose the particular structures used for each speech.

APPLICATION

1. Select a speech from Appendix B and write a thorough critique of its structure. Consider the following questions in your assessment:

   A. Did this speech satisfy the requirements of "good form"? Did it meet the needs of simplicity, balance, and order?

   B. What kind of speech design did it use? Did this design satisfy the principles of similarity, proximity, and closure?

   C. Was supporting material used effectively to strengthen the main points and subpoints?

   D. Did transitions keep the message in focus for listeners as the speech developed?

2. What kinds of introductory and concluding techniques might be most effective for speeches based on the following specific purpose statements?

   A. To inform my audience of the dangers of tanning salons.

   B. To persuade my audience that it is better to marry than to live together.

   C. To inform my audience of the signs of domestic abuse.

   D. To persuade my audience that televising trials subverts the system of justice.

3. The following introduction was used in a speech presented at an honor society recognition conference. Evaluate this introduction in light of the guidelines for preparing effective introductions presented in this chapter and explain how you would revise or reorganize this material to make it more effective.

   Today I'm going to talk about the technology of the future. The theme for your conference is "Preparing for the 21st Century," and getting a grip on the technological changes ahead of us is the best way to prepare for the next century. I'll also tell you a little about Battelle [the speaker's company], and I'll make a few predictions about what our world will be like over the next 10 to 50 years. That has me a little ner-

vous, because any time you start making predictions, you hope no one nearby has a tape recorder.

Here's an example of what I mean. At the Chicago World's Fair way back in 1893, a group of 74 social commentators got together to look 100 years into the future — at the world of 1993. Here are some of their predictions. Many people will live to be 150. The government will have grown more simple, as true greatness tends always toward simplicity. Prisons will decline and divorce will be considered unnecessary. The Nicaraguan canal is as sure to be built as tides are to ebb and flow and the seasons to change.[29]

NOTES

1. Patricia R. Palmerton, "Teaching Skills or Teaching Thinking," *Journal of Applied Communication Research* 20 (1992): 335–341; and Robert G. Powell, "Critical Thinking and Speech Communication: Our Teaching Strategies Are Warranted — Not!" *Journal of Applied Communication Research* 20 (1992): 342–347.

2. Most of the research on the effects of structure was conducted in the 1960s and 1970s. Notable among these studies are Christopher Spicer and Ronald E. Bassett, "The Effect of Organization on Learning from an Informative Message," *Southern Speech Communication Journal* 41 (1976): 290–299; Ernest Thompson, "Some Effects of Message Structure on Listeners' Comprehension," *Speech Monographs* 34 (1967): 51–57; Arlee Johnson, "A Preliminary Investigation of the Relationship Between Organization and Listener Comprehension," *Central States Speech Journal* 21 (1970): 104–107.

3. Patricia Kearney, Timothy G. Plax, Ellis R. Hayes, and Marily J. Ivey, "College Teacher Misbehaviors: What Students Don't Like About What Teachers Say and Do," *Communication Quarterly* 39 (1991): 309–324.

4. J. C. McCroskey and R. S. Mehrley, "The Effects of Disorganization and Nonfluency on Attitude Change and Source Credibility," *Communication Monographs* 36 (1969): 13–21.

5. Saul Kassin, *Psychology* (Boston: Houghton Mifflin, 1995), pp. 208–251.

6. Material in this section is based on the work of the Gestalt psychologists as summarized in Kassin, pp. 78–129.

7. Charles Hulme, Steven Roodenrys, Gordon Brown, and Robin Mercer, "The Role of Long-term Memory Mechanisms in Memory Span," *British Journal of Psychology* 86 (1995): 527–536.

8. Douglas A. Bernstein, Edward J. Roy, Thomas K. Srull, and Christopher D. Wickens, *Psychology*, 2nd ed. (Boston: Houghton Mifflin, 1991), p. 308.

9. Plato, "The Phaedrus," in *The Works of Plato*, ed. Irwin Edman (New York: The Modern Library, 1927), pp. 311–312.

10. Gloria Steinem, *Outrageous Acts and Everyday Rebellions* (New York: Holt, Rinehart & Winston, 1983).

11. Kassin, p. 111.

12. Loren J. Anderson, "A Summary of Research on Order Effects in Communication," *Concepts in Communication,* eds. Jimmie D. Trent, Judith S. Trent, and Daniel J. O'Neill (Boston: Allyn & Bacon, 1973), pp. 129–130.

13. Cited in Arthur M. Schlesinger, Jr., *A Thousand Days: John F. Kennedy in the White House* (Boston: Houghton Mifflin, 1965), p. 733.

14. James Price Dillard, "Persuasion Past and Present: Attitudes Aren't What They Used To Be," *Communication Monographs* 60 (1993): 91.

15. Brock Evans, "The Endangered Species Act: Implications for the Future," in *Vital Speeches of the Day,* 15 Mar. 1993, p. 339.

16. James H. Carr, "Restoring Opportunities for Urban Communities," in *Vital Speeches of the Day,* 15 Jan. 1995, p. 216.

17. Larry N. Landrum, "Mystery, Suspense, and Detective Fiction," *The New Grolier Multimedia Encyclopedia,* Release 6, Grolier Inc. (Novato, CA: Software Toolworks, 1993).

18. Bob Lannom, "Patience, Persistence, and Perspiration," *News Leader* (Parsons, TN), 20 Sept. 1989, p. 9.

19. Donna E. Shalala, "Domestic Terrorism: An Unacknowledged Epidemic," in *Vital Speeches of the Day,* 15 May 1995, p. 450.

20. Takakazu Kuriyama, "Trade Relations: Japan Has Barriers as Does the U.S.," in *Vital Speeches of the Day,* 1 May 1994, pp. 421–422.

21. Sharon S. Brehm and Saul M. Kassin, *Social Psychology,* 2nd ed. (Boston: Houghton Mifflin, 1993), pp. 127–128.

22. R. G. Hass, "Effects of Source Characteristics on the Cognitive Processing of Persuasive Messages and Attitude Change," in R. Petty, T. Ostrom, and T. Brock, eds. *Cognitive Responses in Persuasion* (Hillsdale, NJ: Erlbaum, 1981), pp. 141–172; M. Heesacker, R. E. Petty, and J. T. Cacioppo, "Field Dependence and Attitude Change: Source Credibility Can Alter Persuasion by Affecting Message-Relevant Thinking," *Journal of Personality* 51 (1983): 653–666; J. E. Maddux and R. W. Rogers, "Effects of Source Expertness, Physical Attractiveness, and Supporting Arguments on Persuasion: A Case of Brains Over Beauty," *Journal of Personality and Social Psychology* 39 (1980): 235–244.

23. A. H. Eagly, W. Wood, and S. Chaiken, "An Attribution Analysis of Persuasion," in J. Harvey, W. Ickes, and R. Kidd, eds. *New Directions in Attribution Research* (Hillsdale, NJ: Erlbaum, 1981), pp. 37–62.

24. Brehm and Kassin, pp. 220–221.

25. Kenneth Burke, *A Rhetoric of Motives* (Berkeley and Los Angeles: University of California Press, 1969), pp. 20–23.

26. Donna E. Shalala, "Domestic Terrorism: An Unacknowledged Epidemic," in *Vital Speeches of the Day,* 15 May 1994, p. 453.

27. John Waite Bowers and Michael Osborn, "Attitudinal Effects of Selected Types of Concluding Metaphors in Persuasive Speeches," *Speech Monographs* 33 (1966): 148–155.

28. Melodie Lancaster, "The Future We Predict Isn't Inevitable: Refraining Our Success In the Modern World," in *Vital Speeches of the Day,* 1 Aug. 1992, p. 638.

29. Will Kopp, "Inventing the Future: Battelle's Vision of Tomorrow's Technology," in *Vital Speeches of the Day,* 1 Feb. 1994, p. 244.

CHAPTER 8

Outlining Your Speech

■ understand outlining and why it is important.

■ understand the process involved in developing an effective outline.

■ develop working outlines to help structure your speech.

■ prepare a formal outline following the conventions of coordination and subordination.

■ condense your formal outline into a key-word outline to use as you present your speech.

> **O**ur plans miscarry because they have no aim. When a man does not know what harbor he is making for, no wind is the right wind.
>
> — Seneca

For several years our residential neighborhood was caught up in zoning disputes. We lived in a cove surrounded by undeveloped land that developers wanted to rezone for commercial use. Once when we were at a zoning meeting to protest a proposal to build an automobile dealership next to our home, we learned that a proposal to construct a helicopter port also was on the agenda.

With only minutes to prepare, we organized our arguments against the heliport. Our specific purpose was clear: we wanted to defeat this proposal. Our thesis statement was "A heliport would violate both the law and the tranquility of our neighborhood." We hastily outlined our main arguments on the back of a civil defense bulletin:

I. The applicants had already violated the law.

    A. They had not applied for a license before operating.

    B. They had ignored FAA operating regulations.

II. A heliport would intrude into the tranquility of the neighborhood.

    A. It would disturb the peace and quiet of residents.

    B. It would bother patients in a nearby nursing home.

Armed with this simple outline, which helped us structure our presentation, we defeated both the heliport and the car dealership

in the same afternoon! But if we had tried to speak before the zoning board without first organizing our thoughts, we would never have succeeded.

Developing an outline for a speech is a discipline that helps you get an overall picture of what you want to say. A good outline gives you control over your thoughts. It helps you pinpoint the most important things you want to say, the most effective order in which to say them, and the best way to support them. It helps you plan a speech that is simple, balanced, and orderly. Just as you wouldn't try to build a house without a blueprint, you shouldn't try to prepare a speech without an outline.

Think of outlining as a tool that will help you build the speech structure we discussed in the previous chapter. Outlining both externalizes and objectifies your thinking: it takes ideas out of your head, where they can get all tangled up, and puts them down on paper, where you can sort them, evaluate them, and arrange them in some effective order.[1]

Outlining is both creative and corrective: as you contemplate the relationships of ideas on paper, you may think of new ideas. You can see where you may need more research, whether a point is really relevant and necessary to your specific purpose, and whether the overall structure appears well balanced.[2] You may need to add something here, subtract something there. Outlining helps you find and correct potential problems *before* they become mistakes. Outlining can also help you select an appropriate design pattern for your speech and the right quantity and variety of supporting materials. Finally, the outline can point out where you will need transitions and let you see whether your introduction and conclusion work well with the body of your speech.

Outlining is part of the process of speech preparation. It gives some order to your creative processes. Outlining is especially important when your thoughts are muddled or you are not sure where you are going. Outlining can help you see the way out of your puzzle and may open up new possibilities for your speech.

All you need to outline your speech is a pen or pencil and some paper (plus your research notes). However, outlining is easier if you have access to a computer. With a computer you can type in material, move it around in blocks, and print out several different versions of your outline to help you evaluate them. In this chapter we provide generic outline formats that guide you through the general structure of any speech. You can simply copy these formats and fill in your material in the proper places. In Chapter 12 we offer specific outlining formats that can be used with the major designs for informative speeches: spatial, categorical, comparative, sequential, and causation. In Chapter 13 we show you how to adapt some of these patterns for use in persuasive speeches and provide outlining formats for the major persuasive speech designs: problem-solution, motivated sequence, and refutative.

We think of outlining as a process that evolves from initial working outlines to a formal full-sentence outline to a key-word outline you can use as a prompt during presentation. As you prepare your informative, persuasive, and ceremonial speeches, you will probably develop several working outlines, a formal outline, and a key-word outline for each speech.

DEVELOPING A WORKING OUTLINE

A **working outline** is a tentative plan of the speech you will eventually give. It is a work-in-process outline in which you first lay out the relationships among your ideas and identify potential trouble spots. Why start with a working outline? Why not just begin with the full-sentence formal outline that you will turn in to your instructor? Assume that you plan to present an informative speech on "the greenhouse effect." You have done some reading and thinking on the topic but are not totally sure how your speech will develop. The working outline is a tool "for your eyes only" that can help you to reduce your uncertainty and to structure your speech effectively. *Moreover, while preparing the working outline you often have those moments of creative inspiration that can give your speech an original focus.* Figure 8.1 provides you with a format for developing a working outline for your speech.

You should not think of this format as a rigid structure. Compared to a formal outline, it is quite casual. Adapt it so that it works best for you. In the early stages of developing your speech you need not worry about following the formalities of outline procedure.[3] Your working outline is a disposable tool to help you arrange your first thoughts. You will probably prepare and throw away several working outlines before you find the right approach. The working outline, however, does include your main points and subpoints. Even at this stage you are thinking about the relative importance of ideas, and about their logical relationship to each other and their probable impact on your audience.

A good starting point for your working outline is writing out your topic, specific purpose, and thesis statement. You need to be sure you have these clearly in mind so that you can check how well your main points fit them. Your specific purpose and thesis statement form the foundation for the speech you will build:

Topic:	The greenhouse effect
Specific purpose:	To inform my audience of the causes of the greenhouse effect
Thesis statement:	Today I want to share what I've learned about the greenhouse effect and its causes.

Developing Your Main Points

The next step in preparing your working outline is to sketch the body of your speech. Following the process we discussed in Chapter 7, write out the main points you will develop. You may recall that the process of selecting

FIGURE 8.1

Format for a Working Outline

Topic: _____
Specific purpose: _____
Thesis statement: _____

INTRODUCTION
Attention material: _____
Credibility material: _____
Thesis statement: _____
Preview: _____

(Transition to body of speech)

BODY
First main point: _____
    Subpoint: _____
        Sub-subpoint: _____
        Sub-subpoint: _____
    Subpoint: _____

(Transition to second main point)

Second main point: _____
    Subpoint: _____
    Subpoint: _____
        Sub-subpoint: _____
        Sub-subpoint: _____

(Transition to third main point)

Third Main Point: _____
    Subpoint: _____
    Subpoint: _____

(Transition to conclusion)

CONCLUSION
Summary: _____
Concluding Remarks: _____

main points begins with a research overview. As the process continues, you consider the major themes revealed by this overview in light of the function and purpose of your speech, audience needs, and the time available for you to speak. In our ongoing example of preparing a speech on the greenhouse effect, the first working outline contained the following main points:

First main point:	Industrial emissions accelerate the greenhouse effect.
Second main point:	Increased energy consumption magnifies the greenhouse effect.
Third main point:	The loss of woodlands adds to the greenhouse effect.

Once you have these points in front of you, ask yourself the following questions:

- Will these main points make my message clear to my audience?
- Is this the right order in which to develop them?
- Have I left out anything important?

As you consider these questions, you realize that you have left something out. You remember that all of your sources explained what the greenhouse effect was before discussing its causes. You note that your original list of main points neither explains the greenhouse effect nor gives the audience a reason to be interested in its causes. You also see another potential trouble spot: there is no clear logical or psychological order in your arrangement of main points. But if you put the third point first, the first point second, and the second point third — woodlands, emissions, and consumption — you would be following an order of ascending importance as we discussed in Chapter 7. This would allow your speech to build toward its conclusion, desirable both from the point of view of the logic of the subject and the psychology of the audience. People often like to see a subject develop in order of importance: it holds and builds their interest. You decide to toss out the first working outline and to revise the main points as follows:

First main point:	The greenhouse effect is a gradual warming of the earth caused by human activities.
Second main point:	The loss of woodlands adds to the greenhouse effect.
Third main point:	Industrial emissions accelerate the greenhouse effect.
Fourth main point:	Increased energy consumption magnifies the greenhouse effect.

Developing Your Subpoints

Once you have determined and arranged your main points, you can divide your main points into more specific and concrete statements or buttress them with supporting materials to make them more meaningful and credible. These more concrete statements and supporting materials belong at the **subpoint** level of your outline. Usually each main point will be girded by two or more subpoints that substantiate and clarify it. Each subpoint must relate directly to the main point it follows and should make that point more understandable, believable, or compelling.[4]

To identify the subpoints for each of your main points, imagine a critical listener in front of you. When you state the main point, this listener will ask:

- What do you mean?
- Why should I care?
- How do I know this is true?

The subpoints you arrange for each main point should answer these questions to your listener's satisfaction. If the main points are columns built upon the foundation of the function, purpose, and thesis statement of your speech, the subpoints reinforce these columns so that they will stand under scrutiny. For example, as you develop your working outline, you might list the following subpoints for your first main point:

First main point:	The greenhouse effect is a gradual warming of the earth caused by human activities.
Subpoints:	A. It comes from a high concentration of carbon dioxide in the atmosphere.
	B. It is producing a hole in the ozone layer.
	C. It makes the earth warmer.
	D. It lets more ultraviolet radiation come through.
	E. It can cause climate problems.
	F. It can cause health problems.

As you look back over your first main point, you notice that you have listed six subpoints. Recalling the principles of good form learned in Chapter 7, you say to yourself, "These are *too many* subpoints if I want to keep the structure of this speech simple, balanced, and orderly."

At this point, you should examine your subpoints to see how they relate to each other. Can you collapse any of them into a single subpoint? Do you need to break out the material onto an even more specific and detailed level of **sub-subpoints?** Just as subpoints reinforce and clarify main points, sub-subpoints strengthen and specify subpoints. This process could continue to sub-sub-subpoint level, but the time limitations for short speeches impose some practical limits. In this phase of developing your working outline, you should also include some of the supporting materials you will use and indicate the place for other material. For example, you might expand the first main point in this working outline as follows:

First main point:	The greenhouse effect is a gradual warming of the earth caused by human activities.
Subpoint A:	It comes from a high concentration of carbon dioxide (CO_2) in the air.
Sub-subpoints:	1. Five tons of CO_2 per person per year in the U.S.
	2. 1987: CO_2 at record high [*provide temperature data*].
Subpoint B:	It is producing a hole in the ozone layer.
Sub-subpoints:	1. Chlorofluorocarbons (CFCs) destroy the ozone shield.
	2. More ultraviolet radiation comes through.

Subpoint C: The greenhouse effect can cause serious problems.

Sub-subpoints: 1. It can cause climate problems [*cite possibilities*].

2. It can cause health problems [*describe potential problems*].

Follow this same procedure as you develop each main point in your working outline. Once you have done this, review the working outline of the body of your speech and ask yourself:

- Will a speech based on this outline fulfill my thesis statement for my listeners?
- Will I be able to do all of this in the time available?

Be honest with yourself. It's better to be frustrated now than disappointed later when you present your speech. In addition, be sure your ideas are arranged in an orderly manner that is easy to follow. Make certain that each subpoint relates directly to the main point above it. Be sure that you have enough supporting material to build a sturdy structure of ideas. If you are lacking in any of these areas, now is the time to discover and correct the problem.

Completing Your Working Outline

To complete your working outline, sketch out an introduction that gains attention, establishes your credibility, and focuses and previews your speech, as we discussed in Chapter 7. Next, sketch out a conclusion that includes a summary and concluding remarks. Finally, add the transitions that will tie your speech together into a tidy package. Remember that your transitions should tie the introduction to the body, connect each main point to the next main point, and move the speech from the body to the conclusion.

Now, take a good look at your overall working outline. Figure 8.2 is a sample working outline for a speech on the greenhouse effect.

Review the outline using as a guide the Speaker's Notes 8.1: Checklist for a Working Outline. Then go over the outline with a friend or classmate whose judgment you respect. Another person sometimes can see flaws you might miss because you are too close to the material.

Let your working outline rest for a while, then check to be sure you are still satisfied with it. As you review your working outline, keep the audience at the center of your thinking. Remember the advice given to beginning journalists: *Never overestimate your audience's information, and never underestimate their intelligence!* Ask yourself the following questions:

- Are my main points arranged so that my audience can easily understand and remember them?

Begin the working outline by writing down your topic, specific purpose, and thesis statement so you have them clearly in mind as work progresses.

In your working outline sketch out your introduction, including short notes on attention and credibility materials. However, write out your thesis statement and preview as precisely as possible. Clarity on these points is essential to develop a clear, cohesive speech. As your plannng proceeds, revise these elements as needed.

Include transitions to remind yourself of the need to tie material together and make it flow smoothly.

Labeling the body of the speech points out its importance. Remember, you should develop the body of the speech before developing your introduction and conclusion.

Note that this working outline does not follow the conventional numbering and lettering system of a formal outline. The purpose of the working outline is to allow you to organize ideas and see how they work together.

Topic: The greenhouse effect
Specific purpose: To inform my audience of the causes of the greenhouse effect.
Thesis statement: Today I want to share what I've learned about the greenhouse effect and its major causes.

INTRODUCTION

Attention material: Twain story on "exaggerated death": death of greenhouse effect also exaggerated. Iceberg broke from Larsen Shelf. NASA report proves "human activity causes ozone hole."

Credibility material: Love outdoors and want to see environment safe for future generations. Audience also has vital stake in topic.

Thesis statement: Today I want to share what I've learned about the greenhouse effect and its major causes.

Preview: We need to be concerned, first, about the loss of woodlands, second, about industrial emissions, and third, about overall spectacular increases in world energy consumption.

(**Transition** to body of speech: "First we must understand the greenhouse effect.")

BODY

First main point: The greenhouse effect is a gradual warming of the earth caused by human activities.
   Subpoint A: It comes from a high concentration of carbon dioxide ($CO2$) in the air.
      Sub-subpoints: 1. Five tons of CO_2 per person per year in the U.S.
                      2. 1987: CO_2 at record high [provide temperature data].
   Subpoint B: It is producing a hole in the ozone layer.
      Sub-subpoints: 1. Chlorofluorocarbons (CFCS) destroy the ozone shield.
                      2. More ultraviolet radiation comes through.
   Subpoint C: The greenhouse effect can cause serious problems.
      Sub-subpoints: 1. It can cause climate problems [cite possibilities].
                      2. It can cause health problems [describe potential problems].

(**Transition** to second main point: "Now let's look at causes.")

Second main point: The loss of woodlands adds to the greenhouse effect.
   Subpoint A: Lose woods the size of a football field every second.
      Sub-subpoints: 1. Loss from cutting.
                      2. Loss from burning.
   Subpoint B: Burning adds more CO_2 because of smoke.

(continued)

The working outline serves as your guide and provides a check on the structure of the speech and the adequacy of your preparation.

(Transition to third main point: "But loss of woodlands is just part of the problem.")

Third main point: Industrial emissions accelerate the greenhouse effect.

Subpoint A: More than 20 percent of all air pollution.

Subpoint B: CO_2 and nitrous oxide released when wood, coal, oil, or gas is burned.

Subpoint C: CFCs from refrigeration and air conditioners.

(Transition to fourth main point: "The last cause may be the most important one.")

Since this main point covers the largest single cause of the greenhouse effect, it should be more thoroughly developed than the second and third main points.

Fourth main point: Increased energy consumption magnifies the greenhouse effect.

Subpoint A: Population & prosperity fuel the problem.

Sub-subpoints: 1. More people means more consumption.
2. Rising living standards = rising expectations = more consumption.

Subpoint B: Energy consumption is the single largest cause of the greenhouse effect.

Sub-subpoints: 1. Fossil fuel use has doubled since 1950.
2. Fossil fuel use accounts for 90 percent of America's energy consumption.
3. Transportation-related energy use accounts for half of all air pollution.

(Transition: "In conclusion")

CONCLUSION

Like the introduction, the conclusion is merely sketched in the working outline. Note that this speaker plans to end with a narrative as well as start with one. These opening and closing stories should create a pleasing book-end effect, satisfying audience desires for both balance and closure.

Summary statement: Greenhouse effect threatens our world. It may cause drastic climate changes and serious health problems. Major causes are loss of woodlands, industrial emissions, and increased energy consumption.

Concluding remarks: Gore story about the frog in boiling water.

FIGURE 8.2

Sample Working Outline

▪   Do I have enough supporting material for each main point to satisfy critical listeners?

▪   Do I have a variety of types of supporting materials to make my speech interesting?

Remember, speech preparation often proceeds in fits and starts, periods of frustration followed by moments of inspiration and revision. You may find yourself making and revising several working outlines for each of your major presentations.

Checklist for a Working Outline

_____ 1 My topic, specific purpose, and thesis statement are clearly stated.

_____ 2 My introduction contains attention-getting material, establishes my credibility, and focuses and previews my message.

_____ 3 My main points represent the most important ideas on my topic.

_____ 4 I have an appropriate number of main points to cover my material in the time allotted.

_____ 5 Each subpoint breaks its main point into more specific detail.

_____ 6 My conclusion contains a summary statement and concluding remarks that reinforce and reflect upon the meaning of my speech.

_____ 7 I have planned transitions to use between the introduction and body, following each main point, and between the body and conclusion of my speech.

SPEAKER'S NOTES

DEVELOPING A FORMAL OUTLINE

Once you are satisfied with your working outline, you can go on to prepare a formal outline. The **formal outline** is the final step in a process leading from your first rough draft of ideas through a series of working outlines to the finished product. Developing a formal outline helps ensure that your preparation process reaches a responsible conclusion. This is why your instructor may ask you to turn in a formal outline for your speech as part of your assignment.

The formal outline for a speech follows many of the established conventions of outlining. Figure 8.3 shows a formal speech outline format illustrating these conventions:

1. The identification of speech topic, specific purpose, and thesis statement
2. The separation of speech parts: introduction, body, and conclusion
3. A system of numbering and lettering that displays coordination and subordination
4. The wording of main points and subpoints as declarative sentences
5. A title
6. A list of major sources consulted

In addition, for reasons we will discuss below, _indicate supporting materials and source citations at critical points in the outline._

Topic, Specific Purpose, and Thesis Statement

Some novice speakers make the mistake of repeating their topics, specific purposes, and thesis statements at the beginnings of their speeches as

FIGURE 8.3

Format for a Formal
Outline

TITLE

Topic: _____

Specific purpose: _____

Thesis statement: _____

INTRODUCTION

Attention material: _____
_____

Credibility material: _____
_____

Thesis statement: _____
_____

Preview: _____
_____

(Transition into body of speech)

BODY

I. First main point:
  A. Subpoint or supporting material: _____
  B. Subpoint or supporting material: _____
    1. Sub-subpoint or supporting material: _____
    2. Sub-subpoint or supporting material: _____

(Transition into next main point)

II. Second main point:
  A. Subpoint or supporting material: _____
    1. Sub-subpoint or supporting material: _____
    2. Sub-subpoint or supporting material: _____
  B. Subpoint or supporting material: _____

(Transition into next main point)

III. Third main point:
  A. Subpoint or supporting material: _____
  B. Subpoint or supporting material: _____
    1. Sub-subpoint or supporting material: _____
    2. Sub-subpoint or supporting material: _____
      a. Sub-sub-subpoint or supporting material: _____
      b. Sub-sub-subpoint or supporting material: _____

(Transition into conclusion)

CONCLUSION

Summary statement: _____
_____

Concluding remarks: _____
_____

WORKS CONSULTED

though they were chanting a mantra. "My topic is . . . My specific purpose is . . . My thesis statement is . . ." This is not a good way to begin a speech. Nevertheless, as you are preparing your formal outline, you should write these elements out as you begin the outline. This helps keep them at the forefront of your thinking. It encourages a well focused message that moves purposefully from your opening to closing words. As we noted earlier, identifying the speech topic, specific purpose, and thesis statement in your outline is much like the foundation of a building: although we may never actually see much of it in the speech, we know it must be present before speakers can build an effective structure of ideas. As Figure 8.3 indicates, often the thesis statement, repeated near the end of the introduction, can be the only part of this foundation work that actually appears in the speech.

You will already have written out your topic, specific purpose, and thesis statement as you prepared your working outlines. As you transfer these to your formal outline, be certain that the thesis statement is written as a declarative sentence.

Separation of Speech Parts

Separating the major parts of the speech in the formal outline helps ensure that you give each section the full and careful attention it requires. Only when your introduction, body, and conclusion are fully developed and joined by transitions can they work together to achieve your specific purpose and fulfill the promise of your thesis statement.

Note that in Figure 8.3, only the body of the speech follows an outlining format.[5] As we suggested in Chapters 2 and 7, it is best to plan your introduction and conclusion very carefully to assure that you get into and out of your speech gracefully and effectively. Although there may be times when situational factors necessitate adapting your introduction (we discussed these factors under "Context" in Chapter 4), as a general rule a carefully worded beginning works best. Knowing *exactly* what you want to say and how you want to say it gets you off to a good start and helps build the confidence you need to make the presentation of your ideas effective. At the end of your speech, the exact wording of your concluding remarks can determine whether you make a striking, lasting impression.

Numbering and Lettering Your Outline

Figure 8.3 illustrates a numbering and lettering system that follows the principles of coordination and subordination. It shows you how to use letters, numbers, and indentation to set up a formal outline. The actual number of main points and levels of subpoints you have may vary, but the basic format remains the same. Roman numbers (I, II, III) identify the main points of your speech. Capital letters (A, B, C) identify the subpoints under each main point. Arabic numbers (1, 2, 3) identify the sub-subpoints under any subpoint. Lower case letters (a, b, c) identify any sub-sub-subpoints in your outline.

Outlining brings discipline to structuring your speech. It allows you to check if your main points are adequately developed and if your message flows smoothly from beginning to end.

The principle of **coordination** requires that all statements at a given level belong to the same order and be similar in terms of importance. In other words, your *I*'s and *II*'s, your *A*'s and *B*'s, your *1*'s and *2*'s, and your *a*'s and *b*'s should seem closely related. In Figure 8.4 (Sample Formal Outline) the main points include an explanation of the greenhouse effect and its three major causes. *As* causes and effect, they belong to the same order. Even though the causes differ somewhat in importance, making possible a strategy of arrangement in terms of ascending importance, they still are the most important causes. Think how strange it would seem if a fifth main point, "The greenhouse effect will decrease our recreational opportunities" was added to this outline. That statement would not belong to the order of main points in this speech, nor would it begin to equal them in importance. Nor could you really develop it without violating the time constraints for a short speech. In short, adding such a main point would both violate the principle of coordination and would not be a very practical idea anyway.

The principle of **subordination** requires that related material descend in importance from the more general and abstract main points to the more concrete and specific subpoints, and sub-subpoints related to them, as shown below:

more important	I. Main point	**more general**
	A. Subpoint	
	1. Sub-subpoint	
less important	a. Sub-sub-subpoint	**more specific**

The more important a statement is, the farther to the left it is positioned. If you rotate an outline so that it rests on its right margin, the "peaks" will represent the main points, the most important ideas in your speech, with all other subpoints decreasing according to their significance.

The easiest way to demonstrate the importance of coordination and subordination is to look at an abbreviated sample outline that violates these principles:

I. Computers can help you develop writing skills.
   A. Using PCs can improve your schoolwork.
   B. PCs can be useful for organizing classnotes.

II. Computers can help you keep better financial records.
   A. They can help you plan personal time more effectively.
   B. They can be useful in your personal life.
   C. They can help organize your research notes for class projects.

This collection of thoughts is an outline in name only. It violates the principles of both coordination and subordination in that the levels are not equal in importance, nor are they logically related to each other. To straighten out this problem, let's look first at the main points. In this outline, they are not the most general nor the most important statements. The main points are actually I-A and II-B: the ideas that PCs can improve your schoolwork and can be useful in your personal life. Once we put the main points where they belong, we can easily see where the subpoints go:

I. Computers can improve your schoolwork.
   A. PCs can help you develop writing skills.
   B. PCs can be useful for organizing class notes.
   C. PCs can help organize your research notes for class projects.

II. Computers can be useful in your personal life.
   A. PCs can help you keep better financial records.
   B. PCs can help you plan personal time more effectively.

Wording Your Outline

Each main point and all subpoints in your outline should be worded as declarative sentences. If your points start sprouting clauses, you should reexamine the structure of your speech to simplify it. You may need to break down complex main points into subpoints or complex subpoints into sub-subpoints. For example, the following does not make a good main point sentence:

Bad eating habits endanger health and lower feelings of self-worth, reducing life span and causing personal anguish.

The sentence is too long and complex, and is not entirely clear. It works better if it is expanded and simplified in the following way:

I. Bad eating habits are a threat to our well-being.
  A. Such habits endanger health.
    1. They can result in increased heart disease.
    2. They can shorten the life span.
  B. Such habits can damage self-image.
    1. Obese people sometimes dislike themselves.
    2. They can feel that they have nothing to offer others.

Breaking the complex sentence down into outline form helps you to focus what you are going to say. It simplifies and clarifies both the structure and logic of your speech.

Look for opportunities to use **parallel construction** when wording the main points of your speech. If you were developing a speech on the need for reforms in political campaign financing, you might word your main points as follows:

I. We need reform at the national level.

II. We need reform at the state level.

III. We need reform at the local level.

IV. But first we need to reform ourselves.

You could introduce these statements using these words as you preview your speech. The parallel construction would give listeners a guide to the structure of your speech. You could also repeat the parallel pattern as you summarize your speech, further imprinting its message upon the minds of your listeners.

Parallel construction has many other advantages. Because each sentence has the same basic structure, any variations stand out sharply. The preceding example highlights the words *national, state, local, But first,* and *ourselves* because they are the only words that differ in important ways. Thus parallel construction can become a device for emphasizing important points. In this example, the parallel structure also helps the speech narrow its focus like a zoom lens as it moves from a national to an individual perspective.

Using parallel construction for your main points also helps to distinguish them from your subpoints. It makes possible effective internal summaries as the speech moves toward its conclusion: "Having looked at reform at the national, state, and local levels, we come to the most important part of the problem — ourselves." Since it involves repetition, the structure is easy to remember and may prolong the effect of the speech for your listeners. It satisfies the principles of good form and closure discussed in Chapter 7. Not all material lends itself easily to parallel construction, but look for opportunities to use it when you can.

Supporting Your Main Points

Your formal outline should show precisely how your supporting material fits into the plan of your speech. As we noted in Chapter 6, supporting materials strengthen the points you make in your speech. For example, a sub-point that states "The greenhouse effect is causing climate changes" might rely on a factual example and expert testimony to demonstrate that claim: "According to the National Weather Service, the winter of 1991–92 was the warmest winter in at least ninety-seven years." Be sure that each main point receives the type and amount of supporting material it needs to be effective for your audience. Your audience analysis should provide you with a good idea of where your listeners stand in relation to your subject. In Chapter 6 (p. 196) we offered guidelines for deciding what supporting materials you should use if your ideas will seem controversial, abstract, technical, or distant from the lives of your listeners. We also suggested what type of supporting material you should use if you need to arouse or diffuse emotions. In Chapter 7 (pp. 213) we described how you should work supporting materials into the text of your speech. You should go back and review this material as you prepare your outline.

Title

Outside the classroom, the purpose of a title is to attract audiences. Class-room speeches provide you with an opportunity to practice creating good titles. A good title prepares the audience for the speech. It can arouse curiosity, making people want to come and listen. You may wish to mention your title in your introduction and then refer to it throughout the speech as a reminder of your thesis statement. You don't want to begin your speech, however, by simply stating your title. Rather, find some artful way to weave it into your introduction to help you gain attention.

You should wait until you have outlined your speech before you select a title for it. Your title should not promise too much or deceive the audience. Titles that promise everything from eternal peace of mind to the end of taxation often disappoint or frustrate listeners. Overblown titles can damage your ethos. The speech on the greenhouse effect carries the following title: "Warming Our World and Chilling Our Future." What do you think of this title? Can you come up with a better one?

Changing Your Working Outline to a Formal Outline

Let's look at how you might transform material from your working outline to a formal outline. In the working example provided in Figure 8.2, the fourth main point appears as follows:

Fourth main point: Increased energy consumption magnifies the greenhouse effect.

    Subpoint A: Population and prosperity fuel the problem.

 Sub-subpoints: 1. More people means more consumption.

                    2. Rising living standards = rising expectations = more consumption.

    Subpoint B: Energy consumption is the single largest cause of the greenhouse effect.

 Sub-subpoints: 1. Fuel use has doubled since 1950.

                    2. Fuel use accounts for 90 percent of America's energy consumption.

                    3. Transportation-related energy use accounts for half of all air pollution.

To convert this material into the formal outline format you need to use the proper system of numbering and lettering and to write out your ideas as complete sentences. In the formal outline the fourth main point takes the following form:

IV. Increased energy consumption magnifies the greenhouse effect (National Issues Forums 7).

    A. Both population and prosperity fuel the problem.

       1. More people means more energy consumption.

       2. Improved living standards add to the problem.

    B. Energy consumption is now the single largest cause of the greenhouse effect.

       1. Fossil fuel use has more than doubled since 1950.

       2. Fossil fuels account for 90 percent of America's energy consumption.

       3. Transportation-related energy use accounts for half of all air pollution.

Notice that a source of supporting materials is indicated in parentheses at the end of the statement of the fourth main point. This **source citation** is brief, because it refers to the full listing in "Works Consulted" that appears at the end of the formal outline. Placed at the end of the statement of the main point, this means that this source supports all claims — subpoints and sub-subpoints — that develop below it. If the reference were placed at the end of sub-subpoint B.3, the citation would apply only to that statement.

    The sample formal outline in Figure 8.4 includes a number of source citations. Using them encourages you to apply your research directly to critical points in the speech you are planning. It also reminds you of the

Stating your specific purpose and thesis statement helps you keep them in mind as you outline your speech. The thesis statement is stated as a declarative sentence.

Labeling the introduction shows that it is a distinct and important part of the speech.

Beginning with a humorous anecdote helps gain attention.

Here the speaker provides dramatic evidence of the greenhouse effect to grasp attention and offers an initial definition to establish a beachhead of understanding. A more elaborate explanation and description will develop under the first main point. The use of expert testimony enhances the impact of the facts and figures.

At this point the speaker uses a humorous metaphor to personalize the topic, establish credibility, and involve the audience.

Here the speaker focuses the specific purpose and thesis statement of the speech and previews the form in which it will develop.

The use of transitions helps listeners track the progress of the speech.

TITLE: WARMING OUR WORLD AND CHILLING OUR FUTURE

Topic: The Greenhouse Effect

Specific purpose: To inform my audience of the causes of the greenhouse effect.

Thesis statement: Today I want to share what I've learned about the greenhouse effect and its major causes.

INTRODUCTION

Attention material: When Mark Twain was in London in 1897, a rumor reached the editor of the New York Journal who immediately wired his London correspondent, "HEAR MARK TWAIN DIED, SEND 1000 WORDS." The correspondent showed the telegram to Twain, who wired back this message, "REPORT OF MY DEATH GREATLY EXAGGERATED." This response applies to my speech topic today. Despite the efforts of some to write its obituary, and to erase it from the public agenda, the greenhouse effect is a growing, not declining problem. The reports of its death have been greatly exaggerated.

Almost twenty years ago, environmentalists urged scientists to look to Antarctica for signs of what they called the "greenhouse effect"—the gradual warming of the earth because of human activity (Lemonick, "Iceberg"). During this past winter of 1995 a gigantic iceberg—23 miles wide and 48 miles long, almost as large as the state of Rhode Island—broke off the Larsen Ice Shelf in the Antarctic Peninsula. More than this, the whole Ice Shelf is crumbling. Rodolfo Del Valle, director of geoscience at the Argentine Antarctic Institute, told Newsweek that it "looked liked polystyrene that had been broken by a little boy" (Begley). Such reports simply cannot be ignored. Combined with other recently reported evidence from NASA's Upper Atmosphere Research Satellite which prove that "chemicals generated by human activity cause the ozone hole . . . over the Antarctic," they are ominous signs for our future ("Ozone").

Credibility material: Now I'm what you might call a "country mouse." Living in the outdoors, and loving such activities as hiking, camping, fishing, and hunting for as long as I can remember, it's not hard for me to have a great deal of concern for the environment. But you can be a "city mouse," and still like to breathe clean air and drink good water and not have to worry about the warm sun on your skin. So all of us have a lot at stake here.

Thesis statement: Today I want to share what I've learned about the greenhouse effect and its major causes.

Preview: We need to be concerned, first, about the loss of woodlands, second, about industrial emissions, and third, about overall spectacular increases in world energy consumption.

(**Transition:** "Let's begin by understanding more about the greenhouse effect.")

(continued)

Labeling the body of the speech sets it off as a distinct part of the speech.

The first main point and its subpoints are complete sentences. This point defines the nature of the greenhouse effect and gives the audience good reasons to listen. Placing a source indicator at the end of the first main point ("Monastersky") indicates that the source supplies material for all subpoints and sub-subpoints that develop below it.

Subpoint A is supported with facts and figures. Subpoint B explains how the pollutants bring about the hole in the ozone layer. Subpoint C points out the problems we can expect if the situation continues. It gives the audience a reason to want to learn more about the greenhouse effect.

This transition helps the audience change focus from the explanation to the causes of the greenhouse effect.

The speaker develops the three causes of the greenhouse effect according to their increasing importance. Since the loss of woodlands contributes less than the other points, it receives less attention. It may be underdeveloped. Keep in mind that the outline is not the complete text of a speech, but a guide to its development.

BODY

I. The green house effect is a gradual warming of the earth caused by human activities (Monastersky).

    A. It is characterized by a high concentration of carbon dioxide in the atmosphere (Anthes).
        1. Each year five tons of carbon are pumped into the atmosphere for each person in the United States.
        2. In 1987 the level of carbon dioxide soared to a record high level.
        3. The nine warmest years in this century have all occurred since 1980 (Atkinson).

    B. Carbon pollutants are producing a hole in the ozone layer.
        1. Chlorofluorocarbons act like an atmospheric Pac-Man (National Issues Forums Institute 11).
        2. The hole in the ozone layer reduces the earth's ability to protect us from ultraviolet radiation.

    C. If this problem is not corrected, we may see disastrous results.
        1. There could be dramatic climate changes (Atkinson).
            a. There could be widespread drought in the middle of continents.
            b. There could be increases in the frequency and severity of storms.
            c. There could be rising sea levels that might destroy coastal areas.
        2. There could be serious health problems (Lemonick "Ozone").
            a. There could be an increase in skin cancer.
            b. There could be an increase in cataracts.
            c. There could be weakened immune systems.

   (**Transition:** Now that you understand what the greenhouse effect is and why it is important, let's examine its major causes.)

II. One cause of the greenhouse effect is the loss of woodlands that convert carbon dioxide into oxygen.
    A. One football-field-sized area of forest is lost every second to cutting or burning ("Future" 35).
    B. Burning forests add more carbon dioxide because smoke is produced.

(continued)

This transition announces that the speaker is moving on to another cause.

This third main point is more fully developed than the second. It is rich in facts and figures, but can be more interesting if examples, vivid language, or presentation aids are used. Again the transition signals a change of focus.

Main point IV is more fully developed than the others. Note the use of Roman numerals, capital letters and Arabic numbers for the main point, subpoints, and sub-subpoints. Again, all of the subpoints and sub-subpoints contain only factual information. The speech may need examples or narratives to bring it to life.

Note that the phrase "in short," introducing the summary statement, acts as a transition to cue the audience that the end is coming.

The speaker both begins and ends the speech with a striking story, providing a nice sense of closure. •

(**Transition:** Now let's turn to the second major cause of the greenhouse effect.)

III. Industrial emissions also contribute to the growth of the greenhouse effect (National Issues Forums Institute 6).
  A. Industrial contaminants account for more than 20 percent of our air pollution.
  B. Carbon dioxide is released when wood, coal, and oil are burned.
  C. Chlorofluorocarbons come from refrigeration and air conditioners.
  D. Nitrogen oxides are spewed out of vehicle exhausts and smokestacks.

(**Transition:** The last major cause of the greenhouse effect may be the most important.)

IV. Increased energy consumption magnifies the greenhouse effect (National Issues Forums Institute 7).
  A. Both population and prosperity fuel the problem.
    1. More people means more energy consumption.
    2. Improved living standards add to the problem.
  B. Energy consumption is the single largest cause of the greenhouse effect.
    1. Fossil fuel use has more than doubled since 1950.
    2. Fossil fuels account for 90 per cent of America's energy consumption.
    3. Transportation-related energy use accounts for approximately half of all air pollution.

CONCLUSION

Summary statement: In short, if you want to know why we have a greenhouse effect, listen for the falling trees, watch the industrial smokestacks darkening the sky, and smell the exhaust fumes we are pumping into the air. The greenhouse effect is a monster we all are creating. And if we don't stop, we and our children may face drastic climate changes and serious health problems.

Concluding remarks: Vice-President Al Gore used the following story to illustrate how the greenhouse effect can sneak up on us. In an address to the National Academy of Sciences, he said, "If dropped into a pot of boiling water, a frog will quickly jump out. But if the same frog is put into a pot and the water is slowly heated, the frog will stay put until boiled alive. So it is with pollution . . . If we do not wake up to the slow heating of our environment, we may jump too late" (Gore, "Global"). The more we know about this problem, and the better we understand it, the more likely we are to jump and the less likely we are to be boiled alive.

WORKS CONSULTED

Anthes, Richard A. "Greenhouse Effect." The New Grolier Multimedia Encyclopedia, CD-ROM. Novato, CA: Software Toolworks, 1993.
Atkinson, Rick. "Disputes Heat Global Warming Summit." Commercial Appeal [Memphis] 2 Apr. 1995: A:19.

(continued)

The references in the works consulted follow the format recommended by the Modern Language Association of America. The speaker has used a variety of sources of information to acquire responsible knowledge for the development of the speech.

Begley, Sharon. "Ice Cubes for Penguins." <u>Newsweek</u> 3 Apr. 1995: 56.
Elmer-Dewitt, Philip. "A Season in Hell." <u>Time</u> 19 July 1993: 22.
"The Future Is Here: Earth at the Summit." <u>Newsweek</u> 1 June 1992: 15-43.
Gore, Albert, Jr. <u>Earth in the Balance: Ecology and the Human Spirit</u>. Boston: Houghton Mifflin, 1992.
———. "The Global Environment: A National Security Issue." National Academy of Science. Washington, 1 May 1989.
Lemonick, Michael D. "One Big, Bad Iceberg." <u>Time</u> 20 Mar.1995: 65.
———. "The Ozone Vanishes." <u>Time</u> 17 Feb. 1992: 60.
Monastersky, Richard. "Consensus Reached on Climate Change Causes." <u>Science News</u> 24 Sept. 1994: 198.
National Issues Forums Institute. <u>The Environment at Risk: Responding to Growing Dangers</u>. Dayton: Kettering Foundation, 1989.
"Ozone Mystery Solved." <u>National Wildlife</u> Apr./May 1995: 6.
Schneider, David. "Global Warming is Still a Hot Topic." <u>Scientific American</u> Feb. 1995: 13-14.
Wiltze, Alexandra. "Rush is Wrong." <u>Earth</u> Apr. 1995: 14.

FIGURE 8.4

Sample Formal Outline

importance of documenting points as you speak. These citations tell your instructor that you have not only researched your subject, but that you have also integrated this research into your speech. They help affirm your ethos as a communicator who has met the challenge of responsible knowledge.

Source citations such as we see in Figure 8.4 should be brief and clear cues to the works you list under Works Consulted. The Modern Language Association of America suggests the following procedures for citations in a text:

- List the last name of the author plus the page number when there is more than one page in the work cited. (The Atkinson alone in Figure 8.4 indicates the article cited is complete on one page.)

- The name accompanied by an abbreviated title (Lemonick, "Iceberg") indicates that you include more than one work by the same author in your Works Consulted list, but that again the work cited is complete on one page.

- If the "author" is a corporation, list the name (National Issues Forums), or when the author is not provided, list the first word of the title ("Future" 35).

- If you document your source within the formal outline, the source citation should include pages alone, such as: "*Newsweek*'s 'The Future' says that tropical forests are disappearing (35)."

Remember: documenting your sources carefully within your formal outline does not take the place of oral documentation you must present in your speech. For example, you must say, "In its recent in-depth investigation, 'The Future is Here: Earth at the Summit,' *Newsweek* revealed that one acre of tropical forest disappears every second because of logging or burning." Documenting the source correctly in the formal outline, while important, is not enough. Keep the focus where it belongs: *your formal outline is the completed plan of your speech but not the speech itself.* Your audience will be listening to your speech, not reading the formal outline. Full oral documentation as you present your speech allows you to give credit where credit is due and to enjoy the credit for careful research. Moreover, actually citing expert sources helps prevent any suspicion of plagiarism.

Listing Your References

A list of the major sources you consulted in preparing your speech should appear at the end of your formal outline under the heading, "Works Consulted." Arrange your sources alphabetically by the last name of the author or person interviewed, or by the title of printed materials if the author is not specified. The following guidelines are based on the format suggested by Joseph Gibaldi in *MLA Handbook for Writers of Research Papers* (New York: Modern Language Association of America, 1995). If questions arise concerning these guidelines, consult this book directly. Should your instructor wish you to follow one of the other available formats, he or she will provide additional information.

Books.   For a book by one author, list the author's name (last name first), followed by the title, city of publication, publisher, and date. For example:

> **Damasio, Antonio.** *Descartes' Error.* **New York: Putnam, 1994.**

If the book has two or three authors, list the lead author's name (last name first), followed by the second and third authors (first names first), the title, city of publication, publisher, and date. For example:

> **Combs, James E., and Dan Nimmo.** *The New Propaganda.* **White Plains: Longman, 1993.**

If the book has more than three authors, you can list the lead author's name (last name first), followed by the abbreviation *et al.,* the title, city of publication, publisher, and date. For example:

> **Belenky, Mary Field, et al.** *Women's Ways of Knowing.* **New York: Basic Books, 1986.**

If the book has a corporate author, use the name of the corporation in place of the given name of an author. For example:

> **Boston Women's Health Book Collective.** *Our Bodies, Ourselves.* **New York: Simon and Schuster, 1973.**

If your material comes from a signed article in a reference book, list the author's name (last name first), the title of the article in quotation marks, the title of the reference book, and the edition date. For example:

> Tobias, Richard. "Thurber, James." *Encyclopedia Americana.* 1991 ed.

If your material comes from an unsigned article in a reference book, list the title of the article in quotation marks, the title of the reference book, and the edition number and date. For example:

> "Twyla Tharp." *Who's Who of American Women.* 17th ed. 1991–92.

If your material comes from a government document, list the source of the document, the title of the document, the edition (if given), the city of publication, publisher, and date. For example:

> United States. Cong. House Committee on the Judiciary. *Immigration and Nationality Act with Amendments and Notes on Related Laws.* 7th ed. Washington: GPO, 1980.

Periodicals.   The general format is the same for all periodicals. List the author's name (last name first), followed by the title of the article, name of periodical, volume number if applicable, date of publication, and page numbers. For example:

> Mechling, Elizabeth Walker, and Jay Mechling. "The Atom According to Disney." *Quarterly Journal of Speech* 81 (1995): 436-53.

If the author of the article is not specified, begin with the title of the article. If the magazine is published every month or two months, give the month or months and year, but omit the volume and issue numbers. For example:

> "Ozone Mystery Solved." *National Wildlife* Apr./May 1995: 6.

Materials taken from daily newspapers should include the edition of the paper if applicable, full date of publication, and the section as well as the page numbers. For example:

> Perrusquia, Marc. "Farewell to Innocence: School Kids Take Up Arms." *Commercial Appeal* [Memphis] 5 Nov. 1995, final ed.: A:1.

CD-ROMs, Online Databases, and Computer Networks.   When citing material from these sources you should provide the following types of information: author's name (last name first), article title in quotation marks, periodical title, volume, date, inclusive pages, title of database, publication medium (i.e., CD-ROM, online database), name of vendor or computer service, electronic publication date or date of access.

If your material comes from a CD-ROM, use the following format:

West, Cornel. "The Dilemma of the Black Intellectual." *Critical Quarterly* 29 (1987): 39–52. *MLA International Bibliography.* CD-ROM. SilverPlatter. Feb. 1995.

If your material comes from an online database, use the following format (note that in this example, the plus sign after the page indicates that the article begins on this page but is not printed on consecutive pages):

Gray, John. "The Virtues of Toleration." *National Review* 5 Oct. 1992: 28+. *Magazine Database Plus.* Online. CompuServe. Oct. 1995.

If your material comes from a computer network electronic journal, newsletter, or conference, use the following format:

Schreibman, Vigdor. "Closing the 'Values Gap.' " *FINS* 1.5 (8 March 1993): n.pag. Online. Internet. 10 April 1995.

If your material comes from a computer network electronic mail, use the following format:

Pierson, Michael. "Internet Freedom." 30 April 1995. Online posting: alt.culture. Internet. *Usenet.* 3 May 1995.

Miscellaneous References. You may use other sources of information in your speech such as radio or television programs, films, interviews, advertisements, lectures, or speeches.

For a radio or television show or film use the following format:

"The Hero's Adventure." *Moyers: Joseph Campbell and the Power of Myth.* Prod. Catherine Tatge. PBS. WNET, New York. 23 May 1988.

For an interview use the following format:

Frentz, C. R. Telephone interview. 25 July 1991.

For an advertisement use the following format:

Chevrolet. "Send Yourself to Camp." Advertisement. *National Geographic* July 1995: 142–143.

For a speech or lecture use the following format:

Webb, Lynn. "Presidential Address." Southern States Communication Association Convention. Memphis, 28 March 1996.

Checklist for a Formal Outline

_____ 1   My topic and specific purpose are clearly stated.

_____ 2   My thesis statement is written as a declarative sentence.

_____ 3   My introduction contains material to create attention, establish my credibility, and focus and preview my message.

_____ 4   My main points represent the most important ideas on my topic.

_____ 5   My main points are related in kind and importance.

_____ 6   My main points are stated as declarative sentences.

_____ 7   Each main point is supported by facts, statistics, testimony, examples, or narratives.

_____ 8   My subpoints are divisions of the main points they follow.

_____ 9   My subpoints are more specific than the main points they follow.

_____ 10   My conclusion contains a summary statement that repeats my message, and concluding remarks that reflect on its meaning and significance.

_____ 11   I have provided transitions where they are needed to make my speech flow smoothly.

_____ 12   I have compiled a list of works consulted in the preparation of my speech.

SPEAKER'S NOTES

Once you have completed your formal outline, review it using the Checklist for a Formal Outline in Speaker's Notes 8.2.

DEVELOPING A KEY-WORD OUTLINE

Your formal outline represents a lot of hard work on your part, but remember — it is a blueprint of your speech and not the speech itself. _You should not use your formal outline during the actual presentation of your speech._ If you do, you will be tempted to read it, losing eye contact with listeners, and may miss out on important feedback from them. Rather, you should develop a brief outline that will serve as a prompt and encourage an extemporaneous presentation (see Chapter 11). Prepare a **key-word outline** which reduces your formal outline to a few essential words that will jog your memory and remind you of the sequence of your major points.

Your key-word outline should fit on a few pieces of paper or index cards, the fewer the better to avoid confusion during your speech. Number the pages or cards to help keep them in order. If you are preparing your key-word outline by hand, use a dark felt marker and print your letters large enough to read without straining. If you are preparing it on a computer, choose a large font size, such as fourteen- or eighteen-point. If your printer prints lightly, choose the **BOLD TEXT** command. You may find your key-word outline easier to read if you use all capital letters.

Because it will be used strictly as a memory jogger, you may not want to include the introduction, body, and conclusion headings from the formal outline. However, follow the same format for lettering, numbering, and indentation that you used in the formal outline. If you are preparing your outlines by hand, go through a copy of your formal outline and mark the numbers, letters, and key words with a highlighter. You can then copy these onto another piece of paper or note cards for use as a key-word outline. If you are working on a computer or word processor, make a copy of your formal outline. On the copy, select the numbers, letters, and keywords, change them to **bold**, delete the rest of the material, and save. Just a few stylistic changes will usually suffice to create your key-word outline.

While you reduce much of your formal outline to the essentials for the key-word outline, we recommend that you expand and alter your source citations as needed to help you remember vital details during oral documentation. You may also wish to copy important brief quotations word-for-word so that you can present them accurately.

Let's return to the fourth main point of the formal outline for the greenhouse effect speech to see how it can be turned into a key-word outline format.

IV. **Increased energy consumption** magnifies the greenhouse effect (**National Issues Forums Institute** 7).

    A. Both **population and prosperity** fuel the problem.

        1. **More people** means **more energy** consumption.

        2. **Improved living standards** add to the problem.

    B. Energy consumption is the **single largest cause** of the greenhouse effect.

        1. **Fossil fuel use** has more than **doubled** since **1950**.

        2. Fossil fuels account for **90 percent** of **America's energy consumption.**

        3. **Transportation**-related energy use accounts for approximately **half** of **all air pollution.**

In this example we have highlighted the key words for the main point, each subpoint, and each sub-subpoint. These then convert into the following key-word format:

IV. INCREASED ENERGY CONSUMPTION (ENVIRONMENT)

    A. POPULATION & PROSPERITY

        1. MORE PEOPLE = MORE CONSUMPTION

        2. IMPROVED LIVING STANDARDS = MORE CONSUMPTION

The speaker has made notes on the outline to help during presentation.

The pause can act as a nonverbal transition signaling that a change is coming.

This key-word outline follows the same format of indenting used in the formal outline. It makes it easier for the speaker to check at a glance.

This key-word outline contains just enough information to keep the speaker focused on main points and subpoints. The single words and short phrases keep the speaker from reading the speech.

FIGURE 8.5

Sample Key-Word Outline

GREENHOUSE EFFECT NOT DEAD (TIME/NEWSWEEK '95)   *Make eye contact!*
CONCERN FOR ENVIRONMENT
  GRADUAL WARMING
  LOSS OF WOODLANDS
  INDUSTRIAL EMISSIONS
  RISING ENERGY CONSUMPTION
                                                             Pause!

I. GRADUAL WARMING
   A. HIGH CO_2 IN ATMOSPHERE (<u>SCIENCE NEWS</u> SEPT '94)
   B. HOLE IN OZONE LAYER (NIF, <u>ENVIRONMENT AT RISK</u>)
   C. CONSEQUENCES
      1. CLIMATE CHANGES (<u>CA</u> APR '95)
      2. HEALTH PROBLEMS (<u>TIME</u> MAR '95)
                          Pause and look around room: transition here.
II. LOSS OF WOODLANDS TO CONVERT CO_2 TO O
    A. CUTTING (<u>NEWSWEEK</u> JUNE '92)
    B. BURNING
                                                             Pause!

III. INDUSTRIAL EMISSIONS (<u>ENVIRONMENT</u>)
     A. 20% OF AIR POLLUTION
     B. BURNING WOOD, COAL, & OIL
     C. CFCS: REFRIGERATION AND AIR CONDITIONING
     D. NITROUS OXIDE: VEHICLES & SMOKESTACKS
                                                             Pause!

IV. INCREASED ENERGY CONSUMPTION (<u>ENVIRONMENT</u>)   *Be emphatic!*
    A. POPULATION & PROSPERITY
       1. MORE PEOPLE = MORE CONSUMPTION
       2. IMPROVED LIVING STANDARDS = MORE
          CONSUMPTION
    B. SINGLE LARGEST CAUSE   *Pause and make eye contact!*
       1. FUEL USE <u>DOUBLED</u> — 1950   *Stress these facts!*
       2. <u>90 %</u> OF US ENERGY CONSUMPTION
       3. TRANSPORTATION = HALF ALL AIR POLLUTION

                                        Longer pause/ look around room.

Summary: Problem and Causes
Final remarks: Gore Story: Frog

   B. SINGLE LARGEST CAUSE

      1. FOSSIL FUEL USE DOUBLED — 1950

      2. 90% OF U.S. ENERGY CONSUMPTION

      3. TRANSPORTATION = HALF ALL AIR POLLUTION

As you practice your speech, you may be able to reduce your key-word outline even further. *Remember, the more the speech is outlined in your head rather than on paper, the better.* Start your practice from your formal outline. Go through the speech two or three times, referring to this outline until you feel comfortable with what you are going to say and how you are going to say it. Then practice from your key-word outline until your speech flows smoothly. As you practice, you may want to write in brief notes about presentation, such as "pause here" or "slow down," on your key-word outline. Make such notes with a different color marker or circle them so you don't confuse them with the outline itself during presentation. Put your outlines aside for a while, then rehearse the speech again, using only the key-word outline. If the key words still work as reminders, your preparation has been effective. We provide more suggestions for rehearsing your speech in Chapter 11. Figure 8.5 shows a key-word outline for the speech on the greenhouse effect.

During the actual presentation of your speech you may want to have separate cards for longer quotations or statistics that must be cited exactly. Experiment to find what works best for you.

You should not try to hide the key-word outline during your presentation, nor should you feel self-conscious about using it. Hold your outline in your hand or place it on a lectern so that you minimize the loss of eye contact with listeners when you refer to it. We discuss more about using your key-word outline in Chapter 11, "Presenting Your Speech."

IN SUMMARY

An outline gives you an overview of what you want to say and how you want to say it. It sharpens the logic and improves the structure of your speech, and reminds you of the need to use supporting materials at critical points in your presentation.

Developing a Working Outline. A *working outline* is a tentative plan of your speech. It helps you work out the problems and relationships of your ideas. It brings together the major parts of your speech, showing the relative importance of points and how they fit together. A working outline arranges main points, subpoints, and sub-subpoints in relation to each other. The degree of elaboration depends on your topic, your assessment of audience needs, and time constraints. As working outlines evolve for a particular speech, they indicate how and where you will use supporting materials. They also point up the role of transitions in the speech. By developing working outlines you can judge the effectiveness of your research and determine if you need additional material.

Developing a Formal Outline. The *formal outline* is the final product of the research and planning phase of your speech. It is the most polished and complete outline form. As such, it follows a number of conventions, including coordination and subordination. *Coordination* requires that statements that are alike in kind and importance be placed on the same level in the outline. The support they receive should reflect their importance. *Subordination* requires that statements descend in importance and that each level logically include the level below it. As you descend through the various levels, points become more specific and concrete. The numbering, lettering, and indentation system should be consistent throughout the outline.

The main points in a formal outline should be worded as declarative sentences. *Parallel construction* highlights the main points and helps the audience remember your message. *Source citations*, placed in parentheses at points throughout the outline, provide documentation. They show how you have integrated your research into your speech. A formal outline includes a list of *works consulted*.

Developing a Key-Word Outline. A *key-word outline* can aid in the presentation of a speech. Such an outline reduces the formal outline to a few essential words that remind you of the content, design, and sources of supporting materials as you present the speech. Notes on the key-word outline can also remind you of presentation strategies.

TERMS TO KNOW

working outline	subordination
subpoint	parallel construction
sub-subpoint	source citations
formal outline	works consulted
coordination	key-word outline

DISCUSSION

1. Working in small groups, share a working outline for your next speech. Explain the strategy of your structure and show how your outline satisfies the principles of coordination and subordination. Demonstrate that your supporting materials will be adequate. Revise as appropriate in light of the discussion that follows.

2. Select one of the speeches from Appendix B and prepare a formal outline of it. Does this outline make clear the structure of the speech? Does it reveal any structural flaws? Can you see any different ways the speaker might have developed the speech? Present your thoughts on these questions in class discussion.

APPLICATION

1. Assume that the speeches you give in class this semester will be advertised in the campus newspaper. Develop titles that might help attract an audience.

2. See if you can "unjumble" the following outline of the body of a speech using coordination and subordination appropriately. What title would you suggest for this speech?

Thesis statement: Deer hunting with a camera can be an exciting sport.

I. There is a profound quiet, a sense of mystery.
   - A. The woods in late fall are enchanting.
      1. The "film-hunter" becomes part of a beautiful scene.
      2. Dawn is especially lovely.
   - B. Time that a big doe walked under my tree stand.
      1. When they appear, deer always surprise you.
      2. How a big buck surprised me after a long stalk.

II. Hunting from a stand can be a good way to capture a deer on film.
   - A. The stalk method on the ground is another way to hunt with a camera.
      1. Learn to recognize deer tracks and droppings.
         - a. Learn to recognize deer signs.
         - b. Learn to recognize rubs on trees and scrapes on the ground.
      2. Hunt into the wind and move slowly.
   - B. There are two main ways to hunt with a camera.
      1. Stands offer elevation above the line of sight.
      2. Portable stands are also available.
      3. Locating and building your permanent stand.

III. The right camera can be no more expensive than a rifle.
   - A. Selecting the right camera for film-hunting is essential.
   - B. Certain features — like a zoom lens — are necessary.

IV. Display slide of doe.
   - A. You can collect "trophies" you can enjoy forever.
   - B. Display slide of buck.
   - C. Not all hunters are killers: the film-hunter celebrates life, not death.

NOTES

1. Robert DiYanni, and Pat C. Hoy, II. *The Scribner Handbook for Writers.* (Needham Heights, MA: Allyn & Bacon Publishing Company, 1995), p. 14.
2. Douglas Hunt, *The Riverside Guide to Writing,* 2nd ed. (Boston: Houghton Mifflin Co., 1995), pp. 503–504.
3. Hunt, p. 503.
4. Robert T. Oliver, Harold P. Zelko, and Paul D. Holtzman. *Communicative Speaking and Listening.* (New York: Holt, Reinhart & Winston, 1968), p. 125.
5. This suggestion is consistent with the advice given in English composition texts wherein the authors suggest that the "outline is used primarily to organize the difficult middle portion of an essay," DiYanni and Hoy, p. 14.

WARMING OUR WORLD AND CHILLING OUR FUTURE

Since you have watched the process of developing the "greenhouse effect" speech from its beginnings, we thought you might like to see the final product. Here is a text of the speech as it might be presented. Note how the outlined body of the speech transforms into text that reaches out to its listeners.

Here is an interesting change from the formal outline to the speech text. To communicate sources, the citations must become "oral footnotes." These "oral footnotes" make the speech authoritative and strengthen the speaker's credibility.

In transforming source citations into "oral footnotes," the speech does not emphasize the authors. The speaker correctly assumes that the name of the periodical will be more meaningful than the name of an unknown journalist. Note also how the speech uses repetition and vocal emphasis, indicated by the sentences, to create variety, interest, and excitement during the presentation.

The speaker cites the NASA director. A controversial speech calls for a

When Mark Twain was in London in 1897, a rumor reached the editor of the *New York Journal* who immediately wired his London correspondent: "HEAR MARK TWAIN DIED, SEND 1000 WORDS." The correspondent showed the telegram to Twain, who wired back this message: "REPORT OF MY DEATH GREATLY EXAGGERATED." This response applies to my speech topic today. Despite the efforts of some to write its obituary, and to erase it from the public agenda, the greenhouse effect is a growing, not declining problem. The reports of its death have been greatly exaggerated.

Almost twenty years ago, environmentalists urged scientists to look to Antarctica for signs of what they called the "greenhouse effect" — the gradual warming of the earth because of human activity. During this past winter of 1995, *Time* magazine reported that a gigantic iceberg — 23 miles wide and 48 miles long, almost as large as the state of Rhode Island — broke off the Larsen Ice Shelf in the Antarctic Peninsula. More than this, the whole Ice Shelf is crumbling. Rudolfo Del Valle, director of geoscience at the Argentine Antarctic Institute, told *Newsweek* that it "looked liked polystyrene that had been broken by a little boy." Such reports simply cannot be ignored. Combined with other recently reported evidence from NASA's Upper Atmosphere Research Satellite which prove — according to *National Wildlife* magazine — that "chemicals generated by human activity cause the ozone hole . . . over the Antarctic," they are ominous signs for our future.

Now I'm what you might call a "country mouse." Living in the outdoors, and loving such activities as hiking, camping, fishing, and hunting for as long as I can remember, it's not hard for me to have a great deal of concern for the environment. But you can be a "city mouse," and still like to breathe clean air and drink good water and not have to worry about the warm sun on your skin. So all of us have a lot at stake here. Today I want to share what I've learned about the greenhouse effect and its causes. We need to be concerned, first, about the loss of woodlands, second, about industrial emissions, and third, about overall spectacular increases in world energy consumption.

Let's begin by understanding more about the greenhouse effect. According to *Science News* of September 1994, it is characterized by a high concentration of carbon dioxide in the atmosphere. Each year five tons of carbon are pumped into the atmosphere for each man, woman, and child in the United States. You heard me right: *that's five tons for each and every one of us!* In 1987 the level of carbon dioxide soared to a record high level. By the way, 1987 was the second hottest year on record — 1988 was the hottest year on record. More recently, the summer of 1993 brought record-breaking heat waves and the winter of 1991–92 was the warmest winter in at least 97 years, according to the National Weather Service. In fact, *the nine warmest years in this century have all occurred since 1980!* This is carrying "toasty" a bit too far.

great deal of documentation to defend the validity of information. To keep the speech from being too technical, the speaker ties it to more familiar symbols, such as "mother earth," and to practical lessons for the audience, such as the wisdom (or lack thereof) of investing in beach real estate.

The speaker's direct appeal to listeners' concern for themselves and their offspring might have greater impact if an example or narrative was used.

The use of stylistic touches are important: the phrase "putting the heat on Mother Nature" is apt, and the comparison to a "football field" helps bring the magnitude of the problem into focus. Active verbs like "spew" create ugly pictures in listeners' minds.

The speaker's struggle to bring this technical subject home to listeners makes this speech interesting to analyze for its use of style. Note the dramatic image that compares people to smokestacks, and the analogy to the movie, "Fatal Attraction." There are also clever puns, such as "paying through the nose." We shall discuss such factors in more detail in Chapter 10.

According to Anne Douglas, deputy project director of NASA, the warming effect comes from carbon pollutants which are punching a hole in the ozone layer. Carbon pollutants such as chlorofluorocarbons — CFCs as they are called — act like an atmospheric Pac-Man devouring the ozone shield. This ozone hole reduces the earth's ability to protect us from ultraviolet radiation. If this problem is not corrected, mother earth won't seem quite so motherly.

For instance: There could be dramatic climate changes causing widespread drought in the middle of continents. There could be dangerous and costly increases in the frequency and severity of storms. There could be floods from rising sea levels that might destroy coastal cities and small islands. If even a tenth of Antarctica's ice melts, sea levels would rise 12 to 30 feet. Folks, think twice before you invest in real estate at the seashore. According to *Newsweek* of April 3, 1995, the Caribbean nation Trinidad and Tobago even fears it could turn into a new Atlantis.

Beyond the spectacular effects on the environment, there could be serious health problems as well. These are up-close-and-personal problems for you, more so for your children, even more so for your grandchildren. Skin cancers could increase as much as 26 percent if ozone levels drop by 10 percent. There could be a similar dramatic increase in the number of cataracts. Even our immune systems could be damaged, creating a new problem that could dwarf even the AIDS epidemic. If we don't change the trajectory we're on, if we don't intervene to modify the causes of the greenhouse effect, then all these health problems will result from the increased exposure to ultraviolet radiation.

So what are the causes? Let's examine them, one by one. The first is the loss of woodlands that convert carbon dioxide into oxygen. Without trees to make this conversion, the carbon pollutants escape into the ozone layer. But we are literally putting the heat on Mother Nature to make more room for humans and their activities. One football-field-sized area of forest is lost every second from cutting or burning. The burning of forests further increases the amount of carbon dioxide in the atmosphere because of the smoke that is produced. Forest loss occurs in the rain forests in Cental and South America where teak and mahogany are logged for furniture and houses. It also occurs in the national forests in the United States which are logged by timber companies for use in construction. Much of this native American wood is shipped overseas. Forest loss also comes when land is cleared for development.

An even greater cause of the greenhouse effect is industrial emissions. Here the picture is dramatic — and not very encouraging. The burning of wood, coal, and oil releases large amounts of carbon dioxide into the atmosphere. Industrial refrigeration and air conditioning units add their foul contribution. Nitrogen oxides are spewed out of vehicle exhausts and smokestacks. These industrial contaminants account for more than 20 percent of our air pollution. And this kind of pollution continues to grow! Every day, more and more third world nations become more and more industrialized, and use more and more fuel. But guess what? According to an in-depth report in *Newsweek* in June 1992, we Americans are the worst offenders. We have only 5 percent of the world's population, but we use 26 percent of the world's oil, release 26 percent of the world's nitrogen oxide, and produce 22 percent of the world's carbon dioxide emissions. It's time we did something about it!

All of which leads us to the last major cause of the greenhouse effect, which is also the most important. *Personal energy consumption is the single largest cause of the greenhouse effect.* It's as though each of us was a smokestack, fouling the air. We consume oxygen and emit carbon dioxide into the atmosphere. The more of us there are, especially in industrialized countries, the more energy we consume. And here's another point: as living standards rise around the world, people develop greater expectations — they want to live the good life. One unfortunate result of these expectations is that people use even more energy. If you multiply more people times rising expectations, you can see what this means for energy consumption — and for the greenhouse effect!

According to the National Issues Forums' report, *The Environment at Risk*, fossil fuel use doubled from 1950 to 1990. And according to the U.S. Department of Energy, 90 percent of America's energy consumption comes from fossil fuels. Fossil fuels, such as gas and oil and electricity generated from power plants, heat and cool our homes and provide our transportation. Transportation-related energy use accounts for approximately half of all air pollution in our country. During the summer of 1988 the amount of automotive smog increased to twice its 1987 level in many Eastern states. Moreover, the amount of fuel we use for transportation is growing day by day. In 1950 there were 40 million cars in the U.S. Today there are more than 140 million cars in America. The great American love affair with the car continues, even though this is a "fatal attraction." The American Lung Association has estimated that we spend about $40 billion a year in health care costs related to air pollution. Environmental damage from air pollution costs us another $60 to $100 billion a year. In short, we have to pay through the nose for the problems we create by driving too much and keeping our houses too hot in the winter and too cold in the summer.

In conclusion, if you want to know why we have a greenhouse effect, listen for the falling trees, watch the industrial smokestacks darkening the sky, and smell the exhaust fumes we are pumping into the air. The greenhouse effect is a monster we all are creating. And if we don't stop, we and our children face more and more drastic climate changes and serious health problems.

Vice President Al Gore used the following story to illustrate how the greenhouse effect can sneak up on us. In an address to the National Academy of Sciences, he said, "If dropped into a pot of boiling water, a frog will quickly jump out. But if the same frog is put into a pot and the water is slowly heated, the frog will stay put until boiled alive. So it is with pollution . . . If we do not wake up to the slow heating of our environment, we may jump too late." The more we know about this problem, and the better we understand it, the more likely we are to jump and the less likely we are to be boiled alive.

PART 3

Developing Presentation Skills

CHAPTER 9

Presentation Aids

■ appreciate the advantages of using presentation aids.
■ understand what types of presentation aids work best in different situations.
■ learn how to use presentation aids.
■ plan, design, and prepare presentation aids.

Seeing . . . , most
of all the senses,
makes us know and
brings to light
many differences
between things.
— Aristotle

During your summer vacations you run a small landscaping business. Most of your work has come from neighbors who just want you to mow their grass and carry off trash. This summer you want to expand your operations. You posted notices on community bulletin boards to attract new business. Today you got a call from a small company inviting you to develop a landscape plan for its property and to present it next week at the company's office. This is your big chance to do something you can be proud of and possibly to make enough money to pay your tuition and buy books next fall. You know you will be competing with other, better established landscaping companies.

If you want to have a shot at winning the contract, you will need some well designed presentation aids as you introduce your plan. You could use a model of the property that shows the building and the proposed landscaping. If that isn't feasible, you could use large pictures that demonstrate your landscaping plan for the property. You might want to have these made into slides that you can show as you speak. Or, if you have access to the proper equipment both for preparing and presenting your visual aids, you may wish to make a computer-assisted presentation. Regardless of the method you choose, without presentation aids you won't be able to hold your own against the competition.

U sing presentation aids is not new either to the field of public speaking or even to beginning speakers. Although Columbus did not have access to slides or videos, you can be fairly certain that he spread out a few maps or charts before Queen Isabella to convince her to fund his explorations. Similarly, the first "public speech" you ever gave probably involved the use of a visual aid for "show and tell." You may have brought an object that you were going to talk about — a new toy, something you made, the family pet. The visual aid helped you explain or describe your subject. Presentation aids in later speech situations may go beyond "show and tell" in sophistication, but still serve much the same purpose.

In our world of accelerating technology the ways of generating and using presentation aids are multiplying rapidly. When we wrote the first and second editions of this book, most presentation aids were visual aids, so we concentrated on teaching students how to prepare charts, graphs, maps, and posters. By the third edition we were talking about the possibility of generating such materials with a personal computer. Although the ability to produce and use such traditional visual aids still remains important, technological advances are moving presentation aids into the realm of multimedia. A September 1994 article in *Sales and Marketing Management* suggests that we are at the "beginning of a complete transformation in the way we communicate information on a one-to-one and one-to-many basis."[1] In this chapter we describe the kinds of presentation aids that can be used in speeches, identify the ways in which they can be presented, offer suggestions for preparing them, and present guidelines for their use.

USES AND ADVANTAGES OF PRESENTATION AIDS

Presentation aids give your audience direct sensory contact with your speech. They are useful because words are essentially abstract. Words represent objects and ideas, but they are not the objects and ideas they represent. To understand words, listeners must translate them into mental images, a process that is sometimes difficult and confusing. Imagine how hard it would be to describe through words alone the carburetor system of a car. If described in charts or diagrams, it would still be difficult for many of us to comprehend. It requires both words *and* presentation aids to explain some topics. Presentation aids can help speeches in the following ways:

1. *Presentation aids enhance understanding.* Sometimes presentation aids work better than words to convey meaning. It is easier to give directions when you can trace the route on a map as you describe it. Similarly, if you are comparing the qualities of cassette tapes and CDs, it is more effective to let audiences actually **hear** the differences.

2. *Presentation aids add authenticity.* When you show listeners what you are talking about, you do more than just clarify your message. You authenticate it. You demonstrate that it does indeed exist. This type of sup-

Presentation aids can enhance understanding. Multimedia presentations are frequently used in organizational settings.

port is useful in both informative and persuasive speeches. Research confirms that presentational materials enhance both learning and attitude change.[2] When you can show your audience some aspect of the problem you are talking about, listeners are more likely to accept your solution.

3. *Presentation aids add variety.* Too much of a good thing, even a well-designed fabric of words, can get tiresome. The use of presentation aids at critical points in a speech provides variety. This helps sustain audience interest and attention.

4. *Presentation aids may improve your delivery skills.* Presentation aids force you to move about as you give your speech. It gets you away from the "stand behind the lectern/talking head" mode of presentation that audiences often find boring. Movement energizes your speech. Moreover, if you have problems with "stage fright," purposeful movement such as pointing out the important features of a model gives you a constructive way to use excess energy and redirects your attention from yourself to objects outside yourself.

5. *Presentation aids help your speech have lasting impact.* Presentation aids are easier to remember than words because they are more concrete. The face of a hungry child shown in a photograph may stick in your mind and make you more likely to contribute to a charitable organization. Or you may remember the bright red flags on a map that pinpoint dangerous places better than just the place names.

6. *A neat, attractively designed presentation aid enhances your credibility.* It tells the audience that you put extra effort into preparing your speech. Speakers who use presentation aids are judged more professional, better

prepared, clearer, more credible, more interesting, more concise, and more persuasive than speakers who do not use aids.[3]

Presentation aids are almost mandatory in organizational settings.[4] A wide array of organizations use them in public relations presentations, budget meetings, training and development, and employee orientation programs.[5] They can be seen on the floors of the House and Senate and in the courtrooms of America.[6] Even when meetings are called on short notice, presentation aids such as handouts or transparencies are frequently used.[7] In such business and professional settings, audiences *expect* presentation aids as a matter of course. If you don't have them, you risk disappointing your listeners.

KINDS OF PRESENTATION AIDS

The number and kinds of presentation aids are limited only by your imagination. We shall examine some of the more frequently used types and the speech situations in which they are most helpful and most relevant.

People

People can function as presentation aids. As the speaker, you cannot avoid being a presentation aid for your own speech.[8] Your body, grooming, actions, gestures, voice, facial expressions, and demeanor always provide an added dimension to your speech. Use these factors to help convey your message.

What you wear can function as a presentation aid. If you will be talking about camping and wilderness adventures, blue jeans, a flannel shirt, and hiking boots might be appropriate attire for your speech. What you wear, however, should not be more interesting than what you say. Here, as in all other cases, presentation aids should enhance, not overshadow, your verbal message. We discuss personal appearance in more detail in Chapter 11.

You can also use other people as presentation aids. Neomal Abyskera used two of his classmates to illustrate the line-up positions in the game of rugger as played in his native Sri Lanka. At the appropriate time, Neomal said, "Peter and Jeffrey will show you how the opposing team members line up." While his classmates demonstrated the arm-locked shoulder grip position, Neomal briefly explained when and why the position was assumed. This demonstration was more understandable than if he had tried to describe the position verbally or drawn it on posterboard with stick figures.

If you plan to have classmates act as a presentation aid, be sure that they really want to help you and that they will not distract attention from your speech. Rehearse your presentation with them until all goes smoothly. When you give your speech, have them sit in the front row so that as quickly as possible they can come forward and then sit down again when their part is completed.

Objects and Models

Nothing beats being able to point to exactly what you are talking about. But some objects — those that are extremely large or very small, or those that are exceptionally valuable — simply do not lend themselves for use as presentation aids in speeches. In such cases, reduced or enlarged models may be a better option.

Objects.   If you are speaking about something that can be carried easily to class and that listeners in the back of the room can see without straining, you may decide to use the object itself as a presentation aid. Ideally, it should also be small enough to be kept out of sight until you are ready to use it. If you display the object throughout your speech, you may be upstaged by it. If it is unusual, your listeners may find their attention diverted to it rather than to what you are saying.

One of our students brought six different objects to class to illustrate an informative speech on the Montessori method of preschool education. When it was her turn to speak, she lined up the objects in front of the lectern. They were such a distraction that a student in the front row actually scooted his chair closer to the desk and picked up one of the objects to examine it. She then had to stop and ask him to put it back. She could have

Be careful about the types of objects you select for use as presentation aids. Seeing a snake may upset the audience so much that they can't effectively listen to your message.

handled this situation more effectively by concealing the objects and bringing them forth one at a time.

Inanimate objects make better presentation aids than living things, which you cannot always control. We once had a student bring a six-week-old puppy to use in a speech on caring for young animals. At the beginning of her speech, she removed the lectern from the speaker's table, spread some newspapers on it, and placed the puppy on the table. We are sure you have already guessed what happened. The first thing the puppy did was wet on the papers (including her note cards, which she had put down on the table while trying to control the puppy). The first thing the audience did was giggle. From there it was all downhill. The puppy squirmed and tried to jump on the speaker while yipping and barking throughout the speech. The speaker was totally upstaged by her presentation aid. When this fiasco was over, we asked her why she had brought the puppy to class. She said she thought that because she was talking about young animals, it would be "nice to bring one along."

Another problem arises when using dangerous, illegal, or potentially offensive objects as presentation aids. Such objects might include guns, drugs, or pornography. One of our students used a realistic-looking model of a semiautomatic weapon, which he pulled from beneath the lectern, during the introduction of a speech on gun control. The effect was both dramatic and frightening. Several audience members became quite upset and found it hard to concentrate on his message. Never create these kinds of problems for yourself with a presentation aid! If you have any questions about the appropriateness of an object, check with your instructor.

Objects are frequently used in "how-to" speeches. Indeed, such speeches often cannot succeed without presentation aids. An engaging example of this type of use occurred near Halloween as part of a speech on jack-o'-lanterns, both how to make them and the folklore behind them. The speaker demonstrated how to draw the face on a pumpkin with a magic marker and how to make a beveled cut around the stem so that the top wouldn't fall in. As she was showing her listeners how to do these things, she was also telling stories of the ancient myths surrounding jack-o'-lanterns. Her presentation aid and her words helped each other: the demonstration enlivened her speech, and the stories gave the demonstration depth and meaning. As she came to her closing remarks, she reached inside the lectern and produced a finished jack-o'-lantern, complete with a lighted candle. The effect was memorable.

Models. When an object is too large to carry, too small to be easily seen, very rare, expensive, fragile, or simply unavailable, a model, or scale-sized replica of the object, can serve as a presentation aid. One advantage of a model is that you can provide a cross section or cutaway of the object to show its interior.

George Stacey brought a slightly smaller than life-size model of a person to demonstrate cardiopulmonary resuscitation (CPR). The model folded into a suitcase, so that it could be kept out of sight when not in use. When using a model as a presentation aid, be sure that it is truly representative. It should be constructed to scale, maintaining the proper proportions between parts. The model should also be large enough for all listeners to see from their seats. Any presentation aid that the audience must strain to see will be more of a distraction than a help.

Graphics

Graphics or visual representations of information include sketches, maps, graphs, charts, or textual graphics. Graphics used in speeches may differ from graphics designed for the print media. Because graphics will be displayed for only a short time as you present a speech, they must be immediately understandable.[9] They must be more simple than graphics designed for print, which readers can study at their leisure. Each presentation aid should address only one idea, and there must be a clear focus on that idea. Because presentation aids will be viewed from a distance the colors should be intense and should contrast sharply so that listeners can spot differences easily. Any print on the graphic should stand out sharply from the background so that it can be read without strain. We will cover such considerations more fully in our section on "Preparing Presentation Aids" later in this chapter.

Sketches.   Sketches or diagrams are simplified representations of what you are talking about. Mark Peterson used a sketch to illustrate a speech on buying a bicycle. He placed a poster board containing his sketch of a bicycle on the ledge of the chalkboard (blank side to the audience) before he began his speech. As Mark talked about making bar-to-pedal and seat-to-handlebar measurements, he said, "Let me show you how to take some basic measurements," as he turned the poster around. When he finished his demonstration, he turned the poster board to its blank side so that it would not be a distraction during the rest of his speech.

Maps.   Commercially prepared maps contain too much detail to serve as presentation aids. Much of this detail may be irrelevant to your speech. The best maps are those that you make specifically for your speech so that they are large, simple, relevant to your purpose, and uncluttered. Maps are particularly useful for speeches based on spatial relationships.

The map in Figure 9.1 was used to indicate the distance and routes between major attractions at Yellowstone National Park. Having such a map helps the audience put locations and distances into perspective. Stephen Huff used a map to help his listeners see where a series of earthquakes occurred along the New Madrid Fault and to understand how a recurrence of such earthquakes might endanger them (see his speech and presentation aids at the end of Chapter 12).

How well a map works as a presentation aid depends on how well you can integrate it into your presentation. Elizabeth Walling used a map of the wilderness canoe area in northern Minnesota to familiarize her Memphis

FIGURE 9.1

Map: Yellowstone
Park

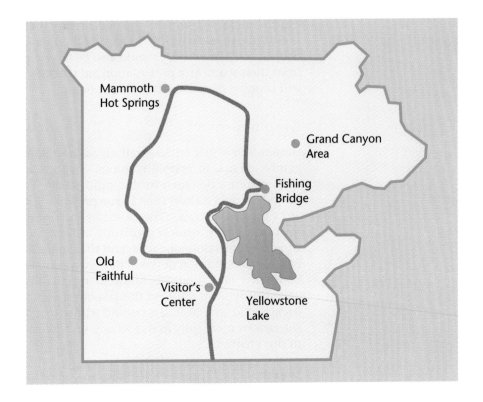

audience with that area. She made a double-sided poster that she was able
to keep hidden behind the speaker's table until she was ready for it. On one
side she highlighted the wilderness canoe area on an outline map of northern Minnesota, pointing out various places of interest to canoers. To illustrate how large the area is, Elizabeth said, "Let me put this in a familiar
context for you." She then turned the poster over, revealing an outline
map of western Tennessee on which she had superimposed the wilderness
area. At a glance we could see that this area would extend from Memphis to
past Jackson, some eighty miles away. By using maps this way, she created a
striking visual comparison. The same type of effect could be obtained by
overlaying transparencies.

Graphs. Mrs. Robert A. Taft once commented, "I always find that statistics are hard to swallow and impossible to digest. The only one I can ever
remember is that if all the people who go to sleep in church were laid end
to end, they would be a lot more comfortable."[10] Many people share Mrs.
Taft's feelings about statistics. As we noted in Chapter 6, masses of numbers presented orally may be confusing or even overwhelming. A well-
designed graph can help make statistical information easier for listeners to
comprehend.

A **pie graph,** or circle graph, shows the size of a subject's parts in relation to each other and to the whole. The circle, or "pie," represents the

FIGURE 9.2

Pie Graph of
Murderer-Victim
Relationships

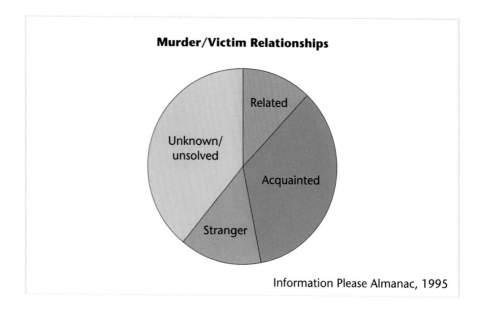

whole, and the segments, or "slices," represent the parts. The pie graph in Figure 9.2 shows the relationships between murderers and victims in the United States in 1992.[11] The most effective pie graphs have five or fewer categories.[12] Too many divisions of the pie make the graph cluttered and difficult to read. The pie graph of religious affiliation shown in Figure 9.3 has too many categories to be used effectively in an oral presentation.

A **bar graph** shows comparisons and contrasts between two or more items or groups. Bar graphs are easy to understand because each item can be readily compared with every other item on the graph. Bar graphs also have a dramatic visual impact. Figure 9.4 is a bar graph illustrating units of

FIGURE 9.3

Religious Affiliations
in the United States

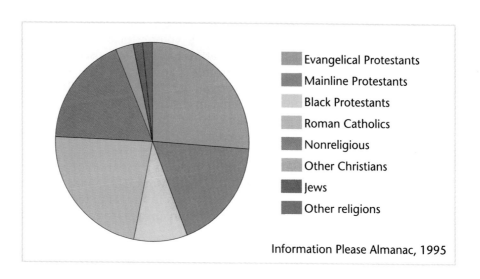

FIGURE 9.4

Bar Graph Indicating Units of Blood Donated by College Classes

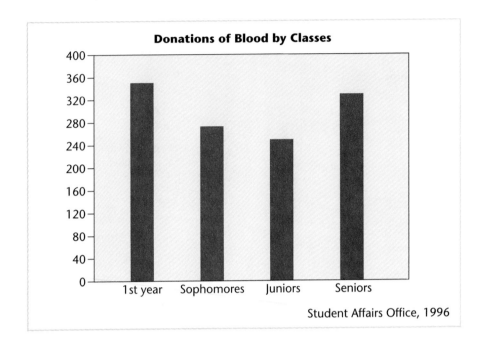

blood donated by undergraduates by class on a certain campus during a recent year.

A **line graph** demonstrates changes across time and is especially useful for indicating trends of growth or decline. Figure 9.5 shows the increases in Olympic shot-put distances for men and women from 1948 to 1988. The upward-sloping lines confirm the dramatic increases in the distances of both men and women across time. But this example also serves as a caution: because men and women throw different weights (16 pounds for men, 8 pounds, 13 ounces for women), you could not conclude from this graph that women have become stronger or more skilled than men in absolute terms. You must not let the dramatic pictorial qualities of presentation aids overrule your critical judgment and tempt you into logical fallacies or unethical claims. We discuss such flaws of reasoning further as we proceed in this chapter and later in Chapter 14.

Whenever you plot more than one line on a graph, you must be certain that listeners can distinguish the lines. Use different colors to designate specific items. Using different colors is preferable to labeling the lines because they keep the graph from becoming cluttered. Never try to plot more than three lines on a graph.

A **mountain graph** is a variation of a line graph that uses different colors to fill in the areas. Mountain graphs are especially effective when there are extreme variations in the data. Figure 9.6 is a line graph charting the amount of snowfall in an area from 1980 through 1996.

Charts.   Charts provide convenient visual summaries of processes and relationships that are not in themselves visible. However, they are difficult to

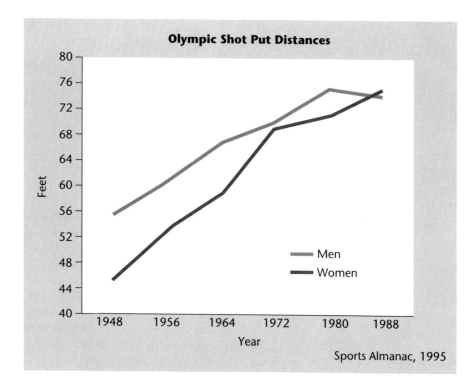

Sports Almanac, 1995

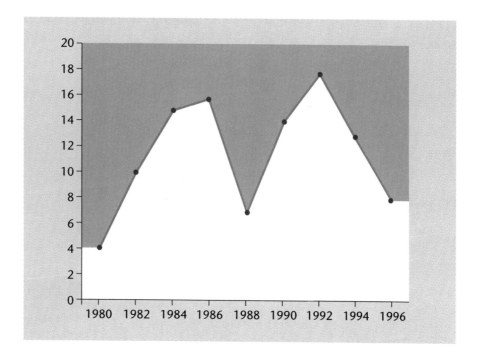

use as presentation aids in speeches because they must often be oversimplified to keep them from being cluttered and distracting. The more frequently used type of chart is a flow chart.

Flow charts detail the steps in a process. The lines and arrows in a flow chart indicate what steps occur simultaneously and what steps occur sequentially. In Chapter 5 we used a flow chart to illustrate the major steps in the preparation of a speech (see Figure 5.1 on page 000). Flow charts are also used to show power and responsibility relationships, such as who reports to whom in an organization. Organizational flow charts usually place the most powerful office or person at the top of the chart, the next most powerful offices or people directly underneath, down through the least powerful offices or people.

One major problem that often arises when using charts in oral presentations is that you may be tempted to load them with too much information. If they become too complex and "busy," they may compete with you for attention or confuse listeners. One way around this problem is to use **sequence charts**, which are presented in succession to show the different stages or phases of a process. Sequence charts create suspense as the audience anticipates what the next chart will reveal. For example, you might choose to illustrate information on the awarding of college degrees by gender in a series of charts. On these charts you could use **pictographs**, which are visually symbolic representations. Figure 9.7 reveals the first and last charts in a series showing degrees by gender across the years. The first chart in Figure 9.7 indicates the figure of a man three times larger than the figure of a woman, representing the 3:1 ratio in earned degrees during 1950. The second chart in Figure 9.7 shows larger pictographs for each gender, indi-

FIGURE 9.7
Sequence Chart

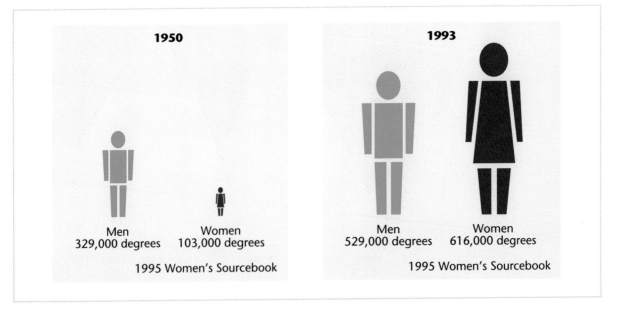

1950

Men
329,000 degrees

Women
103,000 degrees

1995 Women's Sourcebook

1993

Men
529,000 degrees

Women
616,000 degrees

1995 Women's Sourcebook

cating the overall increase of college degrees awarded to both men and women in 1993. It also reveals that the number of degrees awarded to women surpassed those awarded to men. Intermediate charts for decade years could show the more gradual changes in the relative sizes of these figures.

Textual Graphics.   **Textual graphics** are lists of phrases, words, or numbers. Unfamiliar material is clearer and easier for listeners to remember when they can both hear and see the message. Presenting the key words in a message visually can help an audience follow a complicated speech more easily. For example, as you describe a process, you might write on a flipchart or chalkboard the number "1" and by it a key word or phrase, then "2" and "3" as you discuss those ideas. That way you would guide your audience to the main points of your speech. You can present textual graphics using poster board, the chalkboard, transparencies, slides, or handouts.

The most frequently used textual graphics contain **bulleted lists** of information such as that seen in the computer-generated slide shown in Figure 9.8. When you make a bulleted list, begin with a headline or title, then indent and arrange the material under it. Keep the graphic simple. Use intense colors for contrast. Have no more than six lines of information and no more than six words to a line.[13]

Another frequently used type of textual graphic presents an **acronym** composed of the initial letters of words to implant an idea in your audi-

FIGURE 9.8
Bulleted List

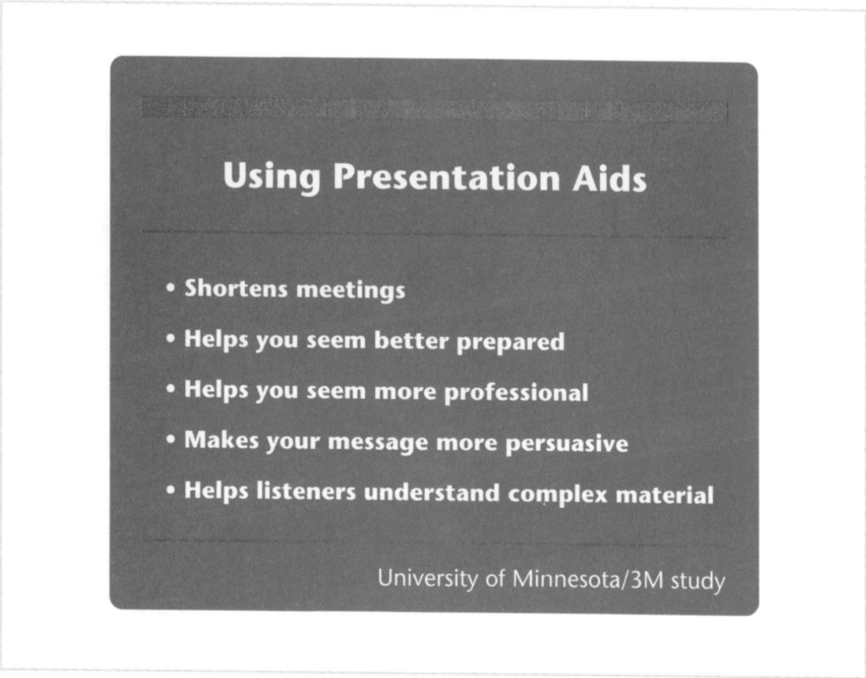

Using Presentation Aids

- Shortens meetings
- Helps you seem better prepared
- Helps you seem more professional
- Makes your message more persuasive
- Helps listeners understand complex material

University of Minnesota/3M study

ence's mind and help them remember your message. The acronym can also help you remember the order of ideas as you present your speech. The computer-generated transparency shown in Figure 9.9 uses the acronym EMILY in a persuasive speech urging students to begin saving early for retirement. When preparing such a graphic, use the acronym as a title, then list the words under it. Make the first letters of the words stand out through size and/or color.

Textual graphics may also be used to present numerical information instead of, or in addition to, the other types of charts discussed earlier in this chapter. When you use a textual graphic to present columns of numbers or other information as a poster, transparency, or slide, you should keep it very simple. Have only two or three columns and no more than five rows of data. Textual graphics designed for handouts can contain more information, but not so much that they will compete with your words for attention. Figure 9.10 illustrates a complicated textual graphic that would be inappropriate for a poster, transparency, or slide. Figure 9.11 shows the same material adapted for such media.

Note that the preferred figure is not only easier to understand but also focuses on the *point* of the display far more effectively.

Pictures

The old Chinese proverb that a picture is worth a thousand words is not always true in public speaking. Pictures or photographs have both ad-

FIGURE 9.9
Acronym Textual Graphic

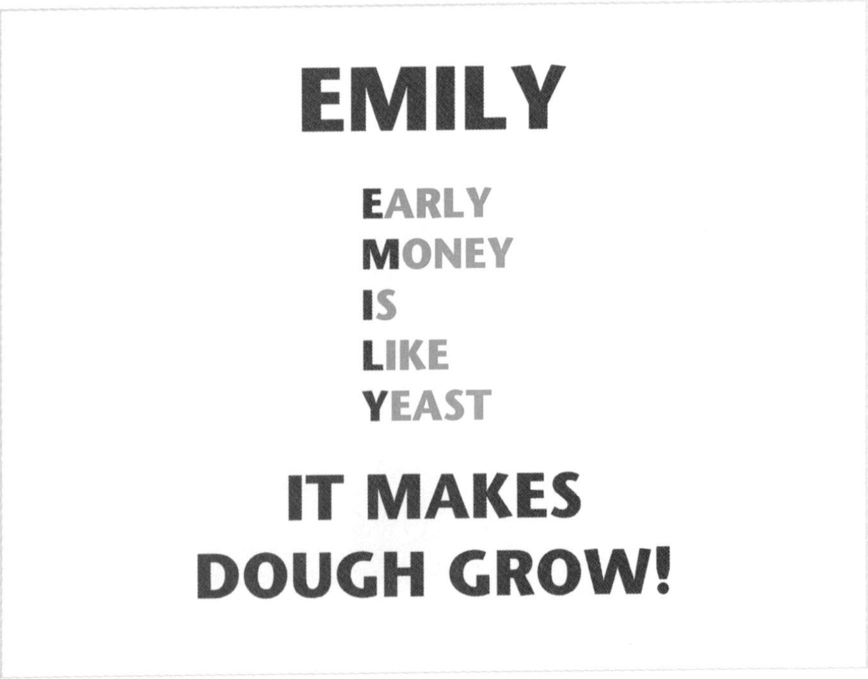

EMILY

EARLY
MONEY
IS
LIKE
YEAST

IT MAKES DOUGH GROW!

FIGURE 9.10

Overly Complicated Textual Graphic

THE MIRACLE OF COMPOUNDING

Here's what happens to $1,000 in an account earning 8 percent a year, compounded annually.

End of Year	Amount	End of Year	Amount
1	$1,080	11	$2,332
2	$1,166	12	$2,518
3	$1,259	13	$2,720
4	$1,360	14	$2,937
5	$1,469	15	$3,172
6	$1,587	16	$3,426
7	$1,714	17	$3,700
8	$1,851	18	$3,996
9	$1,999	19	$4,316
10	$2,159	20	$4,661

Source: Berger, *Feathering Your Nest.* 1993.

vantages and disadvantages. On the plus side, a good photograph can authenticate a point in a speech in a way that words alone cannot. It can make a situation seem more vivid and realistic. For instance, if you were trying to describe the devastation caused by a flood, tornado, or hurricane, photographs could be quite useful.

On the negative side, photographs and pictures frequently include distracting details that are not relevant to your message. Their vividness can also be a disadvantage, especially when speakers rely on them too heavily to make a point, forgetting that spoken words should be the primary means of communication in a speech. Pictures should reinforce, not replace, the speaker's words. If the pictures are too vivid or depict traumatic incidents, they can be very disturbing to the audience. To illustrate her speech concerning child abuse, a student in one of our classes who was also a paramedic showed pictures of child abuse victims that had been taken in a hospital emergency room. Some members of the audience became so upset that they were not able to concentrate on her message.

The major problem with using pictures is their size. A picture must be large enough for everyone in the room to see, or it is useless as a presentation aid. One of our students tried to illustrate a speech on baseball by showing the audience pictures from a book. He marked the pages that contained pictures he wanted to show with paper clips, so that he could open directly to them. Unfortunately, the order of pictures in the book did not match the order of ideas in his speech, so he kept opening to the wrong pages. The pictures in the book also were too small to be seen except by

FIGURE 9.11
Simplified Textual
Graphic

INVESTMENT GROWTH
$1,000 – 8%

5 years	$1,469
10 years	$2,159
15 years	$3,172
20 years	$4,666

Berger, *Feathering Your Nest*, 1995

people in the front row. This presentation aid made his speech less effective and damaged his ethos. Finally, it is hard to resist the temptation to circulate photographs among the audience as you give your speech. The pictures then compete with your words for attention.

Despite their limitations, pictures can work well if they are carefully chosen, controlled, and enlarged. They should be selected for their relevance to your speech. They should be controlled just as you control charts, graphs, and maps — revealed only when they illustrate the point you are making and then put away. Color copiers can now make inexpensive eleven-by-seventeen-inch enlargements from snapshots. These are probably the minimally acceptable size for most classroom speeches. Mount them on poster board for ease of presentation. Museum prints or commercial posters are made to be seen from a distance and are usually large enough to use as presentation aids. In his speech describing an extended camping trip, Michael McDonald used a print of Thomas Moran's painting of the Green River in the American West to convey his feelings about that part of the country. Paintings can often create a mood or feeling, especially when used in combination with eloquent words. You can also use pictures that are made into slides or shown in videotapes or computerized presentations.

PRESENTATION MEDIA

Many media are available for your presentation aids. Speakers most frequently use flip charts, poster boards, handouts, chalk and marker boards, projections, videotapes, and audiotapes. Most corporate conference rooms, school classrooms, and public meeting places are equipped to handle many, if not all, of these forms of presentation aids. In addition, computerized multimedia presentations that can incorporate slides, videotapes, and sound are increasingly being heard and seen in organizational and educational settings.[14]

Flip Chart

A flip chart is a large, unlined tablet. Most flip charts are newsprint pads that measure about two feet wide by three feet high. They are placed on an easel so that pages can be flipped over the top when you are done with them. Flip charts are convenient, inexpensive, and adaptable to most speech settings. They are quite helpful when you want to present a series of visual aids. Business presentations, decision-making groups, and organizational training sessions frequently use flip charts.

With a flip chart you can produce a striking presentation aid because wide-tipped felt markers are available in vivid colors. Because flip charts are portable, you can prepare your materials before your speech. Flip charts can also be used spontaneously should the need arise. This makes them especially useful when subjects come up unpredictably in a meeting that must be explored visually or illustrated before they can be analyzed and understood. Just be certain that you have blank pages in the pad for this purpose and that you bring felt markers.

When preparing presentation aid materials on a flip chart, try to keep each page as simple as possible. Write on every other page because the felt-marker ink may bleed through the paper. Back each page of prepared material with a blank page joined at the bottom with small paper clips. Leave the first page of the flip chart blank so that your written materials are hidden from view until you are ready to flip over the blank page and reveal your message or drawing.

Susan Larson used flip charts effectively to illustrate a speech on nautical navigation. On her first page she used the acronym POSH (Port Out Starboard Home) as a device for demonstrating how to navigate a boat through river channel markers. Susan kept her writing to a minimum so that the material stood out clearly and emphatically. Had she tried to write out the message "Keep the marker buoys to your left (port) as you leave the marina and to your right (starboard) coming home," the flip-chart page would have looked cluttered.

Susan's second and third flip-chart sheets contained color drawings of Coast Guard navigation markers found in the inland waterways. Her fourth sheet, illustrated in Figure 9.12, was a simplified drawing of a navigational chart, showing the placement of channel markers. As she talked, Susan drew the path a boat would have to navigate between the markers, adding an element of spontaneity to her use of this visual aid. The flip-chart technique was less cumbersome than trying to handle four separate posters.

FIGURE 9.12

Flip Chart Used to
Illustrate the Course
a Boat Should Follow
Returning to Home
Port

Poster Board

When you wish to make just one or two highly polished presentation aids or when flip charts are not feasible, poster board can come to your rescue. Using posterboard, you can prepare a professional-looking presentation aid with a minimal investment, even if you are not artistic. Most campus bookstores can provide the materials you need to turn out a polished product: the poster board, a straightedge or ruler, a compass, felt markers, stencils, and stick-on or transfer letters in a variety of colors and sizes. This basic equipment will enable you to prepare sketches, simplified maps, and charts or graphs.

A poster board will not stand by itself, even on the ledge of the chalkboard. Be sure not to roll up your posterboard and secure it with a rubber band to make it easy to carry to class. If you do this you will end up with a crescent moon-shaped poster that is impossible to display effectively. Plan how you will display your poster board at strategic moments in your speech. You may use an easel if one is available, tape it to the chalkboard, or tack it to the cork border on top of the chalkboard. As you make your presentation, be sure to conceal your poster until you need it. Once you are finished with it, get it out of sight. Be sure to rehearse this procedure in advance so it doesn't become a problem while you are speaking. If your materials are simple or if your presentation is being videotaped (see Chapter 11), you may want to cut a large poster board to a smaller size to make it easier to handle. Just be certain that it can be seen by everyone in your audience.

To be certain that things go smoothly, try to practice where you will be giving your speech. Develop effective transitions that introduce the presentation aid ("Let's see how a visual model of these relationships might look") and conclude it ("Now that we've seen a representation of these relationships, let's consider their consequences"). As you practice your presentation, stand to the side of the poster, facing your imaginary audience as much as possible while referring to your aid. Point to each feature as you speak about it. If you cannot get into the classroom for practice, come early on the day of your speech to be sure you can position the poster board just as you want it. Bring masking tape and thumbtacks in case you should need them.

Handouts

Handouts are useful when your subject is complex, your message contains a lot of statistical information, or when you need to introduce new vocabulary. When the speech is concluded, the handout remains to remind listeners of your message.

There is one serious drawback to handouts — they can distract listeners from what you are saying. If you distribute a handout before your speech, it will compete with you for attention. The audience may decide to read the handout instead of listening to your speech. Therefore, distribute handouts before your speech *only* when it is absolutely necessary for listeners to refer to them as you speak and *only* when you are confident of your ability to command attention. Never distribute handouts during your speech: this is a sure-fire way to divert, confuse, and lose listeners.

Dwight Davidson distributed a handout at the beginning of his speech entitled "Job Trends for the Nineties." Dwight's audience was able to follow him as he introduced and explained the statistical tables in the handout. Without such a visual supplement his listeners might have been lost. George Stacey distributed a handout listing the steps involved in CPR *after* he ended his presentation. By waiting until he was finished he avoided a potential distraction during his speech and also helped his audience remember steps in the procedure. Your decision whether to distribute a handout before or after your speech must be based on a consideration of the nature of the subject, how confident you are of your ability to control attention, and how you want your handout to function.

Chalk and Marker Boards

A chalkboard or plastic marker board (used with broad-tipped markers) is a presentation medium available in almost every corporate conference room or classroom. These boards work well when you want to emphasize certain words or ideas, or clear up something the audience doesn't understand by creating a spontaneous presentation aid.

Writing terms or names on the board calls the audience's attention to their importance and helps your listeners remember them. This is especially important if the word or name is spelled differently from the way it is pronounced. For example, if you mentioned the leader of the underground Christianity movement in China, Lin Xiangao, it would be advisable to write the name on the board. As you turn to the board, you might say, "Let me write this name for you." Print the word or words quickly but legibly as you continue speaking, then immediately regain eye contact with your audience.

A chalk or marker board also is a good audience-adaptation tool. Despite your best preparation, there may be moments when you look at your listeners and realize that some of them have not understood what you have just said. You can respond to this feedback by writing a few words on the board or drawing a simple diagram to help reduce their confusion.

Be careful when using chalk or marker boards. When you write on a board, print the words in large letters so that people in the back of the room can read them without straining. Check the chalkboard before your presentation to be certain that it hasn't been waxed by the cleaning crew and be sure that you have chalk. With a marker board, make certain the markers haven't dried out. Don't let the boards get so cluttered with writing that they distract from your speech. Erase any previous words or drawings on the board before you begin. As a courtesy to later speakers, erase the board when you are finished.

Finally, don't overuse or misuse a chalk or marker board. You should not use these media for anything that will take more than a few seconds to write or draw. When you are writing or drawing you lose contact with your audience. We have all had teachers who talked more to the chalkboard than to the class. Talk to the audience, not to the chalk or marker board. Stand to the side of your drawing or writing and maintain eye contact with your listeners. Never use chalk or marker boards simply because you do not want to take the time to prepare a polished presentation aid.

Overhead Projections and Slides

Overhead projections and slides allow audiences to see graphics or photographs more easily or to look at an outline of your main points while you are making them. They help listeners remain on track during long or complicated presentations. Business speakers often prefer overhead projections and slides to posterboards or flip charts because of their professional quality and adaptability. Most personal computers now come packaged with graphics software for the preparation and presentation of projections and slides. Projections are most useful for audiences of up to 50 people; however, slides presented on large screens are better for larger audiences.[15]

Overhead projections are popular because they are easy to make, inexpensive, and adaptable. Transparency projectors transmit an image from a clear acetate original. You can draw, print, or type your material onto plain paper and convert it to a transparency on a copying machine. Transparencies are also one of the best ways to use computer-generated graphics. You can create transparencies directly through your computer printer. If you have access to a color printer, the transparencies can be professional looking and dramatic. Even with a black-and-white printer, once you have made your transparency, you can add color with markers.

Overhead projections lend themselves easily to your needs. You don't have to darken the room completely for overhead projections, and you can continue to face your audience, maintaining direct contact with them. You can revise a transparency while it is being shown, adding flexibility and spontaneity to your presentation. You can use a pencil as a convenient pointer to direct listeners' attention to features you want to emphasize.

To prepare materials for use as projections you should follow the general guidelines presented earlier for the use of graphics. You should frame your transparencies to avoid glare from light showing around the outside edges of the projection. Frames can be purchased at most copy shops or made from construction paper or posterboard.

When using traditional equipment, such as a carousel projector, you will find that slides are somewhat more difficult to handle in public speeches than transparencies. Often the room has to be darkened, and the illuminated screen becomes the center of attention instead of you. When you arrange slides in a carousel, be sure they are in the proper order and that none of them are upside down. Traditional slides also require specialized equipment to prepare. Today, many personal computers are packaged with software that allows you to prepare and present slide presentations. We will discuss this in greater detail as we discuss computer-assisted presentations.

The major disadvantage of overhead projections and slides is that often you must speak from where your equipment is located. Without remote-control equipment, you have to stand behind or in the middle of the audience to run the projector. The result is that you may be talking to someone's back. If you do not have remote-control equipment, your best solution may be to have a classmate change the projections or slides on cue. You will need to practice with this assistant to coordinate the showing of the projections with your words.

If you decide to use overheads or slides, check the equipment ahead of time and become familiar with its operation. You may need a long extension cord to position your equipment where you want it. Check the location of electrical outlets in advance, and be sure the cord fits. Practice using the equipment as you rehearse your speech. In some machines, you must insert slides or transparencies upside down. Be certain you have them in correctly before you make your presentation. Also, be sure you have a spare light bulb for the machine. An upside-down slide or a burned-out light bulb has ruined many a presentation. Finally, don't use too many slides or transparencies in a short speech. A presentation aid should do just that — *aid* your speech, not compete with it or replace it.

Videotapes and Audiotapes

Videotapes and audiotapes can authenticate a speech and add variety to your presentation. Today's audiences, described by Roger Williams, senior writer for *Newsweek Interactive,* as "the first generation that has never watched television without a remote control," may regard such presentation aids as essential to a polished presentation.[16] Videos are especially useful for transporting the audience to distant, dangerous, or otherwise unavailable locations.[17] Although you could verbally describe the scenic wonders of the Grand Canyon, you could reinforce your word-pictures with actual photos of the site or, better still, with living scenes from a videotape. An effective speaker uses video clips for support, but still supplies "the live human touch needed to help move an audience of one, or of hundreds, to the desired conclusion or action."[18]

Using videotapes presents some special problems. Moving images attract more attention than the spoken word, so they can easily upstage you. Moreover, a videotape segment must be carefully cued to begin and end precisely and should be edited so that the splices blend without annoying visual or auditory static. Editing videotapes takes special skill and equipment. Finally, videotapes can be difficult to work into a short speech without consuming all of your time. If not carefully managed, properly cued, and artistically edited, they can become more of a handicap than an aid.

For certain topics, however, carefully prepared videos can be more effective than any other type of presentation aid. A student at Northwest Mississippi Community College who is also a firefighter used videotape to augment his informative speech on fire hazards in the home. By customizing the videotape to fit the precise needs of his speech, he was able to show long shots of a room and then zoom in on various fire hazards.[19] He had prepared the videotape without sound so that his speech provided the commentary needed to interpret and explain the pictures seen by the audience. Using this technique, he made a tired subject come to life in a fascinating way. When in doubt about the wisdom or practicality of using such aids, consult your instructor.

Audiotapes may also be useful as presentation aids and are not as difficult to handle and integrate into your speech. If you wanted to describe the alarm cries of various animals or the songs of different birds, an audiotape could be essential. Consult your instructor about the availability of equipment if you think your speech would benefit from such a tape.

Computer-Generated Materials and Computer-Assisted Presentations

The world of tomorrow has already pushed the world of today into the past. Your speech classroom may not be equipped now for multimedia presentations, but as you move from college into the business world you will encounter more and more sophisticated equipment for use in presentations. In 1994 over 65 percent of all corporations relied on multimedia presentations.[20] Moreover, the present generation is growing up in a multimedia environment. Grade school and middle school students in Louisville and New York City use computers, videos, and digitizers to produce daily news shows.[21] Your audience, and the audience you can expect to address in later business and professional presentations, may be quite attuned to multimedia presentations.

It is one thing to note this trend in the style of presentation aids and quite another to offer useful advice about it. Technology is changing so rapidly that any specific advice we give concerning multimedia presentations will in all likelihood be obsolete by the time you read these words. Because computers are central to such presentations, however, we can offer some helpful general guidelines.

Most personal computers can help you to generate a wide variety of presentation aids. They can be used to develop sketches, maps, graphs, charts, and textual graphics for handouts, transparencies, and slides. More sophisticated computers can also run programs that reproduce pictures, add animation, and edit videotapes. The materials produced on computers are usually much neater and more accurate than those drawn by hand. Unless you have access to a blueprint-size printer, copier, or enlarger, computer graphics are less appropriate for posters.

To make presentation aids on a computer you will need access to spreadsheet, word processing, graphics, and/or presentation software such as ClarisWorks, PowerPoint, Persuasion, or Harvard Graphics. The prototypes for many of the illustrations of presentation aids in this chapter were originally prepared using ClarisWorks and a Macintosh Performa computer. The word processing, spreadsheet, and graphics programs will enable you to produce static visuals for use as presentation aids. The presentation programs allow you both to prepare and present your materials to listeners if you have access to a special projector.

Many of the presentation programs are expensive to purchase. However, Media View, a digital multimedia publication system developed at the Los Alamos National Laboratory, is public domain software and can be downloaded from Internet's World Wide Web.[22] User groups, forums, shareware, and other sources of information and assistance are available from sources such as Internet, CompuServe, and America Online. Specialized publications sponsored by computer and software manufacturers, such as *Presentation Products Magazine,* are available free or for minimal cost.[23] Your campus computer lab may have training programs to help you learn how to access and use these materials.

Computer-assisted presentations can bring together texts, numbers, pictures, and artwork made into slides, videos, animations, and audio materials. Materials such as graphs and charts that are generated with the computer can be changed at any time, even during a presentation. The programs come with a variety of templates that allow you to concentrate on your message rather than worrying about the design and development of your presentation aids.[24] The templates can be adapted to suit your particular needs. To make a computer-assisted presentation you need specialized equipment in addition to the computer and software necessary to prepare the aids. You may need a CD-ROM drive, an audioboard, and a color monitor for use in small group settings. You will need additional special projection equipment for use with large groups.[25] The standard large group projection equipment includes LCD (liquid crystal display) projection panels that connect to the output port on a computer and are then sent through an overhead projector to a screen.

As you move into this new technology for developing preparation aids for use in speeches, be careful not to get so caught up with the glitz and glitter that you lose sight of the fact that *it is your message that is most important.*[26] Using sophisticated technology in your presentation does not excuse you from the usual requirements for speaking.[27] In fact, if your presentation aids draw more attention than your ideas, they may be a hindrance more than a help. Be especially careful not to get caught up with flashy transitions. Remember, it is better to be subtle than sensational. You are giving a speech, not putting on a Disneyland production. Even when you are preparing computer-generated materials or developing computer-assisted presentations, follow the customary guidelines for developing and using presentation aids put forth in this chapter. Don't use new technology just because it is there!

Ethical Considerations

Presentation aids can be powerful, but they can also deceive. They can raise challenging ethical questions. For example, the most famous photographer of the Civil War, Matthew Brady, rearranged bodies on the battlefield to enhance the impact of his pictures. Eighty years later, another American war photographer carefully staged the now celebrated photograph of Marines planting the flag at Iwo Jima.[28] Fifty years after that, *Time* magazine electronically manipulated a cover photograph of O. J. Simpson to "darken it and achieve a brooding, menacing quality."[29] On one hand, these famous images may be fabrications: they pretend to be what they are not. On the other hand, they may bring home more forcefully the reality they represent. In other words, the form of the photos is a lie, but the lie may work to reveal a deeper truth. So are these photographs unethical or are they simply artistic?

Perhaps we can agree that with today's modern technology, the potential for abuse looms quite large. Video editing easily produces illusions of reality. Consider how a recent movie depicts Forrest Gump shaking hands with Presidents Kennedy, Johnson, and Nixon. Or call to mind the image of ten Shaquille O'Neals playing basketball at the same time. Or picture the Statue of Liberty putting down her torch to pick up and examine an American-made car, then smiling over its quality. In movies and television ads such distortions can be amusing. In real life, they can be dangerous. Major television networks and newspapers have "staged" crashes and other visuals to make their stories more dramatic.[30]

All these practices may relate to the ancient adage, "Seeing is believing." We are taught by tradition to be vulnerable to the "reality" revealed by our eyes. Our position on these ethical issues is the following:

- As a speaker, you should alert your listeners to the illusion whenever you manipulate images so that they reveal your message more forcefully.

- You should be prepared to defend the illusion you create as a "better representation" of some underlying truth.

- As a listener, you should cultivate a healthy skepticism for visual images: for you, seeing should no longer be the same as believing.

- Whenever important claims are made, and visual images are offered in support of them, you should ask for further confirmation and for additional evidence.

PREPARING PRESENTATION AIDS

To develop a good presentation aid and use it effectively, you have to go through a process of planning, designing, preparing, and practicing its use. As your speech evolves through your working outlines, you should also consider whether a presentation aid might help your message. To create an effective presentation aid, follow basic principles of design and color.

When using slides as a presentation aid, be sure to maintain eye contact with your audience. Stand to the side and point to specific elements as you talk about them.

Principles of Design

When you apply the basic principles of designing presentation aids — visibility, emphasis, and balance — you have to consider how such aids will function before an audience.

Visibility.   Listeners in the back of the room must be able to see your presentation aid without difficulty. Otherwise, the aid will *not* be an aid. When preparing a large poster or flip-chart presentation aid for speeches in standard classrooms, follow these minimum size guidelines:

Titles:	3 inches high
Subtitles:	2 inches high
Other text:	1½ inches high

If you generate slides or transparencies on a computer, be certain that it can print large letters. Computer print is typically sized in terms of points (pt). Figure 9.13 shows the computer print sizes appropriate for preparing transparencies, slides, or handouts.

Such presentation aids should use the following sizes of letters:

	Transparencies	Slides	Handouts
Title	36 pt	24 pt	18 pt
Subtitles	24 pt	18 pt	14 pt
Other text	18 pt	14 pt	12 pt

Use boldface type when preparing computer-generated materials.

FIGURE 9.13

Standard Computer
Print Sizes

Emphasis. Keep presentation aids simple, so that they emphasize only what your speech emphasizes. Each aid should make only one point. Your listeners' eyes should be drawn immediately to what you want to illustrate. The map of Yellowstone Park (Figure 9.1) eliminates all information except what the speaker wishes to stress. Had the speaker added pictures of bears to indicate grizzly habitat or drawings of fish to show trout streams, the presentation aid would have been more distracting than helpful. Avoid irrelevant cuteness! Graphics prepared for handouts may be more detailed than those used for posters, slides, or transparencies, but they should not contain extraneous material. When in doubt, leave the details out. Let your words provide any necessary elaboration.

Balance. Proper balance, discussed in Chapter 7 as an important requirement for speech structure, is also important for visual materials. Your presentation aid should be balanced so that it is pleasing to the eye. The focal point of the aid can be the actual center of the chart or poster, or it can be deliberately placed off-center for the sake of variety. You should have a margin of at least two inches at the top of poster boards or standard flip charts. The margin at the bottom of such aids should be at least two-and-a-half inches. On computer-generated graphics you should leave at least an inch and a half of blank space at both the top and bottom. You should also have equal side margins. For poster boards and flip charts, these margins should be about one-and-a-half inches wide. On computer-generated graphics they should be at least an inch wide.

FIGURE 9.14

Misleading Bar Graph and Same Material Presented So It Is Not Misleading

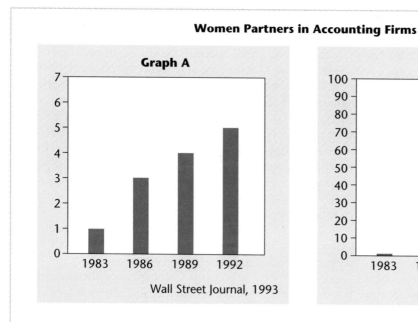
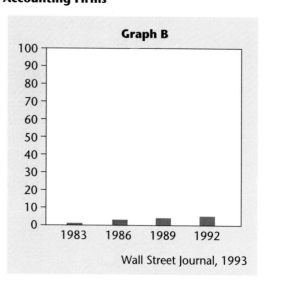

Women Partners in Accounting Firms

Graph A — Wall Street Journal, 1993

Graph B — Wall Street Journal, 1993

Ethical Considerations.   As we noted earlier, photographs and videos can be distorted through electronic manipulation. Graphs and charts can also be rigged so that they misrepresent reality. For example, Figure 9.14 shows how the growth in percentage of women partners in major accounting firms across a recent decade might be misrepresented in bar graph A to make nothing look like something — the advances have gone from pitiful to sorry. Bar graph B in the same figure puts these slight gains into proper perspective.[31] Be careful how you prepare graphs so that they honestly represent a situation.

Another ethical consideration you must keep in mind as you prepare your presentation aids concerns citing your sources of information. Be sure to print your source of information on any presentation aids that you prepare in advance, such as poster boards, slides, transparencies, or handouts. This can be done in smaller letters (still visible to listeners) at the bottom of the aid (see Figure 9.8). Citing your source in this fashion both verifies the data presented and reminds you to mention the source in your oral presentation.

Principles of Color

As many of the illustrations in this chapter show, color adds impact to presentation aids.[32] Clearly, most colored presentation aids can attract and hold attention better than the same images in black and white. Color also is a subtle way to convey or enhance meaning. The striking use of the color red in Figure 9.4 to represent blood donations, and the dramatic contrast of blue and white in Figure 9.6 to highlight annual snowfall, are just two examples. Additionally, a speech detailing crop damage from a drought might use an enlarged outline map showing the least affected areas in green, moderately damaged areas in orange, and severely affected areas in brown. The natural colors would reinforce the message.

Color can also be used to create moods and impressions. For example, the color blue suggests power, authority, and stability (blue chip, blue ribbon, royal blue). Using blue in your graphics can invest them with these qualities. Red signals excitement and may be used to indicate the presence of crisis (in the red, red ink). Line graphs tracing the rise in cases of AIDS could be portrayed in red to convey a sense of urgency. On his map of the New Madrid Fault area, Stephen Huff showed the earthquake epicenters in red, emphasizing their danger. You should avoid using red when presenting financial data unless you want to focus on debts or losses. On the other hand, in the American culture, the color green is associated with both money (greenbacks) and environmental concerns (Green Peace). The use of color in Figure 9.9 resonates with the green of U.S. currency and reinforces the compounded effects of early investments. When selecting colors, you should also be aware of cultural differences. For example, in the United States white is associated with weddings, baptisms, confirmations, and other happy ritual occasions. In Japan white has an entirely different connotation. There it is a funeral color associated with sadness.[33]

Combining colors in particular ways can convey subtle nuances of meaning. An **analogous color** scheme uses colors that are adjacent on the color wheel, such as green, blue-green, and blue. Although this type of color scheme shows the differences among the components represented, it also suggests their connection and compatibility. For example, a pie graph could represent the students, faculty, and administration of a university, using analogous colors. The different colors suggest that these parts are indeed separate, but the analogous color scheme and the inclusion of these parts within a circle imply that they belong together. In this subtle way, the presentation aid itself makes the statement that the components of a university ought to work together.

A **complementary color** scheme uses colors that are opposites on the color wheel, such as red and green. Complementary color schemes suggest tension and opposition among elements in a speech. Because they heighten the sense of drama, they may enliven informative speaking and encourage change in persuasive speaking. For example, one suggestion for developing the map accompanying the speech at the end of Chapter 12 would be to outline and color the New Madrid Fault area dark red and the surrounding area green, further dramatizing the danger of earthquake.

The colors you use for your graphics should always stand out from the background of the poster. It is best to use white or cream-colored poster board and strong, primary colors such as red, blue, and green, for contrast. Or, you might want to use a strong primary color for the background and have the text or other graphic elements printed in white. Color contrast is especially important for computer-generated slides and transparencies, because the colors may wash out and appear less distinct when projected than they do when seen on a monitor. Colors like pink, light blue, and pale yellow may not be strong enough for good graphic emphasis in any type of presentation aid.

Making Presentation Aids

To prepare hand-made charts, graphs, or other poster and flip-chart aids, begin with a rough draft that allows you to see how your aid will look when it is finished. If you will be using poster board, prepare your draft on cheaper paper of the same size. With a light pencil mark off the margins to frame your aid. Divide your planning sheet into four equal sections to help you balance the placement of material. Use a wide-tipped felt marker to sketch in your design and words. Now step back to view your presentation aid from about the same distance as the back row of your audience. Will your most distant listeners be able to read the words without straining? Is everything spelled correctly? Is your eye drawn immediately to the most important elements in the poster? Have you positioned your material so that it will be most effective? Is the poster balanced, or does it look lopsided?

Don't try to crowd too much information into a single presentation aid. Are your margins and borders large enough to provide ample "white space"? Is there anything you can eliminate? If the poster looks cluttered, consider making a series of presentation aids instead of just one.

When you have finished your rough draft, practice presenting your speech using the aid. Does it support your message and purpose? Is it easy

Planning and Preparing Presentation Aids

1 Design a presentation aid that will enhance the meaning or impact of your speech.

2 Limit the number of aids you will use. Keep the focus on your message.

3 Make a rough draft of your presentation aid to see how well it works.

4 Be sure your aid is simple, balanced in design, and easily visible from the back of the room.

5 Use color in your presentation aid to increase its effectiveness.

6 Prepare a neat presentation aid. A sloppy one will damage your credibility and reduce the effectiveness of your speech.

to use? When you have decided on a layout and design, prepare the final polished product. If an art room with equipment is available on campus, seek permission to complete your presentation aid there.

If you use computer-generated graphics to produce slides, transparencies, or handouts, experiment with several different designs. Don't get so caught up with what the program can do that you try to incorporate everything into a single presentation aid. If you do, you will wind up with something that is so "busy" it will detract from your message, rather than enhance it. Simplicity should be your rule of thumb.

USING PRESENTATION AIDS

As we discussed each of the specific kinds of presentation aids, we offered suggestions on how to use them in presentations. Here we review these suggestions and extract some basic guidelines.

- Practice using your presentation aid. Be sure to integrate it smoothly into your speech with transitions.
- Go to the room where you will be speaking to decide where you will place your aid both before and during your speech. Determine what you will need for displaying it (thumbtacks, masking tape, etc.).
- Check out any electronic equipment you will use (slide projector, overhead projector, VCR, etc.) in advance of your presentation. Be certain that you can operate it and that it is working properly.
- Do not display your presentation aid until you are ready to use it. When you have finished with it, cover or remove the aid so that it does not distract your audience.
- Don't stand directly in front of your presentation aid. Stand to the side of it and face the audience as much as possible. Maintain eye contact

with listeners. You want them to see both you and your presentation aid.

- When you refer to something on the presentation aid, point to what you are talking about. Don't leave your audience searching for what you are describing.

- Do not distribute materials during your speech. If you have prepared handouts, distribute them before or after you speak.

- Do not use too many presentation aids in one speech. Remember, they should help your verbal message, not replace it.

IN SUMMARY

Presentation aids are tools to enhance the effectiveness of speeches. They can increase comprehension, authenticate a point, add variety, increase your credibility, and help your speech have lasting impact.

Kinds of Presentation Aids.   Every speech has at least one presentation aid: the speaker. Your appearance, clothing, and body language must all be in concert with your message and appropriate to the audience and situation. Another form of presentation aid is the object itself. Unless an object is large enough to be seen, small enough to be portable, and strictly under your control, you may have to use a model or a sketch instead.

Visual representations of information, or *graphics,* provide a number of options for presentation aids. Maps can be useful in speeches based on spatial designs. Draw them specifically for your speech so that they contain only the material you wish to emphasize. Graphs can help make complex numerical data more understandable to an audience. *Pie graphs* illustrate the relationships between parts and a whole. *Bar graphs* highlight comparisons and contrasts. *Line graphs* show changes over time. *Mountain graphs* are variations of line graphs that use different colors to fill in the areas.

Charts are visual representations that give form to abstract relationships. *Flow charts* may be used to outline the steps in a process or show power and authority relationships within an organization. *Sequence charts* that are presented in succession can be especially effective in speeches to emphasize and illustrate various stages in a process. *Textual graphics* are lists of phrases, words, or numbers. They are often presented as *bulleted lists, acronyms,* or *columnar data.*

Photographs and pictures can add authenticity to a speech if handled correctly. Photographs provide slice-of-life realism but can also include irrelevant detail. Any photograph used in a speech should be enlarged so that everyone in the audience can see it.

Presentation Media.   Speakers may use flip charts, posterboards, handouts, chalk or marker boards, projections, videotapes, and audiotapes to develop presentation aids. Flip charts provide an easy way to present a sequence of visual aids. They are adaptable and inexpensive, and can be colorful and striking. Posterboard can be useful when you want to make one or two polished visual aids. Handouts are effective in explaining complex or unfamiliar material; these should be distributed either before or after a speech. Chalkboards and markerboards should be used sparingly to emphasize points or to clarify questions that can arise during the presentation of a speech.

Overhead projections and slides help audiences see graphics or pictures more clearly. Overhead projections are popular because they are easy to make, inexpensive, and adaptable. Slides may be more difficult to make and handle unless you have access to computerized equipment. Videotapes and audiotapes add variety to a message. They should be used sparingly in presentations because they can easily upstage the speaker.

Most personal computers now have the capacity to generate effective, professional-looking presentation aids such as transparencies, handouts or slides. With specialized equipment you can make computer-assisted presentations.

Preparing Presentation Aids.   As you plan your presentation aids, follow the basic principles of design and color. The presentation aid must be easy for listeners to see. It should emphasize what the speech emphasizes, excluding all extraneous material. It should seem balanced and pleasing to the eye. Plan your layout as you develop the speech itself through the working outlines. Consider using strong colors to add interest and impact.

Using Presentation Aids.   Practice using the presentation aid until it seems a natural part of your presentation. Always talk to your audience, not to your presentation aid, and keep the aid out of sight when not in use. As you consider the use of presentation aids, be sensitive to their potential ethical impact. Be certain that your presentation aid represents its subject without distortion.

TERMS TO KNOW

presentation aids	pictograph
graphics	textual graphics
pie graph	bulleted list
bar graph	acronym
line graph	computer-assisted presentation
mountain graph	analogous colors
flow chart	complementary colors
sequence chart	

DISCUSSION

1. Watch news programs on television or read *USA Today* for several days and observe how graphics and pictures are combined with words to convey meaning. What techniques are most and least useful? Be prepared to discuss examples of effective and ineffective usage in class.

2. Recall classes in which your instructors used presentation aids. Did these aids serve one or more of the basic functions discussed in this chapter:

   ▪ did they aid your understanding?
   ▪ did they authenticate a point?
   ▪ did they enhance your instructors' presentation skills?
   ▪ did they increase their credibility?
   ▪ did they add variety?
   ▪ did they give more impact to messages?

   Why or why not?

3. Describe situations in which speakers either would or would not be effective presentation aids for their own speeches. Have you ever seen examples outside your classroom in which the appearance of speakers worked against their message?

4. Look through a recent popular magazine and analyze the advertisements according to the principles of design discussed here. Do the presentation aspects of the ads work in concert with the words to emphasize the message? Which of the ads seem most balanced and pleasing to the eye? Do any of the ads violate the rules of simplicity and ease of comprehension? Which of the ads use color most and least effectively? Bring the most interesting ads to class and discuss your findings.

APPLICATION

1. Select a speech in Appendix B and prepare the rough draft of a presentation aid that might have been used with it. Would the aid have helped the speech? What other options did you consider?

2. What kinds of presentation aids might be most useful for the following speech topics?

   a. Nuclear-waste disposal sites in the United States
   b. What to do in case of snakebite
   c. History of the stock market over the last decade
   d. How the federal budget is divided into major categories
   e. Administering your university: who has the power to do what to whom?
   f. How we got the modern telephone: the growth of an invention
   g. Poverty in Africa: the human story
   h. The sounds of navigation and what they mean

NOTES

1. Robert L. Lindstrom, "The Presentation Power of Multimedia," *Sales and Marketing Management* (Sept. 1994): 51(7), *Magazine Database Plus,* Online, CompuServe, Nov. 1995.

2. Lindstrom, William J. Seiler, "The Effects of Visual Materials on Attitudes, Credibility, and Retention," *Speech Monographs* 38 (1971): 334; Douglas R.Vogel, Gary W. Dickson, and John A. Lehman, "Persuasion and the Role of Visual Presentation Support: The UM/3M Study," 3M Corporation (1986): 1–20.

3. See studies conducted by Wharton Business School's Applied Research Center and the Management Information Services Department of the University of Arizona, cited by Lindstrom and by Dona Meilach, "Even the Odds with Visual Presentations," *Inc.* Annual (1994): 1(6), *Magazine Database Plus,* Online, CompuServe, Nov. 1995.

4. "The Low-Down on A-V Use," *Sales and Marketing Management,* (Aug. 1991): 25, *Magazine Database Plus,* Online, CompuServe, Nov. 1995; and Jan Ozer, "Presentations Come to Life," *Home Office Computing,* (Dec. 1994): 74, *Magazine Database Plus,* Online, CompuServe, Nov. 1995.

5. Thomas R. King, "Visual Aids: Moving into the 21st Century," Southern States Communication Association Convention, New Orleans, April 1995; Ken Jurek, "Portable Computers: Compact Presentations Receive Rave Reviews," *Presentation Products Magazine,* (Dec. 1992): 32–38; David T. Bottoms, "Multimedia Delivers the Message: Interactivity Livens Up Training, Presentations, and the Budget at TRW," *Industry Week,* 4 Apr. 1994, p. 70, *Magazine Database Plus,* Online, CompuServe, Nov. 1995; James J. McGivney. "Multimedia Educational Systems," *The FBI Law Enforcement Bulletin* (Feb. 1993): 6, *Magazine Database Plus,* Online, CompuServe, Nov. 1995.

6. Michael Barrier, "How He Helps Jurors Stay Awake by Turning Trials into 'Multimedia Events'," *Nations' Business,* (Oct. 1991): p. 18, *Magazine Database Plus,* Online, CompuServe, Nov. 1995.

7. "Low-Down," p. 25.

8. Dona Meilach, "Visually Speaking." Special Advertising Section. *Presentation Products Magazine,* June 1993, sec. J–L.

9. Richard Kern, "Making Visual Aids Work for You," *Sales and Marketing Management,* (Feb. 1989): 45(4), *Magazine Database Plus,* Online, CompuServe, Nov. 1995.

10. Cited in Laurence J. Peter. *Peter's Quotations: Ideas for Our Time* (New York: Bantam, 1979), p. 478.

11. Deborah Prothrow-Stith, "Stop Violence Before It Begins," *USA Today,* 24 Feb. 1994, p. 11A.

12. Kern, p. 45(4).

13. Meilach, "Even the Odds," p. 1(6).

14. Jan Ozer, "Presentations Come to Life," *Home Office Computing,* Dec. 1994, p. 74, *Magazine Database Plus,* Online, CompuServe, Nov. 1995; Lindstrom, p. 51(7); Ripley Hatch, "Making the Best Presentations," *Nation's Business,* August 1992, p. 37(2), *Magazine Database Plus,* Online, CompuServe, Nov. 1995; "The Art of Business Presentations," *Managing Office Technology,* Mar. 1994, p. 83, *Magazine Database Plus,* Online, CompuServe, Nov. 1995; Robert Boroughs, "New Teaching, New Learning," *Electronic Learning* (Jan. 1990): 52(3), *Magazine Database Plus,*

Online, CompuServe, Nov. 1995; Isabelle Bruder, "Multimedia: How It Changes the Way We Teach and Learn," *Electronic Learning* (Sept. 1991): 22(5), *Magazine Database Plus,* Online, CompuServe, Nov. 1995.

15. Meilach, "Visually Speaking," p. B.

16. Todd Oppenheimer, "Exploring the Interactive Future: *Newsweek's* Voyage through Cyberspace," *Columbia Journalism Review* (Nov–Dec 1993): 34(4), *Magazine Database Plus,* Online, CompuServe, Nov. 1995.

17. Lindstrom, p. 51(7).

18. Meilach, "Visually Speaking," p. H.

19. Our thanks for this example go to Professor Mary Katherine McHenry, Northwest Mississippi Community College, Senatobia, MS.

20. Ozer, p. 74.

21. Burroughs, p. 52(3); and Bruder, p. 22(5).

22. Tim Studt, "Multimedia Allows Researchers to Interact With Their Data," *R&D* (July 1994): 35(2), *Magazine Database Plus,* Online, CompuServe, Nov. 1995.

23. For information on subscriptions to *Presentation Products Magazine,* write the Circulation Department, *Presentation Products Magazine,* 23410 Civic Center Way, Suite 10, Malibu, CA 91320.

24. Hatch, p. 37.

25. Philip Bishop, "The World on a Silver Platter: Bring New Power and Flexibility to Your Business with Multimedia," *Home Office Computing* (June 1993), p. 61(3), *Magazine Database Plus,* Online, CompuServe, Nov. 1995.

26. Tom Bunzel, "Content — Not Technology — Is What Counts," *Computer Pictures* (May–June 1993), p. 23, *Magazine Database Plus,* Online, CompuServe, Nov. 1995.

27. John T. Phillips, Jr., "Professional Presentations," *Records Management Quarterly,* Oct. 1994: 44(3), *Magazine Database Plus,* Online, CompuServe, Nov. 1995.

28. Cornelia Brunner, "Teaching Visual Literacy," *Electronic Learning,* Nov.–Dec. 1994: 16(2), *Magazine Database Plus,* Online, CompuServe, Nov. 1995.

29. Arthur Goldsmith, "Digitally Altered Photography: The New Image Makers," *Britannica Book of the Year: 1995* (Chicago: Encyclopaedia Britannica, 1995), p. 135.

30. Gloria Borger, "The Story the Pictures Didn't Tell," *U.S. News and World Report,* 22 Feb. 1993, pp. 6–7; and John Leo, "Lapse or TV News Preview?" *The Washington Times,* 3 Mar. 1993, p. G3.

31. Lee Berton, "Deloitte Wants More Women for Top Posts in Accounting," *Wall Street Journal,* 28 Feb. 1993, p. B1.

32. Meilach, "Even the Odds," p. 1(6).

33. Kern, p. 45(4).

CHAPTER **10**

Using Language
Effectively

THIS CHAPTER WILL HELP YOU

- understand the power of words.
- express your thoughts clearly, simply, and correctly.
- bring your ideas to life through powerful images.
- use symbols to bring listeners together.
- choose words that move an audience to action.

In oratorical imagery the best feature is always its reality and truth.

— Longinus

A legislator was asked how he felt about whiskey. He replied, "If, when you say whiskey, you mean the Devil's brew, the poison scourge, the bloody monster that defiles innocence, dethrones reason, creates misery and poverty — yes, literally takes the bread from the mouths of little children; if you mean the drink that topples Christian man and woman from the pinnacle of righteous, gracious living into the bottomless pit of degradation, despair, shame and helplessness, then certainly I am against it with all my power.

"But if, when you say whiskey, you mean the oil of conversation, the philosophic wine, the ale that is consumed when good fellows get together, that puts a song in their hearts and the warm glow of contentment in their eyes; if you mean Christmas cheer; if you mean the stimulating drink that puts the spring in an old gentleman's step on a frosty morning; if you mean that drink, the sale of which pours into our treasury untold millions of dollars which are used to provide tender care for our crippled children, our blind, our deaf, our dumb, pitiful, aged and infirm, to build highways, hospitals, and schools, then certainly I am in favor of it.

"That is my stand, and I will not compromise."[1]

We often underestimate the power of our own speech. The phrase "mere words" implies that language itself is without real consequence. Yet, as our opening example shows, language can be both deceptive and richly expressive — and at the same time! The wording of a speech can evade questions as it seems to answer them. But as the Roman critic quoted at the head of this chapter reminds us, *when words work ethically as well as effectively, they bring home to listeners the reality and truth of a situation.*

As speakers, we must make many important decisions. We must plan how to overcome fear, suspicion, indifference, and cultural stereotypes. We must decide on a structure for our speeches and select appropriate supporting materials. When speaking on controversial subjects, we must choose the most compelling arguments to advance our position. These decisions make public speaking a fascinating art to practice. However, our understanding of this art is incomplete if we leave out the countless decisions we must make as we fashion the words of our message. The language we select may determine whether our speech succeeds or fails.

This brings us to a third basic metaphor for the skills of public speaking. First, you learn how *to climb* the barriers that separate speakers and listeners. Second, you learn how *to build* the structure of a message. Finally, you learn how *to weave* a fabric of words that expresses your message with clarity, power, and beauty so that listeners will understand and remember what you say and relate it to their lives.

The words you speak are your immediate point of contact with listeners. This chapter describes what oral language can do for you, shows you how to use powerful language techniques, and suggests standards you should follow as you weave the language of your message.

THE POWER OF THE SPOKEN WORD

Our grasp of the power of the spoken word must begin with understanding the differences between oral and written language. One of the most striking differences is that oral language is more spontaneous and less formal than written language. For example, instead of saying, "Eight thousand, three hundred twenty-three cases of measles have been reported in Shelby County," you might say, "More than eight thousand cases of measles have been reported in Shelby County!" It's not really important that listeners remember the exact number of cases — it *is* important that they see the magnitude of the problem. Rounding off numbers helps you make this point emphatically.

Oral language is also more colorful and intense than written language. Sentence fragments and slang expressions are more acceptable in speeches than in essays. Oral language also is more interactive. It depends on audience involvement for its effectiveness. Consider the following quotation from a speech:

> **You want to know what we're going to do? I'll tell you what we're *not* going to do. We're *not* going to play along. This is a rule that deserves to be broken. Yes, broken! And we're going to do the breaking.**

This brief example illustrates many of the spontaneous, informal, intense, fragmentary, and interactive qualities of oral language. The speaker is keenly aware of her audience. Her words reflect the quality of expanded conversation we discussed in Chapter 1. Moreover, in oral communication, pauses, vocal emphasis, and vocal variations act as punctuation marks to clarify and underscore meaning. Such resources are not available to written communication.

In oral communication time considerations are extremely important. Jerry Tarver, professor of speech communication at the University of Richmond, emphasizes three significant time differences between spoken and written language.[2] First, he offers "Tarver's Law of Conciseness: *It takes more words per square idea to say something than to write it.*" Because listeners cannot reread a spoken statement, oral language must be simple and use more repetition. Examples and illustrations are especially important, because they amplify the speaker's point to make sure that listeners get the message.

Tarver's second time difference concerns the *order in which spoken thoughts develop in a sentence.* His example is excellent:

> I recently read in a newspaper column a spirited defense of a public figure. The last line of the column was, "For that he should be congratulated, not chastised." Well and good. The reader gobbles up the line in an instant and digests the contrast between congratulations and chastisement. But when we speak the line we feed it to a listener morsel by morsel. And the last two words prove to be rather bland. We need to *hear* "For that he should not be chastised, he should be congratulated." More words; but more important, a different order. . . . In the slower pace of speech, individual words stand out more, and thus *time* accords a special emphasis to the last idea, the climactic idea in the sentence.
>
> As a rule, then, the stronger, more impressive idea should be saved for the end. And it will often be the case that the punch comes from a positive rather than a negative thought.[3]

Tarver's advice to *build up* to your most important point within a sentence repeats a structural principle discussed in Chapter 7 — that the main points of a speech often work best when arranged in an order of ascending importance.

Tarver's third effect of time is that *"the beat or flow or rhythm of the syllables is even more important in words written to be heard than in words written to be seen."* While the effect is somewhat mysterious, spoken speech often beats on the senses like a drum. The rhythms of oral speech make the meanings of words stick in memory. The beat adds emotionality. Rhythm may also be paired with rhyme to make oral language even more memorable. During the O. J. Simpson murder trial, the prosecution asked Simpson to try on a glove allegedly worn by the killer during the crime. It was a high moment of the trial, but a low moment for the prosecution, when Simpson struggled to put the glove on. Who then can forget how defense attorney Johnny Cochran, in his summary to the jury, impressively intoned: "If it doesn't fit, you must acquit."

Nine Features of Spoken Language

SPEAKER'S NOTES

- ☐ Spoken language is more personal.
- ☐ Spoken language is less formal.
- ☐ Spoken language uses less precise numbers.
- ☐ Spoken language is more colorful and intense.
- ☐ Spoken language uses shorter, more simple, even fragmentary sentences.
- ☐ Spoken language is more repetitious.
- ☐ Spoken language uses more examples and narratives.
- ☐ Spoken language saves important points for the ends of sentences.
- ☐ Spoken language emphasizes the rhythm of speech.

When skillfully used, the spoken word can reach others in ways that the written word cannot. There are four ways that effective oral language can help you influence the lives of listeners:

- ▪ by revealing subjects in certain ways,
- ▪ by arousing intense feelings about subjects,
- ▪ by bringing your listeners together, and
- ▪ by moving your audience to action.[4]

To be an effective and ethical speaker and listener, you must understand how these functions of language can be used or abused.

The Power to Make Listeners See

Speakers and listeners often see subjects in different ways. The artful use of language, however, can close the gap that separates them. Consider, for example, the problem that confronted one of our students, Scott Champlin. As he prepared his self-introductory speech, Scott decided that the most distinctive thing about him was an experience he had undergone in the military. His challenge was deciding how he could share that experience, so that others might understand what it meant to him. One option would be to simply describe the experience matter-of-factly:

> **While I was parachuting into Panama as part of Operation "Just Cause," I was wounded by a tracer bullet.**

The more he thought about that option, the less adequate it seemed. So he began to consider how his words might convey a sense of that experience to his listeners. His depiction of that experience allowed his audience to share his leap into that threatening night:

The darkness of two o'clock in the morning was multiply penetrated by streaks of red marking the paths of tracer rounds as they cut their way through the night. Suddenly, I felt a surge of heat knock me in the right leg with a force that spun me around like a twisted yo-yo at the end of a string.

Here the use of color contrast — between "darkness" and "streaks of red" — paints a vivid picture. Lively verbs such as "penetrated," "cut," "knock," and "spun" fill the picture with action. A brief comparison — "like a twisted yo-yo at the end of a string" — brings the picture into sharp focus. Through his artful choice of words, Scott found the way to communicate the meaning of his message.

This power to shape how an audience sees something is especially important when your subject is unfamiliar or unusual. When listeners don't have a clear perception to compare with the speaker's depiction of a subject, they are quite vulnerable. In such cases, the speaker's words become windows that reveal a subject with startling clarity. The Renaissance scholar Francis Bacon suggested over four hundred years ago that the glass in such windows can be "enchanted." The perspective presented may be distorted by the speaker's interests and values. Words can color and alter subjects, allowing speakers to disguise or obscure reality. The power to make us see also can be a power that can blind. Thus, as critical listeners, we must guard against accepting any speaker's view as THE TRUTH of the matter.

The Power to Awaken Feelings

Language also can arouse intense feelings. It can touch our hearts and change our ways of thinking. Like the power to make people see, the power to make people feel can be used ethically or abused. It is most ethical when it *supplements* sound reasoning and credible evidence as it activates the proof by *pathos* we discuss in Chapter 14. It is abused when speakers *substitute* appeals to feelings for evidence or reasoning. To arouse feelings language must overcome the barriers of time, distance, and apathy.

Overcoming Time.   Listeners live in the present. Therefore, it can be difficult to awaken feeling about events that lie in the remote past or distant future. Fortunately, the language of feeling has a time-machine quality. Speakers can use language skills to bring past and future events into the present and make them seem real.

In many businesses, employees and customers may lack a sense of identification with the company. They may feel that the atmosphere is impersonal and that no one cares about them or their problems. To combat that impression, narratives that recapture feelings from the past are often told at company meetings or used in advertisements. Such narratives help establish a sense of corporate heritage and culture. It is more pleasant to do business with a company that seems to have human qualities. Look how

Martin Luther King, Jr. was famed for his rhetorical style. He made use of many rhetorical techniques such as metaphors and parallel construction in his messages.

the words in the following story awaken feelings. Reconstructed from oft-told legend, these words capture the legend of Federal Express, a pioneer in overnight delivery:

> You know, we take a lot for granted. It's hard to remember that Federal Express was once just a fly-by-night dream, a crazy idea in which a few people had invested — not just their time and their money, but their futures and lives. I remember one time early on when things weren't going so well. We were really up against it. Couldn't even make the payroll that week. It looked like we were going to crash. Fred [Smith, founder of the company] was in a deep funk. Never saw him quite like that before or since. "What the hell," he said, and flew off to Las Vegas. The next day he flew back and his face was shining. "We're going to make it," he said. He had won $27,000 at the blackjack table! And we made it. We met the payroll. Shortly after that things turned around, and Federal Express began to grow into the giant it is today.[5]

This story enlivens the past by emphasizing the contrast of emotions — the "deep funk" versus the "shining" face. "What the hell," and "We're going to make it," express depression and confidence. Such use of dialogue to express feelings recreates the excitement and brings the scene into the present. In using the dialogue, the speaker steps back and gives Fred Smith center stage by letting him voice his own feelings. It would have been less effective if the speaker had simply stated: "Fred was depressed, but after he got back from Las Vegas he was confident." Offering such a summary would have diluted the emotional strength of the scene.

Language can also make the future seem close at hand. Because language can cross the barrier of time, we are able to have both a sense of tradition and a vision of tomorrow to guide us through the present.

Overcoming Distance. The closer anything is to our lives, the easier it is to develop feelings about it. But what if speakers must discuss events that seem distant from their listeners' interests? Language can telescope such subjects and bring them close. Consider how one student reduced the psychological distance between her urban audience and her rural subject through an interesting character and his meaning to her life. Her use of graphic language allows her audience to share her feelings and experiences:

> James Johnson knows the loveliest, most sparkling springs in Perry County. He has lived all eighty-four years of his life there, and he taught me the most important things I know: why the mist rises on a lake at night, how to make the best blackberry jam you've ever tasted, and how to take care of baby wild rabbits that are abandoned. Today, I want to tell you more about James — and about myself through him.

By focusing on the concrete details that helped the audience see the place she was describing — the mist, the blackberry jam, the baby wild rabbits — the speaker conquered distance and aroused feelings about a subject that might otherwise have seemed remote.

Overcoming Apathy. We live in an age of communication overkill. Modern audiences have become jaded by an endless barrage of mass-mediated information, persuasion, and entertainment. The personal contact of public speaking, even when mediated, allows speakers to reach out to listeners and touch them with language. Jesse Jackson stirred the audience of the 1988 Democratic National Convention with the following message:

> America's not a blanket woven from one thread, one color, one cloth. When I was a child growing up in Greenville, South Carolina, and grandmother could not afford a blanket, she didn't complain and we did not freeze. Instead, she took pieces of old cloth — patches, wool, silk, gabardine, crockersack on the patches — barely good enough to wipe off your shoes with.
>
> But they didn't stay that way very long. With sturdy hands and a strong cord, she sewed them together into a quilt, a thing of beauty and power and culture.
>
> Now, Democrats, we must build such a quilt. Farmers, you seek fair prices and you are right, but you cannot stand alone. Your patch is not

big enough. Workers, you fight for fair wages. You are right. But your patch, labor, is not big enough. Women, you seek comparable worth and pay equity. You are right. But your patch is not big enough. Women, mothers, who seek Head Start and day care and pre-natal care on the front side of life, rather than jail care and welfare on the back side of life, you're right, but your patch is not big enough.

Students, you seek scholarships. You are right. But your patch is not big enough. Blacks and Hispanics, when we fight for civil rights, we are right, but our patch is not big enough. Gays and lesbians, when you fight against discrimination and [for] a cure for AIDS, you are right, but your patch is not big enough. Conservatives and progressives, when you fight for what you believe, right-wing, left-wing, hawk, dove — you are right, from your point of view, but your point of view is not enough.

But don't despair. Be as wise as my grandmama. Pool the patches and the pieces together, bound by a common thread. When we form a great quilt of unity and common ground we'll have the power to bring about health care and housing and jobs and education and hope to our nation.[6]

Jackson's references to poverty and his grandmother's loving care aroused sympathetic feelings from many viewers. The image of a quilt — suggesting the warmth of home and the ability to create things of lasting value and beauty from humble materials — gave the audience a vision of unity to guide them. When artfully used, language can overcome the barriers of time, distance, and apathy to make us care about a subject.

The Power to Bring Listeners Together

On many issues, individual action is not enough. In some cases it takes people acting together to bring about or resist change. Therefore, speakers must often remind listeners of the importance of their group memberships. The Jesse Jackson example, while it arouses strong feeling, also reminds listeners that they are part of an important larger group. The farmers, workers, women, students, gays and lesbians, conservatives and progressives — all were *Democrats*. And only if they acted together — as Democrats rather than individual interest groups — would they have a chance to win the election. The quilt metaphor also invoked this sense of belonging to a larger group.

Just as language can unite people, it can also drive them apart. As we write, eight Republican presidential hopefuls are contending in the 1996 New Hampshire primary. During a nationally televised debate these men attacked and belittled each other, especially the frontrunners. The spectacle was not a happy one for the Republican party, for from this group must emerge a leader who can unify and energize the party. One candidate, Rep. Robert Dornan of California, reminded them that their attacks on each other threatened party unity:

I wish the spirit of Ronald Reagan would descend on New Hampshire . . . and [I wish we could remember] his eleventh commandment, that no Republican should speak ill of another Republican. . . . We have to stop tearing at one another, and focus on what I said in Des Moines, Iowa. The target is Clinton [and] the moral crisis in the White House. . . . Gen-tlemen, we're a family here. Let's unify ourselves and make sure we take the White House on November 5th.[7]

Note that as Dornan pleads for unity, he invokes a common hero, Ronald Reagan. He uses the "family" metaphor to invoke an ideal of togetherness. And he reminds listeners of a common enemy and a common goal — their desire to defeat President Clinton.

Heroes and enemies, common goals, shared values, and metaphors of inclusion work together to heighten the value of group membership. We discuss these techniques more closely later in this chapter.

The Power to Encourage Action

Even if your audience members share an identity, they still may not be ready to act. What might stand in their way? For one thing, they may not

When speakers wish to make people act, they often rely on language to express their concerns. Speakers must be sensitive to their audiences so that they can move them to action.

be convinced of the soundness of your proposal. Even if they are, they might hesitate. Listeners may not believe they can do anything about a problem. Action requires energy, commitment, and risk.

Your words must convince your listeners that action is necessary and success is possible. Look at how Anna Aley, whose speech is printed at the end of Chapter 13, dealt with these challenges. Anna wanted her audience to help improve off-campus housing conditions for students at Kansas State University. In her speech, Anna used personal experience combined with factual information to paint vivid word-pictures of deplorable and danger-ous off-campus housing. She also reminded listeners of their group mem-bership — that they were all students, responsible for each other's welfare:

> . . . What can one student do to change the practices of numerous Manhattan landlords? Nothing, if that student is alone. But just think of what we could accomplish if we got all 13,600 off-campus students in-volved in this issue! Think what we could accomplish if we got even a fraction of those students involved!

Anna then offered specific proposals that her listeners might support — proposals that did not call for great energy or risk on their part; in short, she made commitment as easy as possible. Finally, she concluded with a rousing appeal to action:

> Kansas State students have been putting up with substandard living conditions for too long. It's time we finally got together to do some-thing about this problem. Join the Off-Campus Association. Sign my pe-tition. Let's send a message to these slumlords that we're not going to put up with this any more. We don't have to live in slums.

Anna's words expressed both her indignation and the urgency of the prob-lem. Her references to time — "too long" and "it's time" — called for im-mediate action. Her final appeals to join the association and sign the petition were expressed in short sentences that packed a lot of punch and encouraged the impulse to action. Her repetition of "slumlords" and "slums" motivated her listeners to transform their indignation into action.

Anna also illustrated another strategy important to the language of ac-tion. You must be able to depict real-life dramas that reveal what is at stake and challenge listeners to take on certain roles.[8] Such scenarios draw clear lines between right and wrong. In the words of an early union organizing song, the audience may be asked, "Which side are you on?"[9]

Be careful, however, not to go overboard with such techniques. When you script a drama, maintain respect for the humanity of those involved in conflict. As both a speaker and a listener, be wary of melodramas that con-trast unblemished virtue with absolute evil. Such depictions usually distort reality and call your trustworthiness into question.

The power of language is great, ranging from shaping perceptions to in-citing action. How can you harness this power in ways that are both ethical and elevating? We have already pointed out some of the ways as we illustrated the power of words. Now we cover these special techniques in more detail.

USING LANGUAGE RESOURCES

How can you weave powerful language into the fabric of your message? In this section we consider some of the special techniques you can use to help listeners share your perceptions and feelings, connect with you and with each other, and take appropriate action.

Resources that Shape Audience Perceptions

You can close the perceptual gap between yourself and listeners by using techniques that help you make abstract subjects more concrete or complex subjects easier to comprehend.

Abstract Subjects.   Subjects are abstract when listeners do not have direct access to them through their senses. Abstract subjects include ideas, intangible qualities of things, beliefs, and values. Subjects like *justice* or *courage,* for example, can pose special problems. Because such words are not anchored in concrete reality, people may see them in different ways. We may agree that the object before us is a '59 Mustang convertible — here are its lights, its fenders, its hood ornament. But what are the objective, verifiable features of *fairness,* the interior of *honor?* As we talk about such subjects, we often struggle to share our perceptions. To overcome abstraction, remember the three R's of language techniques: relationship, replacement, and representation.

One way to handle an abstraction is to show a **relationship** between the subject and some concrete object of comparison. For example, you might say, "His courage turned on and off like a faucet — first hot, then cold." Here the abstract subject *courage* is related to the concrete object *faucet.* When words such as *like* or *as* are used to connect the abstract and concrete, or the obscure with the well known, the comparison is called a **simile.** Remember Scott Champlin's simile, "a force that spun me around *like* a twisted yo-yo at the end of a string?" Hopefully, not many of us will ever be hit by a tracer bullet while parachuting, but helped by the simile, we can imagine the scene. Similarly, while few of us will ever be president, most of us might understand President Clinton's frustration expressed in the humorous simile, "Being president is like running a cemetery; you've got a lot of people under you and nobody's listening."[10]

Aristotle once warned that what you select for comparison can either enhance or diminish a subject. An ill-advised simile can make your subject (and you!) seem ugly and tasteless. Some critics thought President Clinton was less effective when he suggested that stalling action on health care reform "will make it just like a hangnail or an ingrown toenail. It's just going to get worse."[11] When they work well, vivid similes bring abstract or obscure subjects into the light.

Another technique for overcoming abstraction involves the **replace-ment** of expected words with unexpected words in the form of a **metaphor.** When you use a fresh metaphor, you pull a rabbit out of the lin-guistic hat. A listener's first reaction is apt to be, "Wait a minute, words are not rabbits and language is not a hat." But with a good metaphor, the next reaction is, "Ah, I see what she means!" Good metaphors reveal unex-pected similarities in often dramatic ways. They substitute concrete words for abstractions and bring a subject into focus.

For these reasons, metaphor is perhaps our most useful and versatile lin-guistic tool. Because they invite listeners to explore unusual connections of ideas, good metaphors encourage the constructive listening we discussed in Chapter 3. They advance the informing, instructing function. In this book we have found it impossible to avoid them, especially as we have talked about the *climbing, building,* and *weaving* skills you acquire as you study public speaking. They also offer powerful help to the persuader, as Jesse Jackson's metaphor of the quilt demonstrated.

Because metaphors are so creative and involve an audience in the cre-ation of meaning, they also work well in speeches of celebration. When Martin Luther King, Jr., spoke in Memphis the night before he was assassi-nated, he talked of the "spiritual journey" that his listeners had traveled. He said that he had climbed the mountain ahead of them — that he had "seen the Promised Land." These metaphors of the journey, the mountain, and the grand view of the land beyond lifted his listeners and allowed them to share his vision, just as he had earlier shared his "dream" with them in his famous "I Have a Dream" speech. More than just communicat-ing, such metaphors often allow us to share the soul of the speaker.

Because metaphors can be so powerful, you should select them carefully and use them with restraint. Mixing metaphors, combining images that don't fit well together, can confuse listeners and even create an inappropri-ate comic effect that reflects badly on the speaker's ethos. The speaker who intoned, "Let us *march forward* into the *seas* of prosperity," got a laugh he didn't want and hadn't intended. Finally, avoid trite similes and metaphors, such as "his idea is as dead as a doornail," "she has the courage of a lion," or "our team is on an emotional roller-coaster." Overuse has dimmed these comparisons until people are no longer affected by them. Such clichés can damage your ethos because tired comparisons can suggest a dull mind.

Complex Subjects.   When subjects are very complex you cannot hope to describe them in their entirety. You must select words that focus on the es-sential character of the subject, or that emphasize those aspects that con-vey your point of view and encourage certain attitudes in your listeners. A **synecdoche** focuses on part of a subject as a **representation** of it. It stands for the subject, as in "The *tongue* is mightier than the *sword.*" This synec-doche focuses on representative "parts" of the subject: the tongue as the es-sential producer of speech and the sword as a typical instrument of war. This seven-word sentence expresses in concrete form the complex idea that the power of speech is greater than the force of arms. *Movement* is an im-

How Language Helps Us See: The Three *R*'s and Their Techniques

SPEAKER'S NOTES

1 *Relating* abstract subjects to concrete objects of comparison ("Her heart was as big as a Montana sky" — *simile*).

2 *Replacing* expected, abstract words with unexpected, concrete words ("You may think you're bright, but your bulb has burned out" — *metaphor*).

3 *Representing* complex subjects by focusing on selected features or associations ("There's blood on her hands" — *synecdoche*).

portant synecdoche of our time, often used to characterize campaigns of social change such as the civil and human rights movements or the women's movement. This term focuses on the marching and demonstrating aspects of such campaigns to point up their activity and strength.

In addition to using synecdoche, speakers sometimes simplify complex issues by offering sharp moral contrasts, such as *good-evil* or *right-wrong*. Be careful when using such language, however, because this kind of simplification can invite distortion, creating an ethical problem. And be wary when you are a listener, and speakers try to move you by painting the world in black and white.

The verbal techniques based on relationship, replacement, and representation can help you share with listeners your perceptions of the world.

Resources that Help Arouse Feelings

As we noted in Chapter 3, words have two major types of meaning. The *denotative meaning* of a word is its dictionary definition or generally agreed-upon objective usage. For example, the denotative definition of *alcohol* is "a colorless, volatile, flammable liquid, obtained by the fermentation of sugars or starches, which is widely used as a solvent, drug base, explosive, or intoxicating beverage."[12] How different this is from the two connotative definitions in the opening example of this chapter! *Connotative meaning* invests a subject with emotional coloration. Thus, the "intoxicating beverage" is no longer just a chemical substance but either "the poison scourge" or "the oil of conversation." Connotative language intensifies feelings, whereas denotative language encourages detachment.

Many of the techniques of language that help listeners see subjects can also arouse feelings. Simile and metaphor may kindle emotion by the relationships and similarities they suggest. Synecdoche can arouse by the focus it gives to a subject.

Other techniques, however, are especially suited to stimulate emotions. One such technique is the image with which you create a vivid word picture of your subject. Longinus called the image the natural language of the passions. Writing some two thousand years ago, this Roman rhetorician noted that images intensify feelings when "you think you see what you describe, and you place it before the eyes of your hearers."[13] During the grim days of World War II, when London was bombed every night, the British people needed reassurance of their ability to prevail. Sir Winston Churchill advanced an image of hope for Britons in his frequent radio speeches. Note how he built the image on a metaphor of fire:

> **What he [Hitler] has done is to kindle a fire in British hearts . . . which will glow long after all traces of the conflagration he has caused in London have been removed. He has lighted a fire which will burn with a steady and consuming flame until the last vestiges of Nazi tyranny have been burnt out of Europe.[14]**

Another useful technique to arouse feeling is **onomatopoeia,** the tendency of certain words, like *buzz* or *hiss,* to imitate through their sounds the object or action they signify. This technique often serves to heighten the emotional effect of imagery. Suppose you were trying to describe the desolate scene of multitudes of people fleeing from war and starvation. How could you bring that scene into focus for listeners who are far away? We know now that a representative example can serve as the basis of a vivid image. So you might talk about an old man and his granddaughter, the only survivors of their family, as they *trudge* wearily down a dusty road to nowhere.

The word "trudge" is an example of onomatopoeia. Its sound suggests the weary, discouraged walk of the survivors — we can almost breathe the dust disturbed by their steps. Onamatopoeia can bring us into a scene by allowing us to hear its noises, smell its odors, taste its flavors, or touch its surfaces. As it overcomes distance, it also arouses feeling.

Hyperbole, or purposeful exaggeration, may also arouse feelings. Speakers often use hyperbole to encourage action or force listeners to confront problems. Note the use of hyperbole in Martin Luther King, Jr.'s final speech:

> **Men for years now have been talking about war and peace, but now no longer can they just talk about it. It is no longer the choice between violence and nonviolence in this world, it's nonviolence or nonexistence. . . . And in the human rights revolution, if something isn't done and done in a hurry to bring the colored peoples of the world out of their long years of poverty, their long years of hurt and neglect, the whole world is doomed.[15]**

Are the choices really that simple, the consequences that inescapable? Perhaps not, but King wanted his listeners to understand in their minds *and* hearts what would happen if they neglected their moral responsibility. His use of hyperbole was meant to make his audience think and feel simultaneously. As a speaker you should be careful when using hyperbole. The line between exaggerating and lying is all too easy to cross. Save hyperbole for those moments when it is vital for listeners to get your message.

A final technique that helps awaken feelings, especially when the subject is abstract, is **personification.** Personification involves treating inanimate subjects, such as ideas or institutions, as though they had human form or feeling. In the late spring of 1989, Chinese students demonstrating for freedom marched in Tiananmen Square carrying a statue they called the "Goddess of Liberty." They were borrowing a personification that has long been used in the Western world: the representation of liberty as a woman.[16] When those students then had to confront tanks, and their oppressors destroyed the symbol of liberty, it was easy for many of us, living thousands of miles away in another culture, to feel righteous anger over their wrongs and to identify with their cause. Personification makes it easier to arouse feelings about people and values that might otherwise seem far away.

Both speakers and listeners must be careful in using and responding to the language of feeling. Appeals to feeling can be justified only when you are certain of the ethics of your cause. Such appeals can backfire, and destroy your ethos, if listeners believe you are trying to exploit their emotions. We should be equally careful, however, of **euphemisms,** words that numb our feelings by hiding rather than revealing reality. About a half century ago, the British writer George Orwell warned of a developing language of bureaucracy that can deaden our feelings. Sadly, this danger has materialized in our society. Thus, the medical establishment sometimes describes malpractice as a "therapeutic misadventure" and death as a "terminal episode."[17] Government planners may try to dismiss destructive or costly policy blunders by admitting, "Mistakes were made."[18] In such cases "mistakes" may vastly understate the blunder, and the passive construction, "were made," allows the speaker to avoid taking responsibility or assigning blame. Similarly, "friendly fire" means killing your own troops by mistake, and "collateral damage" means bombs hit civilian targets such as hospitals and schools. As Orwell noted, such language "falls upon the facts like soft snow, blurring the outlines and covering up all the details."[19] Your ethical goal must be to avoid extremes of language that arouse or block feeling without justification.

Resources that Bring People Together

You can create a sense of togetherness by using inclusive pronouns, calling on special words, or evoking universal images.

Inclusive Pronouns.   Successful speakers rarely refer to *my* feelings, *my* plans, or *my* cause, but rather *our* feelings, *our* plans, *our* cause. Similarly, they do not say that *I* will do something or *you* will do something, but that *we* will do it together. These inclusive pronouns help unite speakers and listeners. Their importance can be shown best by a negative example.

When Ross Perot addressed an NAACP convention during the 1992 presidential campaign, he repeatedly referred to his African-American audience as "you people." These words highlighted separation and alienated many listeners.

Special Words. Groups develop a set of special words or **culturetypes** that help specify and sustain their identity. Culturetypes express a group's values and goals. They may do this by referring to its heroes and enemies.[20] The rhetorical critic Richard Weaver called these words "god and devil terms."[21] He suggested that *progress* was the primary "god term" of American culture in the mid-twentieth century. When used in speeches, *progress* became a rallying cry. People were willing to do almost anything to achieve the benefits the word suggested. Other related god terms of the 1950s, according to Weaver, included *science, modern,* and *efficient.* Such expressions, he suggested, had unusual power because they were rooted in American values. On the other hand, words like *Communist* and *un-American* were "devil terms." Devil terms strengthen group ties by pointing out what we are not. Culturetypes can change over time. By the mid-1970s words like *natural, peace,* and *communication* were emerging god terms; *liberal* and *pollution* were emerging devil terms.

Michael Calvin McGee, a rhetorical scholar at the University of Iowa, has written about **ideographs**, those special culturetypes that express a country's basic political beliefs.[22] He suggests that words such as *freedom, liberty,* or *democracy* are especially potent in our culture because they are tied to America's political identity. Expressions like "*freedom* fighters" or "*democracy* in action" have unusual power because they use ideographs.

In addition to national culturetypes, you should also consider whether there may be special culturetypes that express group identity at your school and that might be effective with your classroom audience. In what does your school take pride? Who are its rivals and adversaries? The answers to these questions could alert you to special language that may help advance your purpose. One student at Indiana University strengthened her speech for blood donations by arguing: "Purdue students have done it — why can't we?" Presumably, student speakers at Purdue University could use Indiana in the same culturetypal way.

Culturetypes add strength to a speech when used ethically. They remind us of our heritage, make us proud of who we are, and suggest that we must be true to that identity. They can weave the fabric of mythos, a powerful element of proof discussed in Chapter 14. However, because they are so potent, culturetypes lend themselves to abuse. To avoid problems, demonstrate how culturetypes apply to your topic and defend their relevance to your position. Respect those who may reject the invitation culturetypes offer into group identity. After all, another principle close to the American heart is that individual rights, especially the right to reject conventional values and lifestyles, must be preserved.

Universal Symbols. Some symbols draw on experiences that people share, no matter when or where they live. All of us, for example, may turn away from dark, dangerous places to seek the light. All of us may fear illness and seek to maintain health. Clearly, these basic impulses of attraction and avoidance are closely related to the human needs and motives discussed in Chapter 4. Just as clearly, because they are widely shared, these symbolic associations offer you an opportunity to appeal to people across cultural boundaries as well as touch them deeply. Whenever you are able to relate your topic to these important points of symbolic experience — such as light and darkness, storms, the sea, disease and cure, war and peace, structures, the family, and space — you are making use of **archetypal metaphor.** A brief look at three of these metaphors demonstrates their potential power in communication.[23]

Light and Darkness. From the beginnings of time, people have made negative associations with darkness. The dark is cold, unfriendly, and dangerous. On the other hand, light brings warmth and safety. It restores one's sense of control. When speakers use the light-darkness archetype, they usually equate problems or bad times with darkness and solutions or recovery with light. However, Wuer Kaixi, a leader of the Chinese freedom movement, used the image in a unique way. He expressed his horror over the Tiananmen Square massacre of 1989 by referring to a "black sun that rose on the day in June that should have belonged to a season of fresh flowers."[24] If you can find such creative ways to use this traditional metaphor, your audience will listen with special appreciation.

Storms and the Sea. The storm metaphor is often used when describing catastrophes. Quite often the storm occurs at sea — a dangerous place under the best of conditions. The student speaker who argued that "our society is cut adrift — it has lost its moorings, and we don't see the dark cloud on our horizon" used these archetypes in combination to give dramatic expression to his fears of the future.

Disease and Cure. This archetypal metaphor reflects our fears of illness and our ongoing search for cures. The plague was the great symbolic disease of the past; more recently, cancer is the metaphoric illness that dominates public discourse.[25] The speaker using such a metaphor usually offers a cure. If the disease has progressed too far, radical surgery may be the answer. On the night before he was assassinated, Dr. King warned that "the nation is sick, trouble is in the land, confusion all around." Only the commitment of his listeners to political, economic, and spiritual reform, he suggested, might cure that illness.

Similarly, metaphors of *war* and *peace* reflect our fascination with war and our yearning for peace.[26] *Structural* images, as when we talk about "building" speeches or "laying the foundations" for the future, emphasize the human urge to create and control the conditions of our lives. *Family* metaphors often express the dream of a close, even loving relationship among people through such images as "the family of humanity."[27] And *spatial* metaphors often reflect striving upward and forward toward goals and the desire to avoid falling or retreating into failure.

Culturetypes and archetypal metaphors can help you develop a speech that appeals to our need for togetherness and that sets the stage for group action. *Be careful not to overdo such language.* If you strain to use these metaphors, they will seem artificial. But if such language fits naturally, it can make your speech both unifying and dynamic.

Resources that Encourage Action

Taking action requires time and trouble and often involves cost and risk. Moreover, when we agree to act we often must place our trust in a leader, and leaders can disappoint us. Such barriers may make listeners reluctant to act, even when the need is urgent. There are language resources, however, that can help overcome audience inertia.

Many of the techniques that awaken feelings can also be used to encourage action. Hyperbole, imagery, and personification can picture the possible consequences of *not* acting. Synecdoche can focus our attention and prepare the way for action. For example, "We will win, not with muscle power, but with mind power " could be used to raise education as a national priority and to prepare listeners for changes in policy. Similarly, certain archetypal metaphors, most notably those that connect with illness or war, can prompt action, as when we urge listeners "to join the battle against AIDS" or "to fight the disease of war." Other language techniques that can spur an audience to action include alliteration, parallel construction, inversion, and antithesis. Because these techniques are also part of the language of leadership, they can enhance your ethos.

Alliteration. **Alliteration** is the repetition of initial consonant sounds in closely connected words. One student speaker who criticized lowering educational standards summarized her position this way: "We don't need the *d*octrine of *d*umbing *d*own. What we need are leaders who will *s*trive for the educational *s*tars." Her repetition of sounds was distinctive, and served to reinforce her ideas. Alliteration can be very effective in the introductions and conclusions of action-oriented speeches. It can elevate the speaker in the eyes of listeners. But be careful not to overdo it — if used too frequently, it can distract listeners from your ideas or sound contrived. Save it for the moments that really count.

Parallel Construction. **Parallel construction** is the repetition of the same initial words in a sequence of phrases or sentences. We have already discussed this technique in Chapter 8 as a desirable way to word the main points within the overall structure of a speech. But parallel construction also works in conclusions when it puts the formal seal on thoughts developed in the speech. Senator Dan Coats of Indiana, speaking at the Stony Brook School following a discussion of the Holocaust, used parallel construction very effectively:

Hate is not dead. It does not even sleep.
We see it displayed in racism that finds new victims, and reopens old
wounds.

We see it when a synagogue is desecrated.
We see it when a homosexual is attacked and beaten.
We saw it when flame touched tinder in Los Angeles and Asian shop keepers were assaulted in the riot.
We saw it in Florida when a murder was committed in the name of the pro-life cause.[28]

Inversion. Inversion changes the expected word order to make statements more memorable and emphatic. One student speaker concluded his message with a paraphrase of the poet John Donne: "Ask not for whom the bell tolls. It tolls for me. And it tolls for thee. For all of us who love the Bill of Rights, it tolls." The "ask not" that begins this statement and the concluding sentence are both inverted from their usual order. The unusual order of the words gains attention and makes the statement distinctive.

Antithesis. Antithesis combines opposing ideas in the same or adjoining sentences so that listeners can see their choices clearly. Antithesis suggests that you have a clear grasp of options, an important requirement for leadership. One student used antithesis as she summarized her speech on educational reform:

The lack of funding does not cheat us as much as the lack of leadership. The root of our problem is not small budgets, but small people. Shakespeare put it well: "The fault is not in our stars but in ourselves."

The following quotation from President Kennedy's inaugural address is a famous example that interweaves antithesis, inversion, and parallel construction. See if you can identify these techniques at work together:

And so, my fellow Americans: Ask not what your country can do for you — ask what you can do for your country.

My fellow citizens of the world: Ask not what America will do for you, but what together we can do for the freedom of man.[29]

These language resources can help you use the power of the spoken word to promote good causes. Keep in mind, however, that this power can be abused as well as used. Learn to recognize these techniques so that you can resist their attractiveness when they serve less worthy motives.

USING LANGUAGE EFFECTIVELY

Rhetorical style is the unique way you choose and arrange words in a speech. Your rhetorical style reflects your individuality. Therefore, no one can tell you exactly how you should use language. However, there are certain standards for language usage you should strive to achieve whenever

SPEAKER'S NOTES

The Six C's of Effective Language Use

1 Strive for *clarity* by using familiar words in a simple, direct way.
2 Use *colorful*, vivid language to make your message memorable.
3 Develop *concrete* images so the audience can picture what you're talking about.
4 Check the *correctness* of the words you use.
5 Be *concise*.
6 Be *culturally sensitive*: avoid stereotyping and racist or sexist language.

you communicate. We call these standards the six *C's* of clarity, color, concreteness, correctness, conciseness, and cultural sensitivity.

Clarity

Clarity comes first on our list for good reason: unless you are clear, your speech will fail from the outset. This may seem obvious, but it is often ignored! Many speakers lapse into **jargon**, using technical language before an audience that doesn't understand it. Technical vocabularies are necessary for specialized communication in many professions, but when speakers use these vocabularies with listeners who may not understand their meaning, problems are sure to arise. "Positive vorticity advective" may be a perfectly useful expression at a convention of meteorologists, but for general audiences "It's going to rain" would be much better. Speakers who fall into the jargon trap forget the time and trouble *they* had to spend to acquire a technical vocabulary, so they don't bother to translate the unusual terms into lay language. Therefore they march happily forward into a jungle of unfamiliar verbiage, leaving their bewildered listeners lost behind them.

Closely related to jargon are words that are needlessly overblown. A notorious example occurred at the Barnum museum, when signmakers wanted to tell visitors how they could leave the building. Rather than a simple arrow with "Exit" over it, these wordsmiths came up with "To The Egress." There's no telling how many visitors left the museum by mistake, thinking that they were going to see that rare creature — a living, breathing "Egress."

While misunderstandings may result from such innocent incompetence, at other times jargon can seem purposefully befuddling. Some speakers like to satisfy their egos and intimidate others by displaying their technical vocabularies. The parent of a student in Houston received a message from the high school principal regarding a special meeting on a proposed educational program. The message read:

Our school's cross-graded, multiethnic, individualized learning program is designed to enhance the concept of an open-ended learning program with emphasis on a continuum of multiethnic, academically enriched learning, using the identified intellectually gifted child as the agent or director of his own learning. Major emphasis is on cross-graded, multiethnic learning with the main objective being to learn respect for the uniqueness of a person.

The parent responded:

Dear Principal: I have a college degree, speak two foreign languages and know four Indian dialects. I've attended a number of county fairs and three goat ropings, but I haven't the faintest idea as to what you are talking about. Do you?[30]

While some people seem to take a strange joy in *not* communicating, others may try to hide the truth behind a smokescreen of technobabble that is closely related to the problem of euphemism we discussed earlier. Public television commentator Bill Moyers warned his audience at the University of Texas against such dangers of jargon:

If you would . . . serve democracy well, you must first save the language. Save it from the jargon of insiders who talk of the current budget debate in Washington as "megapolicy choices between freeze-feasible base lines." (Sounds more like a baseball game played in the Arctic Circle.) Save it from the smokescreen artists, who speak of "revenue enhancement" and "tax-base erosion control" when they really mean a tax increase. . . . Save it from . . . the official revisionists of reality, who say that the United States did not withdraw our troops from Lebanon, we merely "backloaded our augmentation personnel."[31]

Fearing what might happen if audiences actually understood their meaning, such speakers attempt to hide behind cloudy technical language. In contrast, ethical speaking is clear and direct.

One way to achieve clarity is through **amplification**, in which you rephrase ideas to emphasize or clarify them. Providing important bits of information or examples that compare and contrast are other ways to amplify an idea. In effect, you tell listeners something, then you expand and repeat what you are saying. Observe the techniques of amplification at work in the following speech sample, in which each sentence expands and repeats the meaning of the sentence that precedes it:

The roadrunner is not just a cartoon character that makes a fool of Wile E. Coyote. It is a member of the cuckoo family and state bird of New Mexico. Still, the cartoon roadrunner and the real roadrunner have much in common. Both are incredibly fast, real roadrunners having been tracked at ground speeds over 15 miles per hour. Neither takes to the air to chase prey or escape a predator. Both look rather awkward as they run, with strides up to 20 inches long — a real feat for a bird that is only 24 inches long with over half its length in its tail.

Color

Color refers to the emotional intensity or vividness of language. Colorful words are memorable because they stand out in our minds. Those who use them also are remembered.

During the 1996 presidential primaries each of the contenders was searching for a way to capture the imagination of voters and to stand out from the pack. In such a contest, those who use language colorfully have an advantage. Patrick Buchanan moved from a long-shot candidate to a leading contender at least partially because of his skill with words. Early in the campaign, Steve Forbes gained a lot of attention through an advertising campaign in which he proposed a flat tax. Senator Phil Gramm, a candidate who later withdrew from the race, criticized Forbes on grounds that his plan would favor the wealthy by eliminating taxes on dividend and interest income. About the flat tax Gramm said, "I reject the idea that income derived from labor should be taxed and that income derived from capital should not."[32]

A nice use of contrast, but look how Buchanan expressed the same idea: "Under Forbes' plan, lounge lizards in Palm Beach would pay a lower tax rate than steelworkers in Youngstown." Later he added that Forbes' plan had been drawn up by "the boys down at the yacht basin." While Gramm's words are a study in abstraction, Buchanan's language is both colorful and concrete. The use of the animal metaphor, "lounge lizards," is striking. So is the use of contrast, setting the "lounge lizards" and the "boys down at the yacht basin" against the steelworkers, Palm Beach against Youngstown. It's sloth and privilege against character and virtue, and we know which side Buchanan is on. These colorful symbols reflected his commitment.

Colorful language can also create sensory images. We saw this technique at work in our earlier excerpt from the student speech about James Johnson: "[He] knows the loveliest, most sparkling springs. . . . He taught me . . . why the mist rises on a lake at night, how to make the best blackberry jam you ever tasted, and how to take care of baby wild rabbits. . . ." This speaker selected her images deliberately to awaken several of her listeners' senses — to make them "see" the mist, "taste" the jam, "feel" the rabbits' fur. She used adjectives sparingly but with striking pictorial result ("sparkling springs" — notice how the alliteration contributes to the pleasing effect). Adjectives should not be strewn about a speech extravagantly but saved so that they really count when you need them.

When you use colorful language effectively, your audience will find *you* to be colorful as well. Your ethos will rise as your listeners assign you high marks for competence and attractiveness. For all these reasons, color is an important standard as you develop your capacity to use language.

Concreteness

It is virtually impossible to discuss anything of significance without using some abstract words. However, if the language in your speech is overly abstract, listeners may lose interest. Moreover, because abstract language is more ambiguous than concrete language, a speech full of abstractions invites misunderstanding. Consider this continuum of terms describing a cat.

Mehitabel is a/an

creature	animal	mammal	cat	Persian cat	gray Persian cat

abstract>————————————————————————————————>concrete

A similar continuum can be applied to active verbs. If we wanted to describe how a person moves, we could use any of the following terms:

Jennifer

moves		walks		strides

abstract>————————————————————————————————>concrete

Again, the more concrete your language, the more pictorial and precise the information you can convey. Concrete words are also easier for listeners to remember. Therefore, your language should be as concrete as the subject permits.

Correctness

Nothing can damage your ethos more quickly than a glaring misuse of language. Mistakes in grammar or word selection can be disastrous because most audiences connect such errors with incompetence. They are likely to reason that anyone who misuses language can hardly offer good advice. When you select your words, be careful that they say exactly what you mean to say.

Occasionally beginning speakers, wishing to impress people with the size of their vocabularies, get caught up in the "thesaurus syndrome." They will look up a simple word to find a synonym that sounds more impressive or sophisticated. What they may not realize is that the words shown as synonyms often have slightly different meanings. For example, the words "disorganize" and "derange" are sometimes listed as synonymous, yet their meanings are different enough that to use them interchangeably could cause serious problems. Just try referring to a disorganized person as deranged, and you will see what we mean. Use your dictionary when you have any doubts about word choice.

People often err when using words that sound similar. Such confusions are called **malapropisms**, after Mrs. Malaprop, a character in an eighteenth-century play by Richard Sheridan. She would say, "He is the very *pineapple* of politeness," when she meant *pinnacle*. Archie Bunker in *All In The Family* also was prone to malapropisms, such as "Don't let your imagination run *rancid*" when he meant *rampant*. William J. Crocker of

Armidale College in New South Wales, Australia, collected the following malapropisms from student speeches in his classes:

> A speaker can add interest to his talk with an *antidote.* [anecdote]
> Disagreements can arise from an unintended *conception.* [Indeed they can!]
> The speaker hopes to arouse *apathy* in his audience. [sympathy? empathy?]
> Good language can be reinforced by good *gestation.* [gestures — but perhaps this relates to the conception mentioned above]
> The speaker can use either an inductive or a *seductive* approach.[33] [deductive — but seductive can work too, especially when it creates a conception!]

Students are not the only ones who make such blunders. A reporter once praised an attorney for his ability to *dissemble* a bicycle. As a colleague observed with heavy irony, no doubt the man could "dissemble"; after all, he was a lawyer. But "dissemble" means to conceal facts, intentions, or feelings by talking around a point. What the unfortunate reporter was praising was the lawyer's ability to "disassemble" the bicycle.[34] Elected officials are also not above an occasional malapropism. One former United States senator declared that he would oppose to his last ounce of energy any effort to build a "nuclear waste *suppository*" [repository] in his state.[35] And a former mayor of Chicago once introduced Carl Sandburg as "the poet *lariat* [laureate] of the United States."[36]

The lesson is clear. To avoid being unintentionally humorous, use a current dictionary to check the meaning and pronunciation of any word you feel uncertain about.

Conciseness

In discussing clarity we talked about the importance of amplification in speeches. Although it may seem contradictory, you must also be concise, even while you are amplifying your ideas. You must make your points quickly and efficiently. Follow the advice on speaking given by President Franklin Delano Roosevelt to his son James: "Be sincere . . . be brief . . . be seated!"

Long, drawn-out speeches lose audience interest. They kill the impulse toward action in persuasive speeches. A concise speech helps listeners see more clearly and feel more powerfully.

To achieve conciseness, work for simple, direct expression. Thomas Jefferson once said, "The most valuable of all talents is that of never using two words when one will do." Use the active voice rather than the passive in your verbs: "We demand action" is more concise — and more direct, colorful, and clear — than "Action is demanded by us."

You can also be concise by using comparisons that reduce complex issues to the essentials. Sojourner Truth, a nineteenth-century human rights activist, once had to counter the argument that society should not educate African-Americans and women because of their alleged "inferiority." She destroyed that then-powerful position with a simple parable: "If my cup won't hold but a pint, and yours holds a quart, wouldn't you be mean not to let me have a little half-measure full?"[37]

The goal of conciseness encourages the use of **maxims**, those wise but compact sayings that summarize the beliefs of a people. During the Chinese freedom demonstrations of 1989, a sign carried by students in Tiananmen Square adapted the maxim of Patrick Henry, "Give Me Democracy or Give Me Death." Sadly, the Chinese authorities took them at their word. In Colorado, demonstrators at a nuclear plant carried a sign reading "Hell No, We Won't Glow!," a variation on a chant often heard in anti-Vietnam war rallies of the 1960s, "Hell no, we won't go!"

As these examples suggest, maxims can have special power in attracting mass-media attention. When printed on signs, they satisfy the hunger of the press for visual messages. Their brevity makes them ideally suited to the rigid time constraints of television news. Of even greater importance, maxims evoke cultural memories and invite identification. When the Chinese students adapted the Patrick Henry maxim and displayed the goddess of liberty, they were in effect both declaring that they shared American values and appealing for our assistance in their desperate struggle. When their cause was crushed, many Americans felt the injustice in a personal way, and the resulting breach between the Chinese government and our own remains to this day.

Maxims serve well within speeches when they focus the message in a compact, memorable statement. Just remember, they cannot substitute for careful, well-supported arguments. Once you have developed a responsible and substantive speech, consider how you might use maxims to reinforce your message.

Cultural Sensitivity

Respect for the power of words reveals how language can lift and unite or wound and hurt different members of your audience. This respect develops into **cultural sensitivity.** If you read the historic writings on human communication, you will find little about cultural sensitivity. The ancient Greeks, for example, worried only about speaking to other male Athenians who were "free men" and citizens. Only in today's world with its emphasis on empowering a wide spectrum of cultures, lifestyles, and races and its pursuit of gender equity, has cultural sensitivity emerged as an important standard for effective language usage.

As we noted in Chapter 4, there is a very high probability that your classroom audience will represent different cultures. As listeners, they may be very sensitive to any negative allusions or clumsy efforts of speakers to identify with folkways that aren't their own. Campaigning for the presidential nomination in his native Southern region in 1992, Bill Clinton was comfortable using such folksy expressions as "my opponents are squealing like a pig caught under a gate." Speaking in Georgia in the same campaign, however, Senator Bob Kerrey from Nebraska, was less adept. At Atlanta's Spelman College, Kerrey declared that if Clinton got the nomination, Bush would open him up "like a soft peanut." Kerrey's listeners looked at each other with puzzled faces. Someone must have spoken with his speechwriters, because in later speeches in that peanut-producing area Kerrey changed the expression to "boiled peanut."[38] The lesson seems clear: don't try to be what you're not, or you may look ridiculous.

A lack of cultural sensitivity almost always has negative consequences. At best, audience members may be mildly offended; at worst, they will be irate enough to reject both you and your message. Cultural sensitivity begins with being attuned to the diversity of your audience, appreciative of the differences between cultural groups, and careful about the words you choose when referring to those who may be different from you. Although you must make some generalizations about your audience, avoid getting caught up in stereotypes that suggest that one group is inferior in any way to another. Stay away from racial, ethnic, religious, or gender-based humor and avoid any expressions that might be interpreted as racist or sexist. (See the Speaker's Notes in Chapter 4, p. 121, for Guidelines on Avoiding Racist and Sexist Language.)

IN SUMMARY

Many of us underestimate the power of our words. The language we select can determine whether we succeed or fail as communicators.

The Power of the Spoken Word.   Oral language is more spontaneous, less formal, and more interactive than written communication. The spoken word is more expansive, alters the structure of sentences, and depends more on the cadence or rhythm of language as it is voiced.

Words can shape our perceptions. They invite us to see and share the world from the speaker's point of view. Words can also distort reality and block certain ways of seeing. Words can arouse intense feeling by overcoming the barriers of time, distance, and audience apathy. The spoken word can bring listeners together in a common identity. Finally, words can prompt us to action.

Language Resources.   Speakers utilize certain techniques to activate the power of language. To help audiences see your point of view, *simile* can clarify abstract subjects by showing their *relationship* to things more concrete and familiar. *Metaphor* offers new perspectives by following the principle of *replacement,* surprising audiences with unexpected uses of words. *Synecdoche* helps simplify complex subjects by *representation,* focusing on essential, strategic features or associations.

To arouse feelings, use words that activate connotative meanings. The *image* creates a stimulating word-picture. *Onomatopoeia* uses words that mime the subjects they refer to. *Hyperbole* uses exaggeration to overcome audience lethargy and kindle powerful feelings. *Personification* attributes human qualities to abstractions or impersonal institutions.

To bring listeners together, use inclusive pronouns such as "our" and "we." You can also use a special vocabulary of symbols. *Culturetypes* express and invoke the values of a group or society, and *archetypal metaphors* remind us of our common heritage as human beings. When properly used, such techniques as *alliteration, parallel construction, inversion,* and *antithesis* can enhance appeals for action.

Using Language Effectively. *Rhetorical style* is the unique way you choose and arrange words. Although style varies with the user and with different topics, audiences, and situations, you should strive to satisfy the six standards of *clarity, color, concreteness, correctness, conciseness,* and *cultural sensitivity.* Clear language is simple and direct and draws its comparisons from everyday life. Amplification promotes clarity by dwelling on important, difficult points.

Color refers to the emotional intensity and vividness of language and is especially vital to the sharing of feeling. The more concrete a word, the more specific the information it conveys. Correctness is vital to ethos because grammatical errors and improper word choices can lower perceptions of your competence. *Malapropisms,* confusions among words based on similarities of sound, can be very damaging. Concise speakers strive for brevity, often using comparisons that reduce complex issues to the essentials. *Maxims* are the ultimate in conciseness. *Cultural sensitivity* demands that a speaker be aware of the diversity within an audience and respectful and appreciative of cultural differences.

TERMS TO KNOW

simile	alliteration
metaphor	parallel construction
synecdoche	inversion
onomatopoeia	antithesis
image	rhetorical style
hyperbole	jargon
personification	amplification
euphemism	malapropism
culturetype	maxim
ideograph	cultural sensitivity
archetypal metaphor	

DISCUSSION

1. The example that opens this chapter presents arguments for and against whiskey, using connotative language. Rephrase these arguments, using denotative language. How does this change affect the power of the appeals? Which speech situations call for more denotative speech? How can connotative words be misused? Under what circumstances are they most appropriate?

2. In the 1950s, Richard Weaver suggested that *progress* was the primary culturetype of American society. What words would you nominate as culturetypes in contemporary society? Why? How are they used now in public communication? Find and share examples from speeches, essays, editorials, cartoons, or advertisements.

3. Look for examples of the use and abuse of specific language techniques in public communication. Report in class and explain why and how they work.

4. Analyze how you used the power of language in your last speech. What, if any, barriers to perception or feeling did you have to overcome, and what techniques did you use? Could you have improved the effectiveness of your language? How?

APPLICATION

1. Use archetypal metaphors to describe the following abstract concepts:

   friendship

   freedom

   justice

   brotherhood

   democracy

   poverty

   opportunity

   Present your descriptions in class. Which work most effectively and why?

2. Study the language used in a contemporary political speech. How is the power of language exercised? What special techniques are used? Evaluate the effectiveness of this usage according to the standards discussed here.

3. Using published pamphlets and speeches, choose one of the following social/political movements and determine its heroes and villains: anti-abortion, civil rights, contract-with-America, environmental, gay rights, and women's liberation. How well does the language of these pamphlets or speeches satisfy the standards of the "six C's": clarity, color, concreteness, correctness, conciseness, and cultural sensitivity?

4. To explore and help develop stylistic techniques, your instructor will assign different language techniques to members of the class and then present a subject. Your task will be to make a statement about this subject using the technique you have been assigned. Share these statements in class. Try this exercise several times, using different subjects and dif-

ferent techniques of language. Evaluate in class what this exercise reveals about the spoken word.

5. Identify and discuss the language techniques used by Elie Wiesel in his Nobel Prize acceptance speech in Appendix B. What techniques were used to reawaken group identity? Did they work for you? Why or why not?

NOTES

1. William Raspberry, "Any Candidate Will Drink to That," *Austin American Statesman,* 11 May 1984, A-10. The "Whiskey Speech," a legend in Southern politics, was originally presented some years ago by N. S. Sweat, Jr., during a heated campaign to legalize the sale of liquor-by-the-drink in Mississippi. Because about half of his constituents favored the question and the other half were vehemently opposed, Representative "Soggy" Sweat decided to defuse the issue with humor.

2. Jerry Tarver, "Words in Time: Some Reflections on the Language of Speech," *Vital Speeches of the Day,* 15 April 1988, p. 410.

3. Tarver, pp. 410–412.

4. These powers of language were first explored in Michael Osborn, *Orientations to Rhetorical Style* (Chicago: Science Research Associates, Inc., 1976), and are developed further in Michael Osborn, "Rhetorical Depiction," in *Form, Genre, and the Study of Political Discourse,* ed. Herbert W. Simons and Aram A. Aghazarian (Columbia: University of South Carolina Press, 1986), pp. 79–107.

5. Based on the account in Claire Perkins, "The Many Symbolic Faces of Fred Smith: Charismatic Leadership in the Bureaucracy," *The Journal of the Tennessee Speech Communication Association* 11 (1985), 22.

6. Jesse Jackson, "Common Ground and Common Sense," *Vital Speeches of the Day,* 15 Aug. 1988, pp. 649–653.

7. From a transcription of the debate, CNN, 15 February 1996.

8. Listeners whose lives seem dull and unrewarding are especially susceptible to such dramas. See the discussion in Eric Hoffer, *The True Believer: Thoughts on the Nature of Mass Movements* (New York: Harper, 1951).

9. Union organizing song written in 1932 by Florence Reece, wife of a leader of the National Miners Union in Harlan County, Kentucky.

10. Speech at Galesburg, Illinois, *U.S. News & World Report,* 23 January 1995, p. 23.

11. "Southern-speak: Clinton Uses It Well," Norfolk *Virginian-Pilot and the Ledger-Star,* 10 April 1994, p. A6.

12. Adapted from *The American Heritage Dictionary,* 2nd ed. (Boston: Houghton Mifflin, 1985), p. 92.

13. Longinus, "On the Sublime," in *The Great Critics: An Anthology of Literary Criticism,* trans. W. Rhys Roberts and ed. James Harry Smith and Edd Winfield Parks (New York: Norton, 1951), p. 82.

14. Winston Churchill, *Blood, Sweat, and Tears* (New York: Putnam, 1941), pp. 367–369.

15. Martin Luther King, Jr., from a transcription of "I've Been to the Mountaintop," delivered in Memphis, TN, 4 Apr. 1968. For complete text, see *Texts in Context: Critical Dialogues on Significant Episodes in American Political Rhetoric,* ed. Michael C. Leff and Fred J. Kauffeld (Davis, CA: Hermagoras Press, 1989), pp. 311–321.

16. Michael Calvin McGee, "The Origins of Liberty: A Feminization of Power," *Communication Monographs* 47 (1980): 27–45.

17. "Stamp Out 'Doublespeak'," *Parade,* 10 January 1988, p. 16.

18. "'To Be' in Their Bonnets: A Matter of Semantics," *Atlantic,* Feb. 1992, p. 20.

19. "Politics and the English Language," *Shooting an Elephant and Other Essays* (London: Secker and Warburg, 1950), p. 97.

20. Osborn, *Orientations to Rhetorical Style,* p. 16.

21. Richard Weaver, "Ultimate Terms in Contemporary Rhetoric," in *The Ethics of Rhetoric* (Chicago: Henry Regnery, 1953), pp. 211–232.

22. Michael Calvin McGee, "The Ideograph: A Link Between Rhetoric and Ideology," *Quarterly Journal of Speech* 66 (1980), 1–16.

23. For further insights into the function of archetypal metaphors, see Michael Osborn, "Archetypal Metaphor in Rhetoric: The Light-Dark Family," *Quarterly Journal of Speech* 53 (1967), 115–126, and "The Evolution of the Archetypal Sea in Rhetoric and Poetic," *Quarterly Journal of Speech* 63 (1977), 347–363.

24. *Time,* 10 July 1989, p. 32.

25. For an insightful discussion of the metaphors we use to construct our ideas about our illnesses, see Susan Sontag, *Illness as Metaphor* (New York: Vintage Books, 1979) and *AIDS and Its Metaphors* (New York: Farrar, Straus, and Giroux, 1988).

26. See Robert Ivie, "Images of Savagery in American Justifications for War," *Communication Monographs* 47 (1980): 279–294.

27. See another side of this image in J. Vernon Jensen, "British Voices on the Eve of the American Revolution: Trapped by the Family Metaphor," *Quarterly Journal of Speech* 63 (1977): 43–50.

28. "The Virtue of Tolerance," *Vital Speeches of the Day,* 21 August 1993, p. 646.

29. Kennedy, "Inaugural Address," p. 11.

30. Ann Landers, "Translate Gobbledygook, Please," *The Commercial Appeal,* 21 August 1992, p. C3.

31. Bill Moyers, "Commencement Address," presented at the Lyndon B. Johnson School of Public Affairs, University of Texas, Austin. Cited in *Time,* 19 June 1985, p. 68.

32. All quotations are from *USA Today,* 18 January 1996, p. 4A.

33. "Malapropisms Live!" *Spectra,* May 1986, p. 6.

34. Memphis *Commercial Appeal,* 24 July 1991, p. A-13.

35. Richard Lacayo, "Picking Lemons for the Plums?" *Time,* 31 July 1989, p. 17.

36. *New York Times,* 30 Jan. 1960. Cited in James B. Simpson, *Simpson's Contemporary Quotations* (Boston: Houghton Mifflin, 1988), p. 208.

37. Sojourner Truth, "Ain't I a Woman?" in *Feminism: The Essential Historical Writings,* ed. Miriam Schneir (New York: Random House, 1972), p. 95.

38. *Time,* 9 Mar. 1992, p. 19.

Presenting Your Speech

> Whosoever hath a good presence and a good fashion carries continual letters of recommendation.
>
> — Francis Bacon

Lou worked very hard preparing his speech. He selected a good topic that he really cared about. He researched and developed his topic carefully and found many good examples to use in his presentation. Despite all of this good work, Lou's speech fell flat. Within the first minute of his presentation he had lost most of his audience.

The trouble began when Lou opened his mouth. His voice did not project the energy and enthusiasm that are necessary to capture an audience's attention and make them want to listen. He spoke in a monotone, never varying his pitch or loudness. He looked down at his notes or up at the ceiling, never making good eye contact with his audience. His soft, hypnotic voice almost lulled them to sleep. Unfortunately, Lou's oral presentation suggested that he was not really interested in his topic or trying to communicate. Little wonder that his listeners found their daydreams more interesting and that his worthy speech never really had a hearing that day.

Successful public speaking involves both *what* you say and *how* you say it. In this chapter we turn our attention to "how you say it," or **presentation**. We consider what makes a presentation effective, the major methods of presentation, adapting for video presentations, responding to audience feedback, handling questions and answers, developing an effective speaking voice, using your body to communicate, and how to practice effectively.

The presentation skills you learn in this class should help you in other communication settings. They will be useful in job interviews, meetings, and even social occasions. Once you gain a sense of presence, it tends to stay with you over the years. It allows you to carry what Francis Bacon called "continual letters of recommendation."

WHAT MAKES AN EFFECTIVE PRESENTATION?

An effective presentation allows you to share your message with your audience. The words *community* and *communication* both stem from the Latin word for *common*. An effective presentation makes it possible for the speaker and audience to hold ideas and feelings in common, even when they come from different cultural backgrounds.

An effective presentation begins with your attitude. You must be committed to your subject and want to share this commitment with your audience. You must want to enlighten listeners, move them, perhaps change the way they think about the topic, or even encourage them to act. The way you speak should convey your enthusiasm, giving energy and force to your speech. Your attitude should assure listeners that you really care about them and your topic.

An effective presentation does not call attention to itself or distract from your message. You want your listeners to focus on what you are saying, not how you are saying it. Consequently, you should avoid pompous pronunciations, artificial vocal patterns, and overly dramatic gestures. Your presentation should be readily intelligible and loud enough to be heard in all parts of the room.

Finally, an effective presentation sounds natural and conversational — as though you were talking *with* your audience, not *at* them. Talking with people instead of at them helps reduce the psychological distance between yourself and an audience. It brings you closer together with your listeners. In this time when we are used to media presentations that bring speakers up close and personal, audiences expect — even demand — such a style. Television has changed the rules of the game.[1]

Immediacy is a term that describes the sense of closeness experienced between speaker and audience in successful communication.[2] James McCroskey, a specialist in the study of immediacy, has written:

> **Immediacy increases the audience's attentiveness; it reduces tension and anxiety for both speaker and audience; it creates greater liking between speaker and audience; and it increases the probability that the speaker's purpose will be accomplished.[3]**

Immediacy relates to the likableness dimension of ethos that we discussed in Chapter 2. It encourages listeners to open their minds to you and to be influenced by what you say.[4]

How, then, can you encourage immediacy? You can often reduce psychological distance by reducing actual distance and by removing physical barriers between yourself and listeners. Step out from behind the lectern and move closer to the audience. Smile at listeners when appropriate, maintain eye contact with them, use gestures to clarify and reinforce ideas, and let your voice express your feelings. Even if your heart is pumping, your hands feel a little sweaty, and your knees feel a bit weak, the self you show to listeners should be a person in control of the situation. Listeners admire and identify with speakers who maintain what Ernest Hemingway once called "grace under pressure."

Your goal should be a speech characterized by an **expanded conversational style**, which we discussed in detail in Chapter 1. An expanded conversational style is direct, spontaneous, colorful, and tuned to the responses of listeners. Such a style, however, is a bit more careful and formal than everyday conversation.

To return to the theme that opened this section: *an effective presentation makes your ideas more effective in the living moments of an actual speech.* The remainder of this chapter will help you move toward this goal of effective presentation.

METHODS OF PRESENTATION

There are four major methods of speech presentation: impromptu speaking, memorized text presentation, reading from a manuscript, and extemporaneous speaking. We cover these major methods in this section and also include suggestions for making video presentations, responding to audience feedback, and handling questions and answers.

Impromptu Speaking

Impromptu speaking is sometimes called "speaking off the cuff," a phrase that suggests you could put all the notes for your speech on the cuff of your shirt. Impromptu speaking is useful when you have little or no time for preparation or practice. The incident we described in Chapter 8, in which we learned during a zoning hearing that developers were proposing a helicopter port in our neighborhood, called for an impromptu speech. At work you might find yourself being asked to make a presentation "in fifteen minutes." In meetings you may want to "say a few words" about something. You can also use impromptu speaking skills in other classes — to answer a question or comment on a point your professor has made.

When you have just a few minutes to prepare, first determine your purpose. What do you want the audience to know? Why is this important? Next, decide on your main points. Don't try to cover too much. Limit yourself to no more than three main points. If you have access to any type of writing material — a note pad, a scrap of paper — jot down a memory-jogging word for each idea, either in the order of importance or as the ideas seem to flow naturally. This skeletal outline will keep you from ram-

Public meetings and hearings often call for impromptu presentations for which people have little or no time for preparation and practice. Standing to speak is a form of emphasis that marks your ideas as important.

bling or forgetting something that is important. Stick to the main points, enumerating them as you go: "My first point is. . . . Second, it is important to. . . . Finally, it is clear that. . . ." Use the **PREP formula:** state a **p**oint, give a **r**eason or **e**xample, then restate the **p**oint. Keep your presentation short and end with a summary of your remarks.

Point:	**The proposal to allow John Clark to operate a helicopter port in the neighborhood is not sound.**
Reason/Example(s):	**The noise generated by helicopters taking off and landing would destroy the tranquility of this quiet residential neighborhood. It would be especially disturbing to the residents of the nursing home one block from the proposed facility.**
Restate Point:	**Therefore, we ask you to vote against this proposal.**

An impromptu speech often is part of a series of such speeches as people express their ideas in meetings. The earlier speeches create the context for your presentation. If others stood at the front of the room to speak, you should do so as well. If earlier speakers remained seated, you may wish to do the same. Much depends on whether earlier speakers have been successful. If these speakers offended listeners while making standing presentations, you may wish to remain seated to differentiate yourself from them. If seated speakers have made trivial presentations, you may wish to stand to signal that what you are going to say is important.

Fortunately, most impromptu speaking situations are relatively casual. No one expects a polished presentation on a moment's notice, but the ability to organize your ideas quickly and effectively and to present them confidently puts you at a great advantage. The principles of preparing speeches that you learn in this course can help you become a more effective impromptu speaker.

Memorized Text Presentation

Memorized text presentations are written out, committed to memory, and delivered word-for-word. Because the introduction and conclusion of a speech are important in gaining audience attention and leaving a lasting impression, their wording should be carefully planned. These are the only parts of most speeches that we would advise you to memorize. You might also want to memorize short congratulatory remarks, a toast, or a brief award acceptance speech. In general, however, you should avoid trying to memorize entire speeches because this method of presentation poses many problems.

Beginning speakers who try to memorize their speeches usually get so caught up with *remembering* that they forget about *communicating*. The result usually sounds stilted or "sing-songy." Speaking from memory also inhibits adapting to audience feedback. It can keep you from clarifying points that the audience doesn't understand or from following up on ideas that seem especially effective. Another problem with memorized speeches is that they must be written out in advance. Most people do not write in an effective oral style. The major differences between oral and written language, covered in Chapter 10, bear repeating. Good oral style uses short, direct, conversational patterns. Even sentence fragments can be acceptable. Repetition, rephrasing, and amplification are more necessary in speaking than in writing. The sense of rhythm, and saving the most forceful idea for the end of the sentence, are more important in oral style. Imagery can be especially useful to help the audience visualize what you are talking about.

If you must memorize a speech, commit the speech so thoroughly to memory that you can concentrate on communicating with your audience. If you experience a "mental block," *keep talking*. Restate or rephrase your last point to put your mind back on track. If this doesn't work, you may find yourself forced into an extemporaneous style and discover that you can express your ideas better without the constraints of exact wording.

Reading from a Manuscript

In a **manuscript presentation** a written text is read to an audience from either a paper script or a teleprompter. Manuscript presentations share many of the same problems of memorized presentations. Speakers are bound to a text, which inhibits adapting to feedback. This problem is worsened with manuscript presentations because speakers must keep their eyes on the script and consequently lose eye contact with listeners. As with memorized presentations, most people have problems writing in a good oral style.

There are some additional problems exclusive to manuscript presentations. Most people do not read aloud well. Their presentations lack variety. Also, when people plan to read a speech, they typically do not practice enough. Unless speakers are comfortable with the material, they end up glued to their manuscripts rather than communicating with their listeners. Other problems may arise if your manuscript pages get out of order, or if you pick up the wrong paper or teleprompter material on your way to a presentation.

Although this last predicament may sound improbable, it can happen, as President Clinton can confirm. In September of 1993 Clinton presented his "Health Care Address to Congress." He had been working on the speech for some time and finished revising it on the ride to the Capitol. The final changes were entered onto computer disks immediately before he was to speak. Here is a report of what happened:

> . . . no one realized that a White House communications aide had already accidentally merged the new speech with an old file of the February 17 speech to Congress. . . . When Clinton took the podium minutes later, he was understandably alarmed to see a seven-month-old speech on the teleprompter's display screens. Clinton told the news to Gore. . . . Gore summoned Stephanopoulos, who scrambled to fix the mistake, eventually downloading the correct version. . . . But for seven minutes, Clinton vamped with just notes.[5]

During the first seven minutes of his presentation, the President was forced into an extemporaneous style — the method of presentation most communication instructors recommend. The speech was received with high acclaim:

> For a man reading the wrong speech off his teleprompter, Bill Clinton spoke with persuasive passion as he addressed Congress and the nation about health care last week. Gone was the Slick Willie. . . . Suddenly Clinton looked the leader millions of Americans hoped they were voting for: decisive, forceful, even visionary.[6]

Manuscript presentations are most useful when accurate wording is important or time constraints are severe, as in formal political speeches, legal announcements, or media presentations that must be timed within seconds. Extemporaneous presentations may include quotations or technical information that should be read to ensure accuracy. Because you may need to make a manuscript presentation at some time, we include some suggestions to help you with this presentation style:

- Use large print to prepare your manuscript so you can see it without straining.
- Use light pastel rather than white paper, to cut down on glare from lights.
- Double- or triple-space the manuscript.
- Mark pauses with slashes.
- Highlight material you want to emphasize.
- Practice speaking from your manuscript so that you can maintain eye contact with your audience.

Figure 11.1 shows a sample manuscript prepared for presentation. Note that two or three slashes together indicate longer pauses. The speaker highlights emphasized material by underlining it.

If possible, videotape your rehearsal, then review the tape to evaluate your presentation. Do you sound as though you are *talking with* someone or *reading?* Did you maintain *eye contact* with the imaginary audience? If you stumbled over phrasing or mispronounced certain words, revise your manuscript to make your presentation flow more smoothly.

Extemporaneous Speaking

Extemporaneous speaking is prepared and practiced but not written out or memorized. When you speak extemporaneously, your wording will differ each time you run through your speech. It will sound spontaneous and natural because it is not written out word for word. An extemporaneous presentation lets you adjust to your audience as you observe listener response.

Extemporaneous speaking involves preparation and practice; therefore, it is more polished than impromptu speaking. This advance preparation shows up in the better organization of material, the greater support you bring to your points, and the smoother flow of your presentation. Most important, extemporaneous speaking allows you to respond to audience feedback and to adapt your presentation accordingly. Because extemporaneous speaking combines the best characteristics of the forms we have discussed, many instructors prefer that you use it for most of your classroom speeches.

Responding to Feedback from Your Audience. As we saw in Chapter 1, **feedback** is the immediate response of listeners to your speech. Since most feedback is nonverbal, you should maintain eye contact with your audience so that you can respond to the signals listeners send. Use feedback to monitor whether listeners understand you, are interested, and

FIGURE 11.1
Sample Speech Script

WE AMERICANS ARE BIG ON MONUMENTS. / WE BUILD MONUMENTS IN MEMORY OF OUR HEROES. // WASHINGTON, JEFFERSON, AND LINCOLN LIVE ON IN OUR NATION'S CAPITAL. // WE ERECT MONUMENTS TO HONOR OUR MARTYRS. / THE MINUTE MAN STILL STANDS GUARD AT CONCORD. / THE FLAG IS EVER RAISED OVER IWO JIMA. / SOMETIMES WE EVEN CONSTRUCT MONUMENTS TO COMMEMORATE VICTIMS. // IN ASHBURN PARK DOWNTOWN THERE IS A MONUMENT TO THOSE WHO DIED IN THE YELLOW FEVER EPIDEMICS. /// HOWEVER, <u>THERE ARE SOME THINGS IN OUR HISTORY THAT WE DON'T MEMORIALIZE</u> // PERHAPS WE WOULD JUST AS SOON FORGET WHAT HAPPENED. /// LAST SUMMER I VISITED SUCH A PLACE — // <u>THE MASSACRE SITE AT WOUNDED KNEE.</u>

agree with what you are saying. Because positive feedback in these areas does not cause problems, we concentrate here on using negative feedback to make on-the-spot adjustments in your presentation.

Feedback that Signals Misunderstanding.   You can usually tell when listeners don't understand by the dumbfounded expressions on their faces. You may need to define an unfamiliar word or rephrase an idea to make it more understandable. You could add an example or story to make an abstract concept more concrete. It might help to compare or contrast an unfamiliar idea with something the audience already knows and understands. You could smile and acknowledge the problem: "You don't understand this, do you? Let me put it another way." Then go on to provide the clearer explanation needed.

Feedback that Signals Loss of Interest. It's easy to spot a bored audience. Listeners wiggle in their seats, drum their fingers, or develop a glazed look. To regain their interest, remind them why your speech is important to them. Provide an example from your own experience or ask a question that calls for a show of hands. Try telling a story that makes your idea come to life. You might even need to startle the audience into attention with an unusual statement. Keep in mind that enthusiasm is contagious. Be more animated. Move from behind the lectern and closer to your listeners. If none of these techniques work, stick with your message, stress your main points, and try to act as though you are satisfied with your presentation. In all likelihood, some people — probably more than you think — will have found the speech interesting.

Feedback that Signals Disagreement. Signs of disagreement include frowns, scowls, or shaking heads. Fortunately, there are a number of techniques you can use to soften disagreement. If you anticipate resistance, work hard to establish your ethos in the introduction of your speech. It is important for your listeners to see you as a competent, trustworthy, and likable person who has their best interests at heart.

To be perceived as competent, you must *be* competent. Arm yourself with a surplus of information, examples, and testimony from sources your audience will respect. Practice your presentation until it is polished. Set the example of tolerance yourself by respecting positions different from your own.

You may find that although you differ with listeners on methods, you may agree with them on goals. Stress the values that you share. Appeal to their sense of fair play and their respect for your right to speak. You should be the model of civility in the situation. Avoid angry reactions and the use of inflammatory language. Think of such listeners as offering an opportunity for your ideas to have impact.

Making Video Presentations

It is quite likely that at some time in your life you will make a video presentation. You may find yourself speaking live on closed-circuit television, videotaping instructions or training materials at work, using community access cable channels to promote a cause, or even appearing on commercial television. Many of these video presentations will be made using a manuscript printed on a teleprompter. At other times you may need to speak impromptu or extemporaneously. With some minor adaptations, the training you receive in this class should serve you well in such situations.[7]

Television brings a speaker close to viewers. It magnifies every visual aspect of you and your message. Therefore, you should dress conservatively, avoiding shiny fabrics, glittery or dangling jewelry, and flashy prints that might "swim" on the screen and distract viewers. You also should not wear white or very light pastels because they reflect glare. Ask in advance about the color of the studio backdrop. If you have light hair or if the backdrop will be light, wear dark clothing for contrast. If you have a dark skin tone, request a light or neutral background and consider wearing light-colored clothes.

Both men and women need make-up to achieve a natural look on television. Have powder available to reduce skin shine or hide a five-o'clock shadow. Women should use make-up conservatively because the camera will intensify it. Avoid glasses with tinted lenses: they will appear even darker on the screen. Even untinted lenses may cause problems, as they reflect glare from the studio lights. Wear contact lenses if you have them. If you can see well enough to read the monitor without glasses, leave them off.

Television requires a conversational mode of presentation. Your audience may be single individuals or small groups assembled in their homes. Imagine yourself talking with another person in an informal setting. While intimate, television is also remote. Since you will have no immediate feedback to help you, your meaning must be instantly clear. Use language that is colorful and concrete so that your audience will remember your material. Use previews and internal summaries to keep viewers on track. You may use visual aids to enhance comprehension, but be sure to confer in advance with studio personnel to be certain your materials will work well in that setting. For example, large posterboards displayed on an easel are more difficult to handle in video presentations than smaller materials. (See related considerations in Chapter 9.)

Vocal variety and facial expressions will become your most important forms of body language. Remember that television will magnify all your movements and vocal changes. Slight head movements and underplayed facial expressions should be enough to reinforce your ideas. Avoid abrupt changes in loudness as a means of vocal emphasis. Rely instead on subtle changes in tempo, pitch, and inflection, and on pauses, to drive your point home.

For most televised presentations, timing is crucial. Five minutes of air time means five minutes, not five minutes and ten seconds. If you run overtime, you may be cut off in midsentence. For this reason television favors manuscript presentations read from a teleprompter. The teleprompter controls timing and preserves a sense of direct eye contact between speakers and listeners. Ask studio personnel how to use the equipment.

Try to rehearse your presentation in the studio with the production personnel. Develop a positive relationship with studio technicians. Your success depends in large part on how well they do their jobs. Provide them with a manuscript marked to show when you will move around or use a visual aid. Practice speaking from the teleprompter if you will be using one. Use the microphone correctly. Don't blow into it to see if it's working. Remember that the microphone will pick up *all* sounds, including shuffling papers or tapping on a lectern. If you use a stand or hand-held microphone, position it about 10 inches below your mouth. The closer the microphone is to your mouth, the more it will pick up unwanted noises like whistled "s" sounds or tongue clicks. Remember that microphones with cords will restrict your movement. Know where the cord is so you don't trip over it if you plan to move about during your presentation.

Don't be put off by distractions as you practice and present your speech. Studio technicians may need to confer with each other while you are speaking. This is a necessary part of their business. They are not being rude. Even though they are in the room with you, they are not your audience. Keep your mind on your ideas and your eyes on the camera. The camera may seem strange at first, but think of it as a friendly face waiting to hear

METHOD	USE	ADVANTAGES	DISADVANTAGES
Impromptu	When you have no time for preparation or practice.	Spontaneity, ability to meet demands of the situation, open to feedback.	Less polished, less use of supporting material, less well researched, less well organized.
Memorized	When you will be making brief remarks such as a toast or award acceptance; when the wording of your introduction or conclusion is important.	Eloquent wording can be planned, can sound well polished.	Focusing on remembering can make you forget to communicate, speech must be written out in advance, style can become sing-songy.
Manuscript	When exact wording is important, time constraints are strict, or your speech will be telecast.	Precise wording can be planned in advance, timing can be down to seconds.	Most people don't read well, inhibits responding to feedback and adapting speech accordingly, may not practice enough.
Extemporaneous	For most public speaking occasions.	Spontaneity, ability to respond to audience feedback, encourages focusing on the essence of your message.	Requires considerable time for preparation and practice, excellence comes through experience.
Video	When you will videotape or make a live televised presentation.	Ability to reach a large audience, can be shown repeatedly to different audiences.	Lack of immediate feedback from audience, may require a manuscript presentation to meet time constraints, strangeness of studio environment.

FIGURE 11.2

Methods of
Presentation

what you have to say. Your eye contact with the camera becomes your eye contact with your audience. Be prepared for lighting and voice checks before the actual taping begins. Use this time to run through your introduction. Before you begin your speech and after you finish, always assume that any microphone or camera near you is "live." Don't say or do anything you wouldn't want your audience to hear or see.

Even though the situation is strange, try to relax. If you are standing, stand at ease. If you are sitting, lean slightly forward as if you were talking to someone in the chair next to you. The floor director will give you a countdown before the camera starts to roll. Clear your throat and be ready to start on cue. Begin with a smile, if appropriate, as you make eye contact with the camera. If several cameras are used, a red light on top will tell you which camera is on. During your presentation the studio personnel may communicate with you using special sign language. The director will tell you what cues they will use.[8]

If you are using a teleprompter script, it will appear directly below or on the lens of the camera. Practice your speech ahead of time until you *almost* have it memorized so that you can glance at the script as a whole. If you have to read it word-for-word, your eyes may be continually shifting (which will make you look suspicious). If you make a mistake, keep going. Sometimes "mistakes" are improvements. Do not stop unless the director says "cut." If appropriate, smile when you finish and continue looking at the camera to allow time for a fade-out.

Handling Questions and Answers

You may need to respond to questions from the audience at the end of your presentation. If you were well prepared for your speech, you should also be well prepared to answer questions on your topic. Because you won't know ahead of time exactly what kind of questions will be asked, your responses will have to be impromptu. The following suggestions should make handling questions and answers easier for you.[9]

First, *prepare for questions in advance.* Be exceptionally thorough in your research so that you are confident of your ability to respond to any rational question on your topic. Try to anticipate the questions you might be asked and think about how you will answer them. Practice your speech before a friend and have him or her ask you tough questions.

Second, *repeat the question or paraphrase what you heard the listener say.* This is especially important if the question was long or complicated and your audience is large. Paraphrasing ensures that everyone in the audience hears the question. It gives you time to think of your answer and it helps you be sure you understood the question. Paraphrasing also enables you to steer the question to the type of answer you are prepared to give.

Third, *maintain eye contact with the audience as you answer.* Note that we said "with the audience," not just "with the questioner." Look first at the questioner, then make eye contact with other audience members, returning your gaze to the questioner as you finish your answer. The purpose of a question-and-answer period should be to extend the understanding of the entire audience, not carry on a private conversation with one person.

Fourth, *defuse hostile questions*. Reword emotional questions in more objective language so that you do not get caught up emotionally yourself. For example, if you are asked, "Why do you want to throw away our money on people who are too lazy to work?" you might respond with something like, "I understand your frustration and think what you really want to know is 'Why aren't our current programs helping people break out of the chains of unemployment?'"

Simply saying "I don't know" can also help defuse a hostile questioner. Roger Ailes, a political media adviser for three U.S. presidents, described how former New York City Mayor Ed Koch once used this technique. Koch had spent three hundred thousand dollars putting bike lanes in Manhattan. Cars were driving in the bike lanes. Cyclists were running over pedestrians. The money seemed wasted. Soon thereafter, when Koch was running for reelection, he appeared on a "meet-the-press" type of show. This is how the questioning went:

> One reporter led off with "Mayor Koch, in light of the financial difficulties in New York City, how could you possibly justify wasting three hundred thousand dollars on bike lanes?. . ." Koch smiled and he said, "You're right. It was a terrible idea." He went on. "I thought it would work. It didn't. It was one of the worst mistakes I ever made." And he stopped. Now nobody knew what to do. They had another twenty-six minutes of the program left. They all had prepared questions about the bike lanes, and so the next person feebly asked, "But, Mayor Koch, how could you do this?" And Mayor Koch said, "I already told you, it was

Handling Questions and Answers

- Practice answering tough questions on your topic before an audience of friends.
- Repeat or paraphrase the question you are asked.
- Maintain eye contact with the audience as you answer. Don't look at just the person who asks the question.
- Defuse hostile questions by rewording them in unemotional language.
- Don't be afraid to say, "I don't know."
- Keep answers short and to the point.
- Handle nonquestions politely.
- Bring the question-and-answer session to a close by reemphasizing your message.

SPEAKER'S NOTES

stupid. I did a dumb thing. It didn't work." And he stopped again. Now there were twenty-five minutes left and nothing to ask him. It was brilliant.[10]

Fifth, *keep your answers short and to the point.* Don't use your answer to a question to give another speech.

Sixth, *handle nonquestions politely.* If someone starts to give a speech rather than ask a question, wait until he or she pauses for breath and then cut in with something like, "Thank you for your comment" or "I appreciate your remarks. Your question, then, is . . ." or "That's an interesting perspective. Can we have another question?" Don't get caught up in a shouting match. Stay in command of the situation.

Finally, *bring the question and answer session to a close.* Call for a final question and summarize the essence of your message to refocus the audience on the major points of your presentation.

USING YOUR VOICE EFFECTIVELY

Your voice plays an important role in the meanings listeners find in your words. By varying the rhythm, pace, emphasis, pitch, or inflection you can easily change these meanings. Consider the following simple sentences:

I don't believe it.

You did that.

Give me a break.

How many different meanings can you create, just by varying the way you say them?

How your message comes across to your audience depends a great deal on the adequacy of your voice. *A good speaking voice conveys your message clearly and enhances your ethos.* It must convey not only the meaning but the feeling of your message. Additionally, the way that you speak has an effect on all dimensions of your ethos. If you sound tentative, people might think you are not very competent. If you mumble, people may think you are trying to hide something and mistrust you. If you are overly loud or strident, listeners may not find you very likable.

Some people resist changing the way they talk. This is natural because how you talk is part of your identity. Your voice even may represent your personality to many people. Someone who talks in a soft, breathy voice may be labeled "sexy"; another, who speaks in a resonant and forceful voice, may be considered "authoritative." Some speakers may wish to maintain a distinct dialect as part of their ethnicity.[11] Listeners may respond positively or negatively to any of these factors. While you may not want to make any drastic changes in your speaking style, minor improvements in the way you talk can bring about positive changes in how others may respond to you. You should work on your voice to eliminate harsh or shrill sounds and to pronounce and enunciate words clearly so that you have the most pleasant and effective speech you are capable of producing.

To speak more expressively, your voice needs careful attention. As one voice specialist put it, "Though speech is a human endowment, how well we speak is an individual achievement."[12] With a little effort and practice, most of us can make positive changes in the way we speak. We caution, however, that simple vocal exercises will not fix serious speech impairments. If you have such a problem, contact the speech pathology clinic on your campus or in your community for professional help.

The first step in learning to use your voice more effectively is to evaluate how you usually talk. Tape-record yourself both speaking spontaneously and reading. When you hear yourself, you may say, "Is that really me?" Most tape recorders will slightly distort the way you sound because they do not exactly replicate the spectrum of sounds made by the human voice. Nevertheless, a tape recording gives you a sample of how your voice may sound to others. Listen to the tape and ask yourself the following questions:

1. Does my voice convey the meaning I intend?
2. Would I want to listen to my voice if I were in the audience?
3. Does my voice present me at my best?

If your honest answers to any of these questions are negative, you may need to work on pitch, rate, loudness, variety, articulation, enunciation, pronunciation, or dialect. Save your original tape so that you can hear yourself improve as you practice.

Pitch

Pitch is the placement of your voice on the musical scale. Vocal pitches can range from low and deep to high and squeaky levels. For effective speaking, you need to find a pitch level that is comfortable for you and others and that allows maximum flexibility and variety. Each of us has a **habitual pitch**, or level at which we speak most frequently. Additionally, we all have an **optimum pitch**, or a level at which we can produce our strongest voice with minimal effort and that allows variation up and down the scale. You can use the following exercise to help determine your optimum pitch:

> Sing the sound *la* down to the lowest pitch you can produce without feeling strain or having your voice break or become rough. Now count each note as you sing up the scale to the highest tone you can comfortably produce. Most people have a range of approximately sixteen notes. Your optimum pitch will be about one-fourth of the way up your range. For example, if your range extends twelve notes, your optimum pitch would be at the third note up the scale. Again, sing down to

The lyrical, melodic writing of Kiowa author N. Scott Momaday offers an opportunity to practice reading for vocal improvement. See if you can make your voice convey the meaning of the passage through variations in pitch and rate.

your lowest comfortable pitch, and then sing up to your optimum pitch level.[13]

Tape-record this exercise, and compare your optimum pitch to the habitual pitch revealed during your first recording. If your optimum pitch is within one or two notes of your habitual pitch, then you should not experience vocal problems related to pitch level. If your habitual pitch is much higher or lower than your optimum pitch, you may not have sufficient flexibility to raise or lower the pitch of your voice for changes in meaning and emphasis. You can change your habitual pitch by practicing speaking and reading at your optimum pitch.

Once you have determined your optimum pitch, use it as a base or point of departure in your practice. Read the following paragraphs from N. Scott Momaday's *The Way to Rainy Mountain* at your optimum pitch level, using pitch changes to provide meaning and feeling. To make the most of your practice, tape-record yourself so you can observe both problems and progress.

> **A single knoll rises out of the plain in Oklahoma, north and west of the Wichita Range. For my people, the Kiowas, it is an old landmark, and they gave it the name Rainy Mountain. The hardest weather in the world is there. Winter brings blizzards, hot tornadic winds arise in the spring, and in the summer the prairie is an anvil's edge. The grass turns brittle and brown, and it cracks beneath your feet. There are green belts along the rivers and creeks, linear groves of hickory and pecan, willow, and witch hazel. At a distance in July or August the steaming foliage seems almost to writhe in fire. . . . Loneliness is an aspect of the land. All things in the plain are isolate: there is no confusion of objects in the eye, but *one* hill or *one* tree or *one* man. To look upon that landscape in the early morning, with the sun at your back, is to lose the sense of proportion. Your imagination comes to life, and this, you think, is where Creation was begun.[14]**

The purpose of this exercise is to explore the full range of variation around your optimum pitch and to make you conscious of the relationship between pitch and effective communication. Tape yourself reading the passage a second time and exaggerate the pitch variations as you read it. Play back both of the taped readings. If you have a problem with a narrow pitch range, you may discover that exaggerating makes you sound more effective.

When you speak before a group, don't be surprised if your pitch seems higher than usual. Your pitch is sensitive to your emotions and will usually go up when you are under pressure. Before beginning to speak, hum your optimum pitch to yourself so you start out on the right note.

Rate

Your **rate,** or the speed at which you speak, helps set the mood of your speech. Serious material calls for a slow, deliberate rate; lighter topics need a faster pace. For a speech to be effective, there should be rate variations that reflect changes in the material being presented. These variations may include the duration of syllables, the use of pauses, and the overall speed of presentation. The rate patterns within a speech produce its **rhythm.** Rhythm is an essential component of all communication.[15] With rhythmic variations you point out what is important and make it easier for listeners to comprehend your message.

Beginning speakers who feel intimidated typically speed up their presentations and run their words together. What this rapid-fire delivery communicates is the speaker's desire to get done and sit down! At the other extreme, some speakers become so deliberate that they almost put themselves and their audiences to sleep. Neither extreme lends itself to effective communication.

As we noted in Chapter 3, the typical rate for extemporaneous speaking is about 125 words per minute. You can check your speed by timing your reading of the excerpt from *Rainy Mountain*. If you were reading at the average rate, you would have taken about sixty seconds to complete that material. If you allowed time for pauses between phrases, appropriate for such formal material, your reading may have run slightly longer. If you took less than fifty seconds, you were probably speaking too rapidly or not using pauses effectively.

Pauses are a very important element in the presentation of speeches. A pause before or after a word or phrase highlights its importance. Pausing also gives your listeners time to contemplate what you have said. They can help build suspense and maintain interest as listeners anticipate what you will say next. Moreover, pauses can clarify the relationships among ideas, phrases, and sentences. They are oral punctuation marks, taking the place of the commas and periods, underlinings and exclamation marks, that occur in written communication.

Beginning speakers often do not use pauses effectively. They may be uncomfortable with silence or think they are not communicating unless their mouths are moving. Effective speakers use pauses to enhance the meanings of their words. Read the following passage aloud again, using pauses (where indicated by the slash marks) and rate changes (faster pace indicated by bold type and slower pace indicated by capital letters) to enhance its meaning and demonstrate mood changes. This exercise will give you an idea of how you can use pauses and rate changes to emphasize and clarify the flow of ideas:

> A single knoll rises out of the plain in Oklahoma / north and west of the Wichita Range // For my people / the Kiowas / it is an old landmark / and they gave it the name Rainy Mountain /// The hardest weather in the world is there // **Winter brings blizzards / hot tornadic winds arise in the spring / and in the summer the prairie is an anvil's edge // The grass turns brittle and brown / and it cracks beneath your feet //** There are green belts along the rivers and creeks / linear groves of hickory and pecan, willow, and witch hazel // At a distance / in July or August / the steaming foliage seems almost to writhe in fire /// LONELINESS IS AN ASPECT OF THE LAND // ALL THINGS IN THE PLANE ARE ISOLATE /// THERE IS NO CONFUSION OF OBJECTS IN THE EYE // BUT ONE HILL // OR ONE TREE // OR ONE MAN /// To look upon that landscape in the early morning / with the sun at your back / is to lose the sense of proportion // Your imagination comes to life // AND THIS / YOU THINK / IS WHERE CREATION WAS BEGUN.

Just as the right use of a pause can work for you, the wrong use of a pause can be a liability. Some speakers habitually use "ers" and "ums," "wells" and "okays," or "you knows" in the place of pauses without being aware of it. These **vocal distractions** may be used to fill in the silence while speakers think about what to say next, or they may be signs of nervousness. To determine if you have such a habit, tape record yourself speaking extemporaneously about one of the main points for your next speech. Often simply becoming aware of such vocal distractions is enough to help you guard against and control them. If you had too many vocal distractions in your recording, retape yourself trying to talk without them. Also, don't use "okay," "well," or "you know" as transitions in your speech. Plan more effective transitions (see Chapter 7). Practice your presentation until the ideas flow smoothly. Finally, don't be afraid of the brief strategic silence that comes when you pause. Make silence work for you.

If your natural tendency is to speak too slowly, you can work to develop a faster rate in practice sessions by reading light material aloud. The following selection by Mark Twain calls for a lively pace. Reading at between 160 and 175 words per minute, you should take about 70 seconds to complete this selection. In the story, the narrator knows absolutely nothing about farming but must write a story to meet a deadline for an agricultural newspaper. In his desperation he fabricates an advice column that causes a farmer to burst into his office.

> "There, you wrote that. Read it to me — quick! Relieve me. I suffer."
> I read as follows:
>
> "Turnips should never be pulled, it injures them. It is much better to send a boy up and let him shake the tree.
>
> "Concerning the pumpkin, the custom of planting it in the front yard with the shrubbery is fast going out of vogue, for it is now generally conceded that the pumpkin as a shade tree is a failure.
>
> "Now, as the warm weather approaches, and the ganders begin to spawn. . . ."
>
> The excited listener sprang toward me and said: "There, that will do. I know I am all right now, because you read it just as I did, word for word. But stranger, when I first read it I said to myself, now I believe I *am* crazy: and with that I fetched a howl that you might have heard for two miles, and started out to kill somebody, because I knew it would come to that sooner or later, and so I might as well begin. I burned my house, crippled several people, and have one fellow up a tree where I can get him if I want him. Then I thought I should stop in here to check with you. I tell you, it is lucky for that chap up in the tree that I did. Good-bye, Sir. *Good-bye.*"[16]

Different cultures and even different subcultures within cultures have different speech rhythms. These differences can involve the overall rate of speaking, such as in the case of Northerners speaking more rapidly than Southerners in the United States. The rhymthic differences also may be more subtle, as when the usual lengths of pauses are different. When the speech rhythms between groups are out of sync, misunderstandings can occur. For example, Californians use longer pauses than New Yorkers. Consequently, Californians may perceive New Yorkers as rude and aggressive, while New Yorkers may see Californians as too laid back or not having much to say.

The ramifications of such rhythm problems can go beyond simple misunderstandings. Ron Scollon, a sociolinguist and communication consultant, reports that Native American Alaskans show deference to authority by slowing down their speech and pausing before speaking or responding to questions. Unfortunately, non-Native law enforcement officials in the area often interpret these rhythmic variations as signs of antagonism or hostility, and the Native Americans typically receive longer jail sentences than do non-Native Americans in the area.[17] Guard against stereotyping individuals on the basis of what may be culturally-based speaking rate variations.

Loudness

No presentation is effective if the audience can't hear you. Similarly, your presentation will not be successful if you overwhelm listeners with a voice that is too loud. When you speak before a group, you usually need to speak louder than you do in general conversation. The size of the room, presence or absence of a microphone, and background noise also may call for adjustments. Take your cues from audience feedback. If you are not loud enough, you may see listeners leaning forward, straining to hear. If you are speaking too loudly, they may unconsciously lean back, pulling away from the noise.

You also should be aware that different cultures have different norms and expectations concerning appropriate loudness. For example, in some Mediterranean cultures a loud voice signifies strength and sincerity, whereas in some Asian and American Indian cultures, a soft voice is associated with good manners and education.[18] When a variety of cultural and ethnic groups is represented in your audience, be especially attentive to feedback on this point.

To speak at proper loudness, you must have good breath control. If you are breathing improperly, you will not have enough force to project your voice so that you can be heard in the back of a room. Improper breathing can also cause you to run out of breath before you finish a phrase or come to an appropriate pause. To check whether you are breathing properly for speaking, do the following:

> **Stand with your feet approximately eight inches apart. Place your hands on your lower rib cage, thumbs to the front, fingers to the back. Take a deep breath — in through your nose and out through slightly parted lips. If you are breathing correctly, you should feel your ribs moving *up and out* as you inhale.**

Improper breathing affects more than just the loudness of your speech. If you breathe by raising your shoulders, the muscles in your neck and throat will become tense. This can result in a harsh, strained vocal quality. Moreover, you probably will not take in enough air to sustain your phrasing, and it will become difficult to control the release of air. The air and sound then all come out with a rush when you drop your shoulders, leading to unfortunate oral punctuation marks when you don't want or need them. To see if you have a problem, try this exercise:

Take a normal breath and see how long you can count while exhaling. If you cannot reach fifteen without losing volume or feeling the need to breathe, you need to work on extending your breath control. Begin by counting in one breath to a number comfortable for you, then gradually increase the count over successive tries. Do not try to compensate by breathing too deeply. Deep breathing takes too much time and attracts too much attention while you are speaking. Use the longer pauses in your speech to breathe, and make note of your breathing pattern as you practice your speech.

You should vary the loudness level of words and phrases in your speech, just as you vary your pitch and your rate of speaking. Changes in loudness are often used to express emotion. The more excited or angry we are, the louder we tend to become. But don't let yourself get caught in the trap of having only two options: loud and louder. Decreasing your volume, slowing your rate, pausing, or dropping your pitch can also express emotion quite effectively.

To acquire more variety in loudness, practice the following exercise recommended by Hillman and Jewell: "First, count to five at a soft volume, as if you were speaking to one person. Then, count to five at medium volume, as if speaking to ten or fifteen people. Finally, count to five, as if speaking to thirty or more people."[19] If you tape-record this exercise, you should be able to hear the clear progression in loudness.

Variety

The importance of vocal variety shows up most in speeches that lack it. Speakers who drone on in a monotone, never varying their pitch, rate, or loudness, send a clear message. They tell us that they have little interest in their topic or in their listeners or that they are afraid of the situation they are in. Variety can make speeches come to life by adding color and interest to a speech. One of the best ways to develop variety is to read aloud materials that demand it to express meaning and feeling. As you read the following selection from *the lives and times of archy and mehitabel,* strive for maximum variation of pitch, rate, and loudness. Incidentally, archy is a cockroach who aspires to be a writer. He leaves typewritten messages for his newspaper-editor mentor but, because he is a cockroach, he can't type capital letters and never uses punctuation marks. His friend mehitabel, whom he quotes in this message, is an alley cat with grandiose dreams and a dubious reputation.

archy what in hell have i done
to deserve all these kittens
life seems to be just one damn litter after another
after all archy i am an artist
this constant parade of kittens
interferes with my career
its not that i am shy on mother love archy

> why my heart would bleed if anything happened to them
> and i found it out
> a tender heart is the cross i bear
> but archy the eternal struggle between life and art
> is simply wearing me out[20]

Tape-record yourself while reading this and other favorite poems or dramatic scenes aloud. Compare these practice tapes with your initial self-evaluation tape to see if you have improved in the use of variety in your presentations.

Patterns of Speaking

People often make judgments about others based on their speech patterns. If you slur your words, mispronounce familiar words, or speak with a dialect that sounds unfamiliar to your audience, you may be seen as uneducated or socially inept. When you sound "odd" to your listeners, their attention will be distracted from what you are saying to the way you are saying it. In this section we cover articulation, enunciation, pronunciation, and dialect as they contribute to or detract from speaking effectiveness.

Articulation. Articulation refers to the way you produce individual speech sounds. Some people have trouble making certain sounds. For example, they may substitute a *d* for a *th,* saying "dem" instead of "them." Other sounds that are often misarticulated include *s, l,* and *r.* Severe articulation problems can interfere with effective communication, especially if the audience cannot understand the speaker or the variations suggest low social or educational status. Such problems are best treated by a speech pathologist, who retrains the individual to produce the sound in a more acceptable manner.

Enunciation. Enunciation refers to the way you pronounce words in context. In casual conversation it is not unusual for people to slur their words — for example, saying "gimme" for "give me." However, careless enunciation causes credibility problems for public speakers. Do you say "Swatuh thought" for "That's what I thought"; "Harya?" for "How are you?"; or "Howjado?" for "How did you do?" These lazy enunciation patterns are not acceptable in public speaking. Check your enunciation patterns on the tape-recordings you have made to determine if you have such a problem. If you do, concentrate on careful enunciation as you practice your speech. Be careful, however, to avoid the opposite problem of inflated, pompous, and pretentious enunciation. Very few speakers can make this work without sounding phony. You should strive to be neither sloppy nor overly precise.

Pronunciation. Pronunciation involves saying words correctly. It includes both the use of the correct sounds and the proper accent on syllables. Because written English does not always indicate the correct pronunciation, we may not be sure how to pronounce words that we first encounter in print. For instance, does the word *chiropodist* begin with an *sh*, a *ch*, or a *k* sound?

If you are not certain how to pronounce a word, consult a dictionary. An especially useful reference is the *NBC Handbook of Pronunciation*, which contains 21,000 words and proper names that sometimes cause problems.[21] When international stories and new foreign leaders first appear in the news, newspapers frequently indicate the correct pronunciation of their names. Check front-page stories in the *New York Times* for guidance with such words.

In addition to problems pronouncing unfamiliar words, you may find that there are certain words you habitually mispronounce. For example, how do you pronounce the following words?

government	library
February	picture
ask	secretary
nuclear	just
athlete	get

Unless you are careful, you may find yourself slipping into these common mispronunciations:

goverment	liberry
Febuary	pitchur
aks	sekaterry
nuculer	jist
athalete	git

Mispronunciation of such common words can damage your ethos. Most of us know what words we chronically mispronounce and are able to pronounce them correctly when we think about it. The time to think about it is when you are practicing and presenting your speech.

Dialect. A dialect is a speech pattern typical of a geographic region or ethnic group. Your dialect usually reflects where you were raised or lived for any length of time or your cultural and ethnic identity.[22] In the United States there are three commonly recognized dialects: eastern, southern, and midwestern. Additionally, there are local variations within the broader dialects. For example, in South Carolina one finds the Gullah dialect from the islands off the coast, the Lowcountry or Charlestonian accent, the Piedmont variation, and the Appalachian twang.[23] And then there's always "*Bah-stahn*" where you buy a "*lodge budded pup con*" at the movies!

There is no such thing in nature as a superior or inferior dialect. However, there can be occasions when a distinct dialect is a definite disadvantage or advantage. Listeners prefer speech patterns that are familiar to their ears. Audiences may also have stereotyped preconceptions about people who speak with certain dialect patterns. For example, those raised in the South often associate a northeastern dialect with brusqueness and abra-

siveness, and midwesterners may associate a southern dialect with slow-
ness of action and mind. You may have to work to overcome these prejudices against your dialect.

Your dialect should reflect the standard for educated people from your
geographic area or ethnic group. You should be concerned about tem-
pering your dialect only if it creates barriers to understanding and identification between you and your audience. Then you may want to work
toward softening your dialect so that you lower these barriers for the sake
of your message.

USING YOUR BODY TO COMMUNICATE

Communication with your audience begins before you ever open your
mouth. Your facial expression, personal appearance, and air of confidence
all convey a message. How do you walk to the front of the room to give
your speech? Do you move with confidence and purpose, or do you stumble and shuffle? As you begin your speech, do you look listeners directly in
the eye, or do you stare at the ceiling as though seeking divine intervention? This **body language** is a nonverbal message that accompanies your
speech. It affects how your audience responds to what you say.[24] For public
speaking to be effective, your body language must reinforce your verbal
language. If your face is expressionless as you urge your listeners to action,
you are sending inconsistent messages. Be sure that your body and words

Reducing the physical distance between the
speaker and audience can
help to increase identification.

both "say" the same thing. Although we discuss separate types of body language in this section, in practice they all work together and are interpreted as a totality by listeners.[25]

Facial Expression and Eye Contact

I knew she was lying the minute she said it. There was guilt written all over her face!

He sure is shifty! Did you see how his eyes darted back and forth? He never did look us straight in the eye!

Most of us believe we can judge character, determine people's true feelings, and tell whether they are honest from their facial expressions. If there is a conflict between what we see and what we hear, we will usually believe our eyes rather than our ears.

The eyes are the most important feature of facial expressiveness. In our culture, frequent and sustained eye contact suggests honesty, openness, and respect. We may think of a person's eyes as windows into the self. If you avoid looking at your audience while you are talking, you are drawing the shades on these windows of communication. A lack of eye contact suggests that you do not care about listeners, that you are putting something over on them, or that you are afraid of them. Other cultures view eye contact differently. For example, in Japan downcast eyes may signal attentiveness and agreement, while Chinese, Indonesians, and rural Mexicans may lower their eyes as a sign of deference, and some American Indians may find direct eye contact offensive or aggressive.[26]

When you reach the podium or lectern, turn, pause, and look at your audience. This signals that you want to communicate and prepares people to listen. During your speech, try to make eye contact with all sectors of your audience. Don't just stare at one or two people. You will make them uncomfortable, and other members of the audience will feel left out. First look at people at the front of the room, then shift your focus to the middle, finally look at those in the rear. You may find that those sitting in the rear of the room are the most difficult to reach. They may have taken a back seat because they don't *want* to listen or be involved. You may have to work harder to gain and hold their attention. Eye contact is one way you can reach them.

Start your speech with a smile unless this is inappropriate to your message. Your face should reflect and reinforce the meanings of your words. An expressionless face in public speaking suggests that the speaker is afraid or indifferent. The frozen face may be a mask behind which the speaker hides. The solution lies in selecting a topic that excites you, concentrating on sharing your message, and having the confidence that comes from being well prepared.

You can also try the following exercise:

Utter these statements, using a dull monotone and keeping your face as expressionless as possible:

I am absolutely delighted by your gift.

I don't know when I've ever been this excited.

We don't need to beg for change — we need to demand change.

All this puts me in a very bad mood.

Now repeat them with *exaggerated* vocal variety and facial expression. You may find that your hands and body also want to get involved. Encourage such impulses so that you develop an integrated system of body language.

Movement and Gestures

Most actors learn — often the hard way — that if you want to steal a scene from someone, all you have to do is move around, develop a twitch, or swing a leg. Before long, all eyes will be focused on that movement. This nasty little trick shows that physical movement sometimes can attract more attention than words. All the more reason that your words and gestures should work in harmony and not at cross-purposes! This also means you should avoid random movements, such as pacing back and forth, hair twirling, or eye rubbing. Once you are aware of such mannerisms, it is easy to control them.

Your gestures and movement should grow out of your response to your material.[27] They should always appear natural and spontaneous, prompted by your ideas and feelings. They should never look contrived and artificial. For example, you should avoid making a gesture fit each word or sequence of words you utter. Perhaps every speech instructor has encountered speakers like the one who stood with arms circled above him as he said, "We need to get *around* this problem." That's not a good way to use gestures!

Effective gestures involve three phases: *readiness, execution,* and *return.* In the readiness phase you must be prepared for movement. Your hands and body should be in a position that does not inhibit free action. For example, you cannot gesture if your hands are locked behind your back or jammed into your pockets, or if you grasp the lectern as though it were a life preserver. Instead, let your hands rest in a relaxed position either at your sides, on the lectern, or in front of you, where they can obey easily the impulse to gesture in support of a point you are making. As you execute a gesture, let yourself move naturally and fully. Don't raise your hand halfway, then stop with your arm frozen awkwardly in the air. When you have completed a gesture, let your hands return to the relaxed readiness position, where they will be free to move again when the next impulse to gesture arises.

Do not assume that there is a universal language of gesture. This can get you in big trouble with a culturally diverse audience. For example, the

American sign for A-OK (thumb and index finger joined in a circle) has an obscene meaning in some cultures, and nodding the head up and down may mean "no" instead of "yes."[28] In an article on the pitfalls of multicultural meetings published in *Training,* management consultant Marc Hequet provided the following additional insight:

> . . . The "Hook 'em, Horns!" hand signal beloved of fans who follow the fortunes of the University of Texas Longhorns college football team once started a brawl in a crowded Italian nightclub when Texans at separate tables merrily flashed each other the sign — hand raised, middle fingers held down by thumb, index and pinky extended. The innocents didn't know it but in Italy the gesture is referred to as cuckold horns. It means, "Your wife is being unfaithful."[29]

From **proxemics,** the study of how humans use space during communication, we can derive two additional principles that help explain the effective use of movement during speeches. The first of these principles suggests that *the physical distance between you as speaker and your listeners will have an impact on the sense of closeness between speakers and listeners.* Bill Clinton made effective use of this principle during the second of the televised debates of the 1992 presidential campaign. In the town meeting setting of that debate, Clinton actually rose from his seat after one question and approached the audience as he answered it. His movement towards his listeners suggested that he felt a special closeness for that problem and for them. Clinton's body language broke the barrier that separated candidates and listeners, and enhanced his identification with the live audience and with the larger viewing audience they represented.

It follows also that the greater the physical distance between speaker and audience, the harder it is to achieve identification. This problem gets worse when a lectern acts as a physical barrier. Short speakers can almost disappear behind it! If this is a problem, try speaking from either beside or in front of a lectern so that your body language can work for you. A different problem arises if you move so close to listeners that you make them feel uncomfortable. If they strain back involuntarily in their chairs, you know you have violated their sense of personal space. You should seek the ideal physical distance between yourself and listeners to increase effectiveness.

The second principle of proxemics suggests that *elevation will also affect the sense of closeness between speakers and listeners.* When you speak, you often stand above your seated listeners in a "power position." Because we tend to associate *above* us with power over us, speakers may find this arrangement stifles identification and immediacy. Often they will sit on the edge of the desk in front of the lectern in a more relaxed and less elevated stance. If your message is informal and requires close identification, you might want to give this a try.

Personal Appearance

Your clothing and grooming affect how you are perceived. These factors also affect how you see yourself and how you behave. A police officer out of uniform may not act as authoritatively as when dressed in blue. A doctor without a white jacket may behave like just another person. You may have a certain type of clothing that makes you feel comfortable and relaxed. You may even have a special "good luck" outfit that raises your confidence.

When you are scheduled to speak, you should dress in a way that puts you at ease and makes you feel good about yourself. Since your speech is a special occasion, you should treat it as such. By dressing a little more formally than you usually do, you emphasize to both yourself and the audience that your message is important. As we noted in Chapter 9, your appearance can serve as a presentation aid that complements your message. Like any other aid, it should never compete with your words for attention or be distracting. Outside the classroom it is best to follow audience custom concerning grooming and dress. Always dress in good taste for the situation you anticipate.

The Importance of Practice

It takes a lot of practice to sound natural. Although this statement may seem contradictory, it should not be surprising. Speaking before a group is not your typical way of communicating. Even though most people seem spontaneous and relaxed when talking with a small group of friends, something happens when they walk to the front of a room and face a larger audience of less familiar faces. They often freeze or become stilted and awkward. This blocks the natural flow of communication.

The key to overcoming this problem is to practice until you can respond fully to your ideas as you present them. Your voice, face, and body should express your feelings as well as your thoughts. On the day of your speech, you become a model for your listeners, showing them how they should respond in turn.

To develop an effective extemporaneous style, practice until you feel the speech is part of you. During practice you can actually hear what you have been preparing and can try out the words and techniques you have been considering. What looked like a good idea on paper may not seem to work as well when it comes to life in spoken words. It is better to discover this fact in rehearsal than before an actual audience.

You will probably want privacy the first two or three times you practice. Even then you should try to simulate the conditions under which the speech will be given. Stand up while you practice. Imagine your listeners in front of you. Picture them responding positively to what you have to say. Address your ideas to them, and visualize your ideas having impact.

If possible, go to your classroom to practice. If this is not possible, find another empty room where the speaking arrangements are similar. Such on-the-site rehearsal helps you get a better feel for the situation you will face, reducing its strangeness when you make your actual presentation. Begin practicing from your formal outline. Once you feel comfortable, switch to your key-word outline, then practice until the outline transfers from the paper to your head.

Keep material to be read to a minimum. Type or print quotations in large letters so you can see them easily. Put each quotation on a single index card or sheet of paper. If using a lectern, position this material so that you can maintain frequent eye contact while reading. If you will speak beside or in front of the lectern, hold your cards in your hand and raise them when it is time to read. Practice reading your quotation until you can present it naturally while only glancing at your notes. If your speech includes presentation aids, practice handling them until they are smoothly integrated into your presentation. They should seem a natural extension of your verbal message.

During practice, you can serve as your own audience by recording your speech and playing it back. If videotaping equipment is available, arrange to record your speech so that you can see as well as hear yourself. It is usually better to review the tape of your speech after some time has passed, when you can be more objective in judging it. If you try to evaluate yourself immediately after you practice, you may hear what you think you said rather than what you actually said. Always try to be the toughest critic you will ever have, but also be a constructive critic. Never put yourself down or give up on yourself. Work on specific points of improvement.

In addition to evaluating yourself, it can be helpful to ask a friend or friends to listen to your presentation. This outside opinion should be more objective than your self-evaluation, and you will get a feel for speaking to real people rather than to an imagined audience. Seek constructive feed-

Practicing for Presentation

- Practice standing up, speaking aloud, if possible in the room where you will be making your presentation.
- Practice first from your formal outline, switching to your key-word outline when you feel you have mastered your material.
- Work on maintaining eye contact with an imaginary audience.
- Practice integrating your presentation aids into your message.
- Check the timing of your speech. Add or cut if necessary.
- Continue practicing until you feel comfortable and confident.
- Present your speech in a "dress rehearsal" before friends. Make final changes in light of their suggestions.

SPEAKER'S NOTES

back from your friends by asking them specific questions. Was it easy for them to follow you? Do you have any mannerisms (such as hair twisting or saying "you know" after every other sentence) that distracted them? Were you speaking loudly and slowly enough? Did your ideas seem clear and soundly supported?

On the day that you are assigned to speak, get to class early enough to look over your outline one last time so that it is fresh in your mind. If you have devoted sufficient time and energy to your preparation and practice, you should feel confident about communicating with your audience.

IN SUMMARY

An effective *presentation* integrates the nonverbal aspects of voice and body language with the words of your speech. It is characterized by enthusiasm and naturalness. Your voice and bearing should project your sincere commitment but should not call attention to themselves. You should sound and look spontaneous and natural, not contrived or artificial.

Methods of Presentation.   The four major methods of speech presentation are impromptu speaking, memorized presentation, reading from a manuscript, and extemporaneous speaking. In *impromptu speaking* you talk with minimal or no preparation and practice. To present an effective impromptu speech, follow the PREP formula: state your *p*oint, give a *r*eason or *e*xample, then restate your *p*oint.

Both *memorized* and *manuscript presentations* require that your speech be written out word for word. Be sure that your speech is written in good oral style. An *extemporaneous presentation* requires careful planning, but the wording is spontaneous. Instructors usually require that you present speeches extemporaneously. Extemporaneous speaking allows you to adapt to feedback from your audience. Be especially alert for signs that your audience doesn't understand, has lost interest, or disagrees with you, then make adjustments to your message to overcome these problems.

When you prepare a video presentation, pay special attention to the visual aspects of your message. Be sure your language is clear and colorful, and remember that timing is crucial. Get comfortable with the setting. Practice using a teleprompter and microphone. Imagine a listener you can see through the eye of the camera. Present your message as though you were speaking to that person in a relaxed setting.

Following any presentation you may need to answer questions about your material and ideas. While your responses will be impromptu, you should prepare for questions in advance and plan appropriate responses.

Using Your Voice Effectively.   A good speaking voice conveys your meaning fully and clearly. Vocal expressiveness depends on your ability to control pitch, rate, loudness, and variety. Your *habitual pitch* is the level at which you usually speak. Your *optimum pitch* is the level at which you can produce a clear, strong voice with minimal effort. Speaking at your optimum pitch gives your voice flexibility. The rate at which you speak can affect the impression you make on listeners. You can control rate to your advantage by using pauses and by changing your pace to match the moods of your material. To speak loudly enough, you need proper breath control. Vary loudness for the sake of emphasis. Vocal variety adds color and interest to a speech, makes a speaker more likable, and encourages identification between speaker and audience.

Articulation, enunciation, pronunciation, and dialect refer to the unique way you give voice to words. *Articulation* concerns the manner in which you produce individual sounds. *Enunciation* refers to the way you utter words in context. Proper *pronunciation* means that you say words correctly. Your *dialect* may identify the area of the country in which you learned language and your cultural or ethnic background. Occasionally, dialect can create identification and comprehension problems between a speaker and audience.

Using Your Body Effectively.   You communicate with *body language* as well as with your voice. Eye contact signals listeners that you want to communicate. Your facial expressions should project the meanings of your words. Movement attracts attention; therefore, your movements and gestures must complement your speech, not compete with it. *Proxemics* is the study of how humans use space during communication. Two proxemic principles, distance and elevation, can affect your identification with an audience as you speak. Be sure your grooming and dress are appropriate to the speech occasion and do not detract from your ability to communicate.

The Importance of Practice.   You should practice your speech until you have the sequence of main points and supporting materials well established in your mind. It is best to practice your presentation under conditions similar to those in which you will give your speech. Keep citations or other materials that you must read to a minimum. Tape-recording or videotaping can be useful for self-evaluation during rehearsal.

TERMS TO KNOW

presentation	optimum pitch
immediacy	rate
expanded conversational style	rhythm
impromptu speaking	vocal distractions
PREP formula	articulation
memorized text presentation	enunciation
manuscript presentation	pronunciation

extemporaneous speaking   dialect

feedback   body language

pitch   proxemics

habitual pitch

DISCUSSION

1. Be part of an audience for a lecture or political speech. Did the speaker read from a manuscript, make a memorized presentation, or speak extemporaneously? Was the speaker's voice effective or ineffective? Why? How would you evaluate the speaker's body language? Discuss your observations with your classmates.

2. Comedians often capture the personalities of public figures by accentuating their verbal and gestural characteristics in comic impersonations. Be alert for such impersonations on late-night television. Which identifying characteristics do the comedians exaggerate? What might this indicate about the "real" speaker's style and ethos? Contribute your observations to a class discussion.

3. You have been invited to present your most recent classroom speech on local public television. How would you adapt your message to that medium? Report your ideas in class. What general conclusions can you draw about the impact of video presentations on public communication?

4. Make a list of questions you think you might be asked following your next speech. Plan and prepare answers to these questions. Working in small groups, distribute your questions to group members to ask of you. Invite them to evaluate your responses.

APPLICATION

1. Exchange your self-evaluation tape with a classmate and write a critique of that person's voice and articulation. Emphasize the positive, but make specific recommendations for improvement. Work on your classmate's recommendations to you, and then make a second tape to share with your partner. Do you hear signs of improvement in each other's performance?

2. Make a list of words you often mispronounce. Practice saying these words correctly each day for a week. See if you carry over these changes into social conversation.

3. As you practice your next speech, deliberately try to speak in as dull a voice as possible. Stifle all impulses to gesture. Then practice speaking with as colorful a voice as possible, giving full freedom to movement and gesture. Notice how a colorful and expressive presentation makes your ideas seem more lively and vivid as you speak.

4. Form small groups and conduct an impromptu speaking contest. Each participant should supply two topics for impromptu speeches, and participants should then draw two topics (not their own). Participants have five minutes to prepare a three-minute speech on one of these topics. Each student then presents the speech to the group, which selects a winner.

NOTES

1. Roger Ailes, *You Are the Message: Getting What You Want by Being Who You Are* (New York: Doubleday, 1988), pp. 15–19.

2. James C. McCroskey, *An Introduction to Rhetorical Communication,* 3rd ed. (Englewood Cliffs, NJ: Prentice-Hall, 1993), pp. 263–264.

3. McCroskey, p. 264.

4. Virginia P. Richmond, James C. McCroskey, and S. K. Payne, *Nonverbal Behavior in Interpersonal Relations,* 2nd ed. (Englewood Cliffs, NJ: Prentice-Hall, 1991), pp. 208–228.

5. Michael Duffy, "Picture of Health," *Time,* 4 October 1993: 28+, *Time Almanac Reference Ed,* CD-ROM, Compact. 1994.

6. "A Letter to Our Readers." *Newsweek,* 4 October 1993, p. 29.

7. The authors are indebted to Professor Roxanne Gee of the television and film area in the Department of Communication at the University of Memphis for her assistance and suggestions in putting together this advice.

8. Illustrations of major video hand signals may be found in Stewart W. Hyde, *Television and Radio Announcing,* 6th ed. (Boston: Houghton Mifflin, 1991), pp. 80–85.

9. These guidelines for handling questions and answers are a compendium of ideas from the following sources: Teresa Brady, "Fielding Abrasive Questions During Presentations," *Supervisory Management,* Feb. 1993, p. 6; Stephen D. Body, "Nine Steps to a Successful Question-and-Answer Session," *Management Solutions,* May 1988, pp. 16–17; J. Donald Ragsdale and Alan L. Mikels, "Effects of Question Periods on a Speaker's Credibility with a Television Audience," *Southern States Communication Journal,* 40 (1975): 302–312; Dorothy Sarnoff, *Never Be Nervous Again* (New York: Ballantine, 1987); Laurie Schloff and Marcia Yudkin, *Smart Speaking: Sixty-Second Strategies* (New York: Holt, 1991); and Alan Zaremba, "Q and A: The Other Part of Your Presentation," *Management World,* Jan.–Feb. 1989, pp. 8–10.

10. Ailes, p. 170.

11. Howard Giles and Arlene Franklyn-Stokes, "Communicator Characteristics," *Handbook of International and Intercultural Communication,* eds. Molefi Kete Asante and William B. Gudykunst (Newbury Park: Sage, 1989), pp. 117–144.

12. Jon Eisenson, *Voice and Diction: A Program for Improvement* (New York: Macmillan, 1974), p. vii.

13. Adapted from Hyde, pp. 80–85.

14. N. Scott Momaday, *The Way to Rainy Mountain* (Albuquerque: University of New Mexico Press, 1969), p. 5.

15. Carole Douglis, "The Beat Goes On: Social Rhythms Underlie All Our Speech and Actions," *Psychology Today* (Nov. 1987), 36(6), *Magazine Database Plus,* online, CompuServe, Nov. 1995.

16. Samuel L. Clemons, adapted from "How I Edited an Agricultural Paper," in *Sketches: Old and New* (Hartford: American, 1901), pp. 307–315.

17. Cited in Douglis, p. 36(6).

18. Larry A. Samovar and Richard E. Porter, *Communication Between Cultures* (Belmont: Wadsworth, 1991), pp. 205–206; Michael L. Hecht, Peter A. Andersen, and Sidney A. Ribeau, "The Cultural Dimensions of Nonverbal Communication," *Handbook of International and Intercultural Communication,* eds. Molefi Kete Asante and William B. Gudykunst (Newbury Park: Sage, 1989), pp. 163–185.

19. Ralph Hillman and Delorah Lee Jewell, *Work for Your Voice* (Murfreesboro: Copymatte, 1986), p. 63.

20. Don Marquis, adapted from "mehitabel and her kittens," in *the lives and times of archy and mehitabel.* Copyright ©1927 by Doubleday and Company, Inc. Reprinted by permission of the publisher.

21. *NBC Handbook of Pronunciation,* 4th ed. (New York: Harper, 1991).

22. William B. Gudykunst et al., "Language and Intergroup Communication," *Handbook of International and Intercultural Communication,* eds. Molefi Kete Asante and William B. Gudykunst (Newbury Park: Sage, 1989), pp. 145–162.

23. Carolanne Griffith-Roberts, "Let's Talk Southern," *Southern Living,* Feb. 1995, p. 82. For a detailed explication of regional dialect variances see Charles K. Thomas, *An Introduction to the Phonetics of American English,* 2nd ed. (New York: Ronald, 1958), pp. 191–260.

24. Samovar and Porter, p. 177.

25. Peter A. Andersen, "Nonverbal Immediacy in Interpersonal Communication." *Multichannel Integrations of Nonverbal Behavior,* eds. A. W. Siegman and S. Feldstein (Hillsdale: Erlbaum, 1985).

26. S. Ishii, "Characteristics of Japanese Nonverbal Communication Behavior," *Communication* (Summer 1973), 163–180; Samovar and Porter 198–200; "Understanding Culture: Don't Stare at a Navajo," *Psychology Today* (June 1974), 107.

27. Charlotte I. Lee and Timothy Gura, *Oral Interpretation,* 8th ed. (Boston: Houghton Mifflin, 1992), pp. 118–119.

28. Mary Munter, "Cross Cultural Communication for Managers," *Business Horizons,* May–June 1993, p. 69(10). For additional insights into cultural differences in nonverbal communication see Roger Axtell, *Gestures: The Do's and Taboos of Body Language Around the World* (New York: Wiley, 1991); E. Hall, *Understanding Cultural Differences* (Yarmouth, ME: Inter-

cultural Press, 1990); J. Mole, *When in Rome . . . A Business Guide to Cultures and Customs in Twelve European Nations* (New York: AMACOM, 1991); D. Ricks, *Big Business Blunders* (Homewood, IL: Dow Jones-Irwin, 1983); C. Storti, *The Art of Crossing Cultures* (Yarmouth, ME: Intercultural Press, 1990).

29. Marc Hequet, "The Fine Art of Multicultural Meetings," *Training* (July 1993), 29(5).

PART 4

Types of Public Speaking

CHAPTER 12

Informative Speaking

- understand the basic functions of informative speaking.
- apply principles of motivation and attention to help listeners learn from your message.
- become familiar with the different types of informative speeches and the designs most appropriate to each.
- prepare and present effective informative speeches.

The improvement of understanding is for two ends: first our own increase of knowledge; secondly, to enable us to deliver that knowledge to others.

— John Locke

In ancient mythology Prometheus was punished by the other gods for showing humans how to make fire. These jealous gods knew that with this ability people could warm themselves, be more safe, cook their food, take advantage of the extended light, and share knowledge as they huddled together around their campfires. Humans could then build civilizations and grow in spiritual stature until they would challenge the gods themselves through the power of their learning. These mythical gods had every right to be angry with Prometheus. He had given the first significant speech of demonstration.

This tale of Prometheus reminds us that information is power. Without the sharing of information there would be no civilization as we know it today. Because we cannot personally experience everything that may be important or interesting to us, we must rely on the knowledge of others to expand our understanding and competence. *Sharing knowledge is the essence of informative speaking.*

Shared information can be important to survival. Early detection and warning systems alert us to impending thunderstorms, hurricanes, and tornadoes. News of medical breakthroughs and information on nutrition and hygiene practices that increase our life span must be communicated so that we can take advantage of them. Beyond simply enabling us to live, information helps us to live better.

We can learn how to work smarter, not harder. Information can help us control the world around us and even manage people.

It follows that people who can deliver information are highly valued. Graduate schools look for students who can help enlarge the range of human knowledge. Companies raid other companies for employees with know-how and creativity. Countries engage in espionage activities to learn what their friends and enemies are doing. An incompetent manager who fears the loss of power may even try to withhold information in an effort to maintain control (a strategy that usually fails).

Throughout our lives we constantly exchange information. In this chapter we look at the functions of informative communication, suggest ways to make it easier for your listeners to learn from your messages, discuss the major types of informative speeches, and explain some basic speech designs that are appropriate to these types. Our objective is to help you bring fire to your listeners.

THE FUNCTIONS OF INFORMATIVE SPEAKING

Informative speaking is defined by its function. In the same speech, you might introduce yourself, provide information, urge action, and celebrate values. *But if your main intention is to share knowledge, then we call the speech informative.*

Sharing knowledge can be vital in four ways. First, informative speaking can empower listeners by sharing information and ideas. Second, informative speaking can shape listener perceptions. Third, informative speaking can help set the agenda of public concerns. Finally, informative speaking can clarify options for action.

Sharing Information and Ideas

An informative speech *gives to* listeners rather than *asks of* them. The demands on the audience are relatively low. Informative speakers want enthusiastic attention from listeners. They want them to understand and use what they learn, but they do not try to make them change values or enact reforms. For example, one student speaker gave an informative speech in which she revealed the dangers of prolonged exposure to ultraviolet radiation, but she did not urge her audience to boycott tanning salons. Although informative speaking makes modest demands on the listener, the demands on the speaker are high. Good informative speakers must have a thorough understanding of their subject. It is one thing to know something well enough to satisfy yourself. It is quite another to know something well enough to assume responsibility for communicating it to others.

By sharing information, an informative speech reduces ignorance. An informative speech does not simply repeat something the audience already knows. Rather, *the **informative value** of a speech is measured by how* *much new and important information or understanding it provides the audience.* As you prepare your informative speech ask yourself the following questions:

Is my topic significant enough to merit an informative speech?

What do my listeners already know about my topic?

What more do they need to know?

Do I have sufficient understanding of my topic to help others understand it better?

The answers to these questions should help you plan a speech with high informative value.

In informative speaking, the speaker functions basically as a teacher. To teach people effectively, you must arouse and sustain attention by adapting your message to their interests and needs. You must make listeners aware of how important the new information is. When you have finished, they should feel enriched by the communication transaction.

Shaping Audience Perceptions

When speakers share information with audiences, they also share their points of view. It is virtually impossible to cover everything there is to know about any significant subject in a short message. Therefore, speakers are always selective in terms of what information they communicate, highlighting ideas and material they believe best represent the subject. When we see the subject through their eyes, we really see their interpretations of the subject. The images they provide are often colored by their feelings. This selective exposure can influence the way we respond to later communications on the subject, especially when this is our first acquaintance with it.

This power of informative speaking to influence our perceptions can serve a **prepersuasive function**, preparing us for later persuasive speaking. Suppose, for example, you heard *one* of two speeches on teaching as a career choice. One was presented by an enthusiastic teacher who described the personal rewards he obtained from teaching and stressed the joys of helping children learn. The other was presented by a teacher suffering from "burn out" who focused on classroom discipline problems and administrative red tape. Neither speaker suggested that you should or should not become a teacher. Each provided what he or she believed was an accurate picture of teaching as a profession. But each created a different predisposition to respond. If you heard only the first speaker, you might be more inclined to consider a message urging you to become a teacher than if you had heard only the second speaker.

If you have strong feelings about your subject, you must work hard *not* to present a distorted perspective. If listeners feel you are massaging the truth or presenting a biased perspective, they will dismiss your message as unreliable and lower their estimation of your character and competence.

Setting the Agenda

The amount of information reaching people today is almost overwhelming. This inundation of information from the mass media serves an **agenda-setting function.**[1] As the media present the "news," they also tell us what we *should* be thinking about. By the amount of coverage allotted to a topic, the media establishes its importance in the public mind.

Informative speaking also performs an agenda-setting role. As it directs our attention to certain subjects, it influences what we feel is important. The informative speech on "The 'Monument' at Wounded Knee," which appears in Appendix B, demonstrates this agenda-setting function, as it shapes perceptions about our country's policy toward Native Americans. Hearing such a message could predispose listeners both to believe the issue is important and to favor better treatment for this group. As you prepare an informative speech, remember the power you have to establish the importance of your topic in the minds of your listeners. Consider the ethical consequences of your words.

Clarifying Options

An informative speech also can reveal and clarify options for action. Information expands our awareness, opens new horizons, and suggests fresh possibilities. Information can also help us discard unworkable options. The better we understand a subject, the more intelligent choices we can make on issues that surround it. For example, what should we know about obesity? Informative speeches may tell us about the consequences of doing something or nothing to correct this condition. They may teach us about the medical soundness of different diets. They may also inform us about

FIGURE 12.1

The Functions of Informative Speaking

Function	Important when
1. Sharing information and ideas	You wish to introduce new ideas and knowledge of a subject.
2. Shaping audience perceptions	You want to prepare listeners for future persuasive messages by revealing a situation they have not been aware of.
3. Setting the agenda	You wish to make listeners realize a topic is important and merits their serious consideration.
4. Clarifying options for action	You want to provide information that makes listeners aware of the positive and negative aspects of options for action so that they can make informed, intelligent decisions.

the roles of exercise and counseling in weight control. Such information would expand our options for dealing with obesity.

Informative speakers carry a large ethical burden to have and communicate responsible knowledge of their topics. A responsible informative speech should cover all major positions on a topic and present all vital information. Although speakers may have strong feelings on a subject, it is unethical to deliberately omit or distort information that is necessary for audience understanding. Similarly, speakers who are unaware of options or information because they have not done the research that will *make* them aware also are irresponsible. As you conduct your research, seek out material from sources that present different perspectives. The two speeches on the teaching profession mentioned earlier demonstrate potential abuses of the option-clarifying function of informative speaking. If the speeches are presented as *representative* of teaching as a career, then both speakers are guilty of overgeneralizing from limited personal experience.

HELPING YOUR AUDIENCE LEARN

The success of an informative speech can be measured by the answer to one simple question, "Does the listener learn from the speech?" As an informative speaker you need to apply basic principles of learning to make your speeches effective. To help your listeners learn and remember your message, you must motivate them by establishing its relevance to their lives, hold their attention throughout your message, and structure your speech so that it is clear and readily understood.

Motivation

To motivate listeners, you must tell them why your message is important to them. In Chapter 4 we discussed motivation as a factor in audience analysis. Now we consider motivation in terms of giving listeners a reason to learn. Go back to the list of twelve needs on page 00 and determine which of these needs might be most relevant to your topic and your audience. Then tie your message to these needs either through direct statements or through interesting examples or narratives. For example, you might relate a speech on how to interview for a job to the needs for control, independence, and success. You could begin by talking about the problem of finding a good job in today's marketplace and provide an example that illustrates how a successful interview can make the difference in who gets hired and who does not. As you preview the body of your speech, you might say, "Today, I'm going to describe four factors that can determine whether you get the job of your dreams. First. . . ." In this case you have given your audience a reason for wanting to listen to the rest of your speech. You have begun the learning process by motivating your listeners.

Informative messages often take place in work settings. Here a ranger demonstrates new techniques for mountain rescue operations.

Attention

Once you have established the importance of your message, you must sustain audience attention throughout your speech. In this section we examine six basic factors that affect attention: *intensity, repetition, novelty, activity, contrast,* and *relevance.* We also explain how to use these factors to sustain interest and promote learning.

Intensity.   Our eyes are drawn automatically to bright lights, and we turn to investigate loud noises. In public communication, intense language and vivid images can be used to attract and hold attention. You can emphasize a point by supplying examples that magnify its importance. You can also achieve intensity through the use of presentation aids and vocal variety. Note how Stephen Huff holds attention through the intensity of his descriptions of the New Madrid earthquakes that struck the south-central area of the United States in the early nineteenth century:

> The Indians tell of the night that lasted for a week and the way the "Father of Waters" — the Mississippi River — ran backwards. Waterfalls were formed on the river. Islands disappeared. Land that was once in Arkansas — on the west bank of the river — ended up in Tennessee — on the east bank of the river. Church bells chimed as far away as New Orleans and Boston. Cracks up to ten feet wide opened and closed in the earth. Geysers squirted sand fifteen feet into the air. Whole forests sank into the earth as the land turned to quicksand. . . . Reelfoot

Lake — over ten miles long — was formed when the Mississippi River changed its course.

Repetition.   Sounds, words, or phrases that are repeated attract our attention and embed themselves in our consciousness. Skillful speakers frequently repeat key words or phrases to stress the importance of points, to help listeners focus on the sequence of ideas, to unify the message, and to help people remember what they have heard.

Repetition is the strategy that underlies the language tools of alliteration and parallel construction. As we saw in Chapter 10, alliteration can lend vividness to the main ideas of informative speeches: "Today, I will discuss how the *M*ississippi River *m*eanders from *M*innesota to the sea." The repetition of the *m* sound catches our attention and emphasizes the statement. In like manner, parallel construction can establish a pattern that sticks in your listeners' minds (see Chapters 7, 8, and 10). When used, for example, as repeated questions and answers such as, "What is our goal? It is to. . . ," parallel construction sustains attention.

Novelty.   We are attracted to anything new or unusual. A novel phrase can fascinate listeners and hold their attention. In the speech reprinted at the end of Chapter 14, Jim Cardoza found a novel way to describe the magnitude of pollution in this country. After documenting that nineteen million tons of garbage are picked up each year along the beaches of the United States, Jim concluded: "And that's just the tip of the wasteberg." His invented word, "wasteberg," was effective because it reminded listeners of "iceberg" and that in turn connoted for them the vastness of the problem. Some famous novel expressions in American history, that have aroused attention for political programs and philosophies are "New Deal," "the New Frontier," "the Great Society," "Star Wars" (Strategic Defense Initiative), "Thousand Points of Light," and "Contract with America." New and startling metaphors often add the element of novelty to speeches and arouse attention.

Activity.   Our eyes are attracted to moving objects, a factor that often gains attention in speeches. Gestures, physical movement, and presentation aids can all add the element of activity to your speech. You can also increase the sense of activity in your speeches by using concrete action words, vocal variety, and a narrative structure that moves your speech along. Note the sense of action and urgency, as well as the invitation to act, in the conclusion of this student's speech:

> I don't know what you're going to do, but I know what I'm going to do. I'm going to march right down tomorrow and register to vote. There's too much at stake not to. Want to join me?

A lively example or an exciting story can also bring a speech to life and engage your listeners.

Contrast.   Opposites attract attention. If you work in a noisy environment and it suddenly becomes quiet, the stillness can seem deafening. Similarly, abrupt changes in vocal pitch or rate of speaking will draw attention. Presenting the pros and cons of a situation creates a sense of conflict and drama that listeners often find arresting. You can also highlight contrasts by speaking of such opposites as life and death, light and dark, or the highs and lows of a situation.

In a speech dramatizing the need to learn more about AIDS, a speaker introduced two or three specific examples with the statement "Let me introduce you to *Death*." Then, as the speech moved to the promise of medical research, she said, "Now let me introduce you to *Life*." This usage combined repetition and contrast to create a dramatic effect.

Surprise is necessary for contrast to be effective. Once people become accustomed to an established pattern, they no longer think about it. They notice any abrupt, dramatic change from the pattern.

Relevance.   Things that are personally related to our needs or interests attract our attention. Research has indicated that sleepers respond with changes in brain-wave patterns when their names are mentioned. Parents have been known to sleep through severe thunderstorms, yet be wakened by the faint sounds of their infant crying. Relevance is essential to public speaking as well.

Darren Wirthwein made a speech on selecting running shoes relevant for his Indiana University audience by stressing the distance between places on campus. Darren pointed out that his early morning speech class was held in a campus building over a mile from the freshman dormitory — that without his running shoes he might have missed his speech! Because his listeners shared his situation, they chuckled, then listened attentively. Follow Darren's lead and increase relevance by using examples close to the lives of audience members.

Retention

Even the best information is useless unless your listeners remember and use it. Repetition, relevance, and structural factors can all be used to help your audience remember your message. The more frequently we hear or see anything, the more likely we are to retain it. This is why advertisers bombard us with slogans to keep their product names in our consciousness. These slogans may be repeated in all of their advertisements, regardless of the visuals or narratives presented. The repetition of key words or phrases in a speech also helps the audience remember. In his famous civil rights speech in Washington, D.C., Martin Luther King's repetition of the phrase "I have a dream . . ." became the hallmark of the speech and is now used as its title.

Relevance is also important to retention. Our minds filter new information as we receive it, associating it with things we already know and unconsciously evaluating it for its potential usefulness or importance. The advice that follows seems simple but is profoundly important. *If you want*

Helping Listeners Learn

1 Approach your topic in a fresh and interesting way.
2 Show listeners how they can benefit from your information.
3 Sustain attention with vivid examples and exciting stories.
4 Organize your material clearly to make it easy to understand.
5 Use strategic repetition to help listeners remember.
6 Provide previews and summaries to aid retention.

SPEAKER'S NOTES

listeners to remember your message, tell them why and how your message relates to their lives.

As we saw in Chapter 7, structural factors also affect how readily a message can be understood and retained. Previews, summaries, and clear transitions can help your audience remember your message. The way you organize your material also has an effect on retention. Suppose you were given the following list of words to memorize:

> north, man, hat, daffodil, green, tulip, coat, boy, south, red, east, shoes, gardenia, woman, purple, marigold, gloves, girl, yellow, west

It looks rather difficult, but see what happens when we rearrange the words:

> north, south, east, west
> man, boy, woman, girl
> daffodil, tulip, gardenia, marigold
> green, red, purple, yellow
> hat, coat, shoes, gloves

In the first example you have what looks like a random list of words. In the second the words have been organized by categories: now you have five groups of four related words to remember. Material that is presented in a consistent and orderly fashion is much easier for your audience to understand and retain. In the remainder of this chapter we look at the major types of informative speeches and the design formats that are most often used to structure informative messages.

TYPES OF INFORMATIVE SPEECHES

As we mentioned earlier, the major purpose of an informative speech is to share knowledge in order to expand your listeners' understanding or competence. To meet this challenge, an informative speech will typically describe, demonstrate, or explain its subject. These different procedures divide informative speaking into types. As we discuss them, we will also consider briefings as an important subtype of informative speaking.

Speeches of Description

Often the specific purpose of a speech is to describe a particular activity, object, person, or place. A **speech of description** should give the audience a clear picture of your subject, such as the one Stephen Huff painted of the New Madrid earthquakes of 1811. An effective speech of description relies heavily on the artful use of language. The words must be clear, concrete, and colorful to carry both the substance and feeling of the message. The speech on the "Monument at Wounded Knee" in Appendix B provides vivid word-pictures. Thus, the landscape is not simply desolate, it is characterized by "flat, sun-baked fields and an occasional eroded gully." The speaker goes on to describe the monument:

> **The monument itself rests on a concrete slab to the right of the grave. It's a typical, large, old-fashioned granite cemetery marker, a pillar about six feet high topped with an urn — the kind of gravestone you might see in any cemetery with graves from the turn of the century. The inscription tells us that it was erected by the families of those who were killed at Wounded Knee. Weeds grow through the cracks in the concrete at its base.**

The topic, purpose, and materials selected for a descriptive speech should suggest the appropriate design. The "Monument" speech follows a spatial pattern. Other designs which may be used for speeches of description include sequential, categorical, and comparative designs, which are discussed later in this chapter.

Speeches of Demonstration

The **speech of demonstration** shows the audience how to do something or how something works. Dance instructors teach us how to waltz or do the Texas two-step. Others may tell us how to access the Internet or how to prepare for the Law School Admission Test or even how to build a fire. The tip-off to the speech of demonstration is the phrase *how to*. What these examples have in common is that they demonstrate a process.

Speeches of demonstration aim either at *understanding* or *application*, introducing listeners to a process or instructing them so that they can perform the process themselves. If your goal is understanding, you can usually demonstrate more complex processes in a short speech than you can if your goal is application. For example, you might be able to prepare a seven-minute speech on how grades are collected, recorded, averaged, and distributed at your university. You could not, however, expect your audience to be able to apply this knowledge and set up a grade-processing system after hearing your presentation. On the other hand, in the short time allotted for a classroom speech, you might be able to teach your classmates how to read a textbook more efficiently. This is a skill they can *apply* to their lives.

The lesson here is clear. Adjust your specific purpose in light of the complexity of your topic and the time allotted for your presentation. Regardless of your specific purpose, most speeches of demonstration follow the sequential design discussed in detail later in this chapter. One final consideration, most speeches of demonstration are helped by the use of presentation aids. The aids can range from yourself as a model performing the activity, to objects used in the process you are demonstrating, to an overhead projection or poster listing the steps in order. Stephen Huff distributed a handout that listed the steps to follow in case of an earthquake (he circulated this *after* his speech so that it would not compete for his listeners' attention). If you are preparing a speech of demonstration, review the materials on presentation aids in Chapter 9 to determine what you could use to help your audience better understand your message. When demonstrating a process, "show and tell" is usually much more effective than just telling.

Speeches of Explanation

The **speech of explanation** informs the audience about subjects that typically are more abstract than the subjects of descriptive or demonstrative speeches. Speeches of explanation may present a challenge to speakers and audiences because abstract subjects are sometimes difficult to understand. To meet this challenge, Katherine Rowan, a communication scholar at Purdue University, suggests that speakers should:

- define the subject in terms of its critical features,
- compare an example with a nonexample (i.e., an instance that may be thought of as an example but is not), and
- provide more examples to reinforce what listeners have learned.[2]

Note how Stephen Lee uses this technique in his speech of explanation on "The Trouble With Statistics." (The complete text of this speech may be found in Appendix B.) Stephen observes that when military personnel were added to the employment pool used to compute unemployment figures, the rate of unemployment went down. But did the actual number of the unemployed? Here is how Stephen handled this technique:

> . . . there is a more important question that needs to be answered. Look at what happened to the number. It changed. Look at what happened to the way the number was computed. It changed, too. But what happened to the very real problem of civilian unemployment, which we all assumed this number to represent? It had not changed at all. It all goes back to what Lester T. Thurow said in his basic theory of economics, "A difference is only a difference if it truly makes a difference." Many times a difference in a number does not represent a difference in the

real world. This also was the case in the late 1970s when housing was taken out of the consumer price index. . . .³

Speeches of explanation face an even greater challenge when the information they offer runs counter to generally accepted beliefs or lay theories of technical phenomena. For example, at one time it was difficult for the Western world to accept that the earth was not the center of the universe. That idea ran counter to religious doctrine and got many scientists in serious trouble. Less than four hundred years ago, Galileo was persecuted and imprisoned by the Inquisition for advancing such a view. Rowan describes a more contemporary case:

> **Perhaps there is no better example of the problems created by lay theories than in research on seat belt safety campaigns. . . . A particularly resilient obstacle to belt use is the erroneous but prevalent belief that hitting one's head on a windshield while traveling at 30 miles per hour is an experience much like doing so when a car is stationary. . . . If people understood that the experience would be much more similar to falling from a three-story building and hitting the pavement face first, one obstacle to the wearing of seat belts would be easier to overcome.⁴**

As her example indicates, dramatic analogies — such as comparing an auto accident at thirty miles per hour to falling out of a building — can help break through our resistance to new ideas that defy folk wisdom. Rowan also recommends that speakers

- state the prevalent view,
- acknowledge its apparent legitimacy,
- demonstrate its inadequacy, and
- show the greater adequacy of the more expert view.

Such a strategy of comparisons and contrasts can help listeners accept the new information and use it in their lives. Speeches of explanation may also use other designs described later in this chapter.

Briefings

A **briefing** is a short informative presentation presented in an organizational setting. Typically it is a speech of description or a speech of explanation. Briefings often take place during meetings when you are called upon to give a status report or update on a project for which you have responsibility. Briefings also take place in one-on-one situations, as when you report to your supervisor at work. Occupational, military, governmental, social, and religious organizations all use oral briefings as an important mode of communication.

Because the stakes are usually highest when you must make a briefing in an occupational setting, most of our suggestions concern how to make effective briefings at work. Most "how-to" books on communicating in organizations stress the importance of brevity, clarity, and directness.[5] When executives in 18 organizations were asked "What makes a poor presentation?" they responded with the following list of factors:

- confusing organization
- poor delivery
- too much technical jargon
- too long
- no examples or comparisons[6]

These observations suggest some clear guidelines as you prepare to make a briefing.

First, a briefing should be what its name suggests: brief. This means you must cut out any extraneous material that is not related directly to your main points. Keep your introduction and conclusions short. Begin with a preview and end with a summary.

Second, organize your ideas before you open your mouth. How can you possibly be organized when you are suddenly called upon in a meeting to "tell us about your project"? The answer is simple. Prepare in advance. (Also, see our guidelines in Chapter 11 for making an impromptu presentation.) *Never go into any meeting in which there is even the slightest possibility that you might be asked to report without a skeleton outline of a presentation.* Select a simple design and make a key-word outline of points you would cover and the order in which you would cover them. Put this outline on a note card and carry it in your pocket. Your supervisors and colleagues will be impressed with your foresight.

Third, rely heavily on carefully verified facts and figures, expert testimony, and short examples for supporting materials. Don't drift off into

Preparing for a Briefing

1 Always be prepared to report in a meeting.
2 Keep your remarks short and to the point.
3 Start with a preview and end with a summary.
4 Have no more than three main points.
5 Use facts and statistics, expert testimony, brief examples, and comparison and contrast for emphasis.
6 Avoid technical jargon.
7 Present your report with assurance.
8 Be prepared to answer tough questions.

SPEAKER'S NOTES

long stories. Use comparison and contrast to make your points clearly and directly.

Fourth, adapt your language to your audience. If you are an engineer reporting on a project to a group of nonengineer managers, use the language of management, not the language of engineering. Tell them what they need to know in language they can understand.

Fifth, present your message with confidence. Be sure everyone can see and hear you. Stand up, if necessary. Look listeners in the eye. Speak firmly with an air of assurance. After all, the project is yours and you are the expert on it.

Finally, be prepared to deal with questions, especially the tough ones. Deal with tough questions forthrightly and honestly. No one likes bad news, but worse news comes when you don't deliver the bad news to those who need to know it *when* they need to know it. Review our suggestions in Chapter 11 for handling question-and-answer sessions.

Speech Designs

There are five major design formats that are appropriate for most informative speeches: spatial, sequential, categorical, comparative, and causation. These designs may also be used in persuasive and ceremonial speeches.

Spatial Design

A **spatial design** is appropriate for speeches that describe places or that locate subjects within a physical arrangement. Such a pattern is based on the principle of proximity discussed in Chapter 7, because the order of discussion is based upon the nearness of things to one another. Suppose someone asked you to name the time zones in the United States. If you live in Washington, D.C., you would probably reply, "Eastern, Central, Mountain, and Pacific." If you live in Washington state, you might answer, "Pacific, Mountain, Central, and Eastern."[7] Either answer would follow a spatial pattern, taking yourself as the point of reference.

Most people are familiar with maps and can readily visualize directions. A speech using a spatial design provides listeners with a verbal map. To develop a spatial design, first select a starting point and determine a direction of movement. Next, take your audience on an *orderly,* systematic journey to some destination. For example, if you wanted to take listeners on a verbal tour of the Napa Valley wine country, you might start with Domaine Chandon at the south end of the valley and move progressively to the Sterling Vineyards at the north end of the valley. Once you begin a pattern of movement for a spatial design, you should stay with it to the end of the speech. If you change directions in the middle, the audience may get lost. Be sure to complete the pattern you are describing so that you satisfy listeners' desire for closure.

The body of a speech using a spatial design might have the following general format:

Preview: When you visit Yellowstone, stop first at the South Entrance Visitor's Center, then drive northwest to Old Faithful, north to Mammoth Hot Springs, and southeast to the Grand Canyon of the Yellowstone.

   I. Your first stop should be at the South Entrance Visitor's Center.

      A. Talk with a park ranger to help plan your trip.

      B. Attend a lecture or film to orient yourself to the park.

      C. Pick up materials and maps to make your tour more meaningful.

  II. Drive northwest through the Geyser Valley to Old Faithful.

      A. Hike the boardwalks in the Upper-Geyser Basin.

      B. Join the crowds waiting for Old Faithful to erupt on schedule.

      C. Have lunch at Old Faithful Inn.

 III. Continue north to Mammoth Hot Springs.

      A. Plan to spend the night at the lodge or in one of the cabins.

      B. Attend the evening lectures or films on the history of the park.

 IV. Drive southeast to the Grand Canyon of the Yellowstone.

      A. Take in the view from Inspiration Point.

      B. Hike down the trail for a better view of the waterfalls.

Sequential Design

While the spatial design moves listeners through space, a **sequential design** moves them through time. Speeches built upon sequential design may present the steps in a process, appropriate to a speech of demonstration, or provide a historical perspective in a speech of explanation.

A sequential design for a speech of demonstration is effective because it allows you to take the audience step-by-step through a process as you talk with them about it. You begin by determining the necessary steps in the process and then decide the order in which they must take place. These steps become the main points of your speech. In a short presentation you should have no more than five steps as main points. If you have more, try to cluster some of them into subpoints. It is also helpful to enumerate the steps as you make your presentation.

The following abbreviated outline illustrates a sequential design for a speech of demonstration:

Preview: The five steps toward efficient textbook reading include skimming, reading, rereading, reciting, and reviewing.

   I. First, *skim* through the chapter to get the "big picture."

      A. Identify from large-print section headings the major ideas that will be covered.

      B. Find and read any summary statements.

    C. Find and read any boxed materials.

    D. Begin a key-word skeleton outline of major topics that will be covered.

II. Second, *read* the chapter a section at a time.

    A. Make notes to yourself in the margins.

      1. Write questions about material you do not understand.

      2. Write a brief summary of ideas you do understand.

      3. Make numbered lists of any materials presented in series.

    B. Look up the definitions of unfamiliar words in the book's glossary or a dictionary.

    C. Go back and highlight the section you have just read.

      1. Highlight only the major ideas.

      2. Highlight no more than 10 percent of the text.

III. Third, *reread* the chapter.

    A. Fill in your skeleton outline with more detail.

    B. Try to answer the questions you wrote in the margin.

    C. Write out questions to ask your instructor on anything that is still not clear.

IV. Fourth, *recite* what you have read.

    A. Use your skeleton outline to make an oral presentation to yourself on the chapter.

    B. Talk about what you have read with someone else.

      1. Ask your roommate, a classmate, or friend to listen.

      2. See if you can explain the material so that your listener understands it.

V. Finally, *review* the material within twenty-four hours.

    A. Review your skeleton outline.

    B. Reread the highlighted material.

    C. See if you can answer any more of your questions now that you have had time to digest the material.

Presenting the steps in this orderly manner helps you "walk and talk" your listeners through the process. They should now understand how to begin and what to do in the proper order.

    The historical variation of a sequential design places a subject in a time perspective and follows an orderly progression. When using a sequential design to provide a historic perspective, you may start with the beginning of an idea or issue and trace it up to the present through its defining moments. Or you may start with the present and trace an issue or situation back to its origins. If you were talking about the Orlando Magic professional basketball team's rapid rise to the NBA championship finals in 1995, you might note that during that year they acquired Horace Grant from the Chicago Bulls, the year before that they drafted Anfernee Hardaway from the University of Memphis, and the year before that — only three years into their franchise — they drafted Shaquille O'Neal from Louisiana State University.

Because of your own time limitations, you must be careful to narrow your topic to manageable proportions. You must be selective, choosing landmark events that are relevant to your purpose and representative of the process you are describing. These landmark events become the main points in your message. Arrange them in their natural order, going either forward or backward in time. A speech on the evolution of the T-shirt using sequential design might be structured as follows:

Preview: The T-shirt began its life as an undergarment, developed into a bearer of messages, and has emerged as high-fashion apparel.

I. The T-shirt originated as an undergarment at the beginning of the twentieth century.

   A. The first undershirts with sleeves were designed for sailors so sensitive people would be spared the sight of hairy underarms.

   B. Sleeved undershirts were first sold commercially by Sears and Hanes in the late 1930s.

   C. During WW II, T-shirts were standard military issue and were used as outerwear in the tropics.

II. After WW II, civilians began using T-shirts as outerwear.

   A. Veterans liked them because they were comfortable and absorbent.

   B. They were popularized in movies like *A Streetcar Named Desire* and *Rebel Without a Cause.*

   C. Parents liked them for children because T-shirts were easy to care for.

III. T-shirts soon became embellished with pictures and messages.

   A. Children's T-shirts had pictures of cartoon characters like Mickey Mouse.

   B. Adult T-shirt designs were usually related to sports team logos.

   C. T-shirts soon became used for "political" statements.

      1. The first "political" T-shirt was made in 1948 and read "Dew-It with Dewey."

      2. Peace symbols were popular during the 1960s.

      3. Ideological slogans such as "A Woman's Place Is in the House (and in the Senate)" appeared during the 1970s.

   D. During the 1980s, T-shirts became walking billboards, especially for sports equipment.

IV. Today you have a choice of unique designs for T-shirts.

    A. T-shirt print shops will customize a message for you.

    B. Craft fairs often offer air-brushed T-shirts.

    C. Your local copy shop will put your picture on a T-shirt.

    D. You can buy dressy T-shirts with rhinestone and pearl decorations.

    E. You can even spend over $800 for a Gianni Versace abstract print of mercerized cotton that feels like silk.

Categorical Design

The **categorical design** is based on the principle of similarity discussed in Chapter 7, and is useful for subjects that have natural or customary divisions. Natural divisions may exist within the subject itself, such as red, white, and blended wines. Customary divisions represent typical ways of thinking about a subject, such as the four food groups that are essential to a healthy diet. Therefore, categories are the mind's way of ordering the world either by seeking the patterns within it or by supplying patterns useful to arrange it. They help us sort out incoming information so that we can make sense of it.

When preparing a speech using a categorical design, each category becomes a main point for development. For a short presentation you should limit the number of categories to four or at most five. Any subject that breaks out into six or more categories will be too complex for most classroom speeches. If you find you have too many categories, see if you can cluster some of them as a single main point. If you cannot condense your categories into a manageable number, you should probably consider another way to design the speech or else rethink your specific purpose to narrow your focus. Also, don't use a categorical design just because you think it is a simple and easy way to organize material. Your categories should represent actual or customary divisions of the topic.

Categorical designs are most effective when you begin and end the body of the speech with the more important categories. The first category gains attention and the final category gives the speech a sense of climax. The following abbreviated outline of a speech on the elements in a healthy diet begins by discussing the importance of eating a substantial amount of complex carbohydrates and ends with the importance of limiting fats in a diet.

Preview: A healthy diet is high in complex carbohydrates, fruits, and vegetables, and low in dairy products, meats and eggs, and fats.

I. You should eat from 6 to 11 servings of whole grain breads, cereals, rice, or pasta a day.

    A. They are a major source of fiber necessary for good digestion.

    B. They provide the complex carbohydrates needed for energy.

    C. They help keep you from feeling hungry.

II. You should eat from 5 to 9 helpings of vegetables and fruits each day.

A. They help fill you up without filling you out.

B. They are a major source of vitamins and minerals.

C. They may help prevent diseases.

III. You should limit dairy products, meats, and eggs to 4 to 6 servings a day.

A. They are too prevalent in American diets.

B. They are high in cholesterol which is related to heart disease.

C. You should choose carefully from this group.

1. Select low-fat or fat-free milk, frozen desserts, and cheeses.

2. Choose chicken and fish over beef and pork.

3. Use egg substitutes or limit eggs to 3 or 4 a week.

IV. You should restrict fat intake to less than 30 percent of your daily calories.

A. Fats make you fat.

B. Saturated fats increase cholesterol in the body.

C. Fat intake can be controlled and limited easily.

1. You can use olive or canola oil, which is low in saturated fats.

2. You can use fat-free salad dressings and mayonnaise.

3. You can use butter-flavored sprays for flavoring and cooking.

4. You can cut back on "fast foods" and "junk foods" which are high in fat and limited in nutritional value.

Comparative Design

A **comparative design** is useful when your topic is new to your audience, abstract, highly technical, or simply difficult to understand. It can also help you describe dramatic changes in a subject. The comparative design aids comprehension by relating the topic to something the audience already knows and understands. Comparative design is especially useful in speeches of description, speeches of explanation, and briefings because it helps bring out meaning more clearly. Speeches of demonstration that use a comparative design can also show the right and wrong ways of doing something.

There are three basic variations of the comparative design. It may be based on (1) a literal analogy, (2) a figurative analogy, or (3) a comparison and contrast format. In a **literal analogy** the subjects compared are drawn from the same field of experience. For example, a student in one of our classes related the game of rugger as played in his native Sri Lanka to the American game of football. Since both rugger and football are contact sports, the comparison between them is literal.

In a **figurative analogy** the subjects compared are drawn from different fields of experience: for example, a speaker might relate the body's struggle

Success on the job may depend on your ability to explain your work to others. If your subject is technical, comparative designs may make it more understandable to a lay audience.

against infection to a military campaign. In such a design the speaker might identify the nature of the armies, the ways the armies fight, and the consequences of defeat and victory. In this book, we have related the challenge of communicating with others to *a climb up an imaginary mountain.* As we discussed structuring a speech, the speaker became *a builder of ideas.* In Chapter 10, as we discussed the arts of language, and in Chapter 14, as we discuss the reasoning process in persuasive speeches, the speaker becomes *a weaver of the fabric of words and of the tapestry of evidence, proof, and argument.* Figurative analogies are basically extended metaphors, which we discussed in Chapter 10. As such, figurative analogies transform a technique of language into a technique of structure. The strength of such design is that it can be insightful and imaginative, helping listeners to see the significance of subjects in often surprising and impressive ways. When well selected, such a design can strengthen the competence dimension of a speaker's ethos. But like any metaphor, an analogy can damage the speaker's ethos and the speech if the comparison seems far-fetched. The advice we gave for metaphor also holds for figurative analogy designs: avoid stretching the comparison too far, or the design will collapse under the strain.

A **comparison and contrast** design points out the similarities and/or differences between subjects or ideas. In the design, each similarity or difference becomes a main point. In the interest of simplicity, you should limit yourself to five or fewer points of similarity and difference in a short presentation. The following example places the emphasis on contrast as it designs the body of a speech:

Preview: Over two decades — from the late 1960s to the late 1980s — the women we saw in advertisements began to change.

I. The products women were used to advertise changed.
   A. In the late 1960s, 75 percent of females shown were in ads for products used in the kitchen or bath.
   B. By the late 1980s only 45 percent of females shown were in ads for products used in the kitchen or bath.
   C. By the late 1980s females were appearing in more ads for alcohol, phone services, automobiles, and other high-ticket products.

II. Women in advertisements began to appear in different roles.
   A. The percentage of women shown in domestic (wife, mother) roles changed.
      1. In the late 1960s two-thirds of women in ads were shown in domestic (wife, mother) roles.
      2. By the late 1980s slightly less than half of the women in ads were shown in domestic roles.
   B. The occupational roles of women in advertisements changed.
      1. In the late 1960s only 9 percent of the females in ads had an identifiable occupation.
      2. By the late 1980s 18 percent of the females in ads had an identifiable occupation.
      3. In the late 1960s working females in ads were restricted to low-paying, traditionally female occupations.
      4. By the late 1980s the majority of females shown in occupation roles were depicted in nontraditional jobs.

III. The apparent ages of women in ads have changed.
   A. In the late 1960s almost 80 percent of the women in ads appeared to be under thirty years of age.
   B. By the late 1980s only about half of the women in ads appeared to be under thirty years of age.

IV. The overall attitude toward women in ads appears to have changed.
   A. In the late 1960s most women were portrayed in demeaning ways, as dumb and dependent sex objects.
   B. By the late 1980s more women were portrayed as intelligent, achieving, and independent individuals.

Causation Design

A **causation design** explains a situation, condition, or event in terms of the causes that led up to it. This design is often used in speeches of explanation that try to make the world understandable. When using a causation design, you may begin with a description of an existing condition, then probe for its causes. The description of the existing condition often becomes the first main point in the body of the speech, with the causes being subsequent main points. The causation design may also be used to predict events or conditions in the future. In that case, the present condition is usually the first main point in the body of the speech and the predictions become the subsequent main points. The causes or predictions may be grouped into categories which can be arranged in order of their importance. They may also be presented sequentially.

Speeches of causation are subject to one very serious limitation — the tendency to oversimplify. Any complex situation will generally have many underlying causes. And any given set of conditions may lead to many different future effects. Be wary of overly simple explanations and overly confident predictions. Such explanations and predictions are one form of faulty reasoning (fallacy) discussed further in Chapter 14.

The speech outline developed extensively in Chapter 8 is a clear example of causation design. Here we present "Warming Our World and Chilling Our Future" in abbreviated form to illustrate the causation pattern. Note that the first main point defines the greenhouse effect, while the second, third, and fourth main points discuss its major causes in an order of ascending importance.

Preview: We need to be concerned, first, about the loss of woodlands, second, about industrial emissions, and third, about overall increases in energy consumption.

    I. The greenhouse effect is the artificial warming of the earth caused by human activities.

       A. It is characterized by a high concentration of carbon dioxide in the atmosphere.

       B. Carbon pollutants are producing a hole in the ozone layer.

       C. If this problem is not corrected, we may see disastrous results.

          1. There could be dramatic climate changes.

          2. There could be serious health problems.

    II. One cause of the greenhouse effect is the loss of woodlands that convert carbon dioxide into oxygen.

       A. One football-field-size area of forest is lost every second to cutting or burning.

       B. Burning forests add more carbon dioxide because smoke is produced.

   III. Industrial emissions also contribute to the growth of the greenhouse effect.

       A. Industrial contaminants account for more than 20 percent of air pollution.

       B. Carbon dioxide is released in large quantities when fossil fuels are burned.

FIGURE 12.2

What Designs to Use When

Design	Use When
Spatial	Your topic can be discussed by how it is positioned in a physical setting or natural environment. It allows you to take your audience on an orderly "oral tour" of your topic as you move from place to place.
Sequential	Your topic can be arranged by time. It is useful for describing a process as a series of steps or explaining a subject as a series of historical landmark developments.
Categorical	Your topic has natural or customary divisions. Each category becomes a main point for development. Useful when you need to organize large amounts of material.
Comparative	Your topic is new to your audience, abstract, technical, or simply difficult to comprehend. Helps make material more meaningful by comparing or contrasting it with something the audience already knows and understands.
Causation	Your topic involves a situation, condition, or event that is best understood in terms of its underlying causes. May also be used to predict the future from existing conditions.

     C. Chlorofluorocarbons come from refrigeration and air conditioners.

     D. Nitrogen oxides are spewed out of vehicle exhausts and smoke-stacks.

  IV. Increased energy consumption magnifies the greenhouse effect.

     A. Both population and prosperity fuel the problem.

       1. More people means more energy consumption.

       2. Improved living standards add to the problem.

     B. Energy consumption is the single largest cause of the greenhouse effect.

       1. Fossil fuel use has more than doubled since 1950.

       2. Fossil fuels account for 90 percent of America's energy consumption.

       3. Transportation-related energy use accounts for about half of all air pollution.

Combined Speech Designs

Although we have presented these designs as simple patterns for speeches, effective speeches sometimes combine two or more of them. If you believe that a combined design will work best for your material, be certain to plan it carefully so that you do not seem to ramble or jump helter-skelter from one design type to another.

Alan Dunnette presented an informative classroom speech, "The Moscow Summer Games," that combined sequential and categorical designs. He opened his speech by providing a historical view of how these "games" originated as a joking response by the citizens of Moscow, Tennessee (population 583), to the American boycott of the 1980 Summer Olympic Games, scheduled for the *other* Moscow. After presenting this historical background, Alan went on to describe the different types of events that make up the games: the serious events, such as the ten-kilometer run and the canoe and kayak races, and the fun events, such as the Women's Skillet Throw and the Invitational Cow Milking Contest ("invitational because Moscow cows are particular about who grabs them and where"). Alan was able to make this combined pattern work effectively because he planned it carefully. He also used a transition to cue the audience to the shift in design by saying, "So that's how the Moscow games got started. Now what kinds of events take place there?"

IN SUMMARY

Sharing knowledge is the essence of informative speaking. It helps us to live better and work smarter. In short, information is power.

Functions of the Informative Speech. Informative speaking serves four basic functions. First, informative speaking empowers listeners by sharing information and ideas. Second, informative speaking shapes listener perceptions for later persuasive speeches. Third, informative speaking sets an agenda of public concerns by suggesting what is important. Finally, informative speaking clarifies options for decision making. In short, informative speaking teaches people something about a subject they need to know better.

Helping Your Audience Learn. From the audience's perspective, an informative speech is a learning experience. To make it easier for listeners to learn, motivate them by showing how your subject is important to them, relating it to their basic needs. You must also hold their attention throughout your speech. To grasp and hold attention, design your message in light of the principles of intensity, repetition, novelty, activity, contrast, and relevance. Help your audience remember your message by organizing your material in an orderly fashion and providing previews and summaries.

Types of Informative Speeches. Informative speeches include speeches of description, demonstration, and explanation. *Speeches of description* create word pictures that help the audience visualize a subject. *Speeches of demonstration* show the audience how something is done. They may give listeners an understanding of a process or teach them how to perform it. Speeches of demonstration are often more effective when presentation aids are used. *Speeches of explanation* inform the audience about abstract and complex subjects, such as concepts or programs. Such speeches normally present a more difficult challenge, especially when their information contradicts folk knowledge or cherished beliefs. Briefings, an important subtype of informative speaking, are presented mainly in organizational settings. Briefings are usually status reports or updates on projects for which you have responsibility.

Speech Designs.   The patterns most frequently employed in informative speeches are spatial, sequential, categorical, comparative, and causation designs. A *spatial design* orders the main points according to the arrangement of a subject in actual space. Spatial designs are especially appropriate for describing objects or places. Most speeches of demonstration use a *sequential design,* which follows a time pattern to present steps in a process as they occur or a series of historical events. *Categorical designs* may represent natural divisions of your subject or traditional ways of thinking. In a short speech you should limit the number of categories to no more than five. *Comparative designs* are especially effective when your topic is new to the audience, when it has undergone dramatic changes, or when you wish to establish right and wrong procedures. These designs are often based on *literal* or *figurative analogies,* depending on whether the compared subjects are drawn from the same or different fields of experience. A *causation design* explains how one condition generates or is generated by another. The causation design is subject to the problem of oversimplification. Sometimes you may decide to incorporate two or more designs into a speech. In that case be certain to provide transitions so that listeners are not confused by the changing patterns.

TERMS TO KNOW

informative value

prepersuasive function

agenda-setting function

speech of description

speech of demonstration

speech of explanation

briefing

spatial design

sequential design

categorical design

comparative design

literal analogy

figurative analogy

comparison and contrast

causation design

DISCUSSION

1. One testimonial to the power of information is the widespread practice of industrial and international espionage. Investigate a specific instance in which such theft of information became widely known. In particular, seek for answers as to why this information was valuable and secret. Ponder this issue: how much secrecy of government information can we tolerate in a society that depends on fully-informed citizens as repositories of political power? Bring your thoughts and findings to class for discussion.

2. You can probably recall one or several outstanding teachers in high school who helped you learn. How did they encourage learning in their classes? Share in class discussion your memories of their techniques for presenting information. What can you learn about communicating information, using them as models of excellence?

3. Over a typical weeks' viewing time, watch tabloid-television programs that purport to be informative. Which informative functions do they fulfill? Are there qualitative differences among them when they are considered as media of information? Are they better characterized as entertainment programs? Do they sometimes serve persuasive purposes as well? Are they ethical providers of information? Discuss your observations and judgments in class.

APPLICATION

1. Analyze the speech by Stephen Lee in Appendix B in terms of its functions, type, and design. Consider how it gains and holds attention and motivates learning. Can you think of different designs for the speech? Would they be more or less effective?

2. Design the informative speech you prepare for class, being sure to include techniques to sustain attention. In the margin of the outline you turn in, specify what attention techniques you will use and why you believe they will be effective.

NOTES

1. D. L. Shaw and M. E. McCombs, *The Emergence of American Political Issues: The Agenda-Setting Function of the Press* (St. Paul, MN: West, 1977).

2. Katherine E. Rowan, "Goals, Obstacles, and Strategies in Risk Communication: A Problem-Solving Approach to Improving Communication About Risks," *Journal of Applied Communication Research,* 19 (1991): 314.

3. Stephen Lee first presented this informative speech of explanation in his public speaking class at the University of Texas, Austin. Later Stephen's speech won the Southern division of the 1991 Houghton Mifflin Public Speaking Contest.

4. Rowan, p. 314.

5. Notable among such books are Milo O. Frank, *How to Get Your Point Across in 30 Seconds or Less* (New York: Simon & Schuster, Inc., 1986); William Parkhurst, *The Eloquent Executive: How to Sound Your Best: High-Impact Speaking in Meetings Large & Small* (New York: Avon, 1988); Joan Detz, *Can You Say a Few Words? How to Prepare and Deliver* (New York: St. Martin's Press, 1991); Sonja Hamlin, *How to Talk So People Listen* (New York: Harper & Row, 1988); Burton Kaplan, *The Manager's*

Complete Guide to Speech Writing (New York: Free Press, 1988); Dorothy Leeds, *PowerSpeak* (New York: Berkeley Books, 1991); Lilly Walters, *Secrets of Successful Speakers: How You Can Motivate, Captivate and Persuade* (New York: McGraw-Hill, 1993); Laurie Schloff and Marcia Yudkin, *Smart Speaking: Sixty-Second Strategies* (New York: Holt, 1991); Jeff Scott Cook, *The Elements of Speech Writing and Public Speaking* (New York: Macmillan, 1989).

6. J. E. Hollingsworth, "Oral Briefings," *Management Review* (Aug. 1968), 2–10.

7. Adapted from material supplied by Randy Scott, Department of Communication, Weber State University, Ogden, Utah.

The New Madrid Earthquake Area
Stephen Huff

Stephen's introduction sets the scene in graphic detail. He opens with a rhetorical question and involves his audience by repeating, "If you're like me." He motivates listeners by tying the San Francisco quake to the New Madrid Fault area where they live. His admission of ignorance allows his audience to identify with him as an attractive and modest person, and suggests his substantial preparation for the speech — both important benefits for his ethos. His central idea provides a preview that promises a categorical design that will combine description, explanation, and demonstration.

Stephen's first main point concerns earthquakes in general and the New Madrid area in particular. The magnitude chart puts the intensity of earthquakes into perspective. His comparisons with the atomic bomb and the recent San Francisco quake help make the numbers meaningful, as do his descriptions of the great New Madrid quakes. He uses facts and statistics as primary supporting material, enlivened by vivid examples and stories.

How many of you can remember what you were doing around seven o'clock on the evening of October 17th? If you're a sports fan like me, you had probably set out the munchies, popped a cold one, and settled back to watch San Francisco and Oakland battle it out in the World Series. Since the show came on at seven o'clock here in Memphis for its pregame hype, you may not have been paying close attention to the TV — until — until — until both the sound and picture went out because of the Bay Area earthquake.

If you're like me, you probably sat glued to the TV set for the rest of the evening watching the live coverage of that catastrophe. If you're like me, you probably started thinking that Memphis, Tennessee, is in the middle of the New Madrid earthquake area and wondering how likely it would be for a large earthquake to hit here. And if you're like me, you probably asked yourself, "What would I do if a major earthquake hit Memphis?"

As I asked myself these questions, I was surprised to admit that I didn't know very much about the New Madrid earthquake area or the probability of a major quake in Memphis. And I was really upset to discover that I didn't have the foggiest idea of what to do if a quake did hit. So I visited the Center for Earthquake Research and Information here on campus; talked with Dr. Arch Johnston, the director; and read the materials he helped me find. Today, I'd like to share with you what I learned about the New Madrid earthquake area, how likely it is that Memphis may be hit by a major quake in the near future, what the effects of such a quake might be, and — most important — what you can do to be prepared.

Let's start with a little history about the New Madrid earthquake area. During the winter of 1811 to 1812, three of the largest earthquakes ever to hit the continental United States occurred in this area. Their estimated magnitudes were 8.6, 8.4, and 8.8 on the Richter scale. [He reveals magnitude chart.] I have drawn this chart to give you some idea of how much energy this involves. To simplify things, I have shown the New Madrid quakes as 8.5. Since a one-point increase in the Richter scale equals a thirtyfold increase in energy release, the energy level of these quakes was over nine hundred times more powerful than the Hiroshima atomic bomb and more than thirty times more powerful than the 7.0 quake that hit San Francisco last October. [He conceals magnitude chart.]

Most of the reports of these early earthquakes come from journals or Indian legends. The Indians tell of the night that lasted for a week and the way the "Father of Waters" — the Mississippi River — ran backwards. Waterfalls were formed on the river. Islands disappeared. Land that was once in Arkansas — on the west bank of the river — ended up in Tennessee — on the east bank of the river. Church bells chimed as far away as New Orleans and Boston. Cracks up to ten feet wide opened and closed in the earth. Geysers squirted sand fifteen feet into the air. Whole forests sank

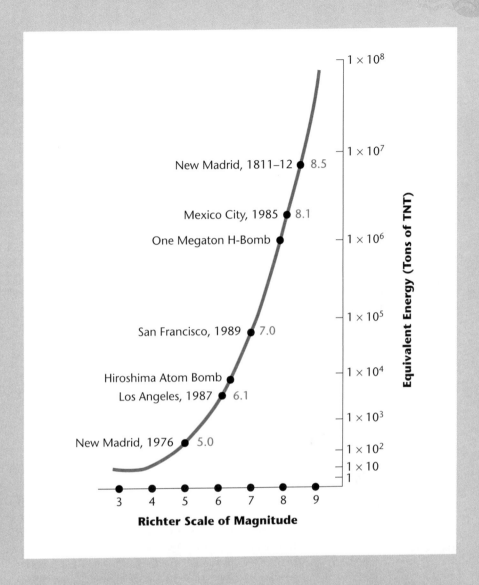

Stephen's simplified map of the New Madrid Fault area helps his audience see the epicenters of earthquake activity in relation to Memphis. He uses contrast between the California and New Madrid earthquakes to maintain attention and motivate listeners. He documents his supporting material carefully.

into the earth as the land turned to quicksand. Lakes disappeared and new lakes were formed. Reelfoot Lake — over ten miles long — was formed when the Mississippi River changed its course. No one is certain how many people died from the quakes because the area was sparsely settled with trappers and Indian villages. Memphis was just an outpost village with a few hundred settlers.

[He shows map of epicenters.] As you can see on this map, Memphis itself is not directly on the New Madrid Fault line. The fault extends from around Marked Tree, Arkansas, northeast to near Cairo, Illinois. This continues to be a volatile area of earthquake activity. According to Robert L. Ketter, director of the National Center for Earthquake Engineering Research, between 1974 and 1983 over two thousand quakes were recorded in the area. About 150 earthquakes per year occur in the area, but only about eight of them are large enough for people to notice. The others are picked up on the seismographs at tracking stations. The strongest quake in recent years occurred here in 1976. [He points to location on map.] This measured 5.0 on the Richter scale.

The New Madrid earthquake area is much different from the San Andreas Fault in California. Because of the way the land is formed, the alluvial soil transmits energy more efficiently here than in California. Although the quakes were about the same size, the New Madrid earthquakes affected an area fifteen times larger than the "great quake" that destroyed San Francisco in 1906.

Although scientists cannot predict exactly when another major quake may hit the area, they do know that the *repeat time* for a magnitude-6 New Madrid earthquake is seventy years, plus or minus fifteen years. The last earthquake of this size to hit the area occurred in 1895 north of New Madrid, Missouri. [He points to epicenter on map.] According to Johnston and Nava of the Memphis Earthquake Center, the probability that one with a magnitude of 6.3 will occur somewhere in the fault area by the year 2000 is 40 to 63 percent. By the year 2035 this probability increases to 86 to 97 percent. The probabilities for larger quakes are lower. They estimate the probability of a 7.6 quake within the next fifty years to be from 19 to 29 percent. [He conceals map of epicenters.]

What would happen if an earthquake of 7.6 hit Memphis? Allan and Hoshall, a prominent local engineering firm, prepared a study on this for the Federal Emergency Management Agency. The expected death toll would top 2,400. There would be at least 10,000 casualties. Two hundred thousand residents would be homeless. The city would be without electricity, gas, water or sewer treatment facilities for weeks. Gas lines would rupture, and fires would sweep through the city. Transportation would be almost impossible, bridges and roads would be destroyed, and emergency supplies would have to be brought in by helicopter. The river bluff, midtown, and land along the Wolfe River would turn to quicksand because of liquification. Buildings there would sink like they did in the Marina area during this past year's San Francisco quake. If the quake hit during daytime hours, at least 600 children would be killed and another 2,400 injured as schools collapsed on them. None of our schools have been built to seismic code specifications.

In fact, very few buildings in Memphis have been built to be earthquake resistant, so it would be difficult to find places to shelter and care for the homeless. The major exceptions are the new hospitals in the suburbs, the Omni Hotel east of the expressway, the Holiday Inn Convention Center, and two or three new office complexes. The only municipal structure built to code is the Criminal Justice Center. The new Memphis Pyramid, being built by the city and county, which will seat over twenty thousand people for the University of Memphis basketball games, is not being built to code. I'd hate to be in it if a major quake hit. The prospects are not pretty.

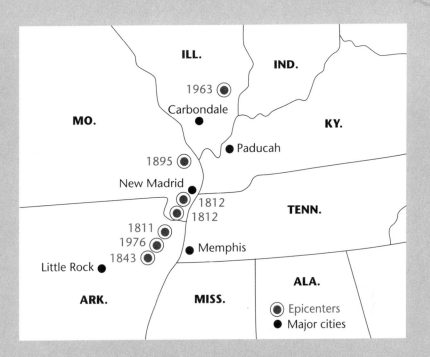

What can we do to prepare ourselves for this possible catastrophe? We can start out by learning what to do if a quake does hit. When I asked myself what I would do, my first reaction was to "get outside." I've since learned that this is not right. The "Earthquake Safety Checklist" published by the Federal Emergency Management Agency and the Red Cross makes a number of suggestions. I've written them out and will distribute them after my speech.

First, when an earthquake hits, if you are inside, stay there. Get in a safe spot: stand in a doorway, stand next to an inside wall, or get under a large piece of furniture. Stay away from windows, hanging objects, fireplaces, and tall unsecured furniture until the shaking stops. Do not try to use elevators. If you are outside, get away from buildings, trees, walls, or power lines. If you are in a car, stay in it; pull over and park. Stay away from overpasses and power lines. Do not drive over bridges or overpasses until they have been inspected. If you are in a crowded public place, do not rush for the exit. You may be crushed in the stampede of people.

When the shaking stops, check for gas, water, or electrical damage. Turn off the electricity, gas, and water to your home. Do not use electrical switches — unseen sparks could set off a gas fire. Do not use the telephone unless you must report a severe injury. Check to see that the sewer works before using the toilet. Plug drains to prevent a sewer backup.

There are also some things you can do in advance to be prepared. Accumulate emergency supplies: at home you should have a flashlight, a transistor radio with fresh batteries, a first-aid kit, fire extinguishers, and enough canned or dried food and beverages to last your family for 72 hours. Identify hazards and safe spots in your home — secure tall heavy furniture; don't hang heavy pictures over your bed; keep flammable liquids in a garage or outside storage area — look around each room and plan where you would go if an earthquake hit. Conduct earthquake drills with your family.

There's one more suggestion that I would like to add. One that is specific to Memphis. Let our local officials know that you are concerned about the lack of preparedness. Urge them to support a building code — at least for public structures — that meets seismic resistance standards.

In preparing this speech, I learned a lot about the potential for earthquakes in Memphis. I hope you have learned something too. I now feel like I know what I should do if an earthquake hits. But I'm not really sure how I would react. Even the experts don't always react "appropriately." In 1971 an earthquake hit the Los Angeles area at about six o'clock in the morning. Charles Richter, the seismologist who developed the Richter scale to measure earthquakes, was in bed at the time. According to his wife, "He jumped up screaming and scared the cat."

Earthquake Preparedness Suggestions

1. If you are inside, stay there. Get in a safe spot: stand in a doorway, stand next to an inside wall, or get under a large piece of furniture. Stay away from windows, hanging objects, fireplaces, and tall, unsecured furniture until the shaking stops. Do not try to use elevators.

2. If you are outside, get away from buildings, trees, walls, or power lines. If you are in a car, stay in it; pull over and park. Stay away from overpasses and power lines. Do not drive over bridges or overpasses until they have been inspected.

3. If you are in a crowded public place, do not rush for the exit. You may be crushed in the stampede of people.

4. When the shaking stops, check for gas, water, or electrical damage. Turn off the electricity, gas, and water to your home. Do not use electrical switches — unseen sparks could set off a gas fire. Do not use the telephone unless you must report a severe injury. Check to see that the sewer works before using the toilet. Plug drains to prevent sewer backup.

There are also some things you can do in advance to be prepared:

1. Accumulate emergency supplies: at home you should have a flashlight, a transistor radio with fresh batteries, a first-aid kit, fire extinguishers, and enough canned or dried food and beverages to last for 72 hours.

2. Identify hazards and safe spots in your home — secure tall, heavy furniture; don't hang heavy pictures over your bed; keep flammable liquids in a garage or outside storage area — look around each room and plan where you would go if an earthquake hit; conduct earthquake drills with your family.

13

Persuasive Speaking

- recognize the characteristics of persuasive speaking.
- understand the steps in the persuasive process.
- adapt persuasion to different audiences.
- learn the major persuasive functions.
- select the designs most useful for your persuasive speeches.

> Because there has been implanted in us the power to persuade each other . . . , not only have we escaped the life of the wild beasts but we have come together and founded cities and made laws and invented arts. . . .
>
> — Isocrates

You awaken to a world of persuasion. On your clock radio you hear a disc jockey selling tickets to a rock concert. The weather forecaster warns you to carry an umbrella. Other students ask you to join their organizations. Stores beg for your business. Politicians plead for your vote. Highway billboards tout everything from bourbon to church attendance. The novels, movies, music, and television shows you see and hear may promote social or political causes.

You are also constantly persuading. You may want your roommate to go out for pizza with you rather than finish an accounting assignment. You think some questions on your last botany test were unfair and would like your instructor to change your grade. You've just met a good-looking guy that you want to date. Your friends are going to Florida for spring vacation and you must convince your parents that you need a break. The history department scholarship you are vying for requires an interview as well as an essay. When job hunting, you must convince a prospective employer of your abilities. If you want to advance at work, you must promote your ideas.

Whatever path your life takes, you can't avoid persuading and being persuaded.

What does it mean to say that we live in a world of persuasion? As we noted in Chapter 5, persuasion is one of the basic functions of speaking. **Persuasion** *is the art of convincing others to give favorable attention to our point of view.* Persuaders typically have specific goals in mind: they want to influence how listeners believe or act on issues they care about. In order to do this they must offer sufficient reasons to accept their advice. To cite an ancient example, while a philosopher might ask, "Should people marry?," a persuader will plead, "Marry me! Here's why . . . "

The range of persuasion is wide, ranging from the ethical to the unethical, the selfless to the selfish, the magnificent to the crass, the inspiring to the degrading. Persuaders can prey upon our vulnerability, or enlighten our minds with reasoning that adds conviction to our commitments. An essential part of being an educated person is learning how to resist the one kind of persuasion and to encourage the other.

Beyond its personal importance to us, persuasion is essential to our society. The right to persuade and be persuaded is the bedrock of the American political system, guaranteed by the First Amendment to the Constitution. According to the late Supreme Court Justice Louis D. Brandeis, "Those who won our independence believed that the final end of the State was to make men free to develop their faculties; and that in its government the deliberative forces should prevail over the arbitrary."[1] Free, open discussion and persuasion are required for these "deliberative forces" to operate.

Deliberation requires that all points of view on an issue be heard before a group reaches a thoughtful decision. The contending factions then agree to accept the majority position. When decisions are arbitrarily imposed, they often need force to be effective. Our political system is based on the premise that persuasion is more ethical and more practical than force. We should make commitments because we are persuaded, not because we are coerced.

Some people, however, object to the very idea of persuasion. They may regard it as an unwelcome intrusion into their lives or as manipulation or domination.[2] While we agree that persuasion can be abusive, we also believe that persuasion can be ethical and valuable. Ethical persuasion is based on sound reasoning that is sensitive to the feelings and needs of listeners. Such persuasion can help us apply the knowledge and wisdom of the past to decisions we now must make. It appeals to our better nature, and can improve the quality and humanity of our commitments.

Although you may object to the expression of opposing views on certain issues, the freedom to voice unpopular views is the heart and soul of liberty. The English philosopher John Stuart Mill put the matter eloquently:

> If all mankind, minus one, were of the one opinion, and only one person were of the contrary opinion, mankind would be no more justified in silencing that one person, than he, if he had the power, would be justified in silencing mankind.
>
> . . . We can never be sure that the opinion we are endeavoring to stifle is a false opinion; and if we were sure, stifling it would be an evil still.[3]

Other reasons for tolerating minority opinions are more practical in nature. Research suggests that exposure to different viewpoints can stimulate listeners and produce better, more original decisions.[4] For example, even though Martha may never agree with Sam's view that we should abolish gun ownership, his arguments may cause her to reexamine her position, to understand her own convictions better, or perhaps even modify her views.

Even though speaking out on public issues is important, many people shy away from persuasion. They may think: "What difference can one person make? I'm not very important, and my words don't carry much weight." Perhaps not, but words make ripples, and ripples come together to make waves. Just ask Anna Aley, a student at Kansas State University, who gave the persuasive speech on substandard student housing reprinted at the end of this chapter. Her speech began as a class assignment and was presented later in a public forum on campus. Anna made such an impression that the text of her speech was reprinted in the local newspaper, the *Manhattan Mercury,* which followed it up with a series of investigative reports and a sympathetic editorial. Brought to the attention of the mayor and city commission, Anna's speech helped promote reforms in the city's rental housing policies. Her words are still reverberating in Manhattan, Kansas.

Perhaps your persuasive speech will not have such a dramatic impact, but be assured that the words we speak constantly affect the conditions of our lives. In this chapter we consider the characteristics of persuasive speaking, the process of persuasion, some of the challenges facing persuasive speakers, the functions of persuasive speeches, and designs appropriate to structure them.

SIX CHARACTERISTICS OF PERSUASIVE SPEAKING

Six characteristics define the nature of persuasive speaking. They are best understood if we view them in contrast with informative speaking:

Informative speakers reveal and clarify options: persuasive speakers urge a choice from among them. Informative speakers expand our awareness. For example, an informative speaker might say, "There are three different ways we can deal with Eastern Europe. Let me explain them for you." In contrast, a persuasive speaker would weigh these options and urge us to support one of them: "Of the three different ways to deal with Eastern Europe, we should pursue *this* policy because it is the best."

Informative speakers provide sound information to enlighten their listeners: persuasive speakers provide such information to justify their recommendations. While both informative and persuasive speaking must be based on responsible knowledge, persuasive speaking uses that knowledge to suggest how we should feel, believe, and act. The persuasive speaker justifies recommendations with **good reasons** for accepting them. Good reasons are based upon responsible knowledge and a sensitive consideration of the best interests of listeners. For example, as President Clinton defended his policy of sending American troops to support the Bosnian peace accords, he could not simply say, "Here is the situation in Bosnia." Rather, he had to argue, "We should support these accords because our vital interests are at stake." He then had to present these vital interests as good reasons justifying his decision.

Persuasive speaking requires more audience commitment than informative speaking. Although there is some risk in exposing ourselves to new information and ideas, there is more at stake when listening to a persuasive speaker. You risk little when you listen to an informative speaker describe off-campus living conditions. A persuasive speaker wants you *to do something* about these conditions. What if the speaker isn't honest? What if the actions you take backfire? *Doing* always involves a greater risk than *knowing*. Your commitment could cost you. Because of the risks involved, audiences for persuasive speeches must practice critical listening skills diligently.

Leadership is a more important issue in persuasive than informative speaking. Because persuaders ask people to assume risks, listeners will weigh the character and competence of these speakers closely. Do they really know what they are talking about? Do they have listeners' interests at heart? Are they willing to place themselves on the line? As you rally others against the slumlords of student housing, your ethos will be on public display and will be scrutinized very carefully.

Appeals to feeling are more appropriate in persuasive than informative speaking. Because a persuasive speaker asks an audience to assume greater risks, listeners may hesitate to accept recommendations, even when they are supported by good reasons. To overcome such inertia, you may have to appeal to feelings.[5] This is why Bonnie Marshall used such a strong emotional opening for her speech advocating living wills (see Appendix B). Similarly, the statement "Studies show that a 10 percent rise in tuition costs will reduce the student population by about 5 percent next fall" may be useful in an informative speech but would not be sufficient in a persuasive speech. Look at another way of putting the matter:

> **The people who want tuition increases have enough money, so they don't think a few hundred dollars more each term will have much effect on us students. They feel most of us can handle a 10 percent rise in tuition costs. They say that the one in twenty who won't be back won't make that much difference!**
>
> **Well, let me tell you about a friend of mine — let's call her Tricia. Both of Tricia's parents lost their jobs last year. Tricia is on the Dean's List, and can look forward to a successful career as a chemist when she graduates. But if this increase in tuition goes through, Tricia won't be back next fall. Her dreams deferred — her dreams denied! What do the legislators care about that? What do they care about Tricia's dreams?**
>
> **Perhaps you are like Tricia. But even if you are not, she is one of us, and she needs our help *now*.**

Emotional language is often needed to help people see the human dimension of problems and move them to action.

The ethical obligation for persuasive speakers is even greater than that for informative speakers. The stirring use of language and strong appeals for action raise ethical questions. As a persuasive speaker, you must assume responsibility for the consequences of your words. You have a special obligation to be sure that your recommendations are sound and well considered. Will your plan for improving off-campus housing result in increased safety, or would it merely raise rents? Are your good reasons compelling? Are they free from logical flaws? Are they built upon responsible knowledge? Are they ethically defensible? Is your plan worth the cost and risk?

To summarize, persuasion asks us to make a choice that will affect how we believe or act. To justify this choice, persuaders must present good reasons drawn from sound knowledge and sensitivity to the audience's values and interests. Persuaders ask listeners to assume the risk of commitment, which in turn raises the issue of their credibility. Can we depend on them? Are they trustworthy? To overcome doubt or hesitation, persuaders often must arouse feelings to make us act. Finally, the potential impact of persuasion on our lives creates a large ethical obligation for persuaders. Persuasion should not be undertaken lightly.

THE PROCESS OF PERSUASION

To understand how Anna Aley stirred her audiences to protest poor housing conditions or how Bonnie Marshall hoped to convince people of the value of living wills, we must look at how persuasion works. William J. McGuire, professor of psychology at Yale University, suggests that effective

Persuasive speeches can help raise support for worthy causes. Here, ex-heavyweight champion George Foreman speaks to at-risk youths at an anti-gang rally in San Antonio, TX.

persuasion is a complicated process involving up to twelve phases.[6] For our purposes, these phases may be grouped into five stages: awareness, understanding, agreement, enactment, and integration. Familiarity with these stages helps us recognize that persuasion is not an all-or-nothing proposition — that a persuasive message may be considered successful if it simply moves people along through the process toward a goal.

The first stage in the persuasive process is raising awareness of an issue. Awareness includes knowing about a problem, paying attention to it, and understanding how it affects our lives. This phase of persuasion is often called **consciousness-raising.** As we noted in Chapter 12, informative speaking can build such awareness and prepare us for persuasion.[7] Creating awareness is especially important when people must be convinced that there actually is a problem. For example, before they could hope for changes in the way females were depicted in children's books, feminists had to make people understand that always showing boys in active roles and girls in passive roles was a serious problem. They had to prove that this could stunt the development of self-esteem in young females.[8] Similarly, Anna Aley had to draw people's attention to the reality of substandard student housing in their town, and Bonnie Marshall had to start her listeners thinking about who might be making life-and-death decisions for them if they did not prepare living wills.

Beyond simply acquainting listeners with a problem, persuasion geared to this stage must convince us of the problem's importance and show how it affects us directly. Persuasive speakers must raise audience awareness before moving on to the next stage in the persuasive process.

The second phase of the persuasive process is developing understanding. Listeners obviously must get the point you are trying to make. Beyond that, they must be moved by your ideas and know how to carry out your proposals. To increase understanding in her speech, Anna Aley pursued an interesting "inside-outside" approach. She carried listeners *inside* the substandard housing problem in Manhattan by describing the basement apartment where she lived in vivid terms. Then she took her audience *outside* the problem by showing them the total picture of the number of students involved, the causes of the problem, and how it might be solved. Helping listeners understand is important when listeners admit there is a problem but don't know what to do about it. Ethical persuasion expands our knowledge of arguments, demonstrates how some arguments are stronger than others, and provides evidence to support a position.[9]

Effective persuasive messages strike sparks in the minds of listeners. For instance, an example may remind listeners of a similar situation they encountered. An argument may generate additional supporting arguments or counterarguments. This interplay engages the audience in *both* critical and constructive listening (described in Chapter 3). It invites listeners to participate in the communication process. Finally, the audience must understand *how* to put the speaker's proposals into effect. Bonnie Marshall clearly spells out the steps she wants her listeners to take, enumerating these as she presents them.

FIGURE 13.1
McGuire's Model of the Persuasive Process

The third stage in the persuasive process is seeking agreement. Agreement depends on listeners accepting recommendations and remembering their reasons for that acceptance. Agreement can range from small concessions to total acceptance. Lesser degrees of agreement could mean success, especially when listeners have to change their attitudes or risk a great deal by accepting your ideas. During the Vietnam War, American speech classrooms were lively arenas for speeches attacking or defending our involvement in that conflict. Feelings ran so high on this issue that just to have one's speech heard without interruption could be considered a victory. If some reluctant listener would nod in agreement, or concede, "I guess you have a point," then one could truly claim a triumph.

Often you achieve agreement by presenting indisputable facts and well-reasoned interpretations of information that make your conclusions seem beyond question. You can help listeners remember their agreement by providing vivid images or telling interesting stories that embody your message. While reasoning is important to secure agreement, stories and images will stay with your audience after they have forgotten the details of your argument.

The fourth stage in the persuasive process is encouraging enactment. It moves listeners beyond agreement to action. It is one thing to get an audience to accept what you say. It is quite another to ask them to put themselves on the line. If you can get listeners to sign a petition, raise their hands, or voice agreement, you give them an active way to express their agreement. *By enacting their agreement, listeners reinforce their commitment.* The student speaker who mobilized his audience against a proposed tuition increase

- brought a petition to be signed,
- distributed a handout containing the addresses and phone numbers of local legislators for students to contact, and
- urged listeners to write letters to campus and local newspapers.

He channeled their agreement into constructive action.

Transforming agreement into action often requires us to touch emotions in ways that make listeners want to act. Stirring stories and examples, vivid images, and colorful language can stir listeners' sympathies. As she told the story of Harry Smith, who died an agonizing death because he had not signed a living will, Bonnie Marshall moved her listeners to act on behalf of themselves and their loved ones. Anna Aley's concluding story of her neighbor's accident helped motivate her audience to undertake the actions she proposed.

The final stage in the persuasive process is *promoting the integration of new attitudes and commitments into enduring patterns of audience beliefs and values.* For your persuasive speech to have a lasting effect, listeners must see the connection between the specific attitudes and actions you propose and the values they already hold dear. You must settle your ideas comfortably within their belief system. As she presented her case for living wills, Bonnie Marshall anchored her appeals in the right to control one's destiny. Anna Aley tied her attack on slumlord housing conditions to the values of fair, respectful treatment from others and safe living conditions.

All of us seek consistency among our values and behaviors. For example, it would be inconsistent for us to march against substandard housing on Monday and contribute to a landlord's defense fund on Tuesday. This is why people sometimes seem to agree with a persuasive message, then change their minds. It dawns on them that this new commitment means they must rearrange the psychological furniture of other behaviors. They may have to give up some cherished beliefs and attitudes. They may even lose friends or social status connected with their previous beliefs.

You are asking a great deal when you invite listeners to undergo dramatic changes. You must offer them compelling reasons, often appealing to the very soul of their humanity. To provide such reasons, point out how the new position is consistent with their cherished values. Show listeners how the change will benefit them and their loved ones. Finally, knowing

Applying McGuire's Model of the Persuasive Process to Your Speeches

SPEAKER'S NOTES

1 Arouse attention with an effective introduction.

2 Involve listeners by relating your message to their interests and needs.

3 Ensure understanding by defining complex terms, using concrete examples, and organizing your material clearly.

4 Build your persuasive efforts on a base of solid information.

5 Be sure listeners know how to carry out your proposal.

6 Help the audience remember your message by using vivid word pictures and a striking conclusion.

7 Ask for a public commitment from your listeners. Start them on the path to change by stirring appropriate feelings.

8 Ensure lasting change by relating it to other enduring beliefs and values.

the inner struggle that some listeners will experience, plan responses to their objections. Help them see a situation in a new way. On some issues before some audiences, it may require an almost biblical conversion — listeners must be "born again." Such a change may be necessary before one can experience that self-growth we described in Chapter 1 as *transformation*. Obviously, this degree of integration is rarely achieved through a single message. Such dramatic changes may require a campaign of persuasion in which any single speech plays its small but vital role.

To conclude: persuasion is a complicated process. Any single persuasive effort must focus on where it can make its most effective contribution: to raise awareness, build understanding, seek agreement, encourage action, or promote the process of integration. To determine where to focus our persuasive efforts, we must carefully analyze our audience and adapt our messages to the specific challenges of the persuasive situation we anticipate.

THE CHALLENGES OF PERSUASION

The challenges that confront persuasive speakers range from enticing a reluctant audience to listen to moving a sympathetic audience to action. As you plan a persuasive speech, you need to consider the audience's position on the topic, how listeners might react to you as an advocate, and the situation in which the speech will be presented. At this point, the information and techniques concerning audience analysis we introduced in Chapter 4 become vital to your success.

Begin preparing your persuasive speech by determining where your listeners stand on the issue. Do they hold varying attitudes about the topic, or are they united? If listeners are divided, you might hope to unify them around your position. If listeners are already united — but in opposition — you might try to divide them and attract some toward your position. Also consider how your listeners might regard you as a speaker on the subject. If you do not have their respect, trust, and good will, use testimony from highly regarded sources to enhance your ethos and improve your chances for success.

Evaluating the relationships among the audience, the topic, and you as speaker will help you determine how far you can go in a particular speech. These relationships also may suggest what strategies you should use and the kind of supporting materials you will need.

Enticing a Reluctant Audience to Listen

When attitudes and beliefs are important to your listeners, they are especially hard to change. If you face an audience that opposes your position, success may be measured in small achievements, such as simply getting thoughtful attention. One way to handle a reluctant audience is to adopt a **co-active approach**, which seeks to bridge the differences between you and your listeners.[10] The major steps in this approach include:

1. *Establish identification and good will early in the speech.* Review the material in Chapter 2 on how to establish favorable ethos. Emphasize experiences, background, beliefs, and values that you share with listeners.

2. *Start with areas of agreement before you tackle areas of disagreement.* Emphasizing points on which you agree often puts listeners in a more receptive frame of mind for your message. Starting out by reminding them of how you differ with them may make them more distant and defensive. Instead of listening, they may sit silently thinking up arguments to refute you.

3. *Emphasize explanation more than argument at the outset.* Reluctant listeners are going to be wary of you and resistant to persuasive efforts. Knowing this, you must create an atmosphere in which your message can have a fair chance to be heard. One indirect approach to persuasion is to say in effect at the outset, "I'm not going to try to persuade you today, but I want you to understand how I came to believe as I do." As you explain the reasons for your position, you will be inviting listeners to consider the merits of your position without risking their own. Such an indirect approach can be very effective in creating awareness and understanding, the early phases of the persuasive process. If you are successful, you can go on in later speeches to show listeners why *they* should also consider agreeing with and committing to your point of view.

4. *Cite authorities the audience will respect and accept.* A good question to ask as you plan your speech is, "Who does my audience respect?" If you can find statements by such authorities favorable to your position, you can make good use of "borrowed ethos." For example, citing "Mr. Conservative" Barry Goldwater, former Arizona senator and Republican presidential nominee, in favor of gay rights before a politically conservative group could be very effective.[11]

5. *Set modest goals for change.* Don't try to push your audience too far too fast. If reluctant listeners have listened to you — if you have raised their awareness and built a basis of understanding — you have accomplished a good deal. Don't risk these gains by being too aggressive. Rome was not built in a day. Nor will most audiences be converted by most speakers on most topics with a single speech. Be content to play your part in the persuasive process.

6. *Offer a multisided presentation in which you compare your position with others to show its superiority.* The **multisided presentation** respects the intelligence of listeners by acknowledging that other positions are possible on your topic. In taking such an approach, you show respect for other positions, but show how they are deficient.

Let's look at how you might apply these steps in a speech against capital punishment. You could *build identification* by pointing out the common beliefs, attitudes, and values you share with the audience, such as "We all respect human life. We all believe in fairness." At the same time you would be *starting with areas of agreement and working toward the acceptance of common values.* It might also help to take an indirect approach in which you present your evidence and reasoning before you announce your purpose.

> **What if I were to tell you that we are condoning unfairness, that we are condemning people to death simply because they are poor and cannot afford a good lawyer? What if I were to show you that we are sanctioning a model of violent behavior in our society that invites more violence and more victims in return?**

As you present evidence, cite authorities that *your audience will respect and accept.* "FBI statistics tell us that if you are poor and black, you are three times more likely to be executed for the crime of murder." *Keep your goals modest.* Ask only for a fair hearing of your position. Your goal might be to give the audience members information that could *eventually* change their minds.

> **I know that many of you may not like to hear what I'm saying, but think about it. If capital punishment does not deter violent crimes, if indeed it may encourage *more* violent crimes, isn't it time we put capital punishment itself on trial?**

Finally, *make a multisided presentation.* Acknowledge the arguments in favor of capital punishment, showing that you respect and understand that position, even though you do not accept it.

> **I know that the desire for revenge can be strong. If someone I love had been murdered, I would want the killer's life in return. I wouldn't care if capital punishment wasn't fair. I wouldn't care that it condones brutality. I would just want an eye for an eye. But that doesn't mean you should give it to me. It doesn't mean that society should base its policy on my anger and hatred.**

A multisided approach is especially effective when an audience initially opposes your position. It helps make those you persuade resistant to later counterattacks, because you show them how to answer and resist such arguments. This is often called the **inoculation effect**, because you "inoculate" your listeners against later exposure to differing messages.[12] When you acknowledge and then refute arguments, you also help your credibility in two ways. First, you enhance your *trustworthiness* by showing respect for your opposition. You suggest that their position merits consideration, even though you have a better option. Second, you enhance your *competence* by showing your knowledge of the opposing position, both of the reasons why people may find it attractive and of how it is defective.

After your speech, you should continue to show respect for the audience. Even if some listeners want to argue or heckle, keep your composure.

Others may be impressed by your self-control and may be encouraged to rethink their positions in light of your example.

There may be times when you and your audience are so far apart that you decide simply to acknowledge your disagreement. You might say that although you do not agree with your listeners, you respect their right to their position and hope they will respect yours. Such openness may help establish the beginnings of trust. Even if audience members do not see you as a supporter, they may at least start to see you as an honest, committed opponent and may give you a hearing. If you emphasize that you will *not* be asking them to change their minds, but simply to hear you out and to listen to the reasons why you believe as you do, you may be able to have your day in court.

We once heard a student speak against abortion to a class that was sharply divided on that issue. She began with a personal narrative, the story of how her mother had been given thalidomide (a drug that was later found to induce birth defects) and was faced with a decision on terminating the pregnancy. The student concluded by saying that if her mother had chosen the abortion route, she would not be there speaking to them that day. She paused, smiled, and said, "Although I know some of you may disagree with my views on abortion, I must say I am glad that you are here to listen and that I am here to speak. Think about it." If your reasons are compelling and your evidence is strong, you may soften the opposition and move "waverers" toward your position.

Another helpful technique for handling opposition involves modifying your specific purpose. Do not try to accomplish too much in a single speech. If too much change is proposed, you may create a **boomerang effect**, in which the audience reacts by opposing your position even more strongly.[13] To hope for a major change on the basis of any single persuasive effort is what McGuire calls the **great expectation fallacy.**[14] Be patient. Try to move your audience a step at a time in the direction you would like them to go.

Do not worry if the change you want does not show up immediately. There often is a delayed reaction to persuasion, a **sleeper effect**, in which change shows up only after listeners have had time to integrate the message into their belief systems.[15] Even if no change is apparent, your message may serve a consciousness-raising function, sensitizing your listeners to the issue and making them more receptive to future persuasion.[16] It may require a series of messages to move people through all the steps in the persuasive process.

Facing a reluctant audience is never easy. But you can't predict what new thoughts your speech might stimulate among listeners or what delayed positive reactions to it there might be. Even if it only keeps alive the American tradition of dissent, it will have served a valuable function. Just as Olympic divers often earn higher scores for attempting difficult dives, persuasive speakers can win added credit by confronting reluctant audiences intelligently, courageously, and constructively.

Removing Barriers to Commitment

Speaking to listeners who have not yet committed to a position also presents a challenge. Listeners may hesitate because they lack important information, or they may not see the connection between their own values and interests and your proposal, or they may not feel certain they can trust what you say. To deal with these challenges you should provide needed information, show listeners how your proposal relates to their values or interests, or strengthen your credibility so that you gain increased trust.

Provide Needed Information. Often a single missing fact or unanswered question can stand in the way of commitment. "I know that many of you agree with me but are asking, 'How much will this cost?'" Anticipating audience reservations and supplying the necessary information can help move listeners toward your position.

Affirm and Apply Values. Persuasive speeches that threaten listener's values are not likely to be effective. You must establish that what you urge agrees with what listeners already believe or with their vital interests. For example, if your listeners resist a proposed educational program for the disadvantaged because they think people ought to take care of themselves, you may have to show them that your program represents "a *hand up,* not a *handout.*" Show the audience how people will be able to take care of themselves once the program goes into effect. Cite examples of previous success. It is also helpful if you can demonstrate that your proposal will lead to other favorable consequences, such as reductions in criminal activities or in the need for public assistance and unemployment compensation programs.

As we noted in Chapter 4, values are often resistant to change. If you can reason from the perspective of your listeners' values, using them as the basis for your arguments, you will create identification and remove a barrier to commitment.

Strengthen Your Credibility. When audiences hesitate because they question your credibility, you can "borrow ethos" by citing expert testimony. Call on sources your listeners trust and respect. Uncommitted audiences will scrutinize both you and your arguments carefully. Reason with such listeners, leading them gradually and carefully to the conclusion you would like them to reach. Provide supporting material each step of the way. Adopt a multisided approach, in which you consider all options fairly, to confirm your ethos as a trustworthy and competent speaker.

When addressing uncommitted listeners, don't overstate your case. Let your personal commitment be evident through your sincerity and conviction, but be careful about using overly strong appeals to guilt or fear. These might backfire, causing listeners to resent and reject both you and your message.[17] It is also important not to push uncommitted listeners too hard. Help them move in the desired direction, but let them take the final step themselves.

Meeting the Challenge of an Uncommitted Audience

1 Provide information needed to prompt a commitment.

2 Show listeners how your proposal will satisfy their needs and strengthen their values.

3 Borrow ethos by citing authorities the audience trusts and respects.

4 Be careful not to overstate your case or rely too heavily on emotional appeals.

SPEAKER'S NOTES

Moving from Attitude to Action

When listeners share your position and accept your leadership, they *may* be ready for a speech proposing action. However, it is one thing to agree with a speaker and quite another to accept all the inconvenience, cost, and risk that action may require. Just as opponents may be reluctant to listen, sympathetic audience members may be reluctant to act. They may believe that the problem does not affect them personally, they may not know specifically what it is they should do, or they may feel that the situation is hopeless.[18] To move people to action, you must present powerful reasons to act. At the least, you may have to remind listeners of their beliefs, demonstrate the need for their involvement, present a clear plan, declare your own personal commitment, and make it easy for them to comply.

Revitalize Shared Beliefs. When speakers and audiences celebrate shared beliefs, the result is often renewed commitment. Such occasions may involve retelling traditional stories and resurrecting heroes, giving them new life and meaning. At political conventions Jefferson, Lincoln, Roosevelt, and Kennedy are often remembered in speeches. Such stories and examples invoke a common heritage and relate it to the present.[19] They can be used to bridge diversity in an audience, bringing differing factions together.

Demonstrate the Need for Involvement. Present vivid images of the *need* for action. Show your listeners how the quality of *their* lives — how even their survival — depends on prompt action. Demonstrate how the results will be satisfying. It often helps if you can associate the change with a vision of the future. In his final speech, Martin Luther King, Jr., said, "I may not get there with you, but I can see the Promised Land." King's vision of the Promised Land helped justify the sacrifice called for in his plan of action.

Unless people believe that a problem will affect them directly, they may be reluctant to act. Use examples and narratives to bring the issue home to them. During the 1992 presidential nominating conventions, both parties featured well-educated, poised, and eloquent women who spoke in support of aggressive action against AIDS. One speaker had contracted the disease from a contaminated blood transfusion, the other from an infected spouse. The message? By their personal witness, they refuted the lingering impression that AIDS was confined to the homosexual population and to the drug-addicted. They illustrated the tragic truth that AIDS was rapidly becoming an equal-opportunity disease. It could happen even to listeners themselves.

Present a Clear Plan of Action. Listeners may resist action by exaggerating the difficulty of a proposal or insisting that it is impossible. To overcome such resistance, show them how others have been successful. Use examples or narratives that picture the audience undertaking the action successfully. Stress that "we *can* do it, and this is *how* we will do it."

To get people to act, you must give them a clear plan. A speaker hoping to persuade classmates to work to defeat a proposed tuition raise said:

> How many of you are willing to help defeat this plan to raise our tuition? Good! I see your heads nodding. Now, if you are willing to sign this petition to protest this injustice, hold up your hands. Hold them higher so I can see you! Okay! Good! I'm going to circulate this petition, and I want each of you to sign it. If we act together, we can make a difference.

The plan you present must show listeners what has to be done, who must do it, and how to proceed. Try to anticipate and refute excuses listeners might offer to avoid responsibility. It often takes strong feelings aroused through vivid images to move people to action. Declare your personal commitment, and invite listeners to join you. Once people have openly voiced their commitment, they are more likely to follow through on it.[20]

Be specific in your instructions. As she urged her audience to support the campaign to defeat a proposed tuition increase, one student speaker said:

> Now, we're going to march on Monday. I'm going to be there, come hell or high water, even if I have to stand alone. But I'm not going to have to stand alone. You're going to be there with me. Together, we're going to line up at noon outside the Student Union, and together we're going to march to the steps of the Administration Building.

She did *not* say, "Let's all do something to defeat this proposal."

Make It Easy for Your Audience to Comply. Instead of merely urging listeners to write their congressional representatives, provide them with legislators' addresses and telephone numbers, a petition to sign, or preprinted addressed postcards to return. During the 1980s, students at the University of North Alabama lobbied the state legislature for additional funding for their school. Volunteers set up tables at the entries of all classroom buildings and the student center. The students had preprinted postcards for others to sign and a list of legislators broken out into the counties they represented. Over three-fourths of the students at the university signed the cards, which were hand-delivered to the state capitol. Result? The school got more money.

MAJOR PERSUASIVE FUNCTIONS

In this section we discuss three major functions that persuasive speeches perform: addressing attitudes and values, urging action, and contending with opposition. Any given persuasive speech may perform all these functions, but it will often emphasize one of them.

Addressing Attitudes and Values

The basic goal of **addressing attitudes and values** is to form, reform, or reinforce how listeners feel and believe about a topic. A persuasive speaker might wish to raise doubt and discontent; for example, in addressing the topic "Have We Played Fair with Haiti?" the speaker might first call into question the history of our relationship with that troubled country. Later in the speech, or in a subsequent speech, the speaker could build on this discontent by outlining and urging a new policy. Thus, speeches addressing attitudes and values often pave the way for speeches urging action.

When they are most ambitious, speeches addressing attitudes aim for a total change of conviction. A speech on the topic "It's time we put football in its place" — urging that we de-emphasize intercollegiate athletics — might attempt such far-reaching influence. Obviously, the greater the change of attitude you aim for, the more difficult it will be to achieve your goal. As we noted in Chapter 4, beliefs, attitudes, and values are an integral part of our personality. Deep changes in any of these can have a radical impact on the way we live, so audiences are usually highly resistant to extreme proposals. Such persuasive efforts might even cause listeners to reject the speaker and cling more stubbornly to their previous beliefs.

To be effective, speeches addressing attitudes must begin on common ground. Betty Nichols's classroom speech on responsible drinking and driving began by assuming that she and her listeners shared the belief that drunk driving is a serious problem. She reinforced that shared belief and then proposed a change in attitude as part of a solution for the prob-

Meeting the Challenge of Moving an Audience to Action

SPEAKER'S NOTES

1 Remove barriers to action by reminding listeners of what they have at stake.
2 Provide a clear plan of action.
3 Use examples and stories that provide models for action.
4 Visualize the consequences of acting and not acting.
5 Demonstrate that you are ready personally to practice what you preach.
6 Ask for on-the-spot commitments.
7 Make it easy for listeners to initiate action.

lem. To encourage such change, offer audience members good reasons for modifying their convictions.[21]

Urging Action and the Support of Policies

Speeches **urging action** go beyond attitude change and encourage listeners to take action either as individuals or as members of a group. Bonnie Marshall asked audience members to take individual action to assure their right to die with dignity: to write their state representatives in support of appropriate legislation, draw up a living will, assign durable power of attorney to a trusted friend or family member, and let their personal physicians know their wishes. When a persuasive speech urges individual commitment, audience members must see the value or necessity of action in personal terms.

In contrast, when a speech advocates group action, the audience must see itself as having common identity and purpose. As we noted in Chapter 10, the speaker can reinforce group identity by using inclusive pronouns (*we, our, us*), telling stories that emphasize group achievements, and referring to common heroes, opponents, or martyrs. Anna Aley used an effective appeal to group identity as she proposed specific actions:

When your goal is to move people to action, you must often remind listeners of what is at stake if they fail to take action.

What can one student do to change the practices of numerous Manhattan landlords? Nothing, if that student is alone. But just think what we could accomplish if we got all 13,600 off-campus students involved in

> **this issue! Think what we could accomplish if we got even a fraction of those students involved!**

By casting students as victims at the hands of unscrupulous landlords, Anna painted the situation she wanted to change in dramatic colors that encouraged her listeners to act.

Speeches advocating action usually involve some risk. Therefore, you must present compelling reasons to overcome listeners' natural caution. The consequences of acting and not acting must be spelled out clearly. **The plan presented must seem practical and reasonable, and listeners should be able to see themselves enacting it successfully.**

Contending with Opposition

When **contending with opposition**, you directly refute opposing arguments to clear the way for attitudes and actions you are proposing. "There are those who say that we cannot afford to land explorers on Mars in the next century," said Marvin Andrews to his public speaking class. "I say we can't afford not to." Marvin then went on to describe the benefits we might expect from such exploration. "But we really have no idea of all the benefits, any more than Queen Isabella could have foreseen all the results of the voyage of Columbus. Fortunately, she did not listen to advisers who said his trip would cost too much," Marvin concluded.

On highly controversial topics such as abortion or the legalization of drugs, you often can't avoid giving such speeches of contention. If some audience members hold opposing views, your criticism of their position could offend them, place them on the defensive, or make them even more difficult to persuade. Why, then, would you risk giving such a speech? In situations when danger threatens and immediate action is needed, indirect approaches to persuasion simply may take too long to be effective. To secure immediate action, you may have to address opposing beliefs directly and discredit the arguments that support them with indisputable facts and figures or expert testimony.

Speeches that contend with opposition may also be the best strategy when your audience is split in terms of attitudes toward the topic. In such cases your primary audience will be uncommitted listeners and reasonable opponents. By presenting tactful, carefully documented counterarguments, you may reach some of them. A refutational approach may also help strengthen the resolve of supporters who need assurance that an opposing position can be effectively countered.

Finally, in some situations that are extremely important to you personally, such as your position on gun control legislation, you may want to give a speech of contention as a last-ditch tactic. You may feel that listeners are so strongly entrenched in their opposition that your only hope is to shock them with a direct, frontal attack that shows them why they are wrong. You hope for a positive delayed effect after their first negative reaction. Or you may even decide that your chances for persuasion are small but that your position deserves to be heard with all the power, reason, and conviction you can muster. You can have your say and feel better for it.

DESIGNS FOR PERSUASIVE SPEAKING

As you consider how you want your persuasive speech to function, you must also decide how to structure your speech. Many of the designs used for informative speeches are also appropriate for persuasive speeches. The categorical design can develop persuasive reasons arranged in familiar patterns, such as arguing that a proposal is *needed,* that it will *work,* and that it offers attractive *benefits.*

The sequential design may be used to outline the steps in a plan of action. If most listeners agree there is a problem, your challenge will be to persuade them that you have a workable plan that they can enact. Visualize the plan in action, showing your audience step-by-step how it will work. The preview for a persuasive speech using the sequential design might state:

> **First, we're going to put the pressure on them. We're going to create an environment for change. Second, we're going to make them want to change this absurd policy. And finally, we're going to help them make the change in a way they will appreciate. Now, let's see how this plan of action will work.**

The comparative design works well for speeches of contention in which you contrast the weaknesses of an opposing argument with the strengths of your own. Using figurative analogy as the basis of this design, as we discussed in Chapter 12, can also stir strong feelings in support of proposals. Recall that this kind of design expands a technique of language, metaphor, into a principle of structure. One student speaker developed a design based on the archetypal metaphor of darkness and light, discussed in Chapter 10, to frame her persuasive speech in an especially moving way. Note the imaginative manner in which she introduced her thesis statement:

> **Those of us suffering from HIV find ourselves lost in a night in which it is hard to see the stars. We need your support to help us find some ray of hope. Today I want to introduce you to our darkness, and show how you might help us light our way out of it.**

As she developed her speech, she repeatedly came back to this basic pattern, often using transitions to make the connections. For example, as she moved to her first main point, she said ironically, "Welcome to our darkness." She then developed facts and figures indicating the magnitude of the AIDS epidemic, and to personalize the problem, she used a narrative to describe the despair of a friend when he learned he had the virus. As she moved to the policy she wished to propose, she asked rhetorically, "Is there any light? Is there any hope?" She went on to outline promising projects in medical research, asking her listeners to support the funding of these projects in legislation before the Congress. In this part of her speech she relied especially on expert testimony. As she offered her concluding remarks she noted:

FIGURE 13.2

What Design to
Use When

Design	Use When
Categorical	Your topic invites thinking in familiar patterns, such as proving a plan will be *safe, inexpensive,* and *effective.* Can be used both to change attitudes and to urge action.
Comparison/ Contrast	You want to demonstrate why your proposal is superior to another. Especially good for speeches in which you contend with opposing views. Use the analogy variation to frame dramatic appeals for action and attitude change, such as presenting your plan to abolish the legal sale of cigarettes as a *cure* for the *national illness.*
Sequential	Your speech presents a clear plan of action that must be carried out in specific order.
Problem-solution	Your topic presents a problem that needs to be solved and a solution that will solve it. Good both for speeches involving attitudes and urging action.
Motivated-sequence	Your topic calls for action as the final phase of a five-step process that also involves, in order, arousing attention, demonstrating need, satisfying need, picturing the results, and calling for action.
Refutative	You must answer strong opposition on a topic before you can establish your position. The major opposing claims become main points for development. Attack weakest points first and avoid personal attacks.

Martin Luther King, Jr., once said, 'Only when it is dark enough can you see the stars.' There are very few stars in our darkness. But you must help us find them. By these stars we shall navigate through this night. Perhaps with your help we can find the dawn.

Other archetypal metaphors that can develop vivid, moving structures for persuasive speeches include death and rebirth, sickness and health, color contrasts, heat and cold, war and peace, and storm and calm. If you can find the right figurative analogy for your design, you may be able to muster considerable emotional force behind your persuasive proposal. But be careful not to strain the analogy too far, or listeners will suspect you of trying to manipulate their feelings.

In the remainder of this chapter, we look at three designs especially suited to persuasive speeches. We shall examine the problem-solution design, the motivated sequence design, and the refutative design.

Problem-Solution Design

The **problem-solution design** first convinces listeners that they face a problem, then shows them how to deal with it. The solution can involve changing an attitude or taking an action. It is sometimes hard to convince listeners that a problem exists or that it is serious. People have an unfortunate tendency to stick their heads in the sand and ignore problems until they reach a critical stage. You can counteract this tendency by depicting in vivid terms the crisis that surely will emerge unless your audience makes a commitment to change.

When you prepare a problem-solution speech, do not overwhelm your listeners with details. Cover the most important features of the problem, then show the audience how your solution will work. A problem-solution speech opposing a proposed tuition increase might build on the following general design:

Thesis statement: We must defeat the proposal to raise tuition next fall.

I. **Problem:** The proposal to raise tuition is a disaster!

    A. The plan will create serious hardships for many students.

        1. Many current students will have to drop out.

        2. New students will be discouraged from enrolling.

    B. The proposed increase will create additional problems for the university and the community.

        1. Decreased attendance will mean decreased revenue.

        2. Decreased revenue will reduce the university's service to the community.

        3. Reduced service will mean reduced support from the contributors.

II. **Solution:** Defeat the proposal to raise tuition!

    A. Sign our petition against the tuition increase.

        1. Write in support as we send copies to state legislators.

        2. Join us as we present our petition to the president of the university.

    B. Write a letter to the local newspaper this week.

    C. Come to our rally on campus next Wednesday.

When the problem can be identified clearly and the solution is concrete and simple, the problem-solution design works well in persuasive speeches. Closely related to it, indeed a variation upon it, is the **stock issues design.** Think of this variation as an elaborate version of the problem-solution design, and use it to check the completeness of your analysis as you develop this format. The stock issues design attempts to answer the major general questions a reasonable person would ask before agreeing to a change in policies or procedures.[22] General questions related to the problem and its solution form the framework for the stock issues design:

I. *Is there a need for change because of some significant problem?*

    A. How did the problem originate?

    B. What caused the problem?

C. How widespread is the problem?

D. How long has the problem persisted?

E. What harms are associated with the problem?

F. Are these harms inherent to the problem?

G. Will these harms continue and grow unless there is change?

II. *What is the solution to this problem?*

A. Will the solution actually solve the problem?

B. Is the solution practical?

C. Would the cost of the solution be reasonable?

D. Might there be additional desirable or undesirable consequences?

III. *Who will put the solution into effect?*

A. Are these people responsible and competent?

B. What role might listeners play?[23]

One advantage of the stock issues variation is that it reminds us of the complex question of inherency (I.F above). Essentially this question asks, first, *whether a particular harmful effect is caused by the problem under consideration, and whether it will disappear when the problem is solved.* For many years, those who defended cigarette manufacturers argued that the magnitude of medical harm attributed to tobacco was not really inherent to its use. A veritable mountain of research now seems to have resolved *that* question of inherency, and as a result, you don't hear the argument used often these days. *A second question prompted by inherency is the extent to which an alleged harm is an inevitable part of a situation and therefore resistant to change.* The folk saying "There's nothing certain but death and taxes" suggests that taxes may be inherent to the human condition. But that doesn't mean that the kind and size of the taxes we pay are beyond our control! To the extent that we can control them, they are not inherent. As you plan your problem-solution speech, decide first how you can prove that the harms you describe are inherent to the problem you reveal. Then, convince listeners that the problem is *not* an inherent part of life, but can be changed by the solution you propose.

Motivated Sequence Design

The **motivated sequence design** also relates to the problem-solution design, but is distinctive enough that we can discuss it separately.[24] This design has five steps, beginning with arousing attention and ending with a call for action. Therefore, it is especially suited for speeches that have action as their goal. The design also emphasizes the role of artfully used language techniques in arousing audience perceptions and feelings. The steps in the motivated sequence are as follows:

1. *Arouse attention.* As in any speech, you begin by stimulating interest in your subject. In Chapter 12 we discussed six factors related to attention: intensity, repetition, novelty, activity, contrast, and relevance. These same techniques may be used to gain attention in persuasive speeches.

2. *Demonstrate a need.* Show your listeners the urgency of the situation you wish to change. Help them understand what they might win or lose if they accept or reject your proposal. To create such understanding, tie your demonstration to the basic needs discussed in Chapter 4.

3. *Satisfy the need.* Present a way to satisfy the need you have demonstrated. Set forth a plan of action and explain how it would work. To encourage agreement, offer examples showing how your plan has worked successfully in other places.

4. *Visualize the results.* You can visualize results with either positive or negative images. You could show your listeners how their lives will be changed for the better when they enact your plan. A positive image of the future can help overcome resistance to action. You could also paint a dire picture of what life could be like if they do not go along with your plan. You might even put these positive and negative verbal pictures side by side to strengthen their impact through contrast.

5. *Call for action.* Your call for action may be a challenge, an appeal, or a statement of personal commitment. The call for action should be short and to the point. Give your listeners something specific that they can do right away to start the process of change. If you can get them to take the first step in the proposal, the next will come more easily.

Let's look at how this model might work in a persuasive speech that appeals to audience motivations for recognition, friendship, and nurturance, using language that activates feelings of sympathy and identification:

1. *Arouse attention*	Have you ever dreamed about being a hero or heroine? Have you ever wished you could do something great, something that would really make a difference in our world? Well, I'm here to tell you how you can, if only you're willing to invest about three hours a week.
2. *Demonstrate need*	Our community needs volunteers to help children who are lonely and neglected. Big Sisters and Big Brothers of Omaha have a program for these children, but only people can make the program work. Last year they had forty-eight student volunteers. This year only thirty have signed up to help. They need at least thirty more. They need you.
3. *Satisfy need*	Volunteering to be a big brother or a big sister will help this program of after-school activities keep going. It will also make you a hero or heroine in the eyes of a child.

4. *Visualize results* Maybe you can have an experience that will be as rewarding as mine has been. Last year I worked with ten-year-old Kevin two afternoons a week. He needed a lot of help with his homework because his grades were just barely passing. I tutored him in math and science. But more than school help, he needed someone to be his friend, someone to talk with, someone who cared about him. The first six weeks his grades went from D–'s to C–'s, and I took him to a basketball game one weekend. The next six weeks his grades went up to C's and C+'s and I took him to a movie. This year Kevin is doing well in school. He's making C's and B's in all his courses, but we still work together and I still have the satisfaction of knowing I'm doing something worthwhile. I'm making a contribution to our community, and I'm a hero in the eyes of an eleven-year-old boy.

5. *Call for action* Won't you join me and become one of the unsung heroines or heroes of our community? If you can give just one or two afternoons a week, you can make a difference in the life of a child and in our future. I've got the applications with me and will be waiting for you to sign up after class.

If you plan to use the motivated sequence, first determine where your listeners stand on the issue, then focus on the steps that will carry persuasion forward. For example, if you were speaking to an audience that was already convinced of the need for a change but lacked a plan to make it work, you could focus on step 3, "satisfy the need." However, if you faced an audience that contested the need, your emphasis should be on step 2, "demonstrate a need."

Refutative Design

In the **refutative design**, used in speeches that contend with opposition, the speaker tries to raise doubt about a competing position by revealing its inconsistencies and deficiencies. To bring off an effective refutation, you must understand the opposition's motivations, arguments, and evidence. It is often wise to take on your opponent's weakest point first. Your refutation then raises doubt about other opposing arguments. The point of attack may be illogical reasoning or flimsy, insufficient evidence, as we shall discuss further in Chapter 14, or even the self-interest of an opposing speaker. However, to keep the dispute as constructive as possible, avoid personal attacks unless credibility issues are central and inescapable.

There are five steps in developing an effective refutation. These five steps should be followed in sequence for each point you plan to refute.

1. State the point you are going to refute and explain why it is important.
2. Tell the audience how you are going to refute this point.
3. Present your evidence using facts and figures, examples, and testimony. Cite sources and authorities the audience will accept as competent and credible.
4. Spell out the conclusion for the audience. Do not rely on listeners to figure out what the evidence means. Tell them directly.
5. Explain the significance of your refutation — show how it discredits or damages the position of the opposition.

For example, you might refute an argument against sex education in public high schools in the following manner:

State the point you will refute and explain its importance.

Tell how you will refute this point.

Present your evidence using credible sources.

State your conclusion.

Explain the significance of your refutation.

> Our well-intentioned friends would have you believe, and this is their biggest concern, that birth-control information increases teen-age sexual activity.
>
> I want to share with you some statistical evidence that contradicts this contention — a contention that is simply not supported by the facts.
>
> The latest study on this issue, conducted in 1995 by the Department of Health, Education, and Welfare, compared sexual activity rates in sixty high schools across the United States — thirty with sex education programs and thirty without. Their findings show that there are no significant differences in sexual activity rates between these two groups of schools.
>
> Therefore, the argument that access to birth-control information through sex education programs increases sexual activity simply does not hold water.
>
> That's typical of the attack on sex education in the schools — to borrow a line from Shakespeare, it's a lot of "sound and fury, signifying nothing."

You can strengthen this design if you follow your refutation by proving a similar point of your own, thus balancing the negative refutation with a positive demonstration. The result supplies the audience with an alternative belief to substitute for the one you have refuted. Use the same five-step sequence to support your position. For example, you might follow the preceding refutation with the following demonstration:

State the point you will support and explain its importance.

Tell how you will support this point.

> I'm not going to try to tell you that birth-control information support reduces sexual activity. But I want to tell you what it does reduce. It reduces teen-age pregnancy.
>
> There is reliable evidence that fewer girls become pregnant in high schools with sex education programs.
>
> The same study conducted by Health, Education, and Welfare demonstrated that in high schools with sex education programs the pregnancy rate dropped from one out of every sixty female students

Present your evidence using credible sources.

State your conclusion.

State the significance of your demonstration.

to one out of ninety within two years of the program's going into effect.

Therefore, sex education is a good program. It attacks a devastating social problem — the epidemic of children having children.

Any program that reduces unwanted teen-age pregnancy is valuable — valuable to the young women involved, valuable to society. We all pay in so many ways for this personal and social tragedy — we should all support a program that works to reduce it. And we should reject the irrational voices that reject the program.

As should now be clear, the study of persuasive speaking is a study of the arts of effective living. Learning how to use persuasion ethically and effectively, and how to avoid being abused by unethical persuaders, are skills central to successful lives. In the next chapter we shall learn more about persuasion by studying patterns of evidence, proof, and argument that drive the persuasive process.

IN SUMMARY

Persuasion is the art of convincing others to give favorable attention to our point of view. Persuasion is vital to our political system, which is based on the principle of rule by *deliberation* and choice rather than by force. The right to express opinions — no matter how unpopular — also serves practical goals. Groups that have been exposed to different positions usually make better decisions because they are stimulated to examine a situation and to think about their options.

Characteristics of Persuasive Speaking. In contrast to informative speaking, persuasive speaking urges a choice among options and asks for a commitment. Ethical persuasive speaking centers on *good reasons* based upon responsible knowledge and a sensitive consideration of audience interests. Persuasive speeches rely more on emotional involvement than do informative speeches, and they carry a heavier ethical burden.

The Process of Persuasion. When persuasion is successful, people listen, learn, agree, and change as a result of what they hear. These behaviors parallel McGuire's categories of awareness, understanding, agreement, enactment, and integration of persuasive material. Awareness suggests that we know of a problem, that it commands our serious attention. Understanding implies that we can see the connection of the problem with our lives, and that we know how to carry out the speaker's proposals. Agreement implies our acceptance of a speaker's interpretations and recommendations. Enactment suggests our commitment and readiness to carry out the speaker's ideas. Integration involves consolidating the new attitudes and commitments into our overall belief and value system.

The Challenges of Persuasion.   Persuading others can pose many challenges. You may have to entice a reluctant audience to listen, remove barriers that block commitment, or move listeners from agreement to action. To encourage reluctant listeners, use a *co-active approach* that seeks to bridge differences and to build identification. Avoid a *boomerang effect* by not pushing listeners too hard in one speech. Remove barriers to commitment by providing vital information, pointing out the relevance to listeners' lives, and building credibility. To move partisan listeners from agreement to action, use vivid language and examples to bring abstract principles to life, prove the need for their involvement, present a clear plan, declare your own commitment as a model, and make it easy for listeners to take the first step into involvement.

Functions of Persuasive Speeches.   Persuasive speeches address attitudes and values, urge action and the support of policies, and contend with opposition. While *addressing attitudes and values,* remember that the more change you ask, the more difficult and risky will be your challenge. You should not commit the *great expectation fallacy,* which asks for more change than one could reasonably expect after one speech. When *urging action,* you ask listeners to take action either as individuals or as members of groups. While *contending with opposition,* you confront contending views by systematically refuting their claims. Speeches that emphasize contention usually do not seek to convert opponents but rather to win over the uncommitted and to influence opinion leaders.

Designs for Persuasive Speaking.   While many of the designs discussed for informative speaking can also serve the purposes of persuasion, three designs in particular serve the needs of persuasive speaking. In a *problem-solution design,* you must first convince the audience that a problem exists, and then advance a solution that corrects it. The *motivated sequence design* has five steps: arousing attention, demonstrating a need, satisfying the need, visualizing results, and calling for action. To use the *refutative design,* state the point you intend to refute, tell how you will refute it, present your evidence, draw a conclusion, and explain the significance of the refutation. Refutation is often followed by demonstration, in which you prove a point to replace the one you have just disproved.

TERMS TO KNOW

persuasion

deliberation

good reasons

consciousness-raising

co-active approach

multisided presentation

sleeper effect

addressing attitudes and values

urging action

contending with opposition

problem-solution design

stock issues design

inoculation effect   motivated sequence design

boomerang effect   refutative design

great expectation fallacy

DISCUSSION

1. Examine magazine ads and newspaper articles for "infomercials" — persuasive messages cloaked as information. What alerts you to the persuasive intent? In what respects does such pseudo-information possess the characteristics of persuasion discussed in this chapter? In what respects does it possess the characteristics of informative speaking discussed in Chapter 12?

2. The letters-to-the-editor section of the Sunday newspaper is often a rich source for the study of persuasive material. Using a recent Sunday paper, analyze the persuasion attempted in these letters. Which do you think are most and least effective and why?

3. The speech on slum housing that appears at the end of this chapter was prepared for a student audience at Kansas State University. What changes might you suggest in this speech if it were to be presented to a luncheon meeting of realtors in Manhattan, Kansas? Why?

4. When should a speaker give up trying to persuade a hostile audience and simply confront listeners directly with the position they oppose? Why would a speaker bother to do this? Is it possible that both speaker and audience might gain something from such a confrontation? Find an example of such a speech. Do you agree with the strategy used in it? Discuss in class.

APPLICATION

1. Keep a diary of your day, identifying all the moments in which you confront and practice persuasion. Evaluate your adventure in persuasion. When were you most and least persuaded and most and least persuasive? Why? Did you encounter (or commit!) any ethical abuses?

2. Read one of the persuasive speeches in Appendix B and identify the following:

   a. the challenge the speaker confronted

   b. the type of persuasive speech

   c. the design of the speech

   Suggest an alternative design for the speech and discuss why you think that approach would work as well or better.

3. Select a controversial subject and outline the persuasive speeches you would present on the subject to

   a. an uncommitted audience.

   b. an audience in agreement.

c. a reluctant audience.

Discuss the differences among your approaches.

NOTES

1. *Whitney* v. *California,* 274 U.S. 357, 375 (1927).

2. Sonja K. Foss and Cindy L. Griffin, "Beyond Persuasion: A Proposal for an Invitational Rhetoric," *Communication Monographs* 62 (1995): 2–18.

3. *On Liberty* (Chicago: Henry Regnery, 1955 [originally published 1859]), p. 24.

4. Charlan Jeanne Nemeth, "Differential Contributions of Majority and Minority Influence," *Psychological Review* 93 (1986): 23–32.

5. Mark A. Hamilton and John E. Hunter, "The Effect of Language Intensity on Receiver Attitudes Toward Message, Source, and Topic," in *Persuasion: Advances Through Meta-Analysis,* ed. M. Allen and R. W. Preiss (Beverley Hills, CA: Sage [in press]).

6. William J. McGuire, "Attitudes and Attitude Change," in *The Handbook of Social Psychology,* ed. Gardner Lindzey and Elliot Aronson (New York: Random House, 1985), I, 258–261.

7. Roger Brown, *Social Psychology* (New York: Free Press, 1965), pp. 709–763.

8. Gloria Steinem, *Revolution From Within: A Book of Self-Esteem* (New York: Little Brown, 1992), p. 120.

9. John C. Reinard, "The Persuasive Effects of Testimonial Assertion Evidence," in *Persuasion: Advances Through Meta-Analysis* (in press). See also J. C. Reinard, "The Empirical Study of the Persuasive Effects of Evidence: The Status After Fifty Years of Research," *Human Communication Research* 15 (1988): 3–59.

10. Here we adapt an approach developed by Herbert W. Simons, *Persuasion: Understanding, Practice, and Analysis,* 2nd ed. (New York: Random House, 1986), p. 138.

11. Barry M. Goldwater, "The Gay Ban: Just Plain Un-American," *The Washington Post,* 10 June 1993, p. 23A.

12. Mike Allen, "Meta-Analysis Comparing the Persuasiveness of One-sided and Two-sided Messages," *Western Journal of Speech Communication* 55 (1991): 390–404; M. Allen et al., "Testing a Model of Message Sidedness: Three Replications," *Communication Monographs* 56 (1990): 275–291; Jerold L. Hale, Paul A. Mongeau, and Randi M. Thomas, "Cognitive Processing of One- and Two-sided Persuasive Messages," *Western Journal of Speech Communication* 55 (1991): 380–389; Carl I. Hovland, Arthur A. Lumsdaine, and Fred D. Sheffield, "The Effects of Presenting 'One Side' versus 'Both Sides' in Changing Opinions on a Controversial Subject," in *Experiments on Mass Communication* (Princeton, NJ: Princeton University Press, 1949), pp. 201–227; William J. McGuire, "Inducing Resistance to Persuasion," in *Advances in Experimental Social Psychology,* ed. L. Berkowitz (New York: Academic Press, 1964), pp. 191–229.

13. N. H. Anderson, "Integration Theory and Attitude Change," *Psychological Review* 78 (1971): 171–206.

14. McGuire, p. 260.

15. Mike Allen and James B. Stiff, "Testing Three Models for the Sleeper Effect," *Western Journal of Speech Communication* 53 (1989): 411–426; T. D. Cook et al., "History of the Sleeper Effect: Some Logical Pitfalls in Accepting the Null Hypothesis," *Psychological Bulletin* 86 (1979): 662–679.

16. M. E. McCombs, "The Agenda-setting Approach," in *Handbook of Political Communication,* ed. D. D. Nimmo and K. R. Sanders (Beverly Hills, CA: Sage, 1981), pp. 121–140.

17. Franklin J. Boster and Paul Mongeau, "Fear-arousing Persuasive Messages," in *Communication Yearbook 8,* ed. R. Bostrom (Beverly Hills, CA: Sage, 1984), pp. 330–377; T. W. Milburn and K. H. Watman, *On the Nature of Threat: A Social Psychological Analysis* (New York: Praeger, 1981).

18. Katherine E. Rowan, "Goals, Obstacles, and Strategies in Risk Communication: A Problem-solving Approach to Improving Communication About Risks," *Journal of Applied Communication Research* 19 (1991): 322.

19. Michael Osborn, "Rhetorical Depiction," in *Form, Genre, and the Study of Political Discourse,* ed. Herbert W. Simons and Aram A. Aghazarian (Columbia: University of South Carolina Press, 1986), pp. 79–107.

20. R. A. Wicklund and J. W. Brehm, *Perspectives on Cognitive Dissonance* (Hillsdale, NJ: Erlbaum, 1976).

21. See Walter R. Fisher, "Toward a Logic of Good Reasons," *Quarterly Journal of Speech* 64 (1978): 376–384; Karl R. Wallace, "The Substance of Rhetoric: Good Reasons," *Quarterly Journal of Speech* 49 (1963): 239–249.

22. J. W. Patterson and David Zarefsky, *Contemporary Debate* (Boston: Houghton Mifflin, 1983).

23. The structure of the stock issues design has been adapted from Charles U. Larson, *Persuasion: Reception and Responsibility,* 6th ed. (Belmont, CA: Wadsworth, 1992), pp. 202–203; and Charles S. Mudd and Malcolm O. Sillars, *Public Speaking: Content and Communication* (Prospect Heights, IL: Waveland, 1991), pp. 100–102.

24. This design was introduced in Alan Monroe's *Principles and Types of Speech* (New York: Scott, Foresman, 1935) and has been refined in later editions.

We Don't Have to Live in Slums

Anna Aley

Slumlords — you'd expect them in New York or Chicago, but in Manhattan, Kansas? You'd better believe there are slumlords in Manhattan, and they pose a direct threat to you if you ever plan to rent an off-campus apartment.

I know about slumlords; I rented a basement apartment from one last semester. I guess I first suspected something was wrong when I discovered dead roaches in the refrigerator. I definitely knew something was wrong when I discovered the leaks: the one in the bathroom that kept the bathroom carpet constantly soggy and molding and the one in the kitchen that allowed water from the upstairs neighbor's bathroom to seep into the kitchen cabinets and collect in my dishes.

Then there were the serious problems. The hot water heater and furnace were connected improperly and posed a fire hazard. They were situated next to the only exit. There was no smoke detector or fire extinguisher and no emergency way out — the windows were too small for escape. I was living in an accident waiting to happen — and paying for it.

The worst thing about my ordeal was that I was not an isolated instance; many Kansas State students are living in unsafe housing and paying for it, not only with their money, but their happiness, their grades, their health, and their safety.

We can't be sure how many students are living in substandard housing, housing that does not meet the code specifications required of rental property. We can be sure, however, that a large number of Kansas State students are at risk of being caught in the same situation I was. According to the registrar, approximately 17,800 students are attending Kansas State this semester. Housing claims that 4,200 live in the dorms. This means that approximately 13,600 students live off-campus. Some live in fraternities or sororities, some live at home, but most live in off-campus apartments, as I do.

Many of these 13,600 students share traits that make them likely to settle for substandard housing. For example, many students want to live close to campus. If you've ever driven through the surrounding neighborhoods, you know that much of the available housing is in older houses, houses that were never meant to be divided into separate rental units. Students are also often limited in the amount they can pay for rent; some landlords, such as mine, will use low rent as an excuse not to fix anything and to let the apartment deteriorate. Most importantly, many students are young and, consequently, naive when it comes to selecting an apartment. They don't know the housing codes; but even if they did, they don't know how to check to make sure the apartment is in compliance. Let's face it — how many of us know how to check a hot water heater to make sure it's connected properly?

Adding to the problem of the number of students willing to settle for substandard housing is the number of landlords willing to supply it. Currently, the Consumer Relations Board here at Kansas State has on file student complaints against approximately one hundred landlords. There are surely complaints against many more that have never been formally reported.

There are two main causes of the substandard student housing problem. The first — and most significant — is the simple fact that it is possible for a landlord to lease an apartment that does not meet housing code requirements. The Manhattan Housing Code Inspector will evaluate an apartment, but only after the tenant has given the landlord a written complaint and the landlord has had fourteen days to remedy the situation. In other words, the way things are now, the only way the Housing Code Inspector can evaluate an apartment to see if it's safe to be lived in is if someone has been living in it for at least two weeks!

A second cause of the problem is the fact that campus services designed to help students avoid substandard housing are not well known. The Consumer Relations Board here at Kansas State can help students inspect apartments for safety before they sign a lease, it can provide students with vital information on their rights as tenants, and it can mediate in landlord-tenant disputes. The problem is, many people don't know these services exist. The Consumer Relations Board is not listed in the university catalogue; it is not mentioned in any of the admissions literature. The only places it is mentioned are in alphabetically organized references such as the phone book, but you have to already know it exists to look it up! The Consumer Relations Board does receive money for advertising from the student senate, but it is only enough to run a little two-by-three-inch ad once every month. That is not large enough or frequent enough to be noticed by many who could use these services.

It's clear that we have a problem, but what may not seem so clear is what we can do about it. After all, what can one student do to change the practices of numerous Manhattan landlords? Nothing, if that student is alone. But just think of what we could accomplish if we got all 13,600 off-campus students involved in this issue! Think what we could accomplish if we got even a fraction of those students involved! This is what Wade Whitmer, director of the Consumer Relations Board, is attempting to do. He is reorganizing the Off-Campus Association in an effort to pass a city ordinance requiring landlords to have their apartments inspected for safety before those apartments can be rented out. The Manhattan code inspector has already tried to get just such an ordinance passed, but the only people who showed up at the public forums were known slumlords, who obviously weren't in favor of the proposed ordinance. No one showed up to argue in favor of the ordinance, so the city commissioners figured that no one wanted it and voted it down. If we can get the Off-Campus Association organized and involved, however, the commissioners will see that someone does want the ordinance, and they will be more likely to pass it

In this section the problem-solution design emerges clearly. Having established the reality of the problem, she turns to the causes, which she must identify before she advances a solution.

Anna appeals to the group identity of her listeners and assures them that there is power in numbers. She spells out what they should do. She might have strengthened her appeal to "join the Off-Campus Association" if she had membership forms and a roster for her listeners to sign.

446

Anna concludes her speech with a true narrative to help her listeners retain her message and integrate it into their belief systems. Her speech ends with a forceful appeal to action.

the next time it is proposed. You can do a great service to your fellow students — and to yourself — by joining the Off-Campus Association.

A second thing you can do to help ensure that no more Kansas State students have to go through what I did is sign my petition asking the student senate to increase the Consumer Relations Board's advertising budget. Let's face it — a service cannot do anybody any good if no one knows about it. Consumer Relations Board's services are simply too valuable to let go to waste.

An important thing to remember about substandard housing is that it is not only distasteful, it is dangerous. In the end, I was lucky. I got out of my apartment with little more than bad memories. My upstairs neighbor was not so lucky. The main problem with his apartment was that the electrical wiring was done improperly; there were too many outlets for too few circuits, so the fuses were always blowing. One day last November, Jack was at home when a fuse blew — as usual. And, as usual, he went to the fuse box to flip the switch back on. When he touched the switch, it delivered such a shock that it literally threw this guy the size of a football player backwards and down a flight of stairs. He lay there at the bottom, unable to move, for a full hour before his roommate came home and called an ambulance.

Jack was lucky. His back was not broken. But he did rip many of the muscles in his back. Now he has to go to physical therapy, and he is not expected to fully recover.

Kansas State students have been putting up with substandard living conditions for too long. It's time we finally got together to do something about this problem. Join the Off-Campus Association. Sign my petition. Let's send a message to these slumlords that we're not going to put up with this any more. We don't have to live in slums.

WORKS CONSULTED

Kansas State University. *K-State! Campus Living*.

Registrar's Office. Kansas State University. Personal interview. 10 March 1989.

Residential Landlord and Tenant Act. State of Kansas. 1975.

Whitmer, Wade. Director, Consumer Relations Board. Personal interview. 10 March 1989.

CHAPTER 14

Evidence, Proof, and Argument

- use supporting materials as powerful evidence.
- develop evidence into persuasive proofs.
- arrange proofs into compelling arguments.
- recognize and avoid defects of evidence, proofs, and arguments.

Speech is power:
Speech is to per-
suade, to convert,
to compel.
— Ralph Waldo
Emerson

I don't think many of us in this room would deny that environ-mental pollution is a problem. We've already heard a speech that pointed out the dangers of the greenhouse effect. Let me add some fuel to the fire.

According to *U.S. News and World Report,* in 1991 six hundred and sixty-seven pounds of garbage was collected for every mile of beach in the United States. There are more than 28,000 miles of beach in the United States, so that's almost nineteen million pounds of garbage. Just from beaches alone! And that's just the tip of the wasteberg. Figures released by the Environmental Protec-tion Agency as reported in the *Environmental Almanac* show that the average U.S. citizen produces more than one-half ton of solid waste each year. With a population of almost 260 million people, that's over 130 million tons of waste per year. Can you picture how much trash that is? The writing paper alone that we throw out each year is enough to build a twelve-foot-high wall from Los Angeles to New York.

The situation with water isn't much better. According to the *1994 Information Please Almanac,* nearly half of our rivers are too polluted to support their intended uses for drinking water, recre-ation, or fisheries. And how about the air we breath? The almanac tells us that this too is getting worse, with cars accounting for over half of all air pollution in the country. Furthermore, *Time* magazine warns us that air pollution can reduce life spans as much as two years, even in areas that meet current federal air quality standards.

As he completed the "problem" phase of the design for his persuasive speech, Jim Cardoza could see from his listeners' faces that he had expanded their awareness of the environmental problem. They frowned and shook their heads as they accepted his *evidence*. He had *proved* his point to their satisfaction. They agreed with his *argument* that environmental recovery should be a high priority. They were prepared now to give serious consideration to his solution (see his entire speech at the end of this chapter).

What do these italicized terms — evidence, proof, and argument — mean? They form the tapestry of reasoning that we see displayed in any successful persuasive speech. They provide the "good reasons" we talked about in the last chapter. They explain why we sometimes listen to speakers with whom we disagree, why we take seriously some facts and testimony that contradict our attitudes, and why we occasionally integrate new convictions into our belief systems. In this chapter we discuss these elements, show how they may be woven together, explain how to use them ethically and effectively, and demonstrate how to avoid some of the mistakes that can rob persuasion of its power.

In this chapter we also extend a theme we introduced in Chapter 10: that in addition to *climbing* and *building,* a third basic metaphor that describes the skills you acquire in a public speaking class is that of *weaving.* Just as you must learn to weave words into the fabric of effective public speeches, so also must you learn how to create a tapestry of good reasons within persuasive speeches by designing an effective pattern of evidence, proof, and argument.

USING EVIDENCE EFFECTIVELY

In Chapter 13 we explained that the good reasons that justify persuasion are based on responsible knowledge of a subject. In persuasive speaking responsible knowledge means having an adequate base of supporting material from which we can draw conclusions. When supporting material serves this persuasive function, we call it **evidence.** In this section we will examine the persuasive functions of evidence to supplement what you learned about supporting materials in Chapter 6.

Consider a hypothetical situation. A speaker says, "We should all sign up as organ donors." A listener asks, "Why?" The speaker replies, "Well, I think we should. That's my opinion." Now consider a different approach. Paul B. Fowler, a student at Alderson-Broaddus College, presented a speech urging his classmates to become organ donors. Instead of just voicing his personal opinion, Paul said:

> According to the *United Network for Organ Sharing,* nearly 200,000 kidney transplants have been performed since 1963. Pittsburgh surgeons alone transplant hundreds of kidneys per year. However, only 25 percent of kidney patients can receive a kidney from a living family member. Many must wait for years for an organ from a donor, and many will die waiting. In the Pittsburgh area alone, nearly one thousand patients

Ethical and effective persuasion brings evidence together into proofs to support a position. This speaker has found a dramatic way to demonstrate the importance of recycling.

are waiting right now for a phone call telling them a kidney has become available. Nationwide, more than 30,000 people are waiting.

The contrast is clear. The person listening to our hypothetical speaker might respond, "You have a right to your opinion, but I have a right to ignore it." Paul's listeners *had* to listen and take his message seriously, even if they did not agree with all his recommendations. The combination of facts and expert testimony lifted his message above personal opinion. His evidence added strength, authority, and objectivity to his speech. *Evidence is basic to the persuasiveness of a speech.*

To better understand the power of evidence, let us look briefly at each of the forms of supporting material identified in Chapter 6 and contrast the work they do in informative and persuasive speeches.

Facts and Statistics

In informative speaking facts and statistics enlarge our understanding; in persuasive speaking they alert us to a situation that we must change. Therefore, facts and figures are especially important during the initial awareness phase of persuasion to prepare listeners for what will follow. Information is an essential fiber in the tapestry of persuasion; without information that fabric will tear when tested by opposing speakers. Juli Pardell, arguing for more effective safety regulations in air travel, showed how the judicious use of facts, interlaced with testimony and examples, can create strong persuasive evidence:

> The Los Angeles airport deserves special attention. The *Christian Science Monitor* of October 29th this year contends that it "exemplifies the growing congestion that decreases safety margins." Thirty other airports lie within a ninety-mile radius of Los Angeles airport, creating a hubbub of planes in the sky. Within a forty-five-mile radius, 197 planes vie for space in the skies at any given moment. Overcongestion only enhances the chance for planes to crash, such as they did last October.

By the time Juli finished presenting such carefully documented facts, her audience felt she had presented compelling evidence for her case.

Examples

In informative speeches, examples illustrate ideas and create human interest. In persuasive speeches, examples also move listeners by exciting emotions such as sympathy, fear, or anger. Factual examples are especially useful. When you can say, "This really happened," you strengthen the example. LaDell Patterson demonstrated the value of factual examples in a speech opposing discrimination against women in news organizations. In her speech she cited the experiences of Laura Stepp, a reporter for the *Washington Post:*

> Ms. Stepp recalled an incident that happened to her. She said while a *Washington Post* lawyer was reading one of her stories, she commented that she hoped it would land on the front page because of its importance. His reply to her was, "All you have to do is shake your little fanny and they'll put it on the front page." When she objected, he said he had no idea that the remark was offensive.

This example, one of many in LaDell's speech, helped arouse the indignation of her listeners against such behavior and prepared them emotionally for the reforms she recommended.

In circumstances in which no one factual example adequately conveys the meaning you wish to communicate, a hypothetical example may work better. Back in Chapter 1, when we wanted to persuade you of the usefulness of the public speaking course, we invented the hypothetical example of "Mary," a composite person who represented all the successful students we have taught. To be ethical, you must let your listeners know when an example has been fabricated to fit the purposes of your persuasive speech.

Narratives

In informative speeches, narratives illustrate the meaning of major points. In persuasive speeches, narratives help create a sense of reality and build identification between listeners and the speech subject. Narratives may also carry listeners to the scene of a problem and engage listeners in a living drama. Kirsten Lientz illustrated these functions when she opened her persuasive speech with the following narrative:

> It's a cold, icy December afternoon. You hear a distant crash, then screams, and finally the unending moan of a car horn fills the silence. You rush the short distance to the scene of the crash, where you find a Ford Bronco overturned with a young woman and two small boys inside. The woman and one of the boys climb from the wreckage unhurt; the other boy, however, is pinned between the dashboard and the roof of the car, unconscious and not breathing. Would you know what to do? Or would you stand there wishing you did? These events are real. Bob Flath saved this child with the skills he acquired at his company's first aid workshop.

After this dramatic narrative introduction, Kirsten's listeners were prepared to listen to her speech urging them to take the course in first aid offered at her university.

Testimony

Testimony is even more critical in persuasive than in informative speaking. When you use testimony in a persuasive speech, you call upon witnesses to confirm your position. Introduce these witnesses carefully, describing their credentials. To support her call for air safety improvements, Juli Pardell cited eight authoritative sources of information. Paul Fowler in his plea for organ donors cited four reputable books. It was not just Juli and Paul speaking — it was all these sources of testimony together.

If the witnesses you cite testify against their self-interest as **reluctant witnesses**, your evidence is even more powerful. For example, if student reform leaders admit that the latest campus demonstrations have gone too far or if government officials confirm that they have made mistakes, their statements provide strong evidence for opposing speakers to use.

In ethical persuasive speaking, you should rely mainly on expert testimony, using prestige and lay testimony as secondary sources of evidence. You can use prestige testimony to stress values you want listeners to embrace. You can use lay testimony to relate your subject to the lives of listeners and increase identification. Keep in mind that when you quote others you are associating yourself with them — for better or for worse. Be careful with whom you associate!

As a matter of fact, select all your evidence carefully. Consider different points of view on a problem, so that you don't simply present one perspective without being aware of others. Gather more research materials than you think you will need so that you have a wide range from which to choose. Be sure you have facts, figures, or expert testimony for each of your main points. Use multiple sources and types of evidence to strengthen your case.

Guidelines for the Ethical Use of Evidence

1 Does my evidence come from credible and trustworthy sources?

2 Have I adequately identified the sources of my evidence?

3 Would my evidence be verified by other expert sources?

4 Is my evidence relevant to the points I wish to make?

5 Is my evidence complete? Has anything been purposely withheld?

6 Is my evidence the most recent available?

7 Have I used testimony properly — i.e., expert testimony to establish facts, prestige testimony to enhance general credibility, lay testimony to humanize a subject and create identification?

8 Have I quoted or paraphrased testimony accurately?

9 Are my examples and narratives representative of the situation and not exceptions to the rule?

SPEAKER'S NOTES

PROVING YOUR POINTS

As we noted in Chapter 13, speakers offer "good reasons" based on responsible knowledge and audience needs to *prove* their points.[1] To prove a point is to present evidence so that listeners find your conclusions undeniable. *Therefore, a* **proof** *weaves evidence into a justification for the advice offered in persuasive speeches.*

The nature of proof has been studied since the Golden Age of Greece. In his *Rhetoric* Aristotle suggested that there are three fundamental types of proof, based on the susceptibilities of audiences. The first, **logos**, recognizes that we are thinking animals who respond to well-reasoned demonstrations. The second, **pathos**, affirms that we are also creatures of emotion who can be touched by appeals to fear, pity, anger, and the like; and the third, **ethos**, recognizes that we respond to leadership qualities in those who speak to us, especially to our perceptions of their competence, character, likableness, and forcefulness. In our time the work of many scholars has confirmed the presence of a fourth dimension of proof, **mythos**, that recognizes that we are also social creatures who seek identity in groups and who respond to appeals to group traditions and values.[2] The dimensions of proof are actually the dimensions of ourselves.

A persuasive speech rarely relies on a single kind of proof. Each type of proof brings its own coloration and strength to the fabric of persuasion, and the design of this fabric may vary as we work through a speech, depending upon the needs of the *particular speech* in the *particular moment* before a *particular audience*. A cloth that combines most, if not all, these strands of proof will be stronger than one which does not. In the sections that follow, we identify the strengths and qualities of these proofs, so that you may become a skilled weaver of your persuasive speech.

Logos

Logos is both practically and ethically important to persuasion. The primary work of logos is to prove that a situation is *real* — that it is not a figment of the speaker's imagination. Therefore, logos relies on facts, statistics, and expert testimony to ground a problem in reality. The second important task of logos is to show the audience what the facts *mean*. This happens when a speaker interprets facts and reasons from them to a conclusion.

How does logos contribute to proof? The process follows a simple basic pattern:

1. An *assertion* is made that must be proved.
2. *Evidence* is provided to support the claim.
3. A *conclusion* is drawn that ties together the assertion and the evidence.

In a classroom speech on drinking and driving responsibly, Betty Nichols wanted to demonstrate that the sense of security people may feel in a car can be dangerous. To prove this assertion, Betty presented these facts:

Drunk driving causes 24,000 deaths per year and 65,000 serious injuries.

Although this evidence is strong, Betty recognized that the facts alone might not be compelling enough to fully support the idea. She would need to interpret them for listeners. Therefore, she added a dramatic contrast to make these figures come to life:

FIGURE 14.1

Weaving the Fabric of Proof

> Let's compare these numbers with the risk of being a homicide victim.
> We have a 1 in 150 chance of being murdered, but we have a 1 in 33
> chance of being killed or crippled in an alcohol-related accident.

Notice that as she draws this contrast, Betty interweaves into her logos a strand of pathos: listeners begin to see the personal threat involved. This appeal to fear, based upon the statistics, becomes even more evident in the following striking conclusion:

> Therefore our car — which makes us feel so safe, so secure, so power-
> ful — can become our assassin, our coffin.

Betty's example demonstrates how logos can work as proof in a speech. An appeal to logos demonstrates the speaker's faith in the audience's intelligence. It implies that if people are offered facts and shown how to interpret them, they will come to the proper conclusion. When interwoven with pathos, *the proof gives listeners a vivid sense of the reality of the message.*[3]

Pathos

Appeals to pathos recognize that we act on feelings as well as information. People usually respond strongly when they feel angry, afraid, guilty, excited, or compassionate toward others. When used ethically, pathos can help change attitudes or advance causes.

When speakers tell personal stories, pathos can be especially effective. Personal examples blend the power of pathos with the authenticity of ethos. During a congressional debate on handgun control legislation, James Brady, the presidential press secretary who was shot during the assassination attempt on President Reagan, testified before the U.S. Senate Judiciary Subcommittee. Speaking from his wheelchair he said:

> There was a day when I walked the halls of this Senate and worked
> closely with many of you and your staffs. There was a wonderful day
> when I was fortunate enough to serve the President of the United
> States in a capacity I had dreamed of all my life. And for a time, I felt
> that people looked up to me. Today, I can tell you how hard it is to have
> people speaking down to me. But nothing has been harder than losing
> the independence and control we all so value in life. I need help get-
> ting out of bed, help taking a shower, and help getting dressed.
>
> There are some who oppose a simple seven-day waiting period for
> handgun purchases because it would inconvenience gun buyers. Well,
> I guess I am paying for their convenience. And I am one of the lucky
> ones. I survived being shot through the head. Other shooting victims
> are not as fortunate.[4]

Often, threads of pathos woven into a proof are the only way to convince people of the human dimensions of a problem or of the need for immediate action. Still, as powerful as emotional appeals may be, they should be used with caution. If the appeal to feeling is too obvious, audiences may suspect you of trying to manipulate them. Appeals to negative emotions such as fear or guilt are especially tricky since they can boomerang, discrediting both the speaker and the speech. When you use pathos, be sure to back up what you say with facts and figures. *Always support pathos with logos.* In your presentation, let your voice and body language understate rather than overstate an emotional appeal. Don't engage in theatrics!

Ethos

Appeals based on ethos recognize that listeners are persuaded by the credibility of message sources. As a speaker, you are one such source. The sources of information you cite in your speech are another.

In Chapter 2 we discussed ways to establish your personal ethos. Here we are concerned with the ethos of your sources of evidence. As they evaluate these sources, critical listeners will apply standards similar to the criteria they employ as they evaluate personal ethos. They especially will consider the sources' reputation for providing authoritative, reliable information. They will also be alert to any bias that might make the source friendly or unfriendly to their interests. If the evaluation of your sources is positive, audiences will be more inclined to accept your proof. Let's look at how Heide Nord used the ethos of her sources to help persuade her listeners to change their attitudes about suntanning. To support the claim "We should avoid prolonged exposure to the sun," Heide emphasized expert testimony supplemented with lay testimony:

> The most recent *Consumer Report* of the Food and Drug Administration tells us that "Prolonged exposure to sunlight without protection is responsible for about 90 percent of skin cancer." It describes the case of Wendell Scarberry, a skin cancer patient with over a hundred surgeries behind him. Wendell talks about the seriousness of the disease and urges that we be careful about sun exposure. "You can't cure skin cancer," he says, "by just having the doc whack it off." Finally, the American Cancer Society in its pamphlet *Fry Now Pay Later* says that skin cancer most often occurs among people who spend a lot of time in the sun, especially if they have been exposed in their teens or twenties. Well, that's where most of us are right now.

This combination of expert and lay testimony helped Heide urge listeners to protect themselves from prolonged exposure to the sun.

Clearly, proof that is based on the testimony of reliable, competent, and trustworthy sources is extremely important in persuasive speaking. *Identify your sources and point out why they are qualified to speak on the subject.* It is also helpful if you can say that their testimony is recent. For maximum effect, quote experts directly rather than paraphrasing them.

Mythos

Mythos has emerged as an important element of proof in contemporary society. *Mythos* appeals to the values, faith, and feelings that make up our social character. It is most often expressed through traditional stories, sayings, and symbols. Proof that emphasizes mythos assumes that people value their membership in a society and share its cultural heritage. Communication scholar Martha Solomon Watson has noted, "Rhetoric which incorporates mythical elements taps into rich cultural reservoirs."[5]

Appeals to mythos call on patriotism, cultural pride, and traditional heroes or enemies for evidence. In the United States we are raised on political narratives, such as those that stress the hardships of Washington's winter at Valley Forge or the triumphs of the suffragists who won women the right to vote. Such stories impress on us the meaning and value of political freedom. We may think of our country as "a frontier" or "the land of opportunity."[6] Appeals to mythos also may be based on economic legends, such as

The Western frontier is a major source of mythos in American speeches. "American Progress," a painting by American artist John Gast, portrays many icons and ideographs. Which ones can you identify?

the American stories of success through hard work and thrift made popular by the Horatio Alger books of the late nineteenth century. The Horatio Alger myth celebrates the rise to power from humble beginnings. It justifies economic power in our society while assuring the powerless that they can make it, if only they have "the right stuff." Appeals to mythos may also draw on religious narratives. Religious documents such as the Bible or the Koran provide a rich storehouse of parables, often used as proof — not just in religious sermons but also in political discourse.[7]

To create mythos, stories need not be retold in their entirety each time they are invoked. Because they are so familiar, allusions to them may be sufficient. The culturetypes discussed in Chapter 10 are often called into service because they compress the myths into a few choice words that are easily recognized throughout the culture. In his speech accepting the Democratic presidential nomination in 1960, John F. Kennedy called on the myth of the American frontier to move Americans to action:

> **The New Frontier of which I speak is not a set of promises — it is a set of challenges. It sums up not what I intend to offer the American people, but what I intend to ask of them.[8]**

This appeal to mythos emerged as a central theme of Kennedy's presidency. He didn't need to refer directly to the legends of Daniel Boone and Davy Crockett or to the tales of wagons pushing west to meet the dangers and challenges that lay ahead — he was able to conjure up those thoughts in listeners with the phrase "the New Frontier." As he ran for the presidency for the first time, Bill Clinton used "the New Covenant" as a theme for his campaign. This phrase echoed Kennedy's "New Frontier" — mythos built on mythos! — and added biblical resonance as well.

How can you use appeals to mythos in a classroom speech? Let us look at how Robert Owens used mythos to urge stronger action against drug traffic in urban slums. In his classroom speech, Robert wanted to establish the thesis "We must win the battle against drugs on the streets of America." He supported this statement by creating a sense of outrage in listeners over the betrayal of the American dream in urban America:

> **Read the latest issue of *Time* magazine, and you'll meet an America you never sang about in the songs we learned in school. It's an America in which hope, faith, and dreams are nothing but a bitter memory. They call America a land of hope, but it's hard to hope when your mother is a cocaine addict on Susquehanna Avenue in North Philadelphia. They call America a land of faith, but what faith can you cling to when even God seems to have abandoned the street corners to the junkies and the dealers! They call America a land of dreams, but what kind of dreams can you have when all you hear at night as you lie in bed are the curses and screams of buyers and dealers.**
>
> **We might be able to redeem the hope, the faith, and the dream Americans like to talk about. But we're going to have to move in a**

hurry. Our president has said that we've got to declare war on drugs, but we need to do more than declare war. We've got to *go* to war, and we've got to win! If we don't, the crack in the Liberty Bell may soon symbolize — not freedom — but a deadly drug that is destroying the American spirit all over this land.

These appeals to a betrayed mythos justified Robert's concluding plea for a broad-based, aggressive campaign to rid America of its drug culture. *The unique function of mythos is to help listeners understand how the speaker's recommendations fit into the total belief and value patterns of their group.* This gives such proof a special role in the persuasive process we discussed in the last chapter. It can help integrate new attitudes and action into the group's culture.

Like appeals to pathos, appeals to mythos can be a great good or a considerable evil. At its best, mythos heightens our appreciation of our social identity and promotes consistency between community values and public policy. However, when misused, appeals to mythos can make it seem that there is only one *legitimate* culture. It can make us forget that the freedom we honor must also affirm the right to practice different lifestyles. American culture is richly diverse. Mythos could be misused to justify action against people who do not conform to dominant group values. Had Robert Owens followed his attack on the drug culture with the conclusion that we ought to muzzle those who wish to see drugs legalized, he would have violated another important social value: freedom of speech. There is a delicate ecology among our social values — they live together in sometimes difficult and fragile harmony. Speakers may do grave damage by careless, ill-considered appeals to mythos.

Weaving the Fabric of Proof

Much of the art of persuasion lies in the way speakers blend the various strands of proof into a convincing demonstration. To weave a powerful fabric of proof, you must (1) determine the type of proof most appropriate to your message, and (2) understand how different types of proof can work together.

When audience awareness or understanding of a problem is uncertain, persuasion should begin with proof by logos. Thereafter, depending on what is crucial, the other elements of proof become important. If a problem calls for human understanding, proof by pathos with moving examples may be needed. If a situation is uncertain or confusing, proof by ethos, based on expert testimony and the speaker's personal witnessing, rises in importance. If traditions and values are relevant to a situation, proof by mythos becomes vital. Mythos can help overcome the differences among people and create a group spirit that is receptive to a message.

Consider again the speech excerpt that begins this chapter. Jim Cardoza believed that his audience accepted the problem phase of his speech: pollution of the environment is a serious problem. The proof he offers is therefore meant simply to strengthen the point before moving into the solution

When and How to Use Proof

1 When you must heighten awareness and promote understanding, use logos (facts and statistics).

2 When you need to help listeners experience the human dimensions of a problem, stir them with pathos (examples and narratives).

3 When situations are complex and much is at stake, emphasize ethos (personal witness and expert testimony carefully documented).

4 When group traditions and values are relevant, stress mythos (group symbols and legends).

SPEAKER'S NOTES

phase of his speech. The strand of logos he weaves into this proof is quite compelling: he offers striking facts to validate the conclusion that the environment is in crisis. Early in his speech, he adds personal ethos to the design of proof by talking about his vital interest in the subject, and borrows ethos from the testimony of expert sources. By reminding listeners that the problem involves the water they drink and the air they breathe, he adds the coloration of pathos. Finally, by his descriptions of nature that definitely are *not* "America the Beautiful," and by his calling listener responsibility "environmental stewardship," Jim adds strands of mythos to his proof fabric. Most of us have been taught pride in our nation's natural beauty as part of the patriotism we learn. Therefore, we should resent and reject those who defile this beauty. Many of us may also learn the value of "stewardship" as selfless service to others as we undergo religious instruction. By connecting his persuasive effort to this religious heritage, Jim strengthens the appeal of his recommendations.

By combining the strengths of these various appeals and kinds of evidence, Jim's tapestry of proof had a striking effect on listeners and moved them to consider his recommendations favorably.

FORMING ARGUMENTS

Just as proofs weave evidence into powerful appeals based upon our nature as thinking and feeling creatures and our needs for leadership and social identity, arguments weave proofs into the tapestry of persuasion in a persuasive speech. **Arguments** combine proofs according to basic patterns of human reasoning. Arguments should provide satisfactory answers to three fundamental questions:

- Is the message based on principles or rules of conduct that I accept?
- Are the conclusions based upon a careful inspection of reality?
- Can we learn something by considering closely related situations?

The three major forms of argument, deductive, inductive, and analogical, correspond to these questions. How well you answer them — by creating a powerful design of deductive, inductive, and analogical arguments that fits the needs of your message and audience — determines your success as a persuasive speaker. In this section we introduce the basic principles of argumentation. Our aim is to help you weave a powerful tapestry of persuasion.

Deductive Argument

As we mature into adulthood and absorb the faiths and beliefs of our culture, we acquire a working set of principles and rules of conduct that guide the way we live. These principles and rules are not necessarily scientifically correct: for example, for a long time, people believed the earth was flat and the sun was the center of the universe. Nevertheless, the assumption was powerful: Columbus had to convince doubters in his own day — especially his sailors — that he was not going to sail off the edge of the world. Rules of conduct are also a part of the working faith of a people: "freedom of speech," for example, is written into the Constitution of the United States as a principle of government.

These principles and rules are basic to persuasion because we *deduce* from them specific lessons to apply in everyday life: hence the name, **deductive argument.** Such argument starts with a generally accepted rule or principle:

"We all believe in freedom of speech."

It then relates a specific issue to that principle:

Obnoxious Melvin would like to speak.

Finally, it reaches a conclusion:

Even though he is obnoxious, we should let Melvin speak.

Because it is based on widely shared principles, deductive argument is especially useful for establishing common ground with reluctant audiences. Deductive argument can also point out inconsistencies between beliefs and behaviors, between what we preach and what we practice. For example, if you can show that the censorship of song lyrics is inconsistent with freedom of speech, then you will have presented a good reason for people to condemn the censorship. We are more likely to change a practice if it is inconsistent with cherished principles than we are to change our principles. Because people like to be consistent and maintain the integrity of their values, deductive argument is a powerful way to change specific attitudes and behaviors.

A deductive argument can be developed *within* a speech or it can *underlie* a speech as an unstated way of thinking. Consider the weather forecaster on a morning television show: after showing the weather map, she says, "You'd better take your umbrella today." That statement is the audible tip of a submerged structure of reasoning which begins with the assumption, "People don't like to get wet." The second element of this argument implies a specific situation, in this case the cell of rain on the weather map that is moving into the area. The third part of the argument is the advice drawn from the hidden pattern of deductive reasoning.

The pattern demonstrated by this example has been recognized for several thousand years as a basic model of human reasoning. Constructing this deductive model was a great intellectual achievement because it permitted the careful investigation of our thinking processes. It includes — in the order described in our weather example — a major premise, a minor premise, and a conclusion.

The **major premise** is the generally accepted belief on which the argument is based. Major premises represent the essence of all we have learned. In their political and social forms, they are the faith by which we live. In our chapter-opening example, the unstated major premise that justifies the reasoning within the speech might be reconstructed as follows: "We have a responsibility to protect the environment in which we live from serious pollution." Similarly, the unstated major premise in Cesar Chavez's "Pesticides Speech," reprinted in Appendix B, might be reconstructed this way: "We should not poison food to grow more of it."

One of the major tasks in understanding arguments is to recognize and evaluate the major premises that support our thinking. One thing we must realize is that some people may not agree with items of faith we accept without question. For example, some researchers discovered that if you read the Bill of Rights to people without telling them it was part of the United States Constitution, an alarming percentage would describe it as "radical" or "communistic." Therefore, when you are devising deductive arguments, you cannot always take your major premises for granted. You may have to defend them and explain them to reinforce your listener's belief in them.

Another problem with deductive reasoning is that people may give lip service to a principle, but not be committed to its meaning. They do not relate to the principle emotionally. In other cases, speakers may base their arguments on major premises that contradict our own basic beliefs. For example, in environmental disputes opposing speakers may argue from the premise, "Society must provide employment for its people." In such cases, you will have to support your major premise to remind people why such principles and rules are important to their way of life. You also may have to show that the apparent contradiction between premises — those you present and those offered by your opponent — does not really exist. You might have to show, for example, that people don't really have to choose between conserving the environment and expanding the economy.

The **minor premise** — which is actually *not* minor in terms of its importance in argument — affirms the reality of some specific relevant situation. Yes, the weather map tells us that rain is moving in. Yes, the evidence presented by Jim Cardozo affirms that pollution of our environment has risen to a serious level. Yes, argued Cesar Chavez, California growers were poisoning food — and agricultural workers and consumers — in order to grow more. As you will quickly discover, the status of the minor premise is often the point of controversy in a dispute. People may not argue passionately about the weather map or the *principle* of environmental protection, but allegations about specific cases of environmental pollution or the agribusiness of California are subject to a great deal of dispute. The proof you weave around your minor premise must support it without question.

Once the audience accepts the major premise, and agrees that the minor premise describes reality, then the **conclusion** logically follows: "Yes, we'd better take our umbrella." "Yes, we'd better assume personal responsibility to improve our environment." "Yes, we'd better boycott grapes." If we accept the major and minor premises, the argument *compels* us to accept its conclusion. To be consistent, we must believe or do what it tells us to.

Yet, as Aristotle implied in his *Rhetoric,* logic and life may be two very different things. When we reason in the real world, we have to account for uncertainty. The weather front might not behave as the forecaster predicts. Jim's proposal to assume personal responsibility for pollution might not help the situation very much. Chavez may have exaggerated the situation to dramatize his plea for action. Because of this uncertainty, a British logician, Stephen Toulmin, recommends that we add a *qualifier* or acknowledge a possible *rebuttal* as we draw conclusions in real-life arguments.[9]

Qualifiers are words like "probably" or "most likely" or "in most cases." They suggest the degree of confidence we have in the conclusion. We use qualifiers to offset possible **rebuttals** that point out conditions under which the conclusion might not hold. Examples of qualifiers might be, "*unless* conditions change rapidly during the next six months, we should adopt the Cardoza plan" or "*unless* growers can prove they have changed the way they do business, we should join the grape boycott." If you carefully qualify your conclusions, recognizing rebuttals when appropriate, you should come across to listeners as a careful persuasive speaker who is not trying to force them into an unreasoned commitment. Rather than a sign of weakness, qualifiers can strengthen your ethos before critical listeners.

As you develop a deductive pattern of reasoning for your speech, keep these cautions in mind:

1. *Be certain your audience will accept your major premise.* If you have any doubt that listeners agree with your major premise, you should support it carefully. Remind listeners *why* they believe as they do. Cite prestige sources who testify to the importance of the premise. Use the pathos of moving examples and the mythos of exciting narratives that stir patriotic feelings about the principle. Weave in threads of logos to show the practical importance of the premise.

2. *Once your major premise is established, concentrate on supporting the minor premise.* This, as we shall see in the next section, is where induc-

tive reasoning joins with deductive reasoning to build a compelling argument.

3. *Demonstrate the relationship between your major and minor premises.* Don't expect your listeners to get the connection automatically. Will listeners see the relationship between environmental conditions and their moral responsibility to maintain the natural beauty of their country? Will they be willing to grant that pesticide poisoning of foods is the result of grower practices? Even if what you say is true, you must establish the connection between your premises. Critical listeners and opponents will demand that you meet this responsibility.

4. *Be certain your reasoning is free from logical errors and fallacies.* We discuss such flaws of argument in the final section of this chapter.

5. *Be sure your conclusion offers a clear direction for your listeners.* Don't leave them foundering without a clear idea as to what you want them to do.

Inductive Argument

As we develop critical listening and thinking abilities, we increasingly demand that persuaders base their conclusions on a careful consideration of conditions that actually exist. While we are still learning to be critical listeners, we often pay a heavy price for gullibility — buying into arguments without checking to see whether claims coincide with reality. We may be burned by those who appeal to us on the basis of tradition and authority. These arguers invite us to live in a strictly deductive world that supplies major premises that predetermine our experiences. For example, we may be taught that "African-Americans are _____" or "White people are _____" (you fill in the blanks). It is just a matter of faith for us to honor these beliefs, regardless of what violence they may bring to fairness or reality. We live in a prison camp of the mind, disciplined — and limited — by the rules we have learned.

These reflections suggest the ethical importance of an inductive orientation. An inductive orientation means that we open ourselves to life as it actually is and that we should be willing to change our conduct and our beliefs based on our experiences. An inductive orientation also means we should ask if conclusions are drawn from a careful observation of reality. It elevates the importance of a second pattern of reasoning, **inductive argument**. While deductive argument is driven by faith in general principles and rules, inductive reasoning emphasizes observation and concrete experiences. Because inductive thinking begins with careful observations, it is the principal method of scientific investigation.

Although these two forms of argument may seem to be opposites, they actually work together. Persuasion based on inductive argument helps verify major premises so that they are no longer simply items of faith. The arguments based on premises which have been justified by inductive investigation lead to more reliable conclusions. For example, if we can demonstrate that "Freedom of discussion results in better public deliberation," then we bring reality and practicality to the support of morality, and we defend our faith in the constitutional premise of freedom of speech.

Beyond simply demonstrating major premises, *the artful joining of deductive and inductive arguments in a speech is essential to persuasive success.* Looking back at deductive reasoning, we see that there is a point at which the facts are critical in the reasoning process. That point is the minor premise which asserts that some situation related to the major premise actually exists. Proving this assertion is sometimes easy, at other times more difficult. In our example of the weather map, the implied minor premise was self-evident: "It looks like it's going to rain." The evidence for that assertion was right there for everyone to see. The problem confronted by Jim Cardoza, to prove that "pollution has reached critical stages in our country," was only slightly more difficult. Jim had good reason to believe that his audience was inclined to accept that assertion. An earlier classroom speech had presented evidence that supported much of what Jim's minor premise claimed, and discussion following the speech indicated that listeners were convinced. Jim's task was to reawaken and strengthen his audience's belief in the minor premise. Therefore, the major focus of his speech was on the conclusion, in which he had to sell his solution as the best answer to the problem. On the other hand, Cesar Chavez faced a different challenge. In his audience, many listeners might question whether growers were actually using pesticides irresponsibly. Chavez had to concentrate on proving that they were.

As these examples indicate, deductive and inductive patterns of reasoning converge at the minor premise. Figure 14.2 shows how this process works.

This model suggests that speakers can lead audiences to accept their conclusions *if* they present a major premise accepted by listeners, and *if* they ver-

FIGURE 14.2

Deductive and Inductive Reasoning in Public Argument

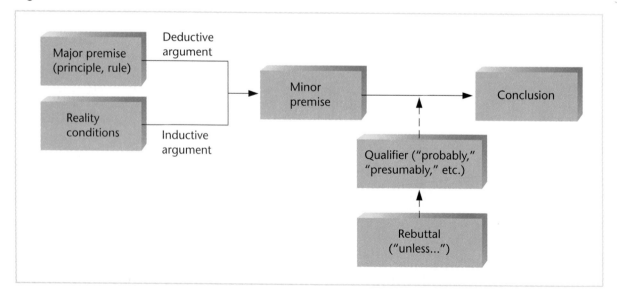

ify the conditions claimed in the minor premise. The major premise grounds the argument in a powerful principle, such as "We should protect our environment." The minor premise presents a claim about the present state of affairs, such as "We are trashing our environment." The minor premise directly depends for verification on inductive argument that highlights the reality, such as "Evidence of environmental abuse abounds." The interaction of the principle and the reality — the interweaving of deductive and inductive arguments — justifies the conclusion, "We need an aggressive policy to restore the environment." The strength of this conclusion may be qualified appropriately by words such as "probably" or "presumably," in light of some possible rebuttal condition such as "unless conditions change dramatically."

It is clear from this model that inductive reasoning is based on concrete instances to prove that a condition actually exists. Therefore, inductive argument is logos-centered. Cesar Chavez, for example, used statistics in striking ways to dramatize and authenticate the severity of conditions in the fields of California.

> **The World Resources Institute reported that over three hundred thousand farm workers are poisoned every year by pesticides. Over half of all reported pesticide-related illnesses involve the cultivation or harvesting of table grapes. They receive *more* restricted-use application permits, which allow growers to spray pesticides known to threaten humans, than *any* other fresh food crop. The General Accounting Office, which does research for the U.S. Congress, determined that *34* of the *76* types of pesticides used *legally* on grapes pose potential human health hazards and could *not be detected* by current multi-residue methods. [The script of the speech supplies the italicized words. They indicate points Chavez particularly wished to emphasize in oral presentations.][10]**

Chavez could bring powerful personal testimony to bear, but sensing that some might suspect him of bias, he also used an abundance of expert testimony, including "reluctant" testimony from sources who might be expected to speak against him.

> **. . . Even the growers' own magazine, *The California Farmer,* admitted that growers were *illegally* using a very dangerous growth stimulator, called *Fix,* which is quite similar to *Agent Orange,* on the grapes.**

Therefore, he wove into the fabric of his proof the authority of both personal and borrowed ethos. As he pointed out examples of the victims of pesticide poisoning — especially among children — he added the coloration of pathos to his tapestry of argument:

> **This is a very technical problem, with very *human* victims. One young body, Felipe Franco, was born without arms or legs in the agricultural town of McFarland. His mother worked for the first three months of her pregnancy picking grapes in fields that were sprayed repeatedly**

with pesticides believed to cause birth defects. . . . *And the children are dying.* They are dying *slow, painful, cruel* deaths in towns called *cancer clusters.* In cancer clusters like McFarland, where the childhood cancer rate is *800 percent* above normal. . . . There are at least *four* other children suffering from cancer and similar diseases which the experts believe were caused by pesticides in the little town of Earlimart, a rate *1200 percent* above normal. In Earlimart, little Jimmy Caudillo died recently from leukemia at the age of three.

The grape vineyards of California have become America's "Killing Fields."

Interestingly, Chavez underplayed mythos, perhaps because he sensed that he and his farm workers did not share the same cultural background of many among his listeners. Perhaps his willingness to appeal to "the court of last resort: the American people" affirms his faith in the essential mythic goodness of American character. What makes this argument inductive is its effort to convince listeners that it pictures reality. By proving his minor premise inductively, Chavez added a powerful sense of this reality to his speech.

Such argument is especially useful in a speech where the major challenge is to establish the reality of a problem. In his speech proposing a national organ transplant program, Paul Fowler first identified and examined three categories of acute need: kidney, heart, and liver transplants. In each category he presented an impressive array of facts and testimony from medical experts to depict the magnitude of the problem. From these particular observations Paul moved to the solution phase of his speech, which included his conclusions and recommendations.

In addition to its special usefulness in problem-solution designs, inductive argument also serves refutative designs in speeches that directly confront the opposition. Refutative speeches closely examine contending positions and criticize specific weaknesses in their evidence or proof. They often argue that opponents have not presented an authentic picture of reality. The usefulness of inductive argument is so widespread that it seems the very foundation of reason in public discussions. Perhaps it is grounded in the common-sense "show-me" and "seeing-is-believing" attitudes of healthy skepticism that many people carry with them when they listen to debate over public issues.

As you plan the inductive phase of your persuasive speech, keep in mind these questions:

- Do your observations adequately justify your conclusions?
- Have you read and observed enough?
- Are your observations recent and reliable?
- Are you objective enough to see the situation clearly?
- Are your observations representative of the situation, reflecting the usual rather than the unusual?
- If your observations are based on peoples' views, have you talked to enough of them to draw responsible inferences?

These are the kinds of questions that critical listeners will ask as they evaluate inductive arguments. Ask them of yourself as you prepare your speech.

Analogical Argument

Analogical argument combines elements of both deduction and induction, but is distinct enough to deserve discussion on its own. The deductive part of analogical thinking is its implied basic premise: *we can learn about a problem, and how to respond to it, by considering a parallel problem closely related to it.* The inductive element in analogical thinking is its close attention to the relevant particulars of parallel problems.

Analogical argument rises out of the need to understand an unfamiliar, abstract, or difficult subject by relating it to something that is familiar, concrete, and easily understood. Used persuasively, analogical argument may associate one subject with another that already has strong positive or negative feelings attached to it. It may also associate a proposed plan with one that either worked or didn't work. One major value of analogical argument is that it can demonstrate that a proposed plan of action will or will not work. For example, some of Chavez's opponents might have argued that the boycott would be ineffective. Chavez anticipated such argument by emphasizing how previous boycotts had worked. Moreover, he presented an analogical argument for his boycott by suggesting its similarity to the Montgomery bus boycott of the Civil Rights movement:

> **I have seen many boycotts succeed. The Reverend Martin Luther King Junior, who so generously supported our first fast, led the way with the bus boycott. And with our first boycott, we were able to get DDT, Aldrin, and Dieldrin banned, in our first contracts with grape growers. Now, even more urgently, we are trying to get deadly pesticides banned.**

In some cases analogical argument can be central to the success or failure of persuasion. For example, in the ongoing debate over our nation's drug policy, those who favor legalizing "recreational" drugs frequently base their arguments on an analogy to Prohibition.[11] They contend that the Prohibition amendment caused more problems than it solved because it led to the rise of a criminal empire. They further suggest that our efforts to outlaw recreational drugs have had the same result. In developing their analogical argument, prolegalization forces claim it is impossible to ban a human desire — that to try to do so simply encourages contempt for the law. Moreover, they assert that legalizing drugs would help put the international drug dealers out of business just as the repeal of Prohibition helped bring about the downfall of the gangsters of the 1930s. Finally, they argue, if drug sales were legal it would be easier to control the quality of drugs, thus reducing the danger to users (parallel to the health problems associated with bootleg whiskey during Prohibition).

As this example shows, analogical argument emphasizes strategic points of comparison between similar situations. People on both sides of an issue will focus on these points, using evidence and proofs to defend or attack them. Opponents to legalizing drugs claim that there are many important differences between drugs and alcohol.[12] They say that alcohol is not as addictive for casual users as heroin or cocaine. They contend that legalization would multiply the drug problem, not reduce it. They further suggest that since many drug abusers are prone to violence, the cost to society would be increased. Moreover, they argue that the campaign against drugs can point to some success, whereas enforcement of the Prohibition laws was a disaster from the beginning. Thus, the public debate rages on, argument clashing with counterargument over these crucial points of comparison.

What makes an analogical argument work? Analogical argument is similar to induction in that we seek insight through careful observation. Analogy differs from induction in that *our observations are concentrated on one similar situation* rather than ranging across many. This means that although analogical argument may seem more concrete and interesting than inductive argument, it also may be less reliable. Before you decide to use analogical argument, be certain that the important similarities between the situations outweigh the dissimilarities. To satisfy critical listeners and to disarm opposition, acknowledge major dissimilarities in your speech, but point out that they don't compromise the analogy. If you must strain to make an analogy fit, rely on the other forms of argument.

The Importance of Defining Terms

All forms of argument depend on clear definitions of terms. Have you ever had a heated discussion with someone, only to discover later that the two

of you were not even talking about the same things? Socrates suggested that all persuasive messages should start with definitions of terms, so that speakers and listeners can share understanding from the beginning. Opening definitions clarify what you mean, reveal your intentions, and show the audience how you see a subject. When the speaker and audience come from different backgrounds, careful definitions are even more important.

Many problems of definition are based more on fundamental disagreements than on simple misunderstanding. Should alcohol be defined as a drug? Should the fetus be defined as a human being? Such questions often lead speakers to argue for *ethical* definitions. In the 1968 Memphis sanitation strike that led to the assassination of Dr. Martin Luther King, Jr., the workers often marched carrying signs that read, "I Am a Man." This simple-looking statement was actually just the tip of a vast underlying moral argument. The strikers, all of whom were African-American, were claiming that they were *not* treated like men, both in social and economic terms. As you develop your arguments, keep in mind that definitions can be the *fundamental issues at the heart of controversies*. Define key terms clearly, and support all controversial definitions with evidence and proof.

AVOIDING DEFECTIVE PERSUASION

It takes hard work to prepare a persuasive speech — analyzing your audience, researching your topic, planning your strategy, and weaving the tapestry of evidence, proof, and argument needed to make your message effective. Do not ruin the effectiveness of all this work by committing errors of reasoning called **fallacies**. Fallacies may crop up in the evidence you use, the proof you develop, or the pattern of your arguments. There are also fallacies particular to some of the speech designs discussed in the previous chapter. In this section we identify some of these major errors so that you can guard against them, as both a producer and a consumer of persuasive messages.

Defective Evidence

Evidence is defective if the speaker misuses facts, statistics, or testimony.

Misuse of Fact.   One major misuse of facts is the **slippery slope fallacy**, which assumes that once something happens it will establish an irreversible trend leading to disaster. During the Vietnam War, government officials who accepted the "domino theory" argued that if Vietnam fell to the Communists, all of Southeast Asia would be lost. Some even suggested that enemy soldiers soon would be landing on the shores of California. The slippery slope fallacy often involves oversimplification and outlandish hyperbole. For example, a prominent religious leader recently suggested that feminism was "a socialist, anti-family political movement that encourages women to leave their husbands, kill their children, practice witchcraft, destroy capitalism, and become lesbians."[13] In the slippery slope fallacy it is not logic that drives the prediction of events, but rather our darkest fears and deepest ignorance.

A second misuse of evidence involves *the confusion of fact and opinion.* A factual statement is objective and verifiable, such as "Many Republicans are supporting the 'Contract with America.' " An opinion is a personal interpretation of information: a statement of belief, feeling, attitude, or value. Normally, factual and opinion statements stay in their proper places. The problem comes when speakers make impassioned claims based on opinions, such as: "The Republicans have done it now! They're violating our Constitution. They're tossing children out into the cold. They're depriving retired people of their right to a secure old age. These are the *facts* of what they're doing." Opinions can be useful in persuasive speeches when they represent careful interpretations that are supported by evidence. However, treating an opinion as a fact, or a fact as an opinion, is the source of many problems. It can make you seem to claim too much or too little and can raise real questions about your competence and ethics.

At one time hunters used to distract their dogs from a trail by dragging a smoked herring across it. In our time, the **red herring fallacy** occurs when persuaders try to draw attention away from the real issues in a dispute, perhaps because they feel vulnerable on those issues or because they see a chance to vilify the opposition. The "red herring" they use is quite pungent — formed by sensational facts dragged across the trail of the discussion. In the current abortion controversy, some "pro-choice" advocates attempt to discredit opposition arguments by suggesting that their opponents are terrorists, associating the entire anti-abortion movement with those who have been convicted of assassinating doctors or bombing clinics. In return, some "pro-life" advocates try to discredit their opponents by arguing that many clinics where abortions are performed were underwritten by "Mafia money." Such charges from both sides divert attention from the central issues of the controversy.

Statistical Fallacies. Audiences are often intimidated by numbers. We've all been taught that "figures don't lie" without being advised that "liars figure." Speakers sometimes exploit this weakness by creating statistical deceptions. For example, consider the **myth of the mean**, or the "illusion of the average." If you've ever vacationed in the mountains, you are well aware that a stream may have an "average depth" of six inches, yet a person could drown in one of its deep pools. A speaker could tell you not to worry about poverty in Plattsville because the average income is well above the poverty level. Yet this average could be skewed by the fact that a few families are very wealthy, creating an illusion of well-being that is not true for many people. Averages are useful to summarize statistical information, but be sure they do not hide the reality of a situation.

Another statistical fallacy occurs when we offer *predictions drawn from statistical comparisons that start from unequal bases.* Many years ago during a college debate, we heard an opponent make a dark prediction: "The gross national product of the United States is growing at an annual rate of only 6 percent, while that of the Soviet Union is growing at a rate of

14 percent. Therefore, the Soviets are rapidly overtaking us." The problem was that the bases of this comparison were radically unequal: a 6 percent rise in the American GNP at that time represented more actual economic growth than a 14 percent rise in the Soviet GNP: 6 percent of $500 billion is greater than 14 percent of $150 billion. It was not the Americans who were losing ground!

Defective Testimony. Testimony can be misused in many different ways. Speakers may omit when a statement was made to hide the fact that the testimony is outdated. They may deceive us when they leave out important facts about their experts, intimidating us instead with titles such as "*Dr.* Michael Jones reported that smoking does not harm health." What the speaker *didn't* reveal was that Dr. Jones was a marketing professor who was writing public relations material for the Tobacco Growers Association. Speakers also abuse testimony when they cite words out of context that are not representative of a person's position. As we noted in Chapter 6, prestige and lay testimony can be misused if they replace expert opinion when facts must be established. Finally, the "voice of the people" can be easily misrepresented, depending on *which* people you choose to quote.

Inappropriate Evidence. Other abuses occur when speakers deliberately use one form of evidence when they should be using another. For example, you might use facts and figures when examples would bring us closer to the human truth of a situation. Welfare statistics are sometimes misused in this way. It is as though the speaker preferred to talk about poverty in the abstract, distancing listeners from its concrete reality. On the other hand, speakers may use examples to arouse emotions when what is needed is a dispassionate picture supported with facts and figures. Testimony is abused when it is used to compensate for inadequate facts. Narratives that create mythos may also be used inappropriately. Calling someone a "Robin Hood who steals from the rich to give to the poor" has been used to justify more than one crime.

Defective Proof

Any element of proof can be defective. We have already pointed out the danger of overreliance on proof by pathos when appeals to feelings overwhelm good judgment and cloud the perception of issues. Speakers might also misuse proof by mythos to promote intolerance, such as "When are Native Americans going to start being *good* Americans?"

In a similar manner, speakers may misuse proof by ethos when they attack the person rather than the argument. This is called an **ad hominem** fallacy. Such persuaders try to avoid issues by calling the opposition derogatory names. Therefore, this fallacy is related to the "red herring" fallacy mentioned earlier. For example, during a recent environmental dispute, one side charged that its opponents were "little old ladies in tennis shoes" and "outside agitators." Not to be outdone, the other side labeled their antagonists as "rapists of public parkland."[14] Senator Jennings Randolph, speaking before the U.S. Senate in the not-so-distant past, dismissed arguments in favor of the Equal Rights Amendment for women on grounds they were offered by a "small band of bra-less bubbleheads."[15] Proof by ethos also can be abused when speakers overuse it — when they try to intimidate listeners by citing an overwhelming number of authorities while neglecting to present information or good reasons for accepting their claims.

Finally, speakers neglect their responsibility to prove their points when they merely assert what they have not proved, thereby committing the fallacy of **begging the question.** Those who "beg the question" usually rely on colorful language to disguise the inadequacy of their proofs, so that the words themselves *seem* to establish the conclusion. Some anti-abortion advocates may be guilty of this practice when they refer to the fetus as the "unborn *child*" without bothering to address first the difficult moral question of when human life actually begins. A similar abuse may occur when the speaker taps into the mythos of the audience without adequate justification or preparation. A conclusion such as "Be *patriotic!* Support the *American way of life!* Speak out against gun control!," tacked onto a speech without further explanation, begs the question because the speaker has not proved that being against gun control is a legitimate form of patriotism.

Defective Arguments

Major fallacies may infest all forms of argument. It is unethical to commit them purposely — irresponsible to commit them accidentally. In your role as critical listener, be on guard against them at all times.

Errors of Deduction.   Because deductive reasoning builds on the major premise, an argument can be only as good as the major premise is sound. *If your major premise is faulty, the entire argument will crumble.* We once heard a student begin with the premise "college athletes don't really want to learn." She was instantly in trouble. When her speech was over, the class assailed her with questions. "How did she define *athletes?*" "Was she talking about intercollegiate or intramural athletes?" "How about the tennis team?" "How did she define learning?" "Was she aware of the negative stereotype at the center of her premise?" "Wasn't she being unfair, not to mention arrogant?" It's safe to say that the speaker did not persuade many people that day. To avoid such a fiasco, be sure that you can defend each word in your major premise and that you are on sound footing as you begin.

Confusing probability and certainty is another fallacy common to deductive argument. Aristotle reminded us that the logic of everyday life is rarely absolutely certain. Suppose a friend from the Tau Beta fraternity calls you to set up a blind date. If the premise "Tau Betas are handsome" holds about 90 percent of the time, in your experience, and if you are about 90 percent certain that your blind date is a Tau Beta, then your conclusion that your date will be attractive is at best an assumption qualified by two factors of uncertainty. There is a 10 percent chance that your date is not a Tau Beta, and even if he is, there is another 10 percent chance he is not one of the handsome ones. If you assert probabilities as though they were certainties, you are guilty of a reasoning error. It is better to use qualifiers that point out the uncertainty: "There is a *good chance* that my date will be handsome." If you point out the uncertainty factor in advance, as you deal with important matters, you may not lose the audience's trust if a prediction does not come true.

Another error common in deductive argument is *reasoning that if something happens after an event, it was therefore caused by the event.* This fallacy, called the **post hoc fallacy** after its abbreviated Latin name, confuses association with causation. It is the basis of many superstitious beliefs. The same people who wear their lucky boots and shirts to ball games may also argue that we should have a tax cut because the last time we had one we avoided war, increased employment, or reduced crime. A speaker always must demonstrate that events are causally connected, not just make the assumption based on association.

Finally, a **non sequitur fallacy** occurs when the minor premise is not related to the major premise, when the conclusion does not necessarily follow from the relationship between premises, or when the evidence presented is irrelevant. House Speaker Newt Gingrich, lecturing students on why men are more suited than women to traditional military combat roles, provided a remarkable example which appears to fit all the conditions of non sequitur reasoning: "If combat means living in a ditch, females have biological problems staying in a ditch for 30 days because they get infections . . . males are biologically driven to go out and hunt for giraffes." Rep. Pat Schroeder responded to this wisdom as follows: "I have been working in a male culture for a very long time, and I haven't met the first one who wants to go out and hunt a giraffe."[16]

In 1989 Joe Foss, then president of the National Rifle Association, argued against pending gun control legislation to the National Press Club in Washington, D.C. See if you can identify the non sequiturs and other fallacies in this excerpt from the speech:

> You see, back when the country was founded — if you look back that far into history you'll find that they needed guns. And they defeated an outfit that was trying to disarm them. And, as a result of our having guns and being able to use them, we won. That was the start of the United States of America. We won a war. And of course, ever since that time we've been involved, and there've been people that would like to take us over. If you've read Marx and Lenin you know that one of their great ambitions is to disarm a nation. And so here you have a reason to be armed: to see to it that no one is going to disarm us, even in today's world. . . .[17]

Errors of Induction. A common error in inductive reasoning is a **hasty generalization** which is based on insufficient or nonrepresentative observations. Suppose a student reasoned: "My big sister in Alpha Chi got a D from Professor Osborn. The guy who sits next to me in history got an F from her. I'm struggling to make a C in her class. Therefore, Professor Osborn is a tough grader." To avoid hasty generalization you would need to know what Professor Osborn's grade distribution looks like over an extended period of time and across courses, plus how her grades compare with those of other professors teaching the same courses.

Defective Analogy.   A **faulty analogy** occurs when the things compared are dissimilar in some important way. If the points of dissimilarity outweigh the similarities, an analogy is in trouble. For example, assume that you have transferred from a college with 1,500 students to a university with 15,000 students. You present a speech proposing new campus security measures, arguing that because they worked well at the college, they should also work well at the university. Would such an analogical argument be valid? That would depend on similarities and dissimilarities between the two schools. Is the size difference important? Are the crime problems similar? Are the schools located in similar settings? Are the students from roughly the same social and economic backgrounds? Dissimilarity on any of these points could raise doubts about the analogy. You would have to overcome these doubts for the analogy to be convincing.

Fallacies Related to Particular Designs

In addition to fallacies of evidence, proof, and argument, there are at least two major fallacies related to particular persuasive designs. **Either–or thinking**, sometimes called *false dilemma,* makes listeners think that they have only two choices — one desirable, the other not. This fallacy is attractive because it is dramatic: it satisfies our yen for conflict and simplicity. It occurs in political behavior when we think we must choose between two political parties. It shows up in policy debates: "Pass our 'Contract With America,'" say the Republicans, "or accept a doomed America." "If you pass the Republican 'Contract *On* America,'" answer the Democrats, "you will sacrifice our basic values." Either–or thinking blinds listeners to other options, such as compromise or creative alternatives not yet considered. Such thinking often infests problem–solution speeches when speakers oversimplify the choices to encourage commitment to their cause. We should be wary of being boxed into either–or decisions by impassioned speakers.

People who have gardens sometimes make up a "straw man" to scare off crows. As the name suggests, the straw is formed into the "likeness" of a man. (Presumably, a "straw woman" would work as well, as far as the crows are concerned!) Whatever the gender, the "straw man" is obviously much less than what it represents. From this name comes the **straw man fallacy,** making up a "likeness" of an opponent's view which makes it seem trivial, ridiculous, or easy to refute. As you might suspect, the straw man fallacy appears most often in speeches that contend with opposition. It understates and distorts the position of opponents, and is unethical. Dismissing Steve Forbes' "flat tax" proposal as simply an effort to reduce his own taxes was the "straw man" of the 1996 Republican primaries, as the candidates trashed each other with negative ads. As an ethical persuasive speaker, you have an obligation to represent an opposing position fairly and fully, even as you refute it. Only then will critical listeners respect you and your arguments. The straw man fallacy is an implicit admission of weakness or desperation and can damage what may well be a legitimate case.

Persuasion is constantly threatened by flaws and deception. In a world of competing views, we often see human nature revealed in its petty as well as its finer moments. As you plan and present your arguments or listen to the arguments of others, be on guard against fallacies.

IN SUMMARY

Evidence, proof, and argument form the substance of reasoning that we see at work in any successful persuasive speech.

Using Evidence Effectively. When supporting materials serve persuasion, it becomes evidence. Evidence is the most basic ingredient in persuasion. Facts and statistics alert us to a situation we must change. Examples move listeners, creating a favorable emotional atmosphere for the speaker's recommendations. Narratives bring a sense of reality, and help listeners identify with the issue. Testimony calls upon witnesses to support a position. When you use evidence, strive for recent facts and figures, emphasize factual examples, engage listeners through stories that make your point, and rely primarily on expert testimony.

Proving Your Points. A *proof* is an arrangement of evidence that provides listeners with good reasons for accepting your advice. The elements of proof, based on deep human qualities, are logos, pathos, ethos, and mythos. *Logos* recognizes that we are thinking animals who respond to well-reasoned demonstrations. *Pathos* affirms that we are creatures of emotion as well. *Ethos* recognizes that we respond to leadership qualities in speakers and are influenced by sources of evidence. *Mythos* relates to our nature as social beings who respond to group traditions and values. A powerful proof will weave a fabric of evidence that appeals to these various dimensions of ourselves. To develop sound proof, you must determine what to emphasize in your particular message, and you must be able to combine the strengths of these different elements.

Forming Arguments. *Arguments* combine evidence and proof into fundamental patterns of reasoning. Deductive argument develops around a *major premise, minor premise,* and *conclusion.* The major premise, often unstated but understood by listeners, is a generally accepted principle, assumption, or rule on which the argument rests. The minor premise focuses on some specific issue relevant to the major premise. The conclusion, drawn from the relationship between major and minor premises, tells us what to believe or do. *Inductive argument* satisfies listeners that the speaker has an adequate grasp of reality by proving the existence of conditions that justify the premises, especially the statement offered in the minor premise. Deductive and inductive patterns of reasoning combine in successful persuasion to build a powerful case. *Analogical argument,* which often relates to the workability of the speaker's plan proposed in the conclusion, compares the plan to parallel, closely related programs already in existence. All three forms of argument depend on clear, persuasive definitions for their effectiveness.

Avoiding Defective Persuasion. Fallacies are errors in reasoning that can damage a persuasive speech. Evidence can be defective when the speaker misuses facts, statistics, and testimony. Common errors include the *slippery slope fallacy,* which assumes that a single instance will establish a trend, the confusion of fact with opinion, and the *red herring,* using irrelevant material to divert attention from the issue. Statistical fallacies include the *myth of the mean,* in which averages create illusions that hide reality, and faulty predictions based upon flawed statistical comparisons. Evidence can also be used inappropriately, featuring facts and figures when the situation calls for examples, examples when the audience needs facts and figures, testimony to hide the weakness of information, or narratives to justify unethical behavior.

Various defects can reduce the value of proof. Speakers misuse proof by ethos when they commit an *ad hominem* fallacy, attacking the person rather than the argument. When speakers merely assert and assume in their conclusion what they have not proved, they commit the fallacy of *begging the question.*

Fallacies are also common in the patterns of argument. If your major premise is faulty, the entire argument will crumble. Other frequent errors occur when probability is passed off as certainty, and when the speaker confuses association with causation, reasoning that if something happened after an event, it therefore was caused by the event. This is called the *post hoc* fallacy. A *non sequitur* fallacy occurs when irrelevant conclusions or evidence is introduced into argument. Inductive reasoning can suffer from a *hasty generalization* drawn from insufficient or nonrepresentative observations. Argument by analogy is defective when important dissimilarities outweigh similarities.

Either–or thinking can be a special problem in speeches calling for action. This fallacy reduces audience options to only two, one advocated by the speaker, the other undesirable. When speeches that contend with opposition understate, distort, or misrepresent an opposing position for the sake of easy refutation, they commit the *straw man* fallacy.

TERMS TO KNOW

evidence	inductive argument
reluctant witnesses	analogical argument
proof	fallacies
logos	slippery slope fallacy
pathos	red herring fallacy
ethos	myth of the mean
mythos	ad hominem fallacy
arguments	begging the question
deductive argument	post hoc fallacy
major premise	non sequitur fallacy
minor premise	hasty generalization
conclusion	faulty analogy

qualifiers

either–or thinking

rebuttals

straw man fallacy

DISCUSSION

1. Bring to class examples of advertisements that emphasize each of the four types of persuasive proof: logos, pathos, ethos, and mythos. What factors in the product, medium of advertising, or intended audience might explain this emphasis in each example? Do the ads make use of other types of proof as well? How effective is each ad?

2. Analyze the tapestry of evidence, proof, and argument that develops in the speech by Bonnie Marshall, reprinted in Appendix B. How powerful is this design of persuasive materials? Might it have been even stronger? How?

3. Look for examples of defective reasoning in the letters-to-the-editor section of your local newspaper. Bring them to class for discussion.

APPLICATION

1. Find a news story that interests you. Taking the information provided, (1) show how you might use this information as evidence in a persuasive speech, (2) structure a proof that would make use of this evidence, and (3) design an argument in which this proof might be functional.

2. In *The Ethics of Rhetoric* Richard Weaver observed that frequent arguments over the definitions of basic terms in the major premises of enthymemes are a sign of social and cultural division. Look for examples of public argument over the definition of one of the following terms:

a. community-based schooling

b. welfare

c. tax fairness

d. abortion

e. gun control

f. alternative lifestyles

g. political correctness

Do the arguments reflect the kind of social division Weaver suggested?

3. Will your next persuasive speech develop both deductive and inductive patterns of argument? Which will it emphasize and why? Will you make any use of analogical argument? Why or why not?

NOTES

1. See Walter R. Fisher, "Toward a Logic of Good Reasons," *Quarterly Journal of Speech* 64 (1978): 376–84; and Karl R. Wallace, "The Substance of Rhetoric: Good Reasons," *Quarterly Journal of Speech* 49 (1963): 239–249.

2. Representative of this scholarship is Ernest G. Bormann. "Fantasy and Rhetorical Vision: The Rhetorical Criticism of Social Reality," *Quarterly Journal of Speech* 58 (1972): 396–407; Walter F. Fisher, "Narration as a Human Communication Paradigm: The Case of Public Moral Argument," *Communication Monographs* 51 (1984): 1–22; Michael C. McGee, "In Search of 'The People': A Rhetorical Alternative," *Quarterly Journal of Speech* 61 (1975): 235–249; Michael Osborn. "Rhetorical Depiction." in *Form, Genre and the Study of Political Discourse,* ed. Herbert W. Simons and Aram A. Aghazarian (Columbia: University of South Carolina Press, 1986), pp. 79–107; Janice Hocker Rushing, "The Rhetoric of the American Western Myth," *Communication Monographs* 50 (1983): 14–32.

3. Antonio R. Damasio, *Descartes' Error: Emotion, Reason, and the Human Brain* (New York: Putnam, 1994).

4. From a brochure distributed by Handgun Control, Inc., 1225 Eye Street NW, Washington, DC 20005, 1990.

5. Martha Solomon, "The 'Positive Woman's' Journey: A Mythic Analysis of the Rhetoric of STOP ERA," *Quarterly Journal of Speech* 65 (1979): 262–274.

6. Rushing, pp. 14–32.

7. Roderick P. Hart, *The Political Pulpit* (West Lafayette, IN: Purdue University Press, 1977).

8. John Fitzgerald Kennedy, "Acceptance Address, 1960," *The Great Society: A Sourcebook of Speeches,* ed. Glenn R. Capp (Belmont, CA: Dickenson, 1969), p. 14.

9. See his discussion in *The Uses of Argument* (London: Cambridge University Press, 1958) and in Stephen Toulmin, Richard Rieke, and Allan Janik, *An Introduction to Reasoning,* 2nd ed. (New York: Macmillan, 1984).

10. Cesar Chavez, "Pesticides Speech," *Contemporary American Speeches: A Sourcebook of Speech Forms and Principles,* ed. Richard L. Johannesen, R. R. Allen, and Wil A. Linkugel, 7th ed. (Dubuque, IA: Kendall/Hunt, 1992), pp. 210–213.

11. Lisa M. Ross, "Buckley Says Drug Attack Won't Work," *Commercial Appeal* (Memphis, TN), 14 Sept. 1989, p. B-2.

12. Mortimer B. Zuckerman, "The Enemy Within," *U.S. News & World Report,* 11 Sept. 1989, p. 91.

13. Gilbert Cranberg, "Even Sensible Iowa Bows to the Religious Right," *Los Angeles Times,* 17 Aug. 1992, p. B-5.

14. Michael M. Osborn, "The Abuses of Argument," *Southern Speech Communication Journal* 49 (1983): 1–11.

15. Howard Kahane, *Logic and Contemporary Rhetoric: The Use of Reason in Everyday Life,* 5th ed. (Belmont, CA: Wadsworth, 1988), p. 38.

16. *Newsweek,* 30 Jan. 1995, p. 17.

17. Joe Foss, "The Right to Bear Arms," speech presented to the National Press Club, Washington, D. C., 14 Mar. 1989 (C-Span transcript of the telecast of the speech).

Reduce, Refuse, Reuse
James Cardoza

Jim Cardoza's clever opening gains attention and creates identification by referring to a shared cultural experience. He invites listeners to confirm from their own experience the urgency of environmental problems. He relies on an unstated major premise which reconstructed might read, "We have a responsibility to protect the environment in which we live from serious pollution."

Jim presents himself as an example of how people can change their environmental habits for the better. His simple formula — Reduce, Refuse, Reuse — is well designed to stick in audience memory.

Jim uses inductive argument to confirm his minor premise, "Pollution of our environment has risen to a serious level." He reminds listeners of the evidence from a previous speech, and adds other facts, statistics, and testimony to prove that the problem is serious. Vivid images, such as picturing the annual amount of discarded pa-

"It isn't easy being green." Recognize this line? Kermit, the frog? Right? One of the Muppets? You got it! Those of us who were raised on Sesame Street know that Kermit's song was all about what it's like to be different — what it's like to be green in a world that isn't. But I want to apply this line in a different context — a context in which it's equally applicable. I want to tell you how "it isn't easy being green" in an ecological, environmental sense.

The environment is very important to me. I enjoy camping and hiking and fishing. To me, being outside and enjoying nature is the ultimate high. But sometimes, being outside has its downside. Have you ever been walking through the woods, thinking you've gotten away from it all — that you've found Nirvana — and then tripped over a beer can? Have you ever wandered down to a river, only to find its beauty spoiled by an old used tire lying on the bottom of the stream? Have you ever gone to the beach for the day, only to find that you couldn't swim because the water was polluted by discarded garbage? Have you ever had trouble seeing the distant mountains because of the smog? Or, worse yet, had trouble breathing the foul air? Well, I have. And it's things like this that have turned me into a budding environmentalist.

At first, it wasn't so "easy being green." I had to break some old, bad habits to stop being part of the pollution problem myself. But then it began to get easier, and by now it's almost become second nature to me. Today I want to share with you why environmental pollution is such a problem and what you can do to help solve it. I want to let you know how you can make it "easier being green" by following what I call "the three R's of environmental stewardship: REDUCE . . . REFUSE . . . REUSE. REDUCE the amount of energy you use. REFUSE to buy products that are environmentally unsound or to shop at stores that aren't environmentally friendly. And REUSE by finding additional uses for things you already have and recycling all that you can.

I don't think that many of us in this room would deny that environmental pollution is a problem. We've already heard a speech that pointed out the dangers of the greenhouse effect. Let me add some fuel to the fire.

According to *U.S. News and World Report,* in 1991 six hundred and sixty-seven pounds of garbage was collected for every mile of beach in the United States. There are more than 28,000 miles of beach in the United States, so that's almost nineteen million pounds of garbage. Just from beaches alone! And that's just the tip of the wasteberg. Figures released by the Environmental Protection Agency as reported in the *Environmental Almanac* show that the average U.S. citizen produces more than one-half ton of solid waste each year. With a population of almost 260 million people, that's over 130 million tons of waste per year. Can you picture how

per as a twelve-foot-high wall stretching from New York to Los Angeles, dramatize the problem.

Jim anticipates audience reactions to his inductive proof as a transition into the solution phase of his speech. As he discusses the first part of his plan, he begins by defining terms. He offers excellent advice on how to "reduce." Missing from his speech is analogical argument that might show how similar programs have been effective in reducing energy consumption. As he concludes the first part of his proposal, he makes good use of prestige testimony.

much trash that is? The writing paper alone that we throw out each year is enough to build a twelve-foot-high wall from Los Angeles to New York.

The situation with water isn't much better. According to the *1994 Information Please Almanac,* nearly half of our rivers are too polluted to support their intended uses for drinking water, recreation, or fisheries. And how about the air we breathe? The almanac tells us that this too is getting worse, with cars accounting for over half of all air pollution in the country. Furthermore, *Time* magazine warns us that air pollution can reduce life spans as much as two years, even in areas that meet current federal air quality standards.

"Enough already," I hear you thinking, "Okay, so we have a problem. What can we do?" Let's look at these "three R's" one at a time — REDUCE, REFUSE, REUSE. [Puts up posterboard with the words REDUCE, REFUSE, and REUSE.] The first "R" of environmental stewardship stands for REDUCE. And I'm not talking about your weight. I'm talking about the amount of energy you consume by driving too much and by using too much gas and electricity in your home.

Driving. Need something from the store four blocks from your apartment? What do you do? Jump in the car and drive over. Drive to campus. Drive to work. Drive when you go out on dates. Drive home for a weekend. Drive out in the country just for the fun of it. Drive, drive, drive, drive, drive! It's our national passion. What are your options? Take the bus to school and you won't have to worry about parking. Carpool with other students or co-workers. Get a bike and use it. Walk anyplace that's closer than a mile or two. Exercise is good for you. Reduce the amount of energy you use by driving sparingly and keeping your car in good repair. And when you're lucky enough to get a new car, get one that's energy efficient and has good pollution controls.

"Well, all right," you may be thinking, "I know I can drive less, but what about electricity and gas. I don't want to be uncomfortable." You don't have to be. Here are some simple things you can do to save energy — and, I might add, money. Set your thermostat a little lower in the winter and a little higher in the summer, then dress for comfort. Keep it no higher than 68° in the winter and no lower than 78° in the summer. When you go to bed or leave your apartment for any length of time — even just for the day at school or work, adjust your thermostat. In the winter, set it down to about 60° and in the summer set it up to about 85°. It will heat back up or cool back down quickly when you return.

Buy a fan. Ceiling fans are especially good because they help move the warm air down in the winter and keep you cooler in the summer. You can buy one for less than $30.00 and install it yourself. Some other things you can do. Turn down the thermostat on your water heater to 130 degrees. It runs all the time, and heating water is generally the second largest energy user in the home. Use that microwave for more than just reheating coffee. It's far more energy efficient than your stove. Turn off the TV unless you are watching a program. Buy energy-efficient light bulbs and turn off the lights when you leave a room. These may sound like little things, but re-

As he moves to the second point, Jim continues to anticipate the reactions of his listeners. His speech is well adapted. He uses examples to illustrate his proposal to buy products with the recycling logo. He "names names" of stores that are committed to saving the environment. Still missing is an analogical argument showing how the reforms might meet the need.

member, little things add up to big savings. The eighteenth-century British statesman Edmund Burke once said, "Nobody made a greater mistake than he who did nothing because he could only do a little."

Now, let's move on to the second "R" of environmental stewardship: REFUSE. Do you remember back in grade school being told, "Just say no!" Well, do it! Just say no to products that are environmentally unsound! Just say no to merchants that don't demonstrate an environmental consciousness! Just say no! Money talks.

For starters, learn to recognize the recycling logo [shows small poster with logo] and buy products that carry this symbol. Buy paper products made from recycled paper. They're not much more expensive. For example, this notebook [shows notebook] made of recycled paper costs just ten cents more than one not made with recycled paper. Think of that dime as your gift to the environment. Learn what companies support environmental causes and choose their products. For example, did you know that Kellogg's has packaged its corn flakes in boxes made from recycled paper since 1906? Buy paper products that are unbleached or bleached without chlorine. Buy products with the least amount of packaging. Don't buy six-packs of drinks with plastic rings.

Be selective about where you spend your money. Find stores that encourage recycling. Anderton's Supermarket will give you three cents for every used grocery bag you return and reuse. That'll make up for that dime you lost on the notebook! Some stores have recycling facilities for bottles, cans, and paper right on the premises. Some even offer shoppers information on consumer and environmental concerns. For example, the Safeway supermarkets in northern California polled customers about the importance of environmentally friendly products and packaging, and whether they'd like more information about steps they could take at home. The result? More people wanted information on recycling than wanted free recipes.

So much for groceries, now on to fast foods places. Watch out for styrofoam. It isn't biodegradable. Patronize places that use paper instead of plastic. And let manufacturers and merchants know your feelings. Money talks. Hit them where it hurts — hit them in the pocketbook.

Jim seems most successful as he presents the "reuse" part of his program of reform. He relates the problem closely to his audience as he discusses the use of disposable cups by "the average college student." Listing universities that have developed successful "use your own mug" programs lays the groundwork for the kind

Now, the third "R" of environmental stewardship — REUSE. Buy and use products that are reusable or recyclable. Did you know that the average American college student goes through 500 disposable cups every year? Carry a mug in your backpack and you can cut that number down to nothing. Other students do it. The University of North Carolina, the University of Vermont, Furman, UCLA, James Madison, and the University of Illinois all have successful "use your own mug" programs. Maintain and repair what you already have rather than replacing it. Rinse out plastic bags and reuse them.

Find innovate ways to reuse. Cut up scrap paper for scratch paper. Use both sides of computer paper when working on rough drafts of term papers. Then save what is left for recycling. Every ton of recycled office paper saves 380 gallons of gas. Read the newspaper at the library. Swap maga-

of analogical argument needed for this speech to be most effective. However, Jim needed to provide more detail on the success of these programs. He uses inductive argument effectively to suggest the possible signficance of his proposal. He points out how recycling a ton of paper means saving 380 gallons of gasoline and significant space in land fills. Perhaps his most striking demonstration comes when he paints the magnitude of improperly disposed of oil each year in this country: equal, he says, "to 35 Exxon Valdez oil spills."

Jim develops an elegant conclusion that repeats his "3 R's" and ties the ending of his speech to its beginning. The poetic conclusion of the speech — Stein's parody of the witches' speech from *Macbeth* — is quite effective.

zines with friends. Donate anything usable that you no longer need to a thrift shop. Someone else may have a good use for it. Another old adage that still holds true, "Waste not, want not."

Finally, recycle your recyclables. According to the *Washington Times*, more than 40 percent of landfill material comes from paper, so recycling paper is the single most effective thing we can do to reduce waste. Each ton of recycled paper saves 3.3 cubic yards of space at the local dump. Recycling paper also saves trees. Wastepaper represents the largest untapped forest in the world. Recycled paper gets reused as newsprint, stationary products, boxes, and insulation. Recycled bottles and cans are redeemable for cash. Recycled plastics show up in cars, carpets, and clothes. Even used tires can be recycled. Over 84 percent of used tires are landfilled, stockpiled, or illegally dumped when they could be retreaded or recycled into asphalt for highway construction or mixed with soil for athletic playing fields. Be sure when you get new tires that your old ones are recycled.

And last, but not least, be sure that when you get an oil change, the old oil is disposed of properly, preferably by being recycled. Do you remember how horrified we were when the Exxon Valdez spilled over 11 million gallons of crude oil in Prince William Sound in Alaska, gravely damaging one of the world's most fragile ecosystems? Well, just listen to this. Each year the amount of improperly disposed of oil in this country is equal to 35 — that's right, 35! — Exxon Valdez oil spills. Each quart of improperly disposed of motor oil can contaminate two million gallons of drinking water.

In closing, let me urge you to do your part in the battle against pollution. REDUCE, REFUSE, AND REUSE. It isn't always easy being green. It may be a little inconvenient, but it will be well worth it in the long run. Let me close by sharing with you a poem from an editorial cartoon I clipped out of the paper several years ago. It drives home the importance of this problem and our need to do something about it. The poem was written by Ed Stein of the *Rocky Mountain News* (with apologies to William Shakespeare):

Double, double toil and trouble, fire burn and cauldron bubble.
Toxic waste and PCBs, bring on suffering and disease.
Acid rain and nuclear spills, infect all with assorted ills.
Leach into the lake and river, poison both the lung and liver.
Spread this waste upon the land, into the flesh of child and man.
By the damage man has done, something wicked this way comes.

WORKS CONSULTED

Browning-Ferris Industries and Earthwatch 3. "One Hundred Things You Can Do For Our Planet." Undated Brochure.

"Database." *U.S. News and World Report*, 15 June 1992: 10.

The Earthworks Group. *Fifty Simple Things You Can Do to Save the Earth*. Berkeley, CA: Earthworks Press, 1989.

Information Please Almanac. Boston: Houghton Miffllin, 1994.

Innerst, Carol. "Students Try Cupfuls of Concern." *The Washington Times* 12 Aug. 1991: A5.

National Issues Forums Institute. *The Environment at Risk: Responding to Growing Dangers.* Dayton: The Kettering Foundation, 1989.

Parfit, Michael. "Troubled Waters Run Deep." *National Geographic,* Nov. 1993: 78–88.

Pisik, Betsy. "Concern for the Environment a Top-Shelf Item for Grocers." *The Washington Times* 23 Mar. 1993: C3.

Wetzstein, Cheryl. "'Waste Not, Want Not' Is Good Advice, Might Soon Be Law." *The Washington Times* 8 Feb. 1991: C3.

World Resources Institute. *The 1992 Information Please Environmental Almanac.* Boston: Houghton Mifflin, 1992.

CHAPTER 15

Ceremonial Speaking

THIS CHAPTER WILL HELP YOU

- appreciate the importance of ceremonial speaking.
- use the techniques of identification and magnification in ceremonial speeches.
- present speeches of tribute, acceptance, introduction, and inspiration.
- prepare a toast or an after–dinner speech.
- act as a master of ceremonies.

[People] who celebrate . . . are fused with each other and fused with all things in nature.

— Ernst Cassirer

Your college has reached a great moment in its history. It has just concluded an ambitious fund-raising campaign to create scholarships and attract outstanding teachers, researchers, artists, and lecturers. As the leader of student volunteers who spent many hours telephoning for contributions, you have been invited to be master of ceremonies at a banquet celebrating the campaign. At the banquet you may both present and listen to many kinds of speeches: speeches of tribute, speeches conferring awards, speeches accepting awards, speeches of introduction, speeches of inspiration, and after-dinner speeches. During the evening there will be moments both of seriousness and of hilarity. They are all part of what we call ceremonial speaking.

There are other occasions when you may be called on to make a ceremonial speech. You may be asked to "say a few words" for a co-worker or former teacher who is retiring, to toast a friend's wedding or anniversary, to welcome newcomers to an organization or community, or to present a eulogy for a dear friend or family member. Although your remarks at such times may be brief, ceremonial speaking is an important part of our lives.

It is very easy to underestimate the importance of ceremonial speaking. After all, informative speaking shares knowledge, and persuasive speaking affects our attitudes and actions. In comparison, ceremonial speaking, with its occasional moments of humor or inspiration, may not seem that significant. Only when we look beneath the surface does the true importance of ceremonial speaking appear. **Ceremonial speaking** stresses the sharing of identities and values that unites people into communities.[1] The philosopher John Dewey observed that people "live in a community in virtue of the things which they have in common; and communication is the way in which they come to possess things in common. What they must have in common . . . are aims, beliefs, aspirations, knowledge — a common understanding. . . ."[2] It is ceremonial speaking that celebrates and reinforces our common aims, beliefs, and aspirations.

Ritual and ceremony are important to all groups because they draw people together.[3] Ceremonial speaking imprints the meaning of a community on its members by providing larger-than-life pictures of their identity and ideals.[4] It answers four basic questions: "Who are we?" "Why are we?" "What have we accomplished?" and "What can we become together?" As it answers these questions, ceremonial speaking provides people with a sense of purpose and helps create an "ordered, meaningful cultural world."[5]

Ceremonial speaking also serves a very practical purpose. As our opening example indicates, ceremonies put the spotlight on the speaker. As you conduct the college's celebration of its fund-raising campaign as master of ceremonies, others will be looking at you and thinking, "Wouldn't he make a good student body president?" or "Wouldn't she be a fine candidate for city council?" From the time of Aristotle, scholars have recognized that ceremonial speaking puts leadership on display.[6]

Ceremonial speeches also serve to establish standards for action or provide the ethical and moral basis for future arguments.[7] Because such speaking centers on the values and beliefs within the traditions of a community, it contributes to the integration phase of persuasion described in Chapter 13. In this chapter we discuss the techniques and major forms of ceremonial speaking.

TECHNIQUES OF CEREMONIAL SPEAKING

Many of the techniques of ceremonial speaking are simply variations on those we have already discussed. Two techniques, however, deserve special attention: identification and magnification.

Identification

We have defined **identification** as the creation of close feelings among the members of the audience and between the audience and the speaker. Because the function of ritual and ceremony is to draw people closer together, identification is the heart of ceremonial speaking. Without it, ceremonial speaking cannot achieve its desired effects. Speakers may promote such identification through the use of narratives, through the recognition of heroes, or through a renewal of group commitment.

The Use of Narrative. Ceremonial speaking is the time for reliving shared golden moments. For example, if you were preparing a speech for the fund-raising celebration, you could recall certain things that happened during those long evenings when student volunteers were making their calls. You might remember moments of discouragement, followed by other moments of triumph, when the contributions were especially large or meaningful. Your story would reflect the meaning of the celebration and would be a tribute both to donors and to the student volunteers who endured frustration and discouragement on their way to success. Stories that have a light touch of humor are especially effective:

> I don't think that any of us will forget the night that John tripped over a phone cord while carrying a tray full of coffee and shorted out the computer network for the phone bank. Although many contributors got "cut off" by the accident, the returned calls netted the highest contributions of any night of the campaign.

Just be certain your humorous stories don't embarrass the people involved.

The Recognition of Heroes and Heroines. As you speak of the trials and triumphs of fund raising, you may want to single out people who made outstanding contributions, but be careful! If everyone worked hard, you risk leaving out people who deserves recognition. This omission could create resentment, a divisive feeling that defeats identification. Therefore, *recognize specific individuals only when they have made truly unusual contributions or when they are representative.* You might say, for instance,

> Let me tell you about Mary Tyrer. She is just one of the many who for the last two months have spent night after night on these phones — talking, coaxing, winning friends for our school, and raising thousands of dollars in contributions. Mary, and all the others like you, we salute you!

Renewal of Group Commitment. Ceremonial speaking is a time both for celebrating what has been accomplished and for renewing commitments to future endeavors. Share with your listeners a vision of what the future can be like for your college if their commitment continues. Plead with them not to be satisfied with present accomplishments. Renew their identity as a group moving toward even greater goals.

In his first inaugural address, delivered on the eve of the Civil War, Abraham Lincoln used the technique of identification in an effort to reunite the nation:

> I am loath to close. We are not enemies, but friends. We must not be enemies. Though passion may have strained, it must not break our bonds of affection. The mystic chords of memory, stretching from every battle-field, and patriot grave, to every living heart and hearthstone, all over this broad land, will yet swell the chorus of the Union, when again touched, as surely they will be, by the better angels of our nature.[8]

Magnification

In the *Rhetoric* Aristotle noted that selecting certain features of a person or event and dwelling on them magnifies them until they fill the minds of listeners and seem to characterize the subject. This technique of **magnification** emphasizes the values the features represent. For example, imagine that you are preparing a speech honoring Jesse Owens's incredible track and field accomplishments in the 1936 Olympic Games. In your research you come up with a variety of facts, such as:

- He had a headache the day he won the medal in the long jump.
- He had suffered from racism in America.
- He did not like the food served at the Olympic training camp.
- He won his four gold medals in front of Adolf Hitler, who was preaching the racial superiority of Germans.
- Some of his friends did not want him to run for the United States.
- After his victories he returned to further discrimination in America.

If you used all this information, your speech might seem aimless. Which of these items should you focus on, and how should you proceed? To make your selection you need to know what themes are best to develop when you are magnifying the actions of a person. These themes include:

1. Overcoming obstacles
2. Unusual accomplishment
3. Superior performance
4. Pure, unselfish motives
5. Benefit to society

As you consider these themes, it becomes clear which items about Jesse Owens you should magnify and how you should go about it. To begin, you would stress that Owens *had to overcome obstacles* such as racism in America to make the Olympic team. Then you would point out that his *accomplishment was unusual*, that no one else had ever won four gold medals in Olympic track and field competition. Moreover, *the performance was superior*, resulting in world records that lasted many years. Because Owens received no material gain from his victories, *his motives were pure*, his performance driven solely by personal qualities such as courage, competitiveness, and determination. Finally, you would demonstrate that because his victories repudiated Hitler's racist ideology, causing the Nazi leader public humiliation, *Owens's accomplishments benefited our society*. The overall effect would be to magnify the meaning of Jesse Owens's great performances both for himself and for his nation.

In addition to focusing on these basic themes, magnification relies on effective uses of language to create dramatic word pictures. *Metaphor* and *simile* can magnify a subject through creative associations, such as, "He seemed like a lightning bolt that day." *Parallel phrasing,* the repetition of key words and phrases that we first discussed in Chapter 7, can also help magnify a subject and embed it in our minds. For example, if you were to say of Mother Teresa, "Whenever there was hurt, she was there. Whenever there was hunger, she was there. Whenever there was human need, she was there," you would be magnifying her dedication and selflessness. This technique should make those qualities seem to resonate in the minds of listeners.

Magnification also favors certain speech designs over others. Comparison and contrast designs promote magnification by making selected features stand out. For example, you might contrast the purity of Owens's motives with those of today's well-paid athletes. Historical designs enhance magnification by dramatizing certain events as stories unfold over time. The causation design serves magnification when a person's accomplishments are emphasized as the causes of important effects: Jesse Owens's victories, a speaker might say, *caused* Nazi propaganda to lose its appeal for many people. Whatever designs ceremonial speeches use, it is important that *they build to a conclusion.* Speakers should save their best stories, their most telling points, until the end of the speech. Ceremonial speeches must never dwindle to a conclusion.

TYPES OF CEREMONIAL SPEECHES

Ceremonial speeches include the speech of tribute (including award presentations, eulogies, and toasts), acceptance speeches, the speech of introduction, the speech of inspiration, and the after-dinner speech.

The Speech of Tribute

Had you developed a speech honoring Jesse Owens's Olympic victories, you would have prepared a **speech of tribute.** The speech of tribute, which may center on a person or an event, recognizes and celebrates accomplishments. For example, you might be called on to honor a former teacher at a retirement ceremony, present an award to someone for an outstanding accomplishment, eulogize a person who has died, or propose a toast to a friend who is getting married.

Accomplishments and events are usually celebrated for two reasons. First, they are important in themselves: the influence of the teacher may have contributed to the success of many of her former students. Second, they are important as symbols. The planting of the American flag at Iwo Jima during some of the most intense fighting of World War II came to symbolize the fortitude of the entire American war effort; it represented commitment and was more important as a symbol than as an actual event. Sometimes the same event may be celebrated for both actual and symbolic reasons. A student speech honoring the raising of $60 million for famine relief celebrated this achievement both as a symbol of global generosity and for the actual help it brought to many starving people. When you plan

FIGURE 15.1

Types of Ceremonial
Speeches

Type	Use When
Tributes	You wish to honor a person, group, occasion, or event. Subtypes include award presentations, eulogies, and toasts. Focuses on contributions or achievements that are unique, superior, and of benefit to society.
Acceptance	You need to acknowledge an award or honor. Acceptances should be made with graciousness and humility.
Introductions	You must introduce a featured speaker in a program. Establish the speaker's ethos without embarrassing him or her.
Inspiration	You want to motivate listeners to appreciate and commit to a goal, purpose, or set of values. May be religious, commercial, political, or social in nature.
After-dinner	You want to entertain the audience while leaving a message that acts as a guide for future behavior. Should be short and contain touches of light humor.
Master of Ceremonies	You must coordinate a program and see that everything runs smoothly. The master of ceremonies sets the mood for the occasion.

a speech of tribute, you should consider both the actual and the symbolic values that are represented.

Developing Speeches of Tribute.　As you prepare a speech of tribute, there are several guidelines that you should keep in mind. First, *do not exaggerate the tribute*. If you are too lavish with your praise or use too many superlatives, you may embarrass the recipient. Second, *focus on the person being honored*, not on yourself. Even if you know what effort the accomplishment required because you have done something similar, don't mention that at this time. It will just seem as though you are tooting your own horn when the focus should be on the honoree. Third, *create vivid, concrete images of accomplishments*. Speeches of tribute are occasions for illustrating what someone has accomplished, the values underlying those accomplishments, and their consequences. Tell stories that make those accomplishments come to life. Finally, *be sincere*. Speeches of tribute are a time for warmth, pride, and appreciation. Your manner should reflect these qualities as you present the tribute.

Award Presentations.　Whenever you present an award, you often accompany it with a speech of tribute. An **award presentation** recognizes the achievements or contributions of those on whom it is bestowed. Most award presentations have two main points that explain: (1) the nature of the award and (2) what the recipient did to qualify for it.

Unless the award is quite well known, such as an Oscar or Nobel Prize, you should always begin an award presentation by talking about the nature of the award. At the very least you should name the award and tell why it is given. For example, you might say:

> Mary Beth Peterson was a graduate assistant in this department who exemplified the best qualities of a teacher: enthusiasm for her subject, the ability to impart it to others, and a real sense of caring for those whom she taught. After her untimely death, her parents and friends endowed the Mary Beth Peterson award, offered each year to the graduate assistant in our department who best exemplifies the qualities Mary Beth brought so generously to the classroom.

The second and most important part of an award presentation involves explaining why the honoree was chosen to receive the award. In talking about the recipient, you should emphasize the uniqueness, superiority, and benefits of his or her achievements. Provide specific examples that illustrate these accomplishments. Finally, you should name the recipient of the award and offer your sincere congratulations and wishes for continued success. The complete text of an award presentation to Olympic track gold medalist Wilma Rudolph may be found at the end of this chapter.

Eulogies. Earlier we asked you to imagine yourself preparing a speech to honor Jesse Owens. Following his death in 1980, many such speeches were actually presented. A speech of tribute presented upon the death of a person is called a **eulogy**. The following comments by Congressman Thomas P. O'Neill, Jr., then Speaker of the House, illustrate how some of the major techniques we have discussed can work in a eulogy:

O'Neill's opening highlights the themes of unusual and superior accomplishment. He begins with the actual value of Owens's victories, and then describes their symbolic value.

> . . . I rise on the occasion of his passing to join my colleagues in tribute to the greatest American sports hero of this century, Jesse Owens. . . . His performances at the Berlin Olympics earned Jesse Owens the title of America's first superstar. . . .
>
> No other athlete symbolized the spirit and motto of the Olympics better than Jesse Owens. "Swifter, higher, stronger" was the credo by which Jesse Owens performed as an athlete and lived as an American. Of his performances in Hitler's Berlin in 1936, Jesse said: "I wasn't running against Hitler, I was running against the world." Owens's view of the Olympics was just that: He was competing against the best athletes in the world without regard to nationality, race, or political view. . . .
>
> Jesse Owens proved by his performances that he was the best among the finest the world had to offer, and in setting the world record in the 100-yard dash, he became the "fastest human" even before that epithet was fashionable. . . .

These comments magnify the values represented by Owens's life and develop the theme of benefit to the community.

> In life as well as on the athletic field Jesse Owens was first an American, and second, an internationalist. He loved his country; he loved the opportunity his country gave him to reach the pinnacle of athletic prowess. In his own quiet, unassuming, and modest way — by example, by inspiration, and by performance — he helped other young people to aim for the stars, to develop their God-given potential. . . .

That Owens remained a patriotic American in the face of racism and indifference magnifies his character.

O'Neill's conclusion emphasizes the symbolic, spiritual values of Owens's life.

As the world's first superstar Jesse Owens was not initially overwhelmed by commercial interests and offered the opportunity to become a millionaire overnight. There was no White House reception waiting for him on his return from Berlin, and as Jesse Owens once observed: "I still had to ride in the back of the bus in my hometown in Alabama."

Can one individual make a difference? Clearly in the case of Jesse Owens the answer is a resounding affirmative, for his whole life was dedicated to the elimination of poverty, totalitarianism, and racial bigotry; and he did it in his own special and modest way, a spokesman for freedom, an American ambassador of good will to the athletes of the world, and an inspiration to young Americans. . . . Jesse Owens was a champion all the way in a life of dedication to the principles of the American and Olympic spirit.[9]

When presented at memorial services, eulogies should also express the pain of loss and offer comfort.[10] At the funeral of young Ryan White, a hemophiliac who had contracted AIDS from a blood transfusion, the Rev. Raymond Probasco comforted mourners with this reflection:

. . . Ryan and his family always believed there would be a miracle. But that didn't happen. I believe God gave us that miracle in Ryan. He healed a wounded spirit in the world and made it whole. . . . He helped us to care and to believe that with God's help, nothing is impossible, even for a kid. . . . With God's help, and each of yours, we'll make AIDS a disease and not a dirty word.[11]

Eulogies presented by family members are usually brief and focus on the personal characteristics of the deceased. At the funeral of the assassinated Israeli Prime Minister Yitzhak Rabin, his teen-aged granddaughter, Noa Ben-Artzi, presented the following eulogy:

The speaker focuses on the personal characteristics of the deceased. Note the use of archetypal metaphors, the Biblical allusion, and the connection to the Holocaust which relate Rabin to the mythos of the Jewish people.

This section reveals the speaker's personal struggle to understand what has happened and to place it somehow meaningfully in her life.

You will forgive me, but I do not want to talk about peace today. I want to talk about my grandfather.

Grandfather, you were the pillar of fire before the camp, and now we are just a camp left alone in the dark, and we're so cold. Very few people knew you truly. They can talk about you, but I feel they know nothing about the depth of the pain, the disaster and, yes, this holocaust, for — at least for us, the family and the friends, who are left only as the camp, without you, our pillar of fire.

People greater than I have already eulogized you, but no one knows the caress that you placed on my shoulder and the warm hug that you saved only for us and your half-smile that always told me so much — the same smile that is no more.

I harbor no feelings of revenge because the pain is too great. The ground was taken from under our feet, and we're trying somehow to make something of this void and have not yet succeeded. Grandpa, you were our hero. I want you to know that everything I did, I always saw you before me.

Your appreciation and your love escorted us through every way and road. You never abandoned us, and here you are, my eternal hero, cold and alone, and there's nothing I can do to save you. We love you, Grandfather, forever.[12]

The speaker concludes with a final good-bye to her grandfather.

The importance of sustaining a sense of community is especially critical after the loss of a valued member of the group. While the eulogy primarily mourns and honors the person who has died, it also celebrates the values of those who remain and helps them rededicate to what that person stood for.

Toasts. A lighter type of tribute is a **toast**, or brief words of praise for people or an occasion. You might be asked to toast a co-worker who has been promoted, a couple at a wedding reception, or simply to celebrate the beginning of a new year. The occasion may be formal or informal, but the message should always be eloquent. It simply won't do to mutter, "Here's to Tony, he's a great guy!" or "Cheers!" Such a feeble toast is "a gratuitous betrayal — of the occasion, its honoree, and the desire [of the audience] to clink glasses and murmur, 'Hear, hear' in appreciation of a compliment well fashioned."[13]

Whenever you think you might be called upon to offer a toast, plan your remarks in advance. Keep your toast brief. Select one characteristic or event that epitomizes your message, illustrate it with a short example, then conclude. You might toast the "coach of the year" in the following way:

I always knew that Larry was destined for greatness from the time he led our junior high basketball team to the city championship. In one game in that tournament, Larry scored twenty-eight points, scrambled for eight rebounds, and dished off thirteen assists. And he was only five feet two inches tall! Here's to Larry, coach of the year!

Because a toast is a speech of celebration, you should refrain from making negative remarks. For example, it would be inappropriate at a wedding reception to say, "Here's to John and Mary. I hope they don't end up in divorce court in a year as I did!" Although most speeches are best presented extemporaneously, a toast should be memorized. Practice presenting your toast with glass in hand until it flows easily. If you have difficulty memorizing your toast, it is probably too long. Cut it. Figure 15.2 presents samples of toasts for different occasions.[14]

Acceptance Speeches

If you are receiving an award or honor, you may be expected to respond with a **speech of acceptance.** A speech of acceptance should express gratitude for the honor and acknowledge those who made the accomplishment possible. In addition, a speech of acceptance should focus on the values the

FIGURE 15.2

Sample Short Toasts

> May you have warm words on a cold evening, a full moon on a dark night, and a road downhill all the way to your door. (Irish Blessing)

> May all your troubles during the coming year be as short-lived as your New Year's resolutions.

> To _____ and _____ (couple's names): May your house be too small to hold all your friends.

> May the hinges of friendship never grow rusty.

> May you live as long as you want and never want as long as you live.

> Here's to the love we give away for it's the only love we keep.

award represents and be presented in language that matches the dignity of the occasion.

Consider a situation in which you are awarded a scholarship by your hometown historical society. The award will be presented at a banquet, and you must make a public acceptance. You would not go amiss if you began with, "Thank you. I appreciate the honor of this award." Let others praise; you should remain modest. When Elie Wiesel was awarded the 1986 Nobel Peace Prize, he began his acceptance speech with these remarks: "It is with a profound sense of humility that I accept the honor you have chosen to bestow upon me."[15] (The complete text of his acceptance speech may be found in Appendix B.) Follow his lead and accept an award with grace and modesty.

In an acceptance speech you should also give credit where credit is due. If your hometown historical society is awarding you a scholarship, it would be appropriate for you to mention some teachers who prepared you for this moment. You might say something like, "This award belongs as much to Mr. Del Rio as it does to me. He opened my eyes to the importance and relevance of history in our world today." When Martin Luther King, Jr., accepted his Nobel Peace Prize in 1964, he did so in these words:

> I accept this prize on behalf of all men who love peace and brotherhood. . . . Most of these people will never make the headlines and their names will not appear in *Who's Who*. Yet when years have rolled past . . . men and women will know and children will be taught that we have a finer land, a better people, a more noble civilization — because these humble children of God were willing to suffer for righteousness' sake.[16]

As you accept an award, express your awareness of its deeper meaning. If you were accepting a history scholarship, you might wish to focus on the values of a liberal arts education and the contributions of history to our understanding of present-day problems. In their acceptance speeches, both

Election night victory celebrations give rise to speeches of acceptance which express gratitude and acknowledge those who made the accomplishment possible. Diane Feinstein celebrated election to the U.S. Senate by thanking her supporters.

Mr. Wiesel and Dr. King stressed the value of freedom and the importance of involvement — of overcoming hatred with loving concern. Finally, be sure the eloquence of your language fits the dignity of the situation. Your remarks should be carefully planned and worded appropriately. Slang and jokes are usually out of place because they might suggest that you do not value the award or take the occasion seriously.

The techniques of magnification are especially useful in speeches of acceptance. Dr. King relied heavily on an extended movement metaphor in his acceptance speech. He spoke of the "tortuous road" from Montgomery, Alabama, to Oslo, Norway, a road on which, in his words, "millions of Negroes are traveling to find a new sense of dignity." In a similar manner Mr. Wiesel told the story of a "young Jewish boy discovering the kingdom of night" during the Holocaust. This personal, metaphorical narrative was introduced early in the speech and repeated in the conclusion when Mr. Wiesel remarked, "No one is as capable of gratitude as one who has emerged from the kingdom of night." Although your rhetorical style may not be as eloquent as these Nobel Prize winners, you should make a presentation that befits the dignity of the occasion.

If an award is presented as part of a larger ceremony involving awards to several people, such as the Academy Awards or at a sports awards banquet, shorter acceptance speeches may be called for. Wilma Rudolph's brief words of acceptance on the National Sports Awards show were appropriate for that situation (see text at end of chapter). Be sure when you make an acceptance speech that you do not try to thank everyone by name you came

Making an Acceptance Speech

1 Be modest.

2 Express your appreciation for the honor.

3 Acknowledge those who made your accomplishment possible.

4 Highlight the values the award represents.

5 Be sure your language fits the formality of the occasion.

SPEAKER'S NOTES

into contact with in the course of your achievement. Such hollow tributes can trivialize the meaning of your speech.

The Speech of Introduction

One of the more common types of ceremonial speeches is the **speech of introduction**, in which you introduce a featured speaker to the audience. The importance of this speech can vary, depending on how well the speaker and listeners know each other. When both the person being introduced and the introducer are very well known, a formal introduction may seem superfluous and a light touch may be called for. For example, when the singer Madonna introduced Muhammad Ali at a recent gathering of New York sports personalities, she simply said:

> **We are alike in many ways. We have espoused unpopular causes, we are arrogant, we like to have our picture taken, and we are the greatest.**[17]

A good introduction will usually meet three goals. It will (1) make the speaker feel welcome, (2) establish or strengthen the ethos of the speaker, and (3) prepare the audience for the speech that will follow. You make a speaker feel welcome by both what you say and how you say it. Let the speaker know that the audience wants to hear the message and feels honored by his or her presence. For example, you might open with, "We feel very fortunate to have Kelvin Andrews as our guest today. We know how busy he is, so it's a special treat and a real compliment to us that he should be here." When such words are delivered with honest warmth and sincerity, the speaker should feel truly welcome.

Once you have welcomed the speaker, you can begin to establish or strengthen the speaker's ethos. As soon as you know you will be introducing a speaker, find out as much as you can about the person. Often guest speakers will provide a resume listing their experiences and accomplishments. Talk with the speaker beforehand to see what he or she would like you to emphasize. If this is not possible, or if the speaker is noncommittal ("Oh, just say anything you want to"), there are still some good guidelines to follow that will help create respect for the speaker and lay the groundwork for speaker-audience identification:

- Create respect by magnifying the speaker's main accomplishments.

- Don't be too lavish with your praise. An overblown introduction can be embarrassing and make it difficult for speakers to get into their messages. One featured speaker was so overcome by an excessive introduction that he responded, "If you do not go to heaven for charity, you will certainly go somewhere else for exaggeration or downright prevarication."[18]

- Mention achievements that are relevant to either the speaker's message, the occasion on which the speech is being presented, or the audience that has assembled.

- Be selective! If you try to present too many details and accomplishments, you may take up some of the speaker's time and make listeners weary. Introducers who drone on too long can create real problems for the speakers who follow.

You can lay the groundwork for speaker-audience identification by mentioning aspects of the speaker's background that are familiar to the audience. The following introduction welcomes the speaker, establishes her ethos, and humanizes her by talking about her family and her connection to the community where the speech is being presented:

> **Tonight's speaker is not only the state's foremost expert on criminal liability. As the mother of two children, Judge Polisky also shares our deep concern for the rights of children. Her grandfather lived in Maryville, and she tells me she still remembers our delicious Maryville strawberries that she enjoyed as a child. Let's welcome back Judge Mary Polisky and share her thoughts on the topic "Law and Disorder."**

The final function of an effective introduction is to tune the audience for the speech that will follow. In Chapter 4 we discussed how preliminary tuning can establish a mood, predisposing an audience to respond positively or negatively to a speech. You can tune the audience as you introduce a speaker by arousing a sense of anticipation in listeners and making them want to listen. However, this does not mean that you should preview the speech in your introduction. Unless you have special knowledge of what the speaker is going to say, previewing can create problems. You might miss the point completely, in which case the speaker may have to begin with a disclaimer. Even if you have seen the speech ahead of time and are aware of its content, leave the presentation to the speaker. *Introduce the speaker; don't present the speech.*

Introducing Featured Speakers

1 Be sure you know how to pronounce the speaker's name.

2 Find out what the speaker would like you to emphasize.

3 Focus on those parts of the speaker's background that are relevant to the topic, audience, and occasion.

4 Announce the title of the speech and tune the audience for it.

5 Make the speaker feel welcome. Be warm and gracious.

6 Be brief!

SPEAKER'S NOTES

The Speech of Inspiration

The **speech of inspiration** arouses an audience to appreciate, commit to, and pursue a goal, purpose, or set of values or beliefs. Speeches of inspiration help listeners see subjects in a new light. Inspirational speeches may be religious, commercial, political, or social. When a sales manager introduces a new product to marketing representatives, pointing up its competitive advantages and its glowing market potential, the speech is both inspirational and persuasive. The marketing reps should feel inspired to push that product with great zeal and enthusiasm. Speeches at political conventions that praise the principles of the party, such as keynote addresses, are inspirational in tone and intent. Major addresses at conferences, such as that presented by Hillary Rodham Clinton to the United Nations Fourth World Conference on Women at Beijing, China, are inspirational as well. So also are commencement addresses, such as that presented by Elizabeth Dole at Radcliffe when she was president of the American Red Cross. (See texts of the speeches by Ms. Clinton and Ms. Dole in Appendix B.) As different as these speech occasions may seem, they have important points in common.

First, speeches of inspiration are enthusiastic. Inspirational speakers accomplish their goals through their personal commitment and energy. Both the speaker and the speech must be active and forceful. Speakers must set an example for their audiences through their behavior both on and off the speaking platform. They must practice what they preach. Their ethos must be consistent with their advice.

Second, speeches of inspiration draw upon past successes and frustrations to encourage future accomplishment. At the 1995 Catalyst Awards Dinner, Sheila W. Welling, the president of that organization, evoked vivid memories of what the past was like for women, as she urged continued progress toward equality in the workplace in the new millennium:

> One hundred years ago, at the dawn of the last millennium, our bustled Victorian great-grandmothers could not run for a bus, let alone for Congress. If the race — as the Victorian poet claimed — went to the swift, women lost. Girdled, corseted, enveloped in yards of gingham and lace, women were balanced precariously on their pedestals.
>
> . . . Women couldn't vote when my mother was born. Every time I think about it, it startles me, even as Edith Wharton wrote her novels, as Helen Keller graduated from Radcliffe with honors, even as women manufactured the arms that led to victory in World War I and the nation's move to global primacy, women still could not vote.[19]

In the later years of his life, when his athletic prowess had faded, Jesse Owens became known as a great inspirational speaker. According to his obituary in the *New York Times*, "The Jesse Owens best remembered by many Americans was a public speaker with the ringing, inspirational delivery of an evangelist. . . . [His speeches] praised the virtues of patriotism, clean living and fair play."[20]

Third, speeches of inspiration revitalize our appreciation for values or beliefs. In the Owens speech that follows, the ideals of brotherhood, tolerance, and fair competition are stressed. Such speeches can strengthen our sense of mythos, the distinctive code of values underlying our society.

Speeches of Inspiration: An Illustration.   In his inspirational speeches to budding athletes, Jesse Owens frequently talked of his Olympic achievements. The following excerpts, taken from a statement protesting America's withdrawal from the 1980 Summer Olympic Games, illustrate his inspirational style. Jesse Owens was unable to deliver this message orally. It was prepared shortly before his death from cancer.

Owens's introduction suggests the larger meaning of his victories and sets the stage for identification.

What the Berlin games proved . . . was that Hitler's "supermen" could be beaten. Ironically, it was one of his blond, blue-eyed, Aryan athletes who helped do the beating.

I held the world record in the broad jump. Even more than the sprints, it was "my" event. Yet I was one jump from not even making the finals. I fouled on my first try, and playing it safe the second time, I had not jumped far enough.

Note the use of graphic detail to recapture the immediacy of the moment.

The broad jump preliminaries came before the finals of my other three events and everything, it seemed then, depended on this jump. Fear swept over me and then panic. I walked off alone, trying to gather myself. I dropped to one knee, closed my eyes, and prayed. I felt a hand on my shoulder. I opened my eyes and there stood my arch enemy, Luz Long, the prize athlete Hitler had kept under wraps while he trained for one purpose only: to beat me. Long had broken the Olympic mark in his very first try in the preliminaries.

Owens's use of dialogue helps listeners feel they are sharing the experience.

This narrative leaves open the meaning of

"I know about you," he said. "You are like me. You must do it all the way, or you cannot do it. The same that has happened to you today happened to me last year in Cologne. I will tell you what I did then."

Owens's "inside" victory: perhaps it was over self-doubt or his own stereotype of Germans. Perhaps it was *both*.

This scene presents an inspirational model of international competition.

Owens shows how individuals can rise above ideologies, as Long's final message invites identification.

Owens ends with a metaphor of the "road to the Olympics."

Luz told me to measure my steps, place my towel 6 inches on back of the takeoff board and jump from there. That way I could give it all I had and be certain not to foul.

As soon as I had qualified, Luz, smiling broadly, came to me and said, "Now we can make each other do our best in the finals."

And that's what we did in the finals. Luz jumped, and broke his Olympic record. Then I jumped just a bit further and broke Luz's new record. We each had three leaps in all. On his final jump, Luz went almost 26 feet, 5 inches, a mark that seemed impossible to beat. I went just a bit over that, and set an Olympic record that was to last for almost a quarter of a century.

I won that day, but I'm being straight when I say that even before I made that last jump, I knew I had won a victory of a far greater kind — over something inside myself, thanks to Luz.

The instant my record-breaking win was announced, Luz was there, throwing his arms around me and raising my arm to the sky. "Jazze Owenz!" he yelled as loud as he could. More than 100,000 Germans in the stadium joined in. "Jazze Owenz, Jazze Owenz, Jazze Owenz!"

Hitler was there, too, but he was not chanting. He had lost that day. Luz Long was killed in World War II and, although I don't cry often, I wept when I received his last letter — I knew it was his last. In it he asked me to someday find his son, Karl, and to tell him "of how we fought well together, and of the good times, and that any two men can become brothers."

That is what the Olympics are all about. The road to the Olympics does not lead to Moscow. It leads to no city, no country. It goes far beyond Lake Placid or Moscow, Ancient Greece or Nazi Germany. The road to the Olympics leads, in the end, to the best within us.[21]

The After-Dinner Speech

Occasions that celebrate special events or that mark the beginning or end of a process often call for an **after-dinner speech.** Political rallies, award banquets, the kickoff for a fund-raising campaign, or the end of the school year may provide the setting for such speaking.

The after-dinner speech is one of the great rituals of American public speaking and public life. In keeping with the nature of the occasion, after-dinner speeches should not be too difficult to digest. Speakers making these presentations usually do not introduce radical ideas that require listeners to rethink their values or that ask for dramatic changes in belief or behavior. Nor are such occasions the time for anger or negativity. They are a time for people to savor who they are, what they have done, or what they wish to do. A good after-dinner speech, however, leaves a message that can act as a vision to guide and inspire future efforts.

The Role of Humor.   Humor is an essential ingredient in most after-dinner speeches. In the introduction humor can place both the speaker and audience

Appropriately used humor can relax audiences. Speakers who tell amusing stories about themselves help build bonds of identification with an audience.

at ease.[22] It can also relieve tension. Enjoying lighter moments can remind us that there is a human element in all situations and that we should not take ourselves too seriously. At least one study has discovered that the use of humorous illustrations helps audiences remember the message of the speech.[23] In addition, humorous stories can create identification by building an "insider's" relationship between speaker and audience that draws them closer together. In sharing humor, the audience becomes a community of listeners.[24]

As we noted in Chapters 6 and 7, humor should not be forced on a speech. If you decide to begin with a joke simply because you think a speech should start that way, the humor may seem contrived and flat. Rather, humor must be functional, useful to make a point.

The humor in a speech is best developed out of the immediate situation. Dick Jackman, the director of corporate communications at Sun Company, opened an after-dinner speech at a National Football Foundation awards dinner with a pointed reference to the seating arrangements, and then warned those in the expensive seats under the big chandelier that it "had been installed by the low bidder some time ago." His speech also contained lighthearted references to well-known members of the audience, including some who were there to receive an award (the complete text appears in Appendix B). In her keynote address at the Democratic National Convention in 1988, Texas state treasurer Ann Richards used pointed humor as she took her party to task for not involving women more directly:

Twelve years ago Barbara Jordan, another Texas woman, . . . made the keynote address to the convention, and two women in 160 years is about par for the course.

> But if you give us a chance, we can perform. After all, Ginger Rogers did everything that Fred Astaire did. She just did it backwards and in high heels.[25]

Humor requires thought, planning, and caution to be effective in a speech. If it is not handled well, it can be a disaster. For example, religious humor is usually dangerous, and racist or sexist humor is absolutely forbidden. The first runs the risk of offending some members of the audience and can make the speaker seem intolerant. The second reveals a devastating truth about the speaker's character and can create such negative reactions from the audience that the rest of the speech doesn't stand a chance. In general, avoid any anecdotes that are funny at the expense of others.

Often the best kind of humor centers on speakers themselves. Speakers who tell amusing stories about themselves sometimes rise in the esteem of listeners.[26] When this technique is successful, the stories that seem to put speakers down are actually building them up. A rural politician once told the following story at a dinner on an urban college campus:

> You know, I didn't have good schooling like all of you have. I had to educate myself for public office. Along the way I just tried not to embarrass myself like another fellow from around here once did. This man wanted to run for Congress. So he came up here to your college to present himself to all the students and faculty. He worked real hard on a speech to show them all that he was a man of vision and high intellect.
>
> As he came to the end of his speech, he intoned very solemnly, "If you elect me to the United States Congress, I'll be like that great American bird, the eagle. I'll soar high and see far! I won't be like that other bird that buries its head in the sand, the oyster!" There was a wonderful reaction from the audience to that. So he said it again — said he wasn't going to be no oyster.
>
> Well, I've tried hard not to be an oyster as I represent you, even though I know there's some folks who'd say, "Well, you sure ain't no eagle, either!"[27]

This story, which led into a review of the politician's accomplishments, was warmly appreciated for both its humor and its modesty. It suggests that humor takes time to develop and must be rich in graphic detail to set up its punch line. The story would not have been nearly as effective had the speaker begun with, "Did you hear the one about the politician who didn't know an ostrich from an oyster?"

Developing an After-Dinner Speech. After-dinner speeches are more difficult to develop than their lightness and short length might suggest. Like any other speech, they must be carefully planned and practiced. They must have an effective introduction that commands attention right away, especially since some audience members may be more interested in talking to table companions than in listening to the speaker. After-dinner speeches should be more than strings of anecdotes to amuse listeners. The stories told must either establish a mood, convey a message, or carry a theme forward. Such speeches should build to a satisfying conclusion that conveys the essence of the message.

Above all, perhaps, after-dinner speeches should be mercifully brief. Long-winded after-dinner speakers can leave the audience fiddling with coffee cups and drawing pictures on napkins. After being subjected to such a speech, Albert Einstein once murmured: "I have just got a new theory of eternity."[28]

Master of Ceremonies

Quite often ceremonial speeches are part of a program of events that must be coordinated with skill and grace if things are to run smoothly. Being the master of ceremonies is no easy task. A speaker who served in such a capacity for a community program once noted:

> Being a master of ceremonies was sort of like having to stand up and juggle a dozen oranges in front of an audience. I just kept standing there, fumbling everything and waiting for the whole thing to be over with.[29]

It takes at least as much careful planning, preparation, and practice to function effectively as a master of ceremonies as it does to make a major presentation. As the **master of ceremonies** you will be expected to keep the program moving along, introduce participants, and possibly present awards. You will also set the tone or mood of the program.

If at all possible, you should be involved in planning the program from the beginning. Then you will have a better grasp of what is expected of you, what events have been scheduled, what the timetable is, who the featured speakers are, and what special logistics (such as meal service) you might have to deal with. The following guidelines should help you function effectively as a master of ceremonies:[30]

- *Know what is expected of you.* Why were you chosen to emcee the program? Remember, as emcee you are not the "star" of the program, but the person who brings it all together and makes it work.
- *Plan a good opener for the program.* Your opening remarks as an emcee are as important as the introduction to a major presentation. You should gain the attention of audience members and prepare them for the program. Be sure that the mood you set with your opener is consistent with the nature of the occasion.
- *Be prepared to introduce the participants.* Be sure you know who they are and can pronounce their names correctly. If you prepare the introductions for them, review the relevant material in this chapter. Find out all you can about them: check *Who's Who* and local newspaper clipping files, and talk to them directly as well as to organizers of the event to see what they want you to emphasize. If the introductions will be

prepared for you, be sure you get them far enough in advance so that you can convert them to your own oral style and practice presenting them (see the guidelines for oral style and manuscript presentations in Chapter 11).

■ *Be sure you know the schedule and timetable so that you can keep the program on track.* Also be sure that the participants get this information. They need to know how much time has been allotted for them to speak. Double check this with them before the program and work out some way to cue them in case they should run overtime. If time restrictions are severe (as in a televised program) be ready to edit and adapt your own planned comments.

■ *Make certain that any prizes or awards are kept near the podium.* You shouldn't be left fumbling around looking for a plaque or trophy at presentation time.

■ *Plan your comments ahead of time.* Develop a key-word outline for each presentation on a running script of the program. Print the name of the person or award in large letters at the top of each outline so that you can keep your place in the program.

■ *Practice your presentation.* Although you are not the featured speaker, your words are important (especially to the person you will introduce or who will receive the award you will present). Practice your comments the same way you would practice a speech.

■ *Make advance arrangements for mealtime logistics.* Speak with the maitre d' before the program to be sure the waiters know the importance of "silent service." If you will be speaking while people are still eating, adapt your message to cope with this distraction by using the attention-gaining techniques discussed in Chapters 7 and 12.

■ *Be ready for the inevitable glitches.* Despite your best efforts, Murphy's Law (If anything can go wrong, it will) will surely prevail. Be ready for problems like microphones that don't work or that squeal, trays of dishes that may be dropped, and people wandering in and out during the course of the program. As you respond to these events, keep your cool and good humor.

■ *End the program strongly.* Just as a speech should not dwindle into nothingness, neither should a program. Review the suggestions for speech conclusions in Chapter 7. Extend thanks to those who made the program possible, then leave the audience with something to remember.

The tribute to Wilma Rudolph (complete text at the end of this chapter) illustrates how one master of ceremonies, Tom Brokaw, performed that role. The text also provides examples of speeches of tribute and acceptance.

As you end this book, we would like to frame our own speech of tribute: this one to you. Public speaking may not have been easy for you. You may have overcome many obstacles to make it to this point. Hopefully, however, you have gained great value from the experience. Perhaps the three

basic metaphors that have emerged in this book have become realities for you, so that:

- you have learned how to climb above the barriers people sometimes initially raise among themselves,

- you have learned to build speeches that are noteworthy for both their power and their integrity, and

- you have learned to weave language into eloquent thoughts and evidence into persuasive patterns of ideas.

We propose a toast: May you use your new speaking skills to improve the lives and lift the spirits of all who may listen to you.

IN SUMMARY

Ceremonial speeches serve important social functions. They reinforce the values that hold people together in a community and give listeners a sense of order and purpose in their lives. They provide the major premises for later arguments and put the spotlight on leadership.

Major Techniques of Ceremonial Speaking. Two major techniques of ceremonial speaking are *identification* and *magnification*. The first creates close feeling, and the second selects and emphasizes those features of a subject that will convey the speaker's message. Themes worthy of magnification include overcoming obstacles, achieving unusual goals, performing in a superior manner, having pure motives, and benefiting the community.

Types of Ceremonial Speeches. *Speeches of tribute* may recognize the achievements of individuals or groups or commemorate special events. Speeches of tribute should help us understand and appreciate the values these achievements represent. Accomplishments and events may be significant in themselves or in what they symbolize. *Award presentations* should explain the nature of the award and what the recipient has done to merit it. *Eulogies* are speeches of tribute presented on the death of a person or persons. *Toasts* are minispeeches of tribute that may be given on special occasions. *Speeches of acceptance* should begin with an expression of gratitude and an acknowledgment of others who deserve recognition. They should focus on the values that the honor represents. Acceptance speeches often call for more formal language than other speeches and for simple eloquence that suits the occasion.

Speeches of introduction should welcome the speaker, establish his or her ethos, and tune the audience for the message to follow. Introductions should focus on information about the speaker that is relevant to the speech topic and the occasion or that has special meaning for the audience. *Speeches of inspiration* help listeners appreciate values and make them want to pursue worthy goals. Such speeches often call on stories of past successes. *After-dinner speeches* should be lighthearted, serving up humor and insight at the same time. Humor should be functional in such speeches, illustrating a point or serving some larger purpose.

The *master of ceremonies* coordinates a program and sees that things run smoothly. He or she sets the mood of the program, introduces the participants, provides transitions, and sometimes presents awards.

TERMS TO KNOW

ceremonial speaking	toast
identification	speech of acceptance
magnification	speech of introduction
speech of tribute	speech of inspiration
award presentation	after-dinner speech
eulogy	master of ceremonies

DISCUSSION

1. The speeches in Appendix B by Hillary Rodham Clinton and Elizabeth Dole are ceremonial addresses. How do they relate to the basic questions of "Who are we?" "Why are we?" "What have we accomplished?" and "What can we become together?" What values do they celebrate?

2. Is there a speech of inspiration you heard some time ago that you still remember? Why do you feel it made such an impression on you?

3. List five heroes or heroines who are often mentioned in ceremonial speeches. Why do speakers refer to them so frequently? What does this tell us about the nature of these admired persons, about contemporary audiences, and about the ceremonial speech situation? Be prepared to discuss this in class.

APPLICATION

1. Select a public figure that you admire and prepare a speech of tribute honoring that person. Discuss the aspects of that person's life you chose to magnify and why.

2. Prepare a toast for a classmate who you feel either (a) has made the most progress as a speaker this semester or (b) has given a speech you will likely remember long after the class is over. Strive for brevity and eloquence in your toast. Be ready to present your toast in class.

NOTES

1. Randall Parrish Osborn, "Jimmy Carter's Rhetorical Campaign for the Presidency: An Epideictic of American Renewal," Southern States Communication Association Convention, Memphis, March 1996; Gray

Matthews, "Epideictic Rhetoric and Baseball: Nurturing Community Through Controversy," *Southern Communication Journal* 60 (1995): 275–291; Richard M. Weaver, *The Ethics of Rhetoric* (Chicago: Henry Regnery, 1953), pp. 164–185; Ch. Perelman and L. Olbrechts-Tyteca, *The New Rhetoric: A Treatise on Argumentation* (South Bend: University of Notre Dame Press, 1971), pp. 47–54; Celeste Michelle Condit, "The Functions of Epideictic: The Boston Massacre Orations as Exemplar," *Communication Quarterly* 33 (1985): 284–299.

2. John Dewey, *Democracy and Education* (New York: Macmillan, 1916), p. 4.

3. Bronislaw Malinowski, "The Problem of Meaning in Primitive Languages," in C. K. Ogden and I. A. Richards, *The Meaning of Meaning: A Study of the Influence of Language upon Thought and of the Science of Symbolism,* 8th ed. (New York: Harcourt, Brace & World, 1946), p. 315.

4. Michael Osborn, *Orientations to Rhetorical Style* (Chicago: Science Research Associates, 1976), p. 32.

5. James W. Carey, "A Cultural Approach to Communication," *Communication* 2 (1975): 6.

6. Walter H. Beale, "Rhetorical Performance Discourse: A New Theory of Epideictic," *Philosophy and Rhetoric* 11 (1978): 221–246; and Bernard K. Duffy, "The Platonic Functions of Epideictic Rhetoric," *Philosophy and Rhetoric* 16 (1983): 79–93.

7. Christine Oravec, "Observation in Aristotle's Theory of Epideictic," *Philosophy and Rhetoric* 9 (1976): 162–174; and Perelman and Olbrechts-Tyteca.

8. From *American Speeches,* ed. Wayland Maxfield Parrish and Marie Hochmuth (New York: Longmans, Green, 1954), p. 43.

9. *Congressional Record,* 1 Apr. 1980, pp. 7459–7460.

10. For a more detailed account of the functions of eulogies see Karen A. Foss, "John Lennon and the Advisory Function of Eulogies," *Central States Speech Journal* 34 (1983): 187–194.

11. "Friends put Ryan White to Rest, But Spirit Lives in AIDS Message," *The Washington Times,* 12 Apr. 1990, p. A5.

12. "'The Pillar of Fire': Excerpts from the Eulogies at the Funeral Yesterday of Yitzhak Rabin," *The Boston Globe,* 7 Nov. 1995, p. A3.

13. Owen Edwards, "What Every Man Should Know: How to Make a Toast," *Esquire,* Jan. 1984, p. 37.

14. Adapted from Wendy Lin, "Let's Lift a Glass, Say a Few Words, and Toast 1996," *The Commercial Appeal* (Memphis), 28 Dec. 1995, p. C3; and Jacob M. Braude, *Complete Speaker's and Toastmaster's Library: Definitions and Toasts* (Englewood Cliffs, NJ: Prentice-Hall, 1965), pp. 88–123.

15. Elie Wiesel, "Nobel Peace Prize Acceptance Speech," 10 Dec. 1986, reprinted in *New York Times,* 11 Dec. 1986, p. A8.

16. Martin Luther King, Jr., "Nobel Peace Prize Acceptance Statement," reprinted in *The Cry for Freedom: The Struggle for Equality in America,* ed. Frank W. Hale, Jr. (New York: Barnes, 1969), pp. 374–377.

17. *The Commercial Appeal* (Memphis), 23 Oct. 1995, p. D2.

18. Cited in Morris K. Udall, *Too Funny to Be President* (New York: Holt, 1988), p. 156.

19. Sheila W. Welling, "Working Women: A Century of Change," presented at the 1995 Catalyst Awards Dinner, New York, 22 Mar. 1995, in *Vital Speeches of the Day,* 15 June 1995, pp. 516–517.

20. *Congressional Record,* 1 Apr. 1980, p. 7249.

21. *Congressional Record,* 1 Apr. 1980, p. 7248.

22. Roger Ailes, *You Are the Message* (New York: Doubleday, 1988), pp. 71–74.

23. Robert M. Kaplan and Gregory C. Pascoe, "Humorous Lectures and Humorous Examples: Some Effects upon Comprehension and Retention," *Journal of Educational Psychology* 69 (1977): 61–65.

24. For more on the social function of laughter, see Henri Bergson, *Laughter: An Essay on the Meaning of the Comic,* trans. Cloudsley Brereton and Fred Rothwell (London: Macmillan, 1911).

25. Ann Richards, "Keynote Address," delivered at the Democratic National Convention, Atlanta, Ga., 18 July 1988, in *Vital Speeches of the Day,* 15 Aug. 1988, pp. 647–649.

26. Christie McGuffee Smith and Larry Powell, "The Use of Disparaging Humor by Group Leaders," *Southern Speech Communication Journal* 53 (1988): 279–292; Charles R. Gruner, "Advice to the Beginning Speaker on Using Humor — What the Research Tells Us," *Communication Education* 34 (1985): 142–147.

27. Thanks for this story go to Professor Joseph Riggs, Slippery Rock University.

28. *Washington Post,* 12 Dec. 1978.

29. Cited in Joan Detz, *Can You Say a Few Words?* (New York: St. Martins, 1991), p. 77.

30. Adapted from Detz, pp. 77–78.

A Tribute to Wilma Rudolph

The following material was presented as part of the National Sports Awards program telecast on NBC, June 20, 1993. The script, transcribed from the telecast of the show and provided by NBC, includes the beginning of the program. Tom Brokaw, NBC Nightly News anchor, was the master of ceremonies. Speeches of tribute were presented by Bill Cosby, entertainer and former college track star; Gail Devers, 1992 Olympic Gold Medal winner in the 100-meter dash; and Ed Temple, Ms. Rudolph's mentor and track coach at Tennessee State University.

Brokaw's general opening remarks set the stage for the program. They are followed by a transition into the tribute which includes the brief introduction of Bill Cosby. Since he could count on Cosby's being well known, he simply notes his relationship to track and field.

Tom Brokaw (Master of Ceremonies): Good evening and welcome. This is such a fitting national celebration because, after all, what would life be without the games that we play? The greatest athletes — the most memorable — are those who gave us a sense of exhilaration off the field as well as on. Heywood Hale Broun once said, "Sports don't build character; they reveal it." What you'll share here tonight is the essence of character as revealed by the lives of these great athletes.

Sports are such an important part of our national culture, our language, our fantasies. Well, tonight the National Sports Awards honors those who played their games at the highest level — and lived their lives at the same heights. They lifted us all by their achievements and by their conduct. Four of them are here in Washington with us tonight; one of them, Ted Williams, has been asked by his doctor not to travel, so he's watching from his home. They were all nominated by a panel of leading sports journalists.

The first that we honor tonight is a woman. When she was born, one of twenty-two children in a Tennessee family, no one could have guessed at that time that her story would echo over the decades, or that it would make even a big impression on the 1962 Middle Atlantic Conference High Jump Champion.

The tribute by Bill Cosby was a multimedia presentation. The first part was presented with Mr. Cosby on camera, the second part was presented as a voice-over for a film showing Wilma Rudolph in action. Note how Cosby's opening words humanize Ms. Rudolph.

This part narrates the film. Cosby begins the

Bill Cosby: She was five foot eleven, she was slender, and she had the manner of a duchess, and you know what they called her in Europe? La Gazelle — La Perle Noire — La Chattanooga Choo-Choo. Wouldn't it be nice to be called "La Chattanooga Choo-Choo?"

I had dreams of being a track star, so I have a particularly vivid memory of this woman who broke barriers, broke records, and brought glory to her country at the 1960 Rome Olympics. Very few Olympians have climbed a bigger mountain than the girl from Clarksville, Tennessee — and her story is one of the most powerful and poignant of the modern Olympics. Madame Choo-Choo, I join the nation in saluting you.

When she was four years old, she contracted polio. Watching other children at play was the cruelest hurt of all. She said, "Only my mother gave me the faith to believe I'd ever walk again." She was the twentieth of twenty-two children. The family scrimped to pay for her therapy at the clinic nearly

90 miles away. But in the end it was her own therapy that did it. She threw away the brace, gritted her teeth, and taught herself to walk . . . to run, to throw herself completely into the Burt High School Basketball team. Then a visiting coach who saw her play suggested she try something else.

She was naturally blessed with burning speed — and the passion to push it. Long-legged — and glamorous, there had never been a woman runner who looked like *this* and ran like *that.*

The Tennessee Tigerbelles made their international debut at the '56 Olympics. She was sixteen and green, and while the team had won a bronze, she missed her golden moment in the 200. It would be four years before the next Olympics. The girls track team was at the bottom of the budget, so Coach Ed Temple picked up the tab. Going into the Rome Olympics she was among the world's fastest but she remembered her failure in '56 — the narrow margin between gold and bronze.

Coach Temple's home movies — occasionally in focus — show the athletes settling in. Here's Wilma, and her new hat . . . and her new friends. Then it got serious. "From the moment I walked into the stadium," she said, "I blocked out everything. Everything." Her first event was the 100 meters. Eleven seconds flat. She was the fastest woman in the world. Then came the 200 — the excruciating demand of speed and stamina. She simply ran away from the rest of the world. Twenty-four flat. An Olympic record. She wasn't done yet. On the last day she ran the anchor leg of the 400-meter relay, and another record fell. It was her third Olympic gold. No American woman had done that in track before.

From out of these Olympic games, Wilma Rudolph entered the company of American heroines. She was honored at every turn. But the greatest reward was in the eyes of her parents. Her hometown set aside old differences. Everyone came out to greet her. That night, for the first time, black and white sat together at the same table. Thirty years ago she gave women a reason to run. She still encourages. She still inspires. It is the simplest, purest athletic endeavor — to run. And oh my — how Wilma could run.

Tom Brokaw: At last summer's Olympic games in Barcelona, we were reminded once again of the power of the human spirit by another American sprinter, gold medal winner Gail Devers.

Gail Devers: I was diagnosed with Graves Disease in 1990, and until I received the proper medication, I had come within two days of having my feet amputated. Long before any of this ever happened, I had heard of a woman named Wilma Rudolph. I read about her in books and I'd watched the Wilma Rudolph stories several times on television and just like Wilma, during my ordeal my first goal was just to walk again. And once I was back on the track running, I thought about her determination.

I knew that she had overcome a very serious illness and still went on to pursue her dream. I felt that if Wilma could do it, I could do it too. Her strong will and her never-give-up attitude had inspired so many of us to keep going despite any obstacles that we may be faced with. And I want to take this opportunity to tell you, Wilma, thank you from the very bottom of my heart. Not just for the example that you've given, not just to me, but to all women in track and field. We love you.

Brokaw provides a transition into the final speech of tribute.

Tom Brokaw: And the man with the movie camera. He has come from Tennessee to present Wilma Rudolph with her award. Her coach and mentor, who retires this fall after forty-two years as coach of the Tennessee State Tigerbelles, Ed Temple, ladies and gentlemen.

Mr. Temple's remarks, though brief, were quite eloquent. Note parallel structure.

Ed Temple: Wilma, you've worked long and hard to achieve these kinds of honors. I've always talked about the adversity that you've had. I tell people that you were able to meet it, to greet it, and defeat it. Wilma, you were an individual who opened up the doors for women's track and field in the United States, and that will always be your greatest legacy. It is an honor for me to be here tonight with you.

Brokaw moves to the award presentation. Note how he refers to her as "the object of our attention and affection."

Tom Brokaw: And on this occasion the great ones do a great walk, so Wilma Rudolph, will you please come forward so that Gail Devers and Ed Temple can present you the first National Sports Award. Ladies and gentlemen, the object of our attention and affection, Wilma Rudolph.

Ms. Rudolph responds with a brief acceptance. Her time was limited because four other award recipients were to receive honors during the show.

Wilma Rudolph: I'm excited. I'll get my breath. I receive this honor, and I dedicate it to the youth of America so they will know that their dreams too can come true. And also to my mother who is eighty-four years old, Blanche Rudolph. Thank you so much for this honor.

Group Communication

When we listen to a speaker present information or make recommendations concerning a problem, what we hear is one person's interpretation of a situation. That point of view may be distorted by bias or self-interest, or it could just be wrong. How can we minimize the risk of listening to just one person's opinion on vital issues?

One solution is to empower a group of people to investigate, analyze, share information and perspectives, and make recommendations about the problem. Group problem solving has a number of advantages. When people from different cultural backgrounds share their unique ways of seeing a problem, they enrich the common understanding.[1] We then see the world through the eyes of others and have the opportunity to learn from them. We may become aware of blind spots in our thinking — biases and misconceptions on which we may base our assumptions. Hearing different points of view can stimulate more creative thinking about the problems that surround us.

In effective problem-solving groups, people on all sides of an issue have an opportunity to discuss the similarities and differences of their perspectives on that issue. Through discussion, the participants may discover some things they can agree on. These areas of agreement can become the foundation for resolving differences. Additionally, people are often more willing to examine their differences in small group meetings than in larger, more public settings. In small groups they may feel freer to explore compromises or new options. For these reasons, organizations often use a small-group approach to problem solving and decision making. In fact, it is estimated that approximately twenty million meetings take place each day in the United States and that the average executive spends "25 to 70 percent of her or his day in meetings — and considers about a third of them to be unproductive."[2]

Although group deliberations have many advantages, there are also some common problems that can make problem-solving groups ineffective. **Cultural gridlock**, an inability to communicate because people don't share basic assumptions and expectations, can impede group deliberations. Cultural gridlock can occur in groups with different racial or ethnic backgrounds. There also can be cultural fault lines between people of different professional backgrounds. For example, people in marketing and lab-cloistered scientists can see the world quite differently. Along with different expectations, participants may also bring to meetings different perspectives on a problem, agendas, priorities, procedures, ways of communicating, and standards for protocol. These differences can cause tension and may sidetrack constructive discussions.

Dealing with cultural gridlock is never easy, but there are some things you can do to minimize its impact:

- Provide a comfortable environment and allow time for people to get acquainted before getting down to the business of the meeting. Remember that personal space requirements differ by cultures. Be sure you have enough room so that people don't feel overly crowded.

- Have a clear agenda for the meeting that lets people know what to expect.
- Be aware of technical language problems. Summarize discussions. Post key points on a chalkboard, markerboard, or flip chart. Avoid colloquialisms or jargon that outsiders may not understand.
- Be sensitive to cultural differences, especially differences in protocol and nonverbal communication. Learn as much as you can about such factors before the meeting, and don't be afraid to ask questions when you are puzzled or to answer questions when your behavior puzzles others.[3]

Another problem inherent to group problem solving is the potential for **groupthink**, or the development of a one-track, uncritical frame of mind that leads to ill-considered decisions.[4] Groupthink is most likely to occur when groups value maintaining strong positive interpersonal relationships more than they value performing competently as decision makers.[5] Consequently they try to avoid any semblance of conflict by discouraging expressions of different opinions or alternative positions. Other major factors that contribute to the development of groupthink include a strong leader preference for a certain course of action and flawed procedures for conducting deliberations. Groupthink is especially dangerous because outsiders are apt to assume that the problem-solving group has deliberated carefully and responsibly when actually it has not.

Preventing groupthink can be difficult, but you can take some steps to guard against it. First, the group needs to be aware of the potential problem. The major symptoms of groupthink include:

- Putting pressure on those who argue against what most of the group believe.
- Censoring one's own thoughts that differ from group beliefs.
- Maintaining an illusion of the group's infallibility.
- Reinforcing an unquestioned belief in the group's moral rightness.
- Attempting as a group to rationalize behaviors and decisions.

The problems that accompany groupthink include (1) incomplete consideration of objectives, (2) poor information retrieval and analysis, and (3) incomplete consideration of alternative solutions.[6]

Once the group becomes aware that there is a potential groupthink problem, members can try to minimize it. First, they should set standards for "vigilant search and appraisal that counter collective uncritical thinking and premature consensus."[7] This suggests that they must have a systematic way to approach the problem. There are other things the group leader can do to help counter groupthink. These include

- reminding everyone that they are to *critically evaluate* whatever is said and proposed;
- not voicing his or her own opinion until others have expressed theirs;
- inviting members to assume the role of "devil's advocate," someone who asks tough, critical questions regarding all proposals and ideas;

- bringing in outsiders to listen and talk with the group about the issues under consideration; and
- encouraging creative conflict in which ideas and issues, but not people, are criticized.

Finally, unless groups have good leadership they can be aimless and unproductive. Ineffective leadership may be one reason why executives often complain that their meetings take too long and accomplish too little.[8] Leaders should remember that their task is to *lead* a group meeting, not *run* it. We give further suggestions for effective group leadership later in this appendix.

GROUP PROBLEM SOLVING

Group deliberations that are orderly, systematic, and thorough help people reach high-quality decisions through consensus.[9] Problem-solving groups can use a variety of methods to achieve their goal.[10] To be effective, groups must decide how they will proceed to assure maximum fairness and efficiency.[11] As we noted earlier, a systematic approach to problem solving can also help forestall a group's tendency toward groupthink.

Reflective-Thinking and Problem Solving

The approach we suggest for most problem-solving groups is a modification of the reflective-thinking technique proposed by John Dewey in 1910.[12] This systematic approach has five steps: (1) defining the problem, (2) generating solution options, (3) evaluating solution options, (4) developing a plan of action, and (5) evaluating the results. The amount of time devoted to each of these steps depends on the depth and complexity of the problem as well as the deadlines faced by the group.

Step 1: Defining the Problem. Groups often mistakenly assume that the "assigned" problem is the real problem. However, sometimes the assigned problem is only a symptom, or just one aspect of the actual problem. So even if a problem may seem obvious, the group needs to define it carefully before looking for solutions. The following questions may help define the problem:

1. Precisely what is the nature of the problem? (Be as concrete and specific as possible.)
2. Why has the problem occurred?
3. What is the history of the problem?
4. Who is affected by the problem and to what degree?
5. If the problem is solved, would things automatically be better? Could they become worse?

6. Does the group have the information it needs to understand the problem completely? If not, how and where can it get this information? (Do not proceed further until this information is in hand.)

7. Has the problem been defined and stated so that everyone understands what the group will work on? (Do not proceed further until such understanding is reached.)

Step 2: Generating Solution Options.   Once a group has determined the nature and extent of the problem, members can begin generating solutions. **Brainstorming**, a technique that encourages all members to contribute freely to the range of options, can help stimulate ideas.[13] Brainstorming aims at producing a large number of potential solutions. It works best in groups of twelve or fewer individuals.[14] At this stage in the problem-solving process, any attempt to evaluate the options or to settle on the right or best option is premature.

The following rules of brainstorming should be communicated to the participants: (1) no criticism during the idea-generating phase, (2) generate ideas without restraint because even something that sounds outrageous may contain the germ of a great approach, (3) go for quantity — the more ideas the better, and (4) combine and improve by building on each other's ideas. The brainstorming process may work through the following steps:

1. The leader asks each member in turn to contribute an idea. If members do not have an idea when it is their turn, they pass.

2. The recorder writes down all the ideas on a flip-chart, markerboard, or chalkboard so that members can see them.

3. Brainstorming continues until all members have offered an idea or have passed.

4. The list of ideas is reviewed for clarification. At this time participants may add additional options or combine related ideas into other alternatives.

5. The participants go over the list again to identify the most useful ideas.

6. The group leader designates one person to receive any additional ideas that members may come up with after the official meeting. These ideas may be added to the list for consideration during the next phase of the problem-solving process.

There are many variations of brainstorming technique that may be helpful for generating ideas.[15] When time for meetings is short or when status differences in the group may stifle ideas, one alternative may be to engage in **electronic brainstorming**. Using this technique, participants generate their ideas on computers before meeting face-to-face.[16] Although specialized networks and software are still quite expensive, group members can use electronic mail or set up forums through existing services such as CompuServe, America Online, or the Internet and achieve similar results.

Step 3: Evaluating Solution Options.   The group should conclude its meeting after generating options and schedule a later meeting to evaluate

them. Group members can then be assigned to develop information between the meetings about the feasibility of each option and determine
whether and how it has been used elsewhere. When the group reconvenes,
it should discuss each of its options using the following guides:

1. How costly is the option?
2. How likely is it to succeed?
3. How hard will it be to make the option work?
4. When would the option take effect?
5. Would the solution solve the problem completely?
6. What additional benefits might the solution produce?
7. What additional problems might the solution cause?

You may wish to use a flip-chart sheet to summarize the answers to
these questions for each option. Post these summaries so that participants
can refer to them as they compare options. As options are evaluated, some
of them will seem weak and be dropped, while others may be strengthened
and refined.

The group also may combine options to generate new alternatives. For
example, if the group is caught between Option A, which promises improved efficiency, and Option B, which promises lower cost, it may be possible to generate hybrid Option C, which combines the best features of
both. This approach is similar to the SIL (Successive Integration of Problem
Elements) Method developed at the Battelle Memorial Institute, a non-
profit research and development think tank. The SIL Method is a six-step
process which includes:

1. A group of four to seven members independently generate solution
   options.
2. Two of the members successively each read one of their ideas to the
   group.
3. The group discusses ways to integrate the two ideas into one solution.
4. A third member reads an idea which the group attempts to integrate
   with the solution generated in step 3.
5. The "add-an-idea" cycle continues until all of the participants' ideas
   have been read aloud and the group has tried to integrate them.
6. The process is complete when the group reaches a consensus on a
   solution.[17]

After each alternative has been thoroughly considered, participants
should rank the solutions in terms of their acceptability. The option receiving the highest overall rank becomes the proposed solution.

During the evaluation step, the leader should focus the discussion on
ideas and not on participants. It is not unusual for group members to become personally caught up with their own solutions. Resist this impulse in
yourself and be tactfully aware of it in others. Discussing the strengths of

an option before talking about its weaknesses can take some of the heat out of the process. Accept differences of opinion and conflict as a natural and necessary part of problem solving.

Step 4: Developing a Plan of Action.   Once the group has selected a solution, it must determine the steps needed to implement it. Developing a plan of action is much like delineating the steps in a process covered under the sequential speech design in Chapter 12. For example, to improve company morale, a group might recommend a three-step plan: (1) better in-house training programs to increase upward mobility of employees, (2) a pay structure that rewards success in the training programs, and (3) increased participation in decision making as employees move into more responsible positions. As the group develops this plan, it should consider what might help or hinder it, the resources needed to enact it, and a timetable for completion.

If the group cannot develop a sequential action plan for the solution, or if insurmountable obstacles appear, the group should return to Step 3 (p. 000) and reconsider its options.

Step 5: Evaluating Results.   Not only must a problem-solving group plan how to implement a solution, it must also set up a system for evaluating the results of the plan. To do this, the group must establish criteria for evaluation concentrating on these three questions:

1. What constitutes success?

2. When can we expect results?

3. What will we do if the plan doesn't work as expected?

The first two questions require the group to specify the desired outcomes and indicate how they can be recognized once the solution goes into effect. To monitor the ongoing success of a solution, such as the three-part plan to improve company morale presented in Step 4, the group would have to decide on a reasonable set of expectations for each stage in the process. That way, the company could detect and correct problems as they occur, before they damage the plan as a whole. Having a scheduled sequence of expectations also provides a way to determine results while the plan is being enacted, rather than having to wait for the entire project to be completed. Positive results along the way can encourage group members by showing them they are on the right track. The third question indicates the importance of contingency plans: what to do if things don't go as expected.

Other Approaches to Group Problem Solving

While the systematic process described above works well in most situations, there are times when a different approach may be called for. When a problem requires the concerted efforts of people from different and separate areas of the public or private sectors, a **collaborative problem-solving approach** may be called for.[18] For example, in many urban areas coalitions of business executives and education professionals have come together to work on plans to educate people for future jobs. In such situations the problems to be addressed are usually acute and the resources are limited. Because there is no prescribed authority structure and because the groups may have different expectations and goals, such groups may have problems accomplishing anything. Consequently, they may need to spend more time defining the problem and exploring each other's perspectives on the situation. Until they recognize and admit their interdependence, they are not likely to be very effective. The participants must come to see themselves, not as members of group A or group B, but as members of group C, the coalition. Leadership is especially difficult in such groups.

One approach that may be useful in such situations is the idea of **dialogue groups.** According to William Isaacs, director of the Dialogue Project at the Massachusetts Institute of Technology's Center for Organizational Learning, "Dialogue is a discipline of collective thinking and inquiry, a process for transforming the quality of conversation, and, in particular, the thinking that lies beneath it."[19] Such groups focus initially, not on solving problems, but on understanding them in terms of the assumptions and embodied meanings that the participants bring to the interaction. The purpose of such groups is to establish a conversation between the participants from which shared meaning based on common ground and mutual trust can emerge.[20]

The role of the group leader or facilitator is critical in dialogue groups. According to Edgar Schein of the MIT Center, the group leader must:

- Organize the physical space to be as nearly a circle as possible. Whether or not people are seated at a table or tables is not as important as the sense of equality that comes from sitting in a circle;
- Introduce the general concept, then ask everyone to think about an experience of dialogue in the sense of "good communication" in their past;
- Ask people to share with their neighbor what the experience was and to think about the characteristics of that experience (this works because people are relating very concrete experiences, not abstract concepts);
- Ask group members to share what it was in such past experiences that made for good communication and write these characteristics on a flip chart.
- Ask the group to reflect on these characteristics by having each person in turn talk about his/her reactions;
- Let the conversation flow naturally once everyone has commented (this requires one-and-a-half to two hours or more);
- Intervene as necessary to clarify or elucidate, using concepts and data that illuminate the problems of communication . . .;
- Close the session by asking everyone to comment in whatever way they choose.[21]

The originators of the dialogue method do not see this as a substitute for other problem-solving techniques, such as the rational-thinking process presented earlier. Instead, they see it as a precursor because they feel

FIGURE A.1

Group Communication
Skills Self-Analysis
Form

		Need to Do Less	Doing Fine	Need to Do More
1.	I make my points concisely.			
2.	I speak with confidence.			
3.	I provide specific examples and details.			
4.	I try to integrate ideas that are expressed.			
5.	I let others know when I do not understand them.			
6.	I let others know when I agree with them.			
7.	I let others know tactfully when I disagree with them.			
8.	I express my opinions.			
9.	I suggest solutions to problems.			
10.	I listen to understand.			
11.	I try to understand before agreeing or disagreeing.			
12.	I ask questions to get more information.			
13.	I ask others for their opinions.			
14.	I check for group agreement.			
15.	I try to minimize tension.			
16.	I accept help from others.			
17.	I offer help to others.			
18.	I let others have their say.			
19.	I stand up for myself.			
20.	I urge others to speak up.			

that discussion and debate work only when "group members understand each other well enough to be 'talking the same language.'"[22] A similar approach may be found in the Kettering Foundation's National Issues Forums.[23]

PARTICIPATING IN SMALL GROUPS

To be an effective group member you must understand your responsibilities as a group participant. First, *you should come to meetings prepared to contribute.* You should have read background materials and performed the tasks assigned by the group leader.

Second, *you should be open-minded* — willing to listen and learn from others. You should be concerned with contributing to the overall effort rather than with dominating the discussion. Although you may have a well-defined point of view, do not be afraid to concede a point when you are wrong and don't become defensive when challenged. Willingness to change one's views is not a sign of weakness, nor is obstinacy a strength.

Third, *be a constructive listener.* Speak only when you need information or can add clarification to an issue. Allow others to complete their points without interruption. Don't be afraid to object if you feel consensus is forming too quickly. You might save the meeting from groupthink. In short, each participant should strive to make a positive contribution to group effectiveness.

Analyzing your group communication skills can help you become a more effective group communicator. Use the self-analysis form (Figure A.1) to steer you toward more constructive group communication behaviors.

As you participate in groups, you should also keep in mind the following questions:

1. What is happening now in the group?
2. What should be happening in the group?
3. What can I do to make this come about?[24]

If you notice a difference between what the group is doing and what it *should be* doing to reach its goals, you have the opportunity to assume group leadership.

LEADERSHIP IN SMALL GROUPS

What does it mean to be a leader? Our natural attraction to leadership, reflected in the importance of ethos as a form of proof (Chapter 14), is very practical: *leaders help get the job done.* For over thirty-five years, social scientists have been studying leadership by analyzing group communication patterns.[25] This research suggests that two basic types of leadership behaviors emerge in most groups. The first is **task leadership behavior,** which directs the activity of the group toward a specified goal. The second is **social leadership behavior**, which builds and sustains positive relationships among group members.

Task leaders initiate goal-related communication, including both giving and seeking information, opinions, and suggestions. A task leader might say, "We need more information on just how widespread grade inflation is on this campus. Let me tell you what Dean Johnson told me last Friday. . . ." Or the task leader might say, "I know Gwen has some important information on this point. Tell us about it, Gwen."

Social leaders initiate positive social communication behaviors, such as expressing agreement, helping the group release tension, or behaving in a generally friendly and supportive manner toward others. The social leader looks for chances to bestow compliments: "I think Gwen has made a very important point. You have really helped us by finding that out." The supportive effect of sincere compliments helps keep members from becoming defensive and helps maintain a constructive communication atmosphere. In a healthy communication climate the two kinds of leadership behavior support each other and work to keep the group moving toward its goal in a positive way. When one person combines both styles of leadership, that person is likely to be highly effective.

As we move into the twenty-first century, a new way of looking at leadership style is emerging. Instead of classifying leaders as having task or social orientation, it suggests that leadership styles are either transactional or transformational. **Transactional leadership** prevails in an environment based on power relationships and relies on reward and punishment to accomplish its ends. **Transformational leadership** appeals to "people's higher levels of motivation to contribute to a cause and add to the quality of life on the planet."[26] The latter style may be the most effective way to bring about collaboration between diverse factions in a group and may be especially important for initiating and sustaining the dialogues that lead to intercultural understanding. It carries with it overtones of stewardship as opposed to management, emphasizing service to others more than controlling them. Transformational leaders manifest the following qualities:

- They have a vision of what needs to be accomplished that is intellectually rich and stimulating.
- They are honest and empathetic so that people feel safe working with them.
- They are trusted because their words and actions are consistent.
- They put others before themselves by giving credit where credit is due.
- They work hard to develop others.
- They share power with others.
- They are willing to take risks, experiment, and learn.
- They have a true passion for their mission.

In short, transformational leaders lead with both their hearts and their heads. According to John Schuster, a management consultant who specializes in transformational leadership training, "the heart is more difficult to develop. It's easier to get smarter than to become more caring."[27] The ideal of transformational leadership appears entirely consistent with the transformational effect of public speaking that we discussed in Chapter 1.

Are only a favored few destined to become leaders? Can you be a leader? To us, the "favored few" theory is primarily an ego trip for those who think they belong to this elite. Most of us have leadership potential that emerges in certain situations. To understand this potential, consider the major components of ethos: central to leadership are competence, trustworthiness, likableness, and forcefulness. In addition, the ideal leader would

- have experience, knowledge, and insight into the problems confronting the group.
- help the group define its problems, set goals, initiate action, and follow through to a successful conclusion.
- be considerate of and sensitive to the needs, talents, and limitations of participants.
- mediate conflicts that can arise during deliberations.
- articulate group consensus as it emerges during discussion.
- adapt to changing circumstances.
- represent the group to others.

Don't be intimidated by these ideal portraits. Most of us have many of these qualities in varying degrees and can use them as the need for leadership arises. To be an effective leader, remember these simple functional goals: *help others be effective and get the job done.* Cultivate an open leadership style that encourages all sides to air their views. Much of the training you have received in this course will help you become a successful leader. You may even find you enjoy the experience.

Planning Meetings

Effective leadership skills include knowing when to call meetings and how to plan and run them.[28] You should call meetings when members need to

- share information and interpret its meaning face-to-face.
- decide on a common course of action.
- plan and lay out a plan of action.
- report on the progress of a plan, evaluate its effectiveness, and revise it if needed.

The following guidelines should help you plan more effective meetings:

1. *Have a specific objective and purpose for holding a meeting.* Unnecessary meetings waste time. If your goal is simply to increase interaction, plan a social event rather than a meeting.

2. *Prepare an agenda for the meeting* and distribute it to participants well before the meeting. Having a list of topics to be covered gives members

time to prepare and assemble any information or materials they might need. Be sure to solicit agenda items from participants.

3. *Keep meetings short and to the point.* After about an hour groups usually grow weary and tempers get short. Don't try to cover too much ground in any one meeting.

4. *Keep groups small.* You will get more participation and interaction in smaller groups. In larger groups people may be inhibited from asking questions or contributing ideas.

5. *Assemble groups that invite open discussions.* In business settings, the presence of an employee's direct supervisor may inhibit honest interaction. You will get better participation if group members come from the same or near the same working level in the organization.

6. *Plan the site of the meeting.* Try to arrange for privacy and freedom from interruptions. A circular table or seating arrangement contributes to member participation because there is no power position in the arrangement. A rectangular table or a lectern and classroom arrangement may inhibit interaction.

7. *Prepare in advance for the meeting.* Have a short form of the agenda available for distribution at the meeting. Be certain that you have all of the supplies the group will need, such as chalk, flip-chart, markers, note pads, and pencils. If you plan to use audio-visual equipment, check in advance to be sure it is in working order.

Conducting an Effective Meeting

Group leaders have more responsibilities than other members. Leaders must understand the problem-solving process the group will use so that deliberations can proceed in an orderly, constructive way. Leaders also should be well informed on the issues involved so that they can answer questions and keep the group moving toward its objective. The following check list should be helpful in guiding your behavior as a group leader.

- Start and end on time.
- Prepare and present background information concisely and objectively.
- Lead, don't run the meeting.
- Be enthusiastic.
- Encourage differences of opinion. Get conflict out in the open so that it can be dealt with directly.
- Urge all members to participate. If group members are reticent, you may have to ask them directly to contribute.
- Keep the discussion centered on the issue.
- Summarize what others have said to keep the group focused on the problem.
- At the close of a meeting, summarize what the group has accomplished.

As group leader, you may need to present the group's recommendations to others. *In this task, you function mainly as an informative speaker.* You should present the recommendations offered by the group, along with the major reasons for these recommendations. You should also mention any opposing reasons or reservations that may have surfaced during group deliberations. Your job in making this report is not to advocate, but to educate. Later, you may join in the discussion that follows your report with persuasive remarks that express your convictions on the subject.

GUIDELINES FOR FORMAL MEETINGS

The larger the group, the more it may need formal procedures to conduct a successful meeting. Also, if a meeting involves a controversial subject, it is often wise to have a set of rules for conducting group business. Such guidelines help keep meetings from becoming chaotic and assure fair treatment of all participants. Many groups operate by **parliamentary procedure.**[29]

Parliamentary procedure establishes an order of business for a meeting and defines the way the group initiates discussions and reaches decisions. Under parliamentary procedure, a formal meeting proceeds as follows:

1. The chair calls the meeting to order.
2. The secretary reads the minutes of the previous meeting, which are corrected, if necessary, and approved.
3. Reports from group officers and committees are presented.
4. Unfinished business from the previous meeting is considered.
5. New business is introduced.
6. Announcements are made.
7. The meeting is formally adjourned.

All business in formal meetings goes forward by means of **motions,** which are proposals set before the group. Consider the following scenario. The chair of a group asks: "Is there new business?" A member responds: "I move that we allot $100 to build a Homecoming float." This member has offered a **main motion,** which proposes to commit the group to some action. Before the motion can be discussed, it must be seconded. If no one volunteers a second, the chair may ask, "Is there a second?" Another member will typically respond, "I second the motion." The purpose of a **second** is to assure that more than one person wishes to see the motion considered. Once a main motion is made and seconded, it is open for discussion. It must be passed by majority vote, defeated, or otherwise resolved before the group can move on to other business. With the exception of a few technical motions (such as "I move we take a fifteen-minute recess" or "Point of personal privilege — can we do anything about the heat in this room?"), the main motion remains at the center of group attention until resolved.

Action	Requires Second	Can Be Debated	Can Be Amended	Vote Required	Function
Main Motion	Yes	Yes	Yes	Majority	Commits group to a specific action or position.
Second	No	No	No	None	Assures that more than one group member wishes to see idea considered.
Move to Amend	Yes	Yes	Yes	Majority	Allows group to modify and improve an existing motion.
Call the Question	Yes	No	No	Two-thirds	Brings discussion to an end and moves to a vote on the motion in question.
Move to Table the Motion	Yes	No	No	Majority	Stops immediate consideration of the motion until a later unspecified time.
Move to Postpone Consideration	Yes	Yes	Yes	Majority	Stops immediate discussion and allows time for the group to obtain more information on the problem.
Move to Adjourn	Yes	No	No	Majority	Formally ends meeting.

FIGURE A.2

Guide to Parliamentary Procedure

Let us assume that as the group discusses the main motion in our example, some members believe the amount of money proposed is insufficient. At this point, another member may say: "I move to amend the motion to provide $150 for the float." The **motion to amend** gives the group a chance to modify a main motion. It also must be seconded and, after discussion, must be resolved by majority vote before discussion goes forward. if the motion to amend passes, then the amended main motion must be considered further.

How does a group come to a decision on a motion? There usually is a time when discussion has pretty well played itself out. At this point the chair might say, "Do I hear a call for the question?" A **motion to call the question** ends the discussion, and requires a two-thirds vote for approval. Once the group votes to end discussion, it must then vote to accept or reject the motion.

At times, discussion of a motion may reveal that the group is deeply confused or sharply divided about an issue. At this point a member may make a **motion to table the motion** or "to lay [the motion] on the table," as it is technically called. This can be a backdoor way to dispose of a troublesome or defective motion without the pain of further divisive or confused discussion. At other times, discussion may reveal that the group lacks vital information needed to come to an intelligent decision. At that point, we might hear from yet another member: "In light of our uncertainty on the cost issue, I move that we postpone further consideration of this motion until next week's meeting." The **motion to postpone consideration,** if approved, gives the chair a chance to appoint a committee to gather the information needed.

These are just some of the important motions and procedures that can help assure that formal group communication remains fair and constructive. For more information on formal group communication procedures, consult the authoritative **Robert's Rules of Order.**

NOTES

1. Marc Hequet, "The Fine Art of Multicultural Meetings," *Training,* July 1993, 29(5), *Business Database Plus,* online, CompuServe, Jan. 1996; William N. Issacs, "Taking Flight: Dialogue, Collective Thinking, and Organizational Learning," *Organizational Dynamics,* Autumn 1993, 24(16), *Business Database Plus,* online, CompuServe, Jan. 1996; Edgar H. Schein, "On Dialogue, Culture, and Organizational Learning," *Organizational Dynamics,* Autumn 1993, 40(12), *Business Database Plus,* online, CompuServe, Jan. 1996.

2. Scot Ober, *Contemporary Business Communication* (Boston: Houghton Mifflin, 1995), p. 498.

3. Adapted from Hequet.

4. Paul R. Bernthal, and Chester A. Insko, "Cohesiveness Without Groupthink: The Interactive Effects of Social and Task Cohesion," *Group and Organization Management,* March 1993, 66(22), *Business Database Plus,* online, CompuServe, Jan. 1996; and Christopher P. Neck and Charles C. Manz, "From Groupthink to Teamthink: Toward the Creation of Constructive Thought Patterns in Self-Managed Work Teams," *Human Relations,* August 1994, 929(24), *Business Database Plus,* online, CompuServe, Jan. 1996.

5. Bernthal and Insko.

6. Neck and Manz.

7. I. L. Janis, *Groupthink: Psychological Studies of Policy Decisions and Fiascoes* (Boston: Houghton Mifflin, 1982), pp. 245–246.

8. Gerald M. Goldhaber, *Organizational Communication* (Dubuque, IA: Brown, 1983), p. 263.

9. Harold Guetzow and John Gyr, "An Analysis of Conflict in Decision–Making Groups," *Human Behavior,* 7 (1954): 367–382; and Norman R. F. Maier and Richard A. Maier, "An Experimental Test of the Effects of 'Developmental' vs. 'Free' Discussion on the Quality of Group Decisions," *Journal of Applied Psychology,* 41 (1957): 320–323.

10. For an overview of other methods, see Patricia Hayes Andrews and Richard T. Herschel, *Organizational Communication: Empowerment in a Technological Society* (Boston: Houghton Mifflin, 1996), pp. 213–218.

11. Donelson R. Forsyth, *Group Dynamics,* 2nd ed. (Pacific Grove, CA: Brooks/Cole, 1990), pp. 286–87.

12. The problem–solving process described here is adapted from William C. Morris and Marshall Sashkin, "Phases of Integrated Problem Solving (PIPS)," *The 1978 Annual Handbook for Group Facilitators,* ed. J. William Pfeiffer and John E. Jones (La Jolla, CA: University Associates, 1978), pp. 109–116.

13. Floyd Hurt, "Better Brainstorming," *Training and Development,* Nov. 1944, 57(3), *Business Database Plus,* online, CompuServe, Jan. 1996.

14. Ron Zemke, "In Search of Good Ideas," *Training,* Jan. 1993: 46(6), *Business Database Plus,* online, CompuServe, Jan. 1996.

15. Hurt, Zemke, and Sivasailam Thiagarajan, "Take Five For Better Brainstorming," *Training and Development Journal,* Feb. 1992, 37(6), *Business Database Plus,* online, CompuServe, Jan. 1996.

16. Srikumar S. Rao, "Meetings Go Better Electronically: Do Hard-Nosed Bosses Stiffle Discussion? Try Conferencing Software," *Financial World,* 14 Mar. 1995, 72(2), *Business Database Plus,* online, CompuServe, Jan. 1996; Gail Kay, "Effective Meetings Through Electronic Brainstorming," *Management Quarterly,* Winter 1994, 15(12), *Business Database Plus,* online, CompuServe, Jan. 1996; Milam Aiken, Mahesh Vanjami, and James Krosp, "Group Decision Support Systems," *Review of Business,* Spring 1995, 38(5), *Business Database Plus,* online, CompuServe, Jan. 1996; and Michael C. Kettelhut, "How to Avoid Misusing Electronic Meeting Support," *Planning Review,* July–Aug. 1994, 34(5), *Business Database Plus,* online, CompuServe, Jan. 1996.

17. Zemke.

18. Jacqueline N. Hood, Jeanne M. Logsdon, and Judith Kenner Thompson, "Collaboration for Social Problem Solving: A Process Model," *Business and Society,* Spring 1993, 1(17), *Business Database Plus,* online, CompuServe, Jan. 1996.

19. William M. Isaacs, "Taking Flight: Dialogue, Collective Thinking, and Organizational Learning," *Organizational Dynamics,* Autumn 1993, 24(16), *Business Database Plus,* online, CompuServe, Jan. 1996.

20. Schein.

21. Schein.

22. Schein.

23. Michael and Suzanne Osborn, *Alliance for a Better Public Voice: The Communication Discipline and the National Issues Forums* (Dayton, OH: National Issues Forums Institute, 1991).

24. Adapted from David G. Smith, "D-I-D: A Three-Dimensional Model for Understanding Group Communication," *The 1977 Annual Handbook for Group Facilitators,* ed. John E. Jones and J. William Pfeiffer (La Jolla, CA: University Associates, 1977), p. 106.

25. Robert F. Bales, *Interaction Process Analysis: A Method for the Study of Small Groups* (Cambridge: Addison-Wesley, 1950); and *Personality and Interpersonal Behavior* (New York: Holt, 1970).

26. John P. Schuster, "Transforming Your Leadership Style," *Association Management,* Jan. 1994, 39(5), *Business Database Plus,* online, CompuServe, Jan. 1996.

27. Schuster.

28. Much of the material in this section is adapted from Robert D. Ramsey, "Making Meetings Work For You," *Supervision,* Feb. 1994, 14(3), *Business Database Plus,* online, CompuServe, Jan. 1966; and Becky Jones, Midge Wilker, and Judy Stoner, "A Meeting Primer," *Management Review,* Jan. 1995, 30(3), *Business Database Plus,* online, CompuServe, Jan. 1996.

29. Darwin Patnode, *Robert's Rules of Order: Modern Edition* (Nashville, TN: Thomas Nelson, 1989).

Speeches for Analysis

SELF-INTRODUCTORY

Rod Nishikawa, "Free at Last"

Laura Haskins, "The Magnificent Juggler"

INFORMATIVE

Cecile Larson, "The 'Monument' at Wounded Knee"

Stephen Lee, "The Trouble with Numbers"

PERSUASIVE

Bonnie Marshall, "Living Wills: Ensuring Your Right to Choose"

Gina Norman, "Secondhand Smoke"

Cesar Chavez, "Pesticides Speech"

CEREMONIAL

Elie Wiesel, "Nobel Peace Prize Acceptance Speech"

Hillary Clinton, "Address to the United Nations Fourth World Conference on Women"

Elizabeth Dole, "Women in Public Life Commencement Address"; Radcliffe University; June 11, 1993

Dick Jackman, "After-Dinner Speech"

John Scipio, "Martin Luther King at the Mountaintop"

Free At Last

Rodney Nishikawa

Rod Nishikawa presented this sensitive and moving self-introductory speech in his public speaking class at the University of California-Davis. Although most of his classmates were aware of prejudice, Rod's personal narrative — about his first encounter with prejudice as a child — introduced many of them to the Japanese-American culture and helped them relate to the problem more closely. Rod's willingness to speak from the heart helped transform his class into a creative, caring community.

Three years ago I presented the valedictory speech at my high school graduation. As I concluded, I borrowed a line from Dr. Martin Luther King's "I Have a Dream" oration: "Free at last, free at last, thank God almighty we're free at last!" The words had only a joyful, humorous place in that speech, but for me personally they were a lie. I was not yet free, and would not be free until I had conquered an ancient enemy, both outside me and within me — that enemy was racial prejudice.

The event in my life that had the greatest effect on me happened over twelve years ago when I was eight years old. I was a shy, naive little boy. I knew I was Japanese, but I didn't consider myself different from my friends, nor did I realize anyone else noticed or even cared. But at least one person did. The "bully" in our class made it a point to remind me by calling me a "Jap." He told me I didn't belong in America, and that I should go back to Japan.

It was hard for me to understand what he meant, because like my parents I was born here in this country. This was my home. I didn't know what to do when I was taunted. All I can remember is going home after school and crying as though my heart were broken. I told my mom that I wished I wasn't Japanese, but that if I did have to be Japanese, why did I have to be born in this country?

Of course my mother knew exactly how I felt. She was about the age I was then when the Japanese attacked Pearl Harbor. She told me how she too had experienced prejudice at school, but that the prejudice she encountered was over a hundred times worse. When my father came home from work, my mom and I told him what had happened. Although my father was understanding, he said that I would never know the meaning of true prejudice because I did not grow up on the West Coast during World War II.

My encounter with the school bully was the beginning of my personal education about prejudice. What I have learned is that prejudice is not a disease that infects only the least educated among us. Rather, it is a bad part of human nature that lies buried deep within all of us. Some people, however, seem to enjoy their prejudice. These people like to feel good by putting others down. But I have also learned how to deal with such problems when they arise. It was the advice from my mother that helped me the most.

My mother explained to me the meaning of the Japanese word *gaman*. *Gaman* means to "bear within" or "bear the burden." It is similar to the American phrase "turn the other cheek," but it means more to "endure" than to "ignore." She told me that when I go back to school, I should practice *gaman* — that even if I am hurt, I should not react with anger or fear, that I should bear the burden within. She said that if I showed anger or fear it would only make things worse, but if I practiced *gaman* things would get better for me. She was right. When I went back to school, I remembered what she had said. I used *gaman*. I bore the burden within. It wasn't easy for an eight-year-old, but I did not show any anger. I did not show any fear to the bully, and eventually he stopped picking on me.

Prejudice has been a bitter teacher in my life, but *gaman* has been an even greater blessing. By learning how to practice it, I feel I have acquired a great deal of inner strength. Whereas Gary (another student in the class) said he is a "competitor," I believe I am a "survivor." I look around my environment, recognize my situation, and cope with it. Because *gaman* has been part of my daily life since I was eight years old, I rarely experience feelings of anger or fear — those negative emotions that can keep a person from really being "free."

Being freed from such negative feelings has also helped me to better understand and accept myself. When I first encountered prejudice, I was ashamed of who I was. I didn't like being different, being a Japanese-American. But as I've grown to maturity, I have realized that I'm really proud to be Japanese-American: Japanese by blood — with the rich culture and heritage of my ancestors behind me — and American by birth — which makes me equal to anyone in this room because we were all born in this country and we all share the same rights and obligations.

Practicing *gaman* has helped me conquer prejudice. Although my Japanese ancestors might not have spoken as boldly as I have today, I am basically an American, which makes me a little outspoken. Therefore, I can talk to you about racial prejudice and of what it has meant to my life. And because I can talk about it, and share it with you, I am finally, truly, "free at last."

The Magnificent Juggler
Laura Haskins

Laura Haskins presented this innovative self-introductory speech in her public speaking class at the University of Memphis. A nontraditional student, Laura decided she was best characterized by the frenetic activity that permeates her life and that she obviously thrives on. She used a "juggler" metaphor as the central theme of her message which imparts a light touch to her message. This metaphor begins in her introduction, "Come one, come all, see the magnificent juggler," and is extended through her transitions, "Toss up the first (or second or third) ball." The most important supporting materials in her speech are the personal narratives that sustain interest and depict her as a genial, clever, and competent person. These narratives helped her audience of younger classmates identify with her.

Come one, come all, see the magnificent juggler. See her juggle family, home, work, college, whatever comes her way. I wasn't always this good. My juggling act began impromptu when I enrolled in nursing school. My children were preschoolers then and I had to learn fast. With experience, practice, and trial and error, I have become a magnificent juggler.

Toss up the first ball. My family and home. Terry's description of her home life sounds just about like mine. The point I'd like to make is that raising a family is juggling their personalities, their needs and desires, and their idiosyncrasies, all of them, all at the same time. My children are as different as night and day. My son Adam, who's twelve, is calm, easygoing, a roll-with-the-punches kind of guy. He came to me recently and said, "Mom, you've got to hear this great new song." I said, "Great, play the tape." He put the tape in. It was "Bohemian Rhapsody" by Queen from 1975, a great new song. I chuckled, went to the attic, dusted off my old album, and said, "Son, this isn't a new song. I knew this song in '75." He looked it over and said, "Cool."

My daughter Sara, who's nine, she is a total opposite. She's energetic and talkative. She does most of the talking in our family, as a matter of fact. Don't take her to the movies. You will not hear the dialogue. I woke her up one morning for school: "Sara, wake up. Aunt Leslie went to the hospital to have her baby today." She sat straight up in bed. "Oh, I hope it's a girl. How big is it going to be? What are they going to name her? When can I hold it? Can I stay home today?" She never stopped to hear one answer. I went next door to wake up her brother: "Adam, wake up. Aunt Leslie went to the hospital today to have her baby." He rolled over and looked at me and said, "Cool." So you see, very different personalities.

Toss up the second ball. I'm a registered nurse in intensive care. I recover open heart surgery patients and I care for critically ill individuals and those who require life support systems or ventilators. That is a juggling act in and of itself. "The doctor wants to see you right away. Critical lab values on line one. This patient's family is really stressed out and this patient's blood pressure is dropping." In the *American Journal of Nursing* last year a physician was quoted as saying, "We doctors don't save the patients' lives, the nurses do."

Toss up ball number three. College. You all know how hard that can be to find time to write papers and prepare speeches. It's a real challenge.

So those are the three main components of my juggling act. When the alarm clock goes off in the morning, I have to look and see what time it is so I'll know what to get up and do. Oh, it's 5:00 AM; I go to work today. Oh, it's 6:30; today is a class day. Dinnertime varies from night to night and sometimes from person to person. Every man for himself. Sundays are a big planning day. Okay, you've got karate Monday night and you've got

Scouts after school Tuesday. Okay, don't forget to go to after-school care those days, and Thursday night I have to work 11:00 to 7:00.

My experience as a juggler has taught me to plan, prioritize, rearrange as necessary, and pass off to my assistant juggler, my husband, without missing a beat. The International Jugglers Association formed in 1947 is reviewing my application for membership. I'm a shoo-in. I may not be June Cleaver, but I am a magnificent juggler.

The "Monument" at Wounded Knee
Cecile Larson

Cecile Larson's classroom speech serves two informative functions. First, it shapes the perceptions of the audience because of the way it describes the "monument" and the perspective it takes on the situation — most of her classmates had had little or no contact with Native Americans, and this might have been their first exposure to this type of information. Second, the speech serves the agenda-setting function in that it creates an awareness of a problem and thus increases its importance in the minds of the audience. The speech follows a spatial design. Cecile's vivid use of imagery and the skillful contrasts she draws between this "monument" and our "official" monuments create mental pictures that should stay with her listeners long after the words of her speech have been forgotten.

We Americans are big on monuments. We build monuments in memory of our heroes. Washington, Jefferson, and Lincoln live on in our nation's capital. We erect monuments to honor our martyrs. The Minute Man still stands guard at Concord. The flag is ever raised over Iwo Jima. Sometimes we even construct monuments to commemorate victims. In Ashburn Park downtown there is a monument to those who died in the yellow fever epidemics. However, there are some things in our history that we don't memorialize. Perhaps we would just as soon forget what happened. Last summer I visited such a place — the massacre site at Wounded Knee.

In case you have forgotten what happened at Wounded Knee, let me refresh your memory. On December 29, 1890, shortly after Sitting Bull had been murdered by the authorities, about 400 half-frozen, starving, and frightened Indians who had fled the nearby reservation were attacked by the Seventh Cavalry. When the fighting ended, between 200 and 300 Sioux had died — two-thirds of them women and children. Their remains are buried in a common grave at the site of the massacre.

Wounded Knee is located in the Pine Ridge Reservation in southwestern South Dakota — about a three-hour drive from where Presidents Washington, Jefferson, Theodore Roosevelt, and Lincoln are enshrined in the granite face of Mount Rushmore. The reservation is directly south of the Badlands National Park, a magnificently desolate area of wind-eroded buttes and multicolored spires.

We entered the reservation driving south from the Badlands Visitor's Center. The landscape of the Pine Ridge Reservation retains much of the desolation of the Badlands but lacks its magnificence. Flat, sun-baked fields and an occasional eroded gully stretch as far as the eye can see. There are no signs or highway markers to lead the curious tourist to Wounded Knee. Even the *Rand-McNally Atlas* doesn't help you find your way. We got lost three times and had to stop and ask directions.

When we finally arrived at Wounded Knee, there was no official historic marker to tell us what had happened there. Instead there was a large, handmade wooden sign — crudely lettered in white on black. The sign first directed our attention to our left — to the gully where the massacre took place. The mass grave site was to our right — across the road and up a small hill.

Two red-brick columns topped with a wrought-iron arch and a small metal cross form the entrance to the grave site. The column to the right is in bad shape: cinder blocks from the base are missing; the brickwork near the top has deteriorated and tumbled to the ground; graffiti on the columns proclaim an attitude we found repeatedly expressed about the Bureau of Indian Affairs — "The BIA sucks!"

Crumbling concrete steps lead you to the mass grave. The top of the grave is covered with gravel, punctuated by unruly patches of chickweed and crabgrass. These same weeds also grow along the base of the broken chain-link fence that surrounds the grave, the "monument," and a small cemetery.

The "monument" itself rests on a concrete slab to the right of the grave. It's a typical, large, old-fashioned granite cemetery marker, a pillar about six feet high topped with an urn — the kind of gravestone you might see in any cemetery with graves from the turn of the century. The inscription tells us that it was erected by the families of those who were killed at Wounded Knee. Weeds grow through the cracks in the concrete at its base.

There are no granite headstones in the adjacent cemetery, only simple white wooden crosses that tell a story of people who died young. There is no neatly manicured grass. There are no flowers. Only the unrelenting and unforgiving weeds.

Yes, Americans are big on monuments. We build them to memorialize our heroes, to honor our martyrs, and sometimes, even to commemorate victims. But only when it makes us feel good.

The Trouble with Numbers
Stephen Lee

Stephen Lee first presented this informative speech of explanation to his public speaking class at the University of Texas-Austin. Later, Stephen's speech won the Southern division of the 1991 Houghton Mifflin speaking contest. The speech is noteworthy for its use of testimony and its illustrative examples. It first gains and holds attention by the novelty of its introduction, as Stephen describes a mythical "average American." The speech is somewhat loosely structured around a categorical design, as Stephen reflects upon the "misuse, abuse, and general overuse" of statistics in various dimensions of modern life. Stephen's presentation skills — his timing, wry sense of humor, eye contact, vocal variety, and gesture — helped bring his speech to life. All in all, he offers a sprightly commentary that critiques our society's over-reliance on one of the basic forms of supporting materials, statistical knowledge.

Name, Bill Smith. Address, 103 Main Street, Smalltown, USA. Height, 5'11", weight, 185 pounds. Who is this person? Why, he's the average American. Bill makes a comfortable $32,000 each year. His car gets 18.9 miles to the gallon. He reads 4.2 novels every year, each with 482.73 pages. He receives 9.7 gifts every Christmas and he brushes his teeth 1.9 times every day. The average American.

Today it seems we hear a lot of this person. Someone who is supposedly like all of us and yet not like any of us. After all, how many men do you know with 2.7 children? No, Bill is by no means real. His composition is not one of flesh and blood. Instead Bill is the product of cold and heartless data. Born of a national almanac, Bill is nothing more than a statistic.

But the characteristics of Bill Smith and the way we interpret them are highly reflective of our society's misuse, abuse, and general overuse of statistics. As Darrell Huff tells us in his essay, *How to Lie With Statistics,* "Americans use statistics like drunks use lamp posts, for support instead of illumination." He was referring to the unfailing dependence that we Americans put on statistics. He continues: "We prefer to record and measure ourselves with numbers and what we can't measure we assume not to exist at all." But what are these mystic symbols and figures? And more importantly, how do they affect us? Humorist Artemus Ward once said, "It ain't so much what we know that gets us in trouble. It's the things we know that ain't so."

Now such was the case in the government. Our government is faulted for many problems. Statistical misuse is perhaps one of the greatest. This was clearly demonstrated in March of 1983 when the computation of the unemployment rate was changed to encompass military personnel. Now this had a significant impact, as the number changed from 10.6% to 10.1%. Some people said this was a political ploy of President Reagan, trying to make himself look good in the public spectrum, while others claimed this was a highly justified move since, after all, military personnel were employed. But I think there is a more important question that needs to be answered. Look at what happened to the number. It changed. Look at what happened to the way the number was computed. It changed, too. But what happened to the very real problem of civilian unemployment, which we all assumed this number to represent? It had not changed at all. It all goes back to what Lester T. Thurow said in his basic theory of economics. "A difference is only a difference if it truly makes a difference." Many times a difference in a number does not represent a difference in the real world. This was the case in the late 1970s when housing was taken out of the consumer price index. Now as contradictory as it might sound, while inflation continued to skyrocket the inflation rate actually stagnated.

In our society we even misuse something as simple as a baseball statistic, denoting one player is good, batting .350, while another one bad, batting .150. But what do these figures tell us about his moral character, his interaction with other players, his leadership abilities — any of which any coach will tell you is necessary for the well-rounded player? While numbers may be convincing, so much of what they imply, as Ward said, simply "ain't so." Perhaps we can all relate to standardized tests, where the quality of one's education is measured by the quantity of correct circles on a piece of paper. You may not be aware of how misleading statistics are on the university level, but look closer when a university advertises that 95% of its needy students receive financial aid. It sounds good, but the truth behind this claim is the fact that the university is the one who determines who is needy, and thereby allocates aid accordingly.

Perhaps the greatest inadequacy surrounding statistics lies not in what is wrong with these numbers, but instead with the way we use them. Numbers are only numbers. Many times we forget this. We forget that there are very real humans and very real human conditions behind these statistics. And yes, we are all affected by them. The only solution to our statistical dilemma is to better understand what a statistic is and what a statistic is not. We need to more adequately comprehend what a statistic can do, but what a number cannot do.

So when you go home today, read your paper. Eat your meal, watch TV. You don't have to go looking for statistics. They're all around us. But this time be aware of them. Train yourself not to passively sit by as seemingly innocent numbers are flashed before your eyes. Learn to question what hides behind those numbers. I think it's interesting, and indeed fascinating, that statistics have come to dominate our decision making in America today. But don't get me wrong. I am not saying that statistics are bad, but that statistics can be misleading. And without careful management they can do more harm than good. Carl Tucker summed it up best in his book, *The Data Game*. He wrote: "Statistics and lists are obviously useful tools. They, in their own way, can tell us what happened, but never why that mattered." And in the end that is the only question worth answering. So as you leave, remember: three-fourths of the people always comprise 75% of the population.

Living Wills: Ensuring Your Right to Choose
Bonnie Marshall

Bonnie Marshall was a student at Heidelberg College in Ohio when she made the following persuasive presentation. Her speech is noteworthy for its use of opening narrative to heighten interest in the problem Bonnie was presenting. The speech is also strong in its use of personal and expert forms of testimony. Clearly, Bonnie had responsible knowledge of her subject. In her conclusion she makes excellent use of anaphora to underscore her message of personal responsibility. She presented the speech with great conviction, and its overall impact led to its selection as a finalist in the Midwest division of the 1991 Houghton Mifflin Public Speaking contest.

Harry Smith was a cranky, obstinate, old farmer. He loved bowling, Glenn Miller music, and Monday night football. He was also dying from cancer of the esophagus, which had metastasized to his lungs. He didn't like doctors and he liked hospitals and modern medicine even less. Harry used to say that he remembered when three square meals, mom's mustard plaster, and an occasional house call from Doc Jones was all anyone ever needed to stay healthy. Harry didn't want to live in pain, and he hated being dependent on anyone else; yet like so many others, Harry never expressed his wishes to his family. When Harry's cancer became so debilitating that he could no longer speak for himself, his family stepped in to make decisions about his medical care. Since Harry never told them how he felt, his children, out of a sense of guilt over the things they had done and the love they hadn't expressed, refused to let Harry die. He was subjected to ventilators, artificial feedings, and all the wizardry that modern medicine can offer. Harry did die eventually, but only after months of agony with no hope of recovery.

Harry's doctor, my husband, agonized too, over the decisions regarding Harry's care. He knew that the children were acting out of grief and guilt, not for Harry's benefit. Yet because Harry had not documented his wishes, his doctor had no choice but to subject Harry to the senseless torture that he didn't want.

We all know of a similar case that gained national attention. On December 26, 1990, Nancy Cruzan died. The tragic young woman who became the focal point for the right-to-die movement was finally allowed to die after eight long years and a legal battle that reached the hallowed halls of the Supreme Court. Nancy's battle is now over, yet the issue has not been resolved and the need for action is more urgent than ever. Since the Supreme Court ruling on June 25, 1990, public interest in this issue has skyrocketed. From July 1990 to November 1990, the last month statistics were available, the Society for the Right To Die answered 908,000 requests for information. By comparison, in November of 1989, the first month that the Society kept monthly statistics, they answered only 21,000 requests.

Today I would like to explore this problem and propose some solutions that we all can implement.

The *Cruzan v. Missouri* decision was significant because it was the first time that the Supreme Court had rendered an opinion on the right-to-die issue. However, the message from the Court is anything but clear and complete. As Justice Sandra Day O'Connor wrote in her concurring opinion, "Today we decide only that one state's practice does not violate the Constitution. . . . The more challenging task of crafting appropriate procedures for safeguarding incompetents' liberty interests is entrusted to the 'laboratory' of the states." So while the Court has for the first time recognized a "constitutionally protected liberty interest in refusing unwanted medical treatment," it has also given the power over this issue back to the states. According to the July 9, 1990, issue of *U.S. News and World Report,* nine states, including Ohio, have no legislation recognizing the legality of living wills. Of the states that do have living will legislation, about one-half do not allow for the withdrawal of nutrition and hydration, even if the will says the patient does not want such treatment, according to Lisa Belken in the June 25th issue of the *New York Times.* Also according to the *Times,* only 33 states have health care proxy laws. Perhaps as a result of all this indecision and inconsistency, desperate patients with terminal illnesses will continue to seek out the "Dr. Deaths" of the medical community, those who, like Dr. Kevorkian of Michigan, are willing to surpass simply allowing the terminally ill to die, to actively bringing about death.

The right-to-die issue may seem far removed from you today, yet the American Medical Association estimates that 80 to 90% of us will die a "managed death." Even today, according to an editorial by Anthony Lewis in the June 29, 1990, *New York Times,* "The problem is far more acute and far-reaching than most of us realize. Almost two million people die in the United States every year, and more than half of those deaths occur when some life-sustaining treatment is ended." The decision to provide, refuse, or withdraw medical treatment should be made individually, personally, with the counsel of family, friends, doctors, and clergy, but certainly not by the state.

More and more, however, these personal decisions are being taken away from patients and their families and instead are being argued and decided in courts of law. Perhaps it began with Karen Ann Quinlan. It certainly continued with Nancy Cruzan, and these decisions could be taken away from you, if we do not act now to ensure that our right to refuse medical treatment is protected. And our right to refuse medical treatment includes the right to refuse artificial nutrition and hydration, just as it includes the right to refuse antibiotics, chemotherapy, surgery, or artificial respiration. According to John Collins Harvey, M.D., Ph.D from the Kennedy Institute of Ethics at Georgetown University, "The administration of food and fluid artificially is a medical technological treatment. . . . Utilizing such medical treatment requires the same kind of medical technological expertise of physicians, nurses, and dietitians as is required in utilizing a respirator for treatment of respiratory failure or employing a renal dialysis machine for the treatment of kidney failure. This medical treatment, however, is ineffective, for it cannot cause dead brain cells to regenerate; it will merely sustain biological life and prolong the patient's dying. Such treatment is considered by many physicians and medical ethicists to be extraordinary." Additionally, the Center for Health Care Ethics of St. Louis University, a Jesuit institution, prepared a brief for the Cruzan case which states that "within the Christian foundation, the withholding and withdrawing of medical treatment, including artificial nutrition and hydration, is acceptable."

So what can we do to protect ourselves and assure that our wishes are carried out? My plan is fourfold. First, we in Ohio must urge our legislators to pass living will legislation. Representative Marc Guthrie, from Newark, Ohio, has drafted a living will bill, House Bill 70. We must urge our legislators to pass this bill, since it is more comprehensive than the Senate version and will better protect our rights on this crucial issue.

Secondly, we must draw up our own living wills stating our philosophy on terminal care. I propose the use of the Medical Directive, a document created by Drs. Linda and Ezekiel Emanuel. This document details twelve specific treatments that could be offered. You can choose different treatment options based on four possible scenarios. You can indicate either that you desire the treatment, do not want it, are undecided, or want to try the treatment, but discontinue it if there is no improvement. This directive, which also includes space for a personal statement, eliminates much of the ambiguity of generic living wills and provides clearer guidelines to your physician and family.

Third, designate a person to make health care decisions for you should you become incompetent. This person should be familiar with your personal philosophy and feelings about terminal care and be likely to make the same decisions that you yourself would make. You should name this person in a Durable Power of Attorney for Health Care, a legal document that is now recognized in the State of Ohio.

Fourth, have a heart-to-heart talk with your doctor and be sure that he or she understands and supports your wishes on terminal care. Have a copy of your living will and Durable Power of Attorney for Health Care placed in your medical file. Finally, for more information on living wills, you can contact: The Society for the Right To Die, 250 West 57th St., New York, NY 10107, or send $1.00 to the Harvard Medical School Health Letter, 164 Longwood Ave., Fourth Floor, Boston, MA 02115 for a copy of the Emanuels' Medical Directive form.

I am interested in this issue because, through my husband, I have seen patients suffer the effects of not having an advance directive. You need to ask yourself how you feel about terminal care, but regardless of your personal response, we all must choose to protect our rights on this issue. WE must choose to pressure our legislators to adopt living will legislation. WE must choose to draw up our own living wills and health care proxies. And most importantly, WE must choose to discuss this most personal and sensitive issue with our families and loved ones, so that in the absence of a legal document, or even with one, they may confidently make the decisions concerning our life and death that we ourselves would make. Not all patients end up like Nancy Cruzan or Harry Smith. Many people are allowed to quietly slip away from the pain and suffering of life. But that can only happen after the careful, painful deliberation of a grieving family,

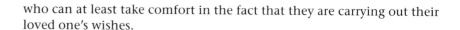

who can at least take comfort in the fact that they are carrying out their loved one's wishes.

Secondhand Smoke
Gina Norman

Gina Norman was a student at the University of Memphis, where she presented this persuasive speech in her public speaking class. The strengths of this speech include her effective introduction and conclusion and the use of a wealth of evidence in the body of the speech. Note how her introductory remarks involve the audience directly and how her conclusion sums up her message in a striking analogy that will be easy for listeners to remember. Note also how Gina integrates her evidence into the speech and works in references to the sources of her information.

Have you ever breathed smoke from someone else's cigarette? Have you ever sat beside someone or behind someone, they light up a cigarette, they take one puff, and then they're either holding it out to the side or they sit it in an ashtray? In my case I feel that I usually end up smoking more of that cigarette than the actual smoker does. As an involuntary smoker, a nonsmoker breathing smoke from others, you are at an increased risk for several diseases. According to former U.S. Surgeon General C. Everett Koop, it is now clear that disease risk due to the inhalation of tobacco smoke is not limited to the individual smoking. According to the American Cancer Society and our own *Fitness and Wellness* book here at Memphis State, undiluted sidestream smoke has higher concentrations of the toxic and carcinogenic compounds than found in mainstream smoke.

For the reason of smokers not being able to control the excess smoke from their cigarettes, cigars, and pipes, I believe smoking should be banned in public places. I'd like to share with you today the reasons for my statement, which include personal experiences and some statistics that I've obtained. My first personal experience was when I was little. I suffered from chronic upper respiratory infections, inner ear infections, and colds. I was in and out of the doctor's office all the time. My father smoked two packs of cigarettes a day. When I moved out, when I got older, I didn't have this problem, although I didn't connect it to cigarette smoking at that time. My other personal experience is where I work. As of last year, our office became nonsmoking. The two years previous that I worked there it was a smoking office. Every month it seemed I was going to the doctor for upper respiratory or inner ear infections. Finally they referred me to an allergist. And the allergist, Dr. Philip Lieberman here in Memphis, said I was allergic to smoke. I told him that our office is huge and I sat on the far, far end in the nonsmoking section. He said that didn't matter. In an enclosed area the air you're breathing is just recirculated. It's the same air that everybody breathes. The air conditioner heating ducts take the air in and then another duct pulls the air back out. So even though you may not be smelling the smoke, you're still breathing the compounds from it.

Our office, as I said, went nonsmoking January of '92. I think I've been maybe twice to the doctor for upper respiratory infections, so it's dropped significantly since our office became nonsmoking. These are just my personal experiences of how smoking aggravates my upper respiratory system, my inner ear, and my sinuses.

Now I'd like to share with you some statistics that I've obtained. According to the American Heart Association, environmental tobacco smoke, ETS, causes an estimated 53,000 deaths annually in the United States — two-thirds from heart disease and 4,000 from lung disease. The *Journal of the American Medical Association* concluded this January that heart disease is an important consequence to the exposure of environmental tobacco smoke. According again to the *Fitness and Wellness* book here at Memphis State, passive smoke aggravates and may precipitate angina. That's chest pain that is a result of diminished supply of blood to the heart. And it also states that secondhand smoke induces small airway dysfunctions in adults. According to the *American Journal of Public Health,* infants born to women who smoke during pregnancy are more likely to die from sudden infant death syndrome. The American Academy of Pediatrics estimates that nine million American children under the age of five may be exposed to environmental tobacco smoke. The American Cancer Society states that children exposed to secondhand smoke have increased risk of respiratory illnesses and infections, impaired development of lung function, and middle ear infections — which is exactly what I had when I was growing up. This is from *Cancer Facts and Figures* 1992. The Environmental Science Advisory Board, in reviewing evidence that environmental tobacco smoke causes excess lung cancer in adults and respiratory illnesses in children, has recommended that environmental tobacco smoke be classified as a Class A, which is a known human carcinogen.

Now this is taken from *Newsweek* 1992 [she refers to chart]. *Newsweek* got this from the Environmental Protection Agency. It's a draft they put out about the dangers of secondhand smoke. The Environmental Protection Agency is saying that secondhand smoke causes 3,000 lung cancer deaths a year; 35,000 heart disease deaths a year; contributes to 150,000 to 300,000 respiratory infections in babies, mainly bronchitis and pneumonia, resulting in 7,500 to 15,000 hospitalizations. It triggers 8,000 to 26,000 new cases of asthma in previously unaffected children and exacerbates symptoms in 400,000 to 1 million asthmatic children. In a study done by the *Journal of the American Medical Association* earlier this year, out of 663 non-smokers who either lived with smokers or worked in a smoking environment, 91 percent had metabolic byproducts of nicotine in their urine, including 162 who reported no exposure to environmental tobacco smoke for four days.

Now I know that this sounds like I have no empathy for the smoker, but I do. Someone I am very close to smokes, my husband. He's tried to quit for me, but he's had a lot of problems. He has a lot of physical withdrawal with quitting smoking. The bottom line, too, is he likes it. He likes to smoke. It helps him to concentrate when he's working, it helps him relax, and it's social. A lot of his friends smoke, and when they get together for a game they like to smoke. I respect his choice for smoking. I respect anybody who smokes; I respect their choice; they have that choice to smoke. However, it's not my choice. And when a smoker smokes in an enclosed area, that smoker takes away the choice for a nonsmoker. I feel that banning smoking in all public places is necessary to protect the health of people who do not smoke.

In closing I'd like to quote Julia Carol — she's with the Americans for Nonsmokers' Rights — when she was quoted in *Newsweek,* June 1992, that separate seating was a nice thought. But sitting in the nonsmoking section of a building is like swimming in the nonchlorinated section of a pool. The difference of course is that a little chlorine won't kill you. Other people's smoke may.

Pesticides Speech
Cesar Chavez

Cesar Chavez was the founder and president of the United Farm Workers union, which organized and led national boycotts of table grapes and iceberg lettuce to protest the misuse of pesticides. The following "generic" speech (dated 1990) was presented to a variety of audiences as Chavez went around the nation speaking to various groups. He would insert names and expand the concluding paragraph depending on the audience. Note the use of statistics in the speech to dramatize the severity of the problem. Consider also how Chavez weaves information and testimony into his message, carefully citing the sources of his information. His citing of "reluctant" testimony from the "grower's own magazine" helps to strengthen his case. Consider also Chavez's use of narratives and analogy to arouse emotion in this speech.

T hank you very much. I am truly honored to be able to speak with you. I would like to thank the many people who made this possible for their kindness and their hospitality (insert names).

Decades ago, the chemical industry promised the growers that pesticides would create vast new wealth and bountiful harvests. Just recently, the experts learned what farm workers, and the truly organic farmers have known for years. The prestigious National Academy of Sciences recently concluded an exhaustive five-year study which showed that by using simple, effective organic farming techniques, *instead of pesticides,* the growers could make *more money,* produce *more crops,* and *protect the environment!*

Unfortunately, the growers are not listening. They continue to spray and inject hundreds of millions of pounds of herbicides, fungicides, and insecticides onto our foods.

Most of you know that the United Farm Workers have focussed our struggle against pesticides on table grapes. Many people ask me "Why grapes?" The World Resources Institute reported that over three hundred thousand farm workers are poisoned every year by pesticides. Over half of all reported pesticide-related illnesses involve the cultivation or harvesting of table grapes. They receive *more* restricted-use application permits, which allow growers to spray pesticides known to threaten humans, than *any* other fresh food crop. The General Accounting Office, which does research for the U.S. Congress, determined that *34* of the *76* types of pesticides used *legally* on grapes pose potential human health hazards and could *not be detected* by current multi-residue methods.

My friends, grapes are the most dangerous fruit in America. The pesticides sprayed on table grapes are *killing America's children*. These pesticides *soak* the fields, *drift* with the wind, *pollute* the water, and are *eaten* by unwitting consumers. These poisons are designed to kill life, and pose a very real threat to consumers and farm workers alike.

The fields are sprayed with pesticides like captan, a fungicide believed to cause cancer, DNA mutation, and horrible birth defects. Other poisons take a similar toll. Parathion and phosdrin are *"nerve gas"* types of insecticides, which are believed to be responsible for the majority of farm worker poisonings in California. The growers spray sulphites, which can trigger asthmatic attacks, on the grapes. And even the growers' own magazine, *The California Farmer,* admitted that growers were *illegally* using a very dangerous growth stimulator, called *Fix,* which is quite similar to *Agent Orange,* on the grapes.

This is a very technical problem, with very *human* victims. One young body, Felipe Franco, was born without arms or legs in the agricultural town of McFarland. His mother worked for the first three months of her pregnancy picking grapes in fields that were sprayed repeatedly with pesticides believed to cause birth defects.

My friends, the central valley of California is one of the wealthiest agricultural regions in the world. In its midst are clusters of children dying from cancer. The children who live in towns like McFarland are surrounded by the grape fields that employ their parents. The children contact the poisons when they play outside, when they drink the water, and when they hug their parents returning from the fields. *And the children are dying.* They are dying *slow, painful, cruel* deaths in towns called *cancer clusters*. In cancer clusters like McFarland, where the childhood cancer rate is *800 percent* above normal.

A few months ago, the parents of a brave little girl in the agricultural community of Earlimart came to the United Farm Workers to ask for our help. Their four-year-old daughter, Natalie Ramirez, has lost one kidney to cancer and is threatened with the loss of another. The Ramirez family knew about our protests in nearby McFarland and thought there might be a similar problem in their home town. Our union members went door to door in Earlimart and found that the Ramirez family's worst fears were true. There are at least *four* other children suffering from cancer and similar diseases which the experts believe were caused by pesticides in the little town of Earlimart, a rate *1200 percent* above normal. In Earlimart, little Jimmy Caudillo died recently from leukemia at the age of three.

The grape vineyards of California have become America's Killing Fields. These *same* pesticides can be found on the grapes you buy in the store. Study after study, by the California Department of Food and Agriculture, by the Food and Drug Administration, and by objective newspapers, concluded that up to *54 percent* of the sampled grapes contained pesticide residues. Which pesticide did they find the most? *Captan,* the same carcinogenic fungicide that causes birth defects.

My friends, *the suffering must end. So many* children are dying, *so many* babies are born without limbs and vital organs, *so many* workers are dying in the fields.

The growers, the supermarket owners, say that the government can *handle* the problem, can *protect* the workers, can *save* the children. It *should,* but it *won't.* You see, agribusiness is *big business.* It is a *sixteen billion* dollar industry in California alone. Agribusiness contributed very heavily to the successful campaign of Republican governor George Deukmajian. He has rewarded the growers by turning the Agricultural Labor Relations Board into a tool for the growers, run by the growers. The governor even vetoed a bill that would have required growers to warn workers that they were entering recently sprayed fields! And only *one percent* of those growers who *are caught* violating pesticide laws were even fined in California.

President Bush is a long-time friend of agribusiness. During the last presidential campaign, George Bush ate grapes in a field just *75 miles* from the cemetery where little Jimmy Caudillo and other pesticide victims are buried, in order to show his support for the table grape industry. He recently gave a speech to the Farm Bureau, saying that it was up to the *growers* to restrain the use of dangerous pesticides.

That's like putting *Idi Amin,* or *Adolph Hitler,* in charge of promoting *peace* and *human rights.*

To show you what happens to pesticides supposedly under government control, I'd like to tell you more about captan. Testing to determine the acceptable tolerance levels of captan was done by Bio-Tech Laboratories, later found *guilty* of falsifying the data to the EPA. The tolerance level set was *ten times* the amount allowed in Canada. Later, government agencies tried to ban captan, but were mysteriously stopped several times. Finally, the government banned captan on 42 crops, but *not on grapes.* Even the General Accounting Office found that the government's pesticide testing is wholly inadequate. The government is *not* the answer, it is part of the problem.

The growers and their allies have tried to stop us with *lies,* with *police,* with *intimidation,* with *public relations agencies,* and with *violence.* But *we cannot be stopped.* In our *life and death struggle* for justice, we have turned to the court of last resort: the American people.

At last we are winning. Many supermarket chains have stopped selling or advertising grapes. Millions of consumers are refusing to buy America's most dangerous fruit. Many courageous people have volunteered to help our cause or joined human chains of people who fast, who go without food for days, to support our struggle. As a result, *grape sales keep falling.* We have witnessed truckloads of grapes being dumped because no one would stoop low enough to buy them. As demand drops, so do prices and profits. This sort of economic pressure is the only language the growers understand.

We are winning, but there is still much work to be done. If we are going to beat the greed and power of the growers, we must work *together.* *Together,* we can end the suffering. *Together,* we can save the children. *Together,* we can bring justice to the killing fields. I hope that you will join our struggle, for it is *your* struggle too. The simple act of boycotting table grapes laced with pesticides is a powerful statement the growers understand. *Please, boycott table grapes.* For your safety, for the workers, *we must act,* and *act together.* (insert additional pitches)

Good night, and God bless you.

Nobel Peace Prize Acceptance Speech
Elie Wiesel

Elie Wiesel delivered the following speech in Oslo, Norway, on December 10, 1986, as he accepted the Nobel Peace Prize. The award recognized his lifelong work for human rights, especially his role as "spiritual archivist of the Holocaust." Wiesel's poetic, intensely personal style as a writer carries over into this ceremonial speech of acceptance. He uses narrative very effectively as he flashes back to what he calls the "kingdom of night" and then flashes forward again into the present. The speech's purpose is to spell out and share the values and concerns of a life committed to the rights of oppressed peoples, in which, as he puts it so memorably, "every moment is a moment of grace, every hour an offering."

It is with a profound sense of humility that I accept the honor you have chosen to bestow upon me. I know: your choice transcends me. This both frightens and pleases me.

It frightens me because I wonder: do I have the right to represent the multitudes who have perished? Do I have the right to accept this great honor on their behalf? I do not. That would be presumptuous. No one may speak for the dead, no one may interpret their mutilated dreams and visions.

It pleases me because I may say that this honor belongs to all the survivors and their children, and through us, to the Jewish people with whose destiny I have always been identified.

I remember: it happened yesterday or eternities ago. A young Jewish boy discovering the kingdom of night. I remember his bewilderment, I remember his anguish. It all happened so fast. The ghetto. The deportation. The sealed cattle car. The fiery altar upon which the history of our people and the future of mankind were meant to be sacrificed.

I remember: he asked his father: "Can this be true? This is the 20th century, not the Middle Ages. Who would allow such crimes to be committed? How could the world remain silent?"

And now the boy is turning to me: "Tell me," he asks. "What have you done with your life?"

And I tell him that I have tried. That I have tried to keep memory alive, that I have tried to fight those who would forget. Because if we forget, we are guilty, we are accomplices.

And then I explained to him how naive we were, that the world did know and remain silent. And that is why I swore never to be silent whenever and wherever human beings endure suffering and humiliation. We must always take sides. Neutrality helps the oppressor, never the victim. Silence encourages the tormentor, never the tormented.

Sometimes we must interfere. When human lives are endangered, when human dignity is in jeopardy, national borders and sensitivities become irrelevant. Wherever men or women are persecuted because of their race, religion or political views, that place must — at that moment — become the center of our universe.

Of course, since I am a Jew profoundly rooted in my people's memory and tradition, my first response is to Jewish fears, Jewish needs, Jewish crises. For I belong to a traumatized generation, one that experienced the abandonment and solitude of our people. It would be unnatural for me not to make Jewish priorities my own: Israel, Soviet Jewry, Jews in Arab lands.

But there are others as important to me. Apartheid is, in my view, as abhorrent as anti-Semitism. To me, Andrei Sakharov's isolation is as much a disgrace as Iosif Begun's imprisonment. As is the denial of Solidarity and its leader Lech Walesa's right to dissent. And Nelson Mandela's interminable imprisonment.

There is so much injustice and suffering crying out for our attention: victims of hunger, or racism and political persecution, writers and poets, prisoners in so many lands governed by the left and by the right. Human rights are being violated on every continent. More people are oppressed than free.

And then, too, there are the Palestinians to whose plight I am sensitive but whose methods I deplore. Violence and terrorism are not the answer. Something must be done about their suffering, and soon. I trust Israel, for I have faith in the Jewish people. Let Israel be given a chance, let hatred and danger be removed from her horizons, and there will be peace in and around the Holy Land.

Yes, I have faith. Faith in God and even in His creation. Without it no action would be possible. And action is the only remedy to indifference: the most insidious danger of all. Isn't this the meaning of Alfred Nobel's legacy? Wasn't his fear of war a shield against war?

There is much to be done, there is much that can be done. One person — a Raoul Wallenberg, an Albert Schweitzer, one person of integrity, can make a difference, a difference of life and death. As long as one dissident is in prison, our freedom will not be true. As long as one child is hungry, our lives will be filled with anguish and shame.

What all these victims need above all is to know that they are not alone: that we are not forgetting them, that when their voices are stifled we shall lend them ours, that while their freedom depends on ours, the quality of our freedom depends on theirs.

This is what I say to the young Jewish boy wondering what I have done with his years. It is in his name that I speak to you and that I express to you my deepest gratitude. No one is as capable of gratitude as one who has emerged from the kingdom of night.

We know that every moment is a moment of grace, every hour an offering; not to share them would mean to betray them. Our lives no longer belong to us alone; they belong to all those who need us desperately.

Thank you Chairman Aarvik. Thank you members of the Nobel Committee. Thank you people of Norway, for declaring on this singular occasion that our survival has meaning for mankind.

Address to the United Nations Fourth World Conference on Women

Hillary Rodham Clinton

Hillary Rodham Clinton received her undergraduate degree from Wellesley College and a law degree from Yale University. She has been active in such causes as child welfare, health care reform, and women's rights. The following speech of inspiration was presented at the United Nations Fourth World Conference on Women, September 5, 1995. In this speech Mrs. Clinton speaks for the unseen and unheard women of the world as she shares the problems that beset them. Her use of parallel structure adds strength to her message. As the First Lady of the United States her presence lends the imprimatur of the U.S. government to her remarks. The speech is strongly embedded in values as it lobbies for human rights for women and protests the violation of such rights.

MRS. CLINTON: Mrs. Mongella, Under Secretary Kittani, distinguished delegates and guests: I would like to thank the Secretary General of the United Nations for inviting me to be part of the United Nations Fourth World Conference on Women. This is truly a celebration — a celebration of the contributions women make in every aspect of life: in the home, on the job, in their communities, as mothers, wives, sisters, daughters, learners, workers, citizens and leaders.

It is also a coming together, much the way women come together every day in every country.

We come together in fields and in factories. In village markets and supermarkets. In living rooms and board rooms.

Whether it is while playing with our children in the park, or washing clothes in a river, or taking a break at the office water cooler, we come together and talk about our aspirations and concerns. And time and again, our talk turns to our children and our families. However different we may be, there is far more that unites us than divides us. We share a common future. And we are here to find common ground so that we may help bring new dignity and respect to women and girls all over the world — and in so doing, bring new strength and stability to families as well.

By gathering in Beijing, we are focusing world attention on issues that matter most in the lives of women and their families: access to education, health care, jobs and credit, the chance to enjoy basic legal and human rights and participate fully in the political life of their countries.

There are some who question the reason for this conference.

Let them listen to the voices of women in their homes, neighborhoods, and workplaces.

There are some who wonder whether the lives of women and girls matter to economic and political progress around the globe.

Let them look at the women gathered here and at Huairou — the homemakers, nurses, teachers, lawyers, policymakers, and women who run their own businesses.

It is conferences like this that compel governments and people everywhere to listen, look and face the world's most pressing problems.

Wasn't it after the women's conference in Nairobi ten years ago that the world focused for the first time on the crisis of domestic violence?

Earlier today, I participated in a World Health Organization forum, where government officials, NGOs, and individual citizens are working on ways to address the health problems of women and girls.

Tomorrow, I will attend a gathering of the United Nations Development Fund for Women. There, the discussion will focus on local — and highly successful — programs that give hard-working women access to credit so they can improve their own lives and the lives of their families.

What we are learning around the world is that if women are healthy and educated, their families will flourish. If women are free from violence, their families will flourish. If women have a chance to work and earn as full and equal partners in society, their families will flourish.

And when families flourish, communities and nations will flourish.

That is why every woman, every man, every child, every family, and every nation on our planet has a stake in the discussion that takes place here.

Over the past 25 years, I have worked persistently on issues relating to women, children and families. Over the past two-and-a-half years, I have had the opportunity to learn more about the challenges facing women in my own country and around the world.

I have met new mothers in Jojakarta, Indonesia, who come together regularly in their village to discuss nutrition, family planning, and baby care.

I have met working parents in Denmark who talk about the comfort they feel in knowing that their children can be cared for in creative, safe, and nurturing after-school centers.

I have met women in South Africa who helped lead the struggle to end apartheid and are now helping build a new democracy.

I have met with the leading women of the Western Hemisphere who are working every day to promote literacy and better health care for the children of their countries.

I have met women in India and Bangladesh who are taking out small loans to buy milk cows, rickshaws, thread and other materials to create a livelihood for themselves and their families.

I have met doctors and nurses in Belarus and Ukraine who are trying to keep children alive in the aftermath of Chernobyl.

The great challenge of this Conference is to give voice to women everywhere whose experiences go unnoticed, whose words go unheard.

Women comprise more than half the world's population. Women are 70 percent of the world's poor, and two-thirds of those who are not taught to read and write.

Women are the primary caretakers for most of the world's children and elderly. Yet much of the work we do is not valued — not by economists, not by historians, not by popular culture, not by government leaders.

At this very moment, as we sit here, women around the world are giving birth, raising children, cooking meals, washing clothes, cleaning houses, planting crops, working on assembly lines, running companies, and running countries.

Women also are dying from diseases that should have been prevented or treated; they are watching their children succumb to malnutrition caused by poverty and economic deprivation; they are being denied the right to go to school by their own fathers and brothers; they are being forced into prostitution, and they are being barred from the bank lending office and banned from the ballot box.

Those of us who have the opportunity to be here have the responsibility to speak for those who could not.

As an American, I want to speak up for women in my own country — women who are raising children on the minimum wage, women who can't afford health care or child care, women whose lives are threatened by violence, including violence in their own homes.

I want to speak up for mothers who are fighting for good schools, safe neighborhoods, clean air and clean airwaves; for older women, some of them widows, who have raised their families and now find that their skills and life experiences are not valued in the workplace; for women who are working all night as nurses, hotel clerks, and fast food cooks so that they can be at home during the day with their kids; and for women everywhere who simply don't have time to do everything they are called upon to do each day.

Speaking to you today, I speak for them, just as each of us speaks for women around the world who are denied the chance to go to school, or see a doctor, or own property, or have a say about the direction of their lives, simply because they are women. The truth is that most women around the world work both inside and outside the home, usually by necessity.

We need to understand that there is no formula for how women should lead their lives.

That is why we must respect the choices that each woman makes for herself and her family. Every woman deserves the chance to realize her God-given potential.

We also must recognize that women will never gain full dignity until their human rights are respected and protected.

Our goals for this Conference, to strengthen families and societies by empowering women to take greater control over their own destinies, cannot be fully achieved unless all governments — here and around the world — accept their responsibility to protect and promote internationally recognized human rights.

The international community has long acknowledged — and recently affirmed at Vienna — that both women and men are entitled to a range of protections and personal freedoms, from the right of personal security to the right to determine freely the number and spacing of the children they bear.

No one should be forced to remain silent for fear of religious or political persecution, arrest, abuse or torture.

Tragically, women are most often the ones whose human rights are violated.

Even in the late 20th century, the rape of women continues to be used as an instrument of armed conflict. Women and children make up a large majority of the world's refugees. When women are excluded from the political process, they become even more vulnerable to abuse.

I believe that, on the eve of a new millennium, it is time to break our silence. It is time for us to say here in Beijing, and the world to hear, that it is no longer acceptable to discuss women's rights as separate from human rights.

These abuses have continued because, for too long, the history of women has been a history of silence. Even today, there are those who are trying to silence our words.

The voices of this conference and of the women at Huairou must be heard loud and clear:

It is a violation of human rights when babies are denied food, or drowned, or suffocated, or their spines broken, simply because they are born girls.

It is a violation of human rights when women and girls are sold into the slavery of prostitution.

It is a violation of human rights when women are doused with gasoline, set on fire and burned to death because their marriage dowries are deemed too small.

It is a violation of human rights when individual women are raped in their own communities and when thousands of women are subjected to rape as a tactic or prize of war.

It is a violation of human rights when a leading cause of death worldwide among women ages 14 to 44 is the violence they are subjected to in their own homes.

It is a violation of human rights when young girls are brutalized by the painful and degrading practice of genital mutilation.

It is a violation of human rights when women are denied the right to plan their own families, and that includes being forced to have abortions or being sterilized against their will.

If there is one message that echoes forth from this conference, it is that human rights are women's rights — and women's rights are human rights. Let us not forget that among those rights are the right to speak freely — and the right to be heard.

Women must enjoy the right to participate fully in the social and political lives of their countries if we want freedom and democracy to thrive and endure.

It is indefensible that many women in nongovernmental organizations who wished to participate in this conference have not been able to attend — or have been prohibited from fully taking part.

Let me be clear. Freedom means the right of people to assemble, organize, and debate openly. It means respecting the views of those who may disagree with the views of their governments. It means not taking citizens away from their loved ones and jailing them, mistreating them, or denying them their freedom or dignity because of the peaceful expression of their ideas and opinions.

In my country, we recently celebrated the 75th anniversary of women's suffrage. It took 150 years after the signing of our Declaration of Independence for women to win the right to vote.

It took 72 years of organized struggle on the part of many courageous women and men. It was one of America's most divisive philosophical wars. But it was also a bloodless war. Suffrage was achieved without a shot being fired.

We have also been reminded, in V-J Day observances last weekend, of the good that comes when men and women join together to combat the forces of tyranny and build a better world.

We have seen peace prevail in most places for a half century. We have avoided another world war.

But we have not solved older, deeply-rooted problems that continue to diminish the potential of half the world's population.

Now it is time to act on behalf of women everywhere.

If we take bold steps to better the lives of women, we will be taking bold steps to better the lives of children and families too.

Families rely on mothers and wives for emotional support and care; families rely on women for labor in the home; and increasingly, families rely on women for income needed to raise healthy children and care for other relatives.

As long as discrimination and inequities remain so commonplace around the world — as long as girls and women are valued less, fed less, fed last, overworked, underpaid, not schooled and subjected to violence in and out of their homes — the potential of the human family to create a peaceful, prosperous world will not be realized.

Let this Conference be our — and the world's — call to action.

And let us heed the call so that we can create a world in which every woman is treated with respect and dignity, every boy and girl is loved and cared for equally, and every family has the hope of a strong and stable future.

Thank you very much.

God's blessings on you, your work and all who will benefit from it.

Women in Public Life
Commencement Address,
Radcliffe University, June 11, 1993
Elizabeth Dole

Elizabeth Hanford Dole received an undergraduate degree from Duke University, a master's degree from Radcliffe, and a law degree from Harvard. Mrs. Dole served as the Secretary of Transportation and the Secretary of Labor during the Reagan and Bush administrations. More recently she has been president of the American Red Cross. As Secretary of Transportation she instituted campaigns against drunken driving and for automobile safety. As Secretary of Labor she worked on programs of job training for at-risk youth, job safety regulations, stricter enforcement of child-labor laws, and ways to shatter the glass ceiling that often precludes women from advancing in organizations. Mrs. Dole's commencement address is a speech of inspiration aimed at getting the female graduates to realize their own potential and value as women. She suggests public service as a viable alternative to the private sector for women. She uses personal examples and narratives to give authenticity to her advice to the young graduates.

I have been asked to share some thoughts this afternoon on women in public policy — an interesting topic, because while there are more women in public leadership roles than in private, there are still relatively few. While there are greater opportunities for women in public leadership than in private, there are still relatively few. While there are greater opportunities for women in government, there obviously remain impediments.

There are many ways to pursue the goal of involving women in shaping public policy. And there are many reasons to pursue this goal. In the first place, it's right. Too many of our number have felt the sting of discrimination. Secondly, women, I believe, have something very special to offer.

And, thirdly, our work force is changing. America must be able to welcome women and minorities into its leadership roles if we are to accommodate that change. Sixty-four percent of the new entrants to the work force over the next 10 years will be women. If the public sector is to attract the best and the brightest, it must be able to attract and reward women.

When I was in law school at Harvard, only 24 of the 550 students were women. There were only a few women, at the time, who had made partner in major law firms. The private sector simply was not a strong option. Public policy beckoned as a rewarding alternative — a call to service, a chance to make a positive difference in people's lives.

There are some observations I could offer [women today] which might smooth the way a little. I could summarize them this way: that our greatest obstacle — that we women are women in a world of men — is really an enormous opportunity.

Remember the question Henry Higgins asked in the film *My Fair Lady,* "Why can't a woman be more like a man?" Because I think it's important to learn the correct lesson from our successes, I believe that further gains do not depend on better answers to the question, "Why can't a woman be more like a man?" The question we should be asking now is "Why can't a woman be more like a woman?"

I'd like to quote for you from a recent article in *Life* magazine: "Women," the article asserts, "are more committed than men to cushioning the hard corners of the country, to making it a safer place. Women want stricter law enforcement against drunk driving and illegal firearms and drug dealing. . . . It's not that men don't care about these issues. It's simply that women care more."

I don't know whether that's true. But perhaps our approach is different. Perhaps our involvement in public policy debates provides a leavening influence. Perhaps more women in public service would result in greater focus on cushioning corners for vulnerable Americans. If that's so, then it is doubly important that we women add our voices to the national debates, that we take our places at the tables of power, that we rise to the challenge of leadership when we believe that to be our calling.

So then, why can't a woman be more like a woman? In other words, progress for women in public policy and private life may indeed hinge on our ability to acknowledge and develop our skills and values as women. It may just be that those are the skills and values our country needs most at this moment.

I have been privileged during my years in public service to work with a number of successful women in public policy and I would like to pass along some of their observations, and some of my own, about drawing on our professional female advantages.

The first is to take full advantage of our trumpeted trait of flexibility — in fact to plan for the unexpected, and relish our ability to think on our feet. Rigid guidelines, set agendas, and line reporting responsibilities all help create the illusion of control in the current management environment. But perhaps a knack for flexibility is more important.

Another observation I have is that to succeed in the public arena, women must learn to trust their instincts. It's not just female intuition — it's a cognitive skill that we are perhaps more open to. Estimation skills are now being taught to children as they come up through elementary and secondary schools, and instinct is oftentimes another word for it. It's an ability to take in a great deal of information and quickly reduce it to a rough but generally accurate picture. It's the soft route to hard data.

Yet too often we women allow ourselves to be intimidated into denying our instincts — whether it's a judgment of people, situations, or the heart of the policy question. The women in the audience have probably all had the experience of sitting across the table from someone — a man, let's say, with whom you disagree. Ask yourselves: how many times, in this situation, has your reaction been to question your own judgment rather than his — only to find out later that you were right on the money?

Over the ages, we women have perfected to a high art form this trait of second-guessing ourselves. Perhaps it stems from our early constant exposure to society's message that female traits and talents are inferior; but we have to get over it. It takes confidence to trust ourselves, and if we don't have confidence, our voices will be lost if ever they're heard.

The third common denominator I've seen among successful women leaders is a commitment to those who follow. About twenty years ago, a group of us formed an organization called "Executive Women in Government," which still flourishes today. Its purpose is twofold: to help younger women who want to follow into public service by giving them information and advice, and to make it easier for women in policy-making positions to relate to one another across government. Networking — women reaching out to other women — is a way of using our special opportunities to overcome obstacles. I have been helped many times in the stages of my career by women who were ahead of me. As a result, my door is always open to young women who are in need of a mentor, and I would encourage other women to do the same.

The final challenge for women is not to let others define success for us. Our lives are complicated, balancing personal and professional goals, loving our families while searching for individual fulfillment. And every woman must find her own answers — answers that are right for her. Women must allow ourselves, and each other, the freedom to choose. Women across America are discovering that feeling in as many ways as there are women — some through public service, some in the world of business or as lawyers and doctors, and some as wives, mothers, and volunteers. No one can or should tell us where we will find that feeling, or how we will come to define our own success. These are decisions we alone can make for ourselves.

In the fairy tales we were read as children, once having been rescued by the prince, the "female lead" lives happily ever after. That was the theme in Cinderella, Snow White, and Sleeping Beauty. But now perhaps we need to read our daughters a new bedtime story — with a heroine who isn't a princess, but a woman who sees that there are things that need to be changed to make life better for herself and others. A woman who is not a victim, and who doesn't need a rescuer. We need a tale about a woman whose talents and abilities are valued and admired, a woman who uses those talents to succeed. A woman who is committed, who feels passionately about her life's decisions. Such a story would not be a fairy tale — there are thousands of examples. And if each of us continues to ask the right question, "Why can't a woman be more like a woman?" there will be hundreds of thousands more tomorrow.

After-Dinner Speech

Dick Jackman

Dick Jackman, an executive with Sun Oil, presented this after-dinner speech at an awards banquet of the National Football Foundation and Hall of Fame in December of 1984. It meets the requirements of a good after-dinner speech in that it is short, light, and lively, yet carries a more serious message — in this case the importance of leadership, teamwork, and optimism in our lives. Note how the humor in this speech arises out of the situation. Note also the use of narratives, complete with dialogue, that create suspense and sustain attention throughout the speech.

Thank you. Sorry I'm so late getting up here. It's about a $2 cab ride from the back row. All of us back there in the cheap seats admire these young athletes, and some of us remarked that we have underwear older than they are.

I'm pleased to be here to share this moment. I look at the logistics here on the dais — Doug Flutie seated alongside Joe Greene. That's like parking a Volkswagen alongside a school bus. And for those of you sitting under the chandelier, you should be aware that it was installed by the low bidder some time ago.

O.K. A football team seems to do best when it produces a combination of leadership and teamwork, and America seems to do best when it produces that same combination. Teamwork being that special quality that helps us look at life not from the standpoint of what's in it for us but from the standpoint of what we can do to help, and leadership being that special quality that helps an awful lot of people in and out of this room stand up on their tiptoes and look over the horizon and lead people there.

You cannot possibly leave this hotel tonight without a great deal of optimism about the future of not only football but America, because there's so much of it in here, and optimism is not meant to be stored. It's meant to be exported. You export it to other people. You make them determined to do that something extra in life that brings a response from others.

Let me mention the finest illustration I've ever heard of doing something extra. We had a teenage neighbor back home, a nice fellow. One day he got home at midnight. His mother said, "Where have you been?" He said, "I was out with my girl." His mother said "I ought to give you a whipping for staying out so late, but you're being honest with me. I admire your honesty. Have some cookies and go to bed." The next night the kid got home at 1:00 AM. His mother said, "Where were you tonight?" He said, "Same place. Out with my girl." His mother said, "I ought to give you the whipping of your life, but since you're being honest with me, have some more cookies and go to bed." The next night, he came home at 2:00 AM. His father was waiting up for him. The kid walked into the house. The father picked up a huge frying pan and turned to face him. The mother leaped to her feet and screamed, "Please don't hit him!" The father said, "Who's going to hit him? I'm going to fry him some eggs. He can't keep this up on cookies." So good people, if you sometimes have difficulty keeping up the pace and the love and the concern for other people on cookies, then let me encourage you to fry some eggs.

By this time we've all learned that, aerodynamically, the bumblebee shouldn't be able to fly. The body is too large. The wings are too small. Every time it takes off it should plunge back to the earth. But fortunately, the bumblebee does not understand its engineering limitations. And it's a good thing it doesn't, or we'd be living in a world of plastic flowers and putting mustard on our pancakes. It's a good thing that Scott Hamilton, at 5'3" and 115 pounds, did not realize that he could not possibly become the world's greatest ice skater, and that Mary Lou Retton, at 4'10", and Doug Flutie, who is here with us tonight, about a foot taller than that, did not realize that they could not possibly become the best at what they do, and that Shakespeare, whose mother could not read or write, did not realize that he couldn't possibly become the world's most honored writer.

And perhaps it's a great thing that 208 years ago, Betsy Ross took out her needle and thread. She did not realize that she could not possibly be sewing together an emblem that would one day umbrella the greatest experiment in human opportunity ever tried on this planet.

Let us not look at our limitations tomorrow morning. Let us pursue our possibilities.

On our track team at the University of Iowa we had a cross-eyed javelin thrower. He didn't win any medals, but he certainly kept the crowd alert. Perhaps part of our mission tonight and all the nights and days to follow is to keep the crowd in our homes, in our schools, and in our country alert to their possibilities and not their limitations.

That's far enough. Have an exciting life. Good night.

Martin Luther King at the Mountaintop
John Scipio

This speech of tribute honoring Dr. Martin Luther King, Jr. was presented by John Scipio in his public speaking class at the University of Memphis. In this speech John uses the technique of magnification by demonstrating that Dr. King had to overcome great obstacles, that his performance was unusual and superior, and that he sacrificed himself for the cause of humanity. Note the colorful use of language in this speech. His graphic descriptions of the stormy April night and of the plight of the sanitation workers in Memphis are good examples. Note that to obtain some of the background information for the speech, John conducted a telephone interview with Dr. Ralph Abernathy of the Southern Christian Leadership Conference. The inclusion of this information increased both the authenticity of the message and the speaker's ethos.

On the stormy night of April 3, 1968, three thousand onlookers came to Mason Temple here in Memphis, Tennessee, to hear what many have considered to be one of the greatest speeches in Martin Luther King, Jr.'s history. The title: "I've Been to the Mountaintop." Richard Lynch in his monograph, "Sixty-five Days in Memphis," describes it as being one of the finest speeches of his career, matching the eloquence of his "I Have a Dream" peroration at the 1963 march on Washington. In it, King seemed to foretell his own death.

Now, King may have used this speech as a medium to predict his forthcoming assassination. But no one really knows. Whether or not he was a prophet, no one can really tell. But in his speech, King constantly refers to death. He often talks about "the Promised Land" and how beautiful it is over there. He also refers, at the ending of his speech, that he may not get to the Promised Land with them, but they as a people will get to the Promised Land.

In order to understand the message that Dr. King was trying to convey in his — to the masses that night, we must look beyond the speech to the conditions and events that were taking place during that time. Dr. King had become the leader of the movement for many years. And many of those that were involved in the actions of the day viewed him as their champion. When injustice raised its ugly head, he would come to the rescue like a mighty warrior. When freedom was being denied, he was there. He was there in Selma, in Montgomery, in Birmingham, and, finally, in Memphis.

But what was it that brought Dr. King to Memphis? The answer — thirteen hundred sanitation workers and their families who thought they had been treated unfairly by the city of Memphis in general and by Mayor Loeb in particular. These workers were angered by the fact that the city refused to recognize their union, the American Federation of State, County, and Municipal Employees, Local 1733. Their frustrations reached a boiling point, and they decided to take action and go on strike. Dr. King came to Memphis to give his support to the workers and to urge others to do the same.

Now, many problems had arisen during the course of the civil rights movement that did nothing insofar as to help the cause, but to cripple it. The violence that erupted during the first march led by Dr. King in Memphis caused many to doubt the effectiveness of his nonviolent movement. Many were tired and weary from this long struggle that they had endured. They were almost to the point of surrender.

Through the speech, Dr. King had to give them some type of motivation — a reason to go on and continue the struggle. With all of the problems that were being put upon him, Dr. King was reluctant to speak that particular night. So, in his stead, he sent his closest friend, Ralph Abernathy. Upon Mr. Abernathy's arrival at Mason Temple and seeing the throngs of people who had come out to hear Dr. King, he immediately phoned him and said, "They're your crowd." They needed a speech that only Dr. King could give.

When asked in a telephone interview what he thought the attraction to Dr. King was, Abernathy stated, "He possessed a power, never before seen in a man of color." What was this power that Abernathy spoke of? It was the power to persuade audiences and change opinions with his words. It was the power of speech. This particular speech is the most evident example of that power. King is a master at using metaphors to dramatize his subject. An example of this is when he states that the nation is sick, there is trouble in the land. He does this to bring life to the suffering that was going on during this time. In his speech, Dr. King had to give these people hope and motivate them to go on. He did this by speaking of the Promised Land and how beautiful it was.

He also makes use of metaphors when he makes reference to the verses of Scripture, which say, "Let justice roll down like waters and righteousness like a mighty stream." King was a master. King's rhetorical style is very effective in conveying his message as well. He uses key phrases time and time again to pound out their meaning. An example of this is when he speaks of a letter, written to him by a little white girl from White Plains. He says that in this letter, she says, "As it should not matter, I am white. I am only writing to say that I read the article in the *New York Times* that stated the blade was so close to your aorta that if you had sneezed, you would have been dead. And I'm just writing to say I'm so happy that you didn't sneeze." Dr. King uses the phrase "if I had sneezed" to backtrack the movement and give us its history.

Another phrase that stands out in this speech is "but I wouldn't stop there." This is a phrase used in the beginning of Dr. King's speech, to give us — take us through — a mental flight of history, up until the present day.

Dr. King's oratorical brilliance is personified in this, his last and greatest speech. Many can be referred to as "speaker," but only a select few have earned the title of "orator." Dr. King was truly an orator.

Glossary

acronym A word composed of the initial letters or parts of a series of words. (9)

addressing attitudes and values A function of persuasive speech that attempts to form, reform, or reinforce audience attitudes. (13)

ad hominem **argument** An attempt to discredit a position by attacking the people who favor it. (14)

after-dinner speech A brief, often humorous, ceremonial speech, presented after a meal, that offers a message without asking for radical changes in attitude or action. (15)

agenda-setting function Employing information to create a sense of what is important. (12)

alliteration The repetition of initial consonant sounds in closely connected words. (10)

amplification The art of developing ideas by strategic repetition in a speech. (10)

analogical argument Creating a strategic perspective on a subject by relating it to something about which the audience has strong positive or negative feelings. (14)

analogous color Colors adjacent on the color wheel; used in a presentation aid to suggest both differences and close relationships among the components represented. (9)

analogy A connection established between two otherwise dissimilar ideas or things. (6, 12)

antithesis A language technique that combines opposing elements in the same sentence or adjoining sentences. (10)

archetypal metaphor A metaphor that draws upon human experience that is common, intense, and enduring, and that arouses group feeling. (10)

argument A combination of evidence and proofs designed to produce a strong case for one side of an issue. (14)

articulation The manner in which individual speech sounds are produced. (11)

assimilation The tendency of listeners to interpret the positions of a speaker with whom they agree as closer to their own views than they actually are. (3)

attitudes Pre-existing complexes of feelings, beliefs, and inclinations that we have toward people, places, events, or ideas. (4)

audience demographics Observable characteristics of listeners, including age, gender, educational level, group affiliations, and sociocultural backgrounds, that the speaker considers when adapting to an audience. (4)

audience dynamics The motivations, attitudes, beliefs, and values that influence the behavior of listeners. (4)

award presentation A speech of tribute that recognizes achievements of the award recipient, explains the nature of the award, and describes why the recipient qualifies for the award. (15)

balance Achieving a balance among the major parts of a presentation. (7)

bar graph A kind of graph that shows comparisons and contrasts between two or more items or groups. (9)

begging the question Assuming that an argument has been proved without actually presenting the evidence. (14)

beliefs Things accepted as true about a subject. (4)

belongingness needs In Maslow's Hierarchy of Needs, the need for group membership, acceptance, friendship, love, nurturance, and enjoyment. (4)

body The middle part of a speech, used to develop the main ideas. (2)

body language Communication achieved using facial expressions, eye contact, movements, and gestures. (11)

boomerang effect An audience's hostile reaction to a speech advocating too much or too radical change. (13)

brainstorming A group technique that encourages all members to contribute freely and creatively to the range of options available for consideration. (Appendix A)

brief example A specific instance illustrating a more general idea. (6)

briefing A short, informative presentation given in an organizational setting. (12)

call the question A motion that proposes to end the discussion on a motion and to bring it to a vote. (Appendix A)

categorical design The use of natural or traditional divisions within a subject as a way of structuring an informative speech. (12)

causation design A pattern for an informative speech that shows how one condition generates, or is generated by, another. (12)

celebratory function The function of a speech designed to mark the importance of an occasion or accomplishment. (5)

ceremonial speech A group of speech types that emphasizes the importance of shared values. Includes the speech of tribute, the speech of acceptance, the speech of introduction, and the after-dinner speech. (3, 15)

closed question In an interview, a question that constrains the interviewee to a brief, yes-or-no response. (5)

co-active approach A way of approaching reluctant audiences in which the speaker attempts to establish good will, emphasizes shared values, and sets modest goals for persuasion. (13)

cognitive restructuring The process of replacing negative thoughts with positive, constructive ones. (2)

collaborative problem solving In group communication, an approach that gathers participants from separate areas of the public or private sectors for their input on a problem. (Appendix A)

communication anxiety Concern or nervousness experienced before or during speaking in public. (2)

communication environment The overall conditions, both physical and psychological, in which communication occurs. (1)

comparative design A pattern for an informative speech that relates an unfamiliar subject to something the audience already knows or understands. (12)

comparison Using supporting material to point out the similarities of an unfamiliar or controversial issue to something the audience already knows or accepts. (6)

comparison and contrast An informative speech design that points out similarities and differences between subjects or ideas. (12)

competence The speaker's appearance of being informed, intelligent, and well prepared. (2)

complementary color Colors opposite one another on the color wheel; used in a presentation aid to suggest tension and opposition among various elements. (9)

computer-assisted presentation The use of commercial presentation software to join audio, visual, text, graphic, and animated components. (9)

concluding remarks The speaker's final reflections on the meaning of the speech. (2, 7)

conclusion The last part of a speech, which should include a summary statement and concluding remarks (2); the proposition that follows the major and minor premises of a syllogism and directs the audience toward the speaker's point of view. (14)

consciousness-raising Making an audience more sensitive to an issue and more receptive to future persuasion. (13)

constructive listening The role of the listener in the creation of meaning. Involves discovering the speaker's intention, tracing out the implications and consequences of the message, and applying the message to one's life. (3)

contending with opposition A function of persuasive speech that confronts the opposition by systematically refuting its claims. (13)

contrast Using supporting materials to emphasize difference between two things. (6)

contrast effect A tendency by listeners to distort the positions of a speaker with whom they disagree and to interpret those positions as even more distant from their own opinions than they actually are. (3)

coordination The requirement that statements equal in importance be placed on the same level in an outline. (8)

critical thinking and listening An integrated way of assessing information, ideas, and proposals that calls not for accepting them at face value, but for exploring the grounds for these views, checking them against previous experience, and discussing them with knowledgeable others. (3)

critique An evaluation of a speech. (3)

cultural gridlock Occurs when the cultural differences in a group are so profound that the varying agendas, priorities, customs, and procedures create tensions that block constructive discussion. (Appendix A)

cultural sensitivity The respectful, appreciative awareness of the diversity within an audience. (10)

culturetype A term expressing the values and goals of a group's culture. (10)

decoding The process by which the listener determines the meaning of the speaker's message and decides the speaker's intent. (1)

deductive argument A kind of proof that begins with a generally accepted truth, connects an issue with that truth, and draws a conclusion based on the connection. (14)

definition A translation of a word an audience may not be familiar with into understandable terms. (6)

deliberation Allowing all sides to express their opinions before a decision is made. (13)

description Vivid "word pictures" to help listeners visualize information. (6)

dialect A speech pattern associated with an area of the country or with a cultural or ethnic background. (11)

dialogue group A group assembled to explore the underlying assumptions of a problem but not necessarily to solve it. (Appendix A)

direct quotation Repeating the exact words of another to support a point. (6)

egocentrism Holding the view that one's own experiences and thoughts are the norm. (1)

either-or thinking A fallacy that occurs when the speaker informs listeners that they have only two options, only one of which is desirable. (14)

encoding The process by which the speaker combines words, tones, and gestures to convey thought and feelings to the audience. (1)

enunciation The manner in which individual words are articulated and pronounced in context. (11)

esteem needs In Maslow's Hierarchy of Needs, the need for a positive self-image and self-respect, and the need to be respected by others. (4)

ethics The moral dimension of human conduct, governing how we treat others and wish to be treated in return. (1)

ethnocentrism The tendency of any nation, race, religion, or organized group to believe that its way of looking at and doing things is right and that other perspectives have less value. (1, 4)

ethos Those characteristics that make a speaker appear honest, credible, and appealing (1); a kind of proof created by a speaker's own favorable impression and by association with credible testimony. (14)

eulogy A speech of tribute presented upon a person's death. (15)

evidence Supporting materials used in persuasive speeches, including facts and figures, examples, narratives, and testimony. (14)

example A verbal illustration of an oral message. (6)

expanded conversational style A speaker's style that, while more formal than everyday conversation, preserves its directness and spontaneity. (11)

expert testimony Information derived from authorities within a field. (6)

explanation A combination of facts and statistics to clarify a topic or process mentioned in a speech. (6)

extemporaneous speaking A form of presentation in which a speech, although carefully prepared and practiced, is not written out or memorized. (3, 11)

extended example A detailed illustration that allows a speaker to build impressions. (6)

fact Verifiable unit of information. (6)

factual example An illustration based on something that actually happened or that really exists. (6)

fallacy An error in persuasion. (14)

faulty analogy A comparison drawn between things that are dissimilar in some important way. (14)

feedback The audience's immediate response to a speaker. (1, 11)

figurative analogy A comparison made between things that belong to different fields. (6, 12)

filtering Listening to only part of a message, the part the listener wants to hear. (3)

flow chart A visual method of representing power and responsibility relationships. (9)

forcefulness A favorable impression created by a speaker's competence, integrity, decisiveness, and confidence. (2)

formal outline The final outline in a process leading from the first rough ideas for a speech to the finished product. (8)

gender stereotyping Generalizations based on oversimplified or outmoded assumptions about gender and gender roles. (4)

general function A speech's overall function. (3, 5)

good form A primary principle of structure, based on simplicity, symmetry, and orderliness. (7)

good reasons The persuasive speaker's justification of a recommendation, based on responsible knowledge and consideration of the listeners' best interests. (13)

graphics Visual representations of information. (9)

great expectation fallacy The mistaken idea that major change can be accomplished by a single persuasive effort. (13)

groupthink Occurs when a single, uncritical frame of mind dominates group thinking and prevents the full, objective analysis of specific problems. (Appendix A)

habitual pitch The level at which people speak most frequently. (11)

hasty generalization An error of inductive reasoning in which a claim is based on insufficient or nonrepresentative information. (14)

hyperbole A technique of language the employs exaggeration to make points and arouse feeling. (10)

hypothetical example A representation of reality, usually a synthesis of actual people, situations, or events. (6)

identification The close involvement of subject, speaker, and listener. (2, 7, 15)

ideograph A word conveying a group's basic political faith or system of beliefs. (10)

image A mental picture created by the use of vivid examples. (10)

immediacy A quality of successful communication achieved when the speaker and audience experience a sense of closeness. (11)

impromptu speaking A talk delivered with minimal or no preparation. (11)

inductive argument The use of specific instances to build general conclusions. (14)

information card A record of facts and ideas obtained from an article or book used in research. (5)

informative function The function of a speech designed to share knowledge with listeners or expand their competence in an area. (5)

informative speech Speech aimed at extending understanding. (3, 12)

informative value A measure of how much new and important information or understanding a speech conveys to an audience. (12)

integrity The quality of being ethical, honest, and dependable. (2)

interest chart A means of finding a speech topic whereby the speaker charts his or her personal interests and those of the audience in order to determine points of convergence. (5)

interference Any physical noise or psychological distraction that impedes the hearing of a speech. (1)

internal summary Reminding listeners of major points already presented in a speech before new ideas are introduced. (7)

introduction The first part of a speech, intended to gain the audience's attention and prepare it for the rest of the presentation. (2)

inversion Changing the normal word order to make statements memorable and emphatic. (10)

jargon Technical language related to a specific field, but often used before an audience that may not understand it. (10)

key-word outline An abbreviated version of a formal outline, used in presenting a speech. (2, 8)

lay testimony Information that is derived from the firsthand experience of ordinary citizens. (6)

likableness The quality of radiating goodness and good will and inspiring audience affection in return. (2)

line graph A visual representation of changes across time; especially useful for indicating trends of growth or decline. (9)

listener A person who interprets the message offered by the speaker to construct its meaning. (1)

literal analogy A comparison made between subjects within the same field. (12)

logos A form of proof that makes rational appeals based on facts and figures and expert testimony. (14)

magnification A speaker's selecting and emphasizing certain qualities about a subject in order to stress the values that they represent. (15)

main motion A proposal that would commit a group to some specific action or declaration. (Appendix A)

main points The most prominent ideas of the speaker's message, and a speech's principal points of focus. (7)

major premise A generally accepted belief upon which an argument is based. (14)

malapropism A language error that occurs when a word is confused with another word that sounds like it. (10)

manuscript presentation A speech read from a manuscript. (11)

marking Adding a gender reference when none is needed — e.g., "a woman doctor." (4)

master of ceremonies A person who coordinates an event or program, sets its mood, introduces participants, provides transitions, and may also present awards. (15)

maxim A brief and particularly apt saying. (10)

medium The channel that transmits the speaker's message, usually the air through which the sound travels. (1)

memorized text presentation A speech that is committed to memory and delivered word for word. (11)

message The fabric of words, illustrations, voice, and body language that conveys the idea of the speech. (1)

metaphor A figure of speech in which anticipated words are replaced by new, surprising language in order to create a new perspective. (7, 10)

minor premise The claim made in an argument that an important idea is related to a generally accepted truth (or major premise). (14)

mirror question A question that includes part of a previous response to encourage further discussion. (5)

motion Formal proposal for group consideration. (Appendix A)

motion to amend A parliamentary move that offers the opportunity to modify a motion presently under discussion. (Appendix A)

motivated sequence design A persuasive speech design that proceeds by arousing attention, demonstrating a need, satisfying the need, visualizing results, and calling for action. (13)

motivation Internal forces that impel action and direct human behavior toward specific goals. (4)

mountain graph A variation of a line graph in which different colors are used to fill in the areas above and below the line(s). (9)

multisided presentation A speech in which the speaker's position is compared favorably to other positions. (13)

myth of the mean The deceptive use of statistical averages in speeches. (14)

mythos A form of proof that connects a subject to the culture and tradition of a group through the use of narratives. (14)

narrative A story used to illustrate some important truth about a speaker's topic. (6)

non sequitur fallacy A deductive error occurring when conclusions are drawn improperly from the premises that preceded them. (14)

onomatopoeia The use of words that sound like the objects they signify. (10)

open question In an interview, questions that encourage substantive responses and discussions. (5)

optimum pitch The level at which people can produce their strongest voice with minimal effort and that allows variation up and down the musical scale. (11)

order A consistent pattern used to develop a speech. (7)

parallel construction Wording an outline's main points in the same way in order to emphasize their importance and to help the audience remember them. (8, 10)

paraphrase A summary of something said or written. (6)

parliamentary procedure A set of formal rules that establishes an order of business for meetings and encourages the orderly, fair, and full consideration of proposals during group deliberation. (Appendix A)

participative communication The shared responsibility of the speaker and the listener for creating meaning. (3)

pathos Proof relying on appeals to personal motives and emotions. (14)

personification A figure of speech in which nonhuman or abstract subjects are given human qualities. (10)

persuasion The art of convincing others to give favorable attention to our point of view. (13)

persuasive function The function of a speech designed to encourage listeners to think and act in a particular way and to give sound reasons for doing so. (5)

persuasive speech Speech intended to influence the attitudes or actions of listeners. (3, 13)

physiological needs In Maslow's Hierarchy of Needs, the most basic needs for food, air, water, and comfort. (4)

pictograph On a chart, a visual image symbolizing the information it represents. (9)

pie graph A circle graph that shows the size of a subject's parts in relation to each other and to the whole. (9)

pitch The position of a human voice on the musical scale. (11)

plagiarism Presenting the ideas and words of others without crediting them as sources. (1)

post hoc **fallacy** A deductive error in which one event is assumed to be the cause of another simply because the first preceded the second. (14)

postpone consideration A motion that defers discussion until some specified time when necessary information will be available. (Appendix A)

precision Using information that is closely and carefully related to the specific purpose; particularly important when a topic varies widely from place to place. (5)

preliminary tuning effect The effect of previous speeches or other situational factors in predisposing an audience to respond positively or negatively to a speech. (4)

prepersuasive function The way in which informative speaking shapes listeners' perceptions, preparing them for later persuasive speeches on a topic. (12)

PREP formula An outlining technique for an impromptu speech: state a **p**oint, give a **r**eason or **ex**ample, and restate the **p**oint. (11)

presentation Utterance of a speech to an audience, integrating the skills of nonverbal communication, especially body language, with the speech content. (11)

presentation aids Supplemental materials used to enhance the effectiveness and clarity of a presentation. (9)

prestige testimony Information coming from a person who is highly regarded but not necessarily an expert on a topic. (6)

preview The part of the introduction that identifies the main points in the body of the speech and presents an overview of the speech to follow. May follow the thematic statement or be part of the thematic statement itself. (5, 7)

principle of closure The need for a satisfactory end or conclusion to a speech. (7)

principle of proximity The idea that things occurring together in time or space should be presented in the order in which they normally happen. (7)

principle of similarity The principle that like things should be grouped together. (7)

probe A question that asks an expert to elaborate on a response. (5)

problem-solution design A persuasive speech pattern in which listeners are first persuaded that they have a problem and then are shown how to solve it. (13)

pronunciation The use of correct sounds and of proper stress or accent on syllables in saying words. (11)

proof An interpretation of evidence that provides reasons for listeners to change their attitudes or behaviors. (14)

proxemics The study of how human beings use space during communication. (11)

qualifier A word suggesting the degree of confidence a speaker has in the conclusion of his or her argument. (14)

quoting out of context An unethical use of a quotation that changes or distorts the original speaker's meaning or intent by not including parts of the quote. (1)

rate The speed at which words are uttered. (11)

rebuttal The pointing out of a condition under which the conclusion of an argument might not hold. (14)

recency Ensuring that the information in a speech is the latest that can be provided. (5)

red herring The use of irrelevant material to divert attention. (14)

refutative design A persuasive speech design in which the speaker tries to raise doubts about, damage, or destroy an opposing position. (13)

reinforcer A comment or action that encourages further communication from someone being interviewed. (5)

reliability The trustworthiness of information critical to the credibility of a speech. (5)

reluctant witness A person cited as evidence whose testimony is against his or her self-interest. (14)

research overview A listing of the main sources of information used in a speech and of the major ideas from each source. (7)

responsible knowledge An understanding of the major features, issues, experts, latest developments, and local applications relevant to a topic. (1, 5)

rhetorical question A question that has a self-evident answer, or that provokes curiosity that the speech then proceeds to satisfy. (7)

rhetorical style The unique way a speaker chooses and arranges words in a presentation. (10)

rhythm Rate patterns within a speech. (11)

Robert's Rules of Order The authoritative, traditional "bible" of parliamentary procedure. (Appendix A)

safety and security needs In Maslow's Hierarchy of Needs, the need to be free from threat and predators, to have control over what happens, and to be able to rely on tradition. (4)

second A motion must receive a "second" before group discussion can proceed. Assures that more than one member wishes to have the motion considered. (Appendix A)

self-actualization needs In Maslow's Hierarchy of Needs, the need to realize one's potential, grow and develop as a person, seek challenges, satisfy curiosity, and enjoy variety. (4)

self-awareness inventory A series of questions that a speaker can ask to develop an approach to a speech of introduction. (2)

sequence chart Visual illustrations of the different stages of a process. (9)

sequential design A pattern for an informative speech that presents the steps involved in the process being demonstrated. (12)

sexism Allowing gender stereotypes to control interactions with members of the opposite sex. (4)

sexist language The use of masculine nouns and pronouns when the intended reference is to both sexes, or the use of derogatory emotional trigger words when referring to women. (4)

simile A language tool that clarifies something abstract by comparing it with something concrete; usually introduced by *as* or *like*. (10)

simplicity A desirable quality of speech structure. Suggests that a speech have a limited number of main points and that they be short and direct. (7)

sleeper effect A delayed reaction to persuasion. (13)

slippery slope fallacy The assumption that once something happens, an inevitable trend is established that will lead to disastrous results. (14)

social leadership behavior Occurs when leaders focus upon building and maintaining positive, productive relationships among group members. (Appendix A)

source card A record kept of the author, title, place and date of publication, and page references for each research source. (5)

source citations Parenthetical references in a speech outline to sources listed in full under *Works Consulted*. (8)

spatial design A pattern for an informative speech that orders the main points as they occur in physical space. (12)

speaker A person who communicates to an audience an oral message intended to inform, persuade, or celebrate. (1)

specific purpose The speaker's particular goal or the response that the speaker wishes to evoke. (5)

speech of acceptance A ceremonial speech expressing gratitude for an honor and acknowledging those who made the accomplishment possible. (15)

speech of demonstration An informative speech aimed at showing the audience how to do something or how something works. (12)

speech of description An informative speech that creates word pictures to help the audience understand a subject. (12)

speech of explanation A speech that is intended to inform the audience about abstract and complex subjects, such as concepts or programs. (12)

speech of inspiration A ceremonial speech directed at awakening or reawakening an audience to a goal, purpose, or set of values. (15)

speech of introduction A ceremonial speech in which a featured speaker is introduced to the audience. (15)

speech of tribute A ceremonial speech that recognizes the achievements of individuals or groups or commemorates special events. (15)

statistics Facts numerically expressed. (6)

stereotype A generalized picture of a race, gender, or nationality that supposedly represents the essential characteristics of that group. (1, 4)

stock issues design A persuasive speech pattern that attempts to answer the major general questions a reasonable person would ask before agreeing to a change in policies or procedures. (13)

straw man fallacy Understating, distorting, or otherwise misrepresenting the position of opponents for the sake of refutation. (14)

subordination The requirement that material in an outline descend in importance from main points to subpoints to sub-subpoints to sub-sub-subpoints. (8)

subpoints The major divisions within a speech's main points. (8)

substance A quality possessed by a speech when it has an important message, a careful plan of development, and adequate facts, examples, and testimony. (3)

sub-subpoints Divisions of subpoints within a speech. (8)

summary statement The speaker's reinterpretation of the speech's main idea at the end of a presentation. (2, 7)

supporting materials The facts and figures, testimony, examples, and narratives that constitute the building blocks of successful speeches. (6)

symbolic racism An indirect form of racism that employs code words and subtle, unspoken contrast to suggest that one race is superior to another. (4)

synecdoche A language technique in which part of a subject is used to represent the whole of it. (10)

table the motion Suspends indefinitely the discussion of a motion. (Appendix A)

task leadership behavior A leadership emphasis that directs the attention and activity of a group towards a specified goal. (Appendix A)

testimony The employment of the observations, opinions, or conclusions of other people or institutions to enhance the credibility of a presentation. (6)

textual graphics Visual presentation of key words in a speech using a chalkboard, posterboard, flip chart, transparency, slide, or handout. (9)

thesis statement The speech's central idea. (2, 5)

thoroughness Providing complete and accurate information about a topic. (5)

toast A short speech of tribute, usually offered at celebration dinners or meetings. (15)

topic area inventory chart A means of determining possible speech topics by listing topics you find of interest and subjects your audience finds of interest, and matching them. (5)

transaction The process by which speaker and listener create each others' identities as they communicate. (1)

transactional leadership A leadership style based on power relationships that relies on reward and punishment to achieve its ends. (Appendix A)

transformation The dynamic effect of successful communication on the identities of the speaker and listener and on public knowledge. (1)

transformational leadership A leadership style based on mutual respect and stewardship rather than on control. (Appendix A)

transitions Connecting elements used in speeches. (7)

trigger word A term or word inspiring positive or negative emotions in listeners. (3)

universal human values Eight values identified by the Institute for Global Ethics that transcend cultural differences: love, truthfulness, fairness, freedom, unity, tolerance, responsibility, and respect for life. (4)

urging action A function of persuasive speech that urges the audience to take action, either as individuals or as a group. (13)

values Standards of desirable or ideal behavior. (4)

verbatim Using the exact words of a source. (6)

verifier A statement by an interviewer confirming the meaning of what has just been said by the person being interviewed. (5)

visualization The process of systematically picturing oneself succeeding as a speaker and practicing a speech with that image in mind. (2)

vocal distractions Filler words, such as *er, um,* and *you know,* used in the place of a pause. (11)

working outline A tentative plan showing the pattern of a speech's major parts, their relative importance, and the way they fit together. (8)

works consulted A bibliography included on the formal outline, listing the major sources for a speech. (8)

Photo Credits

Index